The Princeton Review

Cracking the
NCLEX-RN
with Practice Tests on CD-ROM

BY
JENNIFER A. MEYER, R.N., B.S.N
AND COLLEAGUES

SEVENTH EDITION

RANDOM HOUSE, INC.
NEW YORK

www.PrincetonReview.com

Princeton Review Publishing, L.L.C.
2315 Broadway
New York, NY 10024
E-mail: booksupport@review.com

ISBN 0-375-76302-3
ISSN 1091-9554

Editor: Allegra Burton
Production Coordinator: Ryan Tozzi
Production Editor: Maria Dente

Manufactured in the United States of America.

9 8 7 6 5 4 3 2 1

Seventh Edition

ACKNOWLEDGMENTS

Thanks…

To Celeste Sollod, whose encouragement, reassurance, and expertise were invaluable.

To John Katzman and Chris Kensler, whose vision and guidance said it all: We want to dominate!

To Scott Falk, for your diligence and for putting your heart and soul into this book. Most importantly, thank you for your sense of humor!

To Jeannie Yoon, Melanie Sponholz, and John Fallon, for seeing this project through to the end.

To Editor Allegra Burton, and especially to Maria Dente and Ryan Tozzi.

To my family: Mom and Dad, Doug, Stafford, Grandma, Cedric, and Cody. You put up with "the book" for longer than anyone expected.

To my friends and colleagues, who never stopped believing that "the book" would exist someday: Mimi Mahon, once an advisor; Brooke Wurst, for your brain and the song; Regina Madden and Donna Campbell, for your understanding; Lynn Huzzard and Margaret Crighton, for your dedication and inspiration; Allison Reuter, you rescued me; Ania, you lived it!

To all of the contributing authors and question writers, for your commitment to my cause!

CONTRIBUTORS

Amanda J. Barton, RN, MSN
Nurse Practitioner
Columbia University Health Services

Karen A. Beltran, RN, MS
Nurse Clinician, Transplant/General Surgery
New York University Medical Center

Jennifer M. Brooks, RN, BSN
Nurse Clinician, Pediatrics
New York University Medical Center

Grace E. Brown, RN, BSN
Nurse Clinician, General Surgery
New York University Medical Center

Myrna Buiser, RN, BSN
Nurse Clinician, ICU
New York University Medical Center

Donna Campbell, RN, MSN
Head Nurse, Transplant/General surgery
New York University Medical Center

Marianne Connelly, RN, BSN
Staff Nurse, Pediatric Neuroscience Unit
Beth Israel North Medical Center
New York, New York

Margaret H. Crighton, RN, BSN
Senior Staff Nurse, AIDS Dedicated Unit
New York Hospital-Cornell Medical Center

Jeanne D'Arcangelo Logan, MSN, CRNP
Faculty, University of Pennsylvania

Margot D. Dobies, RN, BSN, BA

Jennifer Eckert, RN, BSN
Staff Nurse, Pediatric Neuroscience Unit
Beth Israel North Medical Center
New York, New York

Genvieve Edmund, RN, BSN
Nurse Clinician, General Surgery
New York University Medical Center

Kristen Fabiszewski, RN, BSN
Nurse Clinician, Pediatrics
New York University Medical Center

Margaret Frank-Bader, RN, MA, ANP, CCRN
Assistant Head Nurse, Transplant/General
    Surgery
New York University Medical Center
Clinical Instructor, New York University School of
    Nursing

Mary Jean Gessner, RN, BSN
Staff Nurse, Cardiovascular Surgery
St. Francis Hospital
Roslyn, New York

Barbara Goldberg-Chamberlain, RN, MSN, CSC,
    CCRN
Assistant Professor of Nursing
Atlantic Community College

Sandra R. Holahan, RN, MSN, CCNP
Pediatric Nurse Practitioner
Alfred I. DuPont Institute

Lynn L. Huzzard, RN, BSN
Senior Staff Nurse, General Medicine
New York Hospital-Cornell Medical Center

Marcia A. Jasper, RN, MS
Faculty Associate, Arizona State University
Perinatal Clinician, Matria (formerly Healthdyne)

Kelly A. Keefe, RN, MSN, CS, CCRN
Pediatric Critical Care Nurse Practitioner
Beth Israel North Medical Center
New York, New York

Carol Klimchak, RN, CS, MS
Clinical Nurse Specialist, Adult Psychiatric
  Nursing
Research Nurse
Long Island Jewish Hospital

Lili-Ann Lidji, MS, RD
New York University Medical Center

Patricia S. Maher, RN, CS, MSN
Senior Nurse Clinician, Psychiatry
New York University Medical Center

Mimi Mahon, PhD, RN, CCNP
Assistant Professor, Nursing of Children
University of Pennsylvania
Coordinator, Sibling Bereavement Program
Children's Hospital of Philadelphia

Mary Maloney, RN, MA, CCRN
Senior Nurse Clinician, ICU
New York University Medical Center

Ellen McCabe, RN, MSN, CCNP
Pediatric Nurse Practitioner
The Milton and Bernice Stern Department of
  Pediatrics
Beth Israel Medical Center

Jacqueline M. McGrath, RN, MSN
Project Director, Neonatal Nutritive Sucking
  Grant
University of Pennsylvania
Neonatal Developmental Nurse Consultant
Clinical Faculty, University of Pennsylvania

Wanda K. Mohr, PhD, RNC
Assistant Professor, Psychiatric Mental Health
  Nursing
University of Pennsylvania

Monica Muzzi, RN, BSN, CCRN
Staff Nurse, Labor and Delivery
New York Hospital-Cornell Medical Center

Lisa M. Nutley, RN, BSN
Staff Nurse, Pediatric Neuroscience Unit
Beth Israel North Medical Center
New York, New York

Roseann Pokoluk, RNC, MA, CNRN
Staff Development Instructor
New York University Medical Center

Laurie A. Pollock, RN, MSN, CRNP
Women's Health Nurse Practitioner
New York Hospital-Cornell Medical Center

Allison C. Reuter, RN, BSN
Nurse Clinician, Pediatrics
New York University Medical Center

Dorothy A. Robinson, RN, MA, ANPC,
  CCRN
Senior Nurse Clinician, Transplant
New York University Medical Center

Crystyna H. Sinclair, MS, RD, CNSD, CS
Senior Pediatric Nutritionist
New York University Medical Center

Julia Stark-Fried, RN, BSN
Cardiac Catheterization Lab, University
  Hospital
State University of New York at Stony Brook

Jo Stecher, MA, RNC
Senior Nurse Clinician
Coordinator, Lung Transplant Program
New York University Medical Center
Independent Lecturer/Consultant

Kerry F. Walsh, RN, BSN
Nurse Clinician, Neurology/Neurosurgery
New York University Medical Center

Anne J .Winkler, RN, MA, CCRN
Staff Nurse, ICU/CCU
Northern Westchester Hospital Center

CONTENTS

PART I: ORIENTATION **1**

Chapter 1   About the NCLEX-RN 3

Chapter 2   Logistics of the NCLEX-RN and Licensure 9

Chapter 3   Cracking the System.. 11

PART II: ADULT PHYSIOLOGICAL INTEGRITY **23**

Chapter 4   The Nervous System.. 25

Chapter 5   The Cardiovascular System 55

Chapter 6   The Respiratory System 77

Chapter 7   The Gastrointestinal System 101

Chapter 8   The Genitourinary System.. 133

Chapter 9   The Musculoskeletal System 163

Chapter 10   The Integumentary System 185

Chapter 11   The Endocrine System 201

Chapter 12   Oncology.. 219

Chapter 13   Human Immunodeficiency Virus (HIV)/
             Acquired Immunodeficiency Syndrome (AIDS)........................ 239

PART III: PEDIATRIC PHYSIOLOGICAL INTEGRITY **251**

Chapter 14   The Hospitalized Child 253

Chapter 15   The Newborn 271

Chapter 16   The Infant.. 305

Chapter 17   Early Childhood.. 329

Chapter 18   Middle Childhood 345

Chapter 19   Adolescence.. 353

Chapter 20   Chronic Health Problems of Childhood 369

Chapter 21   The Child and Family with Special Needs 387

PART IV: HEALTH PROMOTION AND MAINTENANCE **401**

Chapter 22   Growth and Development.. 403

Chapter 23   Maternal/Child Health 421

Chapter 24   Nutrition Through the Life Cycle 447

Part V: Safe, Effective Care Environment 463

Chapter 25   Creating a Safe, Effective Care Environment for Adults 465

Chapter 26   Creating a Safe, Effective Care Environment for Children 479

Chapter 27   Perioperative Nursing 495

Chapter 28   Legal, Ethical, and Professional Issues 513

Part VI: Psychosocial Integrity 523

Chapter 29   Basic Concepts of Psychiatric Nursing and Assessment 525

Chapter 30   Psychiatric Disorders 541

Chapter 31   Psychopharmacology 561

Appendixes

Appendix 1 List of State Boards and Additional Requirements for Licensure 583

Appendix 2 Prefixes and Suffixes 589

Index 597

Using the NCLEX-RN Diagnostic Software 621

About the Author 625

PART I

ORIENTATION

1

ABOUT THE NCLEX-RN

CONGRATULATIONS!

You have successfully completed nursing school and have earned the opportunity to take the NCLEX-RN! Our goal at The Princeton Review is to make this "privilege" a lot less daunting than it may seem now. *Cracking the NCLEX-RN* will walk you through focused preparation for the National Council Licensure Examination for Registered Nurses (NCLEX-RN).

We start with basic information about the NCLEX-RN and computer-adaptive testing, then we outline the logistics of taking the exam and obtaining your license. Finally, we review the content of the exam. While we do not have the power to foresee the exact questions on the exam, we can put you in the frame of mind of an NCLEX-RN question writer and a beginning nurse so that your common sense leads you to the correct answer.

WHAT IS THE NCLEX-RN?

NCLEX-RN stands for National Council Licensure Examination for Registered Nurses. It is defined as "an examination designed to test knowledge, skills, and abilities essential to the safe and effective practice of nursing at the entry level." So, while graduating from nursing school is the first step, your state wants to make sure you can consolidate information and prioritize basic nursing before they let you loose with patients. This is where the NCLEX-RN comes in.

WHO DEVELOPS THIS EXAM, ANYWAY?

The National Council of State Boards of Nursing (NCSBN). This organization conducts a comprehensive study of the activities of beginning graduate/staff nurses all over the country in a variety of health care settings. This is called a job analysis.

Why is the National Council data important to you? Well, the data collected from these studies are used to formulate the NCLEX-RN items or questions. The test questions are reviewed by experts and updated or discarded based on their relevance to current nursing practice of newly licensed nurses. In addition, educators from all over the United States are selected to be item writers. They develop and review new questions to be used on the NCLEX-RN. After these studies have been conducted, the staff of the NCSBN develops a test plan that dictates the types and numbers of questions that will be administered on the exam.

SO, WHAT'S ON THE EXAM?

The following is the test plan effective as of April 2001.

CATEGORIES OF CLIENT NEEDS	Percentage of Questions
A. Safe, Effective Care Environment	
1. Management of Care	7–13%
2. Safety and Infection Control	5–11%
B. Health Promotion and Maintenance	
3. Growth and Development Through the Life Span	7–13%
4. Prevention and Early Detection of Disease	5–11%
C. Psychosocial Integrity	
5. Coping and Adaptation	5–11%
6. Psychosocial Adaptation	5–11%
D. Physiological Integrity	
7. Basic Care and Comfort	7–13%
8. Pharmacological and Parenteral Therapies	5–11%
9. Reduction of Risk Potential	12–18%
10. Physiological Adaptation	12–18%
For more information go to the National Council of State Boards of Nursing website at www.ncsbn.org.	

Client needs was selected as the framework for the exam. It provides a universal structure for defining nursing actions and competencies across all settings for all clients.

An important point to remember, particularly for those of you who have previously worked in a clinical setting, is that NCLEX-RN test questions are written by nurse educators and are based on what is currently being taught in nursing schools. Item (question) writers who develop test questions reference these questions with information provided in commonly used, current nursing textbooks. So, in answering NCLEX-RN questions, **you want to respond with textbook information**, and not what you've learned in clinical practice.

WHAT IS COMPUTER-ADAPTIVE TESTING (CAT)?

In order to understand how to beat the computer-adaptive NCLEX-RN, you have to understand how it works.

Unlike the days of paper-and-pencil standardized tests, which began with an easy question and then got progressively tougher, the CAT always begins by giving you a medium or moderate difficulty question. If you get it right, the computer gives you a slightly harder question. If you get it wrong, the computer gives you a slightly easier question, and so on. The idea is that the computer will zero in on your exact level of ability very quickly, which allows you to answer fewer questions overall, and the computer to make a more finely-honed assessment of your abilities.

CAN I SKIP A QUESTION?

Due to the very nature of computer-adaptive testing, no "skipping" is allowed. So, if you get to a tough question, don't get discouraged. You don't have to get every one correct. Just give it your best shot and move on to the next item.

HOW MANY QUESTIONS WILL I TAKE?

You will take a minimum of 75 questions (15 of which are trial questions and will not count toward your score), and a maximum of 265. The computer screen will go blank when the computer has determined, within a 95 percent confidence level, whether you have passed, or whether you have failed. It is important to note that you can pass or fail after having taken 75 questions, or pass or fail after having taken 265 questions. For example, in 1997 the average candidate completed 120 questions before the computer made a pass/fail determination (National Council Annual Report, 1998). Some students find themselves taking 100 or 120 questions and they think they're failing—they start frantically punching in any answer just to end the exam, and then they really do end up failing. So, don't give up if you find yourself taking up to 265 questions.

Before new questions are integrated into the NCLEX-RN, they are examined to determine if they're valid and reliable. New trial questions are placed, or "seeded", in the exam, but they don't count toward your score. In a 75-question exam, 15 of the questions are trial ones that are being tested for possible future use. If the majority of guinea pigs, sorry, we mean students, sitting for the exam get one of these experimental questions wrong, the test writers will analyze it to determine whether or not it is flawed before adding it (as a scored question) to an actual NCLEX-RN CAT test.

An important note is that you will never get a grade of A, B, C, D or F. In fact, there is no score; you will simply know whether you passed or not. Your state board notifies you of your results.

HOW CAN WE HELP?

While test preparation and review is not painless, your suffering can be minimized with a good, comprehensive manual. What follows is the guide I wish had existed when I took the NCLEX-RN several years ago—so use it to crack the NCLEX-RN. You can do it!

A team of clinical nurses, nurse scholars, and test-prep experts has studied the NCLEX-RN inside and out to provide you with the most straightforward and thorough preparation possible. Cracking the NCLEX-RN will structure your studying and reinforce each piece of information with a multiple choice question and/or drill. Furthermore, at the end of each chapter are sets of NCLEX-style questions which are designed to resemble the real thing. We firmly believe that the best preparation for this kind of test is practicing as many questions as possible, so we are going to do just that.

With all that said, relax, stay focused, and practice, practice, practice...

GOOD LUCK!

LOGISTICS OF THE NCLEX-RN AND LICENSURE

REGISTERING FOR THE NCLEX-RN

As of August 16, 2002, all NCLEX-RN candidates will register through NCS Pearson by phone, mail, or the Internet. And as of October 1, 2002, NCS Pearson will begin conducting NCLEX-RN test administration sessions at Pearson Professional Centers. For more information go to the National Council of State Boards of Nursing website at www.ncsbn.org and the NCS Pearson website at www.ncspearson.com or call the NCSBN at (312) 787-6555 or NCS Pearson at (800) 431-1421.

While each state may be slightly different and your state handbook has the final word, this book can serve as a consolidated, step-by-step guide through registration. Keep detailed records of the information you are requesting, receiving, and submitting. Make copies, record dates and checks, and stay organized. If any of your information is lost, you want to be able to find it easily for resubmission.

THE PROCESS

1. Contact your state board of nursing by phone, mail or the Internet. Request information on, and an application for, licensure. (See Appendix 1 for a list of state board addresses, phone numbers, and requirements for licensure.)

2. Read your state's bulletin thoroughly. Stay on top of each step of the process so your license is not delayed! Send your application via certified mail so you have confirmation of its delivery and receipt.

3. Fill out the "Application for Licensure" and other required forms. Some states have requirements in addition to receipt of your final academic transcript from an accredited registered nursing school and passing the NCLEX-RN. (As we said above, see Appendix 1 for a list of these.) Make sure any educational requirements for licensure specific to your state have been met and that the correct documentation has been filed appropriately.

4. Fill out the "Certification of Nursing Education" form as instructed, then send it to your school with any specified fee. Enclose a stamped, addressed envelope so your school can mail it right out and you know it's going to the correct address. This form is now your school's responsibility, but be sure you have sent it to the correct place and person and that the person knows your time frame.

5. If you are starting work before you take the NCLEX-RN, fill out the "Application for Limited Permit" as instructed. (You may need to submit a recent, signed photograph.) Give this form to your employer with the fee (if your employer does not cover it) and a stamped, addressed envelope. You may have to mail this yourself, depending on your employer.

6. Fill out the NCLEX-RN registration form. Enclose a check for the amount specified and send it via certified mail. You will receive a postcard confirming the delivery of your application.

7. If all goes well, you will receive an "Authorization to Test" card, along with information about making your appointment to take the test. You may wait anywhere from several weeks to three months to receive your authorization card. This is the best time in which to prepare for the exam.

3

CRACKING THE SYSTEM

GO WITH THE EXPERTS

Unlike some other NCLEX-RN review books, we at The Princeton Review have more to say than just a repetition of what you learned in nursing school. We're test-preparation experts, and we've spent years refining our techniques for acing standardized tests. Reviewing the material is only part of what we can do for you; teaching you **how** to take the NCLEX-RN is the other part. Our strategies, outlined in this chapter and referred to throughout this book, will help you understand the test and improve your chances of passing.

In *Cracking the NCLEX-RN*, we briefly review the subjects you will see on the exam. Our goal is not to teach you the material, but to refresh your memory of the subjects you learned in nursing school. More comprehensive discussions of these topics can be found in your textbooks, so refer to them when needed. The key here is to get used to, and good at, answering test questions.

REVIEW QUESTIONS

Each chapter in *Cracking the NCLEX-RN* has dozens of exercises for you to answer. The answers are found at the end of each chapter. You will also find a set of NCLEX-style questions, with the appropriate rationales for arriving at the correct answer, on which to practice.

MAKE A GOOD FIRST IMPRESSION

When you are taking the test, focus on the initial 20 to 30 questions! Your competency level jumps the most in the beginning of the test with each correct answer. Your answers to the first 20 to 30 questions guide the computer to your level; the rest help it narrow in on your specific competency. It's like making a good first impression on a job interview; it's hard to go back and undo the computer's first perception of you.

It takes the computer longer to narrow in on a competency level (the level at which you are getting approximately 50 percent of the questions correct and 50 percent wrong). This is why you could finish after only 75 questions (the minimum number of questions) and the person sitting next to you could require all 265 questions (the maximum) to establish a level. The number of questions you are asked has nothing to do with whether you are passing or failing. You must stay level-headed and think clearly and rationally about each question independently. If your time expires (you have five hours at most to establish a competency level), the computer determines if you are above the pass line.

PROCESS OF ELIMINATION (POE)

One of the major Princeton Review techniques to help you on the NCLEX-RN is **Process of Elimination**, or POE. Using POE can help you improve your chances of answering a question correctly, even if you aren't sure about the answer. Your brain holds years of knowledge from nursing school, a lifetime of common sense, and, after working through this book, a comprehensive understanding of the exam. With all these resources, you should be able to eliminate some incorrect answer choices on questions that stump you.

By eliminating just one answer choice, you improve your chances of guessing correctly and raise your competency level to 33 percent! If you can eliminate two options (e.g., by piecing together words using their roots), you raise your chances of guessing correctly to 50 percent!

If you are left with two choices, here are some criteria for eliminating the remaining incorrect answer choice:

1. In general, choices that contain absolutes (i.e., always, all) are more likely to be incorrect.
2. Choices with qualifiers in them (i.e., commonly, possibly) are more likely to be correct.
3. Information repeated from the question may be repeated in the correct response.

Remember, you must answer every question in order to move on. You might as well make the most of each one!

USE COMMON SENSE

Because the potential scope of information covered on the NCLEX-RN is so wide and varied, you need to be prepared to think on your feet. This requires understanding concepts, not memorizing diseases. Understanding the concepts of safe nursing practice, along with a small amount of memorization, will enable you to pass the NCLEX-RN. Don't panic each time a new question appears on the screen. Just use what you know, along with the information presented, and apply your common sense to each scenario. Remember, the correct answer is always in front of you!

Try the following question:

> A client is admitted to the emergency room in a nonketotic hyperosmolar coma. After ascertaining that her airway is patent and her heart rhythm is sinus, the nurse should assess:
>
> 1. her neurological status
> 2. her urine output
> 3. her family's coping mechanisms
> 4. her skin for breakdown

You might not be able to recall exactly what a nonketotic hyperosmolar coma is. That's okay! You can still eliminate some of the answer choices because you know, using your common sense, that this is hardly the time to assess her family's psychological adaptation to this situation. After a patent airway is established and your client has a stable heart rate, the word "coma" should immediately prompt you to perform a neurological assessment. Urine output is also important, but neurological status is more of a priority. Maintaining skin integrity is a vital nursing function, but you need a viable client to maintain her skin. See, you didn't need to know the details of a nonketotic hyperosmolar coma!

USE PREFIXES AND SUFFIXES

Even if you don't understand the words in the questions at first sight, knowing what prefixes and suffixes mean can help you understand questions and eliminate answer options. Reviewing some of the medical prefixes and suffixes in Appendix 2 may be helpful. You are probably already familiar with many of them, but knowing a few more can help if you are stumped by a question. For example, if a question contains the word hemopoiesis, you do not need to have memorized what it means. Just think about it:

hemo- = blood

-poiesis = making, forming

You have figured out that the question has to do with forming blood. This deduction may help you eliminate some incorrect answers and improve your chances of choosing the correct one. Try to figure out the following questions by breaking down the medical terms:

> A client has returned from the recovery room after a gastrectomy. The nurse anticipates that she will have a(n):
>
> 1. nasogastric (NG) tube
> 2. Hemovac self-contained suction system
> 3. sternal suture line
> 4. cardiac arrhythmia

Gastrectomy and nasogastric are the keys to answering this question. All you need to recall is that gastr- means having to do with the stomach, and you can associate the question with the answer, option 1.

> A female client has recently been diagnosed with osteosarcoma. The nurse knows that clients with this disease usually require:
>
> 1. sedatives
> 2. antibiotics
> 3. chemotherapy
> 4. antipsychotics

Knowing that you can "decode" the medical term, you shouldn't panic! The suffix -sarcoma or just -oma should trigger cancer in your mind. Therefore, the best answer would be chemotherapy, option 3.

USE ALL THE TECHNIQUES TOGETHER

Just to boost your confidence, try the following question, combining all the skills we have just reviewed.

> A 22-year-old male client has been recently diagnosed with pyelonephritis. The immediate nursing interventions include:
>
> 1. encouraging increased fluid intake
> 2. inserting a nasogastric tube
> 3. asking Joe where he feels pain
> 4. encouraging Joe to verbalize his feelings

Let's start with the question. What type of question is it? Intervention! That's right there in the question. Asking the client where he feels pain is an assessment, so eliminate option 3. You have now improved your chances of getting the answer from 1 in 4 to 1 in 3.

Your common sense tells you that encouraging the client to verbalize his feelings is not an immediate concern, so eliminate option 4. Your chances of getting the correct answer are now fifty-fifty.

Now, decipher the parts of "pyelonephritis." Pyelo- refers to the pelvis or the kidney; -nephr indicates kidney; and -itis indicates inflammation. Option 1, encouraging fluid intake, is, therefore, a viable option, as one might want to flush out the urinary system. But don't stop there. Check out option 2 as well. Nasogastric means nose to stomach. This doesn't have anything to do with the kidney or pelvis. Therefore, knowing that stasis of fluid promotes infection (-itis), you can safely assume that option 1 is the correct answer. Increased fluid intake will flush the urinary tract. And you've just raised your competency level.

MORE HELPFUL HINTS

COMMUNICATION QUESTIONS

As you probably already know, a nurse should always serve as a client's advocate. In doing so, communication between the client and nurse becomes an integral part of treatment. Take a look at the example below and see if you select the appropriate response:

On the morning a client is scheduled for surgery, the nurse enters the room. The nurse notices that the client is crying. Which of these responses by the nurse would be most appropriate?

1. "Good morning. Why are you crying?"
2. "I see that you need some private time. I'll come back in five minutes."
3. "It seems that you're crying. Can you tell me what you are feeling?"
4. "You don't need to worry. The surgery will be over in a few hours."

Now, this might seem like an easy question. You might have even encountered this scenario in clinical practice and responded with either choice (1) or (4). But remember you want to respond with textbook information and not what you've learned in clinical practice. The correct answer is (3), because this type of response opens a channel for communication.

There are fundamental principles to follow when communicating with clients, and you should remember them when trying to answer a communication question:

1. Focus on the client.
2. Accept the client as he/she is.
3. Be honest and consistent.
4. Attempt to establish a good relationship (rapport) with the client.
5. Include the family or significant other when appropriate.
6. Allow the client and then the family or significant other to make decisions when possible.
7. Answer according to nursing action.
8. Do not provide a response that implies that the client is unworthy.
9. Select the most comprehensive (global) answer.

DELEGATION QUESTIONS

With today's complex health care system, the reengineering, a.k.a. downsizing, in health care environments has altered the scope of nursing practices. These current changes have led to a reorganization of nursing roles and responsibilities. Nurses, who are qualified, may be involved in coordinating and delegating nursing tasks to others such as Licensed Practical nurses (LPN) or to unlicensed assistive personnel (UAP).

In *delegating*, the registered nurse must use professional judgment to decide what activities can be delegated based on the nurses assessment of the patient's condition and needs.

SOME GUIDELINES

A Registered Nurse May NOT delegate:

- Initial nursing assessment and any other assessments that require professional nursing knowledge, judgment, and skill
- Nursing diagnosis determination
- Development of nursing care plans
- Evaluation of the patient regarding the nursing care plan
- Establishment of nursing care goals
- Patient care activities that require professional nursing knowledge, judgment, and skill

A Registered Nurse MAY delegate:

- Feeding a client
- Taking vital signs
- Hygiene care

Delegation questions can be particularly difficult for nurses who have had clinical experience as a graduate nurse, LPN or aide because they forget to answer with textbook information and not what they have seen in practice. It is also important to note that the even though a UAP's responsibilities vary from institution to institution, the exam will only test on uniformly accepted information.

In a publication entitled *Delegation: Concepts and Decision-Making Process* (1995), the National Council of State Boards of Nursing identified the five rights of delegation. Use them when responding to delegation questions.

The Board of Registration in Nursing presents this framework for the delegation decision-making process. The Five (5) Rights of Delegation delineate professional and legal accountability for nurses at *all* levels.

The Five Rights of Delegation	
1. Right Task	Appropriate activities delegated must fall in the respective scope of practice
2. Right Circumstances	Appropriate patient setting, available resources and other relevant factors conisdered
3. Right Person	Competencies must be established for the person who will carry out the task
4. Right Direction and Communication	Clear, concise description of the task, including its objective, limits, and expectations
5. Right Supervision	Appropriate monitoring, evaluation, intervention as needed, and feedback

Let's try to put all this information to use. Below you will find an example of a delegation question.

Which of the following activities in a high-risk prenatal clinic could the registered nurse delegate to a UAP?

1. Taking the blood pressure of a woman with preeclampsia.

2. Teaching a pregnant woman how to distinguish signs of true labor from Braxton-Hicks contractions.

3. Obtaining weights of pregnant clients before they are examined by a provider.

4. Referring an obese pregnant woman to a dietitian for nutrition counseling.

The best answer is (3). Why? Well, we can eliminate 2 and 4 because a UAP is not authorized to do referrals or instruct/teach the client. Choice 1 is a little less obvious. An RN or LPN should perform blood pressure measurements on clients with preeclampsia because if the blood pressure increases it usually indicates that the preeclampsia is worsening. This is typically the criterion for admission and drug administration, neither of which a UAP is qualified to do.

REMEMBER: If the task requires nursing judgment, it cannot be delegated.

take a few forms on the NCLEX-RN exam. They might ask you:

ost important?

nitial (first) action of the nurse?

best nursing action?

client would the nurse care for first?

er to manage a number of clients simultaneously, nurses must be able to set priorities.
u may see questions that ask you to make an assessment of the types of care needed, and
then evaluate which client would need immediate care. Setting priorities is an important
step in the planning process. Here are a few hints that can help you find the correct answers
to priority questions.

1. Use Maslow's Hierarchy of Needs. The hierarchy includes (in descending order) 1) physiological needs (survival); 2) safety needs (both physical and psychological); 3) psychological needs (care and belonging); and 4) self-actualization. When you see a priority question, you need to choose the response that ranks the highest in the Hierarchy.

2. Use the Nursing Process (APIE) to Establish Priorities. You must first assess, then plan, then implement, and finally evaluate. Select responses in which you assess the client before you implement the care.

3. Use ABCs. When you encounter a question that requires you to establish priorities, think airway, breathing, and then circulation. Your first priority in an emergency situation would be to establish a patent airway.

4. Use RACE. When you see priority questions that deal with fires, think: remove the clients, then sound the alarm, call the fire department, and finally extinguish the fire. The safety of the clients is the first priority.

Physiological needs (survival)
Safety needs
Psychological needs (care & belonging)
Self actualization

assess
implement
evaluate

airway
breathing
circulation

Sound the
R emove the clients
A larm
C all the fire department
E xtinguish the fire

LEGAL/ETHICAL QUESTIONS

Legal/ethical questions can encompass a variety of issues such as substance abuse by a staff member, unsafe practices by a health care provider, or detecting and reporting possible physical abuse. When you see a legal/ethical question bear in mind the following:

1. Your first priority is to the client, not to the provider or the institution
2. Just following orders is not an excuse, legally or ethically
3. Document EVERYTHING!
4. The nurse must be accountable for all actions and be prepared to defend them
5. Confidentiality

Let's take a look at a legal/ethical question:

You and your colleague are having lunch at a nearby restaurant. Your colleague wants to discuss a client from the morning shift. This can lead to which of the following:

A. Discipline by your hospital administrator
B. The loss of your nursing license
C. Nothing, you are not at the hospital
D. Nothing, the patient is not carrying any infectious diseases

The best answer is B. Any disclosure of patient information is strictly prohibited.

SOME FRIENDLY ADVICE

DON'T RUSH

The keys to success on this test are a sharp mind and careful reading! It's that simple. While your time is not limited on any question, once you enter an answer you cannot go back to change it. You must read each word carefully the first time! This is not a race. Work slowly and carefully to get more questions right. You must answer every question, even if it means guessing, and that is where Process of Elimination comes in handy. While there are no deductions for wrong answers, you want to raise your competency level as high as possible to allow for a few errors. Remember, the computer uses **your** answer to determine the next question and, ultimately, to determine your competency level.

WHEN SHOULD I TAKE THE EXAM?

As we mentioned in Chapter 1, one of the nice things about the CAT is that you can schedule your own test-taking time. You know yourself better than anyone else, so this is up to you and your employers (if they have a time frame). Are you a zombie before noon? Do you go into a food coma after lunch? Consider all of your quirks and use the flexibility of the CAT to your advantage in making your test-taking appointment. The Sylvan Technology Center nationwide scheduling phone number is: (800) 800-1123.

WHAT SHOULD I DO IN THE WEEKS LEADING UP TO THE EXAM?

While reviewing content is important, in order to prepare for a standardized test you must simulate exam conditions and practice, practice, practice! Focus your text review early in the preparation process, occasionally doing drills and sample written and CAT questions. Then do test after test, question after question, and review facts as necessary. Practice is helpful only if you review each question, answer, and accompanying rationale after answering the question yourself. Do not get bogged down by the extraordinary amount of information in your review book(s). Know the question types on the exam, recognize them, and answer them using common sense!

Pre-Exam Tips

- The "night before the night before" rule: Get a good night's sleep two nights before the exam and the night before. Some test takers believe the sleep obtained two nights before a big exam is even more important than that obtained the night before. The test can be long and you will need to focus hard for up to five hours. Don't let something as controllable as fatigue be your downfall!

- Do your laundry so you can pick your favorite, most comfortable outfit for the day of the exam. You'll want to dress in layers to be comfortable in any testing climate.

- While you know yourself best, we recommend a mellow, relaxing night before the exam. You shouldn't feel the need to cram. Go to a funny movie. Enjoy dinner with friends who have nothing to do with nursing.

- Eat a normal meal before the exam! Do not stuff yourself—your stomach will be the last thing you want nagging you during the exam. Even if you're not hungry, eat something or you'll be distracted by hunger. Concentrating requires a lot of energy! Take fruit or a light snack to the test in case you get hungry and have a moment to eat.

- Arrive at the Sylvan Technology Center early so you have ample time to relax, register, and get accustomed to your surroundings. Bring the proper identification. You don't want any undue stress just before the exam. If you don't like your testing station, request a change. Are you under a vent blowing hot air? Are you next to an air conditioner? Is there a glare on your computer screen? Are you next to someone who is perpetually coughing or blowing his nose? Once you start the exam you can't change your position, so think about these things before you settle in!

- Tune out your surroundings, get comfortable, and consider each question one at a time. You have years of knowledge stored away, and you know the test!

PART II

ADULT PHYSIOLOGICAL INTEGRITY

"Adult Physiological Integrity" comprises 46–54 percent of the actual test content. This is 130 questions out of the maximum number of questions possible on the CAT (265). When answering these questions, remember:

- Maintaining the client's airway is always your first priority!
- There is always something a nurse can do before calling the provider!

Client needs include:

- Physiological adaptation
- Physiological, psychosocial, and developmental health optimized
- Prevention of complications of medication administration and intravenous therapy
- Provision of basic care

We'll review organ systems from head to toe, starting with the nervous system.

THE NERVOUS SYSTEM

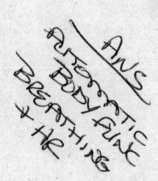
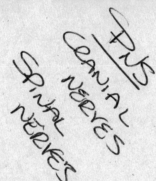
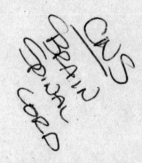

WHAT YOU NEED TO KNOW

Because we are moving from head to toe in our review, the nervous system chapter includes the fundamentals of the eye and the ear. Remember the importance of understanding the general concepts and applying them to specific situations, as we discussed in Chapter 3. Again, we will be briefly reviewing the subjects you will see on the NCLEX-RN to refresh your textbook knowledge. Practicing the questions is the key to passing the NCLEX-RN. Check your answers to the questions at the end of the chapter.

REVIEW OF NEUROANATOMY AND PHYSIOLOGY

The nervous system includes the central nervous system (C.N.S.), the peripheral nervous system (P.N.S.), and the autonomic nervous system (A.N.S.). The **central nervous system** is composed of the brain and spinal cord. The **peripheral nervous system** contains the cranial nerves and the spinal nerves.

The **autonomic nervous system** controls "automatic" body functions, such as breathing and heartbeat. It maintains a stable internal environment for the body. The A.N.S. is divided into the sympathetic and parasympathetic nervous systems.

The Autonomic Nervous System	
Sympathetic	**Parasympathetic**
"Fight or flight"	Maintains normal body functioning
Increases heart rate and blood pressure	Normalizes heart rate and blood pressure
Increases respiratory rate	Normalizes respiratory rate
Decreases peristalsis	Increases peristalsis
Secretes epinephrine and norepinephrine	Secretes acetylcholine
Dilates pulmonary bronchioles	Constricts pulmonary bronchioles

THE NEURON

The **neuron** is the functional unit of the nervous system:

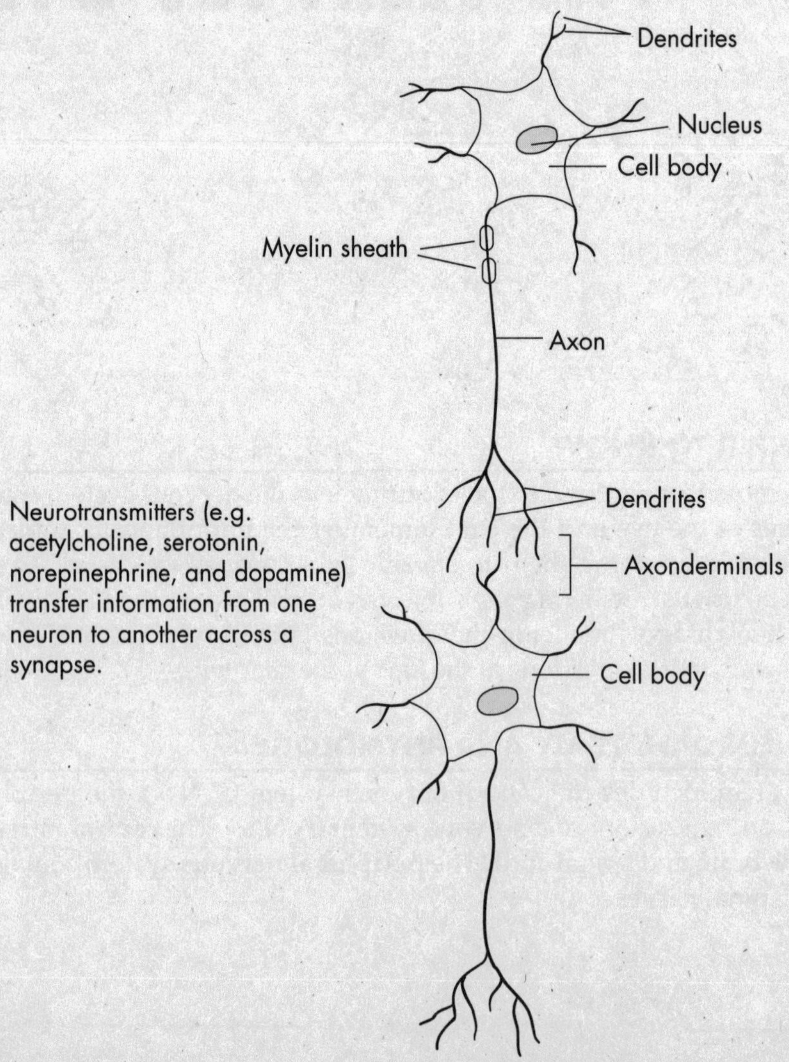

Neurotransmitters (e.g. acetylcholine, serotonin, norepinephrine, and dopamine) transfer information from one neuron to another across a synapse.

- Dendrites
- Nucleus
- Cell body
- Myelin sheath
- Axon
- Dendrites
- Axonderminals
- Cell body

Afferent (sensory) neurons receive information from the periphery of the body and transmit it through the C.N.S. _Efferent_ (motor) neurons conduct information (impulses) from the C.N.S. to muscles and glands.

THE BRAIN

BRAIN

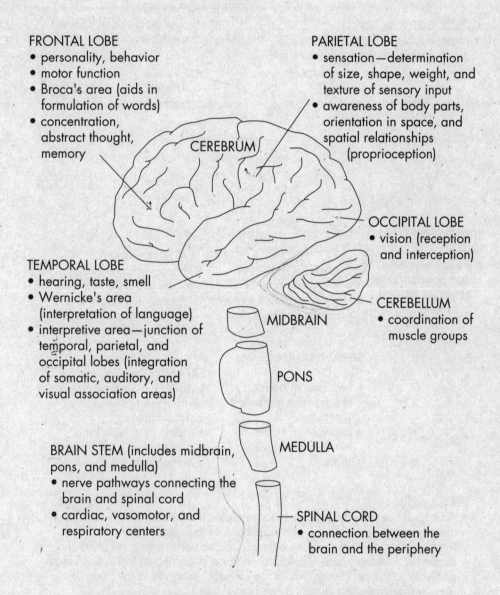

FRONTAL LOBE
- personality, behavior
- motor function
- Broca's area (aids in formulation of words)
- concentration, abstract thought, memory

PARIETAL LOBE
- sensation—determination of size, shape, weight, and texture of sensory input
- awareness of body parts, orientation in space, and spatial relationships (proprioception)

CEREBRUM

OCCIPITAL LOBE
- vision (reception and interception)

TEMPORAL LOBE
- hearing, taste, smell
- Wernicke's area (interpretation of language)
- interpretive area—junction of temporal, parietal, and occipital lobes (integration of somatic, auditory, and visual association areas)

MIDBRAIN

PONS

CEREBELLUM
- coordination of muscle groups

BRAIN STEM (includes midbrain, pons, and medulla)
- nerve pathways connecting the brain and spinal cord
- cardiac, vasomotor, and respiratory centers

MEDULLA

SPINAL CORD
- connection between the brain and the periphery

- The thalamus and hypothalamus are in a region called the DIENCEPHALON, located between the cerebrum and the brain stem.

Thalamus: interpretation of sensation (pain, temperature, touch)

Hypothalamus: temperature control, water metabolism, control of hormonal secretion, heart rate, peristalsis, appetite control, thirst center, sleep-wake cycle

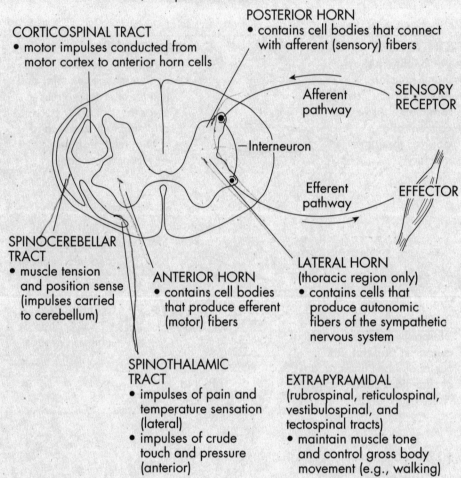

SPINAL CORD

POSTERIOR COLUMN
- impulses of touch, pressure, vibration, and position sense

CORTICOSPINAL TRACT
- motor impulses conducted from motor cortex to anterior horn cells

POSTERIOR HORN
- contains cell bodies that connect with afferent (sensory) fibers

Afferent pathway

SENSORY RECEPTOR

Interneuron

Efferent pathway

EFFECTOR

SPINOCEREBELLAR TRACT
- muscle tension and position sense (impulses carried to cerebellum)

ANTERIOR HORN
- contains cell bodies that produce efferent (motor) fibers

LATERAL HORN
(thoracic region only)
- contains cells that produce autonomic fibers of the sympathetic nervous system

SPINOTHALAMIC TRACT
- impulses of pain and temperature sensation (lateral)
- impulses of crude touch and pressure (anterior)

EXTRAPYRAMIDAL
(rubrospinal, reticulospinal, vestibulospinal, and tectospinal tracts)
- maintain muscle tone and control gross body movement (e.g., walking)

REFLEX ARC
- An impulse received by the sensory receptor (i.e., pain) is carried along the afferent pathway to the posterior horn of the spinal cord. An interneuron creates a synapse between the posterior (sensory) horn and the anterior (motor) horn. The motor impulse is carried along the efferent pathway to the periphery, where the effector responds to the stimulus (i.e., withdrawing hand from a hot stove).

THE TWELVE CRANIAL NERVES

Review the names, order, and basic functions of the twelve cranial nerves here. We will go into more detail about the cranial nerves in the section on neurologic assessment. For now, just associate the cranial nerves with the peripheral nervous system.

The Twelve Cranial Nerves		
Number	Name	Basic Function
I	Olfactory	Smell
II	Optic	Vision
III	Oculomotor	Eye movement
IV	Trochlear	Eye movement
V	Trigeminal	Chewing, facial sensation
VI	Abducent	Eye movement
VII	Facial	Taste, facial movement
VIII	Vestibulocochlear	Hearing, balance
IX	Glossopharyngeal	Taste (posterior tongue), swallowing
X	Vagus	Pharynx, respiratory, cardiac, and circulatory reflexes
XI	Spinal accessory	Shoulders, head movement
XII	Hypoglossal	Tongue movement

Memory tools include remembering that III, IV, and VI (oculomotor, trochlear, and abducent) control eye movement. (On the NCLEX-RN, questions will not require any more detailed knowledge of the cranial nerves.) If VII (facial) controls facial movement and taste, its domain is the anterior tongue, as opposed to the glossopharyngeal nerve (IX) that controls taste on the posterior tongue. XII (the hypoglossal nerve) controls tongue movement.

3 Olfactory
Optic
Oculomotor
2 Trochlear
Trigeminal
Abducent
Facial
Funny Vestibulocochlear
Very Glossopharyngeal
Can Spinal accessory
Spider Hypoglossal
Hurry

Before we review the basic neurologic assessment, quickly assess your retention of neuroanatomy and physiology by filling in the blanks below:

BRAIN

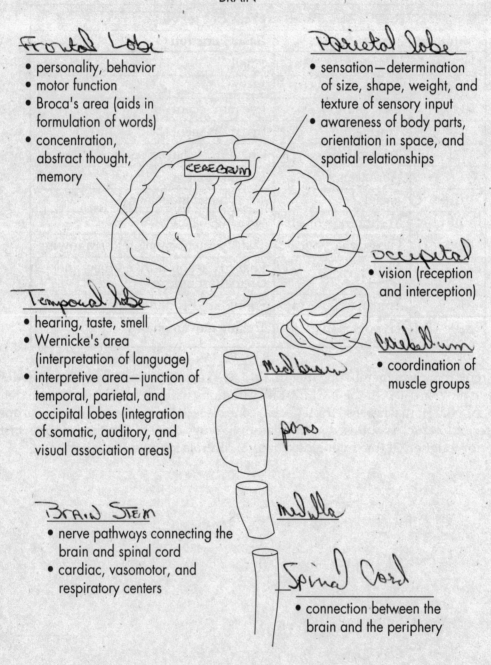

Frontal Lobe
- personality, behavior
- motor function
- Broca's area (aids in formulation of words)
- concentration, abstract thought, memory

Parietal lobe
- sensation—determination of size, shape, weight, and texture of sensory input
- awareness of body parts, orientation in space, and spatial relationships

CEREBRUM

Occipital
- vision (reception and interception)

Temporal lobe
- hearing, taste, smell
- Wernicke's area (interpretation of language)
- interpretive area—junction of temporal, parietal, and occipital lobes (integration of somatic, auditory, and visual association areas)

Midbrain

pons

Cerebellum
- coordination of muscle groups

Brain Stem
- nerve pathways connecting the brain and spinal cord
- cardiac, vasomotor, and respiratory centers

medulla

Spinal Cord
- connection between the brain and the periphery

- The thalamus and hypothalamus are located in a region called the Diencephalon which is located between the cerebrum and the brain stem.

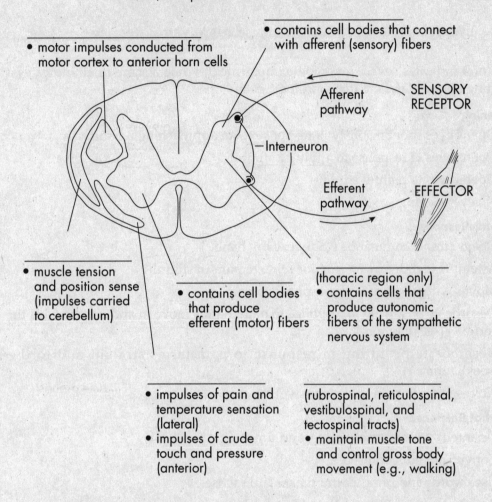

- impulses of touch, pressure, vibration, and position sense

- motor impulses conducted from motor cortex to anterior horn cells

- contains cell bodies that connect with afferent (sensory) fibers

Afferent pathway

SENSORY RECEPTOR

Interneuron

Efferent pathway

EFFECTOR

- muscle tension and position sense (impulses carried to cerebellum)

- contains cell bodies that produce efferent (motor) fibers

(thoracic region only)
- contains cells that produce autonomic fibers of the sympathetic nervous system

- impulses of pain and temperature sensation (lateral)
- impulses of crude touch and pressure (anterior)

(rubrospinal, reticulospinal, vestibulospinal, and tectospinal tracts)
- maintain muscle tone and control gross body movement (e.g., walking)

- An impulse received by the sensory receptor is carried along the afferent pathway to the posterior horn of the spinal cord. An interneuron creates a synapse between the posterior (sensory) horn and the anterior (motor) horn. The motor impulse is carried along the efferent pathway to the periphery, where the effector responds to the stimulus.

NEUROLOGIC ASSESSMENT

1. What is the first thing a nurse should assess to determine the presence of neurological changes? _____LOC_____

Your client's level of consciousness is the best early indicator of neurological status.

Use of the **Glasgow Coma Scale** allows for a consistent and objective assessment of your client's neurological condition and provides an organized summary of a neurological assessment.

The Glasgow Coma Scale
Eye Opening + Best Motor Response + Best Verbal Response = Score

A score of 3 indicates severe neurologic impairment, while a score of 15 indicates a client responding appropriately to the neurologic exam.

Eye Opening

4   Opens eyes spontaneously in response to an approaching person

3   Opens eyes in response to auditory stimuli

2   Opens eyes to painful stimuli

1   No eye opening

Best Motor Response

6   Obeys simple commands ("Squeeze my hand")

5   Attempts to move away from or remove painful stimuli

4   Moves without purpose in response to pain

3   Decorticate posturing in response to pain (hands move in and up, "toward the cortex") (see diagram 1)

2   Decerebrate posturing in response to pain (arms straight and to the side) (see diagram 1)

1   No response to pain (unresponsive)

Best Verbal Response

5   Oriented × 3 (to person, place, and time)

4   Conversant but confused

3   Uses words and phrases, but makes little sense

2   Responds with incomprehensible sounds

1   No verbalization

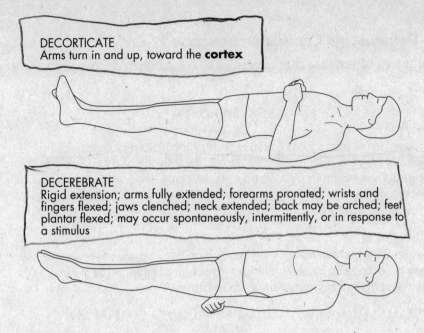

DECORTICATE
Arms turn in and up, toward the **cortex**

DECEREBRATE
Rigid extension; arms fully extended; forearms pronated; wrists and fingers flexed; jaws clenched; neck extended; back may be arched; feet plantar flexed; may occur spontaneously, intermittently, or in response to a stimulus

Diagram 1

CEREBRAL DYSFUNCTION

Cerebral dysfunction is often described using the following terms. Review them and then label the scenarios below with the appropriate term.

Agnosia: The inability to recognize common objects (may be visual, auditory, or tactile)

Apraxia: The inability to perform a skilled motor task, assuming that the client is not paralyzed

Aphasia: The inability to communicate; can be *expressive aphasia* (the inability to speak or difficulty speaking) or *receptive aphasia* (the inability to understand spoken words, to receive information)

2. _C_ A client is able to follow all your commands during physical examination. However, when you ask him about his medical history, his speech is hesitant, his word choice is inappropriate, and he appears extremely frustrated.

3. _A_ While at a client's bedside, you observe a conversation between her and her husband. The husband asks her to pass him a pen (which is on the bedside table directly in front of her). The client stares at the table, but seems unable to recognize the object her husband is requesting.

4. _B_ When asked if he is thirsty, a client nods his head yes. When you hand the client a cup filled with juice, he holds the cup and turns it around in his hands, but never brings the cup to his mouth to drink from it.

5. _D_ A client is awake and alert and seems aware of her surroundings. When you begin physical assessment, she stares at you blankly and is unable to follow any commands.

A. agnosia

B. apraxia

C. expressive aphasia

D. receptive aphasia

RESPIRATORY PATTERNS AND CEREBRAL DYSFUNCTION

Specific respiratory patterns are characteristically found with dysfunction at certain cerebral levels:

VITAL SIGNS

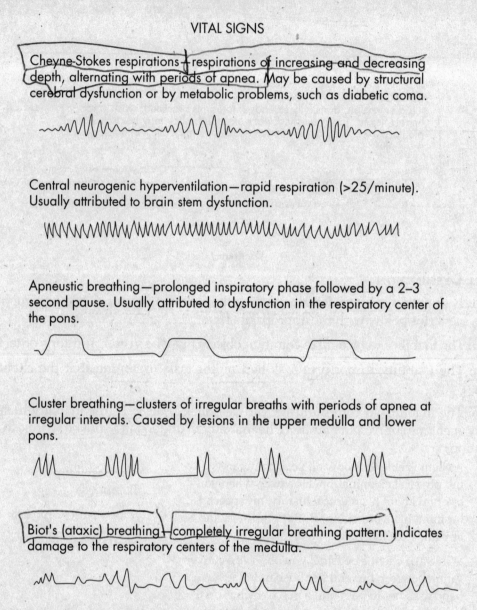

Cheyne-Stokes respirations—respirations of increasing and decreasing depth, alternating with periods of apnea. May be caused by structural cerebral dysfunction or by metabolic problems, such as diabetic coma.

Central neurogenic hyperventilation—rapid respiration (>25/minute). Usually attributed to brain stem dysfunction.

Apneustic breathing—prolonged inspiratory phase followed by a 2–3 second pause. Usually attributed to dysfunction in the respiratory center of the pons.

Cluster breathing—clusters of irregular breaths with periods of apnea at irregular intervals. Caused by lesions in the upper medulla and lower pons.

Biot's (ataxic) breathing—completely irregular breathing pattern. Indicates damage to the respiratory centers of the medulla.

CRANIAL NERVES IN ASSESSING NEUROLOGICAL STATUS

When assessing neurological status, it is important to review which cranial nerves correspond to different impairments as well as any specific nursing interventions that may be indicated. Cranial nerves, remember, are part of the P.N.S. Here we review the basics. Take this knowledge and apply it to the situations presented on the NCLEX-RN. Fill in the name of each cranial nerve in the boxes on the next page.

CN	Fill in the Name	Dysfunction	Interventions
I	*Olfactory*	Decreased sense of smell	Inability to smell is often accompanied by impaired taste and weight loss. Smell serves as a warning for fire, spoiled food, etc.
II	*optic*	Decreased visual acuity and visual fields	Clients require frequent reorientation to environment. Position objects around client in deference to visual field impairment.
III IV VI	*oculomotor* *trochlear* *abducens*	Double vision (diplopia)	Intermittent eye patching for diplopia. Lubricate eyes to protect against corneal abrasions.
V	*trigeminal*	3 (tri-) potential dysfunctions: decreased facial sensation, inability to chew, and decreased corneal reflexes	Caution in shaving and mouth care. Choose easy-to-chew foods with high caloric content. Protect corneas from abrasion by using lubricant.
VII	*Facial*	Facial weakness and decreased taste (anterior tongue)	Cosmetic approach to hiding facial weakness. Oral hygiene. Account for decreased food intake.
VIII	*Vestibular acoustic*	Decreased hearing, imbalance, vertigo (dizziness), tinnitus (ringing in ears)	Safety! Move slowly to prevent nausea and emesis. Assist ambulation.
IX X	*Glossopharyngeal* *Vagus*	Dysarthria (difficulty speaking), dysphagia (difficulty swallowing), cardiac and respiratory instability	Maintain airway. Prevent aspiration. Swallow therapy.
XI	*Spinal accessory*	Inability to turn shoulders or turn head from side to side	Mobility aids. Physical therapy.
XII	*Hypoglossal*	Dysarthria, dysphagia	Maintain airway. Prevent aspiration. Swallow therapy.

ASSESSING MOTOR FUNCTION

Further assessment of motor function includes observing gross motor movement, testing muscle strength, and evaluating the client's gait.

Assessing cerebellar function includes evaluation of balance and coordination. For the NCLEX-RN, know that for *Romberg's test* the client stands erect with feet together, first with eyes open and then closed. If he or she is unable to maintain balance with eyes closed, this is Romberg's sign and indicates cerebellar damage.

Review reflexes that might appear on the NCLEX-RN:

Deep tendon: Reflex response is graded from 0 (no response) to 4 (hyperactive), with 2 being normal (e.g., knee tap).

Superficial: Reflexes elicited by lightly touching a particular area of the skin or mucous membrane. Commonly tested superficial reflexes include corneal, gag, abdominal, and perianal.

Pathological: Babinski's reflex. When the sole of the foot is stroked from the heel to the ball of the foot, the toes should curl downward (negative Babinski's sign). If the toes fan upward, this is termed a positive Babinski's sign and is an abnormal response (after age 2) that suggests brain stem or spinal cord involvement.

ASSESSING SENSORY FUNCTION

In evaluating sensory function, numerous types of sensation awareness may be tested: superficial pain, deep pressure pain, heat and cold sensitivity, vibration sensitivity, texture discrimination, and proprioception (identification of the position of a body part).

The dermatome map below displays areas of spinal nerve innervation and assists in identifying the level of spinal cord damage.

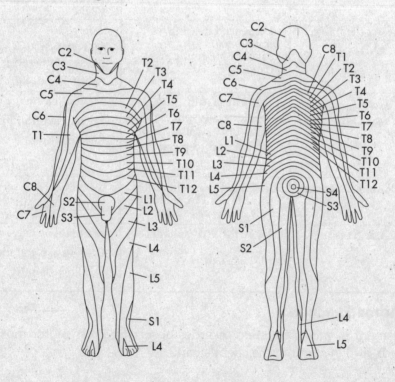

Before we move on to disorders of the nervous system, label the different breathing patterns below and fill in the blank with the associated area of nervous system damage:

VITAL SIGNS

6. *Cheyne Stokes*—respirations of increasing and decreasing depth, alternating with periods of apnea. May be caused by *structural cerebral dysfunction* or by metabolic problems, such as *diabetic coma*.

7. *Central neurogenic hyperventilation*—rapid respiration (>25/minute). Usually attributed to _____ dysfunction.

8. *Apneustic* breathing—prolonged inspiratory phase followed by a 2–3 second pause. Usually attributed to dysfunction in the *resp* _____ center of the _____ .

9. *Cluster* breathing—clusters of irregular breaths with periods of apnea at irregular intervals. Caused by lesions in the upper *medulla* and lower *pons*

10. *Biots breathing* / *Ataxic* breathing—completely irregular breathing pattern. Indicates damage to the respiratory centers of the *medulla*

DISORDERS OF THE NERVOUS SYSTEM

As we review disorders of the nervous system, remember that maintaining a patient's airway is always the primary nursing intervention, unless, of course, there is no risk of airway compromise. Discerning the acuity of the situation (is airway compromise a possibility?) requires basic knowledge of the neurological disorders that may appear on the NCLEX-RN.

Following are some neurologic situations and appropriate nursing interventions. The NCLEX-RN is not limited in its scope of material, so if you are unfamiliar with a scenario, use your common sense to guide your intervention. Remember, the correct answer is always in front of you!

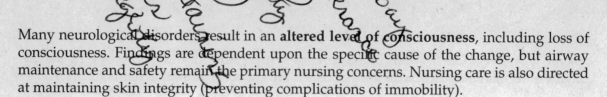

Many neurological disorders result in an **altered level of consciousness**, including loss of consciousness. Findings are dependent upon the specific cause of the change, but airway maintenance and safety remain the primary nursing concerns. Nursing care is also directed at maintaining skin integrity (preventing complications of immobility).

SEIZURES

Seizure disorders are recurrent disturbances in skeletal motor function, sensation, autonomic ("automatic") function, consciousness, or behavior. Epilepsy is the term for chronic, recurrent seizures.

The table below lists the characteristics of each type of seizure.

Type of Seizure	Assessment
Generalized:	
Tonic-clonic (grand mal)	Aura, loss of consciousness, rigidity, repetitive limb movement, postictal lethargy, and confusion
Absence (petit mal)	Brief loss of consciousness, twitching or rolling of eyes
Myoclonic	Brief spasm of a single muscle group
Atonic	Sudden loss of muscle tone, brief loss of consciousness
Partial:	
Simple	Motor, sensory, or autonomic deficits without loss of consciousness
Complex	Cognitive, psychosensory, psychomotor, or affective deficit; may be preceded by aura; brief loss of consciousness

General Intervention for All Seizures
Maintain **safety**; move harmful objects out of the way; protect head.
Do not use a tongue blade or stick anything in the client's mouth.
Allow free movement.
Teach client and family about safety and drug therapy.

The interventions for all seizures are the same. So don't waste your time trying to memorize the specifics of each type, just stick to the basics.

Dilantin (phenytoin sodium) is the most common anticonvulsant drug used to control seizures. For the NCLEX-RN, you need to know that it can only be administered in normal saline, and Dilantin levels are monitored to titrate dosage. The therapeutic Dilantin level is 10–20 mcg/ml. Phenobarbital is a barbiturate used to control seizures. Its main effects and side effects are on the C.N.S. Tegretol (carbamazepine) is used to control seizures that have not responded to other anticonvulsants.

11. With which types of seizures is an aura present?
    A. Tonic clonic
    B. Complex

12. With which types of seizures is there a loss of consciousness?

A. 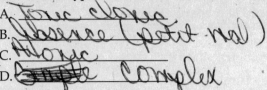 Tonic clonic

B. Absence (petit mal)

C. Atonic

D. ~~Simple~~ Complex

INCREASED INTRACRANIAL PRESSURE

Increased intracranial pressure is caused by tumors, abscesses, edema, hemorrhage, and/or inflammation. Remember, the skull is a fixed space. When one component expands, another part has to give. The client with increased I.C.P. presents with an altered level of consciousness, bradycardia, altered respirations, and projectile vomiting. The following nursing interventions in the presence of increased I.C.P. are directed at minimizing stimuli and promoting venous drainage:

- Maintain airway; limit suctioning to 15 seconds or less.
- Elevate head of bed about 30 degrees.
- Maintain neck in neutral position to promote venous drainage.
- Maintain quiet environment.
- Prevent Valsalva's maneuver by ensuring proper bowel routine.
- Maintain fluid balance (diuretics may be ordered by the provider to decrease fluid volume).

HEADACHES

There are different kinds of **headaches**, each of which requires determination of the cause before treatment is initiated. Careful assessment of the circumstances and characteristics of the headache is imperative, as is environmental control to reduce frequency and acuity of the headache. The nurse is in a prime position to teach the client about alternative methods of pain control.

MENINGITIS

Meningitis is inflammation of the meninges of the brain and spinal cord. It is caused by bacteria (*Haemophilus influenzae, Neisseria meningitidis*, and *Diplococcus pneumoniae*), viruses, or other microorganisms that infect the meninges. Here is a list of symptoms of meningitis and related nursing interventions:

Assessment Findings
- Fever
- Lethargy
- Confusion
- Nuchal rigidity (stiff neck)
- Kernig's sign (see diagram 2)
- Brudzinski's sign (see diagram 2)

Meningitis

Nursing Interventions

- Place client in isolation (depends on hospital protocol).
- Maintain client safety.
- Monitor vital signs and neurological status.
- Prepare client for lumbar puncture.
- (Antibiotics will be ordered by the provider.)

Signs of Meningitis

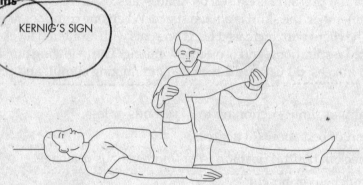

Kernig's sign is present if the lower leg cannot extend due to pain and spasm when a client is lying supine with one leg bent over his abdomen.

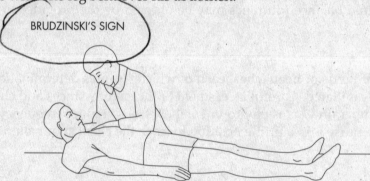

Brudzinski's sign is present if the client's hips and knees flex when he is lying supine with his head lifted towards his chest.

Diagram 2

ENCEPHALITIS

Encephalitis is an inflammation of the brain caused by viruses, bacteria, fungi, or parasites and can occur in connection with diseases such as measles, mumps, or chicken pox. Encephalitis (remember— -itis is inflammation!) presents as a fever, headache, seizures, and stiff neck. Nursing care is the same as for a client with increased intracranial pressure and seizures. Interventions are also similar to those for meningitis.

BRAIN ABSCESS

A **brain abscess** is caused by an infection extending into the cerebral tissue or by organisms carried from other sites in the body (middle ear, mastoid, or sinus). An abscess is always some sort of infection that presents with the typical chills, fever, malaise, and elevated white blood cell count. Because this abscess is in the brain, headache may often times be a symptom. Provide nursing care for the client with an infection and increased intracranial pressure. (Remember, the head has a fixed volume; an abscess takes up unavailable space, thereby increasing the intracranial pressure.) Provide preoperative teaching if the client is to undergo a craniotomy to drain the abscess.

BRAIN TUMORS

Brain tumors are divided into a number of categories, none of which is important for the NCLEX-RN. What is important to remember is that nursing care for brain tumor clients is aimed at treating the deficits experienced by the individual client. In addition, the nurse should also provide the appropriate care for the client with increased intracranial pressure (the head has a fixed volume) and provide teaching applicable to the chosen treatment modality.

CEREBROVASCULAR ACCIDENTS

Cerebrovascular accidents (C.V.A.'s) are characterized by the gradual or rapid, nonconvulsive onset of neurologic deficits that fit a known vascular territory and last for at least 24 hours. They result from reduced cerebral blood flow and oxygen deprivation related to a thrombus (clot), embolism, or hemorrhage (bleeding). Often characterized by facial droop, lateral weakness, or flaccidity, alterations in mental status can also be indicative of a C.V.A. Nursing care is directed at maintaining a patient's airway in the face of mental status changes, and safety! The sensory and motor deficits often experienced by these clients require diligent nursing attention. The list below includes nursing concerns (following airway maintenance and safety) for the client with deficits related to a C.V.A.:

- Potential for aspiration: A swallowing evaluation is imperative to ascertain the extent of dysphagia caused by the C.V.A.; aspiration precautions must be maintained, food should be pureed (no liquid) and calorie-dense
- Altered nutritional status: Encourage pureed, calorie-dense foods; tube feedings may be indicated if nutritional intake is suboptimal
- Altered elimination patterns
- Altered skin integrity
- Impaired communication
- Impaired vision

ANEURYSMS

An **aneurysm** is an outpouching of an artery. A **cerebral aneurysm** is the outpouching of a cerebral artery. Rupture of a cerebral aneurysm results in a subarachnoid hemorrhage. Neurological deficits may also occur if the aneurysm is compressing cranial nerves or is pressing on brain substance. Aneurysm rupture precautions are:

- Quiet, dark environment
- Head of the bed at 30–45 degrees
- Limit visitation to decrease stimuli
- Avoid Valsalva's maneuver
- Avoid rectal temperatures (vagal nerve stimulation)
- Suction only as absolutely necessary

Safe environment

PARKINSON'S DISEASE

Parkinson's disease is a progressive, degenerative disorder caused by dopamine (neurotransmitter) depletion, and resulting in a generalized decline in muscular function. Cardinal signs of Parkinson's disease are:

- Tremor at rest
- Rigidity
- Slow movement
- Shuffling gait
- Mask-like face
- Emotional lability
- Autonomic symptoms: Drooling, sweating, constipation

The nurse's primary responsibility for the client with Parkinson's disease is to maintain a safe environment in deference to the decline in muscular function. In addition, anti-Parkinson's medications have numerous side effects, including constipation, urine retention, blurred vision, and dizziness. It is vital that the client be allowed to maximize his/her independence. A high-calorie diet is recommended in order to minimize the effects of decreased food intake.

MULTIPLE SCLEROSIS

Safety

Multiple sclerosis is a progressive C.N.S. disorder caused by demyelination in the brain and spinal cord. Symptoms vary with the location of demyelination (look back at the anatomy of the brain and spinal cord) but may include visual deficits, diminished sensation, weakness, and paralysis. Nursing interventions are aimed at **safety** and maximizing the client's independence. Clients with multiple sclerosis should be encouraged to follow a diet low in saturated fat.

MYASTHENIA GRAVIS

Myasthenia gravis is an autoimmune disorder (the body is fighting itself) causing disturbances in the transmission of impulses from nerves to muscles resulting in extreme muscle weakness. This chart will help you remember the edophonium chloride (Tensilon) test (the NCLEX-RN loves this test).

Edrophonium Chloride (Tensilon) Test
Differentiates between myasthenia gravis and a cholinergic crisis.
If muscle strength improves with the administration of Tensilon, then mysathenia gravis is diagnosed.

You should know by now that the primary nursing concern is **safety** and maintaining a patent airway when necessary. In a myasthenic crisis, the client will experience sensory deficits, including double vision, difficulty swallowing, ptosis (eye droop), restlessness, and sweating. As always, nutrition is a concern with these clients. Food should be high in calories, and tube (enteric) feedings may be indicated.

Treatment for myasthenia gravis includes rest and anticholinesterase drugs (neostigmine or [Prostigmin], pyridostigmine or [Mestinon]). Observation for signs of a cholinergic crisis (the result of anticholinesterase overdose) is imperative. The following brief chart should help you remember the diagnostic test for, and signs of, a cholinergic crisis.

Cholinergic Crisis
Differentiates by a negative Tensilon test (symptoms worsen with Tensilon administration)
Signs very similar to those of a myasthenic crisis except: • Hypotension   • Bradycardia

DISORDERS OF THE CRANIAL NERVES

Trigeminal neuralgia is a disorder involving the trigeminal nerve (cranial nerve V; tri-) causing severe pain along the sensory distribution of the nerve.

13. Write in the parts of the body that the trigeminal nerve controls:
    A. _facial sensation_
    B. _corneal reflex_
    C. _mastication muscles_

For clients with trigeminal neuralgia, small, frequent meals at lukewarm temperatures are recommended, and environmental temperature extremes should be avoided. Good oral hygiene and protective eyewear are also important.

Bell's palsy is a disorder involving the facial nerve causing facial paralysis on one side.

14. The facial nerve is cranial nerve _VII_.
15. The facial nerve controls _taste_ and _facial movement_

OTHER DISORDERS OF THE NERVOUS SYSTEM

There are certain neurologic disorders you should recognize for the NCLEX-RN. Match the following syndromes with the appropriate definitions:

16. _A_ Possibly an autoimmune disorder characterized by progressive ascending paralysis that most often ceases in approximately 4 weeks, with complete recovery taking 3–6 months. The disease causes motor weakness symmetrically and in an ascending fashion. The client's airway is compromised when the disease reaches the diaphragm.

17. _C_ A progressive, fatal, motor neuron disease causing progressive muscular atrophy.

18. _B_ An inherited disorder causing progressive atrophy of the basal ganglia and portions of the cerebral cortex. Cardinal symptoms include extreme emotional lability, dementia, and uncontrolled limb movements.

A. Guillain-Barré syndrome

B. Huntington's chorea

C. Lou Gehrig's disease

NERVOUS SYSTEM INJURIES

HEAD INJURIES

Head injuries can occur in a variety of different settings. Traumatic injury is most often caused by car accidents, falls, or assaults. Assessment findings are specific to the type of injury.

Type of Injury	Description	Symptoms
Concussion	A blow to the head causes the brain to strike the skull.	Headache, transient loss of consciousness, amnesia, nausea
Contusion	A blow to the head causes a bruise of the brain.	Decreased level of consciousness, aphasia, hemiplegia
Hemorrhage	Blood accumulates in the head; can be anywhere.	Symptoms are specific to location.
Fracture	Skull is cracked or broken.	Headache at site, cerebrospinal fluid (C.S.F.) leakage from nose or ear

SPINAL CORD INJURIES

Spinal cord injuries may be divided into traumatic and nontraumatic (tumors, hematomas, aneurysms, congenital disease) injuries. Assessment findings and treatment are based on the extent and level of the injury. Interventions may be divided into acute/emergency management and chronic management.

Type of Injury	Description	Symptoms	Nursing Interventions
Acute injury	Spinal shock	• Absence of reflexes below the injury • Flaccid paralysis • Urine retention • Hypotension • Bradycardia • Temperature lability	• **Airway**, breathing, circulation (ABC)! • Immobilize client to prevent further injury • Prevent complications of immobility
Chronic injury	Sensory and motor dysfunction may be partial or complete, based on level of spinal cord injury	Traction as indicated: • Gardner-Wells (cervical tongs) • Halo device	• ABC! • Prevent complications of immobility • Meticulous pin site care to prevent infection

Complications of immobility include skin breakdown (turn and position the client every 2–3 hours) and constipation. Increase fiber and fluids in the client's diet unless contraindicated. In addition, the formation of a deep vein thrombosis is a life-threatening complication of immobility. The client may be on low-dose heparin therapy and/or be wearing antiembolic stockings.

ANATOMY OF THE EYE

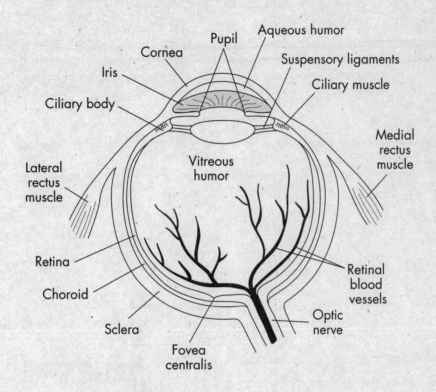

Pupil

Cornea

Iris

Ciliary body

Aqueous humor

Suspensory ligaments

Ciliary muscle

Medial rectus muscle

Lateral rectus muscle

Vitreous humor

Retina

Choroid

Sclera

Fovea centralis

Retinal blood vessels

Optic nerve

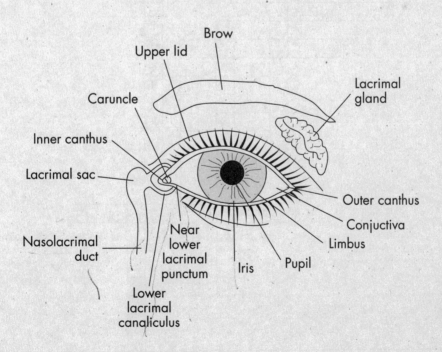

Brow

Upper lid

Caruncle

Inner canthus

Lacrimal sac

Nasolacrimal duct

Lacrimal gland

Near lower lacrimal punctum

Iris

Pupil

Outer canthus

Conjuctiva

Limbus

Lower lacrimal canaliculus

THE EAR

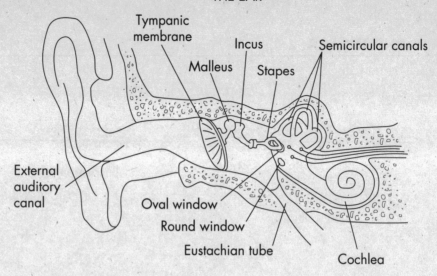

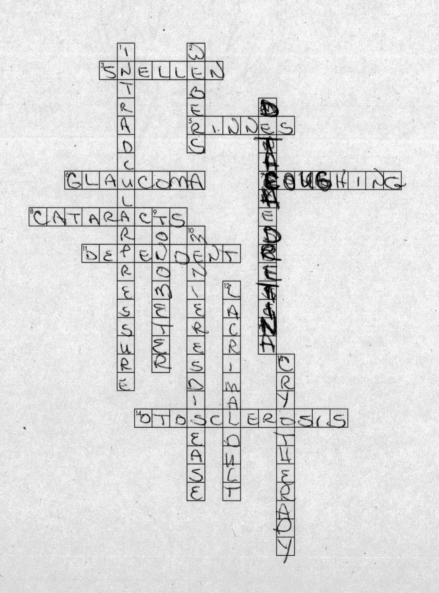

Select words from the following list to fill in the crossword puzzle:

cataracts
coughing
cryotherapy
dependent
detached retina
glaucoma
intraocular pressure

lacrimal duct
Meniere's disease
otosclerosis
Rinne's
Snellen
tonometer
Weber's

ACROSS

3. The _____ chart is used to assess visual acuity.

5. Placing a tuning fork on the mastoid process until sound is no longer heard, and then holding it in front of the ear to test for air conduction is called the _____ test.

6. Tunnel vision, eye pain, and halos around lights are signs of _____.

7. _____ is contraindicated for postoperative eye surgery clients.

8. Signs of _____ include: blurred vision, milky white pupils, progressive vision loss, and a glare in bright light.

11. Nursing care for the client with a detached retina includes bed rest with the head of the bed flat, a bilateral eye patch, and positioning the client with the affected area in a _____ position.

14. _____: The formation of spongy bone in the labyrinth of the ear causing fixation of the stapes in the oval window. Client presents with progressive hearing loss, tinnitus, and conductive hearing loss.

DOWN

1. In order to prevent increased _____, clients should be taught to avoid stooping and lifting, coughing, sneezing, emotional upsets, and excessive fluids.

2. The _____ test uses a vibrating tuning fork placed on the midline of a client's skull to test for conductive vs. sensorineural hearing loss.

4. Flashes of light, floaters, and visual field deficits are signs of _____.

9. Intraocular pressure is measured by a _____; normal pressure is 10–20 mm Hg.

10. Recurrent and progressive vertigo, tinnitus, and hearing loss are indicative of _____.

12. To prevent systemic effects of miotics, pressure should be placed on the _____ after instillation.

13. _____ is a treatment for detached retina which is used to produce a chorioretinal scar to allow the retina to return to its normal position.

CHAPTER 4: EXERCISE ANSWERS

1. What is the first thing a nurse should assess to determine the presence of neurologic changes?
   Level of consciousness

2. **C** **expressive aphasia**—Mr. Jones is able to follow all commands during your physical examination. However, when you ask him about his medical history, his speech is hesitant, his word choice is inappropriate, and he appears extremely frustrated.

3. **A** **agnosia**—While at Ms. Smith's bedside, you observe a conversation between Ms. Smith and her husband. Mr. Smith asks her to pass him a pen (which is on the bedside table directly in front of her). Ms. Smith stares at the table, but seems unable to recognize which object her husband is requesting.

4. **B** **apraxia**—When asked if he is thirsty, Mr. Mark nods his head yes. When you hand Mr. Mark a cup filled with juice, he holds the cup and turns it around in his hands, but never brings the cup to his mouth to drink from it.

5. **D** **receptive aphasia**—Miss Gray is awake and alert and seems aware of her surroundings. When you begin your physical assessment, Miss Gray stares blankly at you and is unable to follow any commands.

6. **Cheyne-Stokes respirations**—respirations of increasing and decreasing depth, alternating with periods of apnea. May be caused by **structural cerebral dysfunction** or by metabolic problems, such as **diabetic coma.**

7. **Central neurogenic hyperventilation**—rapid respiration (>25/minute). Usually attributed to **brain stem** dysfunction.

8. **Apneustic** breathing—prolonged inspiratory phase followed by a 2–3 second pause. Usually attributed to dysfunction in the **respiratory** center of the **pons.**

9. **Cluster** breathing—clusters of irregular breaths with periods of apnea at irregular intervals. Caused by lesions in the upper **medulla** and lower **pons**.

10. **Biot's (ataxic)** breathing—completely irregular breathing pattern. Indicates damage to the respiratory centers of the **medulla**.

11. With which types of seizures is an aura present?

    A. complex partial

    B. tonic-clonic (grand mal)

12. With which types of seizures is there a loss of consciousness?

    A. absence (petit mal)

    B. atonic

    C. complex partial

    D. tonic-clonic (grand mal)

13. Write in the parts of the body that the trigeminal nerve controls: **facial sensation, corneal reflex, mastication muscles**.

14. The facial nerve is cranial nerve **VII**.

15. The facial nerve controls **facial movement** and **anterior taste**.

16. **A Guillain-Barré syndrome**—Possibly an autoimmune disorder characterized by progressive ascending paralysis that most often ceases in approximately 4 weeks, with complete recovery taking 3–6 months. The disease causes motor weakness symmetrically and in an ascending fashion. The client's airway is compromised when the disease reaches the diaphragm.

17. **C Lou Gehrig's disease**—A progressive, fatal, motor neuron disease causing progressive muscular atrophy.

18. **B Huntington's chorea**—An inherited disorder causing progressive atrophy of the basal ganglia and portions of the cerebral cortex. Cardinal symptoms include extreme emotional lability, dementia, and uncontrolled limb movements.

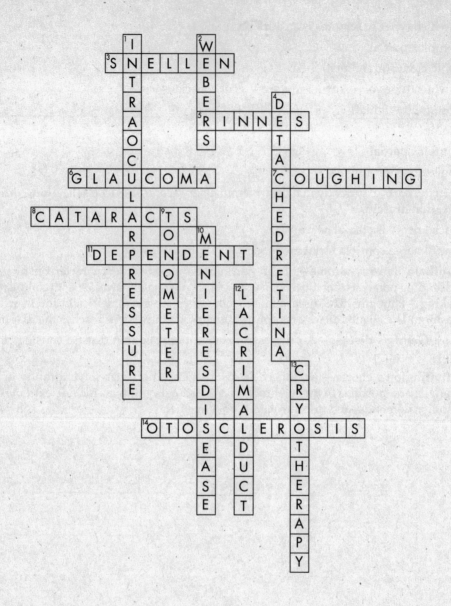

CHAPTER 4: NCLEX-RN STYLE QUESTIONS

1. A head-injured, unconscious child requires skilled nursing care. Which is not a priority when caring for an unconscious child?

   (1) Frequent neurologic checks
   (2) Frequent vital signs
   (3) Everyday weights
   (4) Pain assessment

2. The nurse is performing a neurological assessment on a client with a recent history of head injury. Which of the following is the most sensitive indicator of neurologic functioning?

   (1) Motor ability
   (2) Level of consciousness
   (3) Speech pattern
   (4) Memory

3. Which of the following assessment methodologies is most effective in eliciting a response to pain in a comatose client?

   (1) Using a nail bed pressure
   (2) Pinching the client's nipple
   (3) Squeezing the client's underarm
   (4) Pricking the client with a sharp object

4. A client has been diagnosed with a cerebellar disorder. Which of the following nursing diagnoses is based upon the assessment data for this disorder?

   (1) At risk for injury related to unsteady gait
   (2) Ineffective breathing pattern related to respiratory muscle weakness
   (3) Impaired verbal communication related to cranial nerve dysfunction
   (4) Alteration in body temperature related to damage to the thermoregulatory center

5. The provider has ordered Dilantin IV for a client with severe seizure activity newly admitted to the unit. Which of the following factors are a priority for the nurse's administration of intravenous Dilantin?

   (1) Mix with a solution of D5W piggy-backed with other infusions to ensure prompt administration of all medications needed.
   (2) Monitor carefully for hypertension, muscular excitability, and hyperpnea.
   (3) Expect evidence of increased oxygen demand and uptake of oxygen by the myocardial cells resulting in increased pulse rate.
   (4) Before giving IV Dilantin, assess the client for possible alcohol intake and amount consumed prior to coming to the hospital.

6. The nurse is caring for a client with increased intracranial pressure (I.C.P.). Which of the following nurse interventions is related to the goal of establishing cerebral tissue perfusion?

   (1) Perform passive range-of-motion to the neck.
   (2) Elevate the head of the bed 30 degrees.
   (3) Suction every 2 hours and p.r.n..
   (4) Encourage coughing and deep breathing.

7. When a client has a generalized tonic-clonic seizure, the nursing priority is to

   (1) call the code for cardiac arrest.
   (2) hold the client's extremities down.
   (3) protect the client from immediate injury and allow free movement.
   (4) place an oxygen mask on the client.

8.	The nurse is caring for a client with a head injury. The nurse should be on the alert for signs of increased intracranial pressure, which include	(1) a change in the level of consciousness. (2) bilateral pupil size increase. (3) narrowing pulse pressure. (4) tachycardia.
9.	A client has had a craniotomy to remove a brain tumor. The postoperative orders include maintaining the head of the bed at 45 degrees and turning the client from side to side. In positioning after a craniotomy, which of the following actions is contraindicated?	(1) Placing the client on the side with the head supported in a neutral position and hips flexed. (2) Placing the client on the side with the head supported in a neutral position and a pillow between the client's knees. (3) Placing the client on the back with both arms slightly elevated on pillows. (4) Placing the client on the back with the head supported in a neutral position and the arms slightly elevated.

CHAPTER 4: NCLEX-RN STYLE ANSWERS

1.

(3) CORRECT	Weighing the unconscious child is not a priority.
(1) ELIMINATE	The question asks which is not a priority. Neurologic checks are a priority, as this would detect subtle changes that may require intervention.
(2) ELIMINATE	Vital signs are a priority, as abnormal findings may require intervention.
(4) ELIMINATE	Pain must be assessed very frequently, as it can cause an increase in intracranial pressure.

CATEGORY 10 PHYSIOLOGICAL ADAPTATION

2.

(2) CORRECT	An alteration in the level of consciousness precedes all other neurologic changes, and is more reflective of generalized cerebral function.
(1) ELIMINATE	Motor ability is related to intact upper and lower motor neurons, and to an intact peripheral nervous system. Therefore, changes in motor ability are evidence of narrow and specific deviations.
(3) ELIMINATE	Deterioration in speech is too narrow a parameter upon which to base neurologic function. Alterations in speech may be related to speech centers of the brain, to a cognitive deficit, or simply to localized trauma to the tongue or other structures that influence the quality of speech.
(4) ELIMINATE	Memory changes are related to narrowly prescribed memory centers of the brain.

CATEGORY 09 REDUCTION OF RISK POTENTIAL

3. (1) CORRECT   This method is the least damaging, of the examples given, to skin integrity and is sufficiently effective in eliciting a response to pain.

    (2) ELIMINATE   Pinching the nipple may cause harm to the integrity of the structure of the nipple, which is unnecessary since there are less damaging methods of eliciting response to pain.

    (3) ELIMINATE   Squeezing the underarm may impair the integrity of the sensitive skin located in this area.

    (4) ELIMINATE   In addition to impairing the integrity of the skin, this method places the client at risk of infection, especially if this method is repeated each time the client is assessed.

CATEGORY 04 PREVENTION AND EARLY DETECTION OF DISEASE

4. (1) CORRECT   Cerebellar disorders are characterized by lack of balance and coordination. Ataxia and rhythmic involuntary movements are also characteristic.

    (2) ELIMINATE   Cerebellar dysfunction impairs coordinated voluntary movements. Respiratory muscle weakness is not characteristic.

    (3) ELIMINATE   Cranial nerves originate mostly in the brain stem and not in the cerebellum. Cerebellar disease is related to balance and voluntary movement.

    (4) ELIMINATE   Thermoregulatory centers are located in the hypothalamus and alterations in body temperature are not a characteristic of cerebellar dysfunction.

CATEGORY 09 REDUCTION OF RISK POTENTIAL

5. (4) CORRECT   Alcohol will cause acute potentiation of the central nervous system and will depress effects of Dilantin. Alcohol will also increase the serum level of Dilantin by competing at receptor sites. The provider should be informed if the nurse determines that the client has consumed alcohol. The provider may adjust the dose or select another medication to avoid severe C.N.S. or respiratory complications.

    (1) ELIMINATE   Dilantin must be mixed with normal saline only and is incompatible with all other medications in solution.

    (2) ELIMINATE   Dilantin will cause hypotension and muscle weakness as a side effect.

    (3) ELIMINATE   Administer cautiously in clients with myocardial insufficiency or heart block. Dilantin will cause decreased oxygenation of myocardial cells and depression of myocardial functioning.

CATEGORY 08 PHARMACOLOGICAL AND PARENTERAL THERAPIES

6. (2) CORRECT   Elevation of the head promotes venous return by the jugular veins, which is assisted by gravity. Increased intracranial pressure (I.C.P.) is swelling of the brain, and elevating the head prevents further swelling.

    (1) ELIMINATE   Neck motion causes intermittent flexion of the jugular veins, decreasing venous return and tissue perfusion and increasing intracranial pressure.

    (3) ELIMINATE   Suctioning increases coughing and intra-abdominal pressure, which increases intracranial pressure.

    (4) ELIMINATE   Coughing causes the use of the Valsalva's maneuver, increasing intrathoracic and intracranial pressure.

CATEGORY 09 REDUCTION OF RISK POTENTIAL

7	(3) CORRECT	Safety is always the priority, and the client should be allowed to move freely.
	(1) ELIMINATE	Cardiac arrest codes should not be used for this purpose.
	(2) ELIMINATE	Holding the extremities can lead to injury.
	(4) POSSIBLE	Administration of oxygen is sometimes appropriate after a seizure, but the priority in this situation is safety.

CATEGORY 02 SAFETY AND INFECTION CONTROL

8.	(1) CORRECT	One of the earliest and most sensitive signs of increased intracranial pressure is a change in the level of consciousness.
	(2) ELIMINATE	Unilateral change in pupil size is a sign of increased intracranial pressure.
	(3) ELIMINATE	Widening pulse pressure is a sign of increased intracranial pressure.
	(4) ELIMINATE	Bradycardia is a sign of increased intracranial pressure.

CATEGORY 09 REDUCTION OF RISK POTENTIAL

9.	(2) CORRECT	Proper positioning requires support of the neck in a neutral position to facilitate venous drainage. Pillows should always be placed between the knees. Hip flexion can cause increased intracranial pressure.
	(1) ELIMINATE	This position is not appropriate for a post-op craniotomy patient.
	(3) ELIMINATE	Arms should be slightly elevated to avoid dependent edema.
	(4) ELIMINATE	This position is not appropriate for a post-op craniotomy patient.

CATEGORY 09 REDUCTION OF RISK POTENTIAL

5

THE CARDIOVASCULAR SYSTEM

WHAT YOU NEED TO KNOW

While the cardiovascular system can seem overwhelming when you are not directly applying the concepts to a client, remember that the heart is really just a pump. The NCLEX-RN requires that you know enough to keep that pump pumping! Don't get bogged down in details that you won't retain anyway until you get out into the field.

REVIEW OF CARDIOVASCULAR ANATOMY AND PHYSIOLOGY

Fill in the blanks using the following words:

atria	left	right
diastole	myocardium	systole
endocardium	pericardium	ventricles
epicardium		

The heart is composed of specialized tissue that contracts and relaxes in a coordinated fashion. The outer surface of the heart is known as the (1.) _epicardium_ The (2.) _endocardium_ is the inner surface of the heart that comes in contact with the blood, and the heart muscle itself is the (3.) _myocardium_ The (4.) _pericardium_ is a thin, fibrous sac that surrounds the heart's surface and serves as protection.

Contraction of the heart muscle is referred to as (5.) _systole_, while relaxation of the heart muscle is referred to as (6.) _diastole_. The chambers of the heart are the (7.) _atria_ and the (8.) _ventricles_ The (9.) _left_ ventricle provides blood to the entire body; therefore, its wall is thicker than that of the (10.) _right_ ventricle.

HEART
Interior View

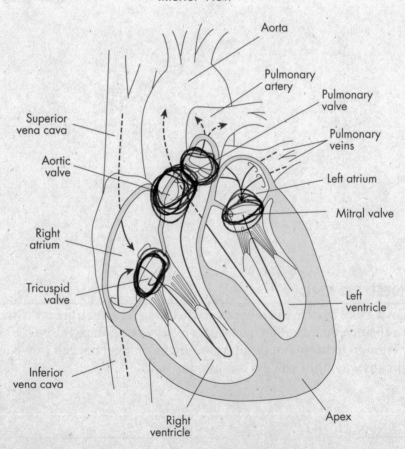

Match the valves with the correct anatomic location:

11. _A_ Located between the right ventricle and the pulmonary artery

12. _C_ Located between the left ventricle and the aorta

13. _D_ Located between the right atrium and the right ventricle

14. _B_ Located between the left atrium and the left ventricle

A. aortic valve

B. mitral valve

C. pulmonary valve

D. tricuspid valve

Specialized cells in the heart conduct electrical impulses to myocardial cells, resulting in contraction. The **sinoatrial node** initiates impulses that are conducted along the myocardial cells to the **atrioventricular node**. The impulse then travels through specialized fibers called the **bundle of His** and terminates in the **Purkinje's fibers**, resulting in **systole** (contraction).

Arrange the following parts of the heart in the order of the conduction pathway of the heart, and then fill in the blanks.

40–60 ——— _2_ atrioventricular node _4_ Purkinje's fibers

60–100 ——— _3_ bundle of His _1_ sinoatrial node

The (15.) _SA node_ is known as the pacemaker of the heart and has an intrinsic rate of (16.) _60-100_ beats per minute. The (17.) _AV node_ has an intrinsic rate of (18.) _40-60_ beats per minute. The (19.) _bundle of his_ are specialized muscle fibers in the septum carrying the impulse to the (20.) _Purkinje fibers_, where it terminates, resulting in contraction of the muscle.

CONDUCTION PATHWAY IN THE HEART

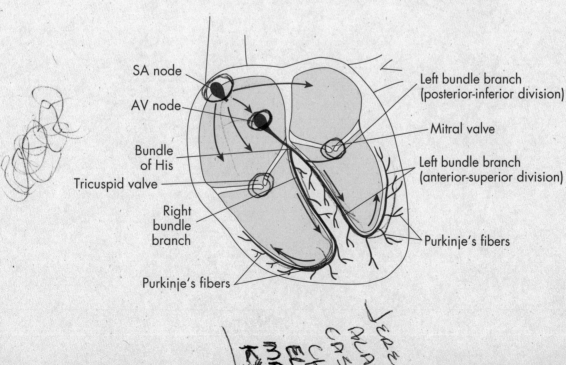

The heart has an anatomic and physiologic pump cycle. Match the parts of the cardiac cycle below with the correct description.

21. _H_ Amount of blood ejected in a heartbeat STROKE VOL

22. _D_ Atrioventricular valves open, returning blood from veins to the atria and the ventricles; ventricles are relaxed DIASTOLE

23. _I_ Atrioventricular valves close and ventricle contracts SYSTOLE

24. _E_ Measure of myocardial contractility, percentage of blood emptied from the ventricle during contraction ejection fraction

25. _F_ End diastolic ventricular volume preload

26. _A_ Tension in the ventricular wall during contraction afterload

27. _C_ The inside of myocardial cells becomes less negative and contraction of the myocardium occurs depolarization

28. _G_ The inside of myocardial cells becomes more negative and relaxation of the myocardium occurs repolarization

29. _B_ Amount of blood pumped by ventricle during a time period; equals stroke volume × heart rate CO

A. afterload
B. cardiac output
C. depolarization
D. diastole
E. ejection fraction
F. preload
G. repolarization
H. stroke volume
I. systole

CARDIOVASCULAR HISTORY AND PHYSICAL ASSESSMENT

A cardiovascular nursing assessment should include the identification of risk factors for **coronary artery disease**.

30. List eight risk factors for coronary artery disease:

    A. SMOKING

    B. ↑ CHOLESTEROL

    C. HTN

    D. DM

    E. PHYSICAL INACTIVITY

    F. HYPERLIPIDEMIA

    G. ↑ AGE

    H. OBESITY

    STESS   USE OF ORAL CONTRACEPTIVES

31. Identify the areas of inspection and palpation of the chest during the physical assessment:

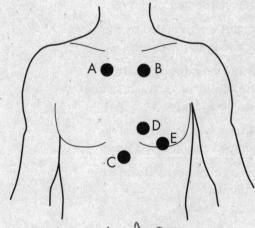

aortic

apical

epigastric

pulmonary

tricuspid

A. AORTIC

B. PULMONARY

C. EPIGASTRIC

D. TRICUSPID

E. APICAL

HEART SOUNDS

Heart sounds are produced by the closure of the **atrioventricular valves**. Assign the following heart sounds to the appropriate description:

32. __F__ Heard during rapid ventricular filling and can be a normal finding in young children; often associated with congestive heart failure and failure of ventricles to eject blood   *S3*

33. __D__ Heard over mitral area; created by closure of the mitral and tricuspid valves   *S1*

34. __G__ Heard during atrial contractions and often associated with ventricular hypertrophy and resistance to filling; also associated with coronary artery disease, hypertension, aortic stenosis   *S4*

35. __E__ Heard at the base of the heart; created by the closure of the aortic and pulmonic valves   *S2*

36. __C__ Created by the flow of blood through narrow valves or incomplete closure of valves, resulting in prolonged sounds   *murmurs*

37. __B__ Transient sounds during systole and diastole, associated with an impedance to blood flow   *gallops*

38. __A__ Caused by the abrasion of pericardial surfaces secondary to inflammation   *friction rubs*

A. friction rubs

B. gallops

C. murmurs

D. S1

E. S2

F. S3

G. S4

ELECTROCARDIOGRAMS

An **electrocardiogram** (E.C.G.) is the visual representation of the heart's conduction system (electrical activity). It is particularly useful in identifying disturbances in the rate and rhythm of the heart, electrolyte imbalances, the presence of myocardial ischemia or infarction, enlargement of heart chambers, and conduction problems.

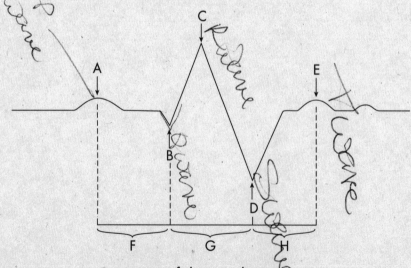

Components of electrocardiogram waves

39. Identify the following parts of the diagram:

~~P wave~~	A.	*P WAVE*
~~P-R interval~~	B.	*Q Wave*
~~Q wave~~	C.	*R Wave*
~~QRS complex~~	D.	*S Wave*
~~R wave~~	E.	*T wave*
~~S wave~~	F.	*P-R interval*
~~S-T segment~~	G.	*QRS complex*
T wave	H.	*S.T seg*

Match the waves and segments to the appropriate statements below:

40. *S Wave* Second negative deflection after the P wave

41. *Q wave* First negative deflection after the P wave

42. *R Wave* First positive deflection after the P wave

43. ~~P-R interval~~ Represents the impulse traveling from the atria through the conduction system

44. *S-T seg* Represents early ventricular repolarization

45. *T wave* Represents ventricular muscle repolarization

46. *P wave* Represents atrial depolarization

47. *QRS complex* Represents ventricular depolarization

RESPIRATORY ASSESSMENT

Because the heart and lungs depend on each other for effective functioning, the respiratory assessment is an important part of the cardiovascular physical assessment. Match the following respiratory terms with the appropriate descriptions:

48. _B_ Noted for apneic periods; often associated with severe left ventricular failure

49. _C_ Indicative of pulmonary edema, characterized by pink or blood-tinged frothy sputum

50. _E_ Rapid, shallow breathing often associated with congestive heart failure, pain, or anxiety

51. _D_ Often noted at the bases of the lungs; progresses upward; associated with congestive heart failure and atelectasis

52. _F_ Compression of small airways associated with pulmonary edema, or in clients taking β-blockers (e.g., propranolol HCl)

53. _A_ Collapse of alveoli or lobule; can be caused by pressure on lung tissue; often associated with pericardial effusion, pleural effusion, or pneumothorax

A. atelectasis

B. Cheyne-Stokes

C. hemoptysis

D. rales

E. tachypnea

F. wheezes

CARDIAC CATHETERIZATION

A **cardiac catheterization** is a diagnostic procedure performed by a physician and is used to determine specific areas of disease in the heart. By threading a catheter through an artery into the heart, the physician is able to visualize the coronary arteries, valves, and great vessels of the heart. The NCLEX-RN examiners love questions regarding this test because of the large role a nurse plays in preventing complications that may arise from this procedure. Nursing considerations for the client undergoing cardiac catheterization or angiography include the following (circle one or more correct answers):

54. The client must be NPO at least (4 hours, 8 hours, 12 hours, 24 hours) prior to the procedure.

55. Prepare the client for sensations such as (cold, heat, palpitations, numbness) when contrast medium is injected into the heart via the catheter.

56. Teach the client of possible entry sites for cardiac catheterization such as the (carotid artery, femoral artery, radial artery, brachial artery).

57. Assess the client for (numbness, sensation, pulses, bleeding) in the affected extremity every 15 minutes for 1 to 2 hours following the procedure.

58. Report to the provider immediately complaints of (chest pain, numbness/tingling of extremity, tachycardia; pain at site; a warm, wet feeling at the site that could signal bleeding).

DISORDERS OF THE CARDIOVASCULAR SYSTEM

ANGINA

Angina is pain resulting from ischemia (decreased blood supply to the heart muscle). It is characterized by substernal (sub- = below) or retrosternal (retro- = behind) pain that can radiate to the inside of one or both arms, the neck, and jaws. Angina is usually described as a squeezing, heavy discomfort or pressure which is precipitated by an event such as emotion, exertion, cold, or eating. Angina usually lasts a few minutes and then subsides. It is often relieved with sublingual nitroglycerin.

MYOCARDIAL INFARCTION

Pain related to a **myocardial infarction** (necrosis of the heart muscle) is often felt substernally or over the precordium and can spread widely across the chest with painful disability of the shoulders and sometimes of the arms and hands. Pain from a myocardial infarction is described as a viselike or crushing pain and is severe and prolonged. It is often associated with dizziness, nausea, and diaphoresis. It occurs spontaneously and is often unrelated to specific events. Pain from a myocardial infarction is usually not relieved by sublingual nitroglycerin. Intravenous nitroglycerin and/or morphine sulfate is usually given for the pain.

PULMONARY EDEMA

Pulmonary edema is an abnormal collection of fluid in the lungs and interstitial spaces and/or alveoli. It occurs when the left side of the heart is not effectively pumping blood out of the heart, so that it backs up into the lungs.

59. List six clinical manifestations of pulmonary edema:

   A. ~~RATE~~ OCCUR AT NIGHT
   B. RALES
   C. RESTLESS / ANXIOUS
   D. COLD / MOIST EXT
   E. SOB / TACHY
   F. CYANOTIC NAIL BEDS / ASHEN SKIN COLOR

Management of pulmonary edema includes increasing oxygenation, diuretic therapy, and cardiac glycosides (e.g., digoxin). Provide a rationale for each intervention used to treat pulmonary edema:

60. Oxygenation _relieve Hypoxia + dyspnea_

61. Diuretics _↓ fluid retention   Vasodilation ↓ venous return_

62. Cardiac glycosides or digoxin _improve contraction ↓ pulm congestion_
   ↑ heart ↑ output of left ventricle ↑ urine output

CONGESTIVE HEART FAILURE

Congestive heart failure is the inability of the heart to pump enough blood to meet the oxygen and nutrient needs of the tissues. It often involves contractile properties of the heart such as decreased cardiac output. Failure of the right ventricle results in a backlog of blood flow that engorges the organs and results in edema. Failure of the left ventricle results in a backlog of blood into the lungs.

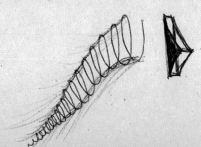

63. For each of the following clinical manifestations, identify whether it is consistent with **left-** or **right-**side failure:

A. _R_ ascites   H. _R_ nocturia

B. _L_ coughing   I. _L_ orthopnea

C. _R_ dependent edema   J. _L_ pulmonary congestion

D. _R_ distended neck veins   K. _L_ S3 heart sounds

E. _L_ dyspnea   L. _L_ tachycardia

F. _L_ hemoptysis   M. _R_ visceral/peripheral congestion

G. _R_ hepatomegaly

Management of congestive heart failure includes administration of ordered cardiac glycosides (e.g., digoxin), diuretics, and vasodilators. Classify the following diuretics as **thiazides**, **loop**, or **potassium sparing**:

64. Spironolactone (aldactone)   _potassium sparing_

65. Furosemide (lasix)   _loop_

66. Hydrochlorothiazide (esidrix)   _thiazide_

67. Ethacrynic acid (edecrin)   _loop_

68. Triamterene (dyrenium)   _potassium sparing_

Hyponatremia and Hypokalemia

Electrolyte imbalances such as **hyponatremia** (decreased serum sodium level) and **hypokalemia** (decreased serum potassium level) are common side effects of diuretic therapy.

69. List three signs and symptoms of hyponatremia (normal serum sodium level is 138–148):

A. _↓ muscle tone_

B. _H/A lethargy_

C. _↓ BP_

      stomach cramps

Answer the following **true** or **false** questions regarding the complications of hypokalemia. (The normal serum potassium level is 3.5–5.5):

70. _F_ leads to ~~increased~~ _dec._ contractility

71. _T_ leads to dangerous and lethal dysrhythmias

72. _T_ can precipitate digoxin toxicity

73. _T_ depresses the myocardium

74. _T_ causes ventricular irritability

Dietary management of hypokalemia is important to the cardiac client. Nursing intervention should include teaching the client which foods to consume that are high in potassium, provided that the client's renal function is adequate.

75. List six food items high in potassium:

A. _bananas_ D. _prunes raisens_

B. _orange juice_ E. _tomatoes_

C. _potatoes_ F. _figs apricots_

Digoxin Therapy

Digoxin is a cardiac glycoside, antiarrhythmic agent used in the treatment of congestive heart failure and tachyarrhythmias (atrial fibrillation, atrial flutter, paroxysmal atrial tachycardia). Digoxin increases cardiac output and slows the heart rate. Nursing considerations in managing the client undergoing **digoxin therapy** include correct administration and monitoring the patient for toxicity. The apical pulse should be monitored for one full minute. Withhold dose and notify physician if pulse < 60.

76. List four signs and symptoms of digoxin toxicity:

A. _anorexia_ C. _halo vision_

B. _nausea vomiting_ D. _PVC_

77. In order to prevent toxicity in digoxin therapy, the nurse must assess for what 3 things?

A. _check pt HR_

B. _check dig level_

C. _check K+ level_

78. Digoxin **increases** or **decreases** the following:

A. _↑_ cardiac output

B. _↓_ heart rate

C. _↓_ venous pressure

D. _↑_ myocardial contractility

Vasodilator Therapy

Vasodilator therapy is important in the management of the client with congestive heart failure. Commonly used drugs include nitroglycerin and sodium nitroprusside (Nipride). These vasodilators reduce or increase specific functions of the heart.

79. Vasodilator therapy **reduces** or **increases** the following (think about the answers, giving consideration to the congestive heart failure disease process!):

A. _reduces_ resistance to left ventricular ejection

B. _increase_ venous capacity

C. _reduces_ left ventricular filling pressure

D. _reduces_ pulmonary congestion

CARDIOGENIC SHOCK

Cardiogenic shock occurs when the heart loses its contractile ability, resulting in inadequate tissue perfusion to the vital organs. Cardiogenic shock is the end stage of heart failure when the left ventricle is severely damaged (often due to myocardial infarction). It has also been associated with cardiac tamponade and pulmonary embolism. Cardiogenic shock is a life-threatening situation in which the nurse must carefully and continually assess the client's hemodynamic status.

Identify the following characteristics associated with cardiogenic shock as **true** or **false**. (Think about left-sided heart failure and what happens when your vital organs lose oxygenation!)

80. _F_ High blood pressure

81. _T_ Low blood pressure

82. _T_ Rapid pulse

83. _F_ Bounding pulse

84. _T_ Confusion

85. _T_ Dysrhythmias

86. _T_ Hypoxia

87. _T_ Reduced cardiac output

88. _T_ Reduced urine output

The damage to the myocardial tissue in cardiogenic shock greatly reduces the heart's ability to act as a pump, thereby reducing cardiac output, arterial blood pressure, and coronary artery flow. This condition is manifested by low blood pressure, rapid weak pulse, decreased urine output, and hypoxia. It continues in a cyclic manner and often leads to death if not immediately treated.

OTHER INFECTIONS AND DISORDERS OF THE CARDIOVASCULAR SYSTEM

There are certain disorders you should recognize for the NCLEX-RN. The purpose of this matching is to get you to use the information provided to choose the best answer. Match the following cardiac infections (-itis) and disorders with the appropriate description:

89. _C_ An infection of the valves and endothelial surface of the heart; a direct invasion of bacteria or other organism leading to deformity of the leaflet valves

90. _F_ Heart damage not infectious in origin; response to streptococcal infection usually seen with polyarthritis; results in formation of nodules that eventually lead to scarring

91. _A_ Caused by inflammatory lesions deforming flaps of the valve resulting in incomplete closure, allowing back flow of blood from the aorta into the left ventricle

92. _D_ Causes high pulmonary arterial pressures resulting from incomplete emptying of left atrium; progressive thickening of valve cusps results, causing obstruction

A. aortic insufficiency

B. cardiomyopathy

C. infective endocarditis

D. mitral stenosis

E. pericarditis

F. rheumatic endocarditis

93. **B** _Disease of the muscle either from unknown etiology or from a systemic disorder; leads to severe heart failure and often death_

94. **E** _Pain most common characteristic, often accompanied by friction rub; refers to inflammation of the membranous sac protecting the heart_

NUTRITION AND THE PREVENTION OF HEART DISEASE

Since nutrition plays such a large role in the prevention of heart disease, education is the key. Primary goals include limiting total fat calories to less than 30 percent of total dietary intake, and limiting saturated fat calories to less than 10 percent of total dietary intake. Cholesterol intake should be less than 300 mg/day. Secondary goals include decreasing saturated fat intake to less than 7 percent/day and cholesterol intake to less than 200 mg/day. Clients should be taught to read labels in the grocery store. All clients with existing heart disease should have a consultation with a nutritionist who can instruct them on the proper diet restrictions to prevent progression of heart disease. Low sodium (2–3 grams), low fat, and low cholesterol are the three major dietary restrictions of which nurses should be aware.

CHAPTER 5: EXERCISE ANSWERS

1. The heart is composed of specialized tissue that contracts and relaxes in a coordinated fashion. The outer surface of the heart is known as the **epicardium**.

2. The **endocardium** is the inner surface of the heart that comes in contact with the blood…

3. …and the heart muscle itself is the **myocardium**.

4. The **pericardium** is a thin, fibrous sac that surrounds the heart's surface and serves as protection.

5. Contraction of the heart muscle is referred to as **systole**…

6. …while relaxation of the heart muscle is referred to as **diastole**.

7. The chambers of the heart are the **atria**…

8. …and the **ventricles**.

9. The **left** ventricle provides blood to the entire body…

10. …therefore, its wall is thicker than that of the **right** ventricle.

11. **C** **pulmonary valve**—Located between the right ventricle and the pulmonary artery.

12. **A** **aortic valve**—Located between the left ventricle and the aorta.

13. **D** **tricuspid valve**—Located between the right atrium and the right ventricle.

14. **B** **mitral valve**—Located between the left atrium and the left ventricle.

15. The **sinoatrial node** is known as the pacemaker of the heart and has an intrinsic rate of…

16. …**60–100** beats per minute.

17. The **atrioventricular node** has an intrinsic rate of…

18. …**40–60** beats per minute.

19. The **bundle of His** are specialized muscle fibers in the septum carrying the impulse to the…

20. **Purkinje's fibers,** where it terminates, resulting in contraction of the muscle.

21. **H** **stroke volume**—Amount of blood ejected in a heartbeat

22. **D** **diastole**—Atrioventricular valves open, returning blood from the veins to the atria and ventricles; ventricles are relaxed

23. **I** **systole**—Atrioventricular valves close and the ventricle contracts

24. **E** **ejection fraction**—Measure of myocardial contractility, percentage of blood emptied from the ventricle during contraction

25. **F** **preload**—End diastolic ventricular volume

26. **A** **afterload**—Tension in the ventricular wall during contraction

27. **C** **depolarization**—The inside of the myocardial cells becomes less negative and contraction of the myocardium occurs

28. **G** **repolarization**—The inside of the myocardial cells becomes more negative and relaxation of the myocardium occurs

29. **B** **cardiac output**—Amount of blood pumped by ventricle during a time period; equals stroke volume heart rate

30. Risk factors for coronary artery disease include:

diabetes, hyperglycemia	obesity
physical inactivity	family history
hyperlipidemia	smoking
hypertension/high blood pressure	stress
increasing age	use of oral contraceptives

31. Answers are shown below:

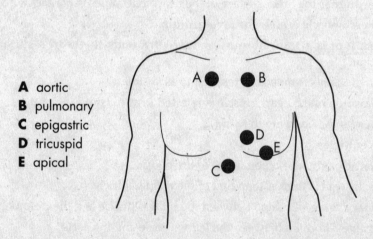

A aortic
B pulmonary
C epigastric
D tricuspid
E apical

32. **F** **S3**—Heard during rapid ventricular filling and can be a normal finding in young children; often associated with congestive heart failure and failure of ventricles to eject blood

33. **D** **S1**—Heard over mitral area; created by the closure of the mitral and tricuspid valves

34. **G** **S4**—Heard during atrial contractions and often associated with ventricular hypertrophy and resistance to filling; also associated with coronary artery disease, hypertension, aortic stenosis

35. **E**   **S2**—Heard at the base of the heart; created by the closure of the aortic and pulmonary valves

36. **C**   **murmurs**—Created by the flow of blood through narrow valves or incomplete closure of valves, resulting in prolonged sounds

37. **B**   **gallops**—Transient sounds heard during systole and diastole, associated with an impedance to blood flow

38. **A**   **friction rubs**—Caused by the abrasion of pericardial surfaces secondary to inflammation

39. Answers are shown below:

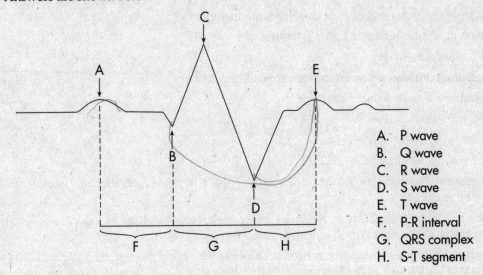

A. P wave
B. Q wave
C. R wave
D. S wave
E. T wave
F. P-R interval
G. QRS complex
H. S-T segment

40. **D**   **S wave**—Second negative deflection after the P wave

41. **B**   **Q wave**—First negative deflection after the P wave

42. **C**   **R wave**—First positive deflection after the P wave

43. **F**   **P-R interval**—Represents the impulse traveling from the atria through the conduction system

44. **H**   **S-T segment**—Represents early ventricular repolarization

45. **E**   **T wave**—Represents ventricular muscle repolarization

46. **A**   **P wave**—Represents atrial depolarization

47. **G**   **QRS complex**—Represents ventricular depolarization

48. **B**   **Cheyne-Stokes**—Noted for apneic periods; often associated with severe left ventricular failure

49. **C**   **hemoptysis**—Indicative of pulmonary edema characterized by pink or blood-tinged frothy sputum

50. **E**   **tachypnea**—Rapid, shallow breathing often associated with congestive heart failure, pain, or anxiety

51. **D**   **rales**—Often noted at the base of the lungs; progresses upward; often associated with congestive heart failure and atelectasis

52. **F**   **wheezes**—compression of small airways associated with pulmonary edema or in clients taking β–blockers (e.g., Propranolol HCl, inderal)

53. **A**   **atelectasis**—Collapse of alveoli or lobule; can be caused by pressure on lung tissue; often associated with pericardial effusion, pleural effusion, or pneumothorax

54. The client must be NPO at least **8 hours** prior to the procedure.

55. Prepare the client for sensations such as **heat** or **palpitations** when contrast medium is injected into the heart.

56. Teach the client of possible catheterization sites such as the **femoral artery** or **brachial artery**.

57. Assess the client for **numbness, sensation, pulses,** and **bleeding** in the affected extremity every 15 minutes for 1 to 2 hours following the procedure.

58. Report to the provider immediately complaints of **chest pain** or **numbness/tingling of extremity**.

59. Clinical manifestations of pulmonary edema include:

   occurs at night after a few hours lying down

   restlessness or anxiety

   coughing with mucoid sputum; sometimes hemoptysis

   cyanotic nail beds, ashen skin color

   cold, moist extremities

   shortness of breath, tachypnea

   rales upon auscultation

60. **Oxygenation** is used to relieve hypoxia and dyspnea. If hypoxia continues, mechanical ventilation may be required.

61. **Diuretics** cause vasodilation, leading to decreased venous return and decreased pulmonary congestion. Increase in urine output is seen.

62. **Cardiac glycosides or digoxin** is used to improve the contraction of the heart and increase the output of the left ventricle. This enhances diuresis and reduces diastolic pressure, subsequently reducing pulmonary capillary pressure.

63. Clinical manifestations of **left**-sided heart failure include:

   B   coughing

   E   dyspnea

   F   hemoptysis

   I   orthopnea

   J   pulmonary congestion

   K   S3 heart sounds

   L   tachycardia

   Clinical manifestations of **right**-sided heart failure include:

   A   ascites

   C   dependent edema

   D   distended neck veins

   G   hepatomegaly

   H   nocturia

   M   visceral/peripheral congestion

64. Spironolactone (aldactone) is a **potassium sparing** diuretic.

65. Furosemide (lasix) is a **loop** diuretic.

66. Hydrochlorothiazide (esidrix) is a **thiazide** diuretic.

67. Ethacrynic acid (edecrin) is a **loop** diuretic.

68. Triamterene (dyrenium) is a **potassium sparing** diuretic.

69. Signs and symptoms of hyponatremia include:

    decreased muscle tone

    headache and lethargy

    low blood pressure

    stomach cramps

70. **False**—Hypokalemia leads to decreased contractility.

71. **True**—Hypokalemia can lead to dangerous dysrhythmias.

72. **True**—Hypokalemia can precipitate digoxin toxicity.

73. **True**—Hypokalemia can depress the myocardium, weakening contractions.

74. **True**—Hypokalemia can cause ventricular irritability.

75. Foods high in potassium include:

apricots	prunes
bananas*	raisins
figs	spinach
orange juice*	tomatoes*
potatoes*	(*Remember these!)

76. Signs and symptoms of digoxin toxicity include:

anorexia	paroxysmal atrial tachycardia
bradycardia	premature ventricular contractions
halo effect on vision	ventricular bigeminy
nausea and vomiting	

77. In order to prevent toxicity in digoxin therapy the nurse must assess for what 3 things?

    A. check client's heart rate

    B. check digoxin level

    C. check potassium level

78. Digoxin:

    A **Increases** cardiac output

    B. **Decreases** heart rate

    C. **Decreases** venous pressure

    D. **Increases** myocardial contractility

79. Vasodilator therapy:

    A. **Reduces** resistance to left ventricular ejection

    B. **Increases** venous capacity

    C. **Reduces** left ventricular filling pressure

    D. **Reduces** pulmonary congestion

80. **False** (Cardiogenic shock reduces blood pressure.)

81. **True** (Low blood pressure is a classic sign of cardiogenic shock.)

82. **True** (Rapid, weak pulse is characteristic of cardiogenic shock.)

83. **False** (Bounding pulses are not seen with cardiogenic shock.)

84. **True** (Confusion may be seen due to hypoxia.)

85. **True** (Dysrhythmias are common due to myocardial hypoxia.)

86. **True** (Hypoxia is often seen in cardiogenic shock.)

87. **True** (Decreased cardiac output is characteristic due to left ventricular damage.)

88. **True** (Decreased urine output is characteristic of cardiogenic shock.)

89. **C** **infective endocarditis**—An infection of the valves and endothelial surface of the heart; a direct invasion of bacteria or other organism leading to deformity of the leaflet valves

90. **F** rheumatic endocarditis—Heart damage not infectious in origin; response to a streptococca infection seen with polyarthritis; results in formation of nodules that eventually lead to scarring

91. **A** **aortic insufficiency**—Caused by inflammatory lesions deforming flaps of the valve resulting in incomplete closure, allowing back flow from the aorta into the left ventricle

92. **D** **mitral stenosis**—Causes high pulmonary arterial pressures resulting from incomplete emptying of left atrium; progressive thickening of valve cusps results, causing obstruction

93. **B** **cardiomyopathy**—Disease of the muscle either from unknown etiology or from a systemic disorder, leads to severe heart failure and often death

94. **E** **pericarditis**—Pain most common characteristic, often accompanied by friction rub; refers to the inflammation of the membranous sac protecting the heart

CHAPTER 5: NCLEX-RN STYLE QUESTIONS

1. A client with congestive heart failure (CHF) has gained 7 pounds since yesterday. In assessing this situation, it would be most important for the nurse to

   (1) ask the client if he or she needs the backrest higher to breathe comfortably.
   (2) check the client's 24-hour intake-output record for the past 2 days.
   (3) auscultate the lungs for a pericardial friction rub.
   (4) examine the client's legs and sacral area.

2. A client returns from a cardiac catheterization with a bandage over the right groin. An unlicensed personnel (UAP) assigned to the client reports that the client's right foot is cool to the touch. The first action of the nurse should be to

   (1) check the foot every 15 minutes.
   (2) call the provider and report the findings.
   (3) loosen the bandage.
   (4) check the client's groin.

3. A client who is admitted with Addison's disease has hyponatremia. Signs and symptoms that the nurse would assess for include

   (1) thirst and dry skin.
   (2) weakness and weight gain.
   (3) restlessness and abdominal cramps.
   (4) tachycardia and headaches.

4. The mother of a child who just returned from a cardiac catheterization asks the nurse why her son has to keep his leg straight for 4–6 hours. The nurse's response includes which of the following statements?

   (1) "This will minimize pain and discomfort."
   (2) "This will facilitate healing of the vessel."
   (3) "This will promote adequate rest for the heart."
   (4) "This will maintain circulation."

5. A client who was hospitalized for congestive heart failure is getting ready to discharge on 40 mg furosemide (Lasix) once a day by mouth (PO). The nurse should include which of the following in the teaching plan?	(1) Signs and symptoms of hypertension (2) Signs and symptoms of hypokalemia (3) Advising client to go to the beach to be exposed to direct sunlight (4) Advising the client to take Lasix before bed
6. The nurse knows that when assessing a client suspected of having a myocardial infarction it is most important to ask which of the following?	(1) "What medications are you currently taking?" (2) "Have you ever had similar symptoms in the past?" (3) "How long ago did these symptoms start?" (4) "Have you been under a lot of stress lately?"
7. Prior to administering morphine IV push to a client with chest pain, the nurse should	(1) evaluate the E.K.G. (2) not administer the drug; it is outside the RN scope of practice. (3) perform the Glasgow coma scale to evaluate neurologic status. (4) check the blood pressure.
8. A client is discharged on digoxin (Lanoxin) 0.25 mg PO daily. Which statement by the client would reflect an understanding of the discharge teaching?	(1) "I will notify the clinic if I experience increased urinary output." (2) "If I experience an increase in heart rate I will notify the clinic." (3) "I will notify the clinic if I experience nausea and vomiting." (4) "If I experience an increase in muscle strength, I will notify the clinic."
9. A client, with a history of congestive heart failure, is admitted to the hospital complaining of changes in vision, nausea, and vomiting. Stat diagnostic studies are ordered. The nurse expects which finding?	(1) Digoxin level of 2.2 ng/mL (2) Digoxin level of 0.5 ng/mL (3) Serum potassium of 5.5 mEq/L (4) Serum potassium of 2.0 mEq/L

CHAPTER 5: NCLEX-RN STYLE ANSWERS

1. (2) CORRECT   Checking the 24-hour intake-output record will be the initial nursing assessment of the weight gain.
    (1) ELIMINATE   This is important for basic care and comfort, but the physiological needs take priority.
    (3) ELIMINATE   There is no reason to auscultate for a pericardial friction rub.
    (4) ELIMINATE   Examining the client for edema would be appropriate.
    CATEGORY 10 PHYSIOLOGICAL ADAPTATION

2.　(4) CORRECT　The first step is for the nurse to always assess the situation and then follow through with any additional actions.

　　(1) *ELIMINATE*　Checking the foot every 15 minutes should only be done after the initial assessment for comparison purposes.

　　(2) *ELIMINATE*　Calling the provider would only be appropriate after the nurse assessed the situation.

　　(3) *ELIMINATE*　Loosening the bandage is probably not necessary but it doesn't cause any harm.

CATEGORY 09 REDUCTION OF RISK POTENTIAL

3.　(2) CORRECT　Muscle weakness and weight gain due to water retention are signs of low sodium levels.

　　(1) *ELIMINATE*　Thirst and dry skin are signs of hypernatremia.

　　(3) *ELIMINATE*　Restlessness is a sign of high sodium levels.

　　(4) *ELIMINATE*　Tachycardia is seen with high sodium levels.

CATEGORY 10 PHYSIOLOGICAL ADAPTATION

4.　(2) CORRECT　Healing the vessel is most important in preventing hemorrhage or hematoma formation at the entry side.

　　(1) *ELIMINATE*　Minimizing pain and discomfort is not the reason to keep the leg straight.

　　(3) *ELIMINATE*　Keeping the leg straight has no effect on the heart.

　　(4) *ELIMINATE*　Keeping the leg straight does not have a relationship to the circulation.

CATEGORY 09 REDUCTION OF RISK POTENTIAL

5.　(2) CORRECT　The client should be instructed about the potassium-wasting properties of furosemide (Lasix).

　　(1) *ELIMINATE*　The client should be instructed about the potential of orthostatic hypotension, not hypertension.

　　(3) *ELIMINATE*　The client should be instructed about photosensitivity.

　　(4) *ELIMINATE*　The client should be instructed to take furosemide (Lasix) early in the day to avoid nocturia and the potassium-wasting properties of Lasix.

CATEGORY 09 REDUCTION OF RISK POTENTIAL

6.   **(3) CORRECT**   Thrombolytic therapy is considered in clients presenting with symptoms of myocardial infarction. One exclusion criteria is chest pain for greater than 6 hours.

     (1) POSSIBLE   It is very important to ascertain a client's medication history. Care should be taken to determine all medications a client is taking, including over-the-counter nonprescription medications. Knowing the client's medication history can give the caregiver important information related to the current complaint; however, when a client complains of chest pain it is more important to determine when the onset of pain occurred. A determination can then be made as to whether the client is a candidate for thrombolytic therapy.

     (2) ELIMINATE   Knowing a client's past medical history is always important; however, in the case of a client suspected of having a myocardial infarction, the most important piece of information the health care provider needs is time related. Thrombolytic therapy is usually not considered for clients having chest pain for more than 6 hours.

     (4) ELIMINATE   Stress is always a factor to consider. It is usually not the cause of a myocardial infarction, although stressful lifestyles have been implicated in the development of cardiovascular disease and are considered to be a risk factor.

CATEGORY 10 PHYSIOLOGICAL ADAPTATION

---

7.   **(4) CORRECT**   Morphine can cause hypotension. When administering it IV, it must be given slowly because rapid administration may lead to hypotension and circulatory collapse.

     (1) ELIMINATE   Evaluating a client's E.K.G. is important; however, it is not a necessary action prior to the administration of morphine.

     (2) ELIMINATE   Administering morphine IV push is within the RN scope of practice.

     (3) ELIMINATE   Evaluating a client's neurologic status with the Glasgow coma scale is not a necessary action prior to the administration of morphine.

CATEGORY 08 PHARMACOLOGICAL AND PARENTERAL THERAPIES

---

8.   **(3) CORRECT**   Nausea and vomiting are classic symptoms of digoxin toxicity.

     (1) ELIMINATE   Digoxin, a positive inotropic, improves cardiac output that enhances tissue perfusion.

     (2) ELIMINATE   It would be important to give the client a specific rate at which he should notify the clinic. Digoxin toxicity can cause cardiac arrhythmias.

     (4) ELIMINATE   Muscle weakness is a symptom of hypokalemia that increases the client's risk for digoxin toxicity.

CATEGORY 08 PHARMACOLOGICAL AND PARENTERAL THERAPIES

---

9.   **(1) CORRECT**   Vision changes, nausea, and vomiting are symptoms of digoxin toxicity.

     (2) ELIMINATE   This would be a normal serum digoxin level.

     (3) ELIMINATE   Hyperkalemia does not have a direct effect on digoxin level.

     (4) POSSIBLE   Hypokalemia would cause the client to be more susceptible to digoxin toxicity.

CATEGORY 10 PHYSIOLOGICAL ADAPTATION

6

THE RESPIRATORY SYSTEM

WHAT YOU NEED TO KNOW

Our review of the respiratory system immediately follows the cardiovascular system not only because we are following a head to toe assessment, but also because the two systems are closely interrelated. Answering questions related to these systems relies heavily on a basic understanding of their mechanics. Because the potential scope of information that can be covered on the NCLEX is so wide and varied, you need to be prepared to think on your feet. This entails understanding concepts, not memorizing diseases. After your review, your common sense should lead you to the correct answer.

REVIEW OF RESPIRATORY ANATOMY AND PHYSIOLOGY

Look at the following diagrams to refresh your knowledge of the respiratory system; then choose from the following list of words to fill in the blanks that follow.

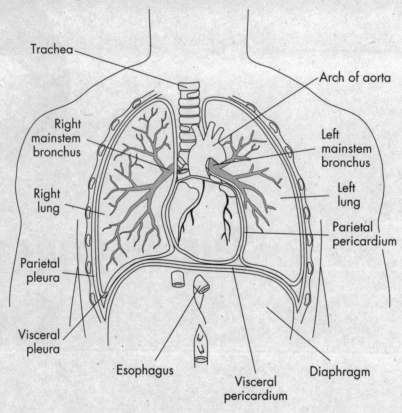

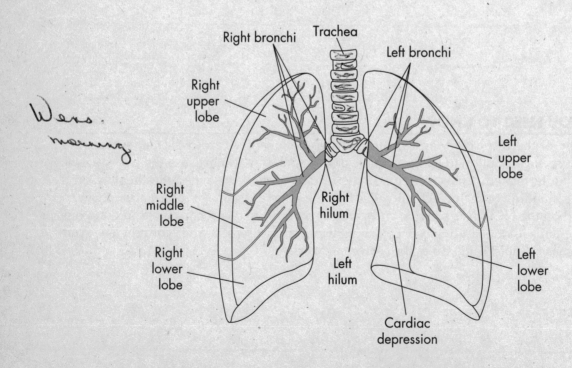

acidos̶is̶   obstruct̶ion   spasm
alkalos̶is̶   pleural̶   surfactant̶
alveolocapi̶llary̶ respira̶tion   swelling
diaphr̶agm̶   slide̶   ventila̶tion
hydro̶gen̶

The pleural membrane covers the lungs. The parietal pleura lines the thoracic cavity. Between these two layers is the pleural space, where a small amount of (1.) *surfactant* fluid fills the space. This fluid allows the two layers to (2.) *slide* over each other without separating. The major respiratory muscles are the (3.) *diaphragm* and the external intercostal muscles.

The alveoli house the (4.) *alveolocapillary* membrane, where oxygen enters the blood and carbon dioxide is removed from the blood. The type II alveolar cells secrete (5.) *surfactant* which coats the inner surface of the alveolus and aids in its expansion during inspiration.

(6.) *respiration* is the mechanical movement of gas or air into and out of the lungs (inspiration and expiration). (7.) *ventilation* is the exchange of oxygen and carbon dioxide during cellular metabolism. The most common causes of airway resistance are (8.) *swelling* *obstruction*, and *spasm*.

Chemoreceptors monitor the pH, PO_2, and pCO_2 of arterial blood. They respond to changes in (9.) *hydrogen* ion concentration. An increased concentration of hydrogen ions causes (10.) *acidosis*. A decreased concentration of hydrogen ions causes (11.) *alkalosis*.

ASSESSMENT OF THE RESPIRATORY SYSTEM

ADVENTITIOUS BREATH SOUNDS

The significance of the different **adventitious breath sounds** is always included somewhere on the NCLEX-RN. We reviewed some of this in the chapters on the nervous and cardiovascular systems. The following exercises should give you more confidence in your ability to assess breath sounds. Match the following types of breath sounds with the correct description on the next page.

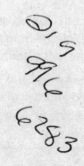

12. __C__ Inflamed surface of the pleura rubbing together

13. __G__ Caused by rapid vibration of bronchial walls (bronchospasm)

14. __D__ Due to obstruction of the large airways with secretions

15. __B__ Due to sudden opening of collapsed alveoli

16. __A__ Due to air passing through airways intermittently occluded by mucus

17. __F__ The usual breath sounds throughout the lungs

18. __E__ Partial obstruction of larynx or trachea

A. coarse crackles (rales)

B. fine crackles (rales)

C. pleural friction rub

D. rhonchi

E. stridor

F. vesicular

G. wheezes

When documenting adventitious breath sounds, include where on the chest they were auscultated; whether they occurred on inspiration, expiration, or both, and if the breath sounds cleared with coughing or deep breathing.

RESPIRATORY PATTERNS

When assessing the respiratory system, it is important to note the client's pattern of respirations. The following exercise will increase your familiarity with the different patterns that may appear on the NCLEX-RN. Match the following breathing patterns with the correct definitions:

19. __J__ Occurs as a result of disorders that stiffen the lungs or chest walls and decrease compliance

20. __D__ Difficulty breathing, shortness of breath

21. __G__ Characterized by slightly increased respiratory rate; often occurs with strenuous exercise and metabolic acidosis

22. __I__ Position dyspnea; in the supine position, abdominal contents exert pressure on the diaphragm

23. __E__ Respiration that exceeds metabolic demands; lungs remove carbon dioxide faster than it is being produced (low pCO_2); associated with severe anxiety and acute head injury

24. __A__ Cessation of respiration

25. __C__ Alternating periods of deep and shallow breathing; apnea may last 15–60 seconds; results from any condition that slows blood flow to the brain stem

26. __H__ Occurs if airways are obstructed as in C.O.P.D.; slow respiratory rate, increased effort, prolonged inspiration or expiration; wheezing or stridor is often present

A. apnea

B. ataxia (Biot's breathing)

C. Cheyne-Stokes respirations

D. dyspnea

E. hyperventilation

F. hypoventilation

G. Kussmaul's respirations (hyperpnea)

H. labored or obstructed respirations

I. orthopnea

J. restricted breathing

27. __F__ Inadequate alveolar ventilation in relation to metabolic demands

28. __B__ Unpredictable irregularity; breaths may be shallow, deep, and stop for short periods of time; associated with respiratory depression and brain damage

Signs of dyspnea include nasal flaring, retraction of intercostal spaces, and use of accessory muscles. Other abnormal clinical manifestations of respiratory problems include (match the terms with the proper definition below):

29. __A__ Commonly associated with diseases that interfere with oxygenation; changes in the appearance of fingernails and toenails

30. __C__ Caused by an increase in the amount of desaturated hemoglobin or a decrease in the amount of hemoglobin. Skin, mucus membranes, and nail beds will become pale, eventually blue secondary to decreased oxygenation. Extremities are affected first.

31. __D__ Coughing up blood or bloody secretions; usually an indication of infection or inflammation that causes damage to the bronchi or lung parenchyma; note amount and duration, which may provide clues to cause; bronchoscopy is used to confirm the site of bleeding

32. __B__ A protective reflex that cleanses the lower airways; if persistent, can indicate the presence of disease

33. __F__ Color, consistency, and amount vary with different pulmonary disorders

34. __E__ Caused by different pulmonary disorders; originates in the pleurae, the lungs, or the chest wall

A. clubbing
B. cough
C. cyanosis
D. hemoptysis
E. pain
F. sputum

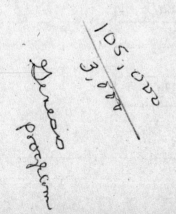

DIAGNOSTIC STUDIES

There are different diagnostic studies used to evaluate pulmonary function and the etiology of respiratory disease. Use the roots of the words to match the study with its correct definition:

35. __E__ Radiographic exam useful in diagnosing pneumonia, neoplasms, abscesses, tuberculosis, atelectasis, and pneumo/hemothorax

36. __A__ Allows for direct inspection of the larynx, trachea, and bronchi

37. __D__ Aspiration of fluid from the pleural cavity; can be used as a diagnostic or therapeutic procedure

38. __C__ Obtained to determine the etiology of and appropriate antibiotic therapy for respiratory infection

39. __B__ Measures lung volume and airway flow; helps in assessing the progression of lung disease and in evaluating a client's response to drug therapy (e.g. bronchodilators) and other interventions

A. bronchoscopy

B. pulmonary function test

C. sputum cultures

D. thoracentesis

E. x-ray

ARTERIAL BLOOD GASES

Arterial blood gases (A.B.G.'s) are diagnostic laboratory tests used to evaluate the etiology of pulmonary disease. A.B.G.'s cause panic among nursing students and beginning nurses. Here we break down the components of an A.B.G. so you know what is important for passing the NCLEX-RN.

An A.B.G. is drawn to assess disturbances in the blood's acid-base balance caused by either a respiratory or metabolic disorder. It also gives a quick indication of the client's oxygenation. Always ensure a patent airway before assessing A.B.G. results!

A.B.G. Component	Normal Value
pH	7.35–7.45
pCO_2	35–45 mmHg
HCO_3	22–26 mEq/L
BE	+2 to –2
Oxygen saturation	>90%
PO_2	>60 mmHg

Select words from the following list to fill in the blanks below:

40. The pH measures the ~~acid-base~~ _____ value.

41. The pCO_2 measures the adequacy of _____ contribution to the acid-base balance.

42. The HCO_3 measures the _____ contribution to acid-base balance.

43. BE (base excess) reflects the deviation of _____ concentration from normal.

44. Oxygen saturation is the percentage of hemoglobin saturated with _____.

45. PO_2 is the pressure that causes oxygen to bind to _____.

A. acid-base

B. bicarbonate

C. hemoglobin

D. metabolic

E. oxygen

F. respiratory

To interpret A.B.G. results, start with the pH. Is it high (alkalosis) or low (acidosis)? Then go to the pCO_2: Is it abnormal (respiratory etiology) or normal? Then assess the HCO_3 and BE: Are they normal (respiratory) or abnormal (metabolic)? Let's sum up:

Acid-Base Imbalance	pH	pCO₂	HCO₃	BE
Respiratory acidosis	low	high	normal	normal
Respiratory alkalosis	high	low	normal	normal
Metabolic acidosis	low	normal	low	low
Metabolic alkalosis	high	normal	high	high

The body will try to compensate for a shift in either direction (acidotic or basic); in these cases the pH should return to normal while the other values do not.

DISORDERS OF THE RESPIRATORY SYSTEM

CHRONIC OBSTRUCTIVE PULMONARY DISEASE

Chronic obstructive pulmonary disease (C.O.P.D.) is a group of diseases that includes emphysema, chronic bronchitis, bronchiectasis, and bronchial asthma. Recurrent obstruction of air flow is the common link among these diseases. C.O.P.D. is a major cause of death and disability in the United States.

Emphysema is the permanent enlargement of the air spaces distal to the terminal bronchioles (i.e., the alveoli). An early symptom of emphysema is dyspnea that becomes progressively more severe. There is minimal coughing with no, or scant amounts of, mucoid sputum. Later in the disease, the anterior-posterior diameter of the chest increases causing a "barrel chest." Clients will demonstrate chest breathing as they use their accessory and intercostal muscles to increase alveolar ventilation. Hypoxemia, especially during exercise, may also be present. Clients usually have weight loss and, in advanced stages, may develop clubbing. Clients with emphysema are often referred to as "pink puffers." Hyperinflation causes adequate oxygenation of tissues and no cyanosis is present. The client with emphysema does not have hypoxia at rest, hypercapnea, and respiratory acidosis until late in the disease.

Chronic bronchitis is caused by a chronic inflammation (-itis) and is characterized by an excessive production of mucus in the bronchi, accompanied by a recurrent cough that persists for at least 3 months of the year, for at least 2 years.

Clients with chronic bronchitis are often referred to as "blue bloaters" because of the hypoxemia and hypercapnia that develop as a result of alveolar hypoventilation. Their skin has a reddish-blue color from increased red blood cells as the body tries to compensate for chronic hypoxemia.

Bronchial asthma is characterized by a hyperresponsiveness of the tracheobronchial tree to a variety of stimuli, such as antigen inhalation, respiratory infection, drug and/or food additives, exercise, and emotional stress. Normally, the bronchioles constrict upon expiration. In an asthma attack, bronchospasm, edema, and increased mucus further narrow the bronchioles, and air then takes longer to move out. These conditions produce the prolonged wheezing associated with asthma. The client may have a nonproductive cough, or one that produces a minimal amount of sputum, which means there is widespread mucus plugging. Dyspnea occurs because of the client's difficulty in moving air in and out of the lungs. During an asthma attack, the client will position himself upright and use his accessory muscles in an attempt to ventilate more effectively. The client may also be restless, anxious, tachycardic, and hypertensive during the attack.

The complications of C.O.P.D. include cor pulmonale (right-sided heart hypertrophy resulting from pulmonary hypertension) and pneumonia. Nutrition is a big issue with these clients, as eating is strenuous and a full stomach decreases the space available for lung expansion. Small, frequent, calorie-dense foods should be encouraged. Overfeeding should be avoided at all costs, especially with carbohydrates, as carbon dioxide is a product of carbohydrate metabolism.

INFECTIOUS PROCESSES

Pneumonia is an inflammatory process of the respiratory bronchioles and the alveolar spaces caused by infection. Because pneumonia is an infectious process, you can anticipate that the physician will order antibiotics for its treatment if the source is isolated as **bacterial**. **Bacterial pneumonia** is often seen in the hospital setting as a complication of surgery or prolonged bed rest due to the stasis of secretions in the distal airways. **Viral pneumonia**, on the other hand, must run its course without antibiotic treatment. The goal of treatment for viral pneumonia is to manage the symptoms.

You may see a question on the NCLEX-RN about *Pneumocystis carinii* pneumonia, the infectious process most commonly associated with the human immunodeficiency virus (HIV). *P. carinii* attacks victims whose immune systems are already compromised and can be fatal unless treated promptly with pentamidine and trimethoprim-sulfamethoxazole (Bactrim) or dapsone with trimethoprim.

Tuberculosis (TB) is an infectious pulmonary process that can be transmitted by inhalation of minute dried droplet nuclei coughed or sneezed into the air by a person whose sputum contains virulent tubercle bacilli. It is more commonly spread to those individuals who have repeated, close contact with an infected person. There is an increased risk for the development of the clinical disease in those clients who are immunosuppressed (e.g., the elderly and clients with AIDS, as well as those on chemotherapy and long-term steroids), diabetic, those under 2 years old, and adolescents. Strict respiratory isolation is indicated as soon as TB is suspected.

Early in the disease the client may be free of symptoms. Systemic manifestations include night sweats and a dry cough. Diagnosis and screening is done through tuberculin skin testing known as the Mantoux skin test.

Purified protein derivative (PPD) of the tuberculin is injected intradermally to detect the delayed hypersensitivity response of the immunocompetent individual. A positive reaction occurs 3 to 10 weeks after the initial infection. The test results are as follows:

Negative	0–4 mm induration after 48 hours
Positive	> 10 mm induration with or without erythema after 48 hours

A positive PPD may not necessarily indicate active TB. A chest x-ray may show calcification at the original site (occurs after several years of infection). Sputum culture is positive for Gram-positive *Mycobacterium tuberculosis* within 2 to 3 weeks of onset of active disease. Sputum culture is negative for mycobacterium in the latent phase, but positive for acid-fast bacilli.

The mainstay of tuberculosis treatment is drug therapy. In active disease, isoniazid (INH) and rifampin are used most frequently. The priority nursing intervention is assuring that the client completes the entire course of TB drug therapy (up to 1 year) to prevent development of drug-resistant strains of TB. Clients infected with the same organism may share a hospital room, if hospitalization is necessary.

STRUCTURAL PROBLEMS

Adult respiratory distress syndrome (A.R.D.S.) occurs when pulmonary capillary permeability increases and fluid enters the lungs. The result is congestion, bleeding, and stiff lungs that cannot perfuse oxygen. Causes of A.R.D.S. include trauma, inhalation of toxins, liquid aspiration, infection, and drug overdose.

Atelectasis is the collapse of airless alveoli. The most common cause is retained secretions. Deep inspiration is needed to open the pores effectively. For this reason, coughing and deep breathing exercises are important in the prevention of atelectasis.

Flail chest results from multiple rib fractures that cause instability of the chest wall. During inspiration, the affected portion is sucked in; during expiration it bulges out. As a result, the injured area of the lung cannot obtain adequate ventilation.

FLAIL CHEST

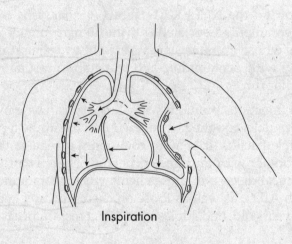

Inspiration

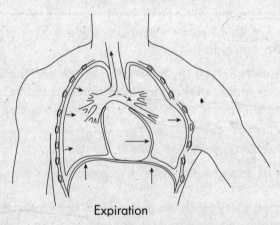

Expiration

A pleural effusion is the collection of fluid in the pleural space. Physical examination reveals dullness on percussion over the affected area and decreased or absent breath sounds as well. The goal of therapy is treatment of the underlying cause (e.g., infection) and a thoracentesis to remove the fluid. Nursing care of the client with pleural effusion includes efforts to maximize ventilation and monitoring for signs of respiratory distress.

A pneumo/hemothorax is the result of a partial or complete collapse of a lung as a result of the accumulation of air or blood in the intrapleural space. A closed pneumothorax has no external wound, whereas an open pneumothorax has an opening in the chest wall through which air enters the pleural space. The client with pneumo/hemothorax will present with respiratory distress, a cough (possible hemoptysis), and chest pain.

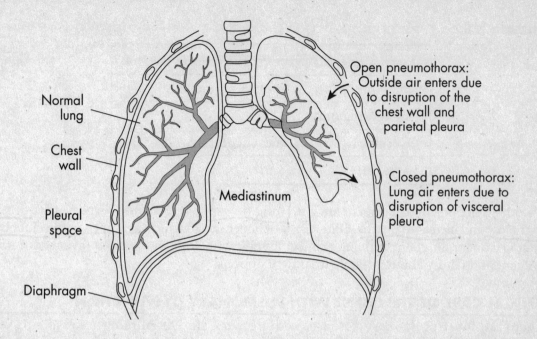

Normal lung

Chest wall

Pleural space

Mediastinum

Diaphragm

Open pneumothorax: Outside air enters due to disruption of the chest wall and parietal pleura

Closed pneumothorax: Lung air enters due to disruption of visceral pleura

Definitive treatment for pneumothorax is chest tube insertion with water seal drainage. In caring for the client with pneumothorax, it is important to monitor for patency of the chest tube and drainage apparatus, as well as to provide supplemental oxygen therapy, pulmonary toileting, and comfort measures. A tension pneumothorax may occur when chest tubes are clamped or become blocked.

MULTISYSTEM PROBLEMS

Pulmonary edema is caused by fluid in the lungs. It occurs when the heart's left ventricle fails or when fluid overload causes fluid to leave the vascular space and go into the interstitial tissues of the lungs. It is characterized by pink, frothy sputum, dyspnea, and confusion.

Pulmonary emboli occur when a pulmonary artery is blocked by a thrombus (clot) originating from peripheral vein. The embolus causes obstruction of the blood supply to the lung tissue and reflex bronchoconstriction occurs. Three factors (Virchow's triad) are related to the development of a venous thrombus:

- Venous stasis (immobilized clients, C.H.F., obesity, venous insufficiency)
- Injury to the vein wall
- Increased blood coagulability

Early ambulation is vital in preventing pulmonary emboli. Clinical manifestations of a pulmonary embolus include dyspnea, cyanosis, unexplained hemoptysis, and apprehension.

Lung Cancer Appears in Various Forms	
Squamous cell	most common (40–50%)
Adenocarcinoma	(25%)
Oat cell	most aggressive (20–25%)
Large cell	(10%)

Like other clients with cancer, clients with lung cancer have generally experienced drastic weight loss and increased fatigue. Other signs of lung cancer include hemoptysis and clubbing. Nursing care for the client with lung cancer involves maximizing ventilation and educating the client and family about possible treatment options.

GENERAL CARE OF THE CLIENT WITH PULMONARY DYSFUNCTION

In general, most pulmonary diseases require very similar nursing assessments and interventions. The following are general guidelines for caring for the client with pulmonary dysfunction. You should know that, after physically stabilizing the client, nursing interventions move to client and family education, ensuring adequate nutrition, and increasing the client's activity tolerance.

A priority nursing function is preventing pulmonary congestion and infection through "pulmonary toileting":

- Chest physiotherapy (C.P.T.) and postural drainage to loosen and remove secretions
- Frequent position changes in bed
- Early ambulation after surgery
- Coughing, deep breathing, and using the incentive spirometer (while splinting) if the client has had surgery

The client with hypoxia and/or respiratory distress requires expedient nursing assessment:

- Assess for signs of hypoxia: restlessness, anxiety, confusion, agitation, cardiac arrhythmias, color of extremities, and circumoral cyanosis.
- Assess for signs of respiratory distress: nasal flaring, cyanosis, intercostal retractions, and use of accessory muscles.
- Auscultate lungs for adventitious breath sounds, assess pulse oximetry.
- Check that patient is wearing oxygen as ordered.

And intervention:

- Position client in the upright position (high Fowler's) to facilitate maximum ventilation.
- Teach pursed lip breathing to facilitate maximum emptying of the alveoli.
- Notify physician.

Oxygen Administration

The NCLEX-RN always includes a question or two on the proper oxygen administration device for different scenarios. The following information will prepare you to choose the best method of oxygen administration for the clients presented on the exam.

Oxygen therapy is an important adjunct to nursing care. The nurse needs a provider's written order to administer oxygen, as it is a drug. Provide the minimum concentration of oxygen possible to prevent oxygen toxicity, atelectasis, and hypoventilation (as in clients with C.O.P.D.). Note the following regarding oxygen masks:

- A non-rebreather mask delivers the highest concentration of oxygen short of intubation.
- A face mask effectively delivers high concentrations of oxygen, but a Venturi mask delivers **exact** oxygen concentrations regardless of the client's respiratory pattern.
- A nasal cannula effectively delivers low concentrations of oxygen and is used frequently in clients with C.O.P.D. so that low oxygen concentration delivery will not compromise respiratory drive.

Pleural Drainage

Chest tubes and pleural drainage are inserted by the provider to remove air and fluid from the intrapleural space to restore the normal negative pressure, allowing the lungs to re-expand.

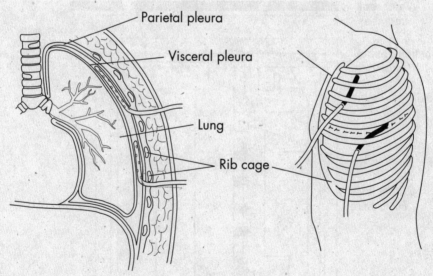

Parietal pleura

Visceral pleura

Lung

Rib cage

Most pleural drainage systems have three compartments:

- **Collection chamber** (collects fluid from the chest)
- **Water seal chamber** (acts as one-way valve to prevent reinhalation of air)
- **Suction control chamber** (regulates amount of suction)

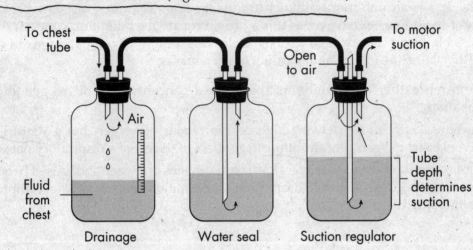

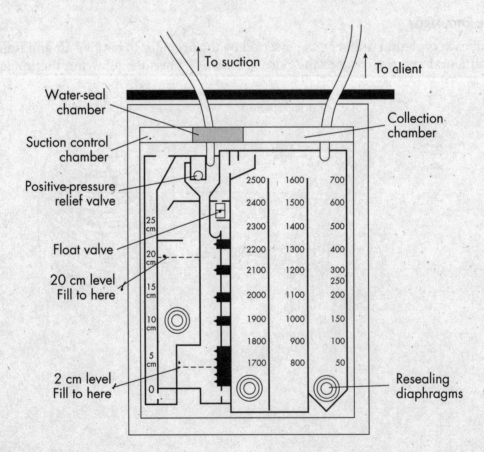

When caring for the client with a chest tube:

- Maintain sterility of the system to prevent infection from developing in the pleural cavity.
- Maintain patency of the system to prevent tension pneumothorax.
- If the chest tube becomes dislodged from the client's chest, the client should exhale forcefully, and a petrolatum jelly gauze dressing should be applied over the site, then notify physician.
- If the drainage compartment (bottle) breaks, clamp the tube nearest to the client until system integrity can be re-established.
- No chest tube should be clamped any longer than is absolutely necessary.
- Note type and amount of drainage.

SURGERY

Often, surgery is indicated to correct a problem with the respiratory system. As we have said before, just be familiar with the terms, and use the roots of the words to guide you to the best answer.

46. _A_ Incision into the thorax to look for injured or bleeding tissues as in chest trauma
47. _C_ Removal of an entire lung
48. _D_ Removal of one or more lung segments
49. _B_ Removal of one lobe of the lung
50. _D_ Removal of a small, localized lesion that occupies only part of a segment of the lung

A. exploratory thoracotomy
B. lobectomy
C. pneumonectomy
D. segmental resection
E. wedge resection

A client who has had a pneumonectomy does not require a chest tube. Fluid gradually fills the space where the lung was removed. Clients may be positioned on their backs or on the operative side with the head of the bed elevated. Positioning the client on the unaffected side can cause respiratory compromise in the remaining lung.

PHARMACOLOGY FOR THE RESPIRATORY SYSTEM

Before we start reviewing specific drugs pertinent to the respiratory system, review the five rights of drug administration:

51. The five rights of drug administration are:
   A. _MED_   D. _ROUTE_
   B. _DOSE_   E. _TIME_
   C. _PATIENT_

Remember, the nurse can only administer drugs according to a written order from the provider! The NCLEX-RN will always give you both the trade and generic name of the drug. Do not waste your time memorizing both names.

Anticholinergics block the action of acetylcholine, resulting in bronchodilation. Side effects include flushed skin and dry mouth. Anticholinergics are contraindicated in clients with glaucoma. Examples of anticholinergics include ipratropium (Atrovent) and atropine sulfate.

Antiinflammatory agents decrease edema in the bronchial airways and decrease mucus secretion. Side effects include cushingoid appearance, skin changes, increased appetite, and immunosuppression (steroids). Names of antiinflammatory agents end in "-one": hydrocortisone (Solu-Cortef), methylprednisolone (Solu-Medrol), prednisone, beclomethasone (Vanceril, Beclovent), and triamcinolone acetonide (Azmacort).

Antihistamines are used to relieve symptoms of the common cold and allergies by blocking the action of histamine at the receptor sites. Side effects include drowsiness (C.N.S. depression), dizziness (C.N.S. depression), dry mouth (anticholinergic effect), and GI irritation (local effect). Examples of antihistamines are diphenhydramine HCl (Benadryl), promethazine HCl (Phenergan), and chlorpheniramine maleate (Chlor-Trimeton).

Antituberculosis drugs include:

- Isoniazid (INH) is used in combination with other drugs, usually rifampin, to treat TB. Significant side effects to know for the boards include vitamin B_6 deficiency and GI upset.

- Rifampin (Rifadin). The client should be told to expect urine, saliva, tears, sweat, and sputum to be orange in color.

Antitussives suppress the cough reflex by acting on the cough center in the medulla. Narcotic antitussives cause drowsiness, drying of respiratory secretions, and constipation. Non-narcotic antitussives cause drowsiness and dizziness and are potentiated by MAO inhibitors, sedatives, tranquilizers, and alcohol. An example of an antitussive is dextromethorphan (Pertussin).

Bronchodilators reverse bronchoconstriction. Side effects include: nervousness, tremors, headaches, palpitations, and tachycardia. Examples include:

- Albuterol (Proventil)

- Epinephrine HCl (Adrenalin)

- Metaproterenol sulfate (Alupent)

- Terbutaline sulfate (Brethine)

Xanthines act directly on bronchial smooth muscle to decrease spasms and relax smooth muscle of the vasculature. Side effects include: dizziness (secondary to decreased blood pressure/relaxed smooth muscle of vasculature), C.N.S. stimulation (sympathetic stimulation), and palpitations (β adrenergic stimulation). Give oral preparations with food to prevent GI upset.

- Aminophylline (Amoline)

- Theophylline (Theo-dur)

Expectorants decrease the viscosity of secretions by increasing fluid in the respiratory tract. Side effects include nausea, vomiting, and gastric irritation.

- Guaifenesin (Robitussin)

Mucolytics decrease mucous viscosity by breaking down its structural bonds (**-lytic**). Adverse effects include bronchospasm (especially in the asthmatic client), rhinitis, and stomatitis.

- Potassium iodide (SSKI)
- Acetylcysteine (Mucomyst); also the antidote for acetaminophen (Tylenol) overdose

CHAPTER 6: EXERCISE ANSWERS

1. The pleural membrane covers the lungs. The parietal pleura lines the thoracic cavity. Between these two layers is the pleural space, where a small amount of **pleural** fluid fills the space.

2. This fluid allows the two layers to **slide** over each other without separating.

3. The major respiratory muscles are the **diaphragm** and the external intercostal muscles.

4. The alveoli house the **alveolocapillary** membrane, where oxygen enters the blood and carbon dioxide is removed from the blood.

5. The type II alveolar cells secrete **surfactant**, which coats the inner surface of the alveolus and aids in its expansion during inspiration.

6. **Ventilation** is the mechanical movement of gas or air into and out of the lungs (inspiration and expiration).

7. **Respiration** is the exchange of oxygen and carbon dioxide during cellular metabolism.

8. The most common causes of airway resistance are **swelling, obstruction,** and **spasm**.

9. Chemoreceptors monitor the pH, PO_2, and pCO_2 of arterial blood. They respond to changes in **hydrogen** ion concentration.

10. An increased concentration of hydrogen ions causes **acidosis**.

11. A decreased concentration of hydrogen ions causes **alkalosis**.

12. **C**   **pleural friction rub**—Inflamed surface of the pleura rubbing together

13. **G**   **wheezes**—Caused by rapid vibration of bronchial walls (bronchospasm)

14. **D**   **rhonchi**—Due to obstruction of the large airways with secretions

15. **B**   **fine crackles**—Due to sudden opening of collapsed alveoli

16. **A**   **coarse crackles**—Due to air passing through airways intermittently occluded by mucus

17. **F**   **vesicular**—The usual breath sounds throughout the lungs

18. **E**   **stridor**—Partial obstruction of larynx or trachea

19. **J**   **restricted breathing**—Occurs as a result of disorders that stiffen the lungs or chest walls and decrease compliance

20. **D**   **dyspnea**—Subjective sensation of breathlessness, shortness of breath

21. **G**   **Kussmaul's respiration (hyperpnea)**—Characterized by slightly increased respiratory rate; often occurs with strenuous exercise and metabolic acidosis

22. **I**   **orthopnea**—Position dyspnea; in the supine position, abdominal contents exert pressure on the diaphragm

23. **E** **hyperventilation**—Respiration that exceeds metabolic demands; lungs remove carbon dioxide faster than it is being produced (low pCO_2); associated with severe anxiety and acute head injury

24. **A** **apnea**—Cessation of respiration

25. **C** **Cheyne-Stokes respirations**—Alternating periods of deep and shallow breathing; apnea may last 15–60 seconds; results from any condition that slows blood flow to the brain stem

26. **H** **labored or obstructed respirations**—Occurs if airways are obstructed as in C.O.P.D.; slow respiratory rate, increased effort, prolonged inspiration or expiration; wheezing or stridor is often present

27. **F** **hypoventilation**—Inadequate alveolar ventilation in relation to metabolic demands

28. **B** **ataxia (Biot's breathing)**—Unpredictable irregularity; breaths may be shallow, deep, and stop for short periods of time; associated with respiratory depression and brain damage

29. **A** **clubbing**—Commonly associated with diseases that interfere with oxygenation; changes in the appearance of fingernails and toenails

30. **C** **cyanosis**—Caused by an increase in the amount of desaturated hemoglobin or a decrease in the amount of hemoglobin

31. **D** **hemoptysis**—Coughing up blood or bloody secretions; usually an indication of infection or inflammation that causes damage to the bronchi or lung parenchyma; note amount and duration, which may provide clues to cause; bronchoscopy is used to confirm the site of bleeding

32. **B** **cough**—A protective reflex that cleanses the lower airways; if persistent can indicate the presence of disease

33. **F** **sputum**—Color, consistency, and amount vary with different pulmonary disorders

34. **E** **pain**—Caused by different pulmonary disorders; originates in the pleurae, the lungs, or the chest wall

35. **E** **x-ray**—Radiographic exam useful in diagnosing pneumonia, neoplasms, abscesses, tuberculosis, atelectasis, and pneumo/hemothorax

36. **A** **bronchoscopy**—Allows for direct inspection of the larynx, trachea, and bronchi

37. **D** **thoracentesis**—Aspiration of fluid from the pleural cavity; can be used as a diagnostic or therapeutic procedure

38. **C** **sputum cultures**—Obtained to determine the etiology of and appropriate antibiotic therapy for respiratory infection

39. **B** **pulmonary function test**—Measures lung volume and airway flow; helps in assessing the progression of lung disease and in evaluating a client's response to drug therapy (bronchodilators) and other interventions

40. **A** The pH measures the **acid-base** value.

41. **F** The pCO_2 measures the adequacy of **respiratory** contribution to the acid-base balance.

42. **D** The HCO_3 measures the **metabolic** contribution to acid-base balance.

43. **B** BE (base excess) reflects the deviation of **bicarbonate** concentration from normal.

44. **E** Oxygen saturation is the percentage of hemoglobin saturated with **oxygen**.

45. **C** PO_2 is the pressure that causes oxygen to bind to **hemoglobin**.

46. **A** **exploratory thoracotomy**—Incision into the thorax to look for injured or bleeding tissues as in chest trauma

47. **C** **pneumonectomy**—Removal of an entire lung

48. **D** **segmental resection**—Removal of one or more lung segments

49. **B** **lobectomy**—Removal of one lobe of the lung

50. **E** **wedge resection**—Removal of a small, localized lesion that occupies only part of a segment of the lung

51. The five rights of drug administration are: **client, dose, drug, route,** and **time**.

1. A postoperative client who has had an open cholecystomy should be encouraged to cough and deep breathe frequently to prevent
   - (1) aspiration pneumonia.
   - (2) atelectasis.
   - (3) spontaneous pneumothorax.
   - (4) pleurisy.

2. Which of the following tests or procedures is the most reliable in diagnosing exposure to tuberculosis?
   - (1) Mantoux test
   - (2) Chest x-ray
   - (3) Auscultation
   - (4) Tine test

3. Your client is at risk for aspiration pneumonia. Which of the following nursing interventions will help prevent aspiration pneumonia?
   - (1) Keeping the head of the bed elevated in at least a 45° angle after delivering enteral feedings
   - (2) Providing vigorous pulmonary toileting immediately after feeding the client.
   - (3) Performing mouth care with the client in the supine position
   - (4) Auscultating breath sounds when ordered

4. The nurse is explaining how tuberculosis (TB) is diagnosed. Of the following, which should the nurse tell the client is the definitive diagnosis for TB?
   - (1) Arterial blood gas
   - (2) Tuberculin skin test
   - (3) Supine chest x-ray
   - (4) Sputum culture for acid-fast bacillus

5. The nurse is caring for a client with respiratory disorders. In assessing oxygenation, it is noted that when the PaO_2 drops below 60 mmHg, the client will probably show signs of
   - (1) wheezing and hypotension.
   - (2) equal expiration and inspiration.
   - (3) diminished breath sounds and cyanosis.
   - (4) restlessness and tachycardia.

6. Clients with tuberculosis may come out of isolation after
   - (1) sputum is negative for acid-fast bacillus.
   - (2) 3–5 days have passed.
   - (3) cough has reduced significantly.
   - (4) fever is reduced.

7. Which of the following arterial blood gas values is consistent with metabolic acidosis?
   - (1) pH 7.35
   - (2) CO_2 48 mmHg
   - (3) Bicarbonate 161
   - (4) PaO_2 90%

8. A blood gas reads as follows: pH 7.48, pCO_2 40 mmHg, HCO_3 34mEq/L. Which of the following is the correct interpretation?
   - (1) Respiratory acidosis
   - (2) Respiratory alkalosis
   - (3) Metabolic acidosis
   - (4) Metabolic alkalosis

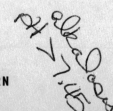

9. A nurse is teaching a client who has chronic obstructive pulmonary disease (C.O.P.D.) about exercise. The nurse teaches the client to

(1) have established rest periods.
(2) exercise strenuously when possible.
(3) use medications during exercise.
(4) avoid exercise.

10. A client's blood gas reads pH 7.32, pCO_2 42 mmHg, and PO_2 55 mmHg. The nurse is aware that the client is exhibiting

(1) tachypnea.
(2) hypoxia.
(3) alkalosis.
(4) hypercapnia.

CHAPTER 6: NCLEX-RN STYLE ANSWERS

1. (2) CORRECT   Coughing and deep breathing prevents atelectasis and pneumonia.
    (1) ELIMINATE   Aspiration pneumonia may occur if the client is vomiting and aspirates vomitus.
    (3) ELIMINATE   Spontaneous pneumothorax occurs when pressure in the intrapleural space occurs. This is not generally related to postoperative cholecystomy clients.
    (4) ELIMINATE   Not a condition that usually occurs postoperatively.

CATEGORY 09 REDUCTION OF RISK POTENTIAL

2. (1) CORRECT   A Mantoux is the most reliable test for determining whether a person was exposed to tuberculosis.
    (2) ELIMINATE   A chest x-ray confirms the disease. It is not a test to determine exposure.
    (3) ELIMINATE   Auscultation findings would not indicate whether a person was exposed to tuberculosis.
    (4) POSSIBLE   A Tine is also a test for exposure to tuberculosis, but it is not as reliable as the Mantoux.

CATEGORY 04 PREVENTION AND EARLY DETECTION OF DISEASE

3. (1) CORRECT   Elevating the head of the client in at least a 45° angle or in a sitting position reduces the risk of regurgitation and pulmonary aspiration.
    (2) ELIMINATE   Providing pulmonary toileting after feeding may promote vomiting and aspiration of gastric contents.
    (3) ELIMINATE   Mouth care should be performed with the client in a lateral position, not in a supine position, in order to prevent aspiration.
    (4) ELIMINATE   Frequent auscultation of breath sounds is essential and is an independent nursing action which does not require an order from the physician.

CATEGORY 04 PREVENTION AND EARLY DETECTION OF DISEASE

4. **(4) CORRECT** Sputum cultures for acid fast bacillus are the definitive diagnosis for tuberculosis.
    (1) *ELIMINATE* Arterial blood gas is not a test for tuberculosis.
    (2) *ELIMINATE* A tuberculine skin test determines if a person has been exposed to the tuberculin bacillus.
    (3) *ELIMINATE* A supine chest x-ray is not a definitive test for tuberculosis.

CATEGORY 04 PREVENTION AND EARLY DETECTION OF DISEASE

---

5. **(4) CORRECT** Tachycardia occurs as the heart compensates by increasing oxygen flow through the body, and restlessness results from decreased oxygen flow to the brain. Cyanosis is a late sign of hypoxemia.
    (1) *ELIMINATE* These symptoms are not necessarily associated with a low oxygen level.
    (2) *ELIMINATE* This phenomenon is not necessarily associated with low oxygenation.
    (3) *ELIMINATE* Cyanosis is associated with low oxygenation, but diminished breath sounds are not always connected to low oxygen.

CATEGORY 10 PHYSIOLOGICAL ADAPTATION

---

6. **(1) CORRECT** The client can come out of isolation when the sputum is clear of the organism.
    (2) *ELIMINATE* There is no time set for removal from isolation.
    (3) *ELIMINATE* Relief of cough does not necessarily sanction removal from isolation.
    (4) *ELIMINATE* Fever reduction does not sanction removal from isolation.

CATEGORY 02 SAFETY AND INFECTION CONTROL

---

7. **(3) CORRECT** In metabolic acidosis, the bicarbonate is low.
    (1) *ELIMINATE* This is a normal pH.
    (2) *ELIMINATE* In metabolic acidosis, the CO_2 is normal. In respiratory acidosis, this value is elevated.
    (4) *ELIMINATE* The PaO_2 is not necessarily part of the assessment of acid/base balance.

CATEGORY 10 PHYSIOLOGICAL ADAPTATION

8. (4) CORRECT   In metabolic alkalosis, the pH is above 7.45, the pCO_2 is normal, and the bicarbonate is above 26.

    (1) *ELIMINATE*   This pH reflects alkalosis, so this choice can be eliminated.

    (2) *ELIMINATE*   Respiratory alkalosis would reveal a pCO_2 below 38.

    (3) *ELIMINATE*   In metabolic acidosis, the pH is below 7.35.

CATEGORY 10 PHYSIOLOGICAL ADAPTATION

---

9. (1) CORRECT   Teaching the client to balance mild exercise, such as walking, with rest helps conserve energy.

    (2) *ELIMINATE*   Strenuous exercise in the C.O.P.D. client must be avoided. If oxygen needs (which are increased with exercise) exceed supply (which is reduced in this disease) it causes hypoxia.

    (3) *ELIMINATE*   Use of medications may help tolerate exercise, but the medications must be given before exercise.

    (4) *ELIMINATE*   Some exercise is beneficial. In the C.O.P.D. client, the exercise depends on the client's general condition.

CATEGORY 07 BASIC CARE AND COMFORT

---

10. (2) CORRECT   Low oxygenation in the blood is evident in this case scenario based on the arterial oxygen level being extremely low.

    (1) *ELIMINATE*   Tachypnea is defined as rapid respirations.

    (3) *ELIMINATE*   Alkalosis is present when the pH is above 7.45.

    (4) *ELIMINATE*   Hypercapnia is not present. This is a normal value.

CATEGORY 10 PHYSIOLOGICAL ADAPTATION

7

THE GASTROINTESTINAL SYSTEM

WHAT YOU NEED TO KNOW

Our approach to the gastrointestinal system is a little bit different from the approach we take in the other chapters. Because the anatomy and physiology of the gastrointestinal system includes many different organs and structures, we will review those organs and structures from head to toe along with the different disorders of the gastrointestinal system. Basic pharmacology is included throughout the chapter.

REVIEW OF GASTROINTESTINAL ANATOMY AND PHYSIOLOGY

Because we consciously use our gastrointestinal system multiple times every day when we eat, it's easier to visualize its anatomy relative to its physiology using a picture. The picture below is a straightforward display of the organs included in the gastrointestinal system. As you proceed with your review, look back at this picture and associate the different organs and structures with their corresponding functions.

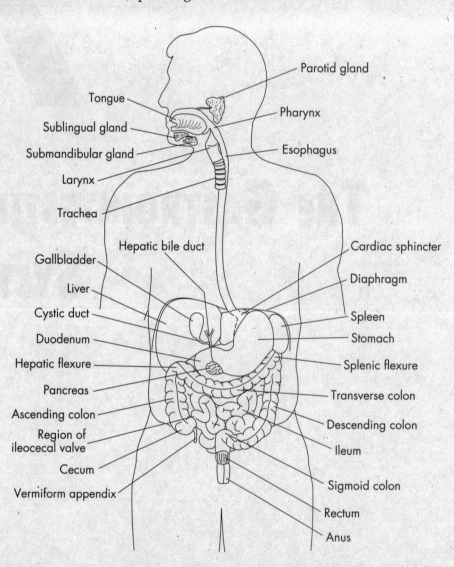

ASSESSMENT OF THE GASTROINTESTINAL SYSTEM

You need to know the four parts of the abdominal assessment for the NCLEX-RN. You should be able to list them, in order:

1. _auscultate inspect_
2. _auscultate_
3. _percussion_
4. _palpate_

Bowel sounds are considered absent if none are heard after auscultating for a minute or two in each quadrant. In order to avoid stimulating bowel sounds, palpation is the last part of abdominal assessment.

Certain diagnostic exams aid in gastrointestinal assessment. Just be familiar with the names. Again, use the roots of the words to guide you to the correct answer. Match the following diagnostic studies with the appropriate definitions:

5. _B_ A flexible fiber-optic scope is used to visualize the entire colon

6. _G_ X-ray exam after oral ingestion of radiopaque dye to determine the patency of the biliary duct

7. _E_ Percutaneous or intraoperative removal of hepatic tissue to confirm diagnosis of hepatocellular diseases

8. _I_ Noninvasive exam using sound waves to determine organ size and shape

9. _A_ Noninvasive radiological exam using tomography to present organ structure at different depths and views; can be used with or without contrast

10. _K_ Observation of contrast medium movement through the esophagus and into the stomach by means of fluoroscopy and x-ray; the contrast dye can cause impaction of stool so keep the client well hydrated; stool may be white for up to 2 days after the test

11. _F_ Radiological observation of contrast medium filling the colon

12. _B_ Flexible fiber-optic scope inserted into the mouth and via the common bile duct and pancreatic ducts to visualize these structures; after the test, observe for hemorrhage

13. _J_ Flexible fiber-optic endoscope that directly visualizes the structures of the upper GI tract; after the test, assess the client's gag reflex before allowing PO intake

14. _H_ Using fluoroscopy, the bile duct is entered percutaneously and injected with dye to observe filling of hepatic and biliary ducts; after the test, observe for hemorrhage

15. _D_ Radiographic exam used to visualize the biliary duct system after intravenous injection of radiopaque dye

A. CAT scan

B. endoscopic retrograde cholangiopancreatography (E.R.C.P.)

C. fiber-optic colonoscopy

D. IV cholangiogram

E. liver biopsy

F. lower GI series (barium enema)

G. oral cholecystogram

H. percutaneous transhepatic cholangiogram (P.T.C.)

I. ultrasound

J. upper GI endoscopy

K. upper GI series (barium swallow)

THE MOUTH

We'll start our review of the gastrointestinal system and its disorders with the mouth. To review, fill in the blanks with words from the list below:

chemical   starch
fifth   starches
mechanical

Gastrointestinal structure and function begins in the mouth with (16.) _Mech_ and (17.) _chem_ digestion. Much of the chewing process is innervated by the (18.) _fifth_ (trigeminal) cranial nerve. Salivary gland secretions begin basic (19.) _starch_ digestion. Salivary amylase begins the chemical breakdown of (20.) _starch_ to maltose.

DISORDERS OF THE MOUTH

As we discuss disorders related to the mouth, think about the roots of the words to guide your answers. You will have to think like this on the NCLEX-RN, as there is no way to know exactly what disease processes will be covered! To continue our review, fill in the blanks with words from the list below:

bland   prolonged NPO status
mouth care   purulent
poor oral hygiene   *Staphylococcus aureus*

Parotitis (think -itis; parotid gland inflammation) is usually caused by (21.) _Poor oral hygiene prolonged NPO Status_ or _____. The client may complain of a variety of symptoms, including ear pain, fever, dysphasia, dry mouth, and gland enlargement. Upon inspection, the nurse may discover (22.) _Purulent_ drainage from the duct. Preventive measures include ensuring adequate fluid intake and proper mouth care.

Stomatitis (mouth inflammation) occurs as a result of trauma or disease. The client should be assessed for excessive salivation and halitosis (bad breath). In caring for the client with stomatitis, the nurse must provide and teach the proper technique for (23.) _mouth care_, as well as dietary instruction on a (24.) _bland_ diet and cool drinks to decrease further irritation.

THE ESOPHAGUS

Select words from the list below to fill in the blanks below:

belching   peristalsis
esophageal sphincter   swallowing
esophageal varices   vomiting

The esophagus consists of muscular layers that contract and propel food into the stomach by (25.) _peristal_ . At the lower end of the esophagus is the (26.) _esophageal sphincter_, which stays constricted except during (27.) _belching_ , _swallowing_ and _vomiting_. Because the lower third of esophageal blood supply drains into the portal system, portal hypertension may lead to the development of (28.) _esophageal varices_

ESOPHAGEAL HERNIA

Select words from the list below to fill in the blanks below:

chest pain   reflux
heartburn   small, frequent meals
muscle weakening   stomach

An **esophageal hernia (hiatal hernia)** is the herniation of a portion of the (29.) _stomach_ through an enlarged esophageal opening in the diaphragm. Factors that contribute to the development of hiatal hernia (like all hernias) include (30.) _muscle weakening_ and anything that increases intra-abdominal pressure such as obesity, pregnancy, tumors, and ascites. The client may be asymptomatic or have complaints of (31.) _reflux_ and _____ . The client may also complain of (32.) _heartburn_ while lying down. Any complaint of (33.) _chest pain_ must be considered cardiac in origin until proven otherwise, so frequent monitoring of vital signs is the nursing priority. In caring for the client with an esophageal (hiatal) hernia, provide (34.) _sm. freq meals_ and maintain the client in an upright position during and after meals to avoid regurgitation.

Listed below are commonly used medications to control symptoms caused by a hiatal hernia.

Drug	Classification	Desired Effect
Aluminum hydroxide (Mylanta) Magnesium hydroxide (Maalox)	Antacid	Decrease heartburn
metoclopramide (Reglan)	Dopamine antagonist	Improve gastric emptying
rantidine (Zantac) famotidine (Pepcid)	Histamine blocker	Decrease gastric acid secretions
cimetidine (Tagamet)	Histamine blocker	Decrease gastric acid secretions
omeprazole (Prilosec)	Protein pump inhibitor	Decrease gastric secretions

If reflux is severe, surgical repair may be performed. **Fundoplication** involves "wrapping" the fundus of the stomach around the lower portion of the esophagus to "reduce" the hernia and tighten the sphincter.

ESOPHAGEAL NEOPLASMS

Esophageal neoplasms predominantly occur in clients with histories of hiatal hernia or alcohol abuse. Clients present with a variety of upper gastrointestinal complaints such as pain, dysphagia, nausea, and vomiting. The nurse must closely monitor the client's nutritional status. The client should take in high-calorie and high-protein liquid supplements and vitamin and mineral supplements. Parenteral nutrition—either total parenteral nutrition (T.P.N.), via a central venous catheter, or peripheral parenteral nutrition (P.P.N.)—can be administered if dysphagia is present. The choice for optimal nutrition is placement of a gastrostomy tube for enteral feedings as soon as possible. This bypasses the affected area of the esophagus but uses the functional stomach and intestines for digestion.

The following surgical procedures are commonly used to treat the client with esophageal neoplasm. Test your ability to use the word to guide you to the definition.

35. __C__ Creating an opening through the abdominal wall and directly into the stomach into which a feeding tube is inserted to bypass the stomach

    A. esophagectomy

    B. esophagogastrectomy

    C. gastrostomy

36. __A__ Removal of part or all of the esophagus, which is replaced by a graft

37. __B__ Resection of part of the esophagus and stomach; the stomach is reconnected to the proximal end of the esophagus

ESOPHAGEAL VARICES

Esophageal varices are blister-like spots in the esophagus caused by portal hypertension and are often associated with liver cirrhosis (think cirrh-, liver; think -osis, disease) and a history of alcohol abuse. The client is usually asymptomatic until the varices rupture and bleed, so clients who are known to have esophageal varices must be monitored for bleeding. The nurse should assess the client for melena stool, tachycardia, and hematemesis (signs of GI bleeding). The rupture of esophageal varices is a life-threatening event associated with a high mortality rate.

Endoscopic sclerotherapy may be done prophylactically, therapeutically, or as an emergency measure for esophageal varices. A sclerosing solution is injected into the varices to cause thrombosis and stop the bleeding.

A Sengstaken-Blakemore tube may be used to mechanically control hemorrhage by balloon tamponade. A client with a Sengstaken-Blakemore tube requires intensive care monitoring, invasive hemodynamic monitoring, and intubation to protect the airway. Since the client is not able to swallow around the tube, frequent mouth care and nutritional support are necessary.

Pharmacological therapy for esophageal varices may include administration of vitamin K, vasopressin (Pitressin), and propranolol HCl (Inderal).

THE STOMACH

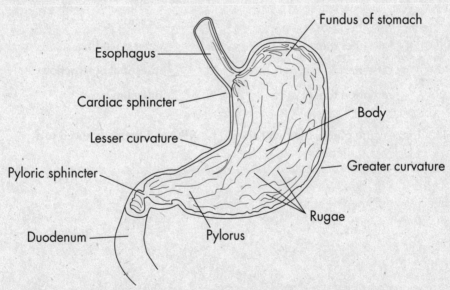

The stomach functions as a reservoir where the mechanical and chemical breakdown of food continues. Ingested food is liquefied and digested by gastric secretions. The vagus and splanchnic nerves innervate the stomach. The vagus nerve is cranial nerve X.

GASTROESOPHAGEAL REFLUX DISEASE

Gastroesophageal reflux disease (G.E.R.D.) is the reflux of stomach contents into the esophagus, causing regurgitation, irritation, and heartburn.

Use your knowledge of G.E.R.D. to fill in the following blanks:

Instruct clients to have small, frequent meals, a lot of liquids, and to avoid (38.) _spicy_, _carbohydrates_, and _citrus juice_ in their diets. The client should be in an (39.) _upright_ position during and after eating. The client should also be advised to avoid activity that increases (40.) _intra-abdominal_ pressure. Pharmacological interventions include the use of (41.) _histamine blockers_, _antacids_, and _dopamine antagonists_, such as metoclopramide (Reglan).

GASTRITIS

Do the following exercise to refresh your knowledge of gastritis. (Think about what might cause inflammation of the stomach lining.)

42. **Gastritis** may be caused by which of the following?

A. ✓ cigarette smoking		H. ✓ chemotherapy	
B. ✓ contaminated foods		I. ___ liver disease	
C. ✓ hypertension		J. ✓ C.N.S. lesions	
D. ✓ alcohol		K. ✓ steroids	
E. ___ low-fiber diet		L. ___ enteral feedings	
F. ✓ caffeine		M. ✓ intestinal obstruction	
G. ✓ radiation therapy		N. ✓ infection	

43. In the acute phase, the client should be NPO and then advanced to a _bland_ diet.

Peptic Ulcer Disease

Peptic ulcer disease always appears in some form on the NCLEX-RN.

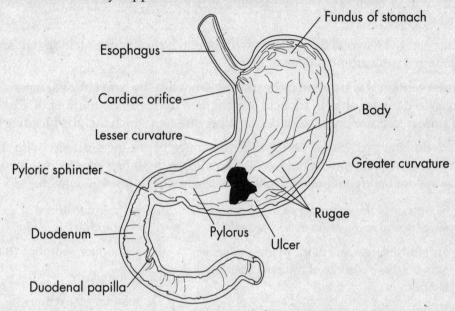

Differences Between Gastric and Duodenal Ulcers		
	Gastric Ulcers	**Duodenal Ulcers**
Most common age	Over 65	Under 65
Sex prevalence	Female	Male
Family history significant?	Yes	Not really
Risk factors	Stress, smoking, alcohol	C.O.P.D., chronic renal failure, chronic pancreatitis, alcohol, and cirrhosis
Location	Stomach antrum	Proximal 1–2 cm of the duodenum
Clinical signs	Upper abdominal pain 1–2 hours after meals; aggravated by food	Upper abdominal pain 2–4 hours after meals; relieved by food and antacids
Clinical course	More likely to be chronic and cause weight loss	Cyclical occurrences with exacerbations and remissions; causes weight gain
Cancer potential	Increased malignancy	Rare malignancy

Pharmacological therapy focuses on antacids, the drugs of choice for peptic ulcer disease. Histamine blockers and anticholinergic drugs are used as well. Sucralfate (Carafate) is prescribed for ulcer healing in the duodenum, as it coats the lining of the stomach to protect it from irritation.

Foods that need to be avoided by clients with peptic ulcer disease include hot, spicy food; alcohol; caffeine; and carbonated beverages.

Surgical intervention is warranted if the ulcer will not heal by conventional means. The goal of surgery is to decrease stimuli for acid secretion, to decrease the number of acid secreting cells, and to correct complications of peptic ulcer disease (which include bleeding).

Match the following procedures performed to manage peptic ulcer disease with the correct definition below. Again, you do not need to memorize these procedures, just increase your confidence in your ability to find the right answer with the information given.

44. __E__ Severance of the vagus nerve, which eliminates neural stimulation of acid secretion

45. __C__ Surgical enlargement of the pyloric sphincter, allowing easy passage of contents from the stomach

46. __D__ Removal of most of the body and all of the antrum of the stomach

47. __B__ Partial gastrectomy with removal of the distal $\frac{2}{3}$ of the stomach and anastomosis of the gastric stump to the duodenum

48. __A__ Partial gastrectomy with removal of the distal $\frac{2}{3}$ of the stomach with anastomosis of the gastric stump to the jejunum

A. gastrojejunostomy (Billroth II)

B. gastroduodenostomy (Billroth I)

C. pyloroplasty

D. subtotal gastrectomy

E. vagotomy

A postoperative complication of gastric resection surgery is "dumping syndrome." This is the result of the stomach's loss of control over emptying its contents into the small intestine. "Dumping syndrome" is generally self-limiting, resolving within one year of surgery. Nursing interventions include monitoring for signs of "dumping syndrome" (palpitations, dizziness, weakness, and abdominal cramping) and instructing the client to eat six small, dry feedings per day that are moderately high in carbohydrates, low in refined sugar, and have a moderate-to-high amount of protein and a moderate amount of fat. Carbonated beverages should be avoided. Milk may not be well tolerated. The client should rest for at least 30 minutes following meals. Fluids should be encouraged between meals.

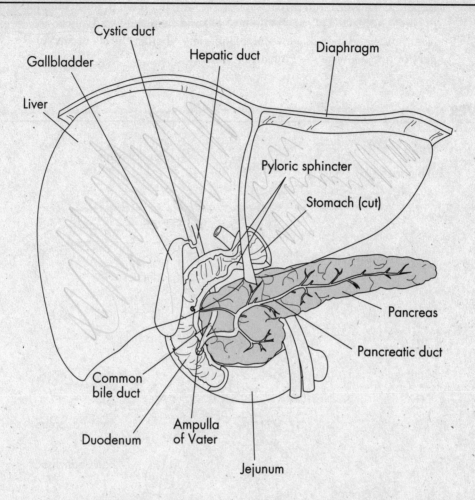

The function of the gallbladder is to concentrate and store bile. The gallbladder contracts and forces bile through the cystic duct into the common bile duct and, hence, into the duodenum. The sphincter of Oddi regulates the one-way flow of bile into the duodenum.

CHOLECYSTITIS

Cholecystitis is the inflammation (-itis) of the gallbladder caused by stones (cholelithiasis). When the common bile duct is completely obstructed by calculi or edema, bile is unable to pass into the duodenum and is, therefore, absorbed into the blood circulation. Certain clients are predisposed to developing cholecystitis. Risk factors include being female, obese, middle-aged, and multiparous. The client usually presents with complaints of right upper quadrant abdominal pain that may radiate to the back. Pain may be severe and is often referred to as biliary colic. Pain sometimes occurs after the client eats a meal consisting of fried or fatty foods. Other complaints include jaundice (in approximately 25 percent of clients) and vomiting.

49. The client may have a cholecystectomy, which is _surgical removal of_ _gallbladder_ (separate the word into its parts to figure out what it is). In the acute phase of cholecystitis, the client should be NPO and then slowly advanced to clear fluids and then to a low-fat, bland diet. Whether the client has surgery or not, a low-fat diet must be followed.

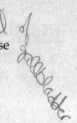

THE LIVER

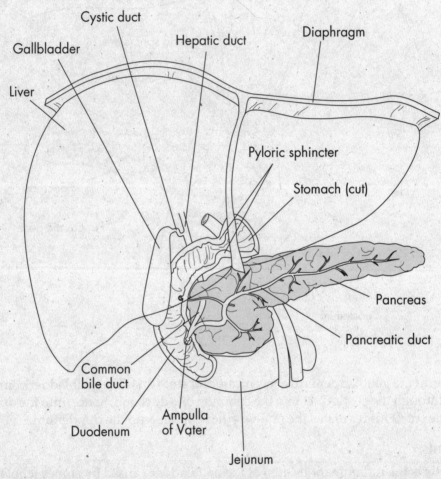

The liver is vital in sustaining life. Use the following chart to review the varied functions of the liver.

Manufacture	Metabolize	Store
Bile	Carbohydrates	Vitamins A, B, D
Fibrinogen	Fat	Iron
Prothrombin	Protein	Copper
Vitamin K	Drugs and alcohol	
Immunoglobins	Hormones	

HEPATITIS

Hepatitis, literally, is inflammation of the liver (hepat- = liver; -itis = inflammation). The **hepatitis virus** invades, replicates, and causes damage only in the liver. What happens when the liver cannot perform the functions listed in the above chart? There are three phases of infection with the hepatitis virus:

- Phase 1: lasts 1–21 days; infectivity is at its height. Gastrointestinal symptoms dominate.

- Phase 2: lasts 2–4 weeks. Symptoms are due to the spread of bilirubin through the tissues: pruritis, dark urine, clay-colored stool, and jaundice.

- Phase 3: lasts 2–4 months, jaundice resolves slowly. The client remains fatigued; hepatomegaly persists.

There is no direct pharmacological treatment for viral hepatitis. Think about bleeding precautions, gastrointestinal support, and client education. Supportive care is provided using vitamin supplements, antiemetics as needed, symptomatic treatment of pain, and rest. The client should be instructed in a proper diet of high-protein, high-calorie foods, and food with low to moderate fat content as tolerated.

Differences Between Hepatitis A, B, and C			
	Hepatitis A	**Hepatitis B**	**Hepatitis C**
Etiology	Hepatitis A virus	Hepatitis B virus	Hepatitis C virus
Transmission	Oral-anal Contaminated food and water	Blood/blood product Body fluids Sexual contact	Blood/blood product Body fluids Sexual contact
Incubation period	2–6 weeks	6 weeks–6 months	2 weeks–6 months
Infectivity period	Latter half of incubation to 1–2 weeks after symptom onset	After symptoms appear; can be a carrier and transmit HBV throughout one's lifetime	After symptoms appear; can be a carrier and transmit HCV throughout one's lifetime
Isolation necessary	Universal precautions	Universal precautions	Universal precautions
Prophylaxis (passive immunity)	Immune globulin before and after exposure	Hepatitis B immunoglobulin (HBIG) after suspected exposure	Immune globulin before and after exposure
Vaccine	Being developed	Recombinant vaccine	None

CIRRHOSIS

Cirrhosis is a chronic and progressive disease that causes extensive destruction of the liver parenchymal cells. The destroyed cells are replaced by scar tissue, which eventually results in poor cellular function, hypoxia, and inadequate blood flow to the liver. Onset of cirrhosis is often insidious, with symptoms including anorexia, weight loss, malaise, altered bowel habits, nausea, and vomiting. Management is directed at avoiding the complications and requires maintaining fluid, electrolyte, and nutritional balance. Proper nutrition for the client with cirrhosis varies and must be individualized. Small, frequent meals are recommended. While protein restriction is the usual dietary recommendation, the threat of malnutrition usually overrides the need to restrict protein.

Complications of cirrhosis include:

- Portal hypertension (obstruction of normal blood flow through the portal and hepatic veins causes hypertension in the portal venous system).

- Esophageal varices (blister-like spots in the esophagus caused by portal hypertension)—Clients who are known to have esophageal varices must be monitored for bleeding. The nurse should assess the client for melena stool, tachycardia, and hematemesis. The rupture of esophageal varices is a life-threatening event associated with a high mortality rate.

- Hepatic encephalopathy/coma (ammonia is a product of protein metabolism normally excreted by the liver; because ammonia is shunted away from the liver, it stays in the bloodstream and crosses into the brain, causing neurological deficits)—lactulose (Cephulac) is the drug of choice as it binds with ammonia and is excreted in the stool.

- Ascites (the accumulation of fluid in the peritoneum as a result of portal hypertension, hypoalbuminemia, and hyperaldosteronism).

THE PANCREAS

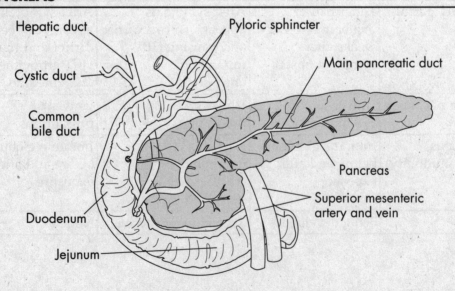

The pancreas has both exocrine and endocrine functions. Exocrine secretions (digestive enzymes) are produced by the acinar cells. Match the following enzymes with the correct substance upon which they act:

50. _____ trypsinogen   A. carbohydrates

51. _____ pancreatic amylase   B. fats

52. _____ pancreatic lipase   C. protein

The endocrine secretions are produced by α, β, and Δ cells of the pancreas. Match each with its proper secretion:

53. _____ α cells   A. glucagon

54. _____ β cells   B. insulin

55. _____ Δ cells   C. somatostatin

56. Alpha cells induce glycogenolysis in the liver when the serum blood sugar falls, while β cells produce _____ when blood sugar rises.

PANCREATITIS

Pancreatitis is a process of autodigestion. Pancreatic enzymes are activated while still in the pancreas, not when they reach the intestines. Pancreatitis is often associated with excessive alcohol ingestion. The client complains of nausea, vomiting, and severe, continuous pain in the left upper quadrant that may radiate to the back. Upon examination, the nurse will note tenderness on palpation of the pancreas and decreased or absent bowel sounds. Diagnostic lab tests include elevated lipase and amylase levels.

The client with pancreatitis is NPO. Nursing interventions are directed at correcting fluid and electrolyte imbalances, providing client and family education about the disease, and providing nutritional support. The client's diet should be advanced slowly from clear liquids and eventually to low-fat with small, frequent meals. Throughout this time, the nurse should be monitoring the client's lipase and amylase levels, and pancreatic enzyme replacements may be indicated.

WHIPPLE OPERATION

Pancreatic cancer is an insidious disease that often goes undetected until its later stages. The goal of treatment is frequently only palliative (to provide relief). If the tumor is less advanced, the goal of treatment is curative. In either case, the treatment of choice is a **Whipple procedure**, the surgical intervention for pancreatic cancer. It may be combined with radiation and/or chemotherapy. Match the parts of a Whipple procedure with the explanations on the right:

57. _____ Proximal pancreatectomy   A. resection of the distal stomach

58. _____ Duodenectomy   B. resection of the duodenum

59. _____ Partial gastrectomy   C. resection of the proximal pancreas

The pancreatic duct, the common bile duct, and the stomach are reanastomosed to the jejunum.

WHIPPLE PROCEDURE (PANCREATODUODENECTOMY)

In this technique, the doctor resects the stomach, duodenum, pancreas, and bile duct. The doctor may also remove the gallbladder. Three anastomoses connect the common bile duct, pancreas, and stomach to the jejunum. The doctor anastomoses the pancreas and bile duct proximal to the gastric anastomosis to neutralize acidic secretions dumped from the stomach into the jejunum. A vagotomy to decrease gastric acid secretion may also be performed.

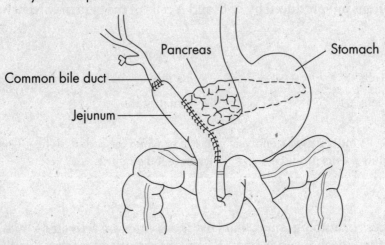

Dietary considerations after a Whipple procedure include a low-fat diet; small, frequent meals; and monitoring the client's blood sugar. Alcohol should be avoided.

THE COLON (SMALL AND LARGE INTESTINE)

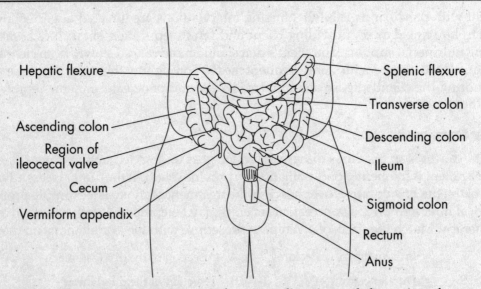

The small intestine has two primary functions: digestion and absorption of the end products of digestion. The small intestine consists of the (60.) _____, _____, and _____.

The most important functions of the large intestine are the absorption of water and electrolytes, and the formation of feces for defecation. The large intestine consists of the (61.) _____, _____, _____, _____, and _____.

The colon is divided into the (62.) _____, _____, and _____ colon.

Transverse colon

Hepatic flexure

Haustra

Taenia coli

Ascending colon

Ileocecal valve

Descending colon

Ileum

Sigmoid colon

Cecum

Appendix

Rectum

Anal canal

Anus

APPENDICITIS

Appendicitis is characterized by periumbilical pain followed by elevated temperature, anorexia, nausea, and vomiting. The pain eventually localizes at McBurney's point, between the umbilicus and the right iliac crest. Rovsing's sign (palpation of the left lower quadrant of the abdomen causes pain in the right lower quadrant) is also present.

DIVERTICULA

Diverticula are outpouchings of the intestinal mucosa through the smooth muscle of the intestinal wall at any point in the gastrointestinal tract. They are most common in the sigmoid colon. **Diverticulosis** is the presence of multiple, noninflamed diverticula. Clients with diverticulosis are often asymptomatic. A high-fiber diet with a lot of liquid is recommended for clients with diverticulosis. Seeds, nuts, and skins are usually restricted (while this is not validated by studies, it is the conventional recommendation). **Diverticulitis** is the inflammation of diverticula and of the surrounding intestine, causing the tissue to become edematous. Deficiency in dietary fiber has been associated with this condition. Complications of diverticulitis are abscess and fistula formation; bleeding; bowel obstruction; and perforation, causing peritonitis. The client with diverticulitis is usually NPO and is advanced slowly to clear liquids and low-fiber to medium-high residue, and, finally, to a high-fiber diet, as tolerated.

CROHN'S DISEASE AND ULCERATIVE COLITIS

Crohn's disease and **ulcerative colitis** always appear on the NCLEX-RN. The following chart summarizes what you need to know to answer these questions correctly.

Differences Between Ulcerative Colitis and Crohn's Disease		
	Ulcerative Colitis	**Crohn's Disease**
Age	Any age; most common 10–50 years old	Any age; most common 10–30 years old
Sex prevalence	Women	Women and men equally
Family history significant?	Not really	Yes
Area affected	Begins in distal large intestine and moves up colon; mucosal and submucosal walls	All layers of bowel wall, from mouth to anus
Distributive	Continuous ulceration	Discontinuous ulceration
Clinical signs	Frequent, bloody diarrhea, abdominal pain	Nonspecific GI complaints; 3–4 semisoft stools/day
Cancer potential	Increased malignancy	No relation

The six goals of management of ulcerative colitis and Crohn's disease are:

1. Control inflammation.
2. Correct metabolic and nutritional deficits. (Total parenteral nutrition is a must! Usual dietary progression is from bowel rest, NPO, to a low-fiber diet, to a regular diet, as tolerated.)
3. Relieve symptoms.
4. Promote healing.
5. Combat infection.
6. Rest the bowel.

Emotional support and education are vital parts of nursing care for these clients, as these conditions can alter lifestyle and body image perception.

Unlike ulcerative colitis, Crohn's disease cannot be cured by surgical interventions. There is a high recurrence rate after surgery. Surgical treatment depends on the affected area and on the general condition of the client. The procedure of choice is conservative resection with anastomosis of healthy bowel.

INTESTINAL OBSTRUCTIONS

Intestinal obstructions include anything that interferes with contents passing through the gastrointestinal tract. The obstruction may be partial or complete. Intestinal obstructions will manifest as abdominal distention and pain, and vomiting that may contain fecal material. The nurse must monitor the client closely for hyperactive bowel sounds and flatus. The client should also be monitored for fluid and electrolyte imbalance and signs of dehydration.

Decompression of the intestine is accomplished using intestinal tubes such as the Cantor tube and the Miller-Abbott tube that remove gas and fluid. Some mechanical obstructions are surgically relieved.

The client with an intestinal tube must be positioned on the right side to facilitate the passage of the tube through the pylorus. After the tube passes the pylorus, the client is placed in a semi-Fowler's position to continue the gradual advancement of the tube into the intestine.

COLON/RECTAL CANCER

Colon/rectal cancer is closely associated with the "Western" diet which consists of foods high in fat and low in fiber. The client is usually asymptomatic until the disease is well advanced. Occult blood in the stool is an early indicator of colon cancer. Many rectal cancers are within reach of the finger upon rectal examination.

Surgery is the only curative treatment of colorectal cancer. Following are the most common surgical procedures performed. Match the procedure with the correct description below:

63. ____ Used for cancer in the cecum, ascending colon, hepatic flexure, or right transverse colon

64. ____ Used for cancer in the left transverse colon, splenic flexure, descending colon, sigmoid colon, or upper portion of the rectum

65. ____ Used for tumors of the rectosigmoid and middle to upper rectum

66. ____ Used for cancer located within 5 cm of the anus (the proximal sigmoid colon is brought through the abdominal wall to form a permanent colostomy; the distal sigmoid, rectum, and anus are removed through a perineal incision)

A. abdominal perineal resection

B. left hemicolectomy

C. low anterior resection

D. right hemicolectomy

HEMORRHOIDS

Hemorrhoids are dilated varicose veins of the anus and rectum. They may be internal or external. Internal hemorrhoids are the most common cause of bleeding upon defecation and, over time, can result in iron deficiency anemia. Causes of hemorrhoids include: pregnancy, constipation, heavy lifting, and prolonged sitting. Treatment includes management of constipation, diet management, and hemorrhoidectomy.

OSTOMIES

In one way or another, **ostomies** are always included on the NCLEX-RN. Teaching clients with ostomies and assessing ostomies are vital nursing functions.

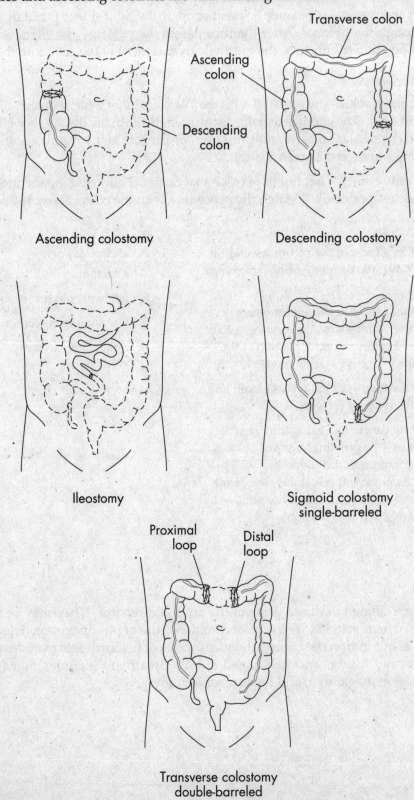

Ascending colostomy

Descending colostomy

Ileostomy

Sigmoid colostomy
single-barreled

Transverse colostomy
double-barreled

Match the following types of ostomies with the correct definition:

67. ____ Opening between the colon and the abdominal wall; often used to temporarily rest the bowel

68. ____ Single stoma from the proximal end of the severed colon with removal of the distal portion of the bowel

69. ____ Loop of bowel is brought out above the skin surface, where it is held in place by a plastic rod

70. ____ Opening from the ileum through the abdominal wall; most commonly used in the surgical treatment of ulcerative colitis. Stool is like liquid. Dietary sodium should be increased in these clients.

71. ____ Colectomy with creation of an internal pouch from the ileum that has a nipple valve to control stool and flatus, thereby maintaining continence; also known as continent ileostomy

A. colostomy

B. ileostomy

C. Kock pouch

D. loop colostomy

E. permanent colostomy

Clients with ostomies may need to increase their fluid intake and avoid gas-producing vegetables, such as onions, beans, and cauliflower.

DISORDERS OF THE ABDOMINAL CAVITY

PERITONITIS

Peritonitis is the inflammation of the peritoneum. It is caused by infection (due to perforation) and also by chemical stress, as in pancreatitis. The client will complain of abdominal pain, elevated temperature, malaise, nausea, and vomiting. On examination, the nurse most often finds rebound tenderness. Complete blood count shows an increase in white blood cells, as in any infection.

HERNIAS

Hernias are the protrusion of the intestine or abdominal organ through a weakening in the abdominal wall (muscle). There are a variety of hernias that nurses encounter. Match the specific hernia type with its clinical presentation:

72. ____ Protrusion that cannot be replaced by manipulation

73. ____ Protrusion through the site of an old surgical incision

74. ____ Intestinal flow is completely obstructed

75. ____ Blood flow to the intestinal wall is completely obstructed

A. femoral

B. incarcerated

C. inguinal

D. irreducible

E. reducible

F. strangulated

G. umbilical

H. ventral

76. ____ Protrusion through the abdominal ring into
the inguinal canal

77. ____ Protrusion through the umbilical ring

78. ____ Protrusion that can be replaced into the
abdominal cavity by manipulation

79. ____ Protrusion through the femoral canal

Hernias can cause general gastrointestinal symptoms and intestinal obstruction. A binder may be used to prevent strangulation. Surgical intervention may be necessary.

GENERAL NURSING CARE AFTER GASTROINTESTINAL SURGERY

When caring for the client who has undergone gastrointestinal surgery, the nurse must look at many factors that could prolong and adversely affect the client's hospital stay. Each physiological system needs to be assessed and interventions initiated in a timely manner to facilitate recovery. The following considerations are crucial in caring for clients following gastrointestinal surgery:

- In the immediate postoperative period, the nursing priority is assessing vital signs until they are stable.

- Pain management: Around-the-clock medication to prevent exacerbations of incisional pain in addition to nonpharmacological pain control methods (the nurse should offer pain management agents, not wait for the client to ask for them; a pain management scale should be used to assess the effectiveness of interventions) Note: Pain medication may decrease peristalsis and cause constipation.

- Client teaching: Pre- and postoperatively, accurate instruction on what the client can expect decreases anxiety surrounding surgery.

- Assessing the suture line: Signs of infection include redness, swelling, drainage, and open areas; if a suture line dehisces, immediately apply moist gauze and call for help.

- Pulmonary toileting: Once pain is managed, the client must be engaged in chest physiotherapy, coughing, and deep breathing, and using the incentive spirometer to prevent pneumonia and atelectasis. After GI surgery, the client has a difficult time taking deep breaths due to the location of the incision. Pain management is a vital component of pulmonary toileting.

- Early ambulation: Increasing activity as soon as possible (after managing incisional pain) helps prevent deep vein thrombosis and pneumonia.

- After lower gastrointestinal surgery, nothing should be inserted per rectum.

- Support nutritional needs: Often, clients with GI problems are malnourished; they need to be started on a clear liquid diet as soon as bowel sounds return (hopefully within five days after surgery), and to be advanced, as tolerated, to a regular diet (or diabetic, or low-fat) depending on preexisting conditions. If a client must be NPO for more than five days, total parenteral nutrition (T.P.N.) must be considered.

In caring for the client after gastrointestinal surgery, the nurse encounters a variety of postoperative drainage devices. Become familiar with them by matching the type of drain with its use from the following list:

80. ____ A collapsible device attached to a drain with multiple openings; exerts negative pressure to withdraw accumulated fluids

81. ____ A nasogastric tube that has a second lumen for air entry that keeps the gastric lining from occluding the drainage holes; often attached to intermittent or low continuous suction; requires frequent irrigation to maintain patency

82. ____ The most common abdominal drain; flat, single lumen withdraws drainage by capillary action

83. ____ Oval, clear, pliable reservoir connected to drainage tubing; reservoir or bulb can be compressed to form negative pressure, often referred to as "self-suction"

84. ____ Single lumen nasogastric tube used to evacuate air and fluid from the stomach; requires frequent irrigation to maintain patency

85. ____ Tube that bypasses the stomach and allows for feedings to maintain or restore a client's nutrition

86. ____ Tube that bypasses the esophagus and allows for feeding to maintain or restore a client's nutrition

87. ____ Thin drainage catheter inserted into the common bile duct during surgery to protect the suture line

A. gastrostomy tube

B. Hemovac self-suctioning device

C. Jackson-Pratt

D. jejunostomy tube

E. Levine tube

F. Penrose drain

G. Salem sump

H. t-tube

PHARMACOLOGY FOR THE GASTROINTESTINAL SYSTEM

88. First, review the five rights of medication administration:

A. _____   D. _____

B. _____   E. _____

C. _____

Antacids provide a protective coating on the stomach lining and increase gastric pH (decrease acidity).

89. Aluminum compounds cause _____, while magnesium compounds cause _____.

Antidiarrheals act by decreasing the fluid in stool (attapulgite [Kaopectate]) or by decreasing intestinal motility (diphenoxylate HCl [Lomotil]). There is a risk of physical dependence with long-term use.

Antiemetics alleviate nausea and vomiting and are also effective in the prevention of motion sickness. (In clients undergoing chemotherapy, antiemetics should be given 30 minutes prior to treatment.)

Histamine antagonists (H_2-**blockers**) inhibit gastric secretion. The most common side effect is confusion in the elderly, as well as headaches and dizziness. Drugs in this category include cimetidine (Tagamet), ranitidine (Zantac), and famotidine (Pepcid). Smoking interferes with the action of H_2-blockers.

Laxatives promote the evacuation of stool. There is a risk of physical dependence, dehydration, and electrolyte imbalance. The following are types of laxatives:

- Intestinal lubricants (mineral oil) hydrate feces and lubricate intestinal tract.
- Stool softeners (docusate sodium [Colace]) allow water and fats to penetrate feces.
- Bulk-forming laxatives (psyllium hydrophilic mucilloid [Metamucil]) increase bulk in the intestinal lumen, causing pressure on the mucosal lining and subsequent stimulation of peristalsis; should be taken with large glasses of water to prevent obstruction.
- Colon irritants (Dulcolax, Senokot) stimulate peristalsis by irritating the intestinal lumen.
- Saline cathartics (magnesium hydroxide [milk of magnesia]) increase osmotic pressure in the intestine, increasing bulk and stimulating peristalsis; side effect is dehydration.

Pancreatic enzymes are used to promote the digestion of proteins, fats, and starch. They replace natural pancreatic enzymes (protease, lipase, amylase). Drugs in this category include pancrelipase (Viokase) and pancreatin. They must be taken with food to minimize gastric irritation.

Miscellaneous drugs you should know for the NCLEX-RN are listed here:

- Sucralfate (Carafate) coats a duodenal ulcer site. A side effect is constipation. The drug may decrease the absorption of other medications, so it should be taken 1–2 hours before other drugs.
- Omeprazole (Prilosec) is a proton pump inhibitor that inhibits gastric acid secretion.
- Metoclopramide (Reglan) enhances gastric motility and gastric emptying.

GO BACK!

Now that you've reviewed the gastrointestinal system, go back to the diagram of the stomach at the beginning of the chapter and view each organ while thinking about its function and associated potential problems. You will be surprised by how much you know!

CHAPTER 7: EXERCISE ANSWERS

The four parts of the abdominal assessment, in order:

1. **inspection**

2. **auscultation**

3. **percussion**

4. **palpation**

5. **C** **fiber-optic colonoscopy**—A flexible fiber-optic scope is used to visualize the entire colon.

6. **G** **oral cholecystogram**—X-ray exam after oral ingestion of radiopaque dye to determine the patency of the biliary duct

7. **E** **liver biopsy**—Percutaneous or intraoperative microscopic exam to confirm diagnosis of hepatocellular diseases

8. **I** **ultrasound**—Noninvasive exam using sound waves to determine organ size and shape

9. **A** **CAT scan**—Noninvasive radiological exam using tomography to present organ structure at different depths and views; can be used with or without contrast

10. **K** **upper GI series (barium swallow)**—Observation of contrast medium movement through the esophagus and into the stomach by means of fluoroscopy and x-ray. The contrast dye can cause impaction of stool so keep the client well hydrated; stool may be white for up to 2 days after the test.

11. **F** **lower GI series (barium enema)**—Radiological observation of contrast medium filling the colon

12. **B** **endoscopic retrograde cholangiopancreatography (E.R.C.P.)**—Flexible fiber-optic scope inserted into the mouth and via the common bile duct and pancreatic ducts to visualize these structures. After the test, observe for hemorrhage.

13. **J** **upper GI endoscopy**—Flexible fiber-optic endoscope that directly visualizes the structures of the upper GI tract. After the test, assess the client's gag reflex before allowing PO intake.

14. **H** **percutaneous transhepatic cholangiogram (P.T.C.)**—Using fluoroscopy, the bile duct is entered percutaneously and injected with dye to observe filling of hepatic and biliary ducts. After the test, observe for hemorrhage.

15. **D** **IV cholangiogram**—Radiographic exam used to visualize the biliary duct system after intravenous injection of radiopaque dye

16. Gastrointestinal structure and function begins in the mouth with **mechanical** and…

17. …**chemical** digestion.

18. Much of the chewing process is innervated by the **fifth (trigeminal)** cranial nerve.

19. Salivary gland secretions begin basic **starch** digestion.

20. Salivary amylase begins the chemical breakdown of **starches** to maltose.

21. Parotitis is usually caused by **prolonged NPO status,** *Staphylococcus aureus***, or poor oral hygiene.**

22. Upon inspection, the nurse may discover **purulent** drainage from the duct.

23. In caring for the client with stomatitis, the nurse must provide and teach the proper technique for **mouth care**…

24. …as well as dietary instruction on a **bland** diet and cool drinks to decrease further irritation.

25. The esophagus consists of muscular layers that contract and propel food into the stomach by **peristalsis.**

26. At the lower end of the esophagus is the **gastroesophageal sphincter**, which stays constricted except during...

27. **swallowing, belching, and vomiting**.

28. Because the lower third of esophageal blood supply drains into the portal system, portal hypertension may lead to the development of **esophageal varices**.

29. An **esophageal hernia** (**hiatal hernia**) is the herniation of a portion of the **stomach** through an enlarged esophageal opening in the diaphragm.

30. Factors that contribute to the development of hiatal hernia (like all hernias) include **muscle weakening** and anything that increases intra-abdominal pressure, such as obesity, pregnancy, tumors, and ascites.

31. The client may be asymptomatic or have complaints of **heartburn and reflux**.

32. The client may also complain of **chest pain** while lying down.

33. Any complaint of **chest pain** must be considered cardiac in origin until proven otherwise, so frequent monitoring of vital signs is the nursing priority.

34. In caring for the client with an esophageal (hiatal) hernia, provide **small, frequent meals** and maintain the client in an upright position during and after meals to avoid regurgitation.

35. **C** **gastrostomy**—Creating an opening directly into the stomach into which a feeding tube is inserted to bypass the stomach

36. **A** **esophagectomy**—Removal of part or all of the esophagus, which is replaced by a graft

37. **B** **esophagogastrectomy**—Resection of part of the esophagus and stomach; the stomach is reconnected to the proximal end of the esophagus

38. Instruct clients to have small, frequent meals, a lot of liquids, and to avoid **caffeine, alcohol, coffee, citrus juices, spicy foods, carbonation, peppermint,** and **chocolate** in their diets.

39. The client should be in an **upright** position during and after eating.

40. The client should also be advised to avoid activity that increases **intra-abdominal** pressure.

41. Pharmacological interventions include the use of **histamine blockers, antacids,** and **dopamine antagonists** such as metoclopramide (Reglan).

42. **Gastritis** may be caused by which of the following?

    A. cigarette smoking

    B. contaminated foods

    D. alcohol

    F. caffeine

    G. radiation therapy

    H. chemotherapy

    J. C.N.S. lesions

    K. steroids

    N. infection

43. In the acute phase of gastritis, the client should be NPO and then advanced to a **bland** diet.

44. **E** **vagotomy**—Severance of the vagus nerve, which eliminates neural stimulation of acid secretion

45. **C** **pyloroplasty**—Surgical enlargement of the pyloric sphincter, allowing easy passage of contents from the stomach

46. **D** **subtotal gastrectomy**—Removal of most of the body and all of the antrum of the stomach

47. **B** **gastroduodenostomy (Billroth I)**—Partial gastrectomy with removal of the distal $\frac{2}{3}$ of the stomach and anastomosis of the gastric stump to the duodenum

48. **A** **gastrojejunostomy (Billroth II)**—Partial gastrectomy of the distal $\frac{2}{3}$ of the stomach with anastomosis of the gastric stump to the jejunum

49. The client may have a cholecystectomy, which is **surgical removal of the gallbladder**.

50. **C** **protein**—trypsinogen

51. **A** **carbohydrates**—pancreatic amylase

52. **B** **fats**—pancreatic lipase

53. **A** **glucagon**—α cells

54. **B** **insulin**—β cells

55. **C** **somatostatin**—Δ cells

56. α cells induce glycogenolysis in the liver when the serum blood sugar falls, while β cells produce **insulin** when blood sugar rises.

57. **C** **resection of the proximal pancreas**—Proximal pancreatectomy

58. **B** **resection of the duodenum**—Duodenectomy

59. **A** **resection of the distal stomach**—Partial gastrectomy

60. The small intestine consists of the **duodenum, jejunum,** and **ileum**.

61. The large intestine consists of the **cecum, appendix, sigmoid, rectum,** and **anus**.

62. The colon is divided into the **ascending, transverse,** and **descending** colon.

63. **D** **right hemicolectomy**—Used for cancer in the cecum, ascending colon, hepatic flexure, or the right transverse colon

64. **B** **left hemicolectomy**—Used for cancer in the left transverse colon, splenic flexure, descending colon, sigmoid colon, or upper portion of the rectum

65. **C** **low anterior resection**—Used for tumors of the rectosigmoid and middle to upper rectum

66. **A** **abdominal perineal resection**—Used for cancer located within 5 cm of the anus (the proximal sigmoid colon is brought through the abdominal wall to form a permanent colostomy; the distal sigmoid, rectum, and anus are removed through a perineal incision)

67. **A** **colostomy**—Opening between the colon and the abdominal wall; often used to temporarily rest the bowel

68. **E** **permanent colostomy**—Single stoma from the proximal end of the severed colon with the removal of the distal portion of the bowel

69. **D** **loop colostomy**—Loop of bowel is brought out above the skin surface, where it is held in place by a plastic rod

70. **B** **ileostomy**—Opening from the ileum through the abdominal wall; most commonly used in the surgical treatment of ulcerative colitis. Stool is like liquid. Dietary sodium should be decreased in clients

71. **C** **Kock pouch**—Colectomy with creation of an internal pouch from the ileum that has a nipple valve to control stool and flatus, thereby maintaining continence; also known as a continent ileostomy

72. **D** **irreducible**—Protrusion that cannot be replaced by manipulation

73. **H** **ventral**—Protrusion through the site of an old surgical incision

74. **B** **incarcerated**—Intestinal flow is completely obstructed

75. **F** **strangulated**—Blood flow to the intestinal wall is completely obstructed

76. **C inguinal**—Protrusion through the abdominal ring into the inguinal canal

77. **G umbilical**—Protrusion through the umbilical ring

78. **E reducible**—Protrusion that can be replaced into the abdominal cavity by manipulation

79. **A femoral**—Protrusion through the femoral canal

80. **B Hemovac self-suctioning device**—A collapsible device attached to a drain with multiple openings; exerts negative pressure to withdraw accumulated fluids

81. **G Salem sump**—A nasogastric tube that has a second lumen for air entry that keeps the gastric lining from occluding the drainage holes; often attached to intermittent or low continuous suction. Requires frequent irrigation to maintain patency

82. **F Penrose**—The most common abdominal drain; its flat, single lumen withdraws drainage by capillary action

83. **C Jackson-Pratt drain**—Oval, clear, pliable reservoir connected to drainage tubing; reservoir or bulb can be compressed to form negative pressure, often referred to as "self-suction"

84. **E Levine tube**—Single lumen nasogastric tube used to evacuate air and fluid from the stomach; requires frequent irrigation to maintain patency

85. **D jejunostomy tube**—Tube that bypasses the stomach and allows for feedings to maintain or restore a client's nutrition

86. **A gastrostomy tube**—Tube that bypasses the esophagus and allows for feeding to maintain or restore a client's nutrition

87. **H t-tube**—Thin drainage catheter inserted into the common bile duct during surgery to protect the suture line

88. The five rights of medication administration: **client, dose, drug, route,** and **time.**

89. Aluminum compounds cause **constipation**, while magnesium compounds cause **diarrhea**.

CHAPTER 7: NCLEX-RN STYLE QUESTIONS

1. The nurse is teaching a parent whose teenage son has hepatitis A. The nurse teaches the mother that the best way to avoid spread of infection is

   (1) wearing a mask.
   (2) wearing gloves.
   (3) hand washing.
   (4) wearing a gown.

2. Nursing care for a client with acute diverticulitis will include

   (1) a high-residue diet.
   (2) bed rest and steroids.
   (3) fluids by mouth and laxatives.
   (4) intravenous fluids and antibiotics.

3. A client has undergone an endoscopy of the upper gastrointestinal tract. The nursing care plan should include which of the following?

   (1) Administering analgesics for pain
   (2) Withholding food until a gag reflex is present
   (3) Positioning the client on the right side
   (4) Observing the client for rectal bleeding

4. A nurse develops a teaching plan for a client diagnosed with hepatitis B. Which diet, when selected by the client, would indicate the teaching has been effective?

   (1) Bacon, eggs, milk
   (2) Shrimp, avocado salad, and skim milk
   (3) Hamburger, cottage cheese, and malted milk
   (4) Carrots, lean beef, and orange juice

5. A nurse is to administer the hepatitis B vaccine to a client. Which of the following accurately describes the recommended dosing interval for the hepatitis B vaccine?

   (1) First dose followed by second dose 3 months later, followed by third dose 6 months later.
   (2) First dose followed by second dose 1 month later, followed by third dose 5 months later.
   (3) First dose followed by second dose 2 months later, followed by third dose 6 months later.
   (4) First dose followed by second dose 6 months later, followed by third dose 6 months later.

6. The nurse is planning care for a client with gastroesophageal reflux. Antacids are the first line of drugs used to treat this disorder, but if these alone are not effective, the nurse may notify the provider to add

   (1) anticholinergics.
   (2) antiemetics.
   (3) calcium channel blockers.
   (4) histamine (H_2) receptor antagonists.

7. A client with a diagnosis of bleeding esophageal varices must be observed for which of the following complications?	(1) Hypovolemic shock (2) Polycythemia vera (3) Hyperglycemia (4) Abscess formation
8. The nurse is teaching a client about treatment of hemorrhoids. In trying to help the client be more comfortable, the nurse teaches nonsurgical treatments for hemorrhoids, which include	(1) Fleet enema. (2) hot packs. (3) stool softeners. (4) hemorrhoidoscopy.
9. The nurse is caring for a client with a duodenal ulcer. The nurse teaches the client that a duodenal ulcer is	(1) most often a chronic ulcer. (2) more likely to cause hemorrhage. (3) related to an increased risk of malignancy. (4) likely to recur seasonally.
10. A 49-year-old man with a duodenal ulcer is admitted to the hospital when his hematocrit was noted to be 18%. He is scheduled for emergency endoscopy. Which diet would be appropriate?	(1) Regular bland diet (2) Full liquid (3) Regular pureed (4) NPO

CHAPTER 7: NCLEX-RN STYLE ANSWERS

1. **(3) CORRECT**   Hand washing is the best method of controlling infection.
   (1) ELIMINATE   Wearing a mask will not reduce the spread of infection.
   (2) POSSIBLE   Wearing gloves will help, but choice #3 is a better answer.
   (4) ELIMINATE   A gown is not necessary.
   CATEGORY 02 SAFETY AND INFECTION CONTROL

2. **(4) CORRECT**   Initial treatment of acute diverticulitis consists of bowel rest. The client with diverticulitis is NPO, and therefore hydration and antibiotics are administered intravenously.
   (1) ELIMINATE   A high-residue diet is recommended for clients with divericular disease, but not in the acute phase.
   (2) ELIMINATE   Steroids are not indicated.
   (3) ELIMINATE   Laxatives are avoided because they increase intestinal mobility.
   CATEGORY 10 PHYSIOLOGICAL ADAPTATION

3. (2) CORRECT   The client undergoing endoscopy has a topical anesthetic agent applied to the back of the throat prior to passage of the endoscope. This facilitates passage of the scope due to the depression of the client's gag reflex. The client can aspirate if food or fluids are given before the gag reflex returns.

    (1) ELIMINATE   This procedure is not usually associated with pain, and analgesia is not usually necessary.

    (3) ELIMINATE   Positioning the client on the right side is not necessary postprocedure.

    (4) ELIMINATE   Assessment for rectal bleeding would be a priority if the client had undergone a colonoscopy.

    CATEGORY 09 REDUCTION OF RISK POTENTIAL

4. (4) CORRECT   A client with hepatitis B should be on a low-fat, cholesterol-restricted diet.

    (1) ELIMINATE   This diet is high in fat.

    (2) ELIMINATE   This diet is high in cholesterol.

    (3) ELIMINATE   This diet is high in calories and fat.

    CATEGORY 07 BASIC CARE AND COMFORT

5. (2) CORRECT   This represents the recommended dosing interval.

    (1) ELIMINATE   The correct sequence is first dose followed by second dose 1 month later, followed by third dose 5 months later.

    (3) ELIMINATE   The correct sequence is first dose followed by second dose 1 month later, followed by third dose 5 months later.

    (4) ELIMINATE   The correct sequence is first dose followed by second dose 1 month later, followed by third dose 5 months later.

    CATEGORY 04 PREVENTION AND EARLY DETECTION OF DISEASE

6. (4) CORRECT   Histamine (H$_2$) blockers (cimetidine, ranitidine, famotidine) inhibit gastric secretion by acting on the histamine receptors in the stomach. Decreased acid production decreases the symptoms of reflux.

    (1) ELIMINATE   Anticholinergics will not relieve the symptoms associated with gastroesophageal reflux.

    (2) ELIMINATE   Antiemetics may reduce nausea, but are not indicated for treatment of hyperacidity.

    (3) ELIMINATE   Calcium channel blockers are indicated in the treatment of cardiac disease and hypertension.

    CATEGORY 08 PHARMACOLOGICAL AND PARENTERAL THERAPIES

7. (1) CORRECT   Hypovolemic shock can develop due to the massive gastrointestinal hemorrhage that can occur with esophageal varices. The client requires fluid volume replacement with normal saline, Ringer's lactate, and blood products.

    (2) ELIMINATE   Polycythemia vera is a condition where blood cells are overproduced, and is not a complication of bleeding varices.

    (3) ELIMINATE   Hyperglycemia is not a complication of bleeding varices.

    (4) ELIMINATE   Abscess formation is not a complication of bleeding varices.

    CATEGORY 07 BASIC CARE AND COMFORT

8. (3) CORRECT   Stool softeners help to relieve pain during defecation. Other treatments include ice packs and sitz baths to help relieve pain and swelling.

    (1) *ELIMINATE*   Inserting a Fleet enema may irritate the hemorrhoids and cause bleeding, which can lead to significant blood loss.

    (2) *ELIMINATE*   Hot packs will increase swelling and increase pain.

    (4) *ELIMINATE*   A hemorrhoidoscopy is diagnostic.

CATEGORY 07 BASIC CARE AND COMFORT

9. (4) CORRECT   Duodenal ulcers are more likely to occur in the spring and fall.

    (1) *ELIMINATE*   Chronic ulcers are usually gastric, and duodenal ulcers tend to occur in exacerbations and remissions (usually in the spring and fall).

    (2) *ELIMINATE*   Gastric ulcers are more likely to cause acute hemorrhage.

    (3) *ELIMINATE*   Gastric ulcers hold an increased risk of malignancies.

CATEGORY 10 PHYSIOLOGICAL ADAPTATION

10. (4) CORRECT   Until the endoscopy is performed, the client should be NPO so that the stomach is empty and the provider can visualize the stomach and the duodenum.

    (1) *ELIMINATE*   Food cannot be taken before this procedure.

    (2) *ELIMINATE*   Fluids cannot be taken before this procedure.

    (3) *ELIMINATE*   Food cannot be taken before this procedure.

CATEGORY 10 PHYSIOLOGICAL ADAPTATION

8

THE GENITOURINARY SYSTEM

WHAT YOU NEED TO KNOW

This system is a killer for most new nurses. We suggest a solid foundation in genitourinary anatomy and physiology to increase your confidence in your ability to work out the details of electrolyte imbalances, fluid balance, acid-base balance, and other anxiety-producing scenarios that might be presented on the NCLEX-RN. Refer to the pictures frequently. You will realize that the root of many words will guide you to the correct answer, provided you know the anatomy.

REVIEW OF GENITOURINARY ANATOMY AND PHYSIOLOGY

The urinary system is composed of two kidneys, two ureters, one bladder, and one urethra. Label them on the picture below:

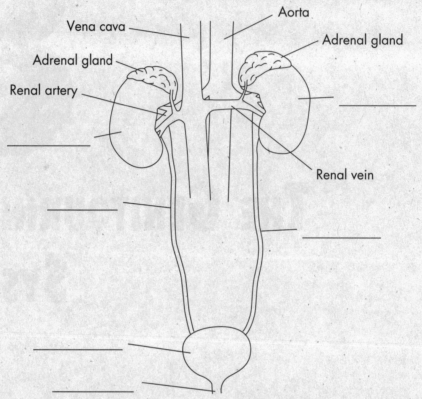

The **kidneys** maintain homeostasis of the blood by forming urine. The functions of the kidneys are:

- arterial blood pressure regulation
- water regulation
- acid-base balance
- electrolyte regulation
- excretion of waste products
- vitamin D and calcium regulation
- erythropoietin regulation
- excretion and detoxification of drugs

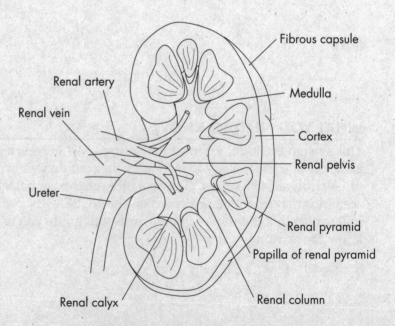

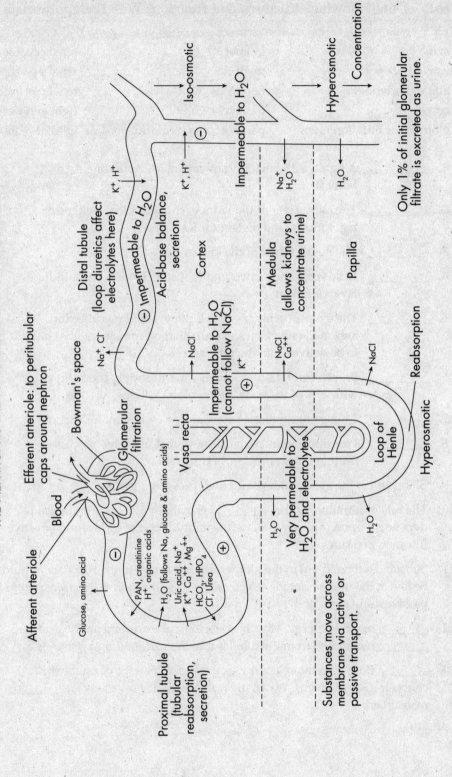

THE NEPHRON IS THE FUNCTIONAL UNIT OF THE KIDNEY

Efferent arteriole: to peritubular caps around nephron

Bowman's space

Glomerular filtration

Blood

Afferent arteriole

Glucose, amino acid

PAN, creatinine H⁺, organic acids

H_2O (follows Na, glucose & amino acids)

Uric acid, Na^+ K^+, Ca^{++}, Mg^{++}

HCO_3^-, HPO_4 Cl^-, Urea

Proximal tubule (tubular reabsorption, secretion)

Distal tubule (loop diuretics affect electrolytes here)

Acid-base balance, secretion

Cortex

K^+, H^+

Na^+, Cl^-

Impermeable to H_2O

Impermeable to H_2O (cannot follow NaCl)

K^+

Vasa recta

$NaCl$ Ca^{++}

$NaCl$

Loop of Henle

Reabsorption

Hyperosmotic

Very permeable to H_2O and electrolytes

H_2O

H_2O

Medulla (allows kidneys to concentrate urine)

Papilla

Substances move across membrane via active or passive transport.

Iso-osmotic

Impermeable to H_2O

Na^+, H_2O

H_2O

Hyperosmotic

Concentration

Only 1% of initial glomerular filtrate is excreted as urine.

Match each of the following structures and functions with the appropriate description below:

actively	glomeruli	renal capsule
active transport	medulla	renal pelvis
afferent arteriole	nephrons	renal pyramids
cortex	passively	right and left renal arteries
glomerular filtration rate	passive transport (diffusion)	tubular reabsorption

1. _____ A tightly adhering, fibrous capsule surrounding each kidney

2. _____ The outer layer of the kidney; contains glomeruli, proximal tubules, and distal tubules

3. _____ The middle layer of the kidney

4. _____ Holds collecting ducts and loops of Henle in the middle layer of kidney

5. _____ The innermost layer of the kidney; a hollow collection area made up of calyces (cup-shaped containers) that hold urine to be delivered to the ureters

6. _____ Branch from the abdominal aorta to supply the kidneys with 20% of the body's total blood volume

7. _____ Clumps of capillaries surrounded by Bowman's capsule

8. _____ Functional units of the kidneys that use three processes: filtration, reabsorption, and secretion

9. Blood enters the glomerulus under high pressure via the _____.

10. The rate of filtration, or the _____, is normally 125 cc/minute and is dependent upon capillary wall permeability, blood pressure, and effective filtration pressures.

11. Substances filtered out in the glomerulus are useful to the body and would be lost in the urine if not for selective _____ through active transport or passive diffusion.

12. _____ requires energy. Most positive ions, glucose, and amino acids are _____ reabsorbed from the tubules into the surrounding capillaries.

13. _____ does not require energy, as it takes advantage of established concentration gradients. Water, urea, and most negative ions are _____ reabsorbed.

The **nephron** of the kidney is made up of several components that carry out certain functions. Match the following nephron structures with their functions and label the picture:

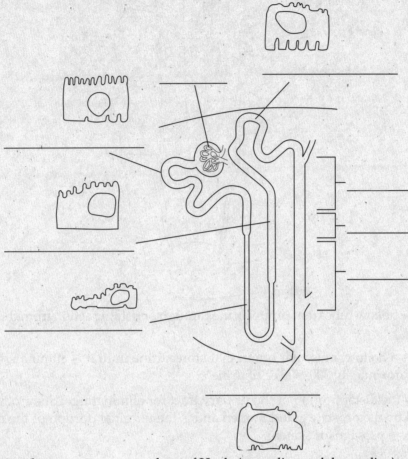

collecting duct   loop of Henle (ascending and descending)
cortex   medulla (inner and outer)
distal tubules   proximal tubules
glomeruli

14. _____ Primary location for reabsorption of glucose, amino acids, and electrolytes

15. _____ Secretion of hydrogen ions (H⁺) to maintain the acid-base balance

16. _____ Reabsorption of water and sodium to concentrate the urine and some electrolytes

17. _____ Primary location for water reabsorption (increases urine concentration)

18. _____ Filtration of water, sodium, potassium, calcium, magnesium, chloride, phosphate, urea, creatinine, glucose, and amino acids occurs here

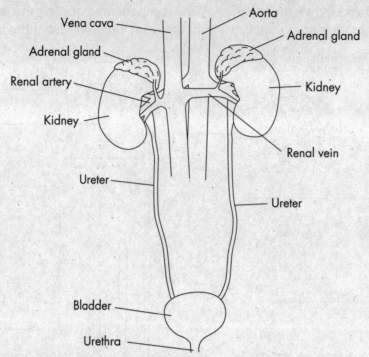

Vena cava
Aorta
Adrenal gland
Adrenal gland
Renal artery
Kidney
Kidney
Renal vein
Ureter
Ureter
Bladder
Urethra

The **ureters** are hollow tubes that propel urine through peristaltic action from the renal pelvis to the bladder.

The **bladder** is a hollow, muscular organ that stores urine until it is eliminated. Its holding capacity is approximately 300–500 cc of urine.

The **urethra** is the distal portion of the urinary tract for eliminating urine from the body. It is surrounded by the prostate gland in men and is the terminal portion of the reproductive tract serving as a passage for semen.

DIAGNOSTIC STUDIES

The *most basic* of **urine** studies is inspection. Upon inspection, including both visual and olfactory, the nurse might suspect an infection in the urinary tract.

19. Which of the following are normal urine findings? (Select all that apply.)
    A. Pale to deep amber in color
    B. Aromatic
    C. Cloudy
    D. More than 30 cc/hour

A **urinalysis** can test for several disorders, including diabetes mellitus, dehydration, a urinary tract infection, kidney trauma, and glomerulonephritis.

A **urine culture and sensitivity** can be collected by a voided specimen (clean catch) or a sterile catheterized specimen. The results identify bacterial count, as well as the infectious agent and its antibiotic sensitivity.

The **creatinine clearance test** is the best indicator of the kidney's filtration function. It measures the amount of creatinine filtered by the glomeruli over a 24-hour period.

SERUM STUDIES

Serum studies can be the most extrordinarily difficult to remember. However, if you have a good understanding of genitourinary anatomy and function, you won't need to memorize them. Think about the system and its mechanisms with each question. Fill in the blanks by choosing from the word list below.

ADH	hypermagnesemia	magnesium
BUN	hypernatremia	osmolality
calcium	hypocalcemia	phosphorus
creatinine	hypokalemia	potassium
hematocrit	hypomagnesemia	sodium
hypercalcemia	hyponatremia	urea
hyperkalemia		

20. _____ is an indicator of the body's water balance; high serum levels indicate dehydration, low serum levels indicate hypervolemia.

21. _____ is either stimulated or inhibited according to these serum levels to regulate the fluid balance.

22. An elevated _____ level, known as _____ (>146 mEq/L), is caused by steroid therapy, renal disease, aldosterone excess, or gain of total body water. Signs and symptoms include water retention, edema, weight gain, and hypertension.

23. An elevated _____ level, known as _____ (>2.5 mEq/L), is caused by renal insufficiency, diabetic ketoacidosis, and excessive intake (usually via antacids). Signs and symptoms include central nervous system and neuromuscular depression, hypotension, sedation, and cardiac arrest.

24. _____ is a specific indicator of renal function, as renal impairment or failure is virtually the only cause for its elevation. Usually viewed with the BUN serum level to obtain a broad view of kidney function. Normal value is 0.7–1.6 mg/dL.

25. A decreased _____ level, known as _____ (<3.5 mEq/L), is caused by diuretic therapy, poor nutritional intake, gastrointestinal loss (via nasogastric tube, nausea, or vomiting), ulcerative colitis, Cushing's syndrome, and alkalosis. Signs and symptoms include muscle weakness, decreased reflexes, flaccid paralysis, C.N.S. depression, lethargy, hypotension, anorexia, and E.C.G. changes.

26. A decreased _____ level, known as _____ (<8.5 mg/dL), is caused by hypoparathyroidism, low vitamin D intake, pregnancy, rickets, and renal disease. Signs and symptoms include tetany, paresthesia of fingers and around the mouth, muscle twitching, cramps, laryngospasms, and elevated phosphorus levels.

27. _____ is inversely proportional to serum calcium levels. Altered levels occur in renal disease, as the kidneys regulate the calcium and _____ balance by activating vitamin D. Normal values: 3.0–4.5 mg/dL.

28. The _____ is a measure of the nitrogen fraction of _____, the end product of protein metabolism. An elevated level results from insufficient secretion and an increase in nitrogenous waste products in the blood. This condition is called azotemia. Sepsis, gastrointestinal bleeding, and certain antibodies may also cause an increase. Normal values: 10–20 mg/dL.

29. An elevated _____ level, known as _____ (>5.5 mEq/L), can be caused by burns, renal failure, acidosis, or excessive intake. Signs and symptoms include skeletal muscle cramps, weakness, bradycardia, arrhythmias, oliguria, diarrhea, and cardiac arrest.

30. A decreased _____ level, known as _____ (<1.5 mEq/L), is caused by alcoholism, malnutrition, and decreased oral intake. Signs and symptoms include tremors, neuromuscular irritability, disorientation, and convulsions.

31. A decreased _____ level, known as _____(<135 mEq/L), is caused by diuretic therapy, burns, gastrointestinal loss, or excess body fluid reducing its ratio to water. Signs and symptoms include decreased blood pressure, poor skin turgor, dehydration, shock, oliguria, and seizures.

32. Decreased _____ levels are seen in clients with renal failure due to low erythropoietin secretion. Normal values range from 40–47%.

33. An elevated _____ level, known as _____ (>10.5 mg/dL), is due to immobility, bone metastasis, excess vitamin D intake, osteoporosis, decreased renal excretion, and parathyroid tumors. Signs and symptoms include skeletal muscle weakness, bone pain, renal calculi, pathological fractures, altered level of consciousness, constipation, nausea, vomiting, anorexia, polyuria, and decreased serum phosphorous levels.

RADIOLOGICAL STUDIES

Match the following **radiological studies** with the appropriate description:

34. ____ A contrast material is injected intravenously. As the kidneys filter and excrete the dye, x-rays are taken at specific time intervals over 1 hour. The kidneys, ureters, and bladder are visualized to evaluate function and identify obstructions present.

- Pretest: Teach client about the test, what he/she will feel, and what is expected following the test. Assess for iodine allergy. Consent is necessary because of the invasive nature of this test and because of the use of dye. The client must be NPO after midnight the evening before.

- Post-test: Assess for dye reactions (edema, itching, wheezing, and dyspnea), encourage fluids, and increase IV fluid rate to wash the dye from the client's system.

A. abdominal x-ray

B. cystoscopy

C. cystourethrogram

D. intravenous pyelogram

E. renal arteriogram

F. renal biopsy

G. renal ultrasound

35. _____ A flat x-ray plate is placed over the abdomen and an x-ray is taken. The kidneys, ureters, and bladder are visualized to assess size and position. Calcified deposits can be identified. This test is painless and requires no preparation.

36. _____ A radioactive isotope is injected via translumbar or femoral catheter and x-rays are taken. Renal circulation is visualized and perfusion insufficiencies can be identified.

- Pretest: Teach client about the test, what he/she will feel, and what is expected following the test. Assess for iodine allergy. Consent is necessary because of the invasive nature of this test and because of the use of dye. The client must be NPO after midnight the evening before.

- Post-test: Maintain bed rest for 8 hours to prevent bleeding and hematoma formation at catheter insertion site; monitor for presence of pulses distal to insertion site.

37. _____ A lighted scope is inserted through the urethra for direct visualization of the bladder. The scope may be used to resect tumors, biopsy the bladder, remove stones, cauterize bleeding areas, or implant radium seeds.

- Pretest: Teach client about the test, what he/she will feel, and what is expected following the test. Consent is necessary because of the invasive nature of this test. The client must be NPO after midnight the evening before.

- Post-test: Assess for blood-tinged urine (hematuria), provide comfort measures, and monitor for fever.

38. _____ An initial x-ray is taken to mark the lower pole of the kidney. The client is positioned prone and bent at the diaphragm. As the client inhales, a needle is inserted into the kidney and a sample is aspirated. The sample is sent to pathology to determine histology.

- Pretest: Assess coagulation status (PT/PTT). Teach client about the test, what he/she will feel, and what is expected following the test. Consent is necessary because of the invasive nature of this test.

- Post-test: Maintain bed rest for 4 hours, monitor urine output, assess needle insertion site for bleeding or hematoma.

39. ____ Sound waves are passed over the abdomen and a computer interprets the tissue density, creating images in print form. The kidneys, ureters, bladder, and renal vessels are visualized to evaluate size, position, and patency. This procedure is not painful or invasive, and requires no preparation.

40. ____ A catheter is inserted via the urethra and radiopaque dye is injected. While the client voids, x-rays are taken. The bladder and urethra are visualized.

- Pretest: Teach client about the test, what he/she will feel, and what is expected following the test. Assess for iodine allergy. Consent is necessary because of the invasive nature of this test and because of the use of dye. The client must be NPO after midnight the evening before.

- Post-test: Encourage fluids to wash dye from client's system, assess for blood-tinged urine (hematuria), provide comfort measures, monitor for fever (sign of infection).

RENAL AND UROLOGICAL DISORDERS

LOWER URINARY TRACT INFECTIONS

Lower urinary tract infections are infectious disorders causing inflammation of the urethra (urethritis) or of the bladder wall (cystitis). Half of the cases are asymptomatic and the remaining half present with urgency, burning upon urination (dysuria), bladder spasms (tenesmus), frequency of urination during the day and night (nocturia), and foul-smelling urine (pyuria).

41. Which of the following are appropriate nursing goals for care of the client with a lower urinary tract infection? (Choose all that apply.)

   A. Nurse demonstrates techniques to prevent reinfection by wiping from front to back.
   B. Client drinks at least 8 glasses of water every day to assist with eradication of the infectious agent.
   C. Client verbalizes understanding of need to drink large quantities of cranberry juice to lower urine pH.
   D. Client holds urine in bladder as long as possible before voiding.
   E. Client drinks large quantities of caffeine products (coffee, tea, and cola).
   F. Client identifies signs and symptoms of infection (chills, fever, dysuria, frequency, urgency, and itching).

Single-dose antibiotics (trimethoprim sulfamethoxazole [Bactrim], ciprofloxacin [Cipro]) are given for 10–14 days. Phenazopyridine HCl (Pyridium) is often ordered to treat urinary tract infections.

42. Which of the following is true concerning phenazopyridine HCl (Pyridium)? (Choose all that apply.)
    A. Stains urine a reddish-orange color
    B. Is a urinary analgesic and antiseptic
    C. Causes bladder spasms
    D. Causes gastrointestinal upset

UPPER URINARY TRACT INFECTIONS

Upper urinary tract infections include pyelonephritis and glomerulonephritis. Remember, -itis is inflammation. By now you should be familiar enough with genitourinary anatomy to identify the location of infection and the potential effects of such infection.

PYELONEPHRITIS

Pyelonephritis is an infectious disease causing inflammation of the kidney tissue (renal parenchyma). Signs and symptoms are the same as those of cystitis, in addition to fever, chills, malaise, flank pain, and costovertebral tenderness. Intervention includes antibiotic therapy, increased fluid intake, urine inspection, daily weights, frequent temperature monitoring, and client teaching to prevent reinfection and to increase compliance.

43. Which of the following abnormal diagnostic findings may occur with pyelonephritis? (Choose all that apply.)
    A. Urinalysis (UA) is positive for bacteria only.
    B. Urine is acidic.
    C. UA is positive for red blood cells, white blood cells, casts, and bacteria.
    D. Intravenous pyelogram reveals enlargement of the involved kidney.

GLOMERULONEPHRITIS

Glomerulonephritis is a nonbacterial inflammation of the glomeruli in both kidneys that involves an antigen-antibody reaction and causes increased membrane permeability, glomerular cell hyperplasia, and scarring with loss of renal function. It frequently follows *Staphylococcus aureus*, group A β-hemolytic streptococcus, or respiratory infection. Signs and symptoms include headache, fever, chills, nausea, vomiting, back pain, oliguria, hematuria, proteinuria, hypertension, edema, azotemia, increased urine specific gravity, and elevated BUN and creatinine.

After careful assessment, planning, and implementation of nursing goals related to glomerulonephritis, the nurse evaluates the following outcomes as positive or negative.

44. Label each outcome below as either **desired** or **undesired**:

A. _____ Client drinks 8 glasses of water every day.

B. _____ Client complies with the prescribed high-calorie, high-carbohydrate, low-protein, and low-sodium diet.

C. _____ Edema is reduced, correlating with daily intake and output and weights.

D. _____ Client takes antibiotics until signs and symptoms of infection are relieved.

E. _____ Blood pressure is controlled with antihypertensives such as clonidine (Catapres), hydralazine (Apresoline), methyldopa (Aldomet), and with diuretics like furosemide (Lasix).

F. _____ Blood urea nitrogen and creatinine levels continue to rise.

G. _____ Bed rest is maintained until hematuria, proteinuria, and hypertension subside.

H. _____ Client discusses the importance of prompt treatment for signs and symptoms of glomerulonephritis, sore throats, and respiratory infections.

Renal Calculi

Renal calculi (urinary stones) often form within the urinary tract, causing pain and damage to surrounding tissues. Stones can consist of calcium, cystine, oxalates, and uric acid. Causes of renal calculi include urinary stasis, hypercalcemia, alkaline urine, gout (elevated uric acid levels), and increased dietary vitamin D, causing increased calcium absorption. Signs and symptoms of renal calculi include: pain (renal colic) radiating from the flank to the abdomen; alternating retention (obstruction) and diuresis (stone passage); nausea; vomiting; hematuria; diaphoresis; restlessness; low-grade fever; urgency; UTI; and pallor.

45. Which diagnostic tests would be utilized to confirm renal stones?

A. _____   D. _____

B. _____   E. _____

C. _____

When caring for a client with renal calculi, it is important to monitor intake and output, strain all urine through gauze to check for passage of stones, take frequent vital signs, prevent infection, and monitor electrolytes, as well as uric acid and calcium levels.

46. All of the following medications are therapeutic for a client with urinary stones EXCEPT (choose two wrong answers):
   A. aluminum hydroxide (phosphate binder)
   B. vitamin D
   C. analgesics like morphine sulfate
   D. antispasmodics such as atropine to relax smooth muscle
   E. allopurinol
   F. diuretics to promote urination

Match the diets below with the conditions listed:

47. ____ Low purine diet with alkaline ash foods such as milk, fruits, rhubarb, and vegetables

48. ____ Reduced dairy products with acid ash foods such as meat, whole grains, cranberry juice, and prunes

A. calcium stones

B. uric acid stones

If the stones do not pass spontaneously, there are invasive procedures that can remove them. Match the following descriptions with the invasive procedure that removes renal calculi:

49. ____ Removal of a stone from the renal pelvis through a flank incision. A urethral catheter and Penrose drain are inserted.

50. ____ An endoscope is passed through a small incision made over the kidney to remove the calculi or disintegrate it with ultrasonic waves.

51. ____ Removal of a kidney is required if extensive damage has occurred to the parenchyma. A Penrose drain is placed in the renal bed.

52. ____ An incision is made into the ureter through an abdominal or flank excision to extract a stone. A Penrose drain is inserted around the ureter to collect extra drainage, and a urethral catheter is inserted to act as a splint that should never be irrigated.

53. ____ Parenchyma of the kidney is cut through a flank incision to extract the stone. A nephrostomy tube is placed to divert the urine away from the kidney.

54. ____ The client is submerged in a large bath of warm water as ultrasonic waves are delivered to the area near the stone to crush or disintegrate it.

A. nephrectomy

B. nephrolithotomy

C. percutaneous lithotripsy

D. pyelolithotomy

E. transcutaneous shock wave lithotripsy

F. ureterolithotomy

ACUTE RENAL FAILURE

Acute renal failure is the sudden and potentially reversible loss of the kidneys' ability to excrete urine and nitrogenous waste products and to maintain fluid and acid-base balance. If inadequately treated, permanent damage can occur and cause chronic renal failure.

Causes of acute renal failure are categorized as pre-renal, renal, and post-renal. Think about the prefixes: Pre-renal causes are outside the kidney and affect structures that supply the kidney; renal causes are structural to the kidney itself; and post-renal causes are mainly due to obstruction within the urinary tract (beyond the kidney). Review the anatomy of the genitourinary system with the causes of acute renal failure in mind.

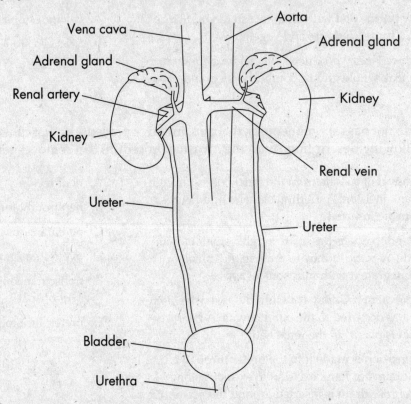

Signs and symptoms of acute renal failure are categorized into three phases:

1. **Oliguric phase**—Urine output is less than 400 cc/day and BUN and creatinine rise, decreasing the normal ratio of BUN:creatinine from 20:1 to 10:1. Hypervolemia, edema, weight gain, and hypertension result. The oliguric phase lasts up to 1–2 weeks.

2. **Diuretic phase**—Urine output is greater than 3 L/day, BUN and creatinine slowly rise, and hypovolemia and weight loss result. The diuretic phase lasts several days to one week.

3. **Recovery phase**—BUN and creatinine are normal and urine output is between 4 and 5 L/day as renal function gradually returns.

The nursing goals and interventions for acute renal failure include:

- Determining the underlying causes of renal failure and preventing them from happening in the future
- Encouraging a diet low in protein, sodium, and potassium; and high in fat, carbohydrates, and calories
- Obtaining daily weights, restricting fluid intake, monitoring the client's intake and output, and assessing for edema in legs, feet, and sacral area
- Instituting bed rest to conserve energy
- Monitoring neurological status and reporting any changes
- Monitoring electrolytes and providing supplements as ordered
- Protecting against infection
- Assessing skin for breakdown, rash, or uremic frost (crystallization of urea on the skin)
- Educating client concerning medications, diet, prevention, and safety

55. During the initial (oliguric) phase of acute renal failure, the nurse would expect to see which of the following abnormal findings? (Choose all that apply.)
    A. Decreased hematocrit, calcium, sodium, and bicarbonate levels
    B. Urine output > 30 cc/hour
    C. High serum pH
    D. Elevated BUN, creatinine, and serum potassium
    E. Urinalysis positive for white blood cells and protein
    F. Peaked T waves on the E.C.G.

Medications often prescribed for treatment of acute renal failure include anti-infectives to treat the organisms, antacids such as aluminum hydroxide (Amphogel) to bind with phosphates, sodium bicarbonate to treat acidosis, antihypertensives, diuretics for fluid overload, such as mannitol (Osmitrol), and potassium-lowering agents (insulin and glucose, sodium polystyrene sulfonate [Kayexalate]). Sometimes a dopamine drip is initiated to increase renal perfusion by activating dopaminergic receptors within the sympathetic nervous system.

CHRONIC RENAL FAILURE

Chronic renal failure is a progressive, irreversible deterioration of renal function that can end in fatal uremia unless dialysis or kidney transplantation is performed. Causes of chronic renal failure include acute renal failure, nephrotoxic agents, metabolic disease, destruction of renal blood vessels due to hypertension or diabetes, and recurrent infections of the urinary tract. Signs and symptoms include: oliguria/anuria, electrolyte imbalances, hypertension, congestive heart failure (retained fluid cannot be pumped sufficiently by the heart), pericarditis, pulmonary edema (retained fluid backs up into the lungs), anorexia, nausea, vomiting, hiccups, ammonia on the breath, mild alteration in sensorium, slurred speech, encephalopathy, potential seizures or coma, peripheral neuropathy, bone pain, pathological fractures, pruritis, dry skin, bruising, petechiae, pallor, brittle hair, dry nails, uremic frost, loss of libido, amenorrhea in women, and infertility. Nursing goals and interventions are similar to those indicated in acute renal failure.

Clients with chronic renal failure have irreversible damage to the renal parenchyma. Dialysis is often used to substitute for lost kidney function. If severe damage occurs, a kidney transplant is indicated.

DIALYSIS

Dialysis is the passage of particles from an area of high concentration to an area of low concentration across a semipermeable membrane. The membrane may be the peritoneum (peritoneal dialysis) or an artificial membrane (hemodialysis).

In peritoneal dialysis (PD), a catheter is placed through the abdominal wall into the peritoneal space. Dialysate flows into the abdominal cavity by gravity, dwells in the abdomen for a specific amount of time, and is then drained into a bag by gravity. Continuous ambulatory peritoneal dialysis requires that dialysate remain in the peritoneum 24 hours per day with several dialysate exchanges each day.

Hemodialysis (HD) involves passage of blood from the client through a semipermeable membrane immersed in dialysate. Diffusion and ultrafiltration occur between blood and dialysate.

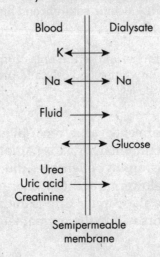

Net Movement of Fluid and Particles
by Osmosis and Diffusion

An arteriovenous (A-V) fistula (or graft) is an internal anastomosis of an artery and a neighboring vein that can be easily accessed for HD.

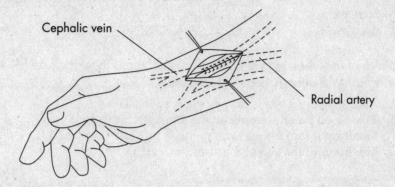

56. Which of the following particles are filtered through the membranes in dialysis? (Choose all that apply.)

    A. Urea
    B. White blood cells
    C. Creatinine
    D. Red blood cells
    E. Sodium
    F. Potassium
    G. Platelets

57. Different types of peritoneal dialysis include: (Choose all that apply.)

    A. intermittent manual
    B. intermittent automatic
    C. continuous automatic
    D. continuous ambulatory

58. The advantages of continuous ambulatory peritoneal dialysis include: (Choose all that apply.)

    A. lowers blood pressure
    B. elevates blood pressure
    C. maintains a more stable hematocrit and hemoglobin
    D. less expensive
    E. promotes weight loss
    F. allows increased freedom for the client
    G. allows for greater number of exchanges per day

59. Nursing considerations during the assessment of a continuous ambulatory peritoneal dialysis client include which of the following? (Choose all that apply.)

    A. Frequent vital signs (especially temperatures)
    B. Monitoring intake only
    C. Monitoring output only
    D. Monitoring both intake and output
    E. Obtaining daily weights
    F. Assessing for exudate or redness around the catheter site

60. As fluid is drained from the peritoneum in peritoneal dialysis, the nurse should expect the client's blood pressure to:

    A. increase
    B. decrease

61. Which of the following are nursing considerations in taking care of a client with an A-V fistula? (Choose all that apply.)

    A. Auscultate for a bruit and palpate for a thrill.
    B. Take blood pressures only on the arm with the fistula.
    C. Monitor for thrombosis formation.
    D. Monitor for infection at the insertion site.

BENIGN PROSTATIC HYPERTROPHY

Benign prostatic hypertrophy (B.P.H.) often appears in some form on the NCLEX-RN because it is so common in men over the age of 50. It is an enlargement of the prostate gland that causes partial or complete obstruction of the urethra. Signs and symptoms include urgency, frequency with alternating hesitancy during urination, nocturia, hematuria, retention, voiding only a small amount at frequent intervals, and an enlarged prostate gland upon palpation and cystoscopic examination. Treatment involves surgical intervention. The four most common procedures to correct B.P.H. are: transurethral resection of the prostate (T.U.R.P.), suprapubic resection, retropubic resection, and perineal (radical) resection.

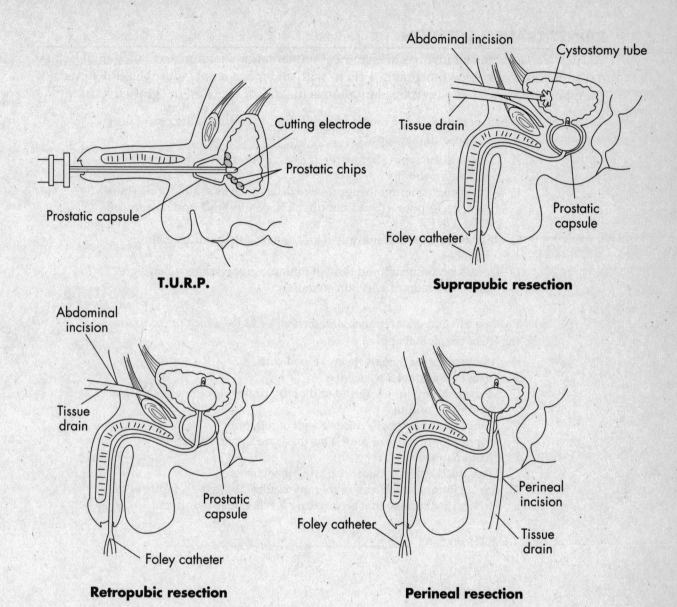

T.U.R.P.

Cutting electrode

Prostatic chips

Prostatic capsule

Suprapubic resection

Abdominal incision

Cystostomy tube

Tissue drain

Prostatic capsule

Foley catheter

Retropubic resection

Abdominal incision

Tissue drain

Prostatic capsule

Foley catheter

Perineal resection

Perineal incision

Foley catheter

Tissue drain

KIDNEY TRANSPLANTATION

Kidney transplantation involves the surgical implantation of a donated (allogenic) kidney to restore normal kidney function in a client with end-stage renal failure (E.S.R.F.). A major complication associated with transplantation is the risk of rejecting the grafted kidney.

62. Which of the following methods are utilized to minimize the risk of rejection? (Choose all that apply.)

   A. Careful tissue typing before the transplant to ensure a high degree of histocompatibility
   B. Administering immunosuppressive drugs such as azathioprine (Imuran), cyclosporine (Sandimmune), FK506 (Prograf), and muromoab-CD3 (OKT3)
   C. Transplanting recipients only if an organ is donated from a family member
   D. Increasing frequency and dose of immunosuppressants when signs and symptoms of infection are noted

63. Postoperative care for a transplanted client includes which of the following? (Choose all that apply.)

   A. Assess urine for hematuria and blood clots
   B. Flush Foley catheter as needed
   C. Measure hourly urine output and notify provider if there is a dramatic drop in output
   D. Monitor for diuresis, as this is a sign of rejection
   E. Monitor for oliguria or anuria, as these are signs of rejection
   F. Hemodialysis
   G. Place the client in a room with any other clients
   H. Ensure immunosuppressive therapy is administered promptly at the scheduled time so that serum drug levels can be monitored

64. T.U.R.P. stands for _____ .

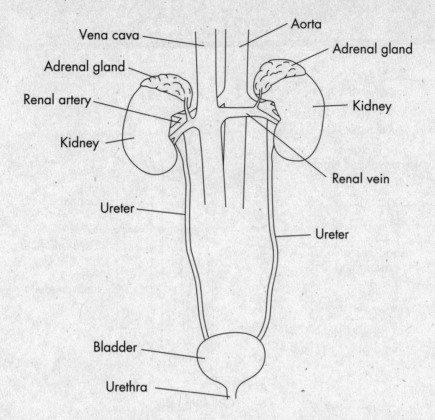

1. **renal capsule**—A tightly adhering, fibrous capsule surrounding each kidney

2. **cortex**—The outer layer of the kidney; contains glomeruli, proximal tubules, and distal tubules

3. **medulla**—The middle layer of the kidney

4. **renal pyramids**—In the middle layer of kidney; hold collecting ducts and loops of Henle

5. **renal pelvis**—The innermost layer of the kidney is a hollow collection area made up of calyces (cup-shaped containers) that hold urine to be delivered to the ureters

6. **left and right renal arteries**—Branch from the abdominal aorta to supply the kidneys with 20% of the body's total blood volume

7. **glomeruli**—Clumps of capillaries surrounded by Bowman's capsule

8. **nephrons**—Functional units of the kidneys that use three processes: filtration, reabsorption, and secretion

9. Blood enters the glomerulus under high pressure via the **afferent arteriole**.

10. The rate of filtration, or the **glomerular filtration rate**, is normally 125 cc/minute and is dependent upon capillary wall permeability, blood pressure, and effective filtration pressures.

11. Substances filtered out in the glomerulus are useful to the body and would be lost in the urine if not for selective **tubular reabsorption** through active transport or passive diffusion.

12. **Active transport** requires energy. Most positive ions, glucose, and amino acids are **actively** reabsorbed from the tubules into the surrounding capillaries.

13. **Passive transport (diffusion)** does not require energy, as it takes advantage of established concentration gradients. Water, urea, and most negative ions are **passively** reabsorbed.

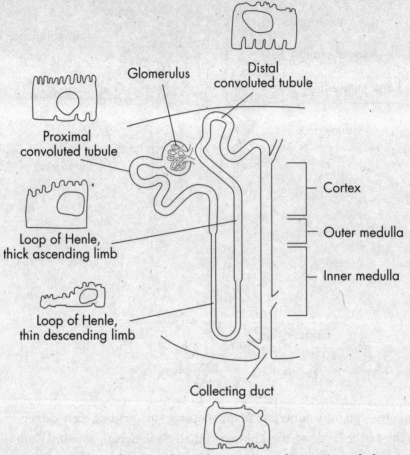

Glomerulus

Distal convoluted tubule

Proximal convoluted tubule

Cortex

Outer medulla

Inner medulla

Loop of Henle, thick ascending limb

Loop of Henle, thin descending limb

Collecting duct

14. **proximal tubules**—Primary location for reabsorption and secretion of glucose, amino acids, and electrolytes

15. **distal tubules**—Secretion of hydrogen ions (H⁺) to maintain the acid-base balance

16. **loop of Henle**—Reabsorption of water and sodium to concentrate the urine and some electrolytes

17. **collecting duct**—Primary location for water reabsorption (increases urine concentration)

18. **glomeruli**—Filtration of water, sodium, potassium, calcium, magnesium, chloride, phosphate, urea, creatinine, glucose, and amino acids occurs here

19. Which of the following are normal urine findings? (Select all that apply.)

    A. Pale to deep amber in color

    B. Aromatic

    C. More than 30 cc/hour

20. **osmolality**—An indicator of the body's water balance; high serum levels indicate dehydration, low serum levels indicate hypervolemia.

21. **ADH** is either stimulated or inhibited according to these serum levels to regulate the fluid balance.

22. An elevated **sodium** level, known as **hypernatremia** (>146 mEq/L), is caused by steroid therapy, renal disease, aldosterone excess, or gain of total body water. Signs and symptoms include water retention, edema, weight gain, and hypertension.

23. An elevated **magnesium** level, known as **hypermagnesemia** (>2.5 mEq/L), is caused by renal insufficiency, diabetic ketoacidosis, and excessive intake (usually via antacids). Signs and symptoms include central nervous system and neuromuscular depression, hypotension, sedation, and cardiac arrest.

24. **Creatinine** is a specific indicator of renal function, as renal impairment or failure is virtually the only cause for its elevation. Usually viewed with the BUN serum level to obtain a broad view of kidney function. Normal value is 0.7–1.6 mg/dL.

25. A decreased **potassium** level, known as **hypokalemia** (<3.5 mEq/L), is caused by diuretic therapy, poor nutritional intake, gastrointestinal loss (via nasogastric tube, nausea, or vomiting), ulcerative colitis, Cushing's syndrome, and alkalosis. Signs and symptoms include muscle weakness, decreased reflexes, flaccid paralysis, C.N.S. depression, lethargy, hypotension, anorexia, and E.C.G. changes.

26. A decreased **calcium** level, known as **hypocalcemia** (<8.5 mg/dL), is caused by hypoparathyroidism, low vitamin D intake, pregnancy, rickets, and renal disease. Signs and symptoms include tetany, paresthesia of fingers and around the mouth, muscle twitching, cramps, laryngospasms, and elevated phosphorous levels.

27. **Phosphoros** is inversely proportional to serum calcium levels. Altered levels occur in renal disease, as the kidneys regulate the calcium and **phosphoros** balance by activating vitamin D. Normal values: 3.0–4.5 mg/dL.

28. The **blood urea nitrogen (BUN)** is a measure of the nitrogen fraction of **urea**, the end product of protein metabolism. An elevated level results from insufficient secretion and an increase in nitrogenous waste products in the blood. This condition is called azotemia. Normal values: 10–20 mg/dL.

29. An elevated **potassium** level, known as **hyperkalemia** (>5.5 mEq/L), can be caused by burns, renal failure, acidosis, or excessive intake. Signs and symptoms include skeletal muscle cramps, weakness, bradycardia, arrhythmias, oliguria, diarrhea, and cardiac arrest.

30. A decreased **magnesium** level, known as **hypomagnesemia** (<1.5 mEq/L), is caused by alcoholism, malnutrition, and decreased oral intake. Signs and symptoms include tremors, neuromuscular irritability, disorientation, and convulsions.

31. A decreased **sodium** level, known as **hyponatremia** (<135 mEq/L), is caused by diuretic therapy, burns, gastrointestinal loss, or excess body fluid reducing the ratio of sodium to water. Signs and symptoms include decreased blood pressure, poor skin turgor, dehydration, shock, oliguria, and seizures.

32. Decreased **hematocrit** levels are seen in clients with renal failure due to low erythropoietin secretion. Normal values range from 40–47%.

33. An elevated **calcium** level, known as **hypercalemia** (>10.5 mg/dL), is due to immobility, bone metastasis, excess vitamin D intake, osteoporosis, decreased renal excretion, and parathyroid tumors. Signs and symptoms include skeletal muscle weakness, bone pain, renal calculi, pathological fractures, altered level of consciousness, constipation, nausea, vomiting, anorexia, polyuria, and decreased serum phosphorous levels.

34. **D** **intravenous pyelogram**—A contrast material is injected intravenously. As the kidneys filter and excrete the dye, x-rays are taken at specific time intervals over 1 hour. The kidneys, ureters, and bladder are visualized to evaluate function and identify obstructions present.

35. **A** **abdominal x-ray**—A flat x-ray plate is placed over the abdomen and an x-ray is taken.

36. **E** **renal arteriogram**—A radioactive isotope is injected via translumbar or femoral catheter and x-rays are taken. The renal circulation is visualized and perfusion insufficiencies can be identified.

37. **B   cystoscopy**—A lighted scope is inserted through the urethra for direct visualization of the bladder. The scope may be used to resect tumors, biopsy the bladder, remove stones, cauterize bleeding areas, or implant radium seeds.

38. **F   renal biopsy**—An initial x-ray is taken to mark the lower pole of the kidney. The client is positioned prone and bent at the diaphragm. As the client inhales, a needle is inserted into the kidney and a sample is aspirated. The sample is sent to pathology to determine histology.

39. **G   renal ultrasound**—Sound waves are passed over the abdomen and a computer interprets the tissue density, creating images in print form. The kidneys, ureters, bladder, and renal vessels are visualized to evaluate size, position, and patency. This procedure is not painful or invasive, and requires no preparation.

40. **C   cystourethrogram**—A catheter is inserted via the urethra and radiopaque dye is injected. While the client voids, x-rays are taken. The bladder and urethra are visualized.

41. Which of the following are appropriate nursing goals for care of the client with a lower urinary tract infection? (Choose all that apply.)

    A. Nurse demonstrates techniques to prevent reinfection by wiping from front to back

    B. Client drinks at least 8 glasses of water every day to assist with eradication of the infectious agent.

    C. Client verbalizes understanding of need to drink large quantities of cranberry juice to lower urine pH.

    F. Client identifies signs and symptoms of infection (chills, fever, dysuria, frequency, urgency, and itching).

42. Which of the following is true concerning phenazopyridine HCl (Pyridium)? (Choose all that apply.)

    A. Stains urine a reddish-orange color

    B. Is a urinary analgesic and antiseptic

    C. Causes bladder spasms

43. Which of the following abnormal diagnostic findings may occur with pyelonephritis? (Choose all that apply.)

    C. UA is positive for red blood cells, white blood cells, casts, and bacteria.

    D. Intravenous pyelogram reveals enlargement of the involved kidney.

44. Label each outcome below as either **desired** or **undesired**:

    A. **Undesired**—Client drinks 8 glasses of water every day.

    B. **Desired**—Client complies with the prescribed high-calorie, high-carbohydrate, low-protein, and low-sodium diet.

    C. **Desired**—Edema is reduced, correlating with daily intake and output and weights.

    D. **Undesired**—Client takes antibiotics until signs and symptoms of infection are relieved.

    E. **Desired**—Blood pressure is controlled with antihypertensives such as clonidine (Catapres), hydralazine (Apresoline), methyldopa (Aldomet), and with diuretics like furosemide (Lasix).

    F. **Undesired**—Blood urea nitrogen and creatinine levels continue to rise.

    G. **Desired**—Bed rest is maintained until hematuria, proteinuria, and hypertension subside.

    H. **Desired**—Client discusses the importance of prompt treatment for signs and symptoms of glomerulonephritis, sore throats, and respiratory infections.

45. Which diagnostic tests would be utilized to confirm renal stones? **Urinalysis, intravenous pyelogram, x-ray, cystoscopy, ultrasound**

46. All of the following medications are therapeutic for a client with urinary stones EXCEPT (choose 2 wrong answers):

    B. vitamin D

    F. diuretics to promote urination

47. **B**   **uric acid stones**—Low purine diet with alkaline ash foods such as milk, fruits, rhubarb, and vegetables

48. **A**   **calcium stones**—Reduced dairy products with acid ash foods such as meat, whole grains, cranberry juice, and prunes

49. **D**   **pyelolithotomy**—Removal of a stone from the renal pelvis through a flank incision; urethral catheter and Penrose drain are inserted

50. **C**   **percutaneous lithotripsy**—An endoscope is passed through a small incision made over the kidney to remove the calculi or disintegrate it with ultrasonic waves.

51. **A**   **nephrectomy**—Removal of a kidney is required if extensive damage has occurred to the parenchyma. A Penrose drain is placed in the renal bed.

52. **F**   **ureterolithotomy**—An incision is made into the ureter through an abdominal or flank excision to extract a stone. A Penrose drain is inserted around the ureter to collect extra drainage, and a urethral catheter is inserted to act as a splint that should never be irrigated.

53. **B**   **nephrolithotomy**—Parenchyma of the kidney is cut through a flank incision to extract a stone. A nephrostomy tube is placed to divert the urine away from the kidney.

54. **E**   **transcutaneous shock wave lithotripsy**—The client is submerged in a large bath of warm water as ultrasonic waves are delivered to the area near the stone to crush or disintegrate it.

55. During the initial (oliguric) phase of acute renal failure, the nurse would expect to see which of the following abnormal findings? (Choose all that apply.)

    A. Decreased hematocrit, calcium, sodium, and bicarbonate levels

    B. Urine output < 30 cc/hour

    C. High serum pH

    D. Elevated BUN, creatinine, and serum potassium

    E. Urinalysis positive for white blood cells and protein

    F. Peaked T waves on the E.C.G.

56. Which of the following particles are filtered through the membranes in dialysis? (Choose all that apply.)

    A. Urea

    C. Creatinine

    E. Sodium

    F. Potassium

57. Different types of peritoneal dialysis include: (Choose all that apply.)

    A. intermittent manual

    B. intermittent automatic

    D. continuous ambulatory

58. The advantages of continuous ambulatory peritoneal dialysis include: (Choose all that apply.)

    A. lowers blood pressure (this depends on fluid states and percent of dialysate used)

    C. maintains a more stable hematocrit and hemoglobin

    D. less expensive

    F. increased freedom for the client

59. Nursing considerations during the assessment of a continuous ambulatory peritoneal dialysis client include which of the following? (Choose all that apply.)

    A. Frequent vital signs (especially temperatures)

    D. Monitoring both intake and output

    E. Obtaining daily weights

    F. Assessing for exudate or redness around the catheter site

60. As fluid is drained from the peritoneum in peritoneal dialysis, the nurse should expect the client's blood pressure to:

    B. decrease

61. Which of the following are nursing considerations in taking care of a client with an A-V fistula? (Choose all that apply.)

    A. Auscultate for a bruit and palpate for a thrill.

    C. Monitor for thrombosis formation.

    D. Monitor for infection at the insertion site.

62. Which of the following methods are utilized to minimize the risk of rejection? (Choose all that apply.)

    A. Careful tissue typing before the transplant to ensure a high degree of histocompatibility

    B. Administration of immunosuppressive drugs such as azathioprine (Imuran), cyclosporine (Sandimmune), FK506 (Prograf), and muromonab-CD3 (Orthoclone OKT3)

63. Postoperative care for a transplanted client includes which of the following? (Choose all that apply.)

    A. Assess urine for hematuria and blood clots.

    C. Measure hourly urine output and notify provider if there is a dramatic drop in output.

    E. Monitor for oliguria or anuria, as these are signs of rejection.

    H. Ensure immunosuppressive therapy is administered promptly at the scheduled time so that serum drug levels can be monitored.

64. T.U.R.P. stands for **transurethral resection of the prostate**.

CHAPTER 8: NCLEX-RN STYLE QUESTIONS

1. The nurse is draining the third exchange of peritoneal dialysis. She needs to call the provider if which of the following is present?

   (1) An amount of outflow equal to the inflow
   (2) Clear, straw-colored fluid
   (3) A 10-minute time span for fluid removal
   (4) Turbid, foul-smelling outflow

2. Nursing care for a client with an arteriovenous (A-V) fistula aimed at maintaining patency includes

   (1) taking blood pressures in the affected arm.
   (2) applying heat to maintain circulation.
   (3) palpating for a bruit.
   (4) keeping the arm free of constriction.

3. A client is about to start the first hemodialysis treatment. Prior to initiating hemodialysis, which of the following actions is most essential?

   (1) Obtaining baseline vital signs and weight
   (2) Reviewing blood chemistries
   (3) Administering all medications
   (4) Administering analgesics

4. The nurse is teaching a client with a renal disease how to restrict dietary potassium. The foods that are high in potassium include

   (1) chocolate.
   (2) caffeine.
   (3) poultry.
   (4) beef.

5. When a client is about to undergo renal transplant surgery, which of the following is necessary to best prepare them preoperatively?

   (1) Hemodialysis
   (2) Fluid restriction
   (3) Administration of diuretics
   (4) Administration of oxygen

6. After transplant surgery, the nurse assesses the client for signs of rejection. These signs include

   (1) clear urinary output of 100 cc/hour.
   (2) BUN 20 mg/dL, creatinine 1.6 mg/dL, potassium 4.0 mEq/L.
   (3) hypotension and rapid pulse.
   (4) Fever above 37.7°C (99.9°F) and red, swollen graft site.

7. Which is the hallmark symptom of acute renal failure (ARF)?

   (1) Hypertension
   (2) Weight gain
   (3) Edema
   (4) Oliguria

8. A nurse is teaching a new hemodialysis client. Hemodialysis is successful in the treatment of end-stage renal disease because it

   (1) mimics renal function.
   (2) restores renal endocrine function.
   (3) restores urinary ability.
   (4) improves immune function.

9. Which of the following diets is appropriate for a client with renal failure on hemodialysis?

(1) High protein, high potassium, and high carbohydrate
(2) Low protein, low potassium, and low phosphate
(3) Low protein, high phosphorus, and high sodium
(4) High protein, high calcium, and low fat

10. When a nurse is giving discharge teaching instructions to a client with pyelonephritis; information on how to prevent reoccurrence should be given. This would include information on

(1) maintenance of perineal hygiene.
(2) discontinuing antibiotic therapy when the client feels better.
(3) limiting fluid intake to 1 liter a day.
(4) monitoring urine output.

CHAPTER 8: NCLEX-RN STYLE ANSWERS

1. (4) CORRECT   Turbid, foul-smelling fluid indicates peritonitis, so the nurse should notify the provider.
   (1) ELIMINATE   This is normal.
   (2) ELIMINATE   This is the normal color of the effluent.
   (3) ELIMINATE   This is the normal time for drainage.
   CATEGORY 09 REDUCTION OF RISK POTENTIAL

2. (4) CORRECT   Circulation must be facilitated to maintain patency in an A-V fistula. The arm should be free from constriction (i.e., tourniquets, blood pressure cuffs, constricting clothing, sleeping on the arm) to allow blood flow.
   (1) ELIMINATE   Taking blood pressures in the arm is contraindicated because it will inhibit blood flow.
   (2) ELIMINATE   Application of heat is not indicated because it serves no specific purpose.
   (3) ELIMINATE   Palpating for a bruit is part of daily assessment, but does not necessarily assist circulation.
   CATEGORY 09 REDUCTION OF RISK POTENTIAL

3. (1) CORRECT   Baseline vital signs and weight help determine effectiveness of the treatment.
   (2) POSSIBLE   Reviewing blood chemistries is important, but choice #1 is more critical.
   (3) ELIMINATE   Not all medications are administered; some are held until after the treatment because they are lost in the dialysate.
   (4) ELIMINATE   There is no need for analgesics.
   CATEGORY 09 REDUCTION OF RISK POTENTIAL

4.   (1) CORRECT   Chocolate is very high in potassium.
  (2) *ELIMINATE*   Caffeine does not contain potassium.
  (3) *ELIMINATE*   Poultry does not contain potassium.
  (4) *ELIMINATE*   Beef does not contain potassium.

CATEGORY 09 REDUCTION OF RISK POTENTIAL

---

5.   (1) CORRECT   Hemodialysis will remove waste products, balance acids and bases, restore electrolytes, and place the client in the best balance possible for facing surgery.
  (2) *ELIMINATE*   Fluid restriction is not a preoperative preparation for this surgery.
  (3) *ELIMINATE*   Diuretics are not part of the preoperative preparation. In fact, if the client has no renal function, there will probably be no output from a diuretic.
  (4) *ELIMINATE*   Administration of oxygen is not as important as hemodialysis in preparing for a transplant.

CATEGORY 09 REDUCTION OF RISK POTENTIAL

---

6.   (4) CORRECT   Signs of rejection include oliguria, anuria, transplanted kidney that is soft and tenderness upon palpation, fever, hypertension, weight gain, and elevated BUN, creatinine, and electrolyte levels.
  (1) *ELIMINATE*   Clear urinary output of 100 cc/hour is a normal postoperative finding.
  (2) *ELIMINATE*   These are normal laboratory values, and would be associated with a successful transplant.
  (3) *ELIMINATE*   Hypotension and tachycardia are not associated with rejection, especially in the immediate postoperative period.

CATEGORY 04 PREVENTION AND EARLY DETECTION OF DISEASE

---

7.   (4) CORRECT   Acute renal failure is an acute deterioration or cessation of renal function. While all of these are symptoms of acute renal failure (ARF), the hallmark sign is oliguria.
  (1) *ELIMINATE*   Hypertension occurs, but is not the hallmark symptom.
  (2) *ELIMINATE*   Weight gain can occur in a number of other conditions. In renal failure it occurs as a result of fluid gain.
  (3) *ELIMINATE*   Edema does occur with renal failure, but is not a hallmark symptom.

CATEGORY 04 PREVENTION AND EARLY DETECTION OF DISEASE

---

8.   (1) CORRECT   Hemodialysis mimics the renal functions of balancing acids/bases and electrolytes, and eliminating fluids and waste products.
  (2) *ELIMINATE*   Hemodialysis does not restore the endocrine functions.
  (3) *ELIMINATE*   Hemodialysis does not restore urinary ability.
  (4) *ELIMINATE*   Hemodialysis does not affect immune function.

CATEGORY 10 PHYSIOLOGICAL ADAPTATION

9.   (2) CORRECT   A low-protein, low-potassium, low-phosphate diet is recommended. The metabolite of protein utilization increases the already elevated blood urea nitrogen [BUN]. Potassium and phosphorus tend to be high in renal failure. High potassium is life threatening, and a high phosphorous causes calcium deposits in soft tissues, so a low-potassium, low-phosphorus diet is indicated.

      (1) *ELIMINATE*   Potassium tends to be high in renal failure, and is therefore restricted.

      (3) *ELIMINATE*   The renal diet is low in phosphorus.

      (4) *ELIMINATE*   The renal diet is low in protein.

CATEGORY 09 REDUCTION OF RISK POTENTIAL

---

10.   (1) CORRECT   Good perineal hygiene will prevent the introduction of microorganisms into the urinary tract. This is the most important component of prevention.

      (2) *ELIMINATE*   Antibiotic therapy must be completed as prescribed, even if symptoms are relieved, or the infection will recur.

      (3) *ELIMINATE*   Fluid intake must be encouraged, not limited, in order to flush the bacteria from the system.

      (4) *ELIMINATE*   There is no need to monitor urinary output in a simple urinary tract infection (UTI).

CATEGORY 09 REDUCTION OF RISK POTENTIAL

THE MUSCULOSKELETAL SYSTEM

WHAT YOU NEED TO KNOW

Before we begin our review of the musculoskeletal system, test your knowledge by filling in the blanks on the next page, choosing from the list of words provided.

bones	movement	red blood cells
calcium	muscle	shape
joints	phosphorus	support
ligaments	protection	tendons
magnesium		cartilage

1. The musculoskeletal system is composed of _____, _____, _____, _____, _____, and _____ that work together to give the body _____, _____, _____, and _____ to the vital organs and tissues. In addition, it provides a place for _____, _____ and _____ storage, and it functions to produce new _____.

REVIEW OF ANATOMY AND PHYSIOLOGY

As you know, the anatomy and physiology of the musculoskeletal system are extremely cumbersome. You do not need to know all the material to pass the NCLEX-RN. Just recognize and think about the following parts and their basic function.

Match the following structures with the appropriate function:

2. ____ bones

3. ____ joint

4. ____ muscle

5. ____ cartilage

6. ____ tendon

7. ____ ligament

A. Connective tissue that cushions bony prominences

B. Dense, fibrous connective tissue; attaches bone to bone

C. Dense, fibrous connective tissue; attaches muscle to bone

D. Formed where two bones touch one another; provides stabilization and movement

E. Form the structure of the skeletal system; store calcium, phosphorus, and magnesium; produce new red blood cells

F. Gives the body shape and form. Includes: cardiac/involuntary; smooth involuntary; striated skeletal/voluntary.

Glance at the following body positions (**abduction** and **adduction**). For the NCLEX-RN, you will want to remember these terms, and the pictures may help:

Abduction 45%

A: While standing or supine, client moves one leg directly away from the other leg.

P: With the client supine, place one hand under the knee and grasp the ankle with the other hand; then move the leg away from the midline.

Adduction 20%

A: Client brings the leg across the midline and then across the opposite leg as far as possible.

P: While supporting the extremity, move it from the abducted position toward the midline and then across the midline.

A = Active
P = Passive

DIAGNOSTIC STUDIES

While it is not necessary to memorize all the laboratory and diagnostic tests related to the musculoskeletal system, you should recognize some names and make certain correlations for the exam. The following exercises are designed to provide a basic understanding of these studies.

Match the following laboratory tests with the appropriate diagnosis:

8. ____ Muscular dystrophy, trauma

9. ____ Rheumatoid arthritis

10. ____ Gout

11. ____ Osteolytic metastatic tumor

12. ____ Most specific test for systemic lupus erythematosus

A. anti-DNA

B. calcium

C. muscle enzymes, including CPK

D. rheumatoid factor

E. uric acid

Match each diagnostic study with the appropriate definition:

13. ____ Fluoroscopic and radiographic examination of the subarachnoid space to help diagnose causes of low back pain. Client must remain NPO for 3-4 hours before the test. The nurse must assess for allergies to iodine and contrast medium. The client must remain supine for 12 hours after the procedure.

14. ____ Microscopic examination of the bone; usually performed after an abnormal bone scan or CAT scan. It helps to distinguish between benign and malignant bone tumors. The client should be NPO for 8 hours before the procedure. The nurse should assess for hypersensitivity to anesthetics. Post procedure, the nurse should assess for signs of infection.

15. ____ Radiological study that senses variations in tissue density and gives a detailed view of bones and tissue. Useful in detecting herniated disks, spinal stenoses, and tumors. The nurse should instruct the client to remain still during the procedure and to remove all metal jewelry. The client should be NPO 4 hours before the procedure.

16. ____ Provides direct visualization of the interior of a joint using an endoscope to evaluate the knee for meniscus cartilage or ligament tears and to diagnose acute and chronic disorders. Corrective surgery may be performed during the procedure. Complications include infection, hemarthrosis, swelling, and joint injury. Client should be NPO after midnight the night before the procedure.

17. ____ Produces sensitive images of soft tissue without contrast dyes. Allows visualization of the spinal cord and locates lesions in the white matter in diseases such as multiple sclerosis.

18. ____ Measures and records electrical currents produced by skeletal muscles. Used in diagnosing cervical or lumbar disk disease, muscular dystrophy, myasthenia gravis, polymyositis, and motor neuron disease. The client must restrict smoking and caffeine intake before the test.

A. arthrography

B. arthroscopy

C. bone biopsy

D. bone scan

E. computed tomography (CT)

F. electromyography

G. magnetic resonance imaging (MRI)

H. myelography

I. radiology/x-ray

19. ____ Imaging with scanning camera after injection of radioactive tracer that collects in tissue having abnormal metabolism, i.e., "hot spots." Increased uptake is found in osteomyelitis, malignant lesions, osteoporosis, fractures, and Paget's disease. The dye is excreted in the urine 6–12 hours after the initial injection.

20. ____ Shows functional or structural changes in bones and joints.

21. ____ Radiographic visualization of joints after injection of a contrast medium. Allows visualization of soft tissues such as ligament and cartilage to detect cause of knee or shoulder pain, joint derangement, and synovial cysts. The nurse should assess for allergies to contrast dyes, seafood, iodine, or local anesthetics. The joint should rest for 12 hours post-procedure.

MUSCULOSKELETAL DISORDERS

Rheumatoid arthritis is an inflammation of the joints (usually the small joints) caused by an external agent. It is characterized by joint pain, warmth, edema, and limited motion and occurs symmetrically.

Osteoarthritis is a noninflammatory degenerative joint disease caused by repeated stress on weight-bearing joints. It occurs asymmetrically and affects only 1 or 2 joints. If the client is overweight, weight loss should be encouraged to reduce pressure on joints.

Gout is a monoarticular arthritis that occurs asymmetrically and is characterized by too much uric acid. Clients report ingestion of too much alcohol or high purine foods. Uric acid crystals precipitate and deposit in the joints and connective tissue, causing swollen, warm, and reddened joints. Diet plays a large role in managing gout. Foods to avoid include organ meats, alcohol, and fat. Beans, lentils, and bran should be limited, and fluids should be encouraged. Diet modification helps prevent excess uric acid formation.

Osteoporosis is the most common metabolic bone disorder, causing decreased bone mass and increased risk of fractures. Causes of osteoporosis include calcium and estrogen deficiency. Post-gastrectomy clients are also susceptible. Calcium and vitamin D supplements are advised.

Osteomalacia occurs when bone does not calcify due to vitamin D deficiency. Bone pain intensifies with activity and is most common in the pelvis and lower extremities.

Osteomyelitis is an acute or chronic bone infection, causing inflammation (osteo- = bone, -itis = inflammation).

Osteitis deformans (Paget's disease) is characterized by accelerated bone resorption. Clients with Paget's disease are prone to fractures, pseudofractures, and bone deformity, especially of the skull, lumbar spine, sacrum, pelvis, and femur.

MUSCULOSKELETAL TRAUMA

You should be familiar with different types of **musculoskeletal trauma** for the NCLEX-RN. Match the type of trauma with its appropriate definition:

22. _____ Displacement of the bone from its normal position in the joint, causing severe pain, change in the length of the extremity, change in the contour and shape of the joint, and inability to move. Treatment includes reduction and immobilization.

23. _____ Injury to the muscle tissue in the form of incomplete tears. Results from overstretching, overuse, or excess stress, causing bleeding into the muscle, pain, swelling, and muscle spasm. Treatment includes ice packs for the first 24 hours followed by moist or dry heat, sling or crutches, and muscle relaxants.

24. _____ Any break in the continuity of the bone occurring in the shaft or diaphysis (complete, incomplete, or bending, open or closed). Treatment includes realignment of bone fragments, maintenance of realignment by immobilization, and restoration of function.

25. _____ Injury to the soft tissue resulting in a rupture of the small blood vessels and ecchymosis (hemorrhage) at the trauma site, manifested by pain, swelling, and discoloration. Treatment includes cold compresses for the first 24 hours, followed by dry heat and elevation of the extremity.

26. _____ Injury involving the ligamentous structures surrounding a joint; tear or stretching of the joint. Immobilization is crucial after swelling has subsided. Treatment includes immobilization, cast application after swelling decreases, cold or heat, and correct positioning.

A. contusion

B. dislocation

C. fracture

D. sprain

E. strain

FRACTURES

Label the following types of fractures:

A. Spiral   E. Greenstick   I. Impacted
B. Transverse   F. Open   J. Depressed
C. Comminuted G. Closed overriding K. Longitudinal
D. Closed   H. Oblique   L. Compressed

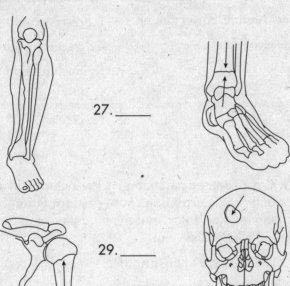

27. _____

28. _____

29. _____

30. _____

31. _____

32. _____

33. _____

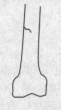

34. _____

35. _____

36. _____

37. _____

38. _____

39. Osteitis deformans is also known as _____. It is characterized by bone **deformity** and accelerated bone resorption.

Potential complications of fractures are listed below. Match each with the associated area of injury:

40. ____ Sciatic nerve damage

41. ____ Profuse bleeding, bladder rupture, bowel trauma

42. ____ Popliteal artery damage, bleeding

43. ____ Popliteal artery damage

44. ____ Nerve damage

45. ____ Injury of peroneal nerve

A. dislocation of fractured knee

B. distal femur

C. fracture of 5th metatarsal

D. fracture of proximal fibula

E. hip

F. pelvic

AMPUTATION

Amputation is the surgical removal of a diseased part or organ. We include it in musculoskeletal disorders but recognize the fact that the determining cause of amputation can be found in many systems. The nursing assessment and interventions in any amputation are the same as those associated with the musculoskeletal system.

Three major nursing concerns related to care of an amputee:

1. Stump care to promote healing and prevent infection
   - Keep stump elevated to decrease swelling.
   - Assess for signs of hemorrhage.
   - Pressure dressing and bandage to prevent edema.
   - Keep site clean and dry.
2. Exercise to maintain tone of unaffected muscle needed for crutch walking or prosthesis physical therapy: active and passive range of motion
3. Psychological support for loss of a body part.
   - Phantom pain may occur.
   - Encourage client to talk about the limitations caused by the amputation and the impact on her life.

GENERAL INTERVENTIONS FOR MUSCULOSKELETAL DISORDERS

Immobilization is the treatment of choice for common musculoskeletal problems including fractures, sprains, strains, and soft tissue injuries. Immobilization is accomplished through traction and casting.

TRACTION

Traction is the application of a pulling force to a specific part of the body to align and immobilize fractured bones, relieve muscle spasm, and correct flexion contractures, deformities, and dislocations. For traction to be effective, there must be a pull in the opposite direction (countertraction).

Nursing care (related to traction) includes the following:

- Five important principles of maintaining traction:
  1. Maintain established line of pull.
  2. Prevent friction.
  3. Maintain countertraction.
  4. Maintain continuous traction unless ordered otherwise.
  5. Maintain correct body alignment.
- Pin care:
  1. Cleanse with hydrogen peroxide or normal saline as ordered.
  2. Maintain proper body alignment.
  3. Turn and position every 2 hours unless contraindicated.
- Skin care:
  1. Monitor for redness and skin breakdown.
  2. Apply antibiotics or antiseptic solution/ointment as ordered.
  3. Monitor for signs and symptoms of infection.
- Documentation:
  1. Length of time in traction (intermittent or continuous)
  2. Client position in bed.
  3. Status of traction setup.
  4. Client response (i.e., pain).

In addition to knowing principles of basic nursing care of the client in traction, it is important to familiarize yourself with the different types of traction outlined below.

Skin Traction (attached to the skin, used intermittently)	
Buck's	Straight line of pull
Russel's	Upward lift
Cervical halter	For sprains and strains to the cervical spine and ruptured cervical disks
Pelvic belt	Relieves lower spine pain

Skeletal Traction (secured into the bone, the skeleton, used continuously)	
Balanced suspension	For femoral fractures; allows movement without disrupting traction pull and alignment
Overhead 90-90 traction	Provides upward pull on upper arm
Cervical tongs	Immobilizes and reduces fractures of cervical spine that may injure spinal cord

Label each of the following pictures with the correct type of traction:

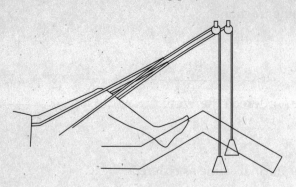

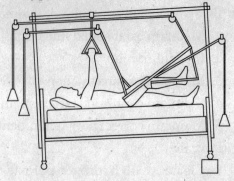

46. _____

47. _____

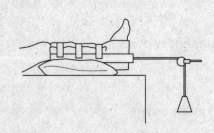

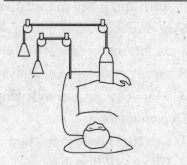

48. _____

49. _____

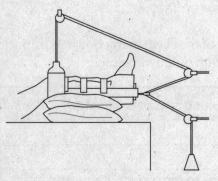

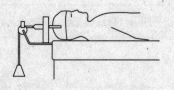

50. _____

51. _____

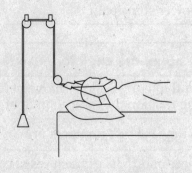

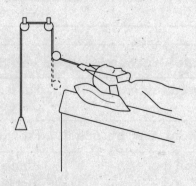

52. _____

Assessment of traction includes:

- Frequent checks for the "5 Ps" of muscle ischemia:
    1. Progressive pain
    2. Pulselessness
    3. Paresthesia
    4. Paralysis
    5. Pallor
- Frequent neurovascular checks:
    1. Pulses
    2. Nail beds (cyanosis, capillary refill)
    3. Skin (blanching, coldness, lack of sensation)
- Frequent assessment for compartment syndrome, the progressive vascular compromise of an extremity due to inability of the fascia surrounding the muscles to expand when edema occurs.

> 53. Assessment of traction includes what three components?
>
>   A. _____
>   B. _____
>   C. _____

CASTS

Casts immobilize fractures after surgical or alternative correction. Types include: short, long, spica, splint, and body cast. Nursing care of the client with a cast includes:

- Checking neurovascular status frequently.
- Noting color of the skin distal to the affected extremity.
- Noting drainage, swelling, irritation, odor, or bleeding.
- Assessing balance and coordination.
- Assessing the 5 Ps of muscle ischemia.

> 54. List the 5 Ps of muscle ischemia:
>
>   A. _____
>   B. _____
>   C. _____
>   D. _____
>   E. _____

- Elevating involved extremity.
- Safety and comfort.
- Emotional support.

Type of Ambulation Aids	
Cane	Instruct client to hold cane in the hand on the opposite side of the affected extremity and advance cane at the same time as the affected extremity.
Walker	Instruct the client to hold upper bars, move walker forward, then step into it.
Crutches	Assure proper length: With the client standing erect, the top of the crutch should be 2 inches below the axilla and the tip of each crutch should be 6 inches in front and to the side of the feet. The client's elbow should be slightly flexed when hand is on hand grip. The client's weight should not be on the axilla.

Match the following types of crutch walking with the appropriate description:

55. ____ Used when weight-bearing is allowed on both extremities. Advance right crutch, step with left foot; advance left crutch, step with right foot.

56. ____ Acceleration of four-point gait. Right crutch moves together with left leg; left crutch moves together with right crutch.

57. ____ Used when weight-bearing is permitted on one extremity only. Advance both crutches and affected extremity several inches; maintaining good balance, advance unaffected leg, supporting weight of body on hands.

58. ____ Used in clients with paralysis of both lower extremities, unable to lift feet from the floor. Place both crutches forward. Client swings forward to the crutches.

59. ____ Used in clients with paralysis of both lower extremities. Both crutches placed forward, client swings body through crutches.

A. four-point gait

B. swing-through gait

C. swing-to gait

D. three-point gait

E. two-point gait

Summary of Nursing Interventions for Musculoskeletal Disorders	
Intervention	Rationale
1. Heat, moist compress, whirlpool bath, ultrasound	Vasodilatation Decrease muscle spasm, edema, joint stiffness and pain in nonacute stage Analgesic effect Increases range of motion
2. Cold packs	Vasoconstriction, decrease swelling, muscle spasm, and pain
3. Joint restriction and immobilization	Decrease weight-bearing and gravitational stresses on the joints
4. Exercises	Range of motion maintains joint mobility and prevents joint stiffness Isotonic exercise increases joint mobility and muscle tone Isometric exercise maintains muscle strength
5. Diversional activities	"Gate control" theory of pain
6. Alternating rest and activity	Fatigue exacerbates joint pain
7. Assistive devices	Decrease weight-bearing load of affected joint Increase self-care ability and self-esteem
8. Good posture and body mechanics	Allow for optimal weight-bearing of joints
9. Verbalization and ventilation	Suppression of feelings may hinder optimal psychological and physiological functioning
10. Client teaching	Knowledge increases self-esteem and client compliance, and decreases client's sense of being out of control
11. Nutrition counseling	Prevent complications of immobility including constipation by increasing fluid and fiber intake

CHAPTER 9: EXERCISE ANSWERS

1. The musculoskeletal system is composed of **bones, joints, muscle, cartilage, tendons**, and **ligaments** that work together to give the body **shape, support, movement**, and **protection** to the vital organs and tissues. In addition, it provides a place for **calcium, magnesium**, and **phosphorus** storage, and it functions to produce new **red blood cells**.

2. **E** **bones**—Form the structure of the skeletal system; store calcium, phosphorus, and magnesium; produce new red blood cells

3. **D** **joint**—Formed where two bones touch one another; provides stabilization and movement

4. **F** **muscle**—Gives the body shape and form. Includes: cardiac/involuntary; smooth involuntary; striated skeletal/voluntary

5. **A** **cartilage**—Connective tissue that cushions bony prominences

6. **C** **tendon**—Dense, fibrous connective tissue; attaches muscle to bone

7. **B** **ligament**—Dense, fibrous connective tissue; attaches bone to bone

8. **C** **muscle enzymes, including CPK**—Muscular dystrophy, trauma

9. **D** **rheumatoid factor**—Rheumatoid arthritis

10. **E** **uric acid**—Gout

11. **B** **calcium**—Osteolytic metastatic tumor

12. **A** **anti-DNA**—Most specific test for systemic lupus erythematosus

13. **H** **myelography**—Fluoroscopic and radiographic examination of the subarachnoid space to help diagnose causes of low back pain. Client must remain NPO for 3–4 hours before the test. The nurse must assess for allergies to iodine and contrast medium. The client must remain supine for 12 hours after the procedure.

14. **C** **bone biopsy**—Microscopic examination of the bone; usually performed after an abnormal bone scan or CAT scan. This procedure helps to distinguish between benign and malignant bone tumors. It should be NPO for 8 hours before the procedure. The nurse should assess for hypersensitivity to anesthetics. Post-procedure, the nurse should assess for signs of infection.

15. **E** **computed tomography (CT)**—Radiological study that senses variations in tissue density and gives a detailed view of bones and tissue. Useful in detecting herniated disks, spinal stenoses, and tumors. The nurse should instruct the client to remain still during the procedure and to remove all metal jewelry. The client should be NPO 4 hours before the procedure.

16. **B** **arthroscopy**—Provides direct visualization of the interior of a joint using an endoscope to evaluate the knee for meniscus cartilage or ligament tears and to diagnose acute and chronic disorders. Corrective surgery may be performed during the procedure. Complications include infection, hemarthrosis, swelling, and joint injury. Client should be NPO after midnight the night before the procedure.

17. **G** **magnetic resonance imaging (MRI)**—Produces sensitive images of soft tissue without contrast dyes. Allows visualization of the spinal cord and locates lesions in the white matter in diseases such as multiple sclerosis.

18. **F** **electromyography**—Measures and records electrical currents produced by skeletal muscles. Used in diagnosing cervical or lumbar disk disease, muscular dystrophy, myasthenia gravis, polymyositis, and motor neuron disease. The client must restrict smoking and caffeine intake before the test.

19. **D** **bone scan**—Imaging with scanning camera after injection of radioactive tracer that collects in tissue having abnormal metabolism, i.e., "hot spots." Increased uptake is found in osteomyelitis, malignant lesions, osteoporosis, fractures, and Paget's disease. The dye is excreted in the urine 6–12 hours after the initial injection.

20. **I** **radiology/x-ray**—Shows functional or structural changes in bones and joints.

21. **A** **arthrography**—Radiographic visualization of joints after injection of a contrast medium. Allows visualization of soft tissues such as ligament and cartilage to detect cause of knee or shoulder pain, joint derangement, and synovial cysts. The nurse should assess for allergies to contrast dyes, seafood, iodine, or local anesthetics. The joint should rest for 12 hours post procedure.

22. **B** **dislocation**—Displacement of the bone from its normal position in the joint, causing severe pain, change in the length of the extremity, change in the contour and shape of the joint, and inability to move. Treatment includes reduction and immobilization.

23. **E** **strain**—Injury to the muscle tissue in the form of incomplete tears. Results from overstretching, overuse, or excess stress, causing bleeding into the muscle, pain, swelling, and muscle spasm. Treatment includes ice packs for the first 24 hours followed by moist or dry heat, sling or crutches, and muscle relaxants.

24. **C** **fracture**—Any break in the continuity of the bone occurring in the shaft or diaphysis (complete, incomplete, or bending, open or closed). Treatment includes realignment of bone fragments, maintenance of realignment by immobilization, and restoration of function.

25. **A** **contusion**—Injury to the soft tissue resulting in a rupture of the small blood vessels and ecchymosis (hemorrhage) at the trauma site, manifested by pain, swelling, and discoloration. Treatment includes cold compress for the first 24 hours, followed by dry heat, and elevation of the extremity.

26. **D** **sprain**—Injury involving the ligamentous structures surrounding a joint; tear or stretching of the joint. Immobilization is crucial after swelling has subsided. Treatment includes immobilization, cast application after swelling decreases, cold or heat, and correct positioning.

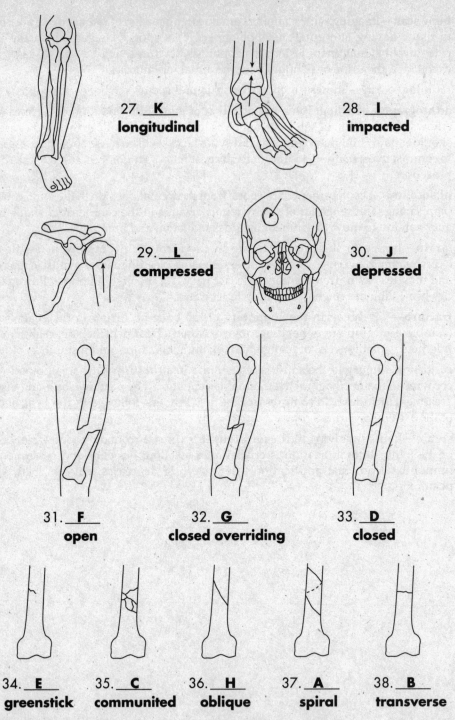

27. **K** longitudinal

28. **I** impacted

29. **L** compressed

30. **J** depressed

31. **F** open

32. **G** closed overriding

33. **D** closed

34. **E** greenstick

35. **C** communited

36. **H** oblique

37. **A** spiral

38. **B** transverse

39. Osteitis deformans is also known as **Paget's disease**. It is characterized by bone **deformity** and accelerated bone resorption.

40. **E** **hip**—Sciatic nerve damage

41. **F** **pelvic**—Profuse bleeding, bladder rupture, bowel trauma

42. **B** **distal femur**—Popliteal artery damage, bleeding

43. **A** **dislocation of fractured knee**—Popliteal artery damage

44. **C** **fracture of 5th metatarsal**—Nerve damage

45. **D** **fracture of proximal fibula**—Injury of peroneal nerve

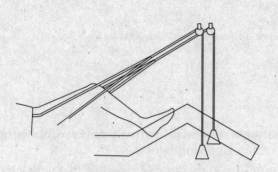

46. Pelvic belt traction (skin)

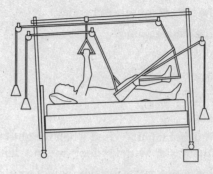

47. Balanced suspension traction (skeletal)

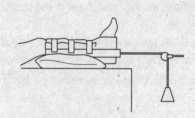

48. Buck's traction (skin)

49. Overhead 90-90 traction (skeletal)

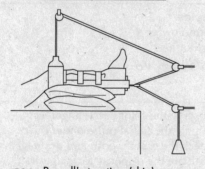

50. Russell's traction (skin)

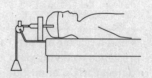

51. Cervical tongs (skeletal)

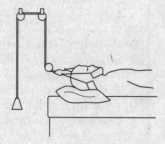

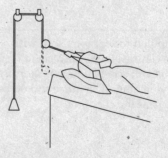

52. Cervical halter (skin)

53. Assessment of traction includes what three components?

    A. the 5 Ps of muscle ischemia

    B. neurovascular checks

    C. assessment for compartment syndrome.

54. List the 5 Ps of muscle ischemia:

    A. Progressive pain

    B. Pulselessness

    C. Paresthesia

    D. Paralysis

    E. Pallor

55. **A**   **four-point gait**—Used when weight-bearing is allowed on both extremities. Advance right crutch, step with left foot; advance left crutch, step with right foot.

56. **E**   **two-point gait**—Acceleration of four-point gait. Right crutch moves together with left leg; left crutch moves together with right crutch.

57. **D**   **three-point gait**—Used when weight-bearing is permitted on one extremity only. Advance both crutches and affected extremity several inches; maintaining good balance, advance unaffected leg, supporting weight of body on hands.

58. **C**   **swing-to gait**—Used in clients with paralysis of both lower extremities, unable to lift feet from the floor. Place both crutches forward. Client swings forward to the crutches.

59. **B**   **swing-through gait**—Used in clients with paralysis of both lower extremities. Both crutches placed forward, client swings body through crutches.

CHAPTER 9: NCLEX-RN STYLE QUESTIONS

1. A client is 1 day postoperative after a total hip replacement. The client should be placed in which of these positions for meals?

    (1) Supine
    (2) Semi-Fowler's
    (3) Orthopneic
    (4) Trendelenburg

2. A client who has had a plaster of Paris cast applied to his forearm is receiving pain medication. To detect early manifestations of compartment syndrome, which of these assessments should the nurse make?

    (1) Observe the color of the fingers.
    (2) Palpate the radial pulse under the cast.
    (3) Check the cast for odor and drainage.
    (4) Evaluate the response to analgesics.

3. After a computed topography scan with intravenous contrast medium, a client returns to the unit complaining of shortness of breath and itching. The nurse should be prepared to treat the client for

    (1) an anaphylactic reaction to the dye.
    (2) inflammation from the extravasation of fluid during injection.
    (3) fluid overload from the volume of infusions.
    (4) a normal reaction to the stress of the diagnostic procedure.

4. While caring for a client with a newly applied plaster of Paris cast, the nurse makes note of all of the following conditions. Which assessment finding requires immediate notification of the physician?

(1) Moderate pain, as reported by the client
(2) Report, by client, that heat is being felt under the cast
(3) Presence of slight edema of the toes of the casted foot
(4) Onset of paralysis in the toes of the casted foot

5. Which nursing intervention is appropriate for a client with skeletal traction?

(1) Pin care
(2) Prone positioning
(3) Intermittent weights
(4) 5-lb weight limit

6. In order for Buck's traction applied to the right leg to be effective, the client should be placed in which position?

(1) Supine
(2) Prone
(3) Sim's
(4) Lithotomy

7. Which of these nursing actions will best promote independence for the client in skeletal traction?

(1) Instruct the client to call for an analgesic before pain becomes severe.
(2) Provide an overhead trapeze for client use.
(3) Encourage leg exercises within the limits of traction.
(4) Provide skin care to prevent skin breakdown.

8. A client presents in the emergency department after falling from a roof. A fracture of the femoral neck is suspected. Which of these assessments best supports this diagnosis?

(1) The client reports pain in the affected leg.
(2) A large hematoma is visible in the affected extremity.
(3) The affected extremity is shortened, adducted, and externally rotated.
(4) The affected extremity is edematous.

9. The nurse is caring for a client with a compound fracture of the tibia and fibula. Skeletal traction is applied. Which of these priorities should the nurse include in the care plan?

(1) Order a trapeze to increase the client's ambulation.
(2) Maintain the client in a flat, supine position at all times.
(3) Provide pin care at least every 8 hours.
(4) Remove traction weights for 20 minutes every 2 hours.

10. To prevent foot drop in a client with Buck's traction, the nurse should

(1) place pillows under the client's heels.
(2) tuck the sheets into the foot of the bed.
(3) teach the client isometric exercises.
(4) ensure proper body positioning.

CHAPTER 9: NCLEX-RN STYLE ANSWERS

1.   **(2) CORRECT**   To prevent dislocation of the hip prothesis, the affected leg should be maintained in abduction, and the hip should not be flexed more than 45 or 60°. In semi-Fowler's position, the head of the bed is raised about 30°, which places the client in a semi-sitting position, is a more natural and safer position for eating.

        (1) POSSIBLE   Although the supine position would not cause dislocation of the hip prosthesis, it may cause the client to aspirate food.

        (3) ELIMINATE   In the orthopneic position, the head of the bed is raised about 90°, which would promote the dislocation of the prosthesis.

        (4) ELIMINATE   In the Trendelenburg position, the head is lower than the feet, which is an unsafe position for both eating and the hip prosthesis.

CATEGORY 09 REDUCTION OF RISK POTENTIAL

2.   **(4) CORRECT**   In compartment syndrome, secondary edema causes an increase in the pressure in the closed spaces of the tissue compartment formed by the nonelastic fascia. As the pressure increases, obstruction of the venous circulation and arterial occlusion occur, which leads to ischemia. The earliest symptom of compartment syndrome is unrelenting, progressive pain distal to the injury that is not relieved by analgesics. The pain characteristic of the syndrome could thus be detected by evaluating the response to analgesics.

        (1) POSSIBLE   Observing the client for a change in skin color could detect pallor, which is a late symptom of the syndrome.

        (2) POSSIBLE   Palpating the radial pulse might allow the nurse to detect pulselessness, which is a late sign of the syndrome.

        (3) ELIMINATE   Odor and drainage on a cast is more indicative of infection.

CATEGORY 09 REDUCTION OF RISK POTENTIAL

3.   **(1) CORRECT**   Clients can be allergic to the intravenous contrast medium, or dye, used in CAT scans and other diagnostic tests, including angiograms. This can be a mild reaction, but it can also be enough to progress to an anaphylactic reaction.

        (2) ELIMINATE   An infiltrated intravenous infusion may cause extravasation of contrast medium, or dye, into tissues, which would cause a local reaction such as swelling and coolness of the skin.

        (3) ELIMINATE   Only a small amount of contrast medium is infused, which is very unlikely to cause fluid overload.

        (4) ELIMINATE   To the contrary, this is an abnormal reaction to the procedure.

CATEGORY 10 PHYSIOLOGICAL ADAPTATION

4.   **(4) CORRECT**   Unrelieved pain, excessive swelling, poor capillary refill, inability to move fingers or toes, and elevated tissue pressure indicate compartment syndrome and must be reported to the physician at once.

     (1) *ELIMINATE*   Moderate pain related to the fracture is a common nursing diagnosis.

     (2) *ELIMINATE*   Heat is produced by the hardening reaction of the plaster.

     (3) *ELIMINATE*   Swelling and edema are expected responses of tissue to trauma.

CATEGORY 01 MANAGEMENT OF CARE

5.   **(1) CORRECT**   Pin care is a critical infection control practice for clients with skeletal traction. It requires cleansing of the insertion sites.

     (2) *ELIMINATE*   Prone positioning is contraindicated, in fact, not possible, when skeletal traction is in use.

     (3) *ELIMINATE*   Weights are not intermittently used.

     (4) *ELIMINATE*   The amount of weight varies with the client.

CATEGORY 02 SAFETY AND INFECTION CONTROL

6.   **(1) CORRECT**   Buck's traction is skin traction for the extremities. To keep the leg in a neutral position, the client must remain in a supine position.

     (2) *ELIMINATE*   Prone position is lying face down and is not effective in maintaining alignment for traction.

     (3) *ELIMINATE*   Sim's position is left side–lying, which would not keep the client's leg in neutral position.

     (4) *ELIMINATE*   Lithotomy position is lying on the back with legs flexed, which would not keep the leg in neutral position.

CATEGORY 09 REDUCTION OF RISK POTENTIAL

7.   **(2) CORRECT**   The trapeze is of great help in assisting the client to move in bed or on and off the bedpan.

     (1) *ELIMINATE*   The client is in a dependent role, depending on the nurse to provide pain medication.

     (3) *ELIMINATE*   Leg exercises are encouraged to decrease venous stasis and help prevent thrombus formation.

     (4) *ELIMINATE*   Frequent repositioning and using skin protective devices are nursing interventions to prevent skin breakdown. They are unrelated to client independence.

CATEGORY 07 BASIC CARE AND COMFORT

8. (3) CORRECT   With fractures of the femoral neck, the leg is shortened, adducted, and externally rotated.

    (1) *ELIMINATE*   Most clients with diseases and traumatic conditions of the muscles, bones, or joints experience pain.

    (2) *ELIMINATE*   Extracapsular fractures, between the base of the femoral neck and lesser trochanter of the femur, are associated with a large hematoma or area of ecchymosis. A femoral neck fracture is an intracapsular fracture.

    (4) *ELIMINATE*   There is a high incidence of hip fracture due to falls associated with medications, treatments, or existing medical conditions.

CATEGORY 09 REDUCTION OF RISK POTENTIAL

9. (3) CORRECT   The pin site is inspected at least every 8 hours for signs of inflammation and evidence of infection.

    (1) *ELIMINATE*   A trapeze is provided to aid the client with bed mobility, not ambulation.

    (2) *ELIMINATE*   Exercises in traction include pulling up on the trapeze, which raises the client into an upright position.

    (4) *ELIMINATE*   Weights should never be removed from skeletal traction unless a life-threatening situation occurs.

CATEGORY 02 SAFETY AND INFECTION CONTROL

10. (3) CORRECT   Isometric exercises can help maintain mobility and muscle tone, thus preventing foot drop. A foot board can also be used.

    (1) *ELIMINATE*   Pillows under the client's heels and proper body positioning can help prevent pressure sores, not foot drop.

    (2) *ELIMINATE*   Sheets should remain untucked to prevent pulling on toes.

    (4) *ELIMINATE*   Proper body positioning does not prevent foot drop.

CATEGORY 09 REDUCTION OF RISK POTENTIAL

10

THE INTEGUMENTARY SYSTEM

WHAT YOU NEED TO KNOW

Luckily, you don't need to know all the details of the integumentary system for this exam. But that doesn't mean you are in the clear. The examiners *love* burns and skin breakdown, so those topics should be your priorities.

REVIEW OF THE INTEGUMENTARY SYSTEM

The integumentary system is composed of skin, hair, nails, and sebaceous and sweat glands. It has the following functions:

1. Protecting the body from dehydration and mechanical injury
2. Maintaining temperature control (e.g., "goose bumps" and sweating)
3. Producing vitamin D; excreting waste materials and toxins
4. Reacting immunologically to microorganisms and chemicals

Do the exercises below to familiarize yourself with the basic concepts related to the integumentary system.

DIAGNOSTIC STUDIES

Assign each of the following studies to its proper definition:

1. __E__ Administration of allergens or antigens on the surface or into the dermis to determine hypersensitivity. There are three types: patch, scratch, and intradermal.

2. __B__ To determine the presence of fungi or bacterial infection of the skin. Nursing care includes explaining the procedure, obtaining samples using aseptic technique, and notifying provider of results so that proper medication or intervention is instituted.

3. __D__ Hemoglobin, hematocrit, red blood cell, and white blood cell counts

4. __C__ Serum calcium, chloride, magnesium, potassium, and sodium

5. __A__ Removal of a sample of tissue (generally 3 mm or more) for examination to determine diagnosis. Nursing care includes maintaining aseptic technique during procedure and while applying dressing; providing client comfort and support.

A. biopsy
B. cultures of the skin
C. electrolytes
D. hematology
E. skin allergy testing

6. List five functions of the integumentary system:
   A. Protect body from dehydration
   B. Temp control
   C. Immunological responses
   D. Produces Vit D
   E. _____

DISORDERS OF THE INTEGUMENTARY SYSTEM

To remind yourself of the terms associated with the integumentary system and some associated skin disorders, do the following matching exercise:

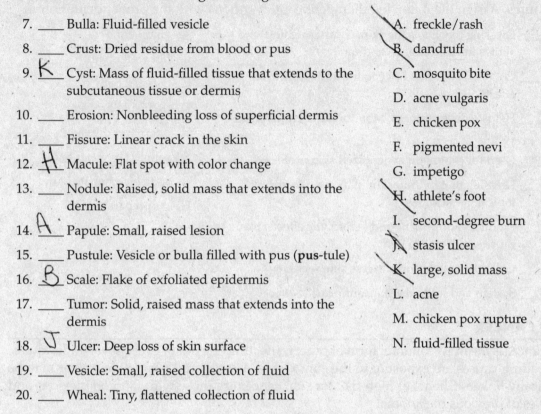

7. ___ Bulla: Fluid-filled vesicle

8. ___ Crust: Dried residue from blood or pus

9. _K_ Cyst: Mass of fluid-filled tissue that extends to the subcutaneous tissue or dermis

10. ___ Erosion: Nonbleeding loss of superficial dermis

11. ___ Fissure: Linear crack in the skin

12. _H_ Macule: Flat spot with color change

13. ___ Nodule: Raised, solid mass that extends into the dermis

14. _A_ Papule: Small, raised lesion

15. ___ Pustule: Vesicle or bulla filled with pus (**pus**-tule)

16. _B_ Scale: Flake of exfoliated epidermis

17. ___ Tumor: Solid, raised mass that extends into the dermis

18. _J_ Ulcer: Deep loss of skin surface

19. ___ Vesicle: Small, raised collection of fluid

20. ___ Wheal: Tiny, flattened collection of fluid

A. freckle/rash
B. dandruff
C. mosquito bite
D. acne vulgaris
E. chicken pox
F. pigmented nevi
G. impetigo
H. athlete's foot
I. second-degree burn
J. stasis ulcer
K. large, solid mass
L. acne
M. chicken pox rupture
N. fluid-filled tissue

Certain specific skin disorders may appear on the exam. We cover them here and include only the points you should associate with each disease for the NCLEX-RN.

Systemic lupus erythematosus is a chronic, systemic, inflammatory disease of collagen tissue. It is an autoimmune skin disorder characterized by a butterfly rash of the face, erythema of the palms, and general malaise. The client must avoid sunlight!

Herpes zoster (shingles) is an acute viral infection (a reactivation of chicken pox virus) that causes painful vesicles along nerve distribution. Prevention of the spread of infection is imperative.

GENERAL INTERVENTIONS FOR INTEGUMENTARY DISORDERS

The primary nursing interventions for disorders of the integumentary system focus on ensuring patient comfort and providing client education regarding medications and procedures. Assign the following therapeutic interventions with the proper definition:

21. ____ Dressing that cools the skin, controls itching, and allows infected lesions to drain

22. ____ Colloidal bath that has cooling and antipruritic effects

23. ____ Helps reduce stiffness. Monitor bath temperature closely!

24. ____ Used for cooling in generalized skin problems

25. ____ Dressing that hydrates the skin; used to apply topical medications

26. ____ Produces antipruritic and keratolytic effects; may cause sensitivity to light

27. ____ Colloidal bath absorbs excess skin secretions

28. ____ Softens and hydrates skin; antipruritic effect

A. emollient

B. hot water bath

C. oatmeal bath

D. occlusive dressing

E. open, wet dressing

F. saline/tap water bath

G. soda bicarbonate bath

H. tar preparation

SKIN CANCER

Skin cancer is the most common form of cancer, affecting one out of every seven individuals. The leading causes are exposure to the sun, x-rays, arsenic, and coal. Skin cancer may be genetically linked. Clients at high risk for skin cancer are those with fair complexions and histories of previous melanoma.

Therapeutic interventions depend on the type of cancer. Melanomas, or malignant tumors, are treated with chemotherapy or immunotherapy. Nonmalignant tumors may be treated with radiation or surgical removal. Regardless, nursing care includes:

- Providing client support and explanation of procedures
- Post surgery: Keeping area dry and clean
- Client teaching: Limit sun exposure, use sun block and protective clothing
- Limit contact with chemical irritants
- Emphasize the need to report lesions that change characteristics
- Monitor appearance of skin lesions

Match the type of skin cancer with its definition:

29. ____ Most serious; may metastasize to blood and other organs. Cancer of the melanocyte cells in the skin. Lesion appearance varies. Any change in size, color, or sensation of a mole may indicate malignancy.

30. ____ Most common; seldom metastasizes; lesions appear small and waxy; may progress to ulcers and crust.

31. ____ May metastasize; lesions appear as rough, scaly tumors with wide edges that frequently bleed and become infected. May develop from precancerous lesions such as actinic keratoses or leukoplakia. Found on mucous membranes, lower lip, neck, and hands.

A. basal cell carcinoma

B. malignant melanoma

C. squamous cell carcinoma

BURNS

Burns are caused by thermal heat, chemical exposure, electrical current, and smoke inhalation. They destroy the epidermis, allowing tissue fluid to escape and leaving the individual vulnerable to infection.

ASSESSMENT

Assessment of burns includes evaluation of the severity of the burn (American Burn Association classification as in the chart below) and determination of the extent of the burn.

Burn severity is determined as follows:

Burn Severity	
Minor	Partial thickness <15% total body surface area (T.B.S.A.) No full thickness burns No involvement of eyes or ears
Moderate	Partial thickness 15–25% T.B.S.A. Full thickness <10% T.B.S.A. No involvement of hands, face, eyes, ears, feet, or genitalia
Major	Partial thickness >25% T.B.S.A. Full thickness >10% True electrical injuries Injury to hands, face, eyes, ears, feet, or genitalia Complications of inhalation injury, fractures, or other (concomitant trauma)

The extent of burn injury is most often determined by the rule of nines. For example, the client's palm equals 1% of T.B.S.A. (see the diagram on the next page).

THE RULE OF NINES

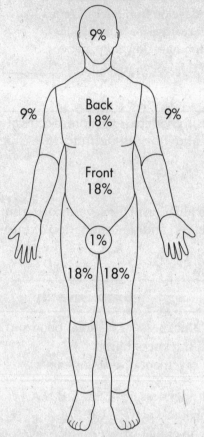

The American Burn Association classifications are as follows:

Classification	Depth	Appearance
First degree burns	Epidermis	Pink, red, dry skin; no blistering
Second degree burns	Epidermis and dermis	Blistered or wet; local edema; very painful
Third and fourth degree burns	Dermis and subcutaneous tissue	Nerves, muscle, tendons, and bones are destroyed; will not be painful because all nerves are destroyed

32. Label the following diagram at the appropriate level with the correct degree of burn injury:

A. first degree (superficial partial thickness burn)
B. second degree (deep partial thickness burn)
C. third degree (full thickness burn)
D. fourth degree (full thickness burn involving subdermal, structures)

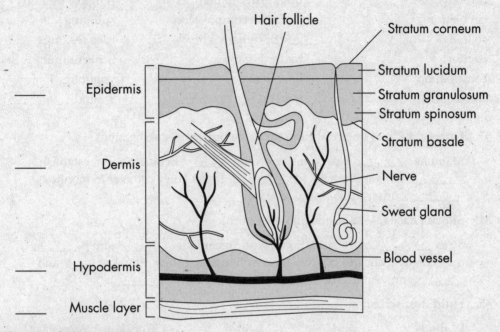

BURN INJURY INTERVENTION

Burn injury is managed in four phases: emergent, shock, diuretic, and convalescent phases. Management is based on five primary objectives:

1. Preserving body function
2. Preventing infection
3. Restoring skin integrity
4. Providing support and comfort
5. Restoring normal living pattern to the patient

Accomplishing these objectives depends on the energy resources of the client that promote healing. Nutritional support is vital as early as possible, yet there is a fine line between overfeeding and underfeeding burn victims. Increased metabolic needs call for increased protein and vitamin and mineral supplements. Enteral nutrition is the route of choice.

Complete the sentences below choosing from the following list of words:

analgesics	Curling's ulcer	nausea
antibiotics	diarrhea	pain
bleeding	dressings	patent airway
calorie	electrolytes	positioning
carbohydrate	fluid resuscitation	range of motion
circulation	gastric decompression	splinting
colloids	gastric hyperacidity	tube feedings
comfort	hydrotherapy	urine output
constipation	infection	vomiting
crystalloids	mineral	wound

33. **Emergent Phase** (removal from source of burn and stabilization):

Maintain _____. Check and control _____. Evaluate and reestablish _____. Obtain IV access for _____. Insert Foley catheter to monitor _____. Insert nasogastric tube for _____.

34. **Shock Phase** (24–48 hours following burn):

Strict _____ control: isolation, aseptic technique. _____ and _____ management: analgesics, relaxation techniques, antipruritics. _____ and _____: prevent loss of motion, active and passive _____.

35. **Fluid Resuscitation**:

IV fluids: _____ and _____. Monitor _____ (30 cc/hour). After client is stabilized, administer remaining fluid required, monitor _____.

36. **Wound Care**:

Premedicate with _____. Cleanse and debride; _____ shower no longer than 30 minutes or wet to dry _____ 3 times per day. Topical _____; skin graft.

37. **Nutrition**:

Monitor _____ and T.P.N. When advanced to oral intake: provide high-_____, high-protein, high-_____ meals with vitamin and _____ supplements for wound healing. Small, frequent meals.

38. **Prevention of Gastrointestinal Complications**:

Nasogastric tube for _____ and _____. Antacids for _____. Magnesium antacids for _____. Aluminum antacids for _____. Bland diet and bed rest for _____.

Skin grafts are applied to burns between the fifth and twenty-first day, depending on the degree of the burn. Nursing care includes:

- Keep affected site elevated; apply warm compresses as ordered; assess for hematoma, fluid accumulation; monitor circulation distal to graft site.

- Monitor for signs of infection: elevated temperature, foul-smelling drainage.

- Administer analgesics as ordered.

- Provide client teaching and discharge planning:

  1. Protect grafted skin from direct sunlight for at least 6 months.

  2. Need to report changes in graft (fluid accumulation, pain, hematoma).

  3. Sensation may or may not return.

PRESSURE ULCERS

Pressure ulcers (decubiti) are breaks in the skin caused by friction or interference with the blood supply to the tissues. Many develop when soft tissues are compressed between a bony prominence and a firm surface for a prolonged period of time. Prevention of decubiti is a priority for any client on bed rest who is immobilized for any period of time. Nursing management of a client with a pressure ulcer includes:

- Turning and positioning the client every 2 hours (most important!)

- Assessing risk factors: Mobility, activity, mental status, continence, nutritional status, age, fluid balance (edema is a risk factor), chronic illness

- Prevention: Inspect pressure points—elbows, sacrum, heels, trochanter/hip

- Wound management: All wounds must be clean to heal; necrotic tissue must be removed either surgically or mechanically with wet to dry dressings; administer antibiotics as ordered, maintain nutrition.

Match the stage of pressure ulcer with the appropriate intervention(s):

      A. Packing with wet to dry dressings of normal saline or Dakin's solution
      B. Surgery requiring myocutaneous flaps to replace missing tissue
      C. Nonabsorptive thin films; absorptive gel wafers; aluminum hydroxide
      D. Surgery that involves rotating normal tissue around the wound to cover it

39. _____ Stage I: Reddened area of skin that returns to normal color after 15–20 minutes of pressure relief

40. _____ Stage II: Top layer of skin is missing; shallow ulcer with a pinkish red base and white or yellow eschar

41. _____ Stage III: Deep ulcers extending into the dermis and subcutaneous tissue; white, gray, or yellow eschar; usually present at bottom of ulcer; purulent drainage common

42. _____ Stage IV: Deep ulcers extending into muscle and bone; foul smelling; presence of black/brown eschar and purulent drainage

1. **E** **skin allergy testing**—Administration of allergens or antigens on the surface or into the dermis to determine hypersensitivity. There are three types: patch, scratch, and intradermal.

2. **B** **cultures of the skin**—To determine the presence of fungi or bacterial infection of the skin. Nursing care includes explaining the procedure, obtaining samples using aseptic technique, and notifying provider of results so that proper medication or intervention is instituted.

3. **D** **hematology**—Hemoglobin, hematocrit, red blood cell, and white blood cell counts

4. **C** **electrolytes**—Serum calcium, chloride, magnesium, potassium, and sodium

5. **A** **biopsy**—Removal of a sample of tissue (generally 3 mm or more) for examination to determine diagnosis. Nursing care includes maintaining aseptic technique during procedure and while applying dressing; providing client comfort and support.

6. Functions of the integumentary system include:

   protecting the body from dehydration and mechanical injury

   maintaining temperature control (e.g., "goosebumps")

   allowing sensory perception

   producing vitamin D; excreting waste materials and toxins

   reacting immunologically to microorganisms and chemicals

7. **I** **second-degree burn**—Bulla: fluid-filled vesicle

8. **G** **impetigo**—Crust: dried residue from blood or pus

9. **N** **fluid-filled tissue**—Cyst: Mass of fluid-filled tissue that extends to the subcutaneous tissue or dermis

10. **M** **chicken pox rupture**—Erosion: nonbleeding loss of superficial dermis

11. **H** **athlete's foot**—Fissure: linear crack in the skin

12. **A** **freckle/rash**—Macule: flat spot with color change

13. **F** **pigmented nevi**—Nodule: raised solid mass that extends into the dermis

14. **D** **acne vulgaris**—Papule: small, raised lesion

15. **L** **acne**—Pustule: vesicle or bulla filled with pus (**pus**-tule)

16. **B** **dandruff**—Scale: flake of exfoliated epidermis

17. **K** **large solid mass**—Tumor: solid, raised mass that extends into the dermis

18. **J** **stasis ulcer**—Ulcer: deep loss of skin surface

19. **E** **chicken pox**—Vesicle: small, raised collection of fluid

20. **C** **mosquito bite**—Wheal: tiny, flattened collection of fluid

21. **E** **open, wet dressing**—Dressing that cools the skin, controls itching, and allows infected lesions to drain

22. **G** **soda bicarbonate bath**—Colloidal bath that has cooling and antipruritic effects

23. **B** **hot water bath**—Helps reduce stiffness. Monitor bath temperature closely!

24. **F** **saline/tap water bath**—Used for cooling in generalized skin problems

25. **D** **occlusive dressing**—Dressing that hydrates the skin; used to apply topical medications

26. **H** **tar preparation**—Produces antipruritic and keratolytic effects; may cause sensitivity to light

27. **C** **oatmeal bath**—Colloidal bath absorbs excess skin secretions

28. **A** **emollient**—Softens and hydrates skin; antipruritic effect

29. **B** **malignant melanoma**—Most serious; may metastasize to blood and other organs. Cancer of the melanocyte cells in the skin. Lesion appearance varies. Any change in size, color, or sensation of a mole may indicate malignancy.

30. **A** **basal cell carcinoma**—Most common; seldom metastasizes; lesions appear small and waxy; may progress to ulcers and crust.

31. **C** **squamous cell carcinoma**—May metastasize; lesions appear as rough, scaly tumors with wide edges that frequently bleed and become infected. May develop from precancerous lesions such as actinic keratoses or leukoplakia. Found on mucous membranes, lower lip, neck, and hands.

32. Label the following diagram at the appropriate level with the correct degree of burn injury:

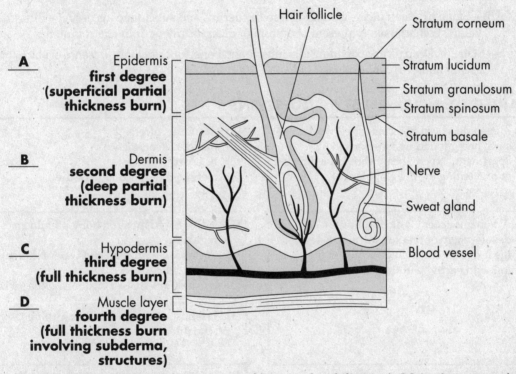

33. **Emergent Phase** (removal from source of burn and stabilization): Maintain **patent airway**. Check and control **bleeding**. Evaluate and reestablish **circulation**. Obtain IV access for **fluid resuscitation**. Insert Foley catheter to monitor **urine output**. Insert nasogastric tube for **gastric decompression**.

34. **Shock Phase** (24–48 hours following burn): Strict **infection** control: isolation, aseptic technique. **Comfort** and **pain** management: analgesics, relaxation techniques, antipruritics. **Splinting** and **positioning**: prevent loss of motion, active and passive **range of motion**.

35. **Fluid Resuscitation**: IV fluids: **colloids** and **crystalloids**. Monitor **urine output** (30 cc/hour). After client is stabilized, administer remaining fluid required, monitor **electrolytes**.

36. **Wound Care**: Premedicate with **analgesics**. Cleanse and debride; **hydrotherapy** shower no longer than 30 minutes or wet to dry **dressings** 3 times per day. Topical **antibiotics**; skin graft.

37. **Nutrition**: Monitor **tube feedings** and T.P.N. When advanced to oral intake: provide high-**calorie**, high-protein, high-**carbohydrate** meals with vitamin and **mineral** supplements for wound healing. Small, frequent meals.

38. **Prevention of Gastrointestinal Complications**: Nasogastric tube for **nausea** and **vomiting**. Antacids for **gastric hyperacidity**. Magnesium antacids for **constipation**. Aluminum antacids for **diarrhea**. Bland diet and bed rest for **Curling's ulcer**.

Match the stage of pressure ulcer with the appropriate intervention(s):

A. Packing with wet to dry dressings of normal saline or Dakin's solution

B. Surgery requiring myocutaneous flaps to replace missing tissue

C. Nonabsorptive thin films; absorptive gel wafers; aluminum hydroxide

D. Surgery that involves rotating normal tissue around the wound to cover it

39. **C**—Stage I: Reddened area of skin that returns to normal color after 15–20 minutes of pressure relief

40. **D**—Stage II: Top layer of skin is missing; shallow ulcer with a pinkish red base and white or yellow eschar

41. **A/B**—Stage III: Deep ulcers extending into the dermis and subcutaneous tissue; white, gray, or yellow eschar; usually present at bottom of ulcer; purulent drainage common

42. **B**—Stage IV: Deep ulcers extending into muscle and bone; foul smelling; presence of black/brown eschar and purulent drainage

CHAPTER 10: NCLEX-RN STYLE QUESTIONS

1. A client has been in a coma for 2 weeks since being found unconscious in his apartment. Nursing care should be directed at preventing the development of
   (1) decubitus ulcers.
   (2) bladder incontinence.
   (3) osteoarthritis.
   (4) increased intraocular pressure.

2. A comatose client is at risk for the development of pressure ulcers; therefore, the nurse should include which of the following activity in the plan of care?
   (1) Massage red areas on bony prominences regularly.
   (2) Wash skin with soap and water frequently to keep well cleaned.
   (3) Use a donut-shaped cushion on the sacral area.
   (4) Establish an individualized turning schedule.

3. The nurse is caring for an elderly client who is at risk for developing a decubitus ulcer due to prolonged bed rest. Which of the following nursing interventions would be most effective in the prevention of this condition?
   (1) Encourage fluid intake.
   (2) Turn and position the client every 2 hours.
   (3) Apply protective padding to bony prominences.
   (4) Apply emollient lotions to sensitive areas of skin.

4. When examining the skin of an elderly client, which of these findings is normal?
   (1) A large purple area, located on the groin, that does not blanch with pressure.
   (2) Spider-like blue markings, about 2 cm in size, located on the lower extremities.
   (3) Dusky red, dome-shaped papules, about 3 mm in diameter, located on the chest and back.
   (4) Reddish blue, linear lesions on the face and trunk.

5. Using the rule of nines, the nurse determines the percentage of the body burned on a client with both arms burned to be

(1) 9%.
(2) 36%.
(3) 18%.
(4) 1%.

6. A child who has been burned is brought to the emergency room. What is the first nursing priority when dealing with burns in children?

(1) Inserting an IV
(2) Inserting a Foley catheter
(3) Comforting the child
(4) Maintaining a patent airway

7. After 48 hours, successful fluid resuscitation of a burn victim can be evaluated by

(1) weight.
(2) urine output.
(3) urine specific gravity.
(4) peripheral perfusion.

8. When caring for a client with a burn, analgesics should be

(1) given 1/2 hour before dressing changes.
(2) given 2 hours before dressing changes.
(3) given due to risk of oversedation.
(4) given 1/2 hour after dressing changes.

CHAPTER 10: NCLEX-RN STYLE ANSWERS

1.

(1)	CORRECT	Since the client is immobilized for an extended period of time, there is an increased incidence of pressure ulcer formation, especially on the bony prominences. Diligent nursing care includes careful skin assessment, frequent turning, positioning, and range of motion exercising.
(2)	*ELIMINATE*	The client most likely will be incontinent of urine, but this is not an issue of prevention. An indwelling Foley catheter may be ordered by the physician to measure output.
(3)	*ELIMINATE*	As musculoskeletal complications, contractures, and osteoporosis may develop, but not osteoarthritis.
(4)	*ELIMINATE*	Given this information, increased intraocular pressure is not related to this client.

CATEGORY 09 REDUCTION OF RISK POTENTIAL

2.

(4)	CORRECT	Turning and positioning interventions, tailored to the client's needs, are designed to reduce pressure and shearing force to the skin.
(1)	*ELIMINATE*	Massage applied directly to a reddened area further promotes skin breakdown.
(2)	*ELIMINATE*	Soap and water cause drying of the skin, which contributes to breaks in skin integrity.
(3)	*ELIMINATE*	A donut-shaped cushion interferes with the oxygenation of the tissue of the sacrum in the center of the donut, thus contributing to decubitus formation.

CATEGORY 07 BASIC CARE AND COMFORT

3.

(2)	CORRECT	Skin cells that are deprived of an adequate supply of oxygen due to interruption in circulation lose viability, and a decubitus ulcer can result. Regular turning and positioning is essential.
(1)	*ELIMINATE*	Not directly associated with decubitus ulcer prevention.
(3)	*ELIMINATE*	While this might help it is not the most effective preventative measure.
(4)	*ELIMINATE*	While this might help it is not the most effective preventative measure.

CATEGORY 07 BASIC CARE AND COMFORT

4.

(3)	CORRECT	This describes a cherry (senile) angioma, a normal change with aging.
(1)	*ELIMINATE*	This describes a port-wine stain that may be associated with a congenital abnormality.
(2)	*ELIMINATE*	This describes a venous star, which is associated with varicose veins.
(4)	*ELIMINATE*	This describes telanglectasia, with is associated with sun exposure, prolonged alcohol intake, systemic scleroderma, and use of potent topical steroids.

CATEGORY 04 PREVENTION AND EARLY DETECTION OF DISEASE

5. (3) CORRECT   Using the rule of nines, each arm is 9%. Both arms would be 18%.

    (1) *ELIMINATE*   Using the rule of nines, the head and neck is 9%.

    (2) *ELIMINATE*   Using the rule of nines, each leg is 18%. Both legs would be 36%. The trunk would also be 36%.

    (4) *ELIMINATE*   Using the rule of nines, the genitalia is 1%.

CATEGORY 10 PHYSIOLOGICAL ADAPTATION

---

6. (4) CORRECT   Maintaining an airway is always the number one priority; IV access, inserting a Foley catheter, and comforting the child are secondary. Use the ABCs (airway, breathing, and then circulation).

    (1) *ELIMINATE*   IV access is secondary to maintaining a patent airway.

    (2) *ELIMINATE*   Inserting a Foley catheter is secondary to maintaining a patent airway.

    (3) *ELIMINATE*   Comforting the child is important but maintaining a patent airway is the priority.

CATEGORY 01 MANAGEMENT OF CARE

---

7. (2) CORRECT   Aside from determining central venous pressure, urine output is the most reliable indicator of fluid balance during the first 24–48 hours after a burn.

    (1) *POSSIBLE*   Weight is another indicator of fluid balance but urine can be measured on an hourly basis.

    (3) *ELIMINATE*   Specific gravity is not an indication of successful fluid resuscitation.

    (4) *ELIMINATE*   Peripheral perfusion, mental status, and vital signs are useful indicators but they are not reliable.

CATEGORY 10 PHYSIOLOGICAL ADAPTATION

---

8. (1) CORRECT   Analgesics should be given 1/2 hour before dressing changes (or any painful procedure) for maximum effectiveness. Around-the-clock pain medication is most effective for any client, and burn clients need a lot of pain medication. The client may need extra medication after the dressing changes.

    (2) *ELIMINATE*   Two hours is too long to wait between pain medication administration and the dressing change, and the client may need extra medication after the dressing change.

    (3) *ELIMINATE*   Pain medication should be given prior to dressing changes.

    (4) *ELIMINATE*   Pain medication should be given 1/2 hour prior to dressing changes, not after dressing changes.

CATEGORY 07 BASIC CARE AND COMFORT

11

THE ENDOCRINE SYSTEM

WHAT YOU NEED TO KNOW

By taking an organ-by-organ approach to the endocrine system, we will simplify the endocrine structures and functions so you can pass the NCLEX-RN. Within the section on each organ, we discuss disorders and associated nursing interventions so you can easily make connections between them.

REVIEW OF ANATOMY AND PHYSIOLOGY

The endocrine system is composed of glands and operates simultaneously with the central nervous system to maintain homeostasis within the body.

ENDOCRINE SYSTEM

The endocrine system consists of a collection of hormone-producing glands, many of which are regulated by trophic (stimulating) hormones secreted by the pituitary, including adrenocorticotropic hormone (ACTH) and thyroid-stimulating hormone (TSH). The pituitary is influenced by hormones secreted by the hypothalamus. Shown are the principal glands, with notes on the hormones they produce.

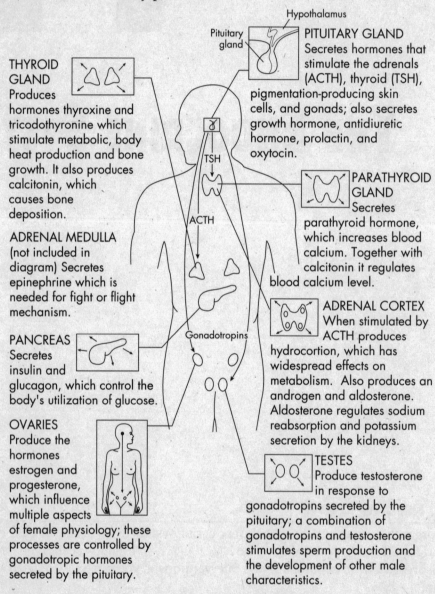

THYROID GLAND Produces hormones thyroxine and tricodothyronine which stimulate metabolic, body heat production and bone growth. It also produces calcitonin, which causes bone deposition.

ADRENAL MEDULLA (not included in diagram) Secretes epinephrine which is needed for fight or flight mechanism.

PANCREAS Secretes insulin and glucagon, which control the body's utilization of glucose.

OVARIES Produce the hormones estrogen and progesterone, which influence multiple aspects of female physiology; these processes are controlled by gonadotropic hormones secreted by the pituitary.

PITUITARY GLAND Secretes hormones that stimulate the adrenals (ACTH), thyroid (TSH), pigmentation-producing skin cells, and gonads; also secretes growth hormone, antidiuretic hormone, prolactin, and oxytocin.

PARATHYROID GLAND Secretes parathyroid hormone, which increases blood calcium. Together with calcitonin it regulates blood calcium level.

ADRENAL CORTEX When stimulated by ACTH produces hydrocortion, which has widespread effects on metabolism. Also produces an androgen and aldosterone. Aldosterone regulates sodium reabsorption and potassium secretion by the kidneys.

TESTES Produce testosterone in response to gonadotropins secreted by the pituitary; a combination of gonadotropins and testosterone stimulates sperm production and the development of other male characteristics.

In the picture above, recognize the glands that make up the endocrine system, especially the hypothalamus and the pituitary gland, the two major endocrine glands. Endocrine function is both directly and indirectly controlled by the hypothalamus.

The endocrine system regulates metabolism, use, and storage of energy through the use of hormones. This diagram is meant to help you associate the overall endocrine process with the associated organs.

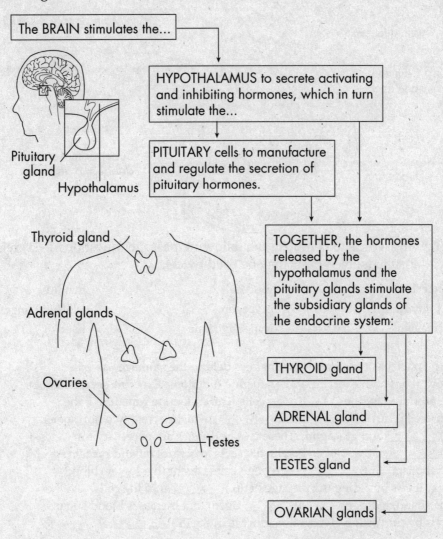

Together, using a negative feedback system, these glands regulate the body's metabolic rate and expenditure of energy.

THE PANCREAS

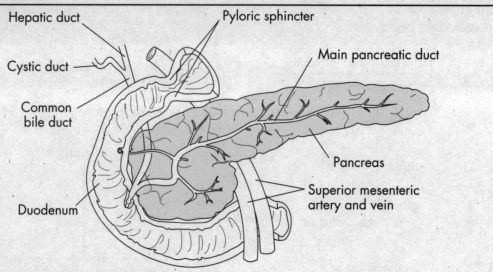

Hepatic duct

Pyloric sphincter

Cystic duct

Main pancreatic duct

Common bile duct

Pancreas

Duodenum

Superior mesenteric artery and vein

Use the following words to complete the following passage (questions 1–11) related to the pancreas and insulin (some words may be used twice):

acinar	glucose	insulin
carbohydrate	glycogen	islets of Langerhans
decreasing	hyperglycemic	liver

The pancreas is a large organ that lies behind the stomach. As you know, it has both exocrine and endocrine functions. Exocrine secretions are produced by the (1.) _____ cells. The endocrine function of the pancreas is carried out by the (2.) _____, which secrete two hormones: (3.) _____ and glucagon. These two hormones are necessary for (4.) _____ metabolism. Insulin also acts to control fat and protein metabolism. (5.) _____ is a hypoglycemic agent that lowers blood sugar levels by aiding the passage of (6.) _____ into the cells. On the other hand, glucagon is a (7.)_____ agent that increases blood sugar levels by converting glycogen to glucose in the (8.) _____.

Insulin has five main functions:

- Promoting the active transport of (9.) _____ into muscle and adipose cells, thus (10.) _____ serum glucose levels
- Regulating the rate at which carbohydrates are expended by the cells
- Converting glucose to (11.) _____ for storage within the liver and to prevent gluconeogenesis
- Promoting the conversion of fatty acids to fat and inhibiting the decomposition of fats into ketone bodies
- Encouraging protein synthesis and preventing the breakdown of proteins to amino acids

DIABETES MELLITUS

Failure of the pancreas to produce an adequate amount of insulin can lead to (12.) _____, a disease characterized by glucose intolerance. There are two types of diabetes: Type I, (13.) _____, and Type II, (14.) _____.

When assessing a client for diabetes mellitus, one should consider family history, age, and weight, as well as evidence of the "3 Ps":

15. ____ Excessive thirst caused by dehydration

16. ____ Excessive urination due to water not being reabsorbed from the renal tubules

17. ____ Excessive hunger caused by tissue wasting

 A. polydipsia

 B. polyphagia

 C. polyuria

There are several diagnostic tools used to assess a potentially diabetic client. Match each diagnostic procedure with its definition below:

18. ____ The presence of ketones indicating that the body is using fat as a major source of energy

19. ____ Random sample taken to determine blood glucose levels

20. ____ The client may not eat 4 hours prior to blood glucose test.

21. ____ Average of blood glucose control over the previous 3 months

22. ____ A blood sample for a fasting glucose level and a urine sample for glycosuria are taken. The client drinks 100 g of glucose. Blood glucose levels are taken at 1-, 2-, and 3-hour intervals.

A. blood glucose

B. fasting blood glucose

C. glucose tolerance test

D. glycosylated hemoglobin

E. urine ketone levels

Once a client is diagnosed with either Type I or Type II diabetes, daily management becomes crucial. Type I diabetes (insulin-dependent) is managed with insulin, diet, and exercise. The nurse should encourage the client to initiate a daily exercise regimen and a diet low in fat and simple sugars. Regular timing and consistency of meals is vital.

Insulin Administration

23. Of the three elements needed to maintain Type I diabetes—_____, _____, and _____—insulin administration is the most crucial.

There are several types of insulin. Match the type below with its proper action time:

24. ____ Short-acting, peaking in 2–4 hours

25. ____ Intermediate-acting, peaking in 6–12 hours

26. ____ Long-acting, peaking in 14–24 hours

  A.   NPH insulin, semilente

  B.   regular insulin, lente

  C.   ultralente insulin

The absorption of insulin is site-dependent. The client should be taught to rotate injection sites to prevent tissue hypertrophy or atrophy.

Sites of insulin injection:

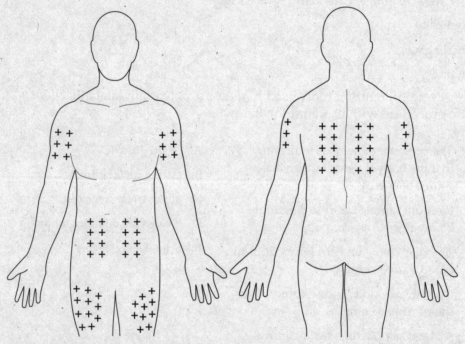

    The client should be instructed on the proper way to mix and administer insulin. When mixing regular and NPH insulin in the same syringe, (27.) _____ insulin is drawn into the syringe first. The insulin should then be injected into (28.) _____ tissue, not muscle.

Complications of Diabetes Mellitus

    Type II diabetes—(29.) _____ is managed with diet, exercise, and oral hypoglycemic agents such as tolbutamine (Orinase), chloropomide (Diabinese), or glyburide (DiaBeta).

    Once pharmacological intervention is initiated, the client should be able to demonstrate adequate knowledge about the side effects of the medication taken. The major side effect of both insulin and oral hypoglycemic agents is (30.) _____. Hypoglycemia is defined as a blood sugar level of (31.) _____ or less.

Early clinical signs of hypoglycemia include:

- headache
- weakness
- irritability
- lack of muscle coordination
- diaphoresis

The most effective means of managing hypoglycemia is by balancing diet, exercise, and hypoglycemic agents. The client should be encouraged to maintain a desirable body weight and to adhere to a low-sugar, low-fat diet. You may see the term "exchanges" used on the NCLEX-RN. It refers to the recommended servings and quantities from each of the six food groups for diabetics: starch, meats, dairy, fruits, vegetables, and fats.

32. Hypoglycemia is not the only complication of diabetes. _____ is characterized by a blood sugar level greater than 120 mg/dL.

Use the following word choices to fill in the other complications of diabetes described below. Complications of diabetes include:

diabetic ketoacidosis   nonketotic
hyperglycemic   retinopathy
hyperosmolar

- neuropathy characterized by the inability to perceive pain

- diabetic (33.) _____ caused by vascular degeneration of the small vessels supporting the eyes

- coronary artery disease related to atherosclerosis

- (34.) _____ , primarily a complication of insulin-dependent diabetes mellitus (IDDM), caused by the accumulation of ketone bodies in the blood leading to metabolic acidosis

- (35.) _____, _____, _____ coma, generally affecting clients with non–insulin-dependent diabetes mellitus (NIDDM), characterized by extreme hyperglycemia and treated with vigorous fluid replacement

THE THYROID GLAND

The thyroid gland plays a large role in the metabolic rate of all tissues. Hormones produced by the thyroid gland (levothyroxine [T4]; and triiodothyronine [T3]) affect the speed of chemical reactions, the volume of oxygen consumed, and the amount of heat produced by the cells.

DISORDERS OF THE THYROID GLAND

There are two categories of thyroid disorders: hypothyroidism and hyperthyroidism.

(36.) _____ is characterized by a deficiency of thyroid hormone resulting in (37.) _____ body metabolism related to decreased oxygen consumption by the tissues. A major complication of hypothyroidism is (38.) _____, a severely hypometabolic state leading to coma.

Hypothyroidism

Hypothyroidism may be caused by congenital deficits (cretinism), defective hormone production, iodine deficiency, drug therapy, or by failure of the (39.) _____ to produce thyroid-releasing hormone (TRH), halting the production of thyroid-stimulating hormone (TSH) by the (40.) _____ gland.

When assessing a client for hypothyroidism, clinical manifestations may include:

- weight gain
- dry skin
- lethargy
- sensitivity to cold
- depression
- constipation
- goiter (an enlarged thyroid gland)

(41.) _____ is characterized by non-pitting edema in the periorbital and facial areas. A client in myxedema coma presents with (42. increased/ decreased) metabolic rate, hypoventilation leading to (43. metabolic/respiratory) acidosis, hypothermia, and hypotension.

Depending on the cause of the hypothyroidism, diagnostic tests used to confirm may include different results. If it is due to lack of iodine there would be (44). (increased/decreased) TRH. (45). (increased/decreased) TSH (46). (increased/decreased) Serum T4 (47). (increased/decreased) serum T3. Once a diagnosis of simple goiter or hypothyroidism is ascertained, treatment is pharmacological with the intention of correcting the thyroid deficiency, reversing symptoms, and preventing further cardiac or arterial damage.

The drug treatment of choice for hypothyroidism is levothyroxine sodium (Synthroid) administered once a day in the morning. Major side effects of Synthroid are caused by increased body metabolism: headache, tremors, tachycardia, and hyperthyroidism.

Hyperthyroidism

Use the following words to fill in the blanks for the following passage on hyperthyroidism (questions 48–56; some words may be used twice):

exophthalmous   hyperthyroidism

Graves' disease   thyroid storm

(48.) _____ is defined as excessive secretion of thyroid hormone commonly caused by overfunctioning of the thyroid gland. The most common form is (49.) _____, which is characterized by hyperthyroidism, goiter, and abnormal protrusion of the eyes, called (50.) _____.

Assessment of the client with hyperthyroidism includes clinical signs of Graves' disease, including weight loss due to increased metabolism, warm smooth skin, thin hair, hyperactivity, goiter, and (51.) _____ due to accumulation of fluid in the fat pads and muscles behind the eyes. Depending on the cause of Grave's disease, diagnostically one would find (52). (increased/decreased) TRH, (53). (increased/decreased) TSH, (54). (increased/decreased) serum T4, and (55). (increased/decreased) serum T3.

The pharmacological treatment of choice for hyperthyroidism is PTU (propylthiouracil), which impairs thyroid hormone synthesis. The major side effect is agranulocytosis. A baseline white blood cell count should be attained prior to administration.

The client with hyperthyroidism may be surgically managed with a total or partial thyroidectomy. Prior to surgery the client is usually treated with radioactive iodine (^{131}I) to decrease the vascularity of the thyroid and prevent a (56.) _____, an acute episode of thyroid overactivity characterized by high fever, severe tachycardia, delirium, dehydration, and extreme agitation. If a thyroid storm occurs, treatment includes fluid replacement, use of a hypothermia blanket, and administration of the radioactive iodine ^{131}I.

The client with hypothyroidism or hyperthyroidism may also exhibit knowledge deficits related to nutrition, activity, elimination, skin integrity, and medications. The client should be instructed in the proper usage and probable side effects of the prescribed medication. The client should also be counseled regarding nutrition and encouraged to return to the pre-illness level of activity. The client with hypothyroidism will find it difficult to achieve and maintain a desirable body weight, so a low-calorie diet should be advised.

THE PARATHYROID GLAND

The parathyroid gland secretes parathyroid hormone which increases bone resorption and maintains calcium and phosphate levels.

Hyperparathyroidism vs. Hypoparathyroidism	
Hyperparathyroidis	Hypoparathyroidism
Increased bone resorption	Decreased bone resorption
Elevated serum calcium levels	Depressed serum calcium levels
Depressed serum phosphate levels	Elevated serum phosphate levels
Hypercalciuria and hyperphosphaturia	Hypocalciuria and hypophosphaturia
Decreased neuromuscular irritability	Increased neuromuscular irritability; may progress to tetany

Parathyroid disorders are usually diagnosed via x-ray and monitoring of serum calcium and phosphorus levels. Treatment of hyperparathyroidism consists of drug therapy that inhibits bone resorption and decreases the release of calcium by the bones along with loop diuretics that promote the urinary excretion of calcium. Treatment of hypoparathyroidism is generally pharmacological, consisting of calcium supplements and vitamin D.

57. The parathyroid gland regulates _____ and _____ levels in the blood.

58. Parathyroid hormone _____ bone resorption.

THE ADRENAL GLANDS

The adrenal cortex of the adrenal glands produces and secretes those hormones necessary to sustain life. There are two types of adrenal gland defects:

- primary adrenal insufficiency, or (59.) _____, resulting from a disorder within the adrenal gland

- adrenal hyperactivity, which generally presents as (60.) _____, excess glucocorticoid production, or (61.) _____, excess aldosterone secretion

The following chart compares adrenal insufficiency and hyperactivity:

	Addison's Disease	Cushing's Syndrome	Conn's Syndrome
Clinical manifestation	Fatigue, weight loss, nausea, vomiting, postural hypotension, hypoglycemia, decreased cardiac output	Steroid psychosis, striae, moon face, trunkal obesity, hirsutism, hypertension, hyperglycemia, osteoporosis	Hypertension, visual changes, heart failure, renal damage, C.V.A.
Diagnostic tests	Decreased plasma ACTH, glucose <50	Increased plasma ACTH, glucosuria, metabolic alkalosis	Metabolic alkalosis
Treatments	Pharmacological: steroid replacement therapy	Surgical: bilateral adrenalectomy followed by lifetime corticosteroid replacement	Pharmacological: Aldactone, potassium sparing diuretic Surgical: Bilateral or unilateral adrenalectomy
Interventions	Instruct client on the side effects of drug therapy, most importantly, symptoms of Cushing's syndrome. Monitor blood pressure for hypotension or hypertension. Monitor blood glucose level for hypoglycemia.	Same as Addison's disease. Protect from injury related to osteoporosis. Promote rest and a stress-free environment. Encourage diet low in sodium, simple sugars, and calories; but high in protein and potassium.	Same as Addison's disease

CHAPTER 11: EXERCISE ANSWERS

1. Exocrine secretions are produced by the **acinar** cells.

2. The endocrine function of the pancreas is carried out by the **islets of Langerhans**, which secrete two hormones:

3. …**insulin** and glucagon.

4. These two hormones are necessary for **carbohydrate** metabolism. Insulin also acts to control fat and protein metabolism.

5. **Insulin** is a hypoglycemic agent that lowers blood sugar levels by aiding the passage of…

6. …**glucose** into the cells.

7. On the other hand, glucagon is a **hyperglycemic** agent that increases blood sugar levels by converting glycogen to glucose in the…

8. …**liver**.

9. Promoting the active transport of **glucose** into muscle and adipose cells, thus…

10. …**decreasing** serum glucose levels

11. Converting glucose to **glycogen** for storage within the liver and to prevent gluconeogenesis

12. Failure of the pancreas to produce an adequate amount of insulin can lead to **diabetes mellitus**, a disease characterized by glucose intolerance. There are two types of diabetes:

13. Type I, or **insulin-dependent diabetes mellitus** and...

14. ...Type II, or **non–insulin-dependent diabetes mellitus**.

15. **A**   **polydipsia**—Excessive thirst caused by dehydration

16. **C**   **polyuria**—Excessive urination due to water not being reabsorbed from the renal tubules

17. **B**   **polyphagia**—Excessive hunger caused by tissue wasting

18. **E**   **urine ketone levels**—The presence of ketones indicating that the body is using fat as a major source of energy

19. **A**   **blood glucose**—Random sample taken to determine glucose levels

20. **B**   **fasting blood glucose**—The client may not eat 4 hours prior to blood glucose test.

21. **D**   **glycosylated hemoglobin**—Average of blood glucose control over the previous 3 months

22. **C**   **glucose tolerance test**—A blood sample for a fasting glucose level and a urine sample for glycosuria are taken. The client drinks 100 g of glucose. Blood glucose levels are taken at 1-, 2-, and 3-hour intervals.

23. Of the three elements needed to maintain Type I diabetes—**insulin therapy, diet,** and **exercise**—insulin administration is the most crucial.

24. **B**   **regular insulin, lente**—Short-acting, peaking in 2–4 hours

25. **A**   **NPH insulin, semilente**—Intermediate-acting, peaking in 6–12 hours

26. **C**   **ultralente insulin**—Long-acting, peaking in 14–24 hours

27. When mixing regular and NPH insulin in the same syringe, **regular** insulin is drawn into the syringe first.

28. The insulin should then be injected into **subcutaneous** tissue, not muscle.

29. Type II diabetes, **non–insulin-dependent diabetes mellitus**, is managed with diet, exercise, and oral hypoglycemic agents such as tolbutamin (Orinase), or glyburide (DiaBeta).

30. The major side effect of both insulin and oral hypoglycemic agents is **hypoglycemia**.

31. Hypoglycemia is defined as a blood sugar level of **60mg/dL** or less.

32. Hypoglycemia is not the only complication of diabetes. **Hyperglycemia** is characterized by a blood sugar level greater than 120mg/dL.

33. Diabetic **retinopathy** caused by vascular degeneration of the small vessels supporting the eyes

34. **Diabetic ketoacidosis**, primarily a complication of insulin-dependent diabetes mellitus (IDDM), caused by the accumulation of ketone bodies in the blood leading to metabolic acidosis

35. **Hyperglycemic, hyperosmolar, nonketotic** coma, generally affecting clients with non–insulin-dependent diabetes mellitus (NIDDM), characterized by extreme hyperglycemia and treated with vigorous fluid replacement

36. **Hypothyroidism** is characterized by a deficiency of thyroid hormone resulting in...

37. ...**decreased** body metabolism related to decreased oxygen consumption by the tissues.

38. A major complication of hypothyroidism is **myxedema**, a severely hypometabolic state leading to coma.

39. Hypothyroidism may be caused by congenital deficits (cretinism), defective hormone production, iodine deficiency, drug therapy, or by failure of the **hypothalamus** to produce thyroid releasing hormone (TRH)...

40. ...halting the production of thyroid stimulating hormone (TSH) by the **pituitary** gland.

41. **Myxedema** is characterized by non-pitting edema most common in the periorbital and facial areas.

42. A client in myxedema coma presents with **decreased** metabolic rate...

43. ...hypoventilation leading to **respiratory** acidosis, hypothermia, and hypotension.

44. Diagnostic tests to confirm hypothyroidism include **increased** TRH...

45. ...**increased** TSH...

46. ...**decreased** serum T4, and...

47. ...**decreased** serum T3.

48. **Hyperthyroidism** is defined as excessive secretion of thyroid hormone commonly caused by overfunctioning of the thyroid gland.

49. The most common form is **Graves' disease** that is characterized by hyperthyroidism, goiter, and...

50. ...abnormal protrusion of the eyes, called **exophthalmous**.

51. Assessment of the client with hyperthyroidism includes clinical signs of Graves' disease, including weight loss due to increased metabolism, warm smooth skin, thin hair, hyperactivity, goiter, and **exophthalmous** due to accumulation of fluid in the fat pads and muscles behind the eyes.

52. Diagnostically, one would find **decreased** TRH...

53. ...**increased** TSH...

54. ...**increased** serum T4, and...

55. ...**increased** serum T3.

56. Prior to surgery the client is usually treated with radioactive iodine (^{131}I) to decrease the vascularity of the thyroid and prevent a **thyroid storm**, an acute episode of thyroid overactivity characterized by high fever, severe tachycardia, delirium, dehydration, and extreme agitation.

57. The parathyroid gland regulates **serum calcium** and **serum phosphate** levels in the blood.

58. Parathyroid hormone **increases** bone resorption.

59. primary adrenal insufficiency, or **Addison's disease**, resulting from a disorder within the adrenal gland

60. adrenal hyperactivity, which generally presents as **Cushing's syndrome**, excess glucocorticoid production, or...

61. ...**Conn's syndrome**, excess aldosterone secretion

1. The nurse is teaching a diabetic client about diet. The client begins to cry and states, "I will no longer be able to cook my traditional Sunday meals." The correct response by the nurse is

   (1) "That's right. You cannot eat any of those foods ever again."
   (2) "You can still have whatever you like, you just cannot eat any more cake."
   (3) "Tell me about these foods, and we will work them into the meal plan."
   (4) "Don't cry. We'll ask the provider to change your diet."

2. A nurse is teaching a diabetic client how to prevent hyperglycemia. The most important food for the client to avoid is

   (1) coffee.
   (2) lollipops.
   (3) bacon.
   (4) bagels.

3. The nurse caring for a diabetic client knows that which of the following clinical manifestations distinguishes a hypoglycemic reaction from ketoacidosis?

   (1) Blurred vision
   (2) Diaphoresis
   (3) Nausea
   (4) Weakness

4. An 18-year-old college student seeking health care at the school infirmary gives a history of "just not feeling right." Upon further questioning, the nurse determines that the client demonstrates symptoms of polyuria, polydipsia, and polyphagia. The nurse knows that these symptoms are indicative of what type of pathology?

   (1) Hyperglycemia
   (2) Hypoglycemia
   (3) Acidosis
   (4) Alkalosis

5. A client experiencing diabetic ketoacidosis is at high risk for which of the following nursing diagnoses?

   (1) High risk for chronic pain
   (2) High risk for impaired gas exchange
   (3) High risk for body image disturbance
   (4) High risk for fluid volume deficit

6. The nurse caring for a client with Type II diabetes mellitus knows that which of the following statements by the client indicates correct knowledge about the characteristics of Type II diabetes mellitus?

   (1) "I have a functioning pancreas but my receptor sites are not sensitive to insulin."
   (2) "My pancreas does not secrete insulin."
   (3) "I'll be okay as long as I take my insulin."
   (4) "If I take my medication, my pancreas will recover."

6. (1) CORRECT   A person with Type II diabetes mellitus has impaired insulin secretion. They may produce too little insulin, adequate levels of insulin, or too much insulin. The problem lies in their impaired ability to utilize the insulin they produce. The Type II diabetic may have peripheral insulin resistance and increased hepatic glucose production. This insulin resistance may result from decreased insulin receptors on cell surfaces or a decreased intracellular response to insulin.

(2) ELIMINATE   The Type II diabetic produces insulin in varying amounts. Their ability to utilize the insulin that they secrete is impaired.

(3) ELIMINATE   The Type II diabetic does not always need insulin. The mainstays of treatment are diet, exercise, and medication. The most commonly utilized medications are the oral hypoglycemics, which help to decrease hepatic glucose production and aid in utilization of endogenous insulin.

(4) ELIMINATE   Diabetes mellitus is not a disease from which a person can recover or be cured. It is manageable, and with proper treatment clients can have positive outcomes and less long-term complications.

CATEGORY 10 PHYSIOLOGICAL ADAPTATION

---

7. (4) CORRECT   This client's complaint is suggestive of peripheral vascular disease. Presence or absence of peripheral pulses is an indicator of adequate circulation to the extremities.

(1) ELIMINATE   This client's complaint is suggestive of peripheral vascular disease. Obtaining the blood sugar level is important to determine his diabetic status but is not related to the present complaint.

(2) ELIMINATE   Obtaining vital signs is an important assessment for all clients but is not related to the present complaint.

(3) POSSIBLE   A client's subjective report of length of walking activity coupled with vascular diagnostic procedures will assist the healthcare provider in determining the extent of vascular disease. Obtaining this information is important, but it is not the primary focus of the nurse at this time.

CATEGORY 10 PHYSIOLOGICAL ADAPTATION

---

8. (3) CORRECT   Warming the fingers causes vasodilatation and an increase in blood supply to the area, thereby increasing the chance of obtaining an adequate blood supply.

(1) ELIMINATE   Cool water may cause vasoconstriction and actually make it more difficult to obtain an adequate blood sample.

(2) ELIMINATE   Holding the hand in a dependent position may assist in obtaining an adequate blood supply.

(4) ELIMINATE   Fluid intake does not affect the adequacy of a blood sample.

CATEGORY 01 MANAGEMENT OF CARE

9.

(1) CORRECT   0.9% is the rehydrating solution that will be ordered for this client. The client in diabetic ketoacidosis is severely dehydrated due to the hypertonic effect of severe hyperglycemia and needs rapid volume replacement. It is not unusual for the client to receive 500–1,000 mL/hour for the first 2–3 hours, then 200–500 mL/hour with a gradual decrease in volume infusion according to client parameters, such as urine output, blood pressure, blood sugar, pulmonary status, etc.

(2) *ELIMINATE*   The administration of intravenous solutions containing glucose is not appropriate at this time. As the client's blood sugar declines, it is necessary to add glucose to the treatment regime so that the blood sugar does not drop too precipitously. This is usually done when the client's blood sugar approaches 250–300 mg/dL.

(3) *ELIMINATE*   Lactated ringers is an appropriate solution. In many instances, it is used as the fluid replacement of choice in burn clients. It is not appropriate for the client in diabetic ketoacidosis.

(4) *ELIMINATE*   The administration of highly concentrated glucose is not appropriate for this client, either as an initial rehydrating solution or as a maintenance solution.

CATEGORY 10 PHYSIOLOGICAL ADAPTATION

10.

(1) CORRECT   The islets of Langerhans perform the endocrine functions of the pancreas. The beta cells secrete insulin, which is essential for protein, carbohydrate, and fat metabolism.

(2) *ELIMINATE*   The alpha islet cells of the pancreas secrete glucagon.

(3) *ELIMINATE*   Glucose is not produced by the pancreas, but the insulin produced by the beta cells of the pancreas is essential for its metabolism.

(4) *ELIMINATE*   Lipase is a lipolytic enzyme found in the blood, pancreatic secretions and tissues.

CATEGORY 10 PHYSIOLOGICAL ADAPTATION

12

ONCOLOGY

WHAT YOU NEED TO KNOW

Cancer is the second leading cause of death in the United States. One in three Americans will suffer from some form of cancer. Before we begin the review, test your general knowledge base with the questions on the next page.

1. The location of cancer with the highest mortality rate is the _____.

2. In males, the two locations with the highest incidence of cancer are:

   A. _____

   B. _____

3. In females, the two locations with the highest incidence of cancer are:

   A. _____

   B. _____

4. Three general signs and symptoms of cancer include:

   A. _____

   B. _____

   C. _____

5. A _____ is a substance that can cause changes in a cell that can lead to cancer.

6. The number one risk factor for developing lung cancer is _____.

7. A diet high in _____ and low in _____ places an individual at increased risk of colon cancer.

8. Infection with the human immunodeficiency virus (HIV) increases the risk of developing which two types of cancer?

   A. _____

   B. _____

9. Three host factors that increase the risk of developing cancer that cannot be controlled include:

   A. _____

   B. _____

   C. _____

10. When a tumor spreads from its primary site, it is called a _____.

11. List the five most common sites of tumor migration:

   A. _____

   B. _____

   C. _____

   D. _____

   E. _____

Nurses can educate their clients to decrease their risk of developing cancer by instructing them to:

- Avoid lung irritants including first- and second-hand smoke
- Eat low-fat, high-fiber diets
- Limit alcohol intake
- Avoid direct exposure to sunlight by using sunscreen and protective clothing
- Practice safe sex (barrier contraception)
- Participate in regular cancer screening programs, based on age and risk groups

CANCER TYPES AND LOCATIONS

It is helpful to recognize types of cancer associated with different tissue types and sites for the NCLEX-RN. Try the exercise below to test your understanding of basic anatomy and physiology. **Remember:** The base/root word of the cancer usually identifies the tissue type, i.e., osteo- = bone.

12. ____ surface epithelial		A.	Osteosarcoma
13. ____ glandular epithelial		B.	Rhabdomyosarcoma
14. ____ fibrous connective tissue		C.	Adenosarcoma
15. ____ adipose tissue		D.	Chondrosarcoma
16. ____ cartilage		E.	Neurolemic sarcoma
17. ____ bone		F.	Fibrosarcoma
18. ____ blood vessels		G.	Leukemia
19. ____ lymph vessels		H.	Squamous cell sarcoma
20. ____ smooth muscle		I.	Hemangiosarcoma
21. ____ striated muscle		J.	Liposarcoma
22. ____ glial tissue		K.	Lymphangiosarcoma
23. ____ nerve sheath		L.	Leiomyosarcoma
24. ____ blood		M.	Glioma

BASIC CANCER SCREENING GUIDE

For the NCLEX-RN, you should be familiar with the general guidelines for cancer screening summarized in the table below:

Test	Who?	Age	Frequency
Pap smear, pelvic examination	Women	Age 18 or when sexually active and beyond	Yearly
Breast self-exam	Women	Age 20 and beyond	Monthly
Breast clinical exam	Women	Age 20 and beyond	Yearly
Testicular self-exam	Men	Age 16 and beyond	Monthly
Sigmoidoscopy	Men and women	Age 50 and beyond	Every 3 years
Stool occult blood	Men and women	Age 50 and beyond	Yearly
Digital rectal exam (prostate check for men)	Men and women	Age 50 and beyond	Yearly
Mammography	Women	Age 35 and beyond	Ages 35–40: one baseline exam Ages 41–50: every 2 years Ages 51 and beyond: yearly

TUMOR STAGING

The TNM system of classification for breast cancer is based on evaluating the spread of disease. T= tumor size. The range is T0–T4, with T0 being no evidence of tumor and T4 being an extensive tumor that extends into the chest wall or skin. N= Lymph node involvement. The range is from N0–N3. N0 indicates that no nodes are involved; N3 indicates that there is extensive involvement in the ipsilateral internal mammary nodes. M= metastasis; M0= no metastasis; M1 signifies that metastases are present.

> 25. When a tumor is staged by the TNM system as T2 N0 M0, it means:
>   _____, _____, and _____.

TUMOR MARKERS

Tumor markers are monitored for decreases or increases that may correlate closely with responses to treatment and reoccurrence or spread of disease. α-fetoprotein is a fetal antigen normally not expressed during adulthood. It can often be detected in the blood of clients with liver cancer and germ cell tumors of the ovary and testes. Carcinoembryonic antigen (CEA) is an embryonic antigen present in 75 percent of clients with colorectal cancer. It can be monitored through simple blood work. A recently popularized tumor marker to follow in men over 40 years old is the prostatic acid phosphatase enzyme. It is usually elevated with prostate enlargement either from cancer or benign prostatic hypertrophy.

> 26. If a 48-year-old male has a routine prostate-specific antigen screening test and there is a significant increase from last year's value, what type of cancer would it most likely indicate? _____

NURSING CARE OF THE CLIENT RECEIVING RADIATION

Approximately 50 percent of clients with cancer receive some form of radiation, especially those with seminoma, Hodgkin's disease, or cancer of the larynx and cervix.

The therapeutic goals of radiation include:

- Cure
- Tumor reduction for comfort
- Maintenance of tumor size during chemotherapy or preparation for surgery

Radiation can immediately kill cells or interrupt cell replication by directly hitting the target cells or by interacting with critical cell components. Since DNA synthesis is inhibited by radiation, rapidly dividing cells are affected the most, including cancer cells, gastrointestinal cells, and bone marrow cells. The vascular changes associated with radiation are dose-dependent. Immediately after radiation, expect the irradiated area to be reddened and dry. After several treatments, the small vessels in the area may be damaged or destroyed. With low-dose radiation, the cells can repair themselves between treatments.

TRUE OR FALSE?

27. _____ The marks indicating the area to be treated with radiation should be washed off immediately after the treatment to avoid skin breakdown.

28. _____ The client should wear light, loose clothing.

29. _____ The client may use moisturizing lotions.

30. _____ Clients should use sunscreen on treated areas when they are outside.

31. _____ Typical side effects of radiation therapy include mucositis, nausea, vomiting, and hair loss.

32. _____ A client receiving internal radiation may have radioactive excretions.

33. _____ A client receiving external radiation may have radioactive excretions.

SIDE EFFECTS OF RADIATION

The adverse effects of radiation therapy vary from client to client. Nutrition must be addressed and an individualized plan followed for each client. For example, clients receiving radiation to their body anywhere from the lung up may experience severe dry mouth at any time during and after the treatment. This can progress and cause dysphagia, thus compromising nutritional intake. Moist, soft foods and a lot of liquid should be encouraged with these clients. Radiation to the lower gastrointestinal tract can cause constipation or diarrhea.

Nutritional Concerns of Lower Gastrointestinal Radiation Therapy	
Constipation	Encourage fluids Increase dietary fiber (unless enteritis is present) Increase physical activity as tolerated
Diarrhea	Low-fiber diet Protect skin from excoriation

NURSING CARE OF THE CLIENT RECEIVING CHEMOTHERAPY

Only nurses trained in handling chemotherapeutic medications should administer them. For the NCLEX-RN, you need to know some general principles for the administration of chemotherapy:

34. All drugs must be mixed using the proper protective gear, including:

    A. _____
    B. _____
    C. _____

35. The five rights of drug administration are:

    A. _____
    B. _____
    C. _____
    D. _____
    E. _____

- Monitor lab values and know when to hold the medication based on white blood cell count, platelet count, or creatinine changes.

- The normal range for white blood cell count is (36.) _____.

- The normal range for platelets is (37.) _____.

- The normal creatinine range is (38.) _____.

- Use a (39.) (large/small) bore needle in the most (40.) (distal/proximal) vein that is accessible and large enough to tolerate the amount of fluid to be delivered.

- Prepare IV site aseptically to avoid infection.

- Frequently ensure proper line placement to avoid tissue infiltration or necrosis.

41. Signs and symptoms of tissue infiltration include:

    A. _____
    B. _____
    C. _____
    D. _____
    E. _____

- Check for signs and symptoms of infection before and after chemotherapy. The risk of infection increases dramatically when the neutrophils fall to 1,000/mL.

- Double check that drugs are mixed properly and the correct amount of fluid is given to the client before, during, and after chemotherapy. Many drugs can be toxic to the kidneys if not diluted enough.

- Monitor for signs and symptoms of chemotherapy-induced toxicity, including a discrepancy in input and output that could signal renal failure, fever, nausea, vomiting, and bone marrow suppression.

- In an oncology client a fever that may signal an underlying infection is one that is over 101.3°F (38°C) for 24 hours or more.

SIDE EFFECTS OF CHEMOTHERAPY

The effects of chemotherapy vary from client to client, and range from mild to severe. Nursing support must be individualized for each client and must include nutritional support. Most of the side effects of the common chemotherapy drugs occur because of the medications' effects on rapidly dividing cells. Though there are many different classes of drugs used in chemotherapy depending on the type and location of the tumor, the side effects vary only in intensity and duration.

42. Anemia and low white blood cell counts occur because of

_____.

43. Alopecia is the result of damage to the rapidly dividing _____.

44. Sterility occurs because of action against the _____.

Other side effects that vary in intensity, duration, and frequency include: stomatositis, dehydration, malnutrition, diarrhea, and paresthesia.

45. Common causes of nausea and vomiting in oncology clients include:

   A. _____

   B. _____

   C. _____

   D. _____

   E. _____

46. Three ways to help manage chemotherapy-induced nausea and vomiting are:

   A. _____

   B. _____

   C. _____

47. List three types of nausea and vomiting related to chemotherapy:

   A. _____

   B. _____

   C. _____

48. Should antinausea medication be given after the first treatment of chemotherapy, when the client asks for it, or before the chemotherapy begins? _____

49. If the chemotherapeutic agent has a long half life, how long should the antinausea medications be continued? _____

50. List three common side effects of the serotonin antagonists granisetron (Kytril) and ondansetron (Zofran):

    A. _____

    B. _____

    C. _____

51. Are Kytril and Zofran used primarily for long-term or acute control of emesis? _____

52. Metoclopramide (Reglan) is a benzamide that is used to control nausea and vomiting. List the three most common side effects:

    A. _____

    B. _____

    C. _____

53. Akathisia is defined as _____.

54. Is prochlorperazine (Compazine) best used for long-term or short-term control of nausea and vomiting? _____

55. Is it best to give medications rectally when a client is complaining of nausea? _____

To support the client who is experiencing nausea and vomiting, instruct him or her not to lie down after meals, to eat odorless, nutrient-dense foods, and to limit liquids taken with meals. In addition, the client should be instructed to avoid greasy, high-fat foods. If the client is constipated, encourage fluids and increase physical activity and fiber as indicated (assess for damage to the lining of the gastrointestinal tract; if present, avoid fiber). Mucositis is a common side effect of chemotherapy, and bland, moist, soft foods should be encouraged. Daily mouth care is imperative in these clients, as mucositis can cause dysphagia and tremendous discomfort.

NURSING CARE OF THE CLIENT UNDERGOING SURGERY

Surgery is used to help diagnose cancer, stage tumor spread, remove solid tumors, and provide palliative relief to clients. General preoperative and postoperative care for an oncology client is essentially the same as it is for other surgical clients. Special attention should be given to the client's psychological condition if it is an exploratory or diagnostic surgery, since many clients will suffer from anxiety and fear.

The following care plan for the client undergoing a mastectomy applies to most forms of cancer and is a good general guide to nursing interventions for the client undergoing any type of surgery.

Nursing Diagnosis *Expected Outcome*	Interventions	Rationale
Preoperative		
Coping related to unknown events surrounding breast • *Client can explain surgical procedure and preoperative routine*	• Assess client's prior surgical experiences • Obtain feedback of client's knowledge of this surgery and perioperative routine • Provide specific information to resolve misconceptions • Allow time for questions and concerns, especially about loss of her breast • Provide emotional support to client and partner	Clients who have knowledge and who are able to cope with their fears or concerns will recover more rapidly
Postoperative		
High risk for infection in wound because of removal of lymph channels and presence of wound drainage system • *Client will have decreased wound drainage and removal of drains about 7–10 days after surgery with no signs of infection*	• Assess drainage system for patency; color, odor, amount, and type of secretions; and proper suctioning • Instruct client on proper care of wound drainage system: cleaning site and catheter insertion site; emptying collection device; recording amount, color, and type of drainage; maintaining suction collection device • Have client demonstrate home care of wound drainage system following instruction • Have client report signs of infection: fever, redness at surgical site, or purulent drainage	Clients who are able to care for themselves recover more rapidly; maintaining suction reduces risk of a seroma; cleaning wound and catheter insertion sites reduces risk of infection
Grieving over body alteration • *Client and partner will adjust normally to altered breast appearance*	• Assess client's ability to inspect her breast after surgery • Assist client in looking at surgical site if needed • Listen attentively to client's and partner's concern to provide emotional support • Request Reach to Recovery visit in-hospital or after discharge	Emotional healing from loss of a breast takes time for most women

Nursing Diagnosis *Expected Outcome*	Interventions	Rationale
Postoperative *cont*.		
Altered tissue perfusion related to removal of some lymph nodes in surgical site • *Client will verbalize care for her arm on surgical side to prevent or control lymphedema*	• Instruct client to avoid heavy lifting; getting blood pressure, intravenous lines, laboratory studies on affected arm	Some clients are prone to develop lymphedema; prevention is less difficult and costly than treating lymphedema
Immobility related to loss of motion while surgical drains are in place • *Client will retain full motion of arm and shoulder on surgical side*	• Instruct client to begin gentle exercises when drains are still in place, such as brushing her hair, hand to shoulder • Instruct to increase exercises after drains are removed to include raising arm above head (using a pulley or climbing the wall) and full rotation of the arm • Request Reach to Recovery volunteer to teach exercises appropriate for post-mastectomy clients	Clients may continue to keep arm immobile after surgical drains are removed; frozen shoulder is very difficult and painful to treat
© Beare P.G., and J. L. Myers, eds. *Principles and Practices of Adult Health Nursing.* 2nd ed. St. Louis: Mosby, 1994.		

MANAGING CANCER PAIN

Adequate pain control can make a significant difference in improving a client's quality of life. Most oncology clients are **under-treated** for pain. As the client advocate, it is the nurse's responsibility to assure that the client is receiving enough pain control medications.

Some helpful hints to remember in managing a client's pain:

- Assess pain using a pain scale or quantifiable system, reassess after giving the appropriate medications.

56. Should pain medication be given around the clock or p.r.n.? _____

57. Should extra pain medications be given before, during, or after painful invasive procedures? _____

- If possible, give clients control of their pain medication through a client-controlled analgesia machine.

- Use different types of pain medication in combination based on the source of the pain (i.e., narcotics, NSAIDs, etc.).

- Do not give aspirin or any other medication to clients on chemotherapy without an order from the oncology team because it can jeopardize the client's ability to form blood clots.

58. Assess for side effects of the pain medications including:

    A. _____

    B. _____

    C. _____

- If a client is experiencing breakthrough pain, consider increasing the dose, or adding a second medication that is either longer-acting or shorter-acting, depending on the timing of the pain. This must be ordered (in writing) by a physician before being administered.

- Clients who are on high doses of narcotics for extended periods of time develop (59.) _____ and need (60.) _____ doses than clients who are being treated episodically.

ONCOLOGY EMERGENCIES

There are several true emergencies for which the nurse must be prepared when working with oncology clients. Complications can occur from damage done by the tumor, metastasis, or the treatment. The following is a chart of the most serious complications. The scenario and description are provided; your job is to decide what action to take as the nurse.

Oncology Complications			
Emergency	Symptoms	Nursing Interventions (fill in)	Rationale
Septic shock	Fever, chills, hypotension, tachycardia, tachypnea		In treating shock, the goal is to maintain life. Priorities are airway, breathing, and circulation (ABCs). Septic shock is caused by systemic infection that requires IV antibiotics
Disseminated Intravascular Coagulation (D.I.C.)	Active bleeding, petechiae, ecchymosis		See ABCs above. D.I.C. is an abnormal clotting condition that rapidly uses up available clotting factors which must be replaced quickly.
Pericardial tamponade	Dyspnea, chest pain, anxiety, tachycardia		See ABCs above. The goal is to support the client until fluid drainage can be performed.
Superior vena cava syndrome	Distention of the neck veins; dyspnea; red, swollen face and neck		See ABCs above. Diuretics, steroids, and tranquilizers decrease the client's anxiety, decrease oxygen consumption, and increase respiratory ease
Hypercalcemia (normal calcium 8.5–10.5 mg/dL)	Fatigue, weakness, abdominal pain, nausea, constipation, confusion, E.C.G. changes, polyuria		Routine monitoring of calcium lab values facilitates early detection and prevents true emergency. Vigorous hydration increases urinary excretion of calcium. Treated only if acute!
Spinal cord compression	Radiating back pain, sensory loss of lower extremities, gait change, loss of bladder and bowel function		Clients will be very anxious. Steroids and radiation therapy are the mainstay treatments to debulk the tumor and relieve pressure on the spinal cord.

1. The location of cancer with the highest mortality rate is the **lung.**

2. In males, the two locations with the highest incidence of cancer are the **lung** and **the prostate.**

3. In females, the two locations with the highest incidence of cancer are the **breast** and **the colon/ rectum.**

4. Three general signs and symptoms of cancer include **anemia, weakness,** and **weight loss.**

5. A **carcinogen** is a substance that can cause changes in a cell that can lead to cancer.

6. The number one risk factor for developing lung cancer is **smoking.**

7. A diet high in **fat** and low in **fiber** places an individual at increased risk of colon cancer.

8. Infection with the human immunodeficiency virus (HIV) increases the risk of developing which two types of cancer? **Kaposi's sarcoma** and **lymphoma**

9. Three host factors that increase the risk of developing cancer that cannot be controlled include **age over 40, being male,** and **race.**

10. When a tumor spreads from its primary site it is called a **metastasis.**

11. List the five most common sites of tumor migration: **lymph system, lungs, bone, liver,** and **brain.**

12. **H surface epithelial**—Squamous cell sarcoma

13. **C glandular epithelial**—Adenosarcoma

14. **F fibrous connective tissue**—Fibrosarcoma

15. **J adipose tissue**—Liposarcoma

16. **D cartilage**—Chondrosarcoma

17. **A bone**—Osteosarcoma

18. **I blood vessels**—Hemangiosarcoma

19. **K lymph vessels**—Lymphangiosarcoma

20. **L smooth muscle**—Leiomyosarcoma

21. **B striated muscle**—Rhabdomyosarcoma

22. **M glial tissue**—Glioma

23. **E nerve sheath**—Neurolemic sarcoma

24. **G blood**—Leukemia

25. When a tumor is staged by the TNM system as T2 N0 M0 it means: **localized lesion with deep penetration into adjacent structures; no lymph node involvement;** and **no metastasis**

26. If a 48-year-old male has a routine prostate-specific antigen screening test and there is a significant increase from last year's value, what type of cancer would it most likely indicate? **Prostate**

27. **False**—The marks indicating the area to be treated with radiation should be washed off immediately after the treatment to avoid skin breakdown.

28. **True**—The client should wear light, loose clothing.

29. **False**—The client may use moisturizing lotions.

30. **True**—Clients should use sunscreen on treated areas when they are outside.

31. **True**—Typical side effects of radiation therapy include mucositis, nausea, vomiting, and hair loss.

32. **True**—A client receiving internal radiation may have radioactive excretions.

33. **False**—A client receiving external radiation may have radioactive excretions.

34. All drugs must be mixed using the proper protective gear including **an exhaust hood, gloves, and goggles**

35. The five rights of drug administration: **drug, client, dose, route,** and **time**.

36. The normal range for white blood cell count is **5,000–10,000/L**.

37. The normal range for platelets is **150,000–400,000/mL**.

38. The normal creatinine range is **0.7–1.6 mg/dL**.

39. Use a **large** bore needle in the most…

40. …**distal** vein that is accessible and large enough to tolerate the amount of fluid to be delivered.

41. Signs and symptoms of tissue infiltration include: **cold, swollen, painful, stiff,** and **reddened area around IV site**.

42. Anemia and low white blood cell counts occur because of **bone marrow suppression**.

43. Alopecia is the result of damage to the rapidly dividing **hair follicles**.

44. Sterility occurs because of action against the **gonads**.

45. Common causes of nausea and vomiting in oncology clients include **bowel obstruction, constipation, fecal impaction, central nervous system metastasis,** and **chemotherapy**.

46. Three ways to help manage chemotherapy-induced nausea and vomiting are: **progressive muscle relaxation, imagery,** and **antiemetic medications**.

47. List three types of nausea and vomiting related to chemotherapy: **acute, delayed,** and **anticipatory**.

48. Should antinausea medication be given after the first treatment of chemotherapy, when the client asks for it, or before the chemotherapy begins? **Before**

49. If the chemotherapeutic agent has a long half life, how long should the antinausea medications be continued? **Up to four days after treatment has ended; give around-the-clock dosing for best relief**

50. List three common side effects of the serotonin antagonists granisetron (Kytril) and ondansetron (Zofran): **Headache, transient elevation in AST and ALT values**

51. Are Kytril and Zofran used primarily for long term or acute control of emesis? **Acute**

52. Metoclopramide (Reglan) is a benzamide that is used to control nausea and vomiting. List the three most common side effects: **Sedation, akathisia,** and **diarrhea**.

53. Akathisia is defined as **a condition of uncontrolled restlessness**.

54. Is (prochlorperazine) Compazine best used for long-term or short-term control of nausea and vomiting? **Long-term**

55. Is it best to give medications rectally when a client is complaining of nausea? **No. IV is the preferred route, especially if the client is on bleeding precautions and nothing should be given rectally**.

56. Pain medication should be given around the clock or p.r.n.? **Around the clock**

57. Give extra pain medications before, during, or after painful invasive procedures? **Before**

58. Assess for side effects of the pain medications including **respiratory depression, constipation,** and **change in level of consciousness**.

59. Clients who are on high doses of narcotics for extended periods of time develop **tolerance** and need…

60. **higher** doses than clients who are being treated episodically.

Oncology Complications			
Emergency	**Symptoms**	**Nursing Interventions (fill in)**	**Rationale**
Septic shock	Fever, chills hypotension, tachycardia, tachypnea	Check vital signs. STAT page provider. Administer oxygen. Ventilate if needed. Increase IV fluids. Monitor fluid balance. Prepare to give IV antibiotics.	In treating shock, the goal is to maintain life. Priorities are airway, breathing, and circulation (ABCs). Septic shock is caused by systemic infection that requires IV antibiotics
Disseminated Intravascular Coagulation (D.I.C.)	Active bleeding, petechiae, ecchymosis	Check vital signs. STAT page provider. Treat for shock. Be prepared to hang blood products, especially platelets and plasma.	See ABCs above. D.I.C. is an abnormal clotting condition that rapidly uses up available clotting factors, that must be replaced quickly.
Pericardial tamponade	Dyspnea, chest pain, anxiety, tachycardia	Check vital signs, including pulsus paradoxus. STAT page provider. Start oxygen if ordered. Set up for bedside pericardiocentesis.	See ABCs above. The goal is to support the client until fluid drainage can be performed.
Superior vena cava syndrome	Distention of the neck veins; dyspnea; red, swollen face and neck	Check vital signs. Page provider. Position for optimal respiratory benefit (high Fowler's). Administer oxygen if ordered. Be prepared to give diuretics, steroids, tranquilizers.	See ABCs above. Diuretics, steroids, and tranquilizers decrease the client's anxiety, decrease oxygen consumption, and increase respiratory ease
Hypercalcemia (normal calcium 8.5–10.5 mg/ dL)	Fatigue, weakness, abdominal pain, nausea, constipation, confusion, E.C.G. changes, polyuria	Monitor calcium value; treat only if acute. Call provider. Be prepared to increase IV hydration and to administer calcitonin (Calcimar), the antidote for high calcium.	Routine monitoring of calcium lab values facilitates early detection and prevents true emergency. Vigorous hydration increases urinary excretion of calcium. Treated only if acute!
Spinal cord compression	Radiating back pain, sensory loss of lower extremities, gait change, loss of bladder and bowel function	Supportive care, including pain and anxiety control. Notify provider. Be prepared to administer steroids Prepare client for radiation therapy.	Clients will be very anxious. Steroids and radiation therapy are the mainstay treatments to debulk the tumor and relieve pressure on the spinal cord.

CHAPTER 12: NCLEX-RN STYLE QUESTIONS

1. As part of a chemotherapy protocol, a female client is to receive cyclophosphamide (Cytoxan). To prevent a side effect of Cytoxan, she should be instructed to

   (1) brush her hair several times a day.
   (2) limit foods high in ascorbic acid in her diet.
   (3) test her urine for glucose before meals.
   (4) drink at least 2,500 mL of fluids each day.

2. A client has pain because of cancer. The client's pain management plan should include which of these recommendations from the World Health Organization?

   (1) The main potential problems of pain medications for cancer are overdose and addiction.
   (2) Meditation and biofeedback should not be suggested because they have been proven to be ineffective in pain relief.
   (3) Pain medications are best absorbed by the oral route.
   (4) The pain ladder concept should be used to decide what medications to use for cancer pain.

3. A client who is receiving chemotherapy for leukemia develops stomatitis. To manage the stomatitis, which of these measures would be appropriate?

   (1) Having the client floss the teeth before and after meals
   (2) Encouraging the client to rinse the mouth with saline q 1–2 hours while awake
   (3) Keeping the client on a clear liquid diet
   (4) Offering the client a citrus fruit juice, high in ascorbic acid, q 4 hours

4. Which of these precautions should staff include in the care of a client who is receiving a sealed source of radiation therapy for uterine cancer?

   (1) Limiting a staff member's time with the client to less than 30 minutes per shift
   (2) Keeping a zinc-lined container and forceps in the client's room
   (3) Instructing visitors to maintain a distance of about 3 feet from the client
   (4) Reminding the client to flush the toilet several times after each use

5. A client who is about to undergo chemotherapy tells you that he or she is more terrified of losing hair than of the drug. The client intends to take an herbal remedy to prevent baldness. The most important nursing intervention is to

   (1) inform the client that herbal remedies will antagonize chemotherapy effects.
   (2) tell the client that he or she must tell the physician, since herbs may or may not be harmful.
   (3) encourage as many herbal remedies as possible, since chemotherapy is so toxic.
   (4) tell the client that being bald and surviving is better than having hair and not being treated.

6. A client with colon cancer tells the nurse, "This is ridiculous. Now they want to stage my tumor? I want to be treated immediately before this spreads. I am sick of tests. I want to be treated now." The best response is

(1) "Do not worry, this cancer spreads slowly."
(2) "You sound angry. Let's talk about this."
(3) "Staging is needed to determine the appropriate treatment."
(4) "I'll call the provider and say that you want to begin treatment."

7. A nurse is teaching a woman who has been diagnosed with breast cancer with axillary node involvement. The nurse's plan of care includes axillary radiation. The nurse should inform the woman that she may experience

(1) lymphangitis.
(2) axillary pain.
(3) lymphedema.
(4) axillary infection.

8. A nurse is caring for a client with an esophageal tumor. As the tumor in a client's esophagus grows, the nurse knows a possible complication is

(1) bowel obstruction.
(2) respiratory distress.
(3) jaundice.
(4) splenomegaly.

9. A client with multiple myeloma has an elevated calcium level. The nurse understands that appropriate nursing care for this client would include

(1) increasing the intake of vitamin D for oral replacement.
(2) handling the client gently to prevent pathologic fractures.
(3) keeping a tracheostomy tray at the bedside for resuscitation.
(4) administering a thiazide diuretic as ordered to foster diuresis.

10. A 72-year-old client has a malignant mass in the sigmoid colon. Nursing care for this client would include assessment for which of the following?

(1) Tachycardia
(2) Hypovolemia
(3) Abdominal pain
(4) Rectal bleeding

CHAPTER 12: NCLEX-RN STYLE ANSWERS

1.
(4) CORRECT		Fluid intake is usually increased to help prevent renal irritation and hemorrhagic cystitis.
(1) *ELIMINATE*		Alopecia occurs in about 33% of clients on Cytoxan. Brushing the hair will not prevent alopecia and, in fact, may cause it to occur sooner.
(2) *ELIMINATE*		Adequate amounts of ascorbic acid (vitamin C) are especially important in the diet.
(3) *ELIMINATE*		Glucosuria is not one of the side effects.

CATEGORY 08 PHARMACOLOGICAL AND PARENTERAL THERAPIES

2.
(4) CORRECT	The pain ladder concept is composed of three steps. For the first step nonopioids, with or without adjuvants, are given. The second step is used when pain has not been controlled and includes the use of opioids (such as codeine) plus nonopioids, with or without adjuvants. If the pain persists or increases, the third step is implemented, which includes opioids (such as morphine), with or without nonopioids, and with or without adjuvants.
(1) *ELIMINATE*	Less than 1% of cancer clients in pain experience overdose or addiction problems.
(2) *ELIMINATE*	Noninvasive techniques, such as meditation, biofeedback, guided imagery, and relaxation, have been proven to be very effective in helping cancer clients control pain.
(3) *ELIMINATE*	The quickest absorption of pain medications is intravenously.

CATEGORY 07 BASIC CARE AND COMFORT

3.
(2) CORRECT	Rinsing the mouth with plain water, or saline, frequently helps to relieve stomatitis (mouth sores). Commercial mouth washes that contain alcohol or other drying agents should be avoided.
(1) *ELIMINATE*	Flossing the teeth may traumatize the oral mucosa further, which could be a serious problem in an immunosuppressed client.
(3) *ELIMINATE*	While the mouth sores may interfere in the client's desire or ability to eat, the client should be encouraged to eat as many nutritious foods as possible. Hot and spicy foods should be avoided. There is no need to keep the client on a clear liquid diet because of the stomatitis.
(4) *ELIMINATE*	Most citrus fruit juices that are high in ascorbic acid (e.g., orange and grapefruit) are tart and would increase mouth pain.

CATEGORY 07 BASIC CARE AND COMFORT

4.

   (1) CORRECT   To protect nurses and others from excessive radiation exposure, the principles of distance, time, and shielding are important. It is recommended that a staff member limits direct care to a client as described to 30 minutes per shift.

   (2) ELIMINATE   Long forceps and a lead-lined container should be available in the event that this sealed radiation source becomes accidently dislodged and must be picked up. Bare hands should not be used.

   (3) ELIMINATE   Visitors, who should be over 18 years old, should be told to maintain a distance of about 6 feet to prevent exposure.

   (4) ELIMINATE   With a sealed source of radiation, the radioisotope cannot circulate through the client's body, nor can it contaminate urine, sweat, blood, vomitus, or excretia. Therefore, the toilet would not need to be flushed more than once.

CATEGORY 02 SAFETY AND INFECTION CONTROL

5.

   (2) CORRECT   The client must understand that the provider must be informed of all medicines (herbal, over-the-counter, prescription medications) because they may not be safe.

   (1) ELIMINATE   This is a generalization that may or may not be true. It is possible that chemotherapy may be antagonized by herbs.

   (3) ELIMINATE   Herbal remedies are not necessarily benign, so this is not a true statement.

   (4) ELIMINATE   This is an inappropriate statement.

CATEGORY 05 COPING AND ADAPTATION

6.

   (3) CORRECT   Staging determines disease progress, and is necessary to determine treatment.

   (1) ELIMINATE   This response is not helpful. The client is expressing fear and anxiety over the diagnosis. Telling him or her the cancer spreads slowly, even if true, will not make him or her feel better.

   (2) POSSIBLE   The client may benefit by talking, but this choice is not as appropriate as choice #3, which provides information.

   (4) ELIMINATE   Calling the provider will not relieve the client's anxiety, and staging is necessary. The intervention should be directed at support and education.

CATEGORY 05 COPING AND ADAPTATION

7.

   (3) CORRECT   Lymphedema may result from removal or damage to axillary nodes. Radiation may obliterate the lymph tissue.

   (1) ELIMINATE   Lymphangitis is an infection in the lymph nodes, and is not necessarily an expectation of radiation.

   (2) ELIMINATE   The procedure is usually not painful.

   (4) ELIMINATE   Infection is not an expectation of radiation.

CATEGORY 07 BASIC CARE AND COMFORT

8.   (2) CORRECT   As the tumor increases in size, it can press on, and even obstruct, the trachea. This causes shortness of breath and respiratory distress.

       (1) ELIMINATE   Bowel obstruction is not usually related to esophageal cancers.

       (3) ELIMINATE   Jaundice may result if liver metastasis occurs, but is not a specific complication of esophageal cancer.

       (4) ELIMINATE   Splenomegaly is not a consequence of esophageal tumor.

CATEGORY 04 PREVENTION AND EARLY DETECTION OF DISEASE

9.   (2) CORRECT   Pathologic fractures occur as a result of calcium being released from the malignant bone, thereby weakening the bone structure.

       (1) ELIMINATE   Vitamin D promotes calcium absorption through the intestines, calcium resorption from the bone and kidney reabsorption of calcium, all of which raise the serum calcium level.

       (3) ELIMINATE   A tracheostomy tray is needed for laryngospasm that occurs with hypocalcemia.

       (4) ELIMINATE   The use of thiazide diuretics are contraindicated because they inhibit calcium excretion.

CATEGORY 02 SAFETY AND INFECTION CONTROL

10.   (4) CORRECT   Tumors in the left side of the colon (sigmoid colon) are likely to cause alteration in bowel habits and passage of blood. Tumors in the right side of the colon are more likely to cause abdominal pain, nausea, and vomiting.

       (1) ELIMINATE   Tachycardia may result due to many factors, but it is not directly related to the medical diagnosis of a mass in the sigmoid colon.

       (2) ELIMINATE   Hypovolemia may occur if the client suffers massive blood or fluid loss.

       (3) ELIMINATE   While assessment for pain is important, it does not occur in all clients diagnosed with colon tumors. Clients often will not experience pain until the later stages of their disease. Rectal bleeding is a classic sign of a malignancy in the bowel.

CATEGORY 10 PHYSIOLOGICAL ADAPTATION

13

HUMAN IMMUNODEFICIENCY VIRUS (HIV)/ACQUIRED IMMUNODEFICIENCY SYNDROME (AIDS)

WHAT YOU NEED TO KNOW

As of the end of 1999, there were 733,374 reported cases of AIDS in the U.S. Every day there are 40,000 new cases. The worldwide statistics are just staggering, with roughly 33 million cases. The nursing care of individuals affected by HIV/AIDS is challenging and complex. In this chapter, we review the basics of how to educate and manage HIV/AIDS patients.

Before we start our review, test your general knowledge of HIV/AIDS by answering the questions below using the words provided:

2	blood	mother-infant
200 mm^3	body fluids	sexual contact
800 mm^3	ELISA	Western blot

1. List three ways that the HIV virus can be transmitted:

   A. _____

   B. _____

   C. _____

2. A normal CD4 count is usually over _____.

3. When the CD4 count falls below _____, the client is considered to have AIDS.

4. The basic screening test for HIV antibodies is the _____. A positive test is confirmed using the more specific _____ test.

5. If a person has ___ or more opportunistic infections, she is considered to have AIDS, regardless of HIV testing status or CD4 count.

LEGAL AND ETHICAL ISSUES CONCERNING HIV/AIDS

Individuals infected with HIV/AIDS are the most discriminated-against patients in the United States. Care must be taken to protect the rights of clients who are or might be infected with HIV/AIDS.

Some important points to remember:

- Strict adherence to client confidentiality is important.

- Many sources recommend that people interested in being tested for HIV antibodies do so anonymously through outside organizations instead of employee health programs or their private doctor's office to protect themselves against discrimination.

- Some states mandate that people who test positive for HIV antibodies be reported by name and social security number.

- The Federal Americans with Disabilities Act of 1990 protects people with HIV/AIDS from being discriminated against in the workplace.

UNIVERSAL PRECAUTIONS

Universal precautions, including personal protective gear, should be used consistently and correctly with every client every time there is a chance of coming into contact with blood or body fluids. A critical part of protecting yourself and others involves the proper disposal of soiled equipment and supplies. The following questions should remind you of the most important aspects of a part of your job that should be second nature.

6. List the four components of personal protective gear:

   A. _____

   B. _____

   C. _____

   D. _____

7. To protect clients from respiratory infections, nurses and visitors who are symptomatic should _____.

MEDICATIONS USED TO TREAT HIV/AIDS

The medications that are used to treat HIV/AIDS focus on slowing down replication of the virus and decreasing the viral load. As of this printing, there is no cure nor vaccination to protect people from HIV/AIDS. Choose from the following list to fill in the blanks below. Remember that AZT (Retrovir, zidovudine) is now referred to as ZDV. You should be able to recognize these drugs and associate them with HIV/AIDS for the NCLEX-RN.

3TC (Zerit)	DDI	nausea
anemia	granulocytopenia	protease inhibitors
d4T	headache	zidovudine
DDC		

8. Antiretrovirals are usually started when the CD4 count falls to 500 or below. List three antiretrovirals used to treat HIV/AIDS:

   A. _____

   B. _____

   C. _____

9. The newer nucleoside analog reverse transcriptase inhibitors used to treat HIV/AIDS in combination with zidovudine include _____ and _____.

10. A medication class that inhibits replication of HIV in chronically infected cells, thereby decreasing the HIV viral load, is _____.

11. List the common side effects of zidovudine:

   A. _____

   B. _____

   C. _____

   D. _____

OPPORTUNISTIC INFECTIONS

12. The leading cause of death in AIDS clients is _____.

13. The best way for nurses to decrease the incidence of nosocomial infections is through _____.

14. An _____ infection is one that a person with an intact immune system would normally not get.

15. List four early signs and symptoms of infection in an HIV/AIDS client:

    A. _____

    B. _____

    C. _____

    D. _____

16. List four opportunistic infections that could be considered AIDS-defining in most clients:

    A. _____

    B. _____

    C. _____

    D. _____

17. A painful opportunistic infection, not listed above, is varicella zoster, also called shingles. Shingles is a reactivation of which childhood illness? _____

18. A potentially disabling consequence of CMV infection is _____.

19. To decrease a client's chance of developing an upper respiratory infection what four things can the client be encouraged to do?

    A. _____

    B. _____

    C. _____

    D. _____

- At the beginning of each shift the nurse should do a head to toe physical assessment of the client, including vital signs, weight if indicated, and assessing IV insertion sites and mental status.

- The early detection of skin breakdown and changes in breath sounds or mucous production could have a major impact on the chances for recovery from opportunistic infections for severely ill clients.

- Invasive procedures should be kept to a minimum with diligent attention to aseptic and sterile techniques to prevent infection.

HEALTH MAINTENANCE

Health maintenance in the HIV/AIDS population is significantly different from that in the general population because of the lethal threat of opportunistic infections. Considerable effort must be made to protect against infections and to detect them early. It is important to remember that HIV/AIDS clients can also be afflicted with diabetes, hypertension, and any other disease for which the general population is at risk, so they must receive the same health maintenance and disease screening that other clients would be encouraged to get, based on age and risk factors.

20. Because of the increased risk of invasive cervical carcinoma, female clients who are HIV positive should have a _____ once every _____.

21. When placing a PPD (purified protein derivative) to test for _____, it is important to read the test between ___ and ___ hours.

22. _____ testing is done to determine a client's ability to respond to TB testing. A control unit of measles or mumps antigen is commonly used.

23. HIV-positive clients should be tested for _____ using a VDRL or RPR blood test.

24. The sexually transmitted disease named in question 23 can cause tertiary side effects that affect which body system? _____

25. Clients should be encouraged to start prophylaxis with co-trimoxazole (Bactrim) against _____ when CD4 counts fall below 200 mm^3.

26. When CD4 counts fall below 100 mm^3, clients should be encouraged to take prophylactic medication against MAC (*Mycobacterium avium* complex). The standard medication given as prophylaxis against MAC is _____.

NUTRITION FOR CLIENTS WITH AIDS

A high-protein, high-calorie diet should be followed for as much time as the client can tolerate it. Nutrient and calorie-dense foods are vital, including nutritional supplements. Many clients with AIDS have a limited tolerance for food by mouth, and a central line or Hickman catheter is often inserted for T.P.N. (total parenteral nutrition).

PAIN

Many clients with HIV/AIDS suffer from considerable muscle aches and pains that need to be mitigated. In addition to pain-relieving medications, care should be taken when moving, lifting, and turning clients. Like oncology clients, AIDS clients in chronic pain may develop a tolerance to the pain medications and may require higher than usual doses for adequate control.

- Some non-pharmacological methods of pain control include massage, imagery, hypnosis, and progressive muscle relaxation.

- All clients benefit from some level of exercise, which can vary from ambulating around the hospital, to physical therapy, to passive range of motion. Without exercise, clients tend to develop painful decubitus ulcers, contractures, and constipation.

CHAPTER 13: EXERCISE ANSWERS

1. List three ways that the HIV virus can be transmitted: **blood** (transfusions prior to mid-1985, sharing IV drug equipment, needle sticks with a contaminated needle), **body fluids/sexual contact** (homosexual and heterosexual), and **mother to infant** (prenatal and through breast milk).

2. A normal CD4 count is usually over **800 mm^3**.

3. When the CD4 count falls below **200 mm^3**, the client is considered to have AIDS.

4. The basic screening test for HIV antibodies is the **ELISA (enzyme-linked immunosorbent assay)**. A positive test is confirmed using the more specific **Western blot** test.

5. If a person has **two** or more opportunistic infections, she is considered to have AIDS, regardless of HIV testing status or CD4 count.

6. List the four components of personal protective gear:

   gloves

   gown

   mask

   face shield

7. To protect clients from respiratory infections, nurses and visitors who are symptomatic should **wear a mask**.

8. Antiretrovirals are usually started when the CD4 count falls to 500 mm^3 or below. List three antiretrovirals used to treat HIV/AIDS:

   ZDV (Retrovir, zidovudine)

   DDC (dideoxycytidine)

   DDI (dideoxyinosine)

9. The newer nucleoside analog reverse transcriptase inhibitors that are used to treat HIV/AIDS in combination with zidovudine include **d4T and 3TC (Zerit)**.

10. A medication class that inhibits replication of HIV in chronically infected cells, thereby decreasing the HIV viral load, is **protease inhibitors**.

11. List the common side effects of zidovudine:

    anemia

    granulocytopenia

    headache

    nausea

12. The leading cause of death in AIDS clients is **infection**.

13. The best way for nurses to decrease the incidence of nosocomial infections is through **diligent hand washing**.

14. An **opportunistic** infection is one that a person with an intact immune system would normally not get.

15. Early signs and symptoms of infection in an HIV/AIDS client include:

    bowel changes

    fever

    restlessness

    increased pulse rate

    productive cough

    change in wound drainage

    lethargy

16. Opportunistic infections that could be considered AIDS defining in most clients include:

    Candidiasis infection of esophagus, trachea, bronchi, or lungs

    Cryptococcus meningitis

    cytomegalovirus (CMV) retinitis

    herpes simplex outbreaks lasting longer than 30 days

    HIV wasting syndrome

    invasive cervical cancer

    Kaposi's sarcoma in clients over age 60

    lymphoma

    Mycobacterium tuberculosis (TB)

    PCP (*Pneumocystis carinii* pneumonia)

    toxoplasmic encephalitis

    toxoplasmosis

17. A painful opportunistic infection, not listed above, is varicella zoster, also called shingles. Shingles is a reactivation of which childhood illness? **Chicken pox**

18. A potentially disabling consequence of CMV infection is **blindness**.

19. To decrease a client's chance of developing an upper respiratory infection, what four things can the client be encouraged to do?

    ambulate

    breathe deeply

    cough

    turn from side to side frequently

20. Because of the increased risk of invasive cervical carcinoma, female clients who are HIV positive should have a **Pap smear** once every **6 months**.

21. When placing a PPD (purified protein derivative) to test for **tuberculosis (TB),** it is important to read the test between **48** and **72** hours.

22. **Anergy** testing is done to determine a client's ability to respond to TB testing. A control unit of measles or mumps antigen is commonly used.

23. HIV-positive clients should be tested for **syphilis** using a VDRL or RPR blood test.

24. The above sexually transmitted disease can cause tertiary side effects that affect which body system? **Nervous system** (this may account for a significant number of AIDS dementia cases)

25. Clients should be encouraged to start prophylaxis with co-trimoxazole (Bactrim) against *Pneumocystis carinii* **pneumonia (PCP)** when CD4 counts fall below 200 mm^3.

26. When CD4 counts fall below 100 mm^3, clients should be encouraged to take prophylactic medication against MAC (*Mycobacterium avium* complex). The standard medication given as prophylaxis against MAC is **rifabutin (Mycobutin).**

1. Which of the following is necessary for nurses to protect themselves from HIV?

   (1) Universal precautions
   (2) Hand washing
   (3) Enteric precautions
   (4) Respiratory precautions

2. Which of the following nursing diagnoses would be most appropriate when planning interventions for a 28-year-old male with a CD4 cell count of 600 mm³ and facial Kaposi's sarcoma (KS) lesions?

   (1) Potential for infection related to open KS lesions
   (2) Body image disturbance related to facial KS lesions
   (3) Potential impaired physical mobility related to lower extremity KS lesions
   (4) Potential sexual dysfunction related to genital KS lesions

3. When managing an AIDS client with weakness and severe vision loss due to CMV retinitis, which of the following nursing interventions is most important?

   (1) Placing a "visually impaired" sign over the head of the bed
   (2) Referring the client to a support group for persons with vision loss
   (3) Instructing the client to call prior to getting out of bed and placing the call bell within reach
   (4) Encouraging the client to verbalize feelings about vision loss

4. When teaching an HIV-positive person about HIV transmission prevention, which of the following should the nurse include?

   (1) The HIV-positive person can share razors and toothbrushes with the other household members.
   (2) The HIV-positive person should have his or her own utensils.
   (3) The HIV-positive person's laundry must be done separately.
   (4) The HIV-positive person can share the same bathroom with the other household members.

5. An HIV-positive client asks the nurse what the best way is to clean up blood spills in the home. The nurse is correct to inform the client to

   (1) remove the excess with a paper towel and clean the remainder with a 1:10 bleach to water solution.
   (2) remove the excess with a paper towel and clean the remainder with rubbing alcohol.
   (3) remove the excess with a paper towel and clean the remainder with soapy water.
   (4) remove the excess with a paper towel and clean the remainder with bleach.

6. An AIDS client with open Kaposi's sarcoma lesions on the upper extremities is admitted to the hospital. When assessing the client's vital signs, the nurse should wear which of the following?

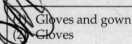

(1) Gloves and gown
(2) Gloves
(3) Gown
(4) Gown and mask

7. An end-stage AIDS client requires suctioning. When performing this task, the nurse is correct to wear

(1) a mask and eye protection.
(2) sterile gloves and eye protection.
(3) a mask and sterile gloves.
(4) a mask, eye protection, and sterile gloves.

8. An AIDS client who is being treated for CMV retinitis asks the nurse why co-trimoxazole (Bactrim) was prescribed. The nurse is correct to respond,

(1) "Bactrim is prescribed to prevent *Pneumocystis carinii* pneumonia (PCP) from developing."
(2) "Bactrim is part of the CMV treatment."
(3) "The order must be incorrect."
(4) "The reason for Bactrim is unclear, and I will check with the provider."

9. The nurse teaches an AIDS client that which of the following are common side effects of zidovudine (Retrovir) therapy?

(1) Hypertension and diarrhea
(2) Hypotension and constipation
(3) Anemia and granulocytopenia
(4) Altered taste and dizziness

10. A client with AIDS and *Pneumocystis carinii* pneumonia (PCP) is receiving IV co-trimoxazole (Bactrim) every 6 hours. The nurse becomes concerned when, during the infusion of the dose on the 7th day of therapy, a red rash is noticed on the client's face, neck, and chest, and the client's respiratory rate has increased to 28/minute. The nurse should

(1) continue the infusion and monitor the client. Because it is day 7 of treatment, the client cannot be having a hypersensitivity reaction.
(2) stop the infusion, assess the client for other hypersensitivity signs and symptoms, and immediately notify the provider of the findings.
(3) ascertain if the client was recently ambulating and auscultate the lungs.
(4) apply lotion to the client's rash and notify the provider of your findings.

1. (1) CORRECT   Universal precautions is a requirement of care to protect both patients and nurses.
    (2) *ELIMINATE*   Hand washing will not stop the spread of HIV.
    (3) *ELIMINATE*   Enteric precautions will not stop the spread of HIV.
    (4) *ELIMINATE*   Respiratory precautions will not stop the spread of HIV.

    CATEGORY 02 SAFETY AND INFECTION CONTROL

2. (2) CORRECT   KS can occur at any time during the course of HIV disease because it is not directly linked to immunosuppression. It often occurs in clients who are relatively well. Body image disturbances are significant issues for clients with dermal KS. Teaching clients to use makeup to cover lesions, and referring them to support groups for people with AIDS-related KS can be significant in improving the client's self-image and overall quality of life.
    (1) *ELIMINATE*   There is not the potential for infection related to KS lesions.
    (3) *ELIMINATE*   There is not a potential for physical immobility related to KS.
    (4) *ELIMINATE*   Sexual dysfunction would not be an appropriate nursing diagnosis.

    CATEGORY 09 REDUCTION OF RISK POTENTIAL

3. (3) CORRECT   This choice puts safety first. Ensuring client safety is of the utmost importance.
    (1) *POSSIBLE*   While this is an acceptable intervention, it is not the most important.
    (2) *POSSIBLE*   While this is an acceptable intervention, it is not the most important.
    (4) *POSSIBLE*   While this is an acceptable intervention, it is not the most important.

    CATEGORY 02 SAFETY AND INFECTION CONTROL

4. (4) CORRECT   Persons sharing households with HIV-positive persons are at very low risk to become infected if good hygiene is performed.
    (1) *ELIMINATE*   Any articles that may come in contact with blood should not be shared.
    (2) *ELIMINATE*   Washing dishes in hot, soapy water kills HIV.
    (3) *ELIMINATE*   Washing clothes in hot, soapy water kills HIV.

    CATEGORY 02 SAFETY AND INFECTION CONTROL

5. (1) CORRECT   The correct cleaning solution is a 1:10 mixture bleach to water.
    (2) *ELIMINATE*   Rubbing alcohol may not effectively kill the virus.
    (3) *ELIMINATE*   Soapy water may not effectively kill the virus.
    (4) *ELIMINATE*   100% bleach is not required.

    CATEGORY 02 SAFETY AND INFECTION CONTROL

6.

(2)	CORRECT	Gloves are the only barrier needed.
(1)	ELIMINATE	A gown is not necessary.
(3)	ELIMINATE	While a gown is not required, gloves are.
(4)	ELIMINATE	Neither a gown nor a mask is indicated.

CATEGORY 02 SAFETY AND INFECTION CONTROL

7.

(4)	CORRECT	When suctioning a client, a mask, sterile gloves, and eye protection must be worn in order to protect the nurse's mucous membranes of the eyes, mouth, and nose.
(1)	ELIMINATE	A mask and eye protection do not provide enough protection.
(2)	ELIMINATE	Sterile gloves and a mask alone are not adequate.
(3)	POSSIBLE	A mask and sterile gloves are not adequate.

CATEGORY 02 SAFETY AND INFECTION CONTROL

8.

(1)	CORRECT	Bactrim is used for PCP prophylaxis.
(2)	ELIMINATE	Bactrim is not effective against CMV.
(3)	ELIMINATE	The Bactrim order is appropriate.
(4)	ELIMINATE	Bactrim is used for PCP prophylaxis.

CATEGORY 08 PHARMACOLOGICAL AND PARENTERAL THERAPIES

9.

(3)	CORRECT	Anemia and granulocytopenia are two frequently occurring side effects of zidovudine therapy. Blood counts should be monitored every 2 weeks. Epoetin alfa recombinant (Epogen) may be prescribed to stimulate red blood cell production, and anemia often requires blood transfusion. Other side effects include headache, nausea, GI pain, skin rash, and fever.
(1)	ELIMINATE	Hypertension and diarrhea are not side effects of Retrovir.
(2)	ELIMINATE	Hypotension and constipation are not side effects of Retrovir.
(4)	ELIMINATE	Altered taste and dizziness are not side effects of Retrovir.

CATEGORY 08 PHARMACOLOGICAL AND PARENTERAL THERAPIES

10.

(2)	CORRECT	Hypersensitivity reactions to co-trimoxazole (Bactrim) occur more frequently in people with AIDS, and can develop several days into the course of therapy. The nurse should stop the infusion, thoroughly assess the client for other signs and symptoms of an allergic response, and immediately notify the provider of the findings.
(1)	ELIMINATE	The nurse should not allow the infusion to continue.
(3)	ELIMINATE	Asking the client these questions has no relevance.
(4)	ELIMINATE	Applying lotion is not an appropriate nursing action.

CATEGORY 01 MANAGEMENT OF CARE

PART III

PEDIATRIC PHYSIOLOGICAL INTEGRITY

Children are not little adults—they differ both physiologically and psychologically from adults. Less detail is spelled out on physical assessment of children because you are expected to build on your knowledge of adults and adapt that to children in the various developmental stages.

This part, "Pediatric Physiological Integrity" and "Adult Physiological Integrity" make up 46–54 percent of the actual test content. This is, at most, 133 questions out of 265, the maximum number of questions possible on the CAT. Again, these 133 questions are divided (not necessarily evenly) between adult and pediatric physiological integrity.

When answering these questions, remember that the nurse is always trying to promote optimal physical health while ensuring physical development within the usual time frame.

This "client need" includes:

- A combination of developmental theory and physical assessment
- Early recognition and treatment of disease
- Incorporating parents into the care of their children
- Extensive education for parents and children, when appropriate
- Always advocating for the child's safety

14

THE HOSPITALIZED CHILD

WHAT YOU NEED TO KNOW

Although every child develops at his own pace, having an understanding of the "normal" levels of a child's cognitive and emotional maturity is essential in deciding how to explain illness, surgery, and procedures to a pediatric client. Each age group has specific attributes that need to be recognized in order to provide safe and effective nursing care.

Throughout your review of pediatric nursing, bear in mind the stages of development as outlined by Erikson. The NCLEX-RN examiners love Erikson, so we'll repeat this information over and over again.

Erickson's Classifications	
Age	**Erickson's Developmental Stage**
Infancy/Toddler (0–18 months)	Trust vs. mistrust
Toddler/Preschooler (1–3 years)	Autonomy vs. shame and doubt
Preschool (3–6 years)	Initiative vs. guilt
School age (6–12 years)	Industry vs. inferiority
Adolescence (12–18 years)	Identity vs. role confusion
Young adult (18–35 years)	Intimacy vs. isolation

This chapter gives you an overview of the physical parameters that should guide your nursing care of children in the hospital. Because it is impossible to separate physiological guidelines from developmental milestones and emotional needs, these concepts are included as well.

Some children may be at risk for excessive emotional stress during hospitalization. Those at risk can include, but are not limited to, children who are admitted to the hospital with inadequate preparation for their developmental needs, children who have "difficult" temperaments or display signs of poor interaction with their parents, and children who have developed fears related to witnessing or experiencing painful procedures.

1. From the following list, circle the descriptions of six children who are at risk for increased stress during and post-hospitalization:

    A. a 2-year-old female admitted emergently for surgical fixation of a broken femur
    B. a preterm infant born at 28 weeks gestation with tetralogy of Fallot
    C. a 15-year-old female undergoing amputation of her right arm following a motor vehicle accident
    D. an 8-year-old girl admitted for a tonsillectomy
    E. an 11-month-old female admitted to the ICU in respiratory distress
    F. a 2-month-old female admitted to your floor for a fever workup
    G. a 16-year-old male newly diagnosed with diabetes mellitus
    H. a 3-year-old female with a planned admission for a cochlear implant
    I. a 7-year-old male with frequent hospital admissions for osteogenic sarcoma of the left tibia

PARENTS' REACTIONS TO A CHILD'S HOSPITALIZATION

In the nursing of children, the client is the child; however, so are his or her parents and family. The more serious the illness, the more likely the parents are to be highly reactive.

The parents will draw upon their previous experience(s) with illness or hospitalization (good or bad) to cope with their child's hospitalization. It is the nurse's job to assess the family's existing and available support systems, the family's coping skills, and any other stressors confronting the family at this time. With culture and religion in mind, the nurse must assess communication patterns within the family and mitigate any misconceptions or feelings of guilt about the child's illness and treatment. Provide emotional support.

TEACHING

The logical beginning of parent and child teaching is with the orientation to the hospital setting. This may be conducted by an interdisciplinary group of health care professionals (e.g., social workers, nurses, and play therapists) or solely by nurses, for children individually and in groups. Teaching needs to be tailored to the intended student, considering the child's cognitive abilities, past experiences, and attention span. Remember the stages of development when considering the best options for teaching methods, length and timing of preparation, and the level of information to be provided. Tours of the hospital facilities can be useful for families and children of most ages. You have to be attentive, however, to the sights, sounds, and smells to which the child may be exposed for the first time in the hospital.

Other methods of teaching can include plays or puppet shows, dolls or toys used to simulate procedures, handouts, and videotapes. Start any teaching session with a simple, honest explanation or demonstration using nonthreatening terminology, and work your way up the developmental ladder from there. Also, when admitting a new client to the pediatric unit, try to collaborate with other caregivers and avoid unnecessary repetition of questions and procedures to lessen the strain on the client and family.

If emergent admission to either a hospital floor or ICU is indicated, and there is little time for an orientation, explain to family members who will be caring for the child and what they can expect to happen next. Be supportive. Try to establish routines for the child, protect the child's needs for privacy, and involve the family in decision-making and client care whenever possible. Prepare the family members and visitors coming to visit the child for the presence of special equipment or any deviations from the child's normal appearance or behavior.

Single-day hospitalization poses another challenge. Although there is less time and less stress when compared to a prolonged hospital stay, careful explanations need to be given so the child and family are not overwhelmed by all the activity. Discharge instructions for these clients need to be explicit due to limited time for preparation.

2. The following list contains suggestions for hospital orientation activities based on the preceding summary. Circle the five most appropriate options:

    A. a group tour of the operating and recovery rooms for a group of 10 preschoolers
    B. deferring orientation to the ICU for the parents of a newly admitted, critically ill child
    C. a puppet show for 5-year-olds explaining the identities of the various staff members
    D. allowing a toddler to play with medical instruments under supervision
    E. reviewing visiting hours and policies with an adolescent client
    F. allowing a tour of facilities exclusively for parents if the child is under 10 years of age
    G. showing a 4-year-old admitted the morning of surgery the location of the playroom and his room when he returns to the floor
    H. explaining to a 6-year-old that the beeps and lights she notices are part of the machines used to make sure she is getting better

Education is the key to alleviating fears and facilitating the family's hospitalization. The nurse must provide careful, education-level–specific information to the child and the family. The child wants to know what she will feel and sense; the parent may want to know more. Their questions are indicative of their readiness to explore issues related to the illness.

FUNCTION OF PLAY IN THE HOSPITAL

Play is the work of kids! It provides diversion and relaxation and helps children feel more secure in a strange environment. In addition, play lessens the stress of separation and the feeling of homesickness experienced when children are hospitalized. It encourages interaction and the expression of feelings, and allows children to make choices, take chances, and be in control. Developmentally appropriate, therapeutic play sessions should be planned in preparation for procedures to lessen fear and anxiety. In general, periods of uninterrupted play should be incorporated into the child's daily schedule.

INFORMED CONSENT

Parents and children need to be made aware of the risks, benefits, and possible outcomes of the many procedures that take place in the hospital setting. Legal aspects of obtaining consent for these procedures vary among institutions and local and state regulations of nursing practice. It is your duty to be aware of your responsibilities and to ensure that anyone signing anything comprehends the document to the fullest extent possible.

REVIEW

Label the following statements regarding pediatric hospitalization as either **true** or **false**:

3. _____ Day surgery clients do not require special preparation, as their hospital stays should be brief.

4. _____ The constant activity and potential disruption of day/night routines in the ICU setting can lead to increased stress in the pediatric client.

5. _____ As children are unable to sign their own informed consents, only parents or guardians need to be informed about procedures.

6. _____ Children in isolation room settings need more opportunities for diversion, as they may feel "punished" in this setting.

7. _____ In choosing a client's roommate, the nurse should consider client ages and diagnoses when possible.

8. _____ In emergent treatment situations, the nurse should limit contact with the client's family until the treatments are completed and/or until further consents are needed.

9. Circle four methods from the list below that you would consider appropriate for play therapy:

   A. holding group meetings for adolescent clients undergoing treatment for cancer

   B. giving a 5-year-old child stickers for every glass of fluid she drinks toward a daily fluid requirement goal

   C. pretending that a medication is a favorite type of candy

   D. withholding play activities if a 9-year-old child cries and screams unnecessarily during a dressing change

   E. giving a 7-year-old child markers to decorate a leg cast

   F. having a 5-year-old child watch the television show "E.R." to let him see what happens in the hospital

   G. encouraging two roommates in a rehabilitative pediatric floor to do exercises together

DISCHARGE PLANNING

For any client, young or old, discharge planning should begin as soon as the client is admitted. The teaching needs to be consistent and simple. Caregivers need ample time to observe and then to demonstrate any necessary procedures. Written materials and videos may be helpful, and referrals to support networks may be indicated. When possible and practical, children and adolescents should be included in all teaching. Pediatric clients, especially adolescents, should be encouraged to take responsibility for themselves.

   10. Which of the following are not useful or realistic techniques in client/family teaching about discharge needs? Circle four options.

   A. Saving teaching for the last day of hospitalization to avoid confusing the parents

   B. Having a family member observe the technique for nasal suctioning, then demonstrate it for you under close supervision

   C. Teaching a parent as well as the adolescent how to monitor blood glucose and administer insulin injections

   D. Encouraging parental contact with support groups and/or parents with similarly diagnosed children for information and support

   E. Alerting the parents of a child beginning chemotherapy to signs and symptoms of thrombocytopenia and neutropenia

   F. Having each nurse caring for a specific client teach a procedure according to her individual style and preferences, so that the family can observe a number of different techniques

   G. Encouraging the parents of a child with cancer to withdraw the child from school and play activities until all treatments are completed

   H. Discouraging family members from researching and reading about a diagnosis, as the information will probably be too technical and difficult for them to understand

VITAL SIGNS

Blood pressure can be affected by the age, weight, and height of the individual child. Activity can increase the child's heart rate and respirations, while rest can decrease these measurements.

"Normal" Vital Sign Ranges			
Age	**Heart Rate**	**Respirations**	**Blood Pressure**
Newborn (0–27 days)	120–160 b.p.m.	30–60/minute Irregular	70/45 mmHg
Infant (1 month–1 year)	100–140 b.p.m.	30–35/minute	80/50 mmHg
Toddler (1–3 years)	90–120 b.p.m.	20–30/minute	100/60 mmHg
Preschooler (3–6 years)	90–110 b.p.m.	20–30/minute	90/65 mmHg
School-age (6–12 years)	80–100 b.p.m.	18–24/minute	100/70 mmHg
Adolescent (12–18 years)	70–100 b.p.m.	12–20/minute	115/80 mmHg

When assessing vital signs, remember that crying can increase body temperature, heart rate, respiratory rate, and blood pressure. Also, sleep slows down the heart and respiratory rates and can lower blood pressure. Unfortunately, vital signs are just something you have to memorize. To help you, we have provided a partially completed table below. Cover the table above and try to fill in the appropriate vital signs.

Age	**Heart Rate**	**Respirations**	**Blood Pressure**
Newborn (0–27 days)	120–160 b.p.m.		
Infant (1 month–1 year)		30–35/minute	
Toddler (1–3 years)	90–120 b.p.m.		
Preschooler (3–6 years)			90/65 mm Hg
School-age (6-12 years)		18–24/minute	
Adolescent (12–18 years)	70–100 b.p.m.		

DEVELOPMENTAL CONSIDERATIONS

As we stated earlier, one cannot separate psychosocial development from physical development. Therefore, the following are items to consider when dealing with children in the different stages of development, in or out of the hospital. Again, these are general considerations to equip you to prioritize and make nursing decisions on the NCLEX-RN.

INFANTS

Infants are physiologically immature and at greater risk for fluid and electrolyte imbalances, hypothermia, infections, and other injuries. They need sensory stimulation and social interaction. Newborns need the initial opportunity for bonding with their primary caregiver. Explanations and preparation aren't going to be as useful with the infant as they are with older children, but you can help to minimize the stress of hospitalization by approaching them in a nonthreatening manner, making sure they are adequately treated for pain, and allowing parents to comfort the infant once an intervention is completed. It is also useful to group interventions together (vital signs, diaper changes, and medication administration, for example) to allow the infant more uninterrupted time, as the infant needs to establish sleeping and feeding patterns.

TODDLERS

Toddlers are best known for their increasing needs for independence, along with their increased separation anxiety. Fears of immobility and isolation and fears of the unknown are likely to appear with illness and/or hospitalization. Preparation for any procedure needs to be brief due to their short attention span—you might explain a procedure by describing any sensations they may feel and how they can cooperate. Familiar routines and opportunities for play can help minimize stress. Regressive behaviors are not uncommon and need to be explained to parents.

Label the following statements about toddlers **true** or **false**:

11. _____ Toddlers should be prepared at least a week prior to a hospitalization.

12. _____ It is normal for a toilet-trained toddler to begin wetting the bed under stressful conditions.

13. _____ It is better to encourage a toddler to take medication by calling it "candy."

PRESCHOOLERS

Preschoolers have greater fears of physical harm than toddlers. Because of their cause-and-effect thinking, preschoolers may believe that illness or hospitalization is a form of punishment because they have done something wrong. They are able to understand more in terms of preparation for procedures, but information should be brief, honest, and in neutral terms. Demonstrating equipment and using play as a method of teaching is most helpful.

SCHOOL-AGE CHILDREN

Children of school age have progressively better self control, increased understanding of time, and a greater comprehension of rules and reasons. Older children also have a more realistic understanding of death. They need more detailed teaching and preparation and should be allowed to make some choices regarding their care. They should be encouraged to develop their independence and their peer relationships, and need to be allowed to ask questions and to share their fears.

ADOLESCENTS

Adolescents have developed abstract thinking and the ability to problem solve. They need full and honest explanations. They need information to enable them to make good choices for their health, especially related to diet, smoking, drugs, alcohol, and sexual activity. Their primary concerns are with the present time as opposed to the future, and they focus on appearances, peer approval, and feelings of normalcy. These priorities, coupled with their need for independence, may lead to noncompliance with health-related behaviors.

REVIEW

Children need different levels of preparation before hospitalization and procedures. Match the appropriate age group on the left with the example on the right.

14. ____ Toddler   A. requires detailed explanations and known outcomes

15. ____ Preschool   B. short attention span; minimal preparation time

16. ____ School-age   C. fears bodily harm; use play to demonstrate

17. ____ Adolescent   D. offer reasons for actions or activities

There are a few key concepts necessary for understanding the potential reactions of a pediatric client and family members to hospitalization. Use the following words or phrases to complete the paragraph, using each word or phrase only once.

adolescents	may believe that they are being punished
bodily injury	need to establish trust
despair	pain
detachment	preschoolers
increased needs for autonomy	protest
infants	school-age children
are very ritualistic	separation anxiety
loss of control	toddlers

18. There are three main issues that arise in most hospitalized children. The first, noted most obviously in the infant or toddler, is _____. It appears in three phases: _____, _____, and _____. The next issue is _____. This can disturb toddlers, who _____; adolescents or school-age children, who are experiencing _____; infants, who _____; or preschoolers, who, because of their egocentric thought processes, _____. The third major concept is fear of _____ and

_____. Younger _____ experience pain, but do not appear to recollect any previous painful experience or show apprehension.

_____ and _____ may be able to deal with pain more effectively, but have increased concerns about cosmetic and functional impairments.

_____ and _____ generally fear any intrusive procedure, regardless of whether it is painful.

TAKE TWO ASPIRIN AND...

Pain medications in children are administered according to weight. Many options are available for analgesics, from a relatively mild drug such as acetaminophen (Tylenol), to narcotics such as morphine sulfate. With narcotic medications, be alert for signs of oversedation and respiratory depression. Have the child rate the amount of pain using a scale appropriate to his or her developmental level, and be alert to signs of pain such as limited mobility, crying, increased heart rate, and increased blood pressure. Also consider nonpharmacological methods of pain relief as appropriate (e.g., relaxation techniques and imagery).

Label the following statements either **true** or **false**:

19. _____ Relaxation techniques such as imagery and deep breathing can be effective with children.

20. _____ A preschooler should be able to accurately rate her/his pain on a numerical scale of 1 to 10.

21. _____ Infants are too neurologically immature to perceive pain.

22. _____ Premedicating children for surgery or invasive procedures is usually worth the trauma of administering an injection to a child.

23. _____ Infants and young children should never receive narcotics.

24. _____ It is helpful to administer analgesics around the clock in some post-operative clients, for example, to maintain adequate levels of pain management and to allow the child to progress with other activities.

25. _____ Narcotic analgesics are only available in injectable form.

SPECIAL CONSIDERATIONS FOR PEDIATRIC NUTRITION

Nutrition therapies for the client unable to maintain adequate oral intake independently include feedings or formula administered in various ways, including via nasogastric, orogastric, or percutaneous gastrostomy tubes. Various kinds of nasogastric tubes can be inserted, e.g., weighted or non-weighted tubes, short- or longer-term usage, and placement sites in the stomach or in the jejunum. For infants, orogastric tubes are generally preferred over nasogastric, as infants are reflexively nasal breathers.

With any tube, always establish placement first and then use the correct apparatus for administration. When feeding infants through a tube, simultaneous use of pacifiers can help develop sucking ability and the association of sucking with feelings of relief from hunger.

This can facilitate later oral feedings. For skin-level gastric devices, find out if decompression is required to alleviate gastric distention. Check for any residuals to determine tolerance of feedings; return any aspirate to the child because it is considered part of the child's intake. If there is a relatively large amount of residual, check with the provider or dietitian to see if you should subtract the volume from the next feed, or if the next feed should be delayed or skipped entirely.

Rates for feeding administration can vary, depending on whether the feeding is to be given continuously or bolused intermittently. The general guidelines for maximum rates are 5 cc/minute in infants and 10 cc/minute in older children. Following completion of the feed, flush and clamp the tube as needed, position small or mobility-impaired children on the right side or the abdomen with the head of the bed raised to 30 degrees to prevent aspiration from regurgitation.

PRIORITIZING

It is important that a nurse be able to prioritize interventions to effectively meet each client's needs. The NCLEX-RN loves to test your ability to prioritize. In the following situations, prioritize the nursing interventions for each case scenario by numbering each 1, 2, or 3:

26. A 5-year-old asthmatic client with a large bruise on his back:

_____ Provide client and parent admission kit.

_____ Administer oxygen.

_____ Call social worker.

27. A 6-year-old postoperative tonsillectomy client with old, dried blood in his mouth:

_____ Fix leaking IV tubing.

_____ Assess client's mouth for further/frank bleeding.

_____ Help client clean/rinse mouth.

28. A 2-year-old girl crying for her mother in her crib with a bloody nose:

_____ Check/change client's diaper.

_____ Assist client to stop bloody nose by applying pressure to her nose.

_____ Hand client her favorite stuffed animal to calm her down.

29. A 4-year-old boy sitting up in his crib, mouth open, drooling with a frog-like croaking noted on inspiration:

_____ Give client oxygen.

_____ Call the provider.

_____ Transfer client into parent's lap.

30. A 5-year-old child needs to have a peripheral IV placed:

_____ Set up supplies.

_____ Assess client for IV access.

_____ Explain procedure to client.

31. You are admitting an alert and awake 3-year-old boy. The client's mother tells you she found him with an empty acetaminophen bottle, but she is not sure if any tablets were ingested. She thinks he may have fed them to the dog:

_____ Reassure client and mother that they were correct in seeking immediate medical attention.

_____ Anticipate administering acetylcysteine/activated charcoal with confirmation of toxicity.

_____ Assess the client while asking the mother more specific questions.

CHAPTER 14: EXERCISE ANSWERS

1. From the following list, circle the descriptions of six children who are at risk for increased stress during and post-hospitalization:

    B. a preterm infant born at 28 weeks gestation with tetralogy of Fallot

    C. a 15-year-old female undergoing amputation of her right arm following a motor vehicle accident

    D. an 8-year-old girl admitted for a tonsillectomy

    G. a 16-year-old male newly diagnosed with diabetes mellitus

    H. a 3-year-old female with a planned admission for a cochlear implant

    I. a 7-year-old male with frequent hospital admissions for osteogenic sarcoma of the left tibia

2. The following list contains suggestions for hospital orientation activities based on the preceding summary. Circle the five most appropriate options:

    C. a puppet show for 5-year-olds explaining the identities of the various staff members

    D. allowing a toddler to play with medical instruments under supervision

    E. reviewing visiting hours and policies with an adolescent client

    G. showing a 4-year-old admitted the morning of surgery the location of the playroom and his room when he returns to the floor

    H. explaining to a 6-year-old that the beeps and lights she notices are part of the machines used to make sure she is getting better

3. **False**—Day surgery clients do not require special preparation, as their hospital stays should be brief.

4. **True**—The constant activity and potential disruption of day/night routines in the ICU setting can lead to increased stress in the pediatric client.

5. **False**—As children are unable to sign their own informed consents, only parents or guardians need to be informed about procedures.

6. **True**—Children in isolation room settings need more opportunities for diversion, as they may feel "punished" in this setting.

7. **True**—In choosing a client's roommate, the nurse should consider client ages and diagnoses when possible.

8. **False**—In emergent treatment situations, the nurse should limit contact with the client's family until the treatments are completed and/or until further consents are needed.

9. Circle four methods from the list below that you would consider appropriate for play therapy:

   A. holding group meetings for adolescent clients undergoing treatment for cancer

   B. giving a 5-year-old child stickers for every glass of fluid she drinks toward a daily fluid requirement goal

   E. giving a 7-year-old child markers to decorate a leg cast

   G. encouraging two roommates in a rehabilitative pediatric floor to do exercises together

10. Which of the following are not useful or realistic techniques in client/family teaching about discharge needs? Circle four options.

   A. Saving teaching for the last day of hospitalization to avoid confusing the parents

   F. Having each nurse caring for a specific client teach a procedure according to her individual style and preferences, so that the family can observe a number of different techniques

   G. Encouraging the parents of a child with cancer to withdraw the child from school and play activities until all treatments are completed

   H. Discouraging family members from researching and reading about a diagnosis, as the information will probably be too technical and difficult for them to understand

11. **False**—Toddlers should be prepared at least a week prior to a hospitalization.

12. **True**—It is normal for a toilet-trained toddler to begin wetting the bed under stressful conditions.

13. **False**—It is better to encourage a toddler to take medication by calling it "candy."

14. **B**   short attention span; minimal preparation time—Toddler

15. **C**   fears bodily harm; use play to demonstrate—Preschool

16. **D**   offer reasons for actions or activities—School-age

17. **A**   requires detailed explanations and known outcomes—Adolescent

18. There are three main issues that arise in most hospitalized children. The first, noted most obviously in the infant or toddler, is **separation anxiety**. It appears in three phases: **protest, despair,** and **detachment**. The next issue is **loss of control**. This can disturb toddlers, who **are very ritualistic**; adolescents or school-age children, who are experiencing **increased needs for autonomy**; infants, who **need to establish trust**; or preschoolers, who, because of their egocentric thought processes, **may believe that they are being punished**. The third major concept is fear of **bodily injury** and **pain**. Younger **infants** experience pain, but do not appear to recollect any previous painful experience or show apprehension. **School-age children** and **adolescents** may be able to deal with pain more effectively, but have increased concerns about cosmetic and functional impairments. **Toddlers** and **preschoolers** generally fear any intrusive procedure, regardless of whether it is painful.

19. **True**—Relaxation techniques such as imagery and deep breathing can be effective with children.

20. **False**—A preschooler should be able to accurately rate her/his pain on a numerical scale of 1 to 10.

21. **False**—Infants are too neurologically immature to perceive pain.

22. **True**—Premedicating children for surgery or invasive procedures is usually worth the trauma of administering an injection to a child.

23. **False**—Infants and young children should never receive narcotics.

24. **True**—It is helpful to administer analgesics around the clock in some postoperative clients, for example, to maintain adequate levels of pain management and to allow the child to progress with other activities.

25. **False**—Narcotic analgesics are only available in injectable form.

26. A 5-year-old asthmatic client with a large bruise on his back:

    3 Provide client and parent admission kit.

    1 Administer oxygen.

    2 Call social worker.

27. A 6-year-old postoperative tonsillectomy client with old, dried blood in his mouth:

    2 Fix leaking IV tubing.

    1 Assess client's mouth for further/frank bleeding.

    3 Help client clean/rinse mouth.

28. A 2-year-old girl crying for her mother in her crib with a bloody nose:

    3 Check/change client's diaper.

    1 Assist client to stop bloody nose by applying pressure to her nose.

    2 Hand client her favorite stuffed animal to calm her down.

29. A 4-year-old boy sitting up in his crib, mouth open, drooling with a frog-like croaking noted on inspiration:

    1 Give client oxygen.

    2 Call the provider.

    3 Transfer client into parent's lap.

30. A 5-year-old child needs to have a peripheral IV placed:

    2 Set up supplies.

    3 Assess client for IV access.

    1 Explain procedure to client.

31. You are admitting an alert and awake 3-year-old boy. The client's mother tells you she found him with an empty acetaminophen bottle, but she is not sure if any tablets were ingested. She thinks he may have fed them to the dog:

    2 Reassure client and mother that they were correct in seeking immediate medical attention.

    3 Anticipate administering acetyclysteine/activated charcoal with confirmation of toxicity.

    1 Assess the client while asking the mother more specific questions.

1. Emergency intervention may need to be instituted if a 2-week-old infant has which of these vital signs?

   (1) Axillary temperature of 99°F (37.2°C)
   (2) Blood pressure of 78/42 mmHg
   (3) Respirations of 48/minute
   (4) Resting heart rate of 70 beats/minute

2. In planning for the care of a child, which statement should guide the nurse in the use of restraints?

   (1) Allow as much mobility as possible while applying the necessary restraint
   (2) Immobilize the child's entire body to prevent any chance of injury
   (3) The child should be restrained only if the parent is unavailable
   (4) Use tape-over sheets to apply the strongest restraint

3. One of the effects of hospitalization for children is separation. At what stage are children most likely to experience separation anxiety?

   (1) Newborn
   (2) Toddler
   (3) Preschool-age
   (4) Adolescent

4. A 16-year-old girl has been admitted for surgery to correct scoliosis. She will probably be hospitalized for 6 days. When should discharge teaching begin?

   (1) Upon admission.
   (2) It is part of preoperative teaching.
   (3) Postoperative day 1.
   (4) The day before discharge.

5. According to Erikson, the developmental stage of a 2-year-old child is

   (1) trust vs. mistrust.
   (2) autonomy vs. shame and doubt.
   (3) initiative vs. guilt.
   (4) preoperational thought.

6. A 30-month-old child has been hospitalized for an acute respiratory infection. The parents have visited regularly, but the child cries whenever they leave. When they visit today the child ignores them. How can the nurse explain this behavior to the parents?

(1) "Your child is having separation anxiety. This behavior is typical, and you should continue to visit and provide support during the hospitalization."
(2) "Your child has adjusted to the hospital environment and is doing fine."
(3) "Your child has become attached to the primary nurse."
(4) "Your child is exhausted from crying whenever you leave."

7. A child is admitted to a coronary care unit (CCU) with a diagnosis of acute myocardial infarction (MI). The provider orders streptokinase (Streptase). The nurse explains to the client that this medication is given to

(1) dissolve the thrombus.
(2) reduce the demand for oxygen by the myocardium.
(3) prevent platelet aggregation.
(4) inhibit further clot formation.

8. An 11-year-old client has been complaining of severe pain since surgery two days ago. The client is currently in the play room, avidly playing video games, and shows no evidence of pain. When the nurse has the client return to bed, the client begins complaining of severe pain again. Which of the following is probably true about this pain?

(1) The client is addicted to pain medication, so pain management must be carefully monitored.
(2) Pain medications wore off as the client went to bed.
(3) The client probably said there was no pain so bedrest wouldn't be indicated.
(4) The distraction of playing video games is an important adjunct to other pain-management techniques.

CHAPTER 14: NCLEX-RN STYLE ANSWERS

1. (4) CORRECT   The normal resting apical pulse rate ranges from 120–140 beats/minute. The
                     infant has bradycardia, which needs immediate intervention.
    (1) POSSIBLE   The normal axillary temperature ranges between 97.9 and 98°F (36.5 and 37°C).
                     The infant's temperature is slightly elevated but would not require emergency
                     intervention.
    (2) ELIMINATE   Normal for an infant.
    (3) ELIMINATE   Normal for an infant.

    CATEGORY 10 PHYSIOLOGICAL ADAPTATION

2. (1) CORRECT   The main purpose of restraining a child is to ensure the child's safety, but the child
                     should be restrained only to the degree necessary to achieve this.
    (2) ELIMINATE   It is the nurse's responsibility to select the most approriate and least restrictive
                     type of restraint.
    (3) ELIMINATE   Using less restrictive restraints is often possible by gaining the cooperation of the
                     parents, but this does not necessarily eliminate the need for restraints.
    (4) ELIMINATE   It is the nurse's responsibility to select the most appropriate and least restrictive
                     type of restraint.

    CATEGORY 02 SAFETY AND INFECTION CONTROL

3. (2) CORRECT   Children of all ages are affected by the separation caused by hospitalization. The
                     manifestations of their reactions to separation differ by age. Separation anxiety
                     usually begins about 6–8 months of age, but it is most acute for toddlers.
    (1) ELIMINATE   Newborns do not experience separation anxiety.
    (3) ELIMINATE   While preschoolers experience separation anxiety, it is much more acute in the
                     toddler.
    (4) ELIMINATE   While separation from home and parents may be difficult for the adolescent, loss
                     of peer-group support may pose a severe emotional threat.

    CATEGORY 03 GROWTH AND DEVELOPMENT THROUGH THE LIFE SPAN

4. (1) CORRECT   Discharge teaching begins upon admission and continues throughout the hospital
                     stay.
    (2) ELIMINATE   Preoperative teaching would focus on a plan for pre- and postoperative care.
    (3) ELIMINATE   The first day postoperative, the client would not physically be able to absorb
                     discharge teaching, nor would it be appropriate.
    (4) ELIMINATE   This is too late to do discharge teaching. It should be an ongoing process during
                     hospitalization.

    CATEGORY 01 MANAGEMENT OF CARE

5.   **(2) CORRECT**   According to Erikson, the developmental stage of children aged 1–3 is autonomy vs. shame and doubt.

       (1) *ELIMINATE*   Trust vs. mistrust is the developmental stage of infants aged 12–18 months.

       (3) *ELIMINATE*   Initiative vs. guilt is the developmental stage of children aged 3–6 years.

       (4) *POSSIBLE*   While preoperational thought is a developmental stage of children aged 2–4, it is Piaget's theory, not Erikson's.

CATEGORY 03 GROWTH AND DEVELOPMENT THROUGH THE LIFE SPAN

6.   **(1) CORRECT**   This is the best answer. A child this age will have separation anxiety.

       (2) *ELIMINATE*   This does not account for the child's behavior.

       (3) *ELIMINATE*   Attachment to the nurse does not account for the child's crying and ignoring his parents.

       (4) *ELIMINATE*   Exhaustion after his parents left will not result in the child's ignoring them on subsequent visits.

CATEGORY 05 COPING AND ADAPTATION

7.   **(1) CORRECT**   Streptokinase is a thrombolytic medication that causes lysis of blood clots; the resultant effect is that the thrombi are destroyed. Streptokinase must be given with 12–14 hours of the clot formation, since it has little effect on organized clots.

       (2) *ELIMINATE*   Beta blockers, nitrates, and calcium channel blockers are used to reduce myocardial oxygen demand.

       (3) *ELIMINATE*   Antiplatelet aggregation medications that are used include acetylsalicylic acid (aspirin) and dipyridamole (Persantine).

       (4) *ELIMINATE*   Anticoagulants, such as heparin, are used to prevent further clot formation.

CATEGORY 09 REDUCTION OF RISK POTENTIAL

8.   **(4) CORRECT**   Nonpharmacologic interventions, including distractions, are an important component of pain-relief modalities.

       (1) *ELIMINATE*   The situation described does not indicate the client is addicted to pain medication.

       (2) *ELIMINATE*   The situation described does not indicate the pain medication wore off.

       (3) *ELIMINATE*   There is a better rationale for why the 11-year-old client complained of pain when returned to bed.

CATEGORY 10 PHYSIOLOGICAL ADAPTATION

15

THE NEWBORN

WHAT YOU NEED TO KNOW

The neonatal period lasts from birth to the 27th day of life. It is a stage of many risks as the newborn adjusts to extrauterine life. The first 24 hours of life are the most critical, because respiratory failure and circulatory failure are most likely to occur rapidly and with little warning during this time. To refresh your memory about the newborn, fill in the blanks below with words from the list on the following page:

breathing   ductus venosus   muscle tone
circulatory   foramen ovale   reflex irritability
color   heart rate   respiratory effort
ductus arteriosus

At birth many physiological changes occur. The most critical is the onset of (1.) _____. Additionally, (2.) _____ changes allow the blood to flow through the newborn's lungs. The transition from fetal circulation to neonatal circulation includes the functional closure of fetal shunts including the (3.) _____, _____, and the _____. During the early neonatal period, functional heart murmurs can be auscultated.

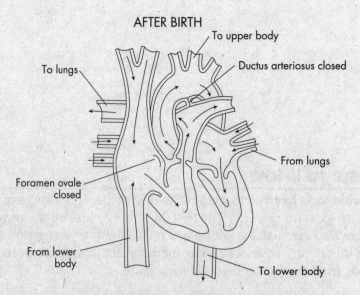

BEFORE BIRTH

To upper body
Ductus arteriosus
Left atrium
Foramen ovale
Right atrium
Left ventricle
Right ventricle
From placenta
To lower body and placenta

AFTER BIRTH

To upper body
To lungs
Ductus arteriosus closed
Foramen ovale closed
From lungs
From lower body
To lower body

These pictures depict the circulatory changes that are supposed to occur at birth

Immediate care of the newborn includes establishing and maintaining respirations, preventing heat loss, and obtaining Apgar assessments at 1 minute and 5 minutes of life. The Apgar assessment rates the neonate's (4.) _____, _____, _____, _____, and _____.

THE NEWBORN ASSESSMENT

Before we start, quickly test your knowledge of newborn nursing care by labeling the following statements **true** or **false**:

5. _____ The usual heart rate of a neonate is 120–160 b.p.m. and regular.

6. _____ A soft cardiac murmur during the first month of life is not normal.

7. _____ A vitamin K injection is given only if the parent decides to have it administered.

8. _____ The yellowish color an infant develops by the third day of life is due to an immature liver.

9. _____ A neonate's breathing pattern is chiefly abdominal and irregular with a rate between 30 and 60 per minute.

10. _____ Periods of apnea up to 15 seconds in duration are normal for a newborn.

11. _____ There is often a brick red stain on the neonate's diaper during the first week.

12. _____ Meconium is black-green in color and is tenacious.

13. _____ The cardiac sphincter of the neonate is not well developed, so regurgitation occurs if the stomach is too full.

14. _____ Neonates normally lose 10 percent of their birth weight by day four of life.

15. _____ Phenylketonuria testing is done after the ingestion of protein.

16. _____ A neonate should be placed on a rigid feeding schedule.

17. _____ Parent-infant relationships can be fostered during feeding times.

There is little time for the nurse to ascertain the health of an infant. Quick, sharp assessment skills are imperative. The neonate's airway is your first priority, which shouldn't be a surprise to you at this point in your review. We summarize what you need to know about the newborn to pass the NCLEX-RN in the following sections and in Chapter 23. While Apgar scoring routinely appears on the NCLEX-RN, there are more objective ways to assess neonates.

Apgar Criteria			
Apgar Score	**0**	**1**	**2**
Color	pale	body pink, extremities blue	totally pink
Heart rate	absent	less than 100 b.p.m.	over 100 b.p.m.
Reflex irritability	no response	grimace	vigorous cry
Muscle tone	limp	some flexion	actively moves
Respiratory effort	absent	slow, irregular	good cry

Total scores of 0 to 3 represent severe distress, scores of 4 to 6 represent moderate compromise, and scores of 7 to 10 indicate the absence of difficulty in adjusting to extrauterine life. Using the Apgar chart above, answer the following questions:

18. At 1 minute of life the nurse assesses the neonate to have an apical heart rate of 90 b.p.m. and an irregular breathing pattern. The neonate is flaccid, cries when the nurse slaps his foot, and his extremities are cyanotic. This infant would receive an Apgar score of ___.

19. At 5 minutes of life the nurse assesses the neonate and finds that the apical heart rate is 110 b.p.m. and his respirations remain irregular and slow. The neonate's extremities are flexed, he cries in response to a slap on the foot, and he is pink all over. The infant's Apgar score is ___.

PHYSIOLOGICAL PARAMETERS FOR THE NEWBORN

The newborn's head circumference should be 33–35 cm, but molding may temporarily decrease this measurement. Head circumference should be 2–3 cm greater than chest circumference. If the head is significantly smaller than the chest, the newborn may have microcephaly (small brain due to impaired growth) or craniostenosis (premature closure of the sutures). Birth weight is generally 2,500–4,000 grams (5 lb. 8oz.–8 lb. 13oz.).

Gestational age assessment parameters include ears, breast tissue, genitalia, and foot creases.

Parameter	**Nursing Action**	**"Term" Infant** Born between 37–42 weeks gestation	**"Preterm" Infant** Born before 37 weeks gestation
Ear	Fold the pinna (auricle) forward	Pinna recoils (springs back)	Pinna opens slowly or stays folded in very premature infants
Breast tissue	Measure it	3 mm	Less than 3 mm
Female genitalia	Observe	Labia majora cover labia minora	Labia minora are more prominent; vaginal opening can be seen
Male genitalia	Observe	Scrotal sac very wrinkled	Fewer shallow rugae on the scrotum
Heel creases	Observe	Extend $\frac{2}{3}$ of the way from the toes to the heel	Soles are smoother, creases extend less than $\frac{2}{3}$ of the wayfrom the toes to the heel

THE HEAD

The infant's head is 25 percent of the total body length. The anterior fontanel is diamond shaped. The posterior fontanel is triangle shaped.

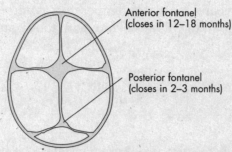

Anterior fontanel
(closes in 12–18 months)

Posterior fontanel
(closes in 2–3 months)

Both the anterior and posterior fontanels should be flat and soft until they close, in 12–18 months (anterior) and 2–3 months (posterior). The anterior fontanel might be smaller than normal due to molding during vaginal delivery. It is a sign of distress or major abnormality if the sutures are fused or if the fontanels are either bulging or depressed when the infant is quiet.

If the head is more than 4 cm larger than the chest and remains this way after several days, the newborn may have one of several causes of increased head circumference such as hydrocephalus (increased cerebrospinal fluid surrounding the brain), cephalohematoma, and caput succedaneum.

Match the following common physiological variations to the head of the newborn with the proper definition on the right:

20. _____ Molding

A. swelling or edema of the head of an infant during labor and delivery; crosses suture lines

21. _____ Cephalohematoma

B. temporary changes in the shape of the head of a neonate as it accommodates to the birth canal during labor

22. _____ Caput succedaneum

C. due to the pressure of the presenting part against the cervix, blood from periosteum accumulates in the tissue of the infant's head, creating a circular swelling that does not cross suture lines

The newborn's face should be symmetrical, even while crying. Observe the eyes for discharge, the pupils for reaction to light, and the equality of eye movements. Infants often have some ocular incoordination. Assess sclera for clarity, jaundice, and hemorrhage. The outer canthus of the eye should be on a horizontal line with the top of the pinna of the ear; low-set ears may be indicative of chromosomal abnormalities.

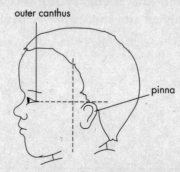

outer canthus

pinna

THE NERVOUS SYSTEM

It is normal for the newborn to sleep erratically for about 20 hours per day. Most neurological functions of the neonate are primitive reflexes. The autonomic nervous system is critical as it stimulates initial respirations and regulates temperature control. Neurological assessment centers on the reflex tests. Fill in the blanks below with the appropriate reflexes:

Babinski	plantar	step
crawl	rooting	sucking
grasp	startle	tonic neck
Moro		

23. A neonate's mother strokes his cheek and he turns his head toward that side. This an example of the _____ reflex.

24. A neonate's mother places an object close to the baby's mouth and he attempts to suck. This is an example of the _____ reflex.

25. A neonate's father places his finger in the palm of the neonate's hand. The neonate flexes his fingers around his father's finger. This is an example of the _____ reflex.

26. A neonate's father runs his thumb up the middle undersurface of the neonate's foot. His toes separate and flare out. This is an example of the _____ reflex.

27. A neonate's father runs his thumb up the lateral undersurface of his son's foot and his toes curl downward. This is an example of the _____ reflex.

28. There is a loud noise in the room and the neonate abducts his arms with flexion of elbows. This is an example of the _____ reflex.

29. A neonate's brother bumps into the bassinet causing a jarring motion. The neonate extends and abducts his extremities and fans his fingers. This is an example of the _____ reflex.

30. The neonate is lying prone and he attempts crawling movements. This is an example of the _____ reflex.

31. A neonate's father supports him under both arms and places his feet on a firm surface. The neonate makes stepping movements. This is an example of the _____ reflex.

32. A neonate's head is turned to the right side by his mother. His right arm and leg extend and his left arm and leg flex. This is an example of the _____ reflex.

NEWBORN REFLEXES

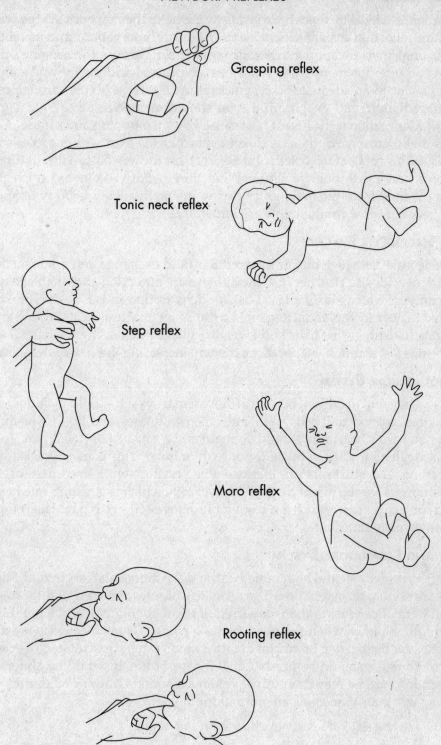

Grasping reflex

Tonic neck reflex

Step reflex

Moro reflex

Rooting reflex

THERMOREGULATION

Heat regulation is critical to a newborn's survival. Due to the newborn's large body surface area to volume ratio, thin layer of subcutaneous fat (heat conservation), and inability to shiver (heat production), they are at great risk for hypothermia. Because the neonate's metabolism and oxygen consumption increases to make heat, to prevent acidosis the nurse must make it a priority to maintain an adequate body temperature. Heat loss occurs through **convection**, **conduction**, **radiation**, and **evaporation** (you should memorize these four words for the NCLEX-RN). Convection is the loss of heat caused by surrounding air currents. Conduction is heat loss that occurs when there is direct contact of the skin with a cooler solid object. Radiation is the loss of heat to cooler solid objects near the newborn without direct contact. Evaporation is heat loss through moisture. When the newborn is cold, too much glucose and oxygen are diverted from the brain and heart to maintain adequate body temperature, so warm blankets and/or warming lights are imperative!

FLUID AND ELECTROLYTE BALANCE

Because the neonate has a high rate of intracellular fluid exchange and a fast metabolic rate, there is a risk of acidosis. Also, because the kidneys are immature and unable to concentrate urine and conserve water, the infant is at risk for dehydration and acidosis. Think about this, as it is related to thermoregulation. Remember, the infant produces heat through an increased metabolic rate (two times that of its body weight), thereby increasing the risk for acidosis. In addition, heat is lost through evaporation, thereby increasing the risk of dehydration.

THE CARDIOVASCULAR SYSTEM

The nurse's assessment of the newborn's cardiovascular system should include the neonate's rate and rhythm, color of nail beds, skin, mucous membranes, and lips. Upon auscultation, the resting newborn's heart rate should be regular at a rate of 120–160 b.p.m. To assess the heart rate, auscultate the apical pulse for one full minute. This is usually easiest when the child is sleeping. The heart rate can increase when crying, while sleep decreases the heart rate. It is abnormal for the infant to have bradycardia, which is a resting rate below 80–100 b.p.m., and/or tachycardia, which is a resting rate above 160–180 b.p.m. Heart murmurs are common and usually transient.

THE CHEST AND RESPIRATORY SYSTEM

The chest of the neonate should be symmetrical, and the thorax almost circular. Slight sternal retractions are normal on inspiration. The neonate's nipples are often slightly engorged due to maternal hormones. Respirations are irregular and abdominal, and should be at a rate of 30–60/minute (higher when the newborn is crying). Usually, crackles are auscultated immediately after birth; later, bronchial breath sounds can be auscultated over most of the chest. A cough reflex should be present at 1–2 days of life. It would be abnormal to find grunting, stridor, marked retractions, unequal breath sounds, and/or wheezing. Periods of apnea lasting less than 15 seconds are normal for the newborn.

33. List five signs of respiratory distress in a newborn:

    A. _____

    B. _____

    C. _____

    D. _____

    E. _____

THE GASTROINTESTINAL SYSTEM

The neonate's abdomen should be soft and slightly rounded. Bowel sounds should be audible on auscultation of all four quadrants 1 hour after birth. The nurse must immediately assess the umbilical cord of the newborn for signs of infection: odor, redness, or discharge. There should be **three vessels** present: **two arteries** and **one vein**.

Neonates are unable to digest polysaccharides and cannot fully absorb fats. Due to the neonate's immature liver, physiological jaundice can occur after 48 hours of life, though it usually disappears by week two. Additionally, the immature liver produces less prothrombin and fewer coagulation factors, predisposing the neonate to hemorrhage.

The newborn should be fed on demand, regardless of whether he is being breast or bottle fed. The infant usually feeds every 3–4 hours. The immature cardiac sphincter promotes regurgitation, therefore a semi-upright feeding position and frequent burping are recommended. Newborns should be positioned on their right side after feedings. This allows the feeding to flow toward the lower portion of the stomach and allows any swallowed air to rise above the liquid and through the esophagus. This position best prevents regurgitation, distention, and choking.

In a properly functioning gastrointestinal tract, there are progressive changes in the neonate's stool. Intestinal obstruction should be suspected if nothing is passed per rectum by 48 hours. The infant's first stool is meconium (thick, black-green stool), the passage of which should occur within the first 48 hours of life. The patency of the anus is confirmed by passage of meconium. After the infant begins to feed, transitional stools follow. These are yellow to greenish-brown in color, thinner, seeding, and less sticky than meconium. By the fourth day of life, milk stools occur. Infants who are breast feeding usually have more frequent stooling.

Newborn's Age	Stool	Appearance
Within 48 hours	Meconium	Thick, black-green, sticky stool
Following meconium passage (in 48 hours)	Transitional	Meconium combined with yellow-brown to greenish-brown milk stools
4–5 days	Milk stools	Yellow to light brown. Breast milk stools are golden yellow and pasty. Cow milk formula stools are pale yellow to light brown, more formed and have a more foul odor.

34. Arrange the following parts of the abdominal assessment in the correct order of implementation: **palpation, auscultation, inspection, percussion**

    A. _____

    B. _____

    C. _____

    D. _____

The Genitourinary System

The newborn's kidneys are immature and cannot properly concentrate urine to correct dehydration. **It is up to the nurse to teach the parents about the high risk of dehydration!** The first void for both males and females should be within 24 hours of life. Other than these facts, genitourinary problems during infancy are not a priority for the NCLEX-RN.

Genitalia

In assessing the male genitalia, observe the position of the external or urethral meatus, which should be at the tip of the glans, and the scrotum for symmetry and size. If the urethral meatus opens on the ventral or underside of the glans or shaft, it is called hypospadias. The scrotum should be markedly wrinkled (rugae) and is usually edematous. Undescended testicles (**cryptorchidism**) are common and can be assessed by palpating the scrotum. A **hydrocele** is characterized by the enlargement or swelling of the scrotum caused by a fluid collection. A hydrocele is diagnosed by the transparent appearance of the scrotum when a flashlight is held to the scrotal sac. It is treated by aspirating the collection of fluid or by surgical removal of the outer tissue.

In assessing the female genitalia, observe the labia and clitoris, which are usually edematous. The labia majora should cover the labia minora in a term infant. There is often vernix caseosa between the labia. Bloody mucoid discharge (pseudomenstruation) from the vagina is normal due to the sudden decrease in maternal hormones.

The Musculoskeletal System

The skeletal system of the neonate is mostly composed of cartilage. Ossification is a continuous process through maturation, but much of it occurs within the first year. The six skull bones are relatively soft and are able to override each other. Both an anterior and posterior fontanel are present at birth and should close in 12–18 months (anterior) and 2–3 months (posterior). (See the illustration on page 275.) The vertebral column should be without separation, masses, or openings. It is abnormal to find a tuft of hair or dimple along the spine. This may indicate an underlying spina bifida.

The hands of a neonate are typically clenched into a fist. The nurse should check the range of motion, number, and variation of fingers. The grasp reflex should be intact when you place your finger in the palm of the infant's hand. At rest, the neonate is often in a flexed position.

Assessing for congenital hip dysplasia should only be done by specially trained, experienced examiners in order to prevent fractures or other damage to the hip.

Ortolani Test—If the femoral head can be felt to slip forward into the acetabulum on pressure from behind, it has been dislocated. Sometimes an audible click can be heard on exit or entry of the femur out of or into the acetabulum.

Barlow's Sign—When pressure is applied from the front, the femoral head "slips" out over the acetabulum and then back, and the hip is said to be dislocatable or unstable.

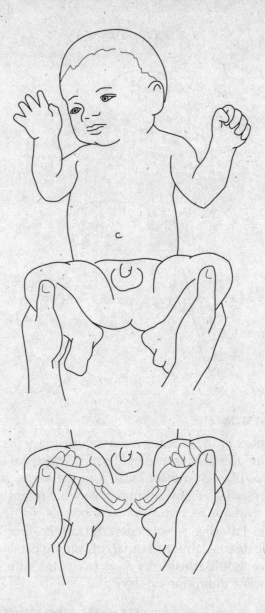

Ortolani's click is present when the hips are dislocated. A "thunk" would be felt as the head of the femur reenters the acetabulum.

In the presence of congenital hip dysplasia, a **Pavlik** harness is prescribed to maintain proper positioning and hopefully to stabilize the hip. The harness is worn continuously until the hip becomes "stable" (usually about 3–6 months). If this does not work, more aggressive treatment may be necessary such as a hip spika cast or brace.

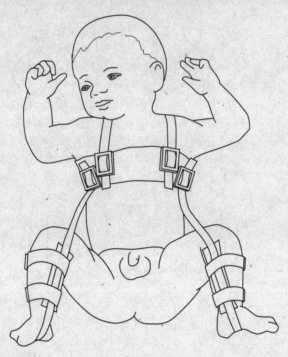

THE INTEGUMENTARY SYSTEM

The skin and mucous membranes are the neonate's primary barriers against infection. The two layers of the skin are the dermis and epidermis. These are loosely bound together and are very thin. Sebaceous glands (mostly located in the scalp, face, and genitalia) produce the vernix caseosa (cheeselike substance) that covers the infant at birth. The neonate's skin is normally pink with cyanotic extremities (acrocyanosis) for the first 24 hours of life, due to sluggish circulation. Jaundice is abnormal during the first 24 to 48 hours of life (and may indicate hemolytic disease), but after that, physiological jaundice is normal due to the immature liver. Jaundice should subside by week two. Match the common newborn findings below with the appropriate definition on the right:

35. ____ Lanugo

A. dark spots on the lumbar region in the newborn children of non-Caucasian races

36. ____ Mongolian spots

B. white, evanescent, pinhead-sized papules that occur on the face and less often on the trunk

37. ____ Acrocyanosis

C. soft, fine, downy hair found on both preterm and term newborns

38. ____ Erythema toxicum

D. pink, papular rash that may have purulent vesicles

39. ____ Harlequin sign

E. cyanosis of the hands and feet

40. ____ Milia

F. outlined color change as an infant lies on one side; the lower half of the body becomes pink and the upper half pales

It is important to assess the newborn's skin for abrasions, rashes, crackling, and elasticity, which are indicators of tissue hydration. Forceps marks are sometimes present as bruises. Abnormal findings include progressive jaundice (especially in the first 24 hours), cracked or peeling skin, pallor, poor skin turgor, generalized cyanosis, hemorrhage and ecchymosis, or petechiae that persist past the first few hours of life.

OTHER PHYSICAL CONSIDERATIONS

Infants are generally not capable of producing antibodies until approximately 2 months of life. They receive passive immunity, immunoglobulin G (IgG), from maternal circulation and human milk. They are protected from most childhood diseases during this time. Infants start receiving immunizations at 2 months.

The endocrine system in the term infant is sufficiently developed, but functions immaturely. Maternal sex hormones may have physiological effects on the neonate, including hypertrophied labia, engorged breasts, and pseudomenstruation (a bloody secretion) in females.

NURSING CARE OF THE NEWBORN

Health promotion of the neonate includes maintenance of homeostasis. The most important nursing functions are:

- Maintaining a patent airway
- Maintaining stable body temperature
- Protecting the newborn from infection
- Ensuring optimal nutrition
- Teaching care of the infant to the parents

To ascertain a patent airway, the nurse must suction mucus from the mouth and nose as needed, position the newborn lying on his side, and observe for signs of respiratory distress, such as grunting, nasal flaring, and sternal retractions. To provide warmth, the nurse should keep the newborn in a heated crib until body temperature is stable. The neonate's skin should be kept clean and dry. To protect the newborn from infection, the nurse must administer the ordered eye drops (usually erythromycin or tetracycline) to prevent **ophthalmia neonatorum**. Ophthalmia neonatorum is a purulent conjunctivitis usually contracted from infected secretions in the mother's vagina. Maternal *Chlamydia trachomatis* and *Neissepia gonorrhoea* are two possible causes of ophthalmia neonatorum.

PARENTAL TEACHING

Because maternity hospital stays are so short, it is important that the parents can adequately care for their infant on discharge. Teaching is a primary nursing intervention, the outcome of which should be evaluated through return demonstrations by the parents.

Basic Teaching Needs of New Parents	
Cord care	• Cleanse the cord with alcohol and sometimes triple dye once a day • Keep the area clean and dry • Keep the newborn's diaper below the cord to prevent irritation • Signs of infection: Redness, drainage, swelling, odor • Notify physician for signs of infection
Circumcision care (Circumcision is optional!)	• Observe for bleeding, first urination • Apply diaper loosely to prevent irritation • Signs of infection: Redness, drainage, swelling, odor, and/or fever • Notify physician for signs of infection
Bonding	• Encourage the parents to talk to, hold, and sing to the infant • Promote skin-to-skin contact between parent and infant • Feedings are good opportunities for parent-infant bonding • Notify physician for signs of infection

COMMON HEALTH PROBLEMS OF THE NEWBORN

Before we begin, test your knowledge by labeling the following statements either **true** or **false**:

41. _____ A newborn is labeled "preterm" when it is born before 37 weeks of gestation.

42. _____ A low birth weight infant is one who weighs less than 2,500 grams (5.5 pounds) at birth.

43. _____ Preterm infants have lanugo on the face, less subcutaneous fat, and ears that are less supported by cartilage than term infants.

44. _____ In the preterm infant, respirations are efficient and the neonate is not at greater risk than a full-term infant for respiratory distress.

45. _____ Heat regulation is poorly developed in the neonate due to poor development of the central nervous system.

RESPIRATORY DISTRESS SYNDROME

Respiratory distress syndrome (R.D.S.) often results from a developmental delay in lung maturation and a deficiency in **surfactant**. Surfactant functions to maintain adequate lung inflation and ventilation by promoting elasticity of the lung tissues. R.D.S. is almost always seen in preterm infants who are born before the lungs are fully prepared to serve as efficient organs for gas exchange. R.D.S. is common following cesarean births and in low birth weight infants due to the interrupted development of surfactant. Common signs of R.D.S. include: cyanosis, dyspnea, sternal and/or costal retractions, tachypnea, grunting, and nasal flaring.

To correct R.D.S., the nurse should maintain a patent airway, place the infant in a warm isolette with oxygen, administer antibiotics as prescribed by the provider, and correct the acidosis. Respiratory acidosis is treated with assisted ventilatory support. Metabolic acidosis is treated with IV sodium bicarbonate as ordered by the physician.

Meconium aspiration syndrome is another condition that compromises the newborn's airway. It is caused when the fetus passes meconium into the amniotic fluid and it is inhaled into the nasooropharynx on initiation of the first breath. Meconium is sticky in nature and adheres to airway and alveoli, causing uneven ventilation perfusion and decreased lung compliance, which leads to respiratory distress. In postterm infants or in compromised mothers, it is often necessary to suction meconium and amniotic fluid from the infant's nasopharynx and oropharynx immediately after delivery to prevent meconium aspiration syndrome. Quick intervention is imperative, so the nurse must pay careful attention to the appearance of the amniotic fluid to see if it is stained with meconium.

CRANIAL BIRTH INJURIES

Signs of increased **intracranial pressure** (I.C.P.) include abnormal respirations; cyanosis, a high pitched shrill cry; flaccidity; restlessness; poor sucking; and convulsions. In the neonate, the fontanels will bulge and become firm in the presence of increased intracranial pressure. The head of the newborn's bed should be elevated to 30 degrees and the newborn's head maintained in a neutral position without neck flexion to prevent further increases in I.C.P.

Increased I.C.P. can be caused by an **intracranial hemorrhage**. This is manifested by a sudden deterioration in the neonate condition. Remember, neonates have immature livers that produce insufficient vitamin K and clotting factors. Therefore, they are more prone to hemorrhage. Besides intervening for increased I.C.P., the nurse may also administer vitamin K to promote clotting.

Hydrocephalus also causes increased I.C.P. Hydrocephalus is characterized by an excess of cerebrospinal fluid (C.S.F.) in the ventricular system of the brain. This buildup can be caused by either an obstruction to the flow of C.S.F. or by abnormal absorption of C.S.F., either of which can be congenital. It is characterized by rapidly increasing head circumference, enlarged fontanels, and "sunsetting" eyes (see illustration on page 286). Treatment is the same as for increased I.C.P., but includes surgical insertion of a shunt to drain the C.S.F. from the ventricle into the peritoneal cavity.

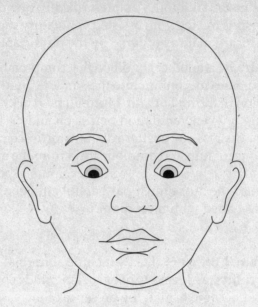

HYDROCEPHALUS

The large cranium and sunsetting
eyes of hydrocephalus

Hemolytic Disease

Hemolytic disease resulting from ABO or Rh incompatibility causes rapid red blood cell destruction in the neonate. The common signs of hemolytic disease include jaundice in the first 24 hours of life, signs of anemia (restlessness, fatigue, anorexia), enlargement of liver and spleen, and increased bilirubin levels.

To prevent hemolytic disease, **Rh$_o$(D) immune globiuyin (RhoGAM)** is given to the Rh-negative mother at the 28th week of pregnancy and after delivery. Following delivery, the infant with hemolytic disease may be given an exchange transfusion. Exchange transfusions are composed of type O Rh-negative blood that has been matched with the mother's blood to prevent the neonate's antibodies from attacking it. Bilirubin encephalopathy or kernicterus is severe brain damage caused by a toxic accumulation of bilirubin in CNS tissue. Signs of **kernicterus** develop without an exchange transfusion. The nurse must be aware of the potential for kernicterus, which can occur when hyperbilirubinemia is left untreated. Symptoms of kernicterus include absence of the Moro reflex, apnea, lethargy, high-pitched cry, assumption of opisthotonos position (head and heels bent backward, the body forms a bow), tremors, and convulsions.

Hyperbilirubinemia

Hyperbilirubinemia is defined as serum bilirubin greater than 15 mg/dL. Jaundice spreads from the infant's face to feet. Jaundice and elevated bilirubin levels occurring within the first 24–36 hours of life are alarming and must be treated to prevent kernicterus. Primary treatment for hyperbilirubinemia is **phototherapy**, for which the infant must be unclothed except for eye and genitalia protection. Phototherapy uses fluorescent light to accelerate the excretion of bilirubin in the skin. The infant undergoing phototherapy requires frequent bilirubin levels (every 4 to 12 hours) to evaluate effectiveness.

Physiological hyperbilirubinemia is less alarming because it is due to immature hepatic function. This jaundice peaks at 72 hours. Physiological hyperbilirubinemia should decrease on its own by days 5–7 of life.

COLIC

There are many theories as to the causes of colic. It is believed that colic may be caused by random spasms of the intestine. Colic usually occurs within the first 3 months of life. Babies with colic tend to cry constantly and frequently tuck their knees up to their abdomens. Infants with colic typically have soft, yellow stools and flatus due to the abdominal cramping. Colic does not seem to affect the infant's growth, as these infants usually gain weight and thrive. The nurse should instruct the parents to burp the infant frequently since most of the discomfort is associated with air in the stomach and intestines. Babies with colic should be held upright when feeding. The nurse can provide support and assure the parents that colic usually disappears by the age of 3 months.

INFECTION

Neonates with infection are at high risk for fluid and electrolyte imbalance, dehydration, hypothermia, and altered nutrition. Infection causes one's metabolism to speed up, so oxygen and sugar get diverted from the brain, and more fluid evaporates through the skin.

Thrush is a mouth infection caused by *Candida albicans* and can be transmitted via the vaginal canal and unclean feeding utensils. Thrush is characterized by white spots on the tongue that do not wash off. Treatment is with the antifungal medication **nystatin** (**Mycostatin**), applied topically as ordered by the physician.

Use the following scenario about the neonate to label the statements that follow as **true** or **false**:

A female neonate is 1 week old and is brought into the hospital by her parents. She is lethargic, febrile, and irritable; her mother reports she has not been feeding well, has been vomiting, and has had diarrhea.

46. _____ The nurse should first assess the neonate's hydration status.

47. _____ The neonate will, most likely, require IV antibiotic treatment.

48. _____ It is important to assess the neonate's vital signs.

49. _____ Sepsis (infection) in infants is difficult to determine because there are no definitive signs.

NEONATES BORN TO DIABETIC MOTHERS

Neonates born to diabetic mothers produce increased levels of insulin to compensate for the maternal hyperglycemic state. At birth, the hyperglycemic state ends for the newborn, and **hyperinsulinism** and **hypoglycemia** result. Infants of poorly controlled diabetic mothers are usually large for gestational age (macrosomia). Feedings of breast milk or formula should begin within 1 hour after birth (this may be a question on the NCLEX-RN!). Blood glucose levels of the newborn are closely monitored.

PROBLEMS CAUSED BY ALTERED PHYSICAL DEVELOPMENT

With any congenital malformation, it is important to encourage the parents to hold and talk to the infant to promote bonding. Parents often feel guilty for the infant's defect, and it is the nurse's job to reassure parents, allow them to grieve for their "imperfect" baby, and to educate them about their child's condition. Remember, bonding is a primary goal of the neonatal stage, and any defect or extended hospitalization may inhibit this effort.

NERVOUS SYSTEM ANOMALIES

We discussed **increased intracranial pressure** (I.C.P.) and **hydrocephalus** earlier in this Chapter. Refresh your memory by labeling the following statements as either **true** or **false**:

50. _____ To correct hydrocephalus and decrease intracranial pressure, a ventricular-peritoneal shunt is often placed. Postoperative care includes monitoring for signs of cerebrospinal fluid infection and increased intracranial pressure.

51. _____ Postoperative care for a ventricular-peritoneal shunt includes placing the infant on the non-operated side with the head of the bed elevated.

52. _____ Hydrocephalus is often associated with myelomeningocele.

53. _____ The earliest signs of hydrocephalus include increased head circumference and bulging fontanels.

54. _____ Hydrocephalus is characterized by an accumulation of cerebrospinal fluid in the ventricles.

55. _____ Increased intracranial pressure can be caused by any matter that tries to take up some of the fixed space of the cranium.

Myelomeningocele (a.k.a. meningomyelocele) is a type of **spina bifida** in which the spinal cord and associated membranes protrude through a gap in the laminae of the vertebrae. This spinal cord defect produces varying degrees of paralysis and sensory loss below the level of the lesion. Babies with myelomeningocele often have hydrocephalus. Surgical repair and a multidisciplinary approach (neurology, urology, orthopedics, rehabilitation, and physical therapy) to management is required.

MYEOCELE

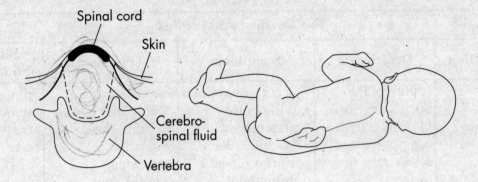

Spinal cord
Skin
Cerebro-
spinal fluid
Vertebra

MENINGOCELE

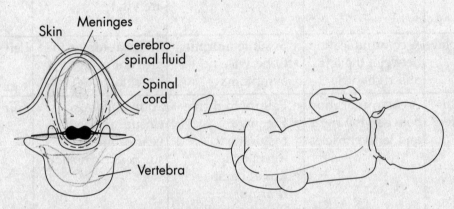

Skin Meninges
Cerebro-
spinal fluid
Spinal
cord
Vertebra

Label the following statements about myelomeningocele **true** or **false**:

56. ___T___ Myelomeningocele is a soft sac containing spinal fluid, meninges, spinal cord, and/or nerve roots protruding through a bony defect in the spine.

57. ___F___ If a client has a lumbar myelomeningocele there is no effect on the lower extremities.

58. _____ Overflow incontinence with constant dribbling is common in infants with myelomeningocele. Applying pressure to the suprapubic area is the best way to facilitate emptying of the bladder.

Families of the neonates with myelomeningocele need information and emotional support to deal with the multitude of problems associated with this disability.

		The Cardiac Anomalies		
Condition	Description	Symptoms	Treatment	Blood Shunting
Patent ductus arteriosus	Failure of the ductus arteriosus to close; often a complication of severe respiratory distress	• Recurrent apnea • Wide pulse pressure • Machine-like murmur, heard throughout systole and most of diastole	Spontaneous closure at 3 weeks, but until then, fluid regulation, respiratory support, and surgical ligation to constrict the ductus are vital	From pulmonary artery to aorta
Atrial septal defect (A.S.D.)	A communication between the left and right atria	• Systolic murmur • Otherwise no symptoms	Surgical repair to prevent congestive heart failure	Left to right
Ventricular septal defect (V.S.D.)	A communication between the right and left ventricles	• Failure to thrive • Frequent respiratory infections • Loud, harsh murmur • Systolic thrill	Spontaneous closure in the first year of life or surgical correction	Left to right
Tetralogy of Fallot (T.O.F.)	1. V.S.D. 2. Pulmonary stenosis 3. Right ventricular hypertrophy 4. Overriding aorta	• Cyanotic newborn • Cyanosis increases with age	Surgical repair between 18–36 months	Right to left

PATENT DUCTUS ARTERIOSUS

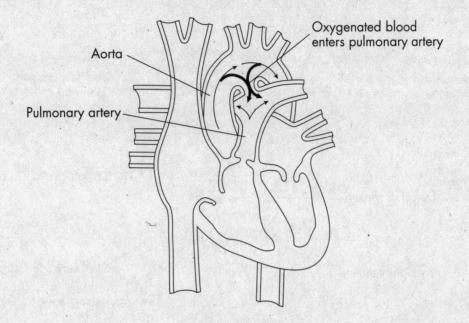

Aorta

Pulmonary artery

Oxygenated blood
enters pulmonary artery

ATRIAL SEPTAL DEFECT (A.S.D.)

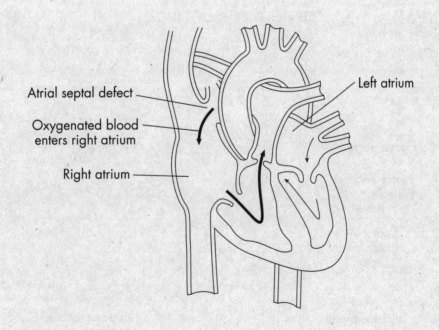

Atrial septal defect

Oxygenated blood
enters right atrium

Right atrium

Left atrium

VENTRICULAR SEPTAL DEFECT (V.S.D.)

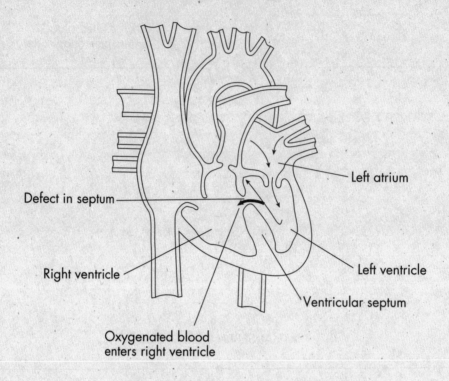

Left atrium

Defect in septum

Right ventricle

Left ventricle

Ventricular septum

Oxygenated blood
enters right ventricle

TETRALOGY OF FALLOT (T.O.F.)

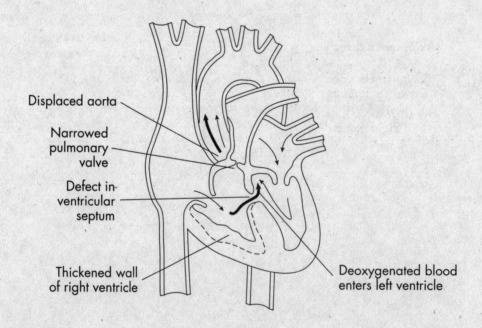

Displaced aorta

Narrowed
pulmonary
valve

Defect in
ventricular
septum

Thickened wall
of right ventricle

Deoxygenated blood
enters left ventricle

GASTROINTESTINAL ANOMALIES

Cleft lip and **palate** are defects in embryonic development that can occur independently or, more frequently, together. The cleft lip and palate make feeding and sucking extremely challenging, so nutrition is a nursing concern. Food can also leak through the infant's nose. Because of the extreme physical malformation, it is imperative to allay the fears of the parents and promote parent-infant bonding. The nurse should lead by example by displaying acceptance and composure around the baby. The cleft lip is usually repaired before the cleft palate, both of which are repaired surgically. An interdisciplinary team of specialists (orthodontist, speech therapist, otolaryngologist) is required to facilitate normal growth and development. As with any physical deformity, there may be problems with emotional and social adjustments of both the child and parents.

Label the following statements **true** or **false**:

59. _____ Cleft lip and palate are facial malformations including a defect in the lip and soft and/or hard palate.

60. _____ Infants with cleft palate who are fitted with special prosthetics can use bottles for feeding.

61. _____ Infants with cleft palate tend to swallow large amounts of air during feeding and therefore should be burped frequently.

62. _____ After cleft lip repair, a rubber-tipped syringe should be used for feeding.

Tracheoesophageal fistula (T.E.F.) is a rare malformation in which the trachea and esophagus do not separate into distinct structures. Clinical manifestations of a T.E.F. include excessive salivation, choking, drooling, coughing after feeding, cyanosis, and feedings returning through the nose. Nursing intervention may require oropharyngeal suctioning to correct cyanosis secondary to laryngospasm from an overflow of saliva. Gastric distention will occur as a result of air entering the stomach through the fistula. The infant should be placed with the head of the bed elevated to alleviate pressure from the stomach on the diaphragm and to prevent reflux. Prior to T.E.F. repair, the infant often has a gastrostomy tube placed for decompression and later for feeding. During gastrostomy feeds, the infant should be given a pacifier to promote sucking.

TRACHEOESOPHAGEAL FISTULA (T.E.F.)

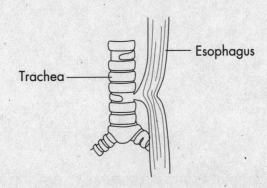

Esophagus

Trachea

Imperforate anus is suspected when a newborn fails to pass his first meconium. There is a bulging membrane at the place where the anus should be. Usual correction includes incision of the membrane, at which point the bowel and sphincter return to normal. In many cases, the newborn will have associated anal stenosis and require daily anal dilations by the nurse and continued by the parents at home. Checking for patency of the anus and rectum is a routine part of the newborn assessment.

IMPERFORATE ANUS

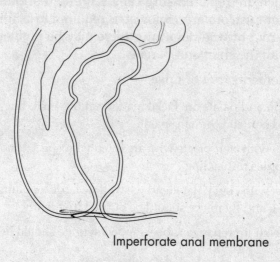

Imperforate anal membrane

Pyloric stenosis is a malformation of the pyloric sphincter (the stomach outlet) that impedes expulsion of stomach contents into the small intestine. The typical complaint of parents with an infant with pyloric stenosis is projectile vomiting (anywhere from 1 to 4 feet). The infant is at risk for dehydration and metabolic alkalosis due to excessive loss of potassium, hydrochloric acid, and chloride in the emesis. The vomitus typically contains stomach contents, mucus, and streaks of blood and is nonbilious. The infant fails to gain weight or may lose weight. Nursing care includes assuring fluid and electrolyte balance, controlling pain due to gastric distention, and supporting the parents. The infant can begin to take oral fluids approximately 6 hours after surgical correction, which usually takes place within 2 months of life.

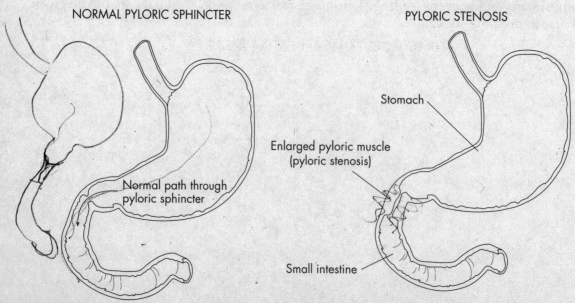

NORMAL PYLORIC SPHINCTER

PYLORIC STENOSIS

Normal path through pyloric sphincter

Stomach

Enlarged pyloric muscle (pyloric stenosis)

Small intestine

Necrotizing enterocolitis (N.E.C.) is an acute inflammatory disease of the bowel with increased incidence in preterm infants. The exact cause is uncertain, but N.E.C. seems to occur in infants whose gastrointestinal tract has been vascularly compromised. Intestinal ischemia occurs often secondary to asphyxia due to decreased cardiac output. Clinical signs include distended abdomen, gastric retention, and blood in stool or gastric contents. Onset is 4–10 days after birth. Treatment begins with prevention, therefore oral feedings are withheld for 24–48 hours for infants with believed asphyxia at birth. Treatment includes discontinuing oral feedings, initiating parenteral nutrition, abdominal decompression, IV antibiotics, and treating electrolyte imbalances. Surgery may be necessary to remove the necrotic areas of the bowel.

GENITOURINARY ANOMALIES

Inguinal hernias are very common in infancy—more so in males. They are characterized by inguinal swelling, which often disappear during rest periods and are reducible with gentle pressure. Inguinal hernias are, therefore, more prominent when the infant cries or strains. Surgical repair is the treatment of choice. Postoperatively, frequent diaper changes are important to keep the suture line clean, dry, and free of infection. Parents are instructed to give sponge baths instead of tub baths for 2–5 days.

Children with **undescended testicles (cryptorchidism)** are often given a trial dose of human chorionic gonadotropic hormone to promote descension of the testicles. This requires a series of injections over a few weeks. Otherwise, if the testicles do not fall spontaneously, surgical repair or orchiopexy is done before the child's second birthday.

UNDESCENDED TESTICLES

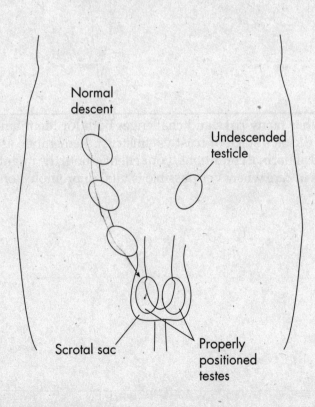

Normal descent

Undescended testicle

Scrotal sac

Properly positioned testes

You should be familiar with the following terms for the NCLEX-RN. Use the roots of the words to help you match them with the proper definition on the right:

63. C Cryptorchidism

A. urethra opens on the ventral surface of the penis or perineum

64. D Hydrocele

B. fibrous band of tissue that extends from the scrotum up the penis and pulls it ventrally into an arc

65. A Hypospadias

C. undescended testicles

66. B Congenital chordae

D. collection of fluid in the tunica vaginalis of the testicle or along the spermatic cord

HYPOSPADIAS

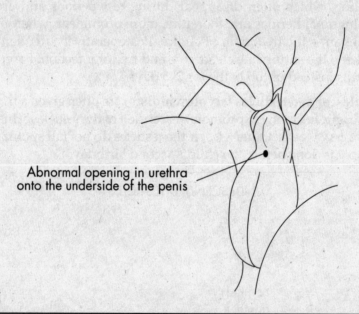

Abnormal opening in urethra onto the underside of the penis

KEEP IN MIND

The newborn period has many risks and challenges both for the infant and the parents. It is the beginning of Erikson's stage of trust vs. mistrust. Remember, as the nurse of babies with both normal and abnormal conditions, your client is both the infant and the parent, and including the parents in care whenever possible is vital to promote bonding and trust.

CHAPTER 15: EXERCISE ANSWERS

1. At birth many physiological changes occur. The most critical is the onset of **breathing**.

2. Additionally, **circulatory** changes allow the blood to flow through the newborn's lungs.

3. The transition from fetal circulation to neonatal circulation includes the functional closure of fetal shunts, including the **foramen ovale, ductus arteriosus,** and the **ductus venosus**. During the early neonatal period, functional heart murmurs can be auscultated.

4. Immediate care of the newborn includes establishing and maintaining respirations, preventing heat loss, and obtaining Apgar assessments at 1 minute and 5 minutes of life. The Apgar assessment rates the neonate's **heart rate, muscle tone, respiratory effort, color,** and **reflex irritability**.

5. **True**—The usual heart rate of a neonate is 120–160 b.p.m. and regular.

6. **False**—A soft cardiac murmur during the first month of life is not normal.

7. **False**—A vitamin K injection is given only if the parent decides to have it administered.

8. **True**—The yellowish color an infant develops by the third day of life is due to an immature liver.

9. **True**—A neonate's breathing pattern is abdominal and irregular with a rate between 30 and 60 per minute.

10. **True**—Periods of apnea up to 15 seconds in duration are normal for a newborn.

11. **True**—There is often a brick red stain on the neonate's diaper during the first week.

12. **True**—Meconium is black-green in color and is tenacious.

13. **True**—The cardiac sphincter of the neonate is not well developed, so regurgitation occurs if the stomach is too full.

14. **True**—Neonates normally lose 10 percent of their birth weight by day four of life.

15. **True**—Phenylketonuria testing is done after the ingestion of protein.

16. **False**—A neonate should be placed on a rigid feeding schedule.

17. **True**—Parent-infant relationships can be fostered during feeding times.

18. At 1 minute of life, the nurse assesses the neonate to have an apical heart rate of 90 b.p.m. and an irregular breathing pattern. The neonate is flaccid, cries when the nurse slaps his foot, and his extremities are cyanotic. This infant would receive an Apgar score of **5**.

19. At 5 minutes of life the nurse assesses the neonate and finds that the apical heart rate is 110 b.p.m. and his respirations remain irregular and slow. The neonate's extremities are flexed, he cries in response to a slap on the foot, and he is pink all over. The infant's Apgar score is **8**.

20. **B** Molding—**temporary changes in the shape of the head of a neonate as it accommodates to the birth canal during labor**

21. **C** Cephalohematoma—**due to the pressure of the presenting part against the cervix, blood from periosteum accumulates in the tissue of the infant's head, creating a circular swelling that does not cross suture lines**

22. **A** Caput succedaneum—**swelling or edema of the head of an infant during labor and delivery; crosses suture lines**

23. A neonate's mother strokes his cheek and he turns his head toward that side. This an example of the **rooting** reflex.

24. A neonate's mother places an object close to the baby's mouth and he attempts to suck. This is an example of the **sucking** reflex.

25. A neonate's father places his finger in the palm of the neonate's hand. The neonate flexes his fingers around his father's finger. This is an example of the **grasp** reflex.

26. A neonate's father runs his thumb up the middle undersurface of the neonate's foot. His toes separate and flare out. This is an example of the **Babinski** reflex.

27. A neonate's father runs his thumb up the lateral undersurface of his son's foot and his toes curl downward. This is an example of the **plantar** reflex.

28. There is a loud noise in the room and a neonate abducts his arms with flexion of elbows. This is an example of the **startle** reflex.

29. A neonate's brother bumps into the bassinet, causing a jarring motion. The neonate extends and abducts his extremities and fans his fingers. This is an example of the **Moro** reflex.

30. A neonate is lying prone and attempts crawling movements. This is an example of the **crawl** reflex.

31. A neonate's father supports him under both arms and places his feet on a firm surface. The neonate makes stepping movements. This is an example of the **step** reflex.

32. A neonate's head is turned to the right side by his mother. His right arm and leg extend, and his left arm and leg flex. This is an example of the **tonic neck** reflex.

33. Signs of respiratory distress in a newborn include:

    Grunting

    Retractions

    Stridor

    Unequal breath sounds

    Wheezing

34. Arrange the following parts of the abdominal assessment in the correct order of implementation:

    A. Inspection

    B. Auscultation

    C. Percussion

    D. Palpation

35. **C** Lanugo—**soft, fine, downy hair found on both preterm and term newborns**

36. **A** Mongolian spots—**dark spots on the lumbar region in the newborn children of non-Caucasian races**

37. **E** Acrocyanosis—**cyanosis of the hands and feet**

38. **D** Erythema toxicum—**pink, papular rash that may have purulent vesicles**

39. **F** Harlequin sign—**outlined color change as an infant lies on one side; the lower half of the body becomes pink and the upper half pales**

40. **B** Milia—**white, evanescent, pinhead-sized papules that occur on the face and less often on the trunk**

41. **True**—A newborn is labeled "preterm" when it is born before 37 weeks gestation.

42. **True**—A low birth weight infant is one who weighs less than 2,500 grams (5.5 pounds) at birth.

43. **True**—Preterm infants have lanugo on the face, less subcutaneous fat, and ears that are less supported by cartilage than term infants.

44. **False**—In the preterm infant, respirations are efficient and the neonate is not at greater risk than a full-term infant for respiratory distress.

45. **True**—Heat regulation is poorly developed in the neonate due to poor development of the central nervous system.

46. **True**—The nurse should first assess the neonate's hydration status.

47. **True**—The neonate will, most likely, require IV antibiotic treatment.

48. **True**—It is important to assess the neonate's vital signs.

49. **True**—Sepsis (infection) in infants is difficult to determine because there are no definitive signs.

50. **True**—To correct hydrocephalus and decrease intracranial pressure a ventricular-peritoneal shunt is often placed. Postoperative care includes monitoring for signs of cerebrospinal fluid infection and increased intracranial pressure.

51. **True**—Postoperative care for a ventricular-peritoneal shunt includes placing the infant on the non-operated side with the head of the bed elevated.

52. **True**—Hydrocephalus is often associated with myelomeningocele.

53. **True**—The earliest signs of hydrocephalus include increased head circumference and bulging fontanels.

54. **True**—Hydrocephalus is characterized by an accumulation of cerebrospinal fluid in the ventricles.

55. **True**—Increased intracranial pressure can be caused by any matter that tries to take up some of the fixed space of the cranium.

56. **True**—Myelomeningocele is a soft sac containing spinal fluid, meninges, spinal cord, and/or nerve roots protruding through a bony defect in the spine.

57. **False**—If a client has a lumbar myelomeningocele there is no effect on the lower extremities.

58. **True**—Overflow incontinence with constant dribbling is common in infants with myelomeningocele. Applying pressure to the suprapubic area is the best way to facilitate emptying of the bladder.

59. **True**—Cleft lip and palate are facial malformations including a defect in the lip and soft and/or hard palate.

60. **True**—Infants with cleft palate who are fitted with special prosthetics can use bottles for feeding.

61. **True**—Infants with cleft palate tend to swallow large amounts of air during feeding and therefore should be burped frequently.

62. **True**—After cleft lip, repair a rubber-tipped syringe should be used for feeding.

63. **C** Cryptorchidism—**undescended testicles**

64. **D** Hydrocele—**collection of fluid in the tunica vaginalis of the testicle or along the spermatic cord**

65. **A** Hypospadias—**urethra opens on the ventral surface of the penis or perineum**

66. **B** Congenital chordae—**fibrous band of tissue that extends from the scrotum up the penis and pulls it ventrally into an arc**

1. A premature newborn is being observed for manifestations of respiratory distress syndrome, which include

(1) nasal flaring.
(2) clubbing of the fingers.
(3) tracheal deviation.
(4) bradypnea.

2. A 6-week-old male infant is admitted to the pediatric floor for persistent and forceful vomiting. On examination of the abdomen, an olive-shaped mass is palpated in the right upper quadrant. The emesis will most likely consist of

(1) bile.
(2) blood.
(3) mucous.
(4) breast milk or formula.

3. Which of the following reflexes would alert the nurse to a possible problem in an otherwise normal newborn?

(1) Positive rooting reflex
(2) Negative Babinski's reflex
(3) Positive Moro reflex
(4) Positive corneal reflex

4. A parent calls a nurse and is very upset because her newborn daughter is having loose, frequent (5 per day), yellow stools. What should be the nurse's response to this parent?

(1) Send the client and her newborn to the emergency room for rehydration.
(2) Ask if the baby has tears to assess hydration status.
(3) Frequent diarrhea is normal, but ask questions about fluid intake and urine output to assess hydration.
(4) Ask questions about accompanying signs of pain.

5. Which of the following situations would alert the nurse to a possible problem with an infant in the newborn nursery?

(1) Eating 1.5 ounces every 3 hours
(2) Circumoral cyanosis during feeding
(3) Wet burping after feeding
(4) Stooling during feeding

6. A new father observes the nurse instilling eye drops in his newborn's eyes and angrily asks, "Why are you doing that?" The nurse responds, "To protect the eyes because

(1) the exposure to light may cause swelling and irritation."
(2) they may have come into contact with bacteria during birth."
(3) newborns don't have tears for about 2 months."
(4) it is mandated by state and federal law."

7. A breast-feeding mother is concerned because her newborn daughter has lost 6 ounces in the first 2 days of life. Which of the following responses by the nurse would be most therapeutic?	(1) "Maybe you should bottle-feed her until she starts to gain weight." (2) "Perhaps we should review breast-feeding procedures." (3) "Most infants lose some of their birth weight in the first few days." (4) "How many wet diapers has your daughter had today?"
8. Since infants are at risk for hypothermia, the nurse should do which of the following when examining an infant?	(1) Place the infant in an incubator. (2) Place the infant under a radiant heat source. (3) Undress and dress the newborn quickly. (4) Undress only the body area being examined.
9. The flexion of the newborn's elbows with abduction of the arms and hands clenched in response to a sudden loud sound is known as the	(1) Moro reflex. (2) doll's eye reflex. (3) placing reflex. (4) startle reflex.

CHAPTER 15: NCLEX-RN STYLE ANSWERS

1.

(1) CORRECT — Nasal flaring, grunting, intercostal retractions, duskiness or cyanosis are some of the manifestations of respiratory distress syndrome.

(2) *ELIMINATE* — Although clubbing of the fingers indicates chronically decreased arterial oxygen levels, it is most often associated with a compensatory polycythemia—which takes a long time to develop.

(3) *ELIMINATE* — Among the causes of tracheal deviation are pneumothorax, large pleural effusion, mediastinal mass, and neck tumor.

(4) *ELIMINATE* — Tachypnea, not bradypnea, is seen in respiratory distress syndrome.

CATEGORY 10 PHYSIOLOGICAL ADAPTATION

2.

(4) CORRECT — Due to outlet obstruction in pyloric stenosis, the emesis consists primarily of oral feedings.

(1) *ELIMINATE* — Bile would indicate a lower obstruction.

(2) *ELIMINATE* — Not associated with an abdominal mass.

(3) *ELIMINATE* — Not associated with an abdominal mass.

CATEGORY 10 PHYSIOLOGICAL ADAPTATION

3. | (2) CORRECT | A Babinski's reflex should be positive (fanning of the toes) until 2 years of age.
| (1) ELIMINATE | A positive rooting reflex is normal in a newborn.
| (3) ELIMINATE | A positive Moro reflex is normal in a newborn.
| (4) ELIMINATE | A positive corneal reflex is normal in a newborn.

CATEGORY 04 PREVENTION AND EARLY DETECTION OF DISEASE

4. | (3) CORRECT | While such stools would be a cause for concern in older children and adults, loose, frequent, yellow stools are normal in newborns. The nurse should ask questions about intake and urine output to assess hydration. However, most parents just need to be reassured of the normalcy of these stools.
| (1) ELIMINATE | There is nothing in the question to indicate that the baby is dehydrated.
| (2) ELIMINATE | Not a proper way to assess hydration.
| (4) ELIMINATE | Parent has given you no indication that the baby is in pain.

CATEGORY 03 GROWTH AND DEVELOPMENT THROUGH THE LIFE SPAN

5. | (2) CORRECT | Periorbital cyanosis is the symptom of possible cardiac problems.
| (1) ELIMINATE | Eating 1.5 ounces every 3 hours is a normal finding.
| (3) ELIMINATE | Burping after feeding with some formula being expelled is normal.
| (4) ELIMINATE | Newborns often have a bowel movement during a feeding.

CATEGORY 04 PREVENTION AND EARLY DETECTION OF DISEASE

6. | (2) CORRECT | Eye prophylaxis is necessary to protect against exposure to gonorrhea and chlamydia.
| (1) ELIMINATE | Birth trauma rather than exposure to light is responsible for edema of the eyelids following delivery.
| (3) ELIMINATE | While this statement is true, the installation of eye drops at birth is prophylaxis against infection.
| (4) POSSIBLE | Eye prophylaxis is mandated by law, but this response does not provide the parent with an adequate rationale for the mandate.

CATEGORY 04 PREVENTION AND EARLY DETECTION OF DISEASE

7. | (3) CORRECT | Initial weight loss of 5–10% of birth weight is normal because of loss of extracellular fluid and the passage of meconium.
| (1) ELIMINATE | Breast feeding should not be discouraged because both bottle-feeding and breast-feeding infants experience weight loss in the first few days of life.
| (2) POSSIBLE | Reviewing breast-feeding techniques may be reassuring to the mother but would not help her to understand that weight loss is expected in the first few days of life.
| (4) ELIMINATE | While this statement would provide information about intake, it would not address the client's concern about weight loss.

CATEGORY 07 BASIC CARE AND COMFORT

8.   **(4) CORRECT**   By undressing only the area to be examined, the nurse conserves body heat and helps to safeguard against hypothermia.

     (1) *ELIMINATE*   It is not necessary to place the infant in an incubator.

     (2) *ELIMINATE*   It is not necessary to place the infant under a radiant heat source.

     (3) *ELIMINATE*   This technique promotes rushing through the examination, and the infant may become hypothermic while undressed.

CATEGORY 03 GROWTH AND DEVELOPMENT THROUGH THE LIFE SPAN

---

9.   **(4) CORRECT**   The startle reflex is elicited with a sudden loud noise. The infant abducts his arm, flexes his elbows, and fans his fingers.

     (1) *POSSIBLE*   The Moro reflex is elicited with the sudden jarring of the infant. The extremities extend and abduct while the fingers fan.

     (2) *ELIMINATE*   The doll's eye reflex is an abnormal neurological reflex. The eyes lag behind when the head is turned from side to side.

     (3) *ELIMINATE*   The placing reflex is elicited when the foot is placed next to a solid object and the infant is held upright. The infant will raise up his leg as if to step up.

CATEGORY 03 GROWTH AND DEVELOPMENT THROUGH THE LIFE SPAN

16

THE INFANT

WHAT YOU NEED TO KNOW

The stage of infancy lasts from 28 days to 1 year of life. This period of growth is characterized by Erikson's developmental stage of trust vs. mistrust. As you progress through this chapter, bear in mind that the physical assessment cannot be separated from developmental assessment in children.

To put you in the proper mindset to review infancy, label the following characteristics as appropriate for an **infant**, a **toddler**, or a **preschooler**:

1. _____ Has imaginary friends

2. _____ Can sit with support

3. _____ Self-blends with environment

4. _____ Parallel play

5. _____ Toilet training

6. _____ Handedness is established

7. _____ Well-developed pincer grasp

8. _____ Separation anxiety begins

9. _____ Magical thinking

10. _____ Recognizes own name

ASSESSMENT OF THE INFANT

The importance of the infant examination in providing the opportunity for early recognition of problems is very critical. Initially, the inexperienced examiner will find physical assessment time-consuming and frustrating, but with experience and repetition the infant will be viewed as a whole being, and not as a crying set of systems.

Before performing any component of the physical examination, the nurse must obtain a thorough history of genetics, neurological problems, maternal medical problems, use of medication, and alcohol and drug use during pregnancy.

Some of the following concepts will be familiar to you, as there are similarities with the newborn assessment.

HEAD, EYES, EARS, NOSE, AND THROAT (HEENT)

Examination of the head and neck requires visual inspection, palpation, use of an ophthalmoscope, auscultation, and, occasionally, transillumination. The occipital-frontal circumference (OFC) of the head is measured with an inelastic tape. The OFC is plotted on the growth chart at every well-child visit up to 36 months. **Microcephaly** is an OFC below the 10 percent for gestational age. **Macrocephaly** is diagnosed when the OFC is above 50 percent, but the infant's weight and length are normal for gestational age.

Inspection and palpation of the infant's skull are necessary to identify bones, sutures, and fontanels. Sutures separate the skull bones, and fontanels occur where two sutures meet. The anterior fontanel is normally described as flat and soft. A tense or bulging fontanel may be a sign of increased intracranial pressure or may occur with crying. A sunken fontanel is a sign of dehydration.

11. The anterior fontanel normally closes by _____.

12. The posterior fontanel is small and closes by approximately _____.

13. Facial movement must be _____, even when the infant is crying.

The ear is assessed for shape, symmetry, and auditory function. Also assess the presence and patency of the auditory canal. The infant should start to cry, stiffen, or exhibit the startle (Moro) reflex at the sound of a loud noise during early office visits.

Nystagmus is a rapid, searching movement of the eyeballs that usually disappears by 3–4 months of age. Persistence may indicate a neurological problem.

The nose should be symmetrical and placed vertically on the midline. Examination of the mouth is easiest when the infant is crying. The cry should be assessed during the exam for quality, strength, pitch, and hoarseness. White patches on the tongue and mucous membranes may be residual milk. If not easily removed, these lesions are usually **candidiasis** (oral **thrush**).

14. Thrush is best treated with the medication _____.

NEUROLOGICAL ASSESSMENT

Evaluation of muscle tone involves examination of resting power, passive tone, and active tone of all major muscle groups. **Hypotonia** (poor head control, limp extremities) is the most consistent abnormality observed in the neurological examination. **Hypertonia** (jittery, startles easily, arms and hands are tightly flexed, legs stiffly extended) is a less common finding in infancy. The infant should have the ability to hold his head erect momentarily and turn his head from side to side in prone position in early office visits. Assessment of the sensory system includes a response to touch and pain.

Cranial nerves II–XII are also tested. Cranial nerve I is rarely tested because disturbances in olfaction are not usually correlated with neurological dysfunction.

Quickly review cranial nerves here by filling in the names of each nerve:

CN	Fill in the Name	Dysfunction	Interventions
I	_____	Decreased sense of smell	• Inability to smell is often accompanied by impaired taste and weight loss. • Smell serves as a warning for fire, spoiled food, etc.
II	_____	Decreased visual acuity and visual fields	• Clients require frequent reorientation to environment. • Position objects around client in deference to visual field impairment.
III IV VI	_____ _____ _____	Double vision (diplopia)	• Intermittent eye patching for diplopia. • Lubricate eyes to protect against corneal abrasions.
V	_____	3 (tri-) potential dysfunctions: decreased facial sensation, inability to chew, and decreased corneal reflexes	• Caution in shaving and mouth care. • Choose easy-to-chew foods with high caloric content. • Protect corneas from abrasion by using lubricant.
VII	_____	Facial weakness and decreased taste (anterior tongue)	• Cosmetic approach to hiding facial weakness. • Oral hygiene. • Account for decreased food intake.
VIII	_____	Decreased hearing, imbalance, vertigo (dizziness), tinnitus (ringing in ears)	• **Safety!** • Move slowly to prevent nausea and emesis. • Assist ambulation.
IX X	_____ _____	Dysarthria (poor speech), dysphagia (inability to swallow), cardiac and respiratory instability	• Maintain **airway**. • Prevent aspiration. • Swallow therapy.
XI	_____	Inability to turn shoulders or turn head from side to side	• Mobility aids. • Physical therapy.
XII	_____	Dysarthria, dysphagia	• Maintain **airway**. • Prevent aspiration. • Swallow therapy.

FUNCTIONS OF CRANIAL NERVES

Some cranial nerves function principally to deliver sensory information from organs, such as the ears, nose, and eyes, to the brain. Others carry messages that move the tongue, eyes, facial, and other muscles, or stimulate glands such as the salivary glands. A few have both sensory and motor functions. One of the nerves—the tenth cranial, or vagus nerve—is one of the most important components of the parasympathetic nervous system. It functions to maintain the rhythmic automatic function of the internal body machinery. It has branches to all the main digestive organs, the heart, and the lungs.

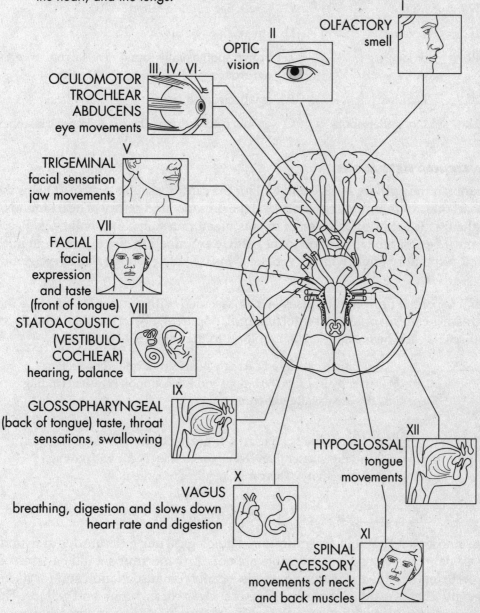

I
OLFACTORY
smell

II
OPTIC
vision

III, IV, VI
OCULOMOTOR
TROCHLEAR
ABDUCENS
eye movements

V
TRIGEMINAL
facial sensation
jaw movements

VII
FACIAL
facial
expression
and taste
(front of tongue)

VIII
STATOACOUSTIC
(VESTIBULO-
COCHLEAR)
hearing, balance

IX
GLOSSOPHARYNGEAL
(back of tongue) taste, throat
sensations, swallowing

X
VAGUS
breathing, digestion and slows down
heart rate and digestion

XI
SPINAL
ACCESSORY
movements of neck
and back muscles

XII
HYPOGLOSSAL
tongue
movements

SKIN ASSESSMENT

A complete examination of the skin involves both inspection and palpation under bright, natural lighting in a warm room. Observe the skin and note size, color, and placement of any discoloration or markings. Palpation permits examination of the underlying dermis, thickness of skin, presence of edema, and irregularities of texture.

Poor skin turgor may indicate dehydration or poor nutritional status. Review some of the terminology of skin lesions below by matching with the definitions on the right:

15. ____ Papule   A. small, raised, whitish lesion; usually on the face

16. ____ Macule   B. superficial inflammatory condition; redness, itching

17. ____ Milia   C. small, flat, colored lesion

18. ____ Eczema   D. streak, line

19. ____ Striae   E. brown spot; usually found near sacrum in certain ethnic groups

20. ____ Jaundice   F. small, elevated lesion

21. ____ Mongolian spots   G. yellow coloring, usually due to hepatic insufficiency

CARDIOVASCULAR ASSESSMENT

Auscultation is the primary assessment tool for the cardiovascular system. It helps the nurse assess heart rate, rhythm, and regularity, and the presence and clarity of heart sounds. Again, inspect the infant's skin color, color of mucus membranes, lips and nail beds. Respiratory activity must be observed in relation to the cardiac examination. For example, an infant with unlabored respiratory effort who is cyanotic is most likely cyanotic due to congenital heart disease.

The character of the peripheral pulses is best assessed with a quiet infant. Use the index finger to assess carotid, brachial, radial, femoral, popliteal, posterior tibial, and the dorsalis pedis pulses. Is each heartbeat perfusing blood to the infant's extremities?

22. _____ is defined as a heart rate less than normal for age. For infants, it is usually less than 80 b.p.m. and is a common transient finding. These episodes are usually self-correcting.

23. _____ is defined as a heart rate greater than normal for age. For infants, it is usually greater than 180 b.p.m. It may occur with crying, feeding, fever, or activity. This rarely requires treatment.

24. _____ are caused by turbulent blood flow.

There are innocent and pathological **murmurs**. Pathological murmurs are due to an underlying cardiovascular disease, innocent murmurs are not. Any murmur should be assessed for its time of occurrence in the cardiac cycle, for its location on auscultation and for its loudness and intensity. There are other abnormal sounds such as clicks, hums, and gallops. The nurse should become familiar with normal infant heart sounds and refer any other auscultated sounds for further evaluation.

CHEST AND RESPIRATORY SYSTEM ASSESSMENT

Inspection of the infant's chest should begin with an overall assessment of the infant's color, tone, and activity. The color should be pink and well-perfused with deviations including cyanosis, ruddiness, and paleness.

The infant should appear relaxed with symmetrical abdominal respirations. The infant uses the abdomen as the primary muscle of respiration. Asymmetrical breathing may result from a diaphragmatic hernia, cardiac lesion, pneumothorax, or phrenic nerve damage.

The infant should have a flexed posture and active movement of all four limbs.

Inspect the rate, quality, and pattern of respirations.

25. Tachypnea of an infant is defined as respirations greater than ___/minute.

26. Bradypnea of an infant is defined as respirations less than ___/minute.

To auscultate breath sounds, use the bell of a warmed stethoscope. Breath sounds are usually more coarse in the infant than in the adult because an infant has less subcutaneous tissue to muffle transmission. Adventitious sounds include rales (high-pitched or moist sound that results from the passage of air through fluid), rhonchi (loud, low, coarse sounds like a snore), and wheezes (musical sound, like a squeak, which is produced as air passes through narrowed passageways).

ABDOMINAL AND GASTROINTESTINAL SYSTEM ASSESSMENT

27. List, in proper order, the four components of an abdominal assessment:
    A. _____
    B. _____
    C. _____
    D. _____

Normal abdominal movements are synchronous with chest movements. The normal full-term infant has a slightly rounded, soft, and symmetrical abdomen. An **omphalocele** is the herniation of the umbilicus through which abdominal contents and other organs may protrude. The difference between an omphalocele and an umbilical hernia is the omphalocele is covered only with a thin, translucent sac. Nursing intervention includes covering the area with a moist dressing until the infant can be taken to the operating room. Complications may include rupture and infection. **Gastroschisis** is also a herniation of abdominal contents, but is usually located to the right of the midline without involvement of the umbilicus and is not enclosed in a protective sac. Surgical intervention is required to correct the evisceration. The liver can be palpated in the infant. Don't panic about these big words, just recognize them. Refer to the list of word roots to help tackle this kind of vocabulary. Chances are there will be words like these on the NCLEX-RN that you've never seen before. Practice dealing with them now!

GENITOURINARY SYSTEM ASSESSMENT

Fill in the blanks below with the correct word from our review of the newborn:

28. _____ is present when one or both testes have not descended completely into the scrotum.

29. _____ is a scrotal mass containing clear fluid. This usually resolves by 6 months of age.

30. _____ is the condition in which the urethra opens on the underside of the penis.

MUSCULOSKELETAL SYSTEM ASSESSMENT

A thorough evaluation of the musculoskeletal system involves inspection and palpation. One must evaluate posture and positioning while looking for gross anomalies, discomfort from bone or joint movement, and range of motion. The nurse is also looking at the configuration and mobility of the back. Early diagnosis of musculoskeletal disorders and early intervention lead to favorable outcomes. Disorders that affect the musculoskeletal system may also originate from the nervous system.

The examiner should be able to accurately describe skeletal positions and muscle movements during the examination, i.e., flexion: bending a limb at a joint; pronation: turning face-down. These movements are summarized in the illustration below.

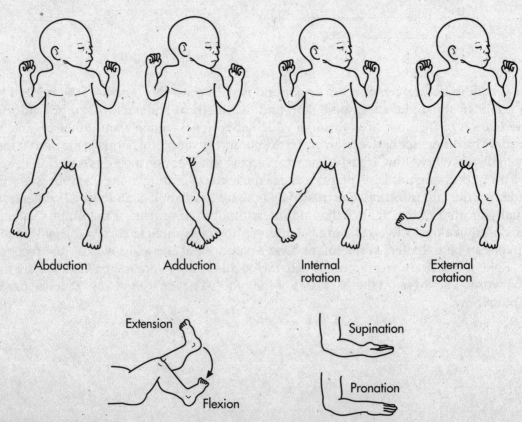

Abduction   Adduction   Internal rotation   External rotation

Extension   Flexion   Supination   Pronation

General inspection includes observation for symmetry of movement, and for size, shape, alignment, and position of muscles and joints. Asymmetry in range of motion may indicate weakness, paralysis, fractures, or infection. Failure to move an extremity may indicate a brachial plexus palsy or a spinal cord injury.

The spine should be examined with notation of any skin disruption, tufts of hair, soft or cystic masses, hemangiomas, a pilonidal dimple, cysts, or sinus tracts. One of these conditions may be a sign of a congenital spinal or neurological anomaly (e.g., spina bifida).

31. _____ is used to evaluate hip stability. The infant's knee and hip is flexed, then the thigh is grasped with the third or fourth finger placed over the greater trochanter. The leg is first abducted with a lifting motion and then adducted.

32. _____ should be suspected when an audible or palpable "clunk" is noted as the femoral head passes over the acetabulum.

HEALTH PROMOTION DURING INFANCY

Parental education is the primary method of promoting health during infancy. New parents need an abundance of instruction before leaving the hospital following the birth of their child. Constant reinforcement is necessary, and nurses are in a perfect position to provide it. Following are some issues you should be aware of as you put parents in the best position possible to raise their babies.

NUTRITION DURING INFANCY

While we discuss this topic in detail in Chapter 24, we highlight some specifics here as well.

- Human milk is the most desirable food for the infant for the first 6 months of life.

- Human milk can be expressed by hand or pump and safely refrigerated for 48 hours or frozen in plastic bottles for up to 6 months.

- An acceptable alternative to breast feeding is commercial, iron-fortified formula. The only supplementation needed is fluoride if the local water supply is not fluoridated. Fluoride is recommended for all infants 2 weeks of age or older who live in areas with suboptimal levels of fluoride in the local water supply (i.e., well water). Fluoride is also recommended for exclusively breast-fed infants regardless of the fluoride content of their water, and infants who consume relatively little fluoridated tap water (i.e., those who receive ready-to-eat formula).

- Solid foods should be introduced between 4–6 months of age. Give one new food at a time over a few days to determine allergy or intolerance.

- Feeding an infant solid foods too soon may expose the infant to antigens that may induce food protein allergies.

- Developmentally, infants are not ready for solids until 4 months of age because of the presence of the **extrusion reflex,** which pushes food out of the mouth.

Between the ages of 6 and 12 months, human milk/formula remain the primary source of nutrition, but the gastrointestinal tract is now mature enough to handle complex nutrients and is less sensitive to potentially allergenic foods. In addition, tooth eruption facilitates chewing and the extrusion reflex has disappeared by this time. Improved head control, grasping, and improved eye-hand coordination also allow self-feeding.

Rice cereal is suggested as the initial food because of its easy digestibility and low allergenic potential. Rice can be followed by barley, oatmeal, and high-protein, ready-to-serve infant dry cereal. Cereal can be mixed with formula, breast milk, water, or fruit juice. The vitamin C content of the juice enhances the absorption of iron in the cereal.

Weaning the infant from the breast or bottle to a cup is usually best accomplished during the latter part of the first year of life, at approximately 8 months. Weaning should progress gradually by replacing one bottle or breast feeding at a time with a covered cup with a spout. The nighttime feeding is usually the last to be weaned.

SLEEP

Remember the newborn who slept for about 20 hours a day? Well, by the time the infant weighs 10–12 pounds or is around 3 months old, sleep takes up only about 9 to 11 hours of the night. The total daily sleep should be about 14 hours, including naps. The number of naps varies but the infant usually takes two a day by the end of the first year.

IMMUNIZATIONS

Since the advent of immunizations there has been a dramatic reduction in infectious diseases in children. However, with success, both complacency and unwarranted fears have ensued. Practitioners are required to fully inform families of the risks and benefits of each vaccine, to record certain information, and to report selected post-vaccine events such as anaphylaxis, encephalopathy, or paralytic poliomyelitis.

Immunizations are introduced in the nursery, starting with the hepatitis B vaccine. Children born prematurely should receive the full dose of each vaccine at the appropriate chronological age. This 1996 schedule of immunizations is taken from the American Academy of Pediatrics recommendations:

Recommended Immunization Schedules Initiated During Infancy										
	Months								Years	
	0	1	2	4	6	12	15	18	4–6	11–12
Hepatitis B	#1		#2			#3				If not yet taken
Diphtheria Tetanus Pertussis (DTP)			#1	#2	#3		#4			
H. influenzae Type B			#1	#2	#3		#4			
Polio			#1	#2	#3				#4	
Measles Mumps Rubella (MMR)						#1			#2	
Varicella zoster virus						#1				If not yet taken and no history of chicken pox
Tuberculin test (Td)						Test				Frequency of testing depends on individual's risk of developing TB.

The inactivated polio vaccine is recommended for routine infant vaccination.

INJURY PREVENTION

Throughout childhood, constant supervision is essential to prevent injury. During infancy, as the child learns to roll over and crawl and develops eye-hand coordination, the risk for injury increases exponentially.

COMMON HEALTH PROBLEMS OF INFANCY

SUDDEN INFANT DEATH SYNDROME

Sudden infant death syndrome (S.I.D.S.) is defined as the sudden, unexpected death of an infant under 1 year of age that remains unexplained after an autopsy. It is **the leading cause of death** in children between the ages of 1 month and 1 year. The nurse's role is to assist the parents in coping with the sudden death of their child.

Infants at the greatest risk for S.I.D.S. include those who:

- Have a family history of S.I.D.S. (especially siblings)
- Have a history of seizures
- Are born prematurely

A history of apnea does not appear to be a factor in the occurrence of S.I.D.S. Parents should be instructed that infants should sleep on their backs or propped on their sides until they are able to roll over on their own.

APNEA OF INFANCY

Apnea of infancy refers to a pathological apnea (cessation of respirations ≥ 20 seconds with accompanying cyanosis, pallor, bradycardia or hypotonia), which is an apparent life-threatening event. It can be a symptom of many disorders including sepsis, seizures, upper airway abnormalities, gastroesophageal reflux, hypoglycemia, or other metabolic problems. Treatment usually involves continuous home monitoring of cardiorespiratory rhythms and/or the use of methylxanthines (theophylline or caffeine).

The nurse can be a major source of knowledge and support to the family in terms of education about the disease, the equipment, observation of the infant, and immediate intervention, including cardiorespiratory intervention.

33. Apnea lasting longer than ___ seconds is abnormal in children of any age.

SKIN DISORDERS

A number of skin disorders manifest themselves during infancy. **Diaper dermatitis** peaks between the ages of 9 and 12 months. It may be associated with decreased frequency of diaper changes and diet changes. It is caused by prolonged and repetitive contact with an irritant, principally urine, feces, soaps, detergents, ointments, and friction. Treatment is related to the source. Occasionally, low-potency topical steroids are used. *Candida* infections are treated with nystatin ointment.

Parents need to be educated to change the diaper as soon as it becomes wet. Removing the diaper and exposing the buttocks to light and air promotes healing, but good hygiene is essential in prevention.

Seborrheic dermatitis is an inflammatory, scaling eruption most commonly found on the scalp (**cradle cap**), though it can involve the eyelids (**blepharitis**), external ear canal (**otitis externa**), nasolabial folds, and inguinal region. The etiology is unknown. Although it occurs in an area with a large number of sebaceous glands, there is no proof that it is caused by increased sebum production. Seborrheic dermatitis also occurs in adolescents. On examination, the nurse finds evidence of pruritis, flaking of the scalp, and dandruff. Cradle cap can be treated by rubbing baby oil into the scalp to soften crusts 20 minutes before shampooing. The parents should be instructed to shampoo their child's scalp daily with baby shampoo, using a soft brush. Toddlers or adolescents may use an antiseborrheic shampoo (Selsun or Sebulex) every other day.

Atopic dermatitis (**eczema**) usually begins during infancy and is associated with an allergy. The disorder can be controlled but not cured, so the goals of management are to:

- Relieve the pruritis
- Hydrate the skin
- Reduce inflammation
- Prevent secondary infection

Management includes avoiding exposure to skin irritants like overheating, overdrying, and administration of medications such as antihistamines and topical steroids.

Laryngotracheobronchitis (most common form of croup)

Croup is a general term applied to a symptom complex. It is an inflammation of the larynx, trachea, and bronchi. It is characterized by a narrowing of the air passages, which causes edema of the respiratory mucosa. Croup is most often seen in children ages 3 months to 3 years, and is usually of viral origin. Croup is usually preceded by a upper respiratory infection.

Symptoms observed in the child with croup include: irritability, "brassy" or "barking" cough, hoarseness, restlessness, inspiratory stridor, anorexia, fever, nausea and vomiting, and rales, wheezing, or rhonchi on auscultation.

At home management involves observing for signs of respiratory obstruction, bed rest, cool, humidified air, fluids, and antipyretic measures (if needed). This is the disorder in which you tell the parents to put the child in a steamy bathroom to alleviate acute croup episodes.

Nurses need to perform assessments with careful observations of respiratory pattern: are nasal flaring, retractions, or grunting present? These are signs of respiratory distress, as we've discussed. Observation of pallor or cyanosis, association of dyspnea with pain, rest, or exertion may also be noted. Observe for any signs or symptoms of infections, a cough, the presence of adventitious breath sounds, and appearance of sputum.

Epiglottitis

Epiglottitis is an inflammation of the supraglottis and epiglottis generally caused by *Haemophilus influenzae* bacteria. It has an abrupt onset and progresses rapidly. The child will insist on sitting forward, leaning forward with chin and mouth open, and tongue protruding. The child may appear irritable, anxious, or apprehensive, and have a "muffled" voice. The throat is red and inflamed with a large cherry-red, edematous epiglottis. The throat of a child with epiglottitis should only be examined by a trained professional under extreme care. Emergency endotracheal equipment or tracheostomy equipment should be available. Antibiotics are used to eradicate bacterial organisms.

THE CHILD WITH EPIGLOTTITIS

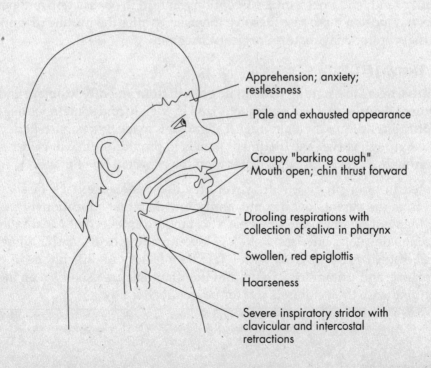

Apprehension; anxiety; restlessness

Pale and exhausted appearance

Croupy "barking cough"
Mouth open; chin thrust forward

Drooling respirations with collection of saliva in pharynx

Swollen, red epiglottis

Hoarseness

Severe inspiratory stridor with clavicular and intercostal retractions

GASTROINTESTINAL DIFFICULTIES

Spitting up refers to the dribbling of unswallowed formula after a feeding. **Regurgitation** refers to the return of undigested food from the stomach, usually accompanied by burping. Helpful measures to prevent both conditions include burping the infant frequently and minimizing handling after feeding.

Colic is characterized by bouts of abdominal pain in which the infant has a shrill cry and pulls his knees up to his abdomen. The colicky infant places a major emotional strain on parent-child attachment and family relationships. The nurse must stress to parents that, despite the crying and obvious pain, the infant is doing well. In addition, it is important to allow time for parents to verbalize their frustration with their colicky infant. Colic usually disappears by 3 months of age. Encourage the parent to arrange for "free time."

Diarrhea is a sudden increase in the number of stools with an increasingly watery consistency. Any part of the gastrointestinal (GI) tract can be involved: gastroenteritis, enteritis, enterocolitis, and colitis. The stools may be green in color. **Acute diarrhea** occurs with an infection to the GI tract, a toxic reaction to poisons, introducing certain foods too early, or an infectious process outside of the GI tract. **Chronic diarrhea** may be associated with a malabsorption disorder, an anatomic defect, abnormal gastric motility, or an inflammatory response.

The water and electrolyte loss that accompanies diarrhea places the infant at high risk for dehydration and acid-base imbalance. Signs of dehydration will vary, depending on the degree of diarrhea and other symptoms: vomiting, sunken fontanel, decreased or absent tearing, sunken eyeballs, irritability, lethargy, decreased cry, mild (5 percent) to marked (15 percent) weight loss, pallor, decreased urination, and dry mucous membranes. Oral rehydrating solutions such as **Pedialyte** help to replace the necessary liquid and electrolytes, but the cause of the diarrhea must be addressed.

Intussusception is the condition in which part of the intestine falls forward into an adjoining part. The cause is usually unknown, but it is most common in infants 3–12 months of age. Symptoms include currant jellylike stools (know this for the NCLEX-RN!) and abdominal pain, distention, and tenderness. Intussusception can lead to obstruction and perforation of the intestine, but most of these cases resolve themselves after the routine diagnostic barium enema. Intussusception may require surgical correction.

FAILURE TO THRIVE (F.T.T.)

Failure to thrive refers to a state of inadequate growth from inability to obtain and/or use the calories required for growth. F.T.T. is characterized by weight and sometimes height that falls below the fifth percentile for the child's age. Diagnosis is made by a persistent deviation from an established growth curve. The treatment goal is to provide sufficient calories to support "catch-up" growth: a rate of growth greater than the expected rate for age.

Factors related to poor prognosis are severe feeding resistance, lack of awareness and cooperation from the parent, low-income family, low maternal educational level, and early onset F.T.T. Many of these children possess substandard intellectual capabilities and have poorer language development, less well-developed reading skills, and a higher incidence of behavioral disturbance. The child with F.T.T. has a history of difficult feeding, vomiting, sleep disturbance, and irritability. Parents and their families are usually at an increased risk for poor bonding with their children and for potential abuse.

Specific nursing care depends on the identified cause of the F.T.T. If the etiology is organic, care is directed at the problem. If the problem is one of inadequate knowledge regarding child rearing, parental education and a social service referral are required. When serious psychosocial factors exist, hospitalization is required.

URINARY TRACT INFECTION (U.T.I.)

A U.T.I. is an infection of any part of the urinary tract: urethritis, cystitis, ureteritis, and pyelonephritis. A bacterium invades the urinary structures (usually the bladder, but possibly the upper collecting system and kidney). In children under age 21 the nurse may observe vomiting, diarrhea, poor feeding, failure to thrive, strong-smelling urine, and/or persistent diaper rash.

Treatment is with antibiotics, usually penicillins or sulfonamides. Fluids should be encouraged to help flush the bacteria out of the system. Education should be given to the family as to skills in caring for the child with a U.T.I., such as wiping the child from front to back and keeping diapers clean and dry.

REVIEW

Assess your knowledge of the following newborn and infant-related terminology by matching the word on the left with the correct description on the right:

34. ____ Cryptorchidism	A.	an irretractable foreskin
35. ____ Cyanosis, central	B.	the appearance of crossed eyes in the newborn due to muscular incoordination
36. ____ Hydrocephalus	C.	chronic inflammatory lipogranuloma of a meibomian gland in the upper or lower eyelid
37. ____ Lanugo	D.	failure of one or both testes to descend into the scrotum
38. ____ Phimosis	E.	an infant whose weight, length, and/or occipital-frontal circumference falls above the 90th percentile for gestational age when plotted on the growth curve
39. ____ Measles	F.	a circumscribed collection of clear fluid in the scrotum; may resolve spontaneously by 6 months of age
40. ____ Chalazion	G.	the turning of the body or body part face-down
41. ____ Nystagmus	H.	intestinal obstruction caused by invagination of a portion of the intestine onto itself; manifested by vomiting and currant jelly stools
42. ____ Colic	I.	a procedure for evaluating hip stability in a newborn

43. ____ Red retinal reflex

44. ____ Patent ductus arteriosus

45. ____ Strabismus

46. ____ Edema

47. ____ Hydrocele

48. ____ Large for gestational age

49. ____ Intussusception

50. ____ Fontanel

51. ____ Ortolani's click

52. ____ Pronation

53. ____ Rhonchi

J. adventitious breath sounds; lower in pitch and more musical than rales

K. acute, highly contagious viral illness; incubation period is 10–12 days; can be transmitted from 5th day of incubation

L. paroxysmal crying lasting several hours in an otherwise healthy baby

M. reflection of clear, red color from the retina when a bright light is directed at the newborn's lens

N. abnormally large amounts of fluid in the intercellular spaces of the body, usually in subcutaneous tissue

O. bluish discoloration of the skin and mucous membranes due to significant arterial desaturation

P. a membrane-covered space in the infant's skull reflecting incomplete ossification; occurs where two sutures meet

Q. accumulation of cerebrospinal fluid in the skull due to obstruction of cerebrospinal fluid pathways

R. a fine, soft, downy hair covering the fetus in utero and sometimes covering the neonate

S. a cardiac abnormality marked by failure of the ductus arteriosus to close after birth

T. a rapid, searching movement of the eyeballs seen in some newborns until 3–4 months of age

KEEP IN MIND

The nursing focus during infancy is on promotion of normal physical growth and psychosocial development. Think about the newborn and the infant: The small body size plays a major role in things that go wrong. Smaller passages mean it takes less to clog things up. The nurse is in a prime position to educate parents on prevention and early intervention for common problems.

CHAPTER 16: EXERCISE ANSWERS

1. **Preschooler**—Has imaginary friends
2. **Infant**—Can sit with support
3. **Infant**—Self-blends with environment
4. **Toddler**—Parallel play
5. **Toddler**—Toilet training
6. **Preschooler**—Handedness is established

7. **Infant**—Well-developed pincer grasp
8. **Infant**—Separation anxiety begins
9. **Preschooler**—Magical thinking
10. **Infant**—Recognizes own name
11. The anterior fontanel normally closes by **12–18 months**.
12. The posterior fontanel is small and closes by approximately **2–3 months**.
13. Facial movement must be **symmetrical**, even when the infant is crying.

	Cranial Nerve	**Dysfunction**	**Nursing Considerations**
I	**Olfactory**	Decreased sense of smell	• Inability to smell is often accompanied by impaired taste and weight loss.
II	**Optic**	Decreased visual acuity and visual fields	• Clients require frequent reorientation to environment. • Position objects around client in deference to visual field impairment.
III IV VI	**Oculomotor Trochlear Abducens**	Double vision (diplopia) Inability to blink (ptosis)	• Intermittent eye patching for diplopia. • Lubricate eyes to protect against corneal abrasions.
V	**Trigeminal**	3 (tri-) potential dysfunctions: decreased facial sensation, inability to chew, and decreased corneal reflexes Inability to turn shoulders	• Caution in shaving and mouth care. • Choose easy-to-chew foods with high caloric content. • Protect corneas from abrasion by using lubricant.
VII	**Facial**	Facial weakness and decreased taste (anterior tongue)	• Cosmetic approach to hiding facial weakness. • Oral hygiene.
VIII	**Vestibulocochlear**	Decreased hearing, imbalance, vertigo (dizziness), tinnitus (ringing in ears)	• Safety! • Move slowly to prevent nausea and emesis. • Assist ambulation.
IX X	**Glossopharyngeal** **Vagus**	Dysarthria (poor speech), dysphagia (inability to swallow), cardiac and respiratory instability	• Maintain airway. • Prevent aspiration. • Swallow therapy.
XI	**Accessory**	Inability to tilt head or turn head from side to side	• Mobility aids. • Physical therapy.
XII	**Hypoglossal**	Dysarthria, dysphagia	• Maintain airway. • Prevent aspiration. • Swallow therapy

14. Thrush is best treated with the medication **nystatin (Mycostatin)**.

15. **F**   Papule—**small, elevated lesion**

16. **C**   Macule—**small, flat, distinctly colored lesion**

17. **A**   Milia—**small, raised, whitish lesion; usually on the face**

18. **B**   Eczema—**superficial inflammatory condition; redness, itching**

19. **D**   Striae—**streak, line**

20. **G**   Jaundice—**yellow coloring, usually due to hepatic insufficiency**

21. **E**   Mongolian spots—**brown spot; usually found near sacrum in certain ethnic groups**

22. **Bradycardia** is defined as a heart rate less than normal for age. For infants, it is usually less than 80 b.p.m. and is a common transient finding. These episodes are usually self-correcting.

23. **Tachycardia** is defined as a heart rate greater than normal for age. For infants, it is usually greater than 180 b.p.m. It may occur with crying, feeding, fever, or activity. This rarely requires treatment.

24. **Murmurs** are caused by turbulent blood flow.

25. Tachypnea of an infant is defined as respirations greater than **60/minute**.

26. Bradypnea of an infant is defined as respirations less than **30/minute**.

27. List, in proper order, the four components of an abdominal assessment: **inspection, auscultation, percussion, palpation**.

28. **Cryptorchidism** is present when one or both testes have not descended completely into the scrotum.

29. **Hydrocele** is a scrotal mass containing clear fluid. This usually resolves by 6 months of age.

30. **Hypospadias** is the condition in which the urethra opens on the underside of the penis.

31. **Ortolani's click** is used to evaluate hip stability. The infant's knee and hip is flexed, then the thigh is grasped with the third or fourth finger placed over the greater trochanter. The leg is first abducted with a lifting motion and then adducted.

32. **Congenital hip dysplasia** should be suspected when an audible or palpable "clunk" is noted as the femoral head passes over the acetabulum.

33. Apnea lasting longer than **15 seconds** is abnormal in children of any age.

34. **D**   Cryptorchidism—**failure of one or both testes to descend into the scrotum**

35. **O**   Cyanosis, central—**bluish discoloration of the skin and mucous membranes due to significant arterial desaturation**

36. **Q**   Hydrocephalus—**accumulation of cerebrospinal fluid in the skull due to obstruction of cerebrospinal fluid pathways**

37. **R**   Lanugo—**a fine, soft, downy hair covering the fetus in utero and sometimes covering the neonate**

38. **A**   Phimosis—**an irretractable foreskin**

39. **K**   Measles—**acute, highly contagious viral illness; incubation period is 10–12 days; can be transmitted from 5th day of incubation**

40. **C**   Chalazion—**chronic inflammatory lipogranuloma of a meibomian gland in the upper or lower eyelid**

41. **T**   Nystagmus—**a rapid, searching movement of the eyeballs seen in some newborns until 3–4 months of age**

42. **L**   Colic—**paroxysmal crying lasting several hours in an otherwise healthy baby**

43. **M**   Red retinal reflex—**reflection of clear, red color from the retina when a bright light is directed at the newborn's lens**

44. **S**   Patent ductus arteriosus—**a cardiac abnormality marked by failure of the ductus arteriosus to close after birth**

45. **B**   Strabismus—**the appearance of crossed eyes in the newborn due to muscular incoordination**

46. **N**   Edema—**abnormally large amounts of fluid in the intercellular spaces of the body, usually in subcutaneous tissue**

47. **F**   Hydrocele—**a circumscribed collection of clear fluid in the scrotum; may resolve spontaneously by 6 months of age**

48. **E**   Large for gestational age—**an infant whose weight, length, and/or occipital-frontal circumference falls above the 90th percentile for gestational age when plotted on the growth curve**

49. **H**   Intussusception—**intestinal obstruction caused by invagination of a portion of the intestine onto itself; manifested by vomiting and currant-jelly stools**

50. **P**   Fontanel—**a membrane-covered space in the infant's skull reflecting incomplete ossification; occurs where two sutures meet**

51. **I**   Ortolani's click—**a procedure for evaluating hip stability in a newborn**

52. **G**   Pronation—**the turning of the body or body part face down**

53. **J**   Rhonchi—**adventitious breath sounds; lower in pitch and more musical than rales**

1. An infant is about to receive her first oral polio vaccine (OPV). Administration of the OPV would be contraindicated if

   (1) the infant weighed 5.5 kg.
   (2) the infant had a family history of milk allergy.
   (3) the sister had diarrhea.
   (4) the primary caretaker was HIV-positive.

2. According to the recommended childhood immunization schedule, an infant should receive the first dose of oral poliovirus vaccine at how many months of age?

   (1) 1 month
   (2) 2 months
   (3) 3 months
   (4) 4 months

3. In counseling a teenage mother on the first solid food to introduce to her 5-month-old child, which of the following foods should be recommended?

   (1) Eggs
   (2) Pureed chicken
   (3) Bananas
   (4) Rice cereal

4. The mother of a 6-month-old infant calls the nurse 24 hours after the child received a diphtheria, pertussis, and tetanus (DTP) immunization because there is mild swelling and tenderness at the injection site. The nurse's response to the mother's concern would be

   (1) "Swelling and tenderness are normal side effects of the vaccine."
   (2) "Take the infant to the emergency room immediately."
   (3) "Withhold feeding for 8 hours."
   (4) "Immerse the extremity in cool water."

5. When counseling a parent about the side effects of the varicella vaccine (Varivax), the nurse is correct to include which of the following in the teaching plan?

   (1) The child may cry inconsolably for 24 hours after the vaccination.
   (2) A lump may appear at the site of injection and persist for weeks to months.
   (3) Vaccine-induced paralysis may occur.
   (4) A mild maculopapular rash may appear.

6. Which of the following situations would alert the nurse to a possible problem with an infant?

   (1) Drinking 1.5 ounces of milk every 3 hours
   (2) Circumoral cyanosis during feedings
   (3) Wet burping after feedings
   (4) Stooling during feedings

7. When teaching the mother of an infant with a cold, the nurse instructs the mother to seek further treatment if

(1) the cold lasts for more than 5 days.
(2) a high fever develops.
(3) rhinorrhea develops.
(4) the infant becomes increasingly irritable.

8. The mother of a 14-month-old infant has called the primary care clinic. She describes the following symptoms: barking cough, a hoarse cry, and a rectal temperature of 100.2°F (37.9°C). The nurse would realize that these were symptoms of

(1) croup.
(2) asthma.
(3) epiglottitis.
(4) aspiration.

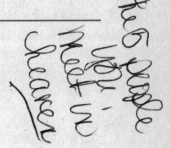

CHAPTER 16: NCLEX-RN STYLE ANSWERS

1. (4) CORRECT   OPV is a live virus that is shed in the stool. The caretaker would be at risk for developing polio due to the compromised immune response.
   (1) ELIMINATE   The first dose of OPV is given when the infant is 2 months old. The infant weighs 5.5 kg, or about 12 lbs, which would not be a contraindication.
   (2) ELIMINATE   A family history of milk allergy would not preclude administering OPV.
   (3) ELIMINATE   Although her sister has diarrhea, there is no indication that the infant is sick.

   CATEGORY 04 PREVENTION AND EARLY DETECTION OF DISEASE

2. (2) CORRECT   The first dose of oral poliovirus vaccine (OPV) is given at 2 months of age
   (1) ELIMINATE   The second dose of hepatitis B vaccine is usually given at 1 month of age.
   (3) ELIMINATE   If the child has been on the recommended immunization schedule, no immunization is due on the third month.
   (4) ELIMINATE   At 4 months, three vaccines are due. These vaccines are diphtheria, tetanus and pertussis (DTP), *H. influenzae*, Type B (Hib), and the second dose of OPV.

   CATEGORY 04 PREVENTION AND EARLY DETECTION OF DISEASE

3. (4) CORRECT   Rice cereal should be fed first, followed by noncitrus fruits, to reduce the risk of food allergies. Waiting 3 to 5 days between the introduction of each new food assists in identification of possible allergens.

    (1) *ELIMINATE*   Eggs are highly allergenic and should be avoided until after 1 year.

    (2) *ELIMINATE*   Pureed meat may be introduced at a later time.

    (3) *ELIMINATE*   Noncitrus fruits are usually the second food recommended.

CATEGORY 07 BASIC CARE AND COMFORT

---

4. (1) CORRECT   Swelling and tenderness after a DPT injection can be expected.

    (2) *ELIMINATE*   This is not an emergency situation.

    (3) *ELIMINATE*   Nutritional intake is not related to the DPT injection.

    (4) *ELIMINATE*   There is no need to immerse the extremity in cool water.

CATEGORY 04 PREVENTION AND EARLY DETECTION OF DISEASE

---

5. (4) CORRECT   A varicella-like or maculopapular rash can occur not only at the site of injection, but also anywhere on the body.

    (1) *ELIMINATE*   Inconsolable crying is associated with diphtheria vaccination.

    (2) *ELIMINATE*   Local pain and tenderness may occur, but a lump is not common.

    (3) *ELIMINATE*   Paralysis is associated with the OPV.

CATEGORY 04 PREVENTION AND EARLY DETECTION OF DISEASE

---

6. (2) CORRECT   Cyanosis is an indication of a possible cardiac defect.

    (1) *ELIMINATE*   This is a normal feeding pattern.

    (3) *ELIMINATE*   Wet burping is normal after feedings.

    (4) *ELIMINATE*   Stooling during feedings is not abnormal.

CATEGORY 04 PREVENTION AND EARLY DETECTION OF DISEASE

7.   **(2) CORRECT**   A high fever is an indication of a complication or other disease and warrants further examination.

    (1) *ELIMINATE*   A cold may linger more than 5 days.

    (3) *ELIMINATE*   Rhinorrhea may develop with a cold.

    (4) *ELIMINATE*   The infant may become irritable with a cold.

CATEGORY 04 PREVENTION AND EARLY DETECTION OF DISEASE

---

8.   **(1) CORRECT**   Croup is a viral infection with these symptoms.

    (2) *ELIMINATE*   The barking cough and hoarse cry are not symptoms of asthma.

    (3) *ELIMINATE*   Epiglottitis would include symptoms of respiratory distress.

    (4) *ELIMINATE*   The barking cough, hoarse cry, and slightly elevated rectal temperature would not be signs of aspiration.

CATEGORY 02 SAFETY AND INFECTION CONTROL

17

EARLY CHILDHOOD

WHAT YOU NEED TO KNOW

The accurate physical assessment of a pediatric client requires knowledge and understanding of childhood development. This combination establishes the base on which a nurse builds effective pediatric nursing interventions. The stage of early childhood is composed of two parts: toddlerhood (1–3 years of age) and preschool age (3–6 years). This chapter focuses on assessment skills of both the toddler and the preschooler, as well as health promotion and health problems of each age group.

Get your mind going by labeling the following characteristics as appropriate to a **toddler**, a **preschooler**, or **both**:

1. _____ T _____   Age 1 to 3 years
2. _____ T _____   Physical growth slows down considerably
3. _____ B _____   Intensely active and curious
4. _____ T _____   Normal blood pressure ranges between 105/66 mmHg and 95/53 mmHg
5. _____ P _____   Age 3 to 6 years
6. _____ P _____   To assess this child's ears, pull the pinna (auricle) up and back
7. _____ T _____   To assess this child's ears, pull the pinna (auricle) down and back
8. _____ B _____   The S3 heart sound is a normal finding during this stage
9. _____ P _____   Erikson's psychosocial stage of initiative vs. guilt
10. _____ P _____   Spends the majority of time in pretend play
11. _____ T _____   Has difficulty compromising with others during play
12. _____ T _____   Anterior fontanel closes
13. _____ B _____   Hearing, smell, taste, and touch become increasingly well developed, coordinate with each other, and are associated with other experiences
14. _____ P _____   Can tie shoelaces but may not be able to tie bow
15. _____ P _____   Identifies strongly with parent of same sex
16. _____ T _____   Toilet training occurs
17. _____ P _____   Enjoys parallel and associative play

Now label the following statements concerning early childhood either as **true** or **false**:

18. _____ T _____   Imitative play is common during toddler years.
19. _____ F _____   By the age of 9 months a child should be able to feed himself.
20. _____ T _____   A purse would be considered an appropriate gift for a female toddler.
21. _____ T _____   A 24-month-old child should know her first name and refer to herself by name.
22. _____   Ignoring is considered an effective type of discipline for the early childhood years.

Now that you have thought about and reviewed the general principles of early childhood development, we will move on to the physiological integrity of the toddler and preschooler.

EARLY CHILDHOOD ASSESSMENT

Physical changes during early childhood are mostly due to general physical growth, not to changes in the actual organs. Therefore, assessment findings may be closer to what you reviewed in Part II on adult physiological integrity.

Children learn about their world and how to deal with their environment through experimentation with various objects and people. At the same time, they learn about themselves operating within their environment—what they can do, how to relate to things and situations, and how to adapt themselves to the demands of society. By the beginning of the second year, the toddler starts to think and reason things out. This is evident during play as the toddler repeats trial and error to achieve a specific result. Another cognitive achievement of early childhood is the acquisition of language, which involves mental symbolism.

- Toilet training may occur at 18 months and older. (Physiologic and psychologic readiness is usually complete at 18 to 24 months.)

Special skills and patience are required to assess the child between the ages of 1 and 6 years. Often, complete assessment cannot occur in an orderly fashion. The following table assesses your creativity in working with children.

23. Write in the space provided the most appropriate nursing intervention based on the assessment and rationale given:

Assessment	Nursing Intervention	Rationale
Auscultation of heart and lungs	_Let child hold & tone tool, listen to own heart_	The child becomes familiar with assessment tools and reduces the threat that is often associated with such equipment.
Administration of medication by mouth		Involves the child by offering choices, allowing her some measure of control.
Giving an intramuscular injection		A child who is occupied with an interesting activity is less likely to focus on the procedure.
Postoperative dressing change		Explanation of procedure helps to decrease anxiety and gives the child a sense of control.

Separation anxiety peaks between the ages of 1 and 3, so parents should be encouraged to stay with their children during your assessment.

Some landmark events to look for are the following:

- The anterior fontanel closes between the ages of 1 and 3.
- Full set of baby teeth should be present at around 30 months ($2\frac{1}{2}$ years)
- Handedness may become apparent at around age 2.
- Toddlers usually have a "pot belly," which subsides by age 3.

- Large muscle groups are well developed around 18 months.
- Fine motor skills begin to develop at 18 months.
- Bowlegs are normal around ages 2–3.
- Between the ages of 3 and 6, children should gain about 4–6 pounds/year.

When explaining things to a child, the nurse must make careful word choices to allay fears. Match the word or phrase to avoid (on the left) with the more appropriate words for use with a pediatric client:

24. _C_ Incision   A. make better

25. _A_ Cut, fix   B. TV screen

26. _B_ Monitor   C. special opening

27. _E_ Electrodes   D. puffiness

28. _D_ Edema   E. stickers

Many experts believe that play is the work of the child. In the following examples, choose the inappropriate play activity, the one which would NOT facilitate the given procedure:

29. Deep breathing
    A. You and the child blow bubbles.
    B. The child plays a band instrument.
    C. Tell the child to breathe deeply or he can't go home.
    D. Ask the child to try blowing up a balloon.

30. Range of motion
    A. Play "Simon Says."
    B. Position the bed so child must turn to view TV.
    C. Organize wheelchair races.
    D. Play catch with a foam ball.

31. Soaks/baths
    A. Allow child to bathe alone.
    B. Wash dolls or toys during soak.
    C. Play with small objects (e.g., cups, syringes without needles) in the water.
    D. Read or sing to child while bathing.

32. Injections
    A. Allow the child to pretend to give you an injection using syringe without needle.
    B. Provide the child with a colorful bandage and stickers after the injection.
    C. Have a parent assist in holding the child down.
    D. Take the child to the treatment room.

PROMOTING HEALTH DURING EARLY CHILDHOOD

These principles are similar to the ones discussed in the chapter on infancy. Education of parents and children, when appropriate, is the most important function of the nurse in health promotion during early childhood.

CHILDHOOD INJURIES

Injuries are the leading cause of death in children over the age of 1 year. Injuries cause more deaths and disabilities in children than all causes of disease combined. Listed below are common preventable injuries associated with early childhood. Match the injury on the left with the associated developmental ability of early childhood:

33. __E__	Hit by car	A.	able to explore if left unsupervised
34. __D__	Choking	B.	pulls objects
35. __E__	Falls	C.	cannot read
36. __C__	Poisoning	D.	explores by putting things in mouth
37. __B__	Burns	E.	walks, runs, climbs
38. __F__	Drowning	F.	depth perception unrefined

POISONING

Poisoning causes a considerable number of injuries in children under 4 years of age. Examples of common poisons ingested by children include lead, acetaminophen (Tylenol), overdose, and cleaning supplies. Poison episodes can be reduced by instructing parents to use child safety locks on cabinets containing potential hazards and to seek immediate medical attention if they think their child has ingested a poison. Instruct parents to keep the telephone number of the poison control hotline near phone and keep syrup of Ipecac in the home to use as directed.

Poisoning Symptoms by System	
Central nervous system	Dizziness Sudden loss of consciousness Seizures
Respiratory/circulatory system	Depressed respirations Unexpected cyanosis Shock
Gastrointestinal system	Abdominal pain Vomiting Diarrhea

CHILD MALTREATMENT

Child maltreatment is one of the most significant social problems affecting children. Physical neglect is characterized by the deprivation of necessities such as food, clothing, shelter, supervision, medical care, personal hygiene, and education. Emotional neglect refers to the failure to meet the child's need for affection, attention, and emotional nurturing. Physical abuse is a clinical condition in which children have received serious physical injury, sometimes leading to death, usually from a parent or caretaker.

To help solidify these definitions in your mind, indicate whether the following clinical manifestations are symptomatic of **physical neglect**, **emotional neglect**, or **physical abuse**:

39. ___*PAN*___ Signs of malnutrition

40. ___*EN*___ Feeding disorders

41. ___*EN*___ Overcompliant

42. ___*PA*___ Bruises and welts

43. ___*PA*___ Burns

44. ___*PAN*___ Dirty, inappropriate dress

The nurse must remember that even **suspected** child abuse must be reported to the proper authorities outside the hospital.

COMMON HEALTH PROBLEMS OF EARLY CHILDHOOD

Toddlers and preschoolers are prone to certain health problems related to the short, straight structures of their ears and throat, such as otitis media, tonsillitis, and upper respiratory infections. In addition, the lymphoid tissue of the tonsils and adenoids continues to be large, leaving it open to infection.

OTITIS MEDIA

Otitis media is one of the most common health problems in childhood due to the short, straight eustachian tubes of children aged 6–24 months. The child feels that the affected ear is "full" and may experience decreased hearing in that ear. The client may feel pain in the ear and exhibit some signs of infection such as fever, malaise, and irritability. Systemic antibiotics are the treatment of choice. It is imperative to instruct the parents to complete the entire course of antibiotics!

Label the following statements either **true** or **false**:

45. __F__ The most frequent cause of otitis media is trauma to a child's ear.

46. __T__ The peak incidence of otitis media occurs between 6 and 24 months.

47. __T__ Passive smoking has been established as a significant factor in the development of otitis media.

48. __F__ Children who are fed formula as infants have a lower incidence of otitis media compared with those who are breast-fed.

RESPIRATORY PROBLEMS

It is important to be familiar with the clinical manifestations and treatments associated with common pediatric respiratory problems. Two specific respiratory problems, **croup** and **epiglottitis**, can lead to potentially fatal respiratory distress.

Croup is an acute obstruction at the larynx usually caused by viral infection. The hacking, barking cough can be a scary experience for both parent and child. Mild cases can often be treated by putting the child in a steamy bathroom. More severe cases may require intubation.

Epiglottitis is a bacterial infection that causes acute inflammation of the epiglottis and surrounding structures. It is characterized by inspiratory stridor with marked retractions. Often, the child will sit bolt upright with his tongue protruding, leaning forward on his knees for support to facilitate breathing.

THE CHILD WITH EPIGLOTTITIS

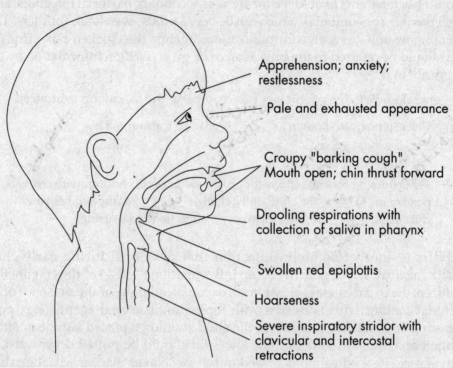

Apprehension; anxiety; restlessness

Pale and exhausted appearance

Croupy "barking cough"
Mouth open; chin thrust forward

Drooling respirations with collection of saliva in pharynx

Swollen red epiglottis

Hoarseness

Severe inspiratory stridor with clavicular and intercostal retractions

Decide whether each characteristic below belongs to either **croup** or **epiglottitis**:

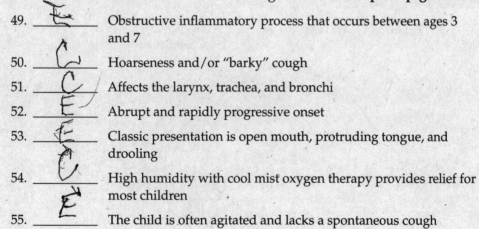

49. _____ Obstructive inflammatory process that occurs between ages 3 and 7

50. _____ Hoarseness and/or "barky" cough

51. _____ Affects the larynx, trachea, and bronchi

52. _____ Abrupt and rapidly progressive onset

53. _____ Classic presentation is open mouth, protruding tongue, and drooling

54. _____ High humidity with cool mist oxygen therapy provides relief for most children

55. _____ The child is often agitated and lacks a spontaneous cough

INFECTIONS

Chicken pox is a common infectious health problem of early childhood. The incubation period (between exposure and clinical symptoms) is 11–21 days, and the vesicles dry after about 7 days. When caring for a pediatric client with chicken pox, maintenance of strict isolation is important, especially in a hospital setting where other children are susceptible to infections. At home, isolation should be maintained until vesicles are dry.

Nurses should teach parents to observe for signs of secondary bacterial infections associated with chicken pox (e.g., pneumonia), which can be very serious, even fatal. Toddlers (12 months and older) are now able to receive immunizations against the chicken pox virus (varicella zoster) and should be referred to the physician or be given written information by the nurse to learn more about it.

With your general knowledge of chicken pox, complete the following sentences:

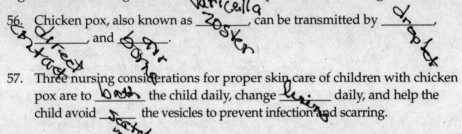

56.   Chicken pox, also known as ___varicella zoster___, can be transmitted by ___droplet___, ___direct contact___, and ___air borne___.

57.   Three nursing considerations for proper skin care of children with chicken pox are to ___bath___ the child daily, change ___linin___ daily, and help the child avoid ___scratching___ the vesicles to prevent infection and scarring.

Conjunctivitis is another common infection that develops during early childhood. Conjunctivitis, also known as pink eye, is an inflammation ("-itis") of the conjunctiva of the eye. In children, the usual cause is either viral, bacterial, allergic, or the presence of a foreign body. Bacterial conjunctivitis is treated with topical antibacterial agents (e.g., polymyxin and polysporin). To instill eye mediation, the child should be placed supine or sitting with head extended and asked to look up. The lower lid should be pulled downward, forming a conjunctival sac. The medication is placed in the sac. Never place medication directly on the eyeball.

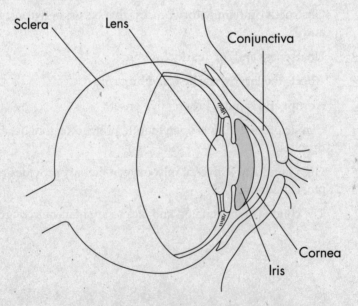

Sclera   Lens   Conjunctiva   Cornea   Iris

The conjunctiva is inflamed in conjunctivitis

Complete the following sentences about conjunctivitis:

58. The two main clinical manifestations of conjunctivitis are _Viral_ and _bacterial_

59. It is important for the nurse to keep the eye _____ and to administer medication as ordered to avoid persistence of the infection.

60. The proper method of wiping the child's eye is to start from the _____ and wipe in a/an _____ and _____ direction, away from the opposite eye.

KEEP IN MIND

Remember, the toddler (age 1–3) is in Erikson's stage of autonomy vs. shame and doubt, and the preschooler (age 3–6) is in Erikson's stage of initiative vs. guilt. The years from 1 to 6 are a generally healthy period for most children, in which growth is steady and the world becomes more and more manageable with each new discovery.

CHAPTER 17: EXERCISE ANSWERS

1. **Toddler**—Age 1 to 3 years
2. **Toddler**—Physical growth slows down considerably
3. **Both**—Intensely active and curious
4. **Toddler**—Normal blood pressure ranges between 105/66 mmHg and 95/53 mmHg
5. **Preschooler**—Age 3 to 6 years
6. **Preschooler**—To assess this child's ears, pull the pinna (auricle) up and back
7. **Toddler**—To assess this child's ears, pull the pinna (auricle) down and back
8. **Both**—The S3 heart sound is a normal finding during this stage
9. **Preschooler**—Erikson's psychosocial stage of initiative vs. guilt
10. **Preschooler**—Spends the majority of time in pretend play
11. **Toddler**—Has difficulty compromising with others during play
12. **Toddler**—Anterior fontanel closes
13. **Both**—Hearing, smell, taste, and touch become increasingly well developed, coordinate with each other, and are associated with other experiences
14. **Preschooler**—Can tie shoelaces but may not be able to tie bow
15. **Preschooler**—Identifies strongly with parent of same sex
16. **Toddler**—Toilet training occurs
17. **Preschooler**—Enjoys parallel and associative play
18. **True**—Imitative play is common during toddler years.
19. **False**—By the age of 9 months a child should be able to feed himself.
20. **True**—A purse would be considered an appropriate gift for a female toddler.
21. **True**—A 24-month-old child should know her first name and refer to herself by name.
22. **True**—Ignoring is considered an effective type of discipline for the early childhood years.
23. Provide the most appropriate nursing intervention based on the assessment and rationale given:

Assessment	Nursing Intervention	Rationale
Ascultation of heart and lungs	Allow child to play with the stethoscope and try it on the nurse.	The child becomes familiar with assessment tools and reduces the threat that is often associated with such equipment.
Administration of medication by mouth	Provide child with the choice of taking the medication with juice or with milk.	Involves the child by offering choices, allowing them some measure of control.
Giving an intramuscular injection	Divert the child's attention by singing a song the child knows.	A child who is occupied with an interesting activity is less likely to focus on the procedure.
Postoperative dressing change	Honestly explain what the child will feel during the procedure.	Explanation of procedure helps to decrease anxiety and gives the child a sense of control.

24. **C** Incision—**special opening**

25. **A** Cut, fix—**make better**

26. **B** Monitor—**TV screen**

27. **E** Electrodes—**stickers**

28. **D** Edema—**puffiness**

29. Deep breathing

    C. Tell the child to breathe deeply or he can't go home.

30. Range of motion

    C. Organize wheelchair races.

31. Soaks/baths

    A. Allow child to bathe alone.

32. Injections

    C. Have a parent assist in holding the child down.

33. **E** Hit by car—**walks, runs, climbs**

34. **D** Choking—**explores by putting things in mouth**

35. **F** Falls—**depth perception unrefined**

36. **C** Poisoning—**cannot read**

37. **B** Burns—**pulls objects**

38. **A** Drowning—**able to explore if left unsupervised**

39. **Physical neglect**—Signs of malnutrition

40. **Emotional neglect**—Feeding disorders

41. **Emotional neglect**—Overcompliant

42. **Physical abuse**—Bruises and welts

43. **Physical abuse**—Burns

44. **Physical neglect**—Dirty, inappropriate dress

45. **False**—The most frequent cause of otitis media is trauma to a child's ear.

46. **True**—The peak incidence of otitis media occurs between 6 and 24 months.

47. **True**—Passive smoking has been established as a significant factor in the development of otitis media.

48. **False**—Children who are fed formula as infants have a lower incidence of otitis media compared with those who are breast-fed.

49. **Epiglottitis**—Obstructive inflammatory process that occurs between ages 3 and 7

50. **Croup**—Hoarseness and/or "barky" cough

51. **Croup**—Affects the larynx, trachea, and bronchi

52. **Epiglottitis**—Abrupt and rapidly progressive onset

53. **Epiglottitis**—Classic presentation is open mouth, protruding tongue, and drooling

54. **Croup**—High humidity with cool mist oxygen therapy provides relief for most children

55. **Epiglottitis**—The child is often agitated and lacks a spontaneous cough

56. Chicken pox, also known as **varicella zoster**, can be transmitted by **direct contact, droplet,** and **air.**

57. Three nursing considerations for proper skin care of children with chicken pox are to **bathe** the child daily, change **linens** daily, and help the child avoid **scratching** the vesicles.

58. The two main clinical manifestations of conjunctivitis are **drainage** and **redness.**

59. It is important for the nurse to keep the eye **clean** and to administer medication as ordered to avoid persistence of the infection.

60. The proper method of wiping the child's eye is to start from the **inner canthus** and wipe in a **downward** and **outward** direction, away from the opposite eye.

CHAPTER 17: NCLEX-RN STYLE QUESTIONS

1. A 4-year-old child with a new arm cast is going back to the day care center. Which age-appropriate instruction should the nurse give this child?

   (1) "Don't chew the cast edges."
   (2) "Be careful. Your cast can break if you fall on it."
   (3) "Don't use the cast to hammer pegs into holes."
   (4) "Other people won't see the cast if you wear long sleeves."

2. A 4-year-old boy is scheduled for an angiogram. What can the nurse tell the child to better prepare him for this procedure?

   (1) Tell the child that he will go for the test in 2 hours.
   (2) Explain that the doctor will look at his heart through a hole in his leg.
   (3) Explain that the room will be cold and the table will feel hard.
   (4) Promise him that he will be fine.

3. When counseling parents about the nutritional habits of toddlers, the nurse should include which of the following?

(1) If toddlers state that they don't want a food, it should be substituted for one that they request.
(2) Toddlers should be given the same utensils and dishes every day.
(3) Between-meal snacks should be avoided.
(4) Food should be designated as a reward.

4. When counseling parents about lead poisoning prevention, the nurse should include which of the following in her teaching plan?

(1) Dry cleaning techniques are helpful.
(2) Toys and pacifiers should be cleaned weekly.
(3) Water should be run for 5 minutes prior to use.
(4) Cold water should be used for consumption.

5. When counseling parents about accidental poisoning, the nurse should include which of the following in the teaching plan?

(1) The parents should administer syrup of ipecac immediately.
(2) The parents should give the child milk.
(3) The poison control center should be contacted immediately.
(4) The child should be taken to the emergency room.

6. A toddler is brought to the emergency department with a fractured arm. The nurse obtains the old chart and notes the child has previously been diagnosed with a fractured clavicle and several urinary tract infections. What would be the initial action by the nurse?

(1) Confront the parents about the suspected child abuse.
(2) Descriptively document the present assessment findings.
(3) Following the institution's protocol for reporting child abuse.
(4) Notify the supervisor.

7. A child has chicken pox. The younger sister has not had the disease. What helpful advice can the nurse give the mother?

(1) Keep the sister separated from the infected child as much as possible.
(2) The rash will be more severe in the sister.
(3) Start giving the sister acetaminophen (Tylenol) now to decrease the length of the illness.
(4) The sister may have a low-grade fever before the vesicles break out.

8. The nurse teaches parents that the most important factor for successful toilet training is which of the following?

(1) Parents' willingness to stick to a schedule
(2) Developmental readiness of the child
(3) Age of child and onset of training
(4) Toilet sitting at scheduled times

9.	The mother of a 4-year-old child calls the clinic, saying that her child has been wetting the bed at night. What would be an appropriate response by the nurse?	(1) "There is probably a physical problem causing the bedwetting." (2) "Stress is probably contributing to your child's bedwetting." (3) "Children of this age are not expected always to be dry at night." (4) "You may want to contact your child's teacher to discuss this with her as well."
10.	The parents of a 5-year-old child speak to the nurse regarding their concern about the language development of their child. Which of the following statements would guide the action of the nurse?	(1) The nurse should do a Denver Developmental Screening (DDS) test. (2) Parents are usually accurate in their assessments or impressions of language development. (3) Behavioral assessment should precede assessment for language development. (4) Concerns about language should not be addressed until at least school age.

CHAPTER 17: NCLEX-RN STYLE ANSWERS

1.
(2) CORRECT	There is a fear for pre-schoolers that if an injury occurs, all their "insides" can leak out. Reminding the child of this age group of safety factors is important.
(1) ELIMINATE	Infants experience the world using tactile senses such as touch and taste. Biting is a common behavior in this age group.
(3) ELIMINATE	Toddlers will test the strength and durability of a new toy or object.
(4) ELIMINATE	School-aged children are acutely aware of body deviation from the norm.

CATEGORY 03 GROWTH AND DEVELOPMENT THROUGH THE LIFE SPAN

2.
(3) CORRECT	Piaget described the preoperational thinking of a 2–7 year old as concrete and tangible.
(1) ELIMINATE	At a 4-year-old's developmental level, time is still incompletely understood; the child interprets it according to his own frame of reference.
(2) ELIMINATE	Preschoolers believe in the power of words and accept their meaning literally.
(4) ELIMINATE	The nurse does not know for a fact that the child will be fine.

CATEGORY 03 GROWTH AND DEVELOPMENT THROUGH THE LIFE SPAN

3.   (2) CORRECT   Toddlers' needs for routine/ritualism should be incorporated into feeding practices.

        (1) *ELIMINATE*   Substitution should be made sparingly in order to avoid catering to the changing whims of toddlers.

        (3) *ELIMINATE*   Toddlers enjoy grazing, and the provision of nutritious snacks can help to maximize nutrition.

        (4) *ELIMINATE*   The use of food as reward encourages overeating.

CATEGORY 03 GROWTH AND DEVELOPMENT THROUGH THE LIFE SPAN

4.   (4) CORRECT   Lead concentrations are lower in cold water than in hot water.

        (1) *ELIMINATE*   Wet cleaning methods more effectively remove lead-containing dust.

        (2) *ELIMINATE*   Toys and pacifiers should be cleaned frequently in order to minimize dust consumption.

        (3) *ELIMINATE*   Tap water should be run from 30 seconds to 2 minutes prior to use.

CATEGORY 09 REDUCTION OF RISK POTENTIAL

5.   (3) CORRECT   In the event of a poisoning, the poison control center should be contacted immediately. The telephone number for the center should be posted near each telephone in the house.

        (1) *ELIMINATE*   Syrup of ipecac should only be given if it is ordered by the provider or the poison control center.

        (2) *ELIMINATE*   Nothing should be given to the child unless directed by the provider or the poison control center.

        (4) *ELIMINATE*   Prior to taking the child to the emergency room, the poison control center should be contacted.

CATEGORY 02 SAFETY AND INFECTION CONTROL

6.   (2) CORRECT   Documentation of the present assessment findings would be the most appropriate initial action by the nurse.

        (1) *ELIMINATE*   The nurse should not confront the parents, but rather follow hospital protocol.

        (3) *POSSIBLE*   The nurse should follow hospital protocol, but after documenting current assessment findings.

        (4) *POSSIBLE*   The nurse would notify the supervisor after documenting the assessment findings.

CATEGORY 06 PSYCHOSOCIAL ADAPTATION

7.   (4) CORRECT   The sister may have a low-grade fever before the vesicles break out.

      (1) *ELIMINATE*   The sister would have been infected by the time the chicken pox lesions appeared on the sibling.

      (2) *ELIMINATE*   It is not a true statement that the rash would be more severe in the sibling.

      (3) *ELIMINATE*   Giving the sister Tylenol will not decrease the length of the illness.

CATEGORY 04 PREVENTION AND EARLY DETECTION OF DISEASE

8.   (2) CORRECT   Unless the child is developmentally ready, toilet training may be very ineffective and may serve only the parents' desire to train the child.

      (1) *ELIMINATE*   The parents must be willing to stick to a schedule but this is not the most important factor.

      (3) *ELIMINATE*   Developmental level, not age, is the most important factor.

      (4) *ELIMINATE*   Toilet sitting at scheduled times is a factor but not the most important.

CATEGORY 03 GROWTH AND DEVELOPMENT THROUGH THE LIFE SPAN

9.   (3) CORRECT   Children achieve nighttime bladder control after daytime bladder control. Nighttime bladder control may not be until 5–7 years of age.

      (1) *ELIMINATE*   At 4 years of age a child may not physically be able to achieve nocturnal bladder control.

      (2) *ELIMINATE*   Stress may not be the problem; rather, the child is not physically mature.

      (4) *ELIMINATE*   The teacher should not be contacted because the child is not having daytime problems but, rather, is wetting the bed at night.

CATEGORY 03 GROWTH AND DEVELOPMENT THROUGH THE LIFE SPAN

10.   (2) CORRECT   Parents are usually fairly accurate in their assessment of language problems. A 5-year-old child would be expected to use more than 2,000 words. A referral to a speech therapist might be appropriate, depending on the circumstances.

      (1) *ELIMINATE*   The Denver Developmental Screening Test (DDS) is not a good screening tool for language delay in that there are a number of false negatives.

      (3) *ELIMINATE*   This is not an appropriate statement.

      (4) *ELIMINATE*   The nurse should not wait to refer this child until school age.

CATEGORY 03 GROWTH AND DEVELOPMENT THROUGH THE LIFE SPAN

18

MIDDLE CHILDHOOD

WHAT YOU NEED TO KNOW

Middle childhood begins at the age of 6 and extends until the age of 12. Children at this age are most often referred to as **school-aged** because they are in grade school. During this time, children are exposed to the world outside their immediate neighborhoods, and new experiences greatly influence their development and relationships.

School-aged children identify with peers of the same sex and initiate independence from their parents. During this period, they make their first real attempts to form and be a part of social groups outside the family. Their play involves increased physical skill, intellectual ability, and fantasy, and is dominated by ritual and conformity. The majority of their play is highly active and includes team sports.

Middle childhood is characterized as a time of gradual growth and development, with continual progress in physical, mental, and social development. Overall, this age group is generally healthy. Common conditions include asthma attacks, gastrointestinal upset, dental problems, and behavior disorders. Most children have been immunized against or have already contracted the communicable diseases of childhood. Their hearty appetites and active play further influence their general good health.

ASSESSMENT OF THE SCHOOL-AGED CHILD

Between the ages of 6 and 12 years, a child's deciduous teeth will fall out. Permanent teeth grow in by age 12. Vision should be almost perfect by this stage. The child gains deliberate hand-eye coordination during these years.

Further understanding of the school-aged child's health requires complete knowledge of the child's growth and development. Think about each of the following statements and label them **true** or **false**:

1. _F_ According to Erikson, school-aged children have already developed trust, autonomy, and identity.

2. _T_ Even though increased independence is a developmental goal of the school-aged child, parental rules and family values should prevail.

3. _F_ During middle childhood, sleepwalking replaces the nightmares of preschool children.

4. _F_ Because school-aged children are prone to injury, the most appropriate intervention for a sleepwalking child is to wake him up and lead him back to bed.

5. _T_ Middle childhood is an opportune time for the school nurse to inform students about issues of sexuality.

6. _F_ Eight-year-old children who look like 11-year-old children will think and act like 11-year-olds.

7. _T_ According to Erikson, failure to develop a sense of accomplishment during middle childhood results in a sense of inferiority.

8. _T_ You unexpectedly discover four neighborhood children, both males and females, unclothed and playing "doctor." Your best response is to provide reassurance that this behavior is normal and open yourself to any questions they may have.

9. _F_ During middle childhood, it is uncommon for children to lie, cheat, and/or steal.

10. _T_ Children riding bicycles should always wear helmets.

COMMON HEALTH PROBLEMS OF MIDDLE CHILDHOOD

Bear in mind the implications of smaller airways and passages in the body; there is less room for imperfection! There is increased risk of rapid deterioration and poor outcomes!

TONSILLITIS

The tonsils (and the adenoids) are part of the lymph tissue that surrounds the pharynx. A tonsillectomy is one of the most common surgical procedures of childhood, and is indicated for sleep apnea, chronic and recurrent otitis media, and recurrent tonsillitis. *Streptococcus* is the most common bacterial cause of tonsillitis. If antibiotic treatment does not control tonsillitis, a tonsillectomy is indicated. Pre- and postoperative care should be aimed at the developmental stage of the child. For the school-aged child, this means honest, accurate definitions with outcomes described. The nurse's interventions regarding tonsillectomy should include reducing anxiety, keeping child calm, and maintaining adequate hydration since they are at risk for dehydration secondary to reluctance to swallow. The client should be allowed to make some choices regarding their care at this point. Continue to provide parents with information and support.

PROBLEMS WITH THE SKIN

Skin assessment is important for children of all ages because they are so susceptible to bacterial infections. You should be aware of the potential skin disorders and infections, as well as the various terms used to describe skin lesions. Match the following terms with the definitions on the right:

11. _D_ Erythema   A. caused by spirochete, transmitted by ticks

12. _C_ Ecchymosis   B. wheals

13. _F_ Petechiae   C. localized red or purple discoloration

14. _B_ Urticaria   D. reddened area

15. _G_ Psoriasis   E. hair loss

16. _E_ Alopecia   F. tiny, nonraised, pinpoint spots

17. _A_ Erythema migrans   G. round, thick, dry, reddish patches covered with coarse, silvery scales

18. _H_ Contact dermatitis   H. an inflammatory reaction of the skin that triggers a hypersensitivity response; constant itching

BEHAVIORAL PROBLEMS

Behavioral problems seen in middle childhood include attention deficit disorder (ADD), enuresis, school phobia, and recurrent abdominal pain. See if you can correctly fill in the blanks using the words provided below:

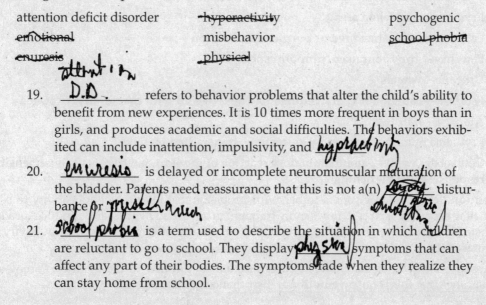

attention deficit disorder   ~~hyperactivity~~   psychogenic

~~emotional~~   misbehavior   ~~school phobia~~

~~enuresis~~   ~~physical~~

19. _A.D.D._ refers to behavior problems that alter the child's ability to benefit from new experiences. It is 10 times more frequent in boys than in girls, and produces academic and social difficulties. The behaviors exhibited can include inattention, impulsivity, and _hyperactivity_.

20. _enuresis_ is delayed or incomplete neuromuscular maturation of the bladder. Parents need reassurance that this is not a(n) _____ disturbance or _misbehavior_.

21. _School phobia_ is a term used to describe the situation in which children are reluctant to go to school. They display _physical_ symptoms that can affect any part of their bodies. The symptoms fade when they realize they can stay home from school.

22. Recurrent abdominal pain is an example of a somatic complaint of childhood that is usually attributed to a *psychogenic* etiology. Diagnosis is confirmed when physical exams and lab results remain negative.

Remember, the school-aged child is in Erikson's stage of industry vs. inferiority. Like early childhood, this is a generally healthy stage in which parents and children should be focused on sibling rivalry and peer relationships. Establishing routines and order while recognizing the child's accomplishments help the school-aged child emerge from this stage with **industry** on top!

CHAPTER 18: EXERCISE ANSWERS

1. **False**—According to Erikson, school-aged children have already developed trust, autonomy, and identity.

2. **True**—Even though increased independence is a developmental goal of the school-aged child, parental rules and family values should prevail.

3. **True**—During middle childhood, sleepwalking replaces the nightmares of preschool children.

4. **False**—Because school-aged children are prone to injury, the most appropriate intervention for a sleepwalking child is to wake him up and lead him back to bed.

5. **True**—Middle childhood is an opportune time for the school nurse to inform students about issues of sexuality.

6. **False**—Eight-year-old children who look like 11-year-old children will think and act like 11-year-olds.

7. **True**—According to Erikson, failure to develop a sense of accomplishment during middle childhood results in a sense of inferiority.

8. **True**—You unexpectedly discover four neighborhood children, both males and females, unclothed and playing "doctor." Your best response is to provide reassurance that this behavior is normal and open yourself to any questions they may have.

9. **True**—During middle childhood it is uncommon for children to lie, cheat, and/or steal.

10. **True**—Children riding bicycles should always wear helmets.

11. **D** Erythema—**reddened area**

12. **C** Ecchymosis—**localized red or purple discoloration**

13. **F** Petechiae—**tiny, nonraised, pinpoint spots**

14. **B** Urticaria—**wheals**

15. **G** Psoriasis—**round, thick, dry, reddish patches covered with coarse, silvery scales**

16. **E** Alopecia—**hair loss**

17. **A** Erythema migrans—**caused by spirochete, transmitted by ticks**

18. **H** Contact dermatitis—**an inflammatory reaction of the skin that triggers a hypersensitivity response; constant itching**

19. **Attention deficit disorder** refers to behavior problems that alter the child's ability to benefit from new experiences. It is 10 times more frequent in boys than in girls, and produces academic and social difficulties. The behaviors exhibited can include inattention, impulsivity, and **hyperactivity**.

20. **Enuresis** is delayed or incomplete neuromuscular maturation of the bladder. Parents need reassurance that this is not an **emotional** disturbance or **misbehavior**.

21. **School phobia** is a term used to describe the situation in which children who are reluctant to go to school. They display **physical** symptoms that can affect any part of their bodies. The symptoms fade when they realize they can stay home from school.

22. Recurrent abdominal pain is an example of a somatic complaint of childhood that is usually attributed to a **psychogenic** etiology. Diagnosis is confirmed when physical exams and lab results remain negative.

CHAPTER 18: NCLEX-RN STYLE QUESTIONS

1. For which of the following would you initiate a dental referral?

   (1) A 3-year-old with brown spots on his teeth
   (2) An 18-month-old unable to brush her teeth
   (3) A 2-month-old with white patches on her buccal mucosa
   (4) A 4-month-old with drooling so copious that it soaks his shirt

2. A 5-year-old has recently developed straining with bowel movements that produce hard, firm stools. The mother asks the nurse for a recommendation as to what to do about her child's constipation. The nurse's best response would be

   (1) to refer the child to a gastroenterologist.
   (2) to instruct the mother to give 2 tablespoons of mineral oil per day.
   (3) to reassure the mother that most 5-year-olds have occasional constipation.
   (4) to educate the mother regarding high-fiber foods and fluids.

3. According to Freud, school-aged children are in which of the following developmental stages?

   (1) Oral
   (2) Anal
   (3) Genital
   (4) Latent

4. A 6-year-old child has chicken pox and the mother is asking when the child can return to school. The nurse should respond

   (1) "In 14 days, once the virus has passed the incubation period."
   (2) "In 7 days, after the lesions have all crusted."
   (3) "In 3 days, after new vesicles have stopped appearing."
   (4) "After the antibiotics have been given for 2 full days."

5. A 6-year-old child has head lice. The nurse should instruct the parents to do which of the following?

   (1) Keep the child home from school for 3 days.
   (2) Discard combs and brushes.
   (3) Get the child a haircut.
   (4) Place all stuffed toys in a black plastic bag for 24 hours.

6. Which of the following questions is best to ask when determining whether a child has primary or secondary enuresis?

(1) "Has the child ever achieved full bladder control?"
(2) "Has the child ever achieved full bowel control?"
(3) "Has the child ever been able to go through the night without being incontinent?"
(4) "Has the child ever been able to tell you when he needs to urinate?"

CHAPTER 18: NCLEX-RN STYLE ANSWERS

1.
(1) CORRECT   This could be indicative of bottle caries, which results from being habitually put to bed with a sugar-containing liquid.
(2) ELIMINATE   The nurse should initiate oral hygiene teaching.
(3) ELIMINATE   This is not an appropriate dental referral.
(4) ELIMINATE   This is not an appropriate dental referral.
CATEGORY 04 PREVENTION AND EARLY DETECTION OF DISEASE

2.
(4) CORRECT   Modifying the diet to include high-fiber foods and fluids is essential in preventing constipation.
(1) ELIMINATE   Referral to a gastroenterologist would be appropriate only if the constipation were chronic or present with another condition.
(2) ELIMINATE   Mineral oil can be effective but dietary modification should be attempted first.
(3) ELIMINATE   Five-year-olds do have occasional constipation but this is not the best answer.
CATEGORY 03 GROWTH AND DEVELOPMENT THROUGH THE LIFE SPAN

3.
(4) CORRECT   The latent stage applies to school-aged children and is characterized by sexual indifference.
(1) ELIMINATE   The oral stage applies to infants.
(2) ELIMINATE   The anal stage applies to toddlers.
(3) ELIMINATE   The genital phase applies to adolescents.
CATEGORY 03 GROWTH AND DEVELOPMENT THROUGH THE LIFE SPAN

4. (2) CORRECT   Children may return to school once all of the lesions have crusted over, generally 7–10 days after the onset of rash.
    (1) *ELIMINATE*   The incubation period is 14–21 days prior to onset of rash.
    (3) *POSSIBLE*   Children may not return to school until all of the lesions have crusted over.
    (4) *ELIMINATE*   Antibiotics are not indicated for the treatment of varicella.

CATEGORY 02 SAFETY AND INFECTION CONTROL

5. (4) CORRECT   All stuffed toys should be placed in a black plastic bag for 24 hours so that the nits that could be on them are killed.
    (1) *ELIMINATE*   Children may return to school the first day after initial treatment.
    (2) *ELIMINATE*   Combs and brushes should be soaked in a pediculocidal agent for 15 minutes.
    (3) *ELIMINATE*   Hair cuts are not required.

CATEGORY 02 SAFETY AND INFECTION CONTROL

6. (1) CORRECT   Secondary enuresis is when a child who has achieved full bladder control begins to regress.
    (2) *ELIMINATE*   Enuresis has nothing to do with bowel control.
    (3) *ELIMINATE*   This question does help to distinguish between primary and secondary enuresis.
    (4) *ELIMINATE*   Again, this does not help to differentiate between primary and secondary enuresis.

CATEGORY 03 GROWTH AND DEVELOPMENT THROUGH THE LIFE SPAN

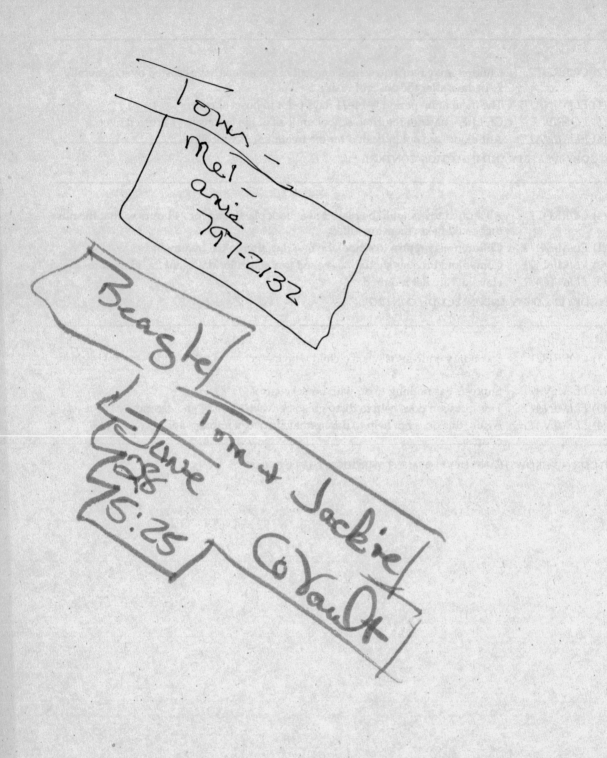

19

ADOLESCENCE

WHAT YOU NEED TO KNOW

Adolescence is the gateway between childhood and the world of an adult. A multi-step process of changes occurs on emotional, physiological, and social levels.

This transitional time differs slightly between girls and boys. For example, girls usually have their growth spurt earlier than boys. Puberty generally lasts from the age of 10 to age 18. Both girls and boys shift their priorities during this stage—their foci become peers, vocational goals, appearance, and social awareness. The physiological changes that take place are a natural progression of a female's or male's body awakenings. As in early and middle childhood, adolescence is a generally healthy period of life, but the hormonal and growth effects of the reproductive organs can hamper both physical and emotional progress.

ASSESSMENT OF THE ADOLESCENT

Establishing a trusting and confidential relationship is of the utmost importance in meeting an adolescent's health care needs. The nurse must act in a simple, honest fashion to eliminate any threat to the client. This may determine the success or failure of the physical assessment.

At the beginning of the assessment, the nurse should inform the teenager of what to expect. Being warm and friendly is much more inviting to the adolescent client than trying to speak to her on an adolescent level.

Before the physical exam, an interview is necessary. The following dialogue is an example of the initial interview with a 15-year-old boy.

1. Assess your knowledge by using these words or phrases to fill in the blanks in the conversation:

alcohol	foods	seat belt
career	frequent waking	sexually
confidential	health	sleeping
contraception	insomnia	testicular self-examination
drugs	meals	tobacco

"Hi, I'm Lisa. I am going to ask you some personal questions. This is not because I want to snoop, but it may be important to your _____. I assure you that what we talk about is _____, just between the two of us. Okay, how many _____ do you eat daily and what types of _____? Do you have any difficulty _____, either _____ or _____, that would affect your daily life? When you drive do you wear your _____? What grade are you in in school? What are your long-term goals concerning your _____? Do you use _____ or _____? How often and what types? Have you ever experimented with _____? Are you _____ active? Do you use any type of _____? Do you perform _____ regularly?"

Questions should be matter-of-fact, and the nurse's responses should be free of judgment; active listening is vital in validating the adolescent's comments. At the conclusion of the interview the nurse should provide the teenager with a gown and a private changing area. During the physical exam, many teenagers are shy and modest, especially if examined by a person of the opposite sex. The examiner should address this verbally prior to the start and provide careful explanations throughout the exam.

During the physical exam, be sure to note the adolescent's grooming, hygiene, posture, coordination, and interest in body image and health. A disheveled appearance may be indicative of depression.

General Notes on the Physical Characteristics of an Adolescent from Head to Toe	
Hair and skin	• Sebaceous glands activate • Dandruff or oily hair • Acne on the face, back and chest (acne vulgaris) • Body hair assumes distribution and texture change (axillary and perineal hair grows)
Vision	• Acuity should be that of a normal adult • Hereditary myopia may occur
Lymph nodes	• Palpable lymph nodes usually indicate infection or other abnormalities
Musculoskeletal	• Body mass reaches that of an adult • Muscle represents a large percentage of body weight • Bone density increases • Females grow 2–8 inches, gain 15–55 pounds, and fat is distributed to the shoulders, hips, breasts, and thighs • Males grow 4–12 inches, gain 15–65 pounds, and legs lengthen while shoulders broaden
Breasts and genitalia	• Males may develop **gynecomastia** (excessive growth of mammary glands; may become functional) • Females show breast enlargement • **Menarche** (menstruation) usually occurs $2\frac{1}{2}$ years after puberty begins (from years 10 through 15)
Elimination	• Adolescents are usually aware of their normal urine quality and bowel patterns. They need to be instructed to report any abnormalities

The Tanner staging of genitalia and pubic hair development during puberty is a useful tool for following normal growth and discerning any growth deficiencies. View it on the following pages, noting the stages and associated expectations.

BOYS' GENITAL DEVELOPMENT

STAGE 1
Preadolescent. Testes, scrotum, and penis are of about the same size and proportion as in early childhood.

STAGE 2
Enlargement of scrotum and testes. Skin of scrotum reddens and changes in texture. Little or no enlargement of penis at this time.

STAGE 3
Enlargement of penis that occurs at first mainly in length. Further growth of testes and scrotum.

STAGE 4
Increased size of penis with growth in breadth and development of glans. Testes and scrotum larger, scrotal skin darkens.

STAGE 5
Genitalia adult in size and shape.

GIRLS' BREAST DEVELOPMENT

STAGE 1
Preadolescent. Elevation of papilla only.

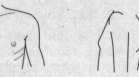

STAGE 2
Breast bud stage. Elevation of breast and papilla as small mound. Enlargement of areola diameter.

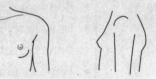

STAGE 3
Further enlargement and elevation of breast and areola with no separation of their contours.

STAGE 4
Projection of areola and papilla to form a secondary mound above level of the breast.

STAGE 5
Mature stage: Projection of papilla only, due to recession of the areola to the general contour of the breast.

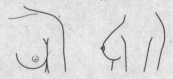

BOTH SEXES: PUBIC HAIR DEVELOPMENT

STAGE 1
Preadolescent. The vellus over the pubis is not further developed than that over the abdominal wall, i.e., no pubic hair.

STAGE 2
Sparse growth of long, slightly pigmented, downy hair. Straight or slightly curled at the base of the penis or along labia.

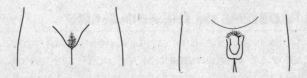

STAGE 3
Considerably darker, coarser, and more curled. The hair spreads sparsely over the symphysis of the pubis.

STAGE 4
Hair now adult in type, but area covered is still considerably smaller than in adult. No spread to medial surface of thighs.

STAGE 5
Adult in quantity and type; distribution of the horizontal (or classically "feminine") pattern. Spread to medial surface of thighs or above base of the inverse triangle occurs late (stage 6).

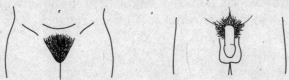

HEALTH PROMOTION FOR ADOLESCENTS

Adolescents can think in more abstract terms and can associate cause and effect, so education is a prime method of promoting good health practices in them. It is imperative that whole peer groups be informed, as the adolescent makes most of his choices based on acceptance by his peer group.

The nutritional needs of adolescents correspond to the speed of their growth at any given time. More energy is required when the adolescent is engaged in a physically active schedule, but the child's appetite should also increase and demand that energy. Eating habits will be greatly influenced by the adolescent's peers, and snacking provides most of an adolescent's caloric intake. One can expect that, due to the rapid growth experienced during puberty, an adolescent will sleep a lot.

Accidents are the leading cause of death in adolescents, so prevention is imperative. The sense of immortality and associated risk-taking behaviors can be curbed through education.

COMMON HEALTH PROBLEMS OF THE ADOLESCENT

Though this may be a physically healthy stage, a number of physical problems may be associated with the biological development of the body. None of them may prove life-threatening, but they are problems the nurse, adolescent, and parents should be aware of.

ACNE VULGARIS

Acne vulgaris is caused by the obstruction and inflammation of the sebaceous glands. Experiencing some degree of acne is almost inevitable during adolescence due to the naturally increased activity of the sebaceous glands. Poor hygiene does not cause acne, but can exacerbate it. The degree to which an individual is affected may range from a small amount only occurring intermittently, to a severe inflammatory reaction creating a serious body image problem. The usual places for acne are the face, upper back, shoulders, and chest.

| Acne Vulgaris Lesions ||
Non-inflamed	Inflamed
• Closed	• Papules (small, raised lesion)
• Whiteheads with no visible openings	• Pustules (small, raised lesions containing pus)
• Blackheads with visible, discolored openings	• Nodules

Treatment is available to control acne and improve personal appearance. The treatment approach combines improving the overall health of an adolescent (e.g., sleep, exercise, nutrition) and topical and/or systemic medications. Throughout treatment, it is vital for the nurse to validate the adolescent's concerns about body image.

SCOLIOSIS

Scoliosis is a lateral curvature of the spine that can present at any time during childhood but is most commonly diagnosed after age 10. People with scoliosis will appear to have poor posture, one shoulder and hip higher than the other, and an uneven waistline. Back pain is **not** a routine finding with scoliosis. The goal of treatment of scoliosis is to halt the progression of the curvature, usually using a brace (e.g., Milwaukee brace) 23 hours per day for several years. Exercise therapy has proven to be helpful. If this is not successful, surgical correction is necessary.

The issues of scoliosis are mostly psychological for adolescents, whose self-esteem is often associated with being just like their peers. In addition, maintaining skin integrity is a priority. Under the brace, a thin t-shirt may be worn to reduce direct abrasions to the skin.

DEFECTS OF THE SPINAL COLUMN

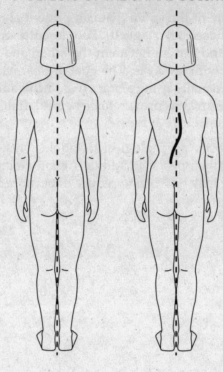

The normal spine in the upright position is vertically aligned, not twisted.

Mild to moderate spinal curvature (the upright spine has a marked serpentine twist) may benefit from corrective bracing or surgery.

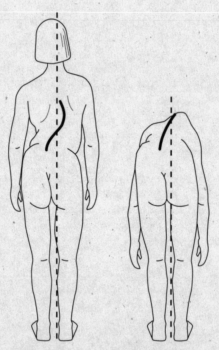

The rib hump, a hallmark of severe scoliosis, is accentuated when the client bends forward. Severe curvature is generally treated with surgery.

SEXUAL ACTIVITY IN ADOLESCENTS

Sexually transmitted disease (S.T.D.) represents one of the leading causes of adolescent morbidity. Teenagers are at high risk because of their growing interest in relations with the opposite sex and because of their general feeling of invulnerability. A large percentage of the adolescent population engages in sexual activity at a young age. Experimentation is a large part of this developmental stage. Adolescence is the time in which one's identity is separated from the family and the individual emerges as a sexual being. It is extremely important that adolescents are educated and aware of the potential outcomes of their sexual behavior. The use of condoms is the best way to prevent S.T.D.'s in sexually active individuals!

Nursing interventions for adolescents with S.T.D.'s include education, prevention, and treatment. The adolescent and his or her partner should be treated simultaneously with the appropriate regimen. They should be closely followed because poor compliance with treatment is common in this age group. It is extremely important to emphasize abstinence until both partners complete treatment to prevent reinfection or further spread of infection. Possible complications of recurrent infection include problems with fertility and ectopic pregnancy.

SEXUALLY TRANSMITTED DISEASES

Gonorrhea is a common, highly contagious bacterial infection that causes inflammation and pus production of the mucus membranes of the genital organs. It is associated with cervicitis in females and urethritis in males, and is diagnosed from a smear or culture. It is either asymptomatic or is characterized by dysuria (painful urination), possible vaginal discharge, and/or urethral discharge. Gonorrhea is treated with a single injection of either penicillin or spectinomycin, but reinfection is possible as no immunity is established.

Chlamydia is often called the "silent S.T.D." because it is often asymptomatic but transmittable. Those with symptoms will experience meatal erythema, tenderness, itching, and dysuria. Males will have a watery urethral discharge, and, in women, mucopurulent cervical exudate may be present. Treatment is usually a 10–14 day course of doxycycline for both the client and his/her sexual partner.

Human papillomavirus (H.P.V.) can be found in any part of male or female genitalia. After an incubation period of up to 8 months, clusters of lesions may progress to become vesicles and ulcers. Two different types of lesions are described: raised, polypoid masses that have a cauliflower appearance, and single flat condyloma (or warts). Symptoms of H.P.V. include itching, burning, and reddened areas. Treatment includes topical chemical agents, freezing agents (liquid nitrogen), and laser surgery for larger lesions.

Herpes simplex is an acute viral disease characterized by blisters on the genitalia (also on the lips). The lesions will burn and itch, but outbreaks are often self-limiting. When known, active herpes simplex is present, contact isolation is necessary to prevent the spread. There is no cure for herpes, but preferred treatment of intermittent outbreaks is with acyclovir (Zovirax), an antiviral medication. Nursing interventions for clients with herpes include emotional support and education. The lesions should be kept clean and dry, and loose clothing will help prevent irritation.

Syphilis is a contagious bacterial S.T.D. The first sign of syphilis is a painless **chancre**, a hard, red, nontender lesion with a raised border and yellow discharge. Chancres are usually found on the cervix, penis, and vulva. Treatment is with antibiotics such as penicillin or tetracycline. Pregnant women with syphilis can pass it on to their unborn children, but treatment (with erythromycin) before the fifth month of pregnancy can prevent transmission.

Human immunodeficiency virus (HIV) is the cause of AIDS and is transmitted through blood, body fluids (semen), and from mother to unborn child. Prevention is the key, because there is no cure for HIV and it is always fatal. Abstinence is the number one way to prevent HIV, but if the adolescent is sexually active, condoms are the best way to prevent infection. Education is imperative, as adolescents need to know that one can have the HIV virus for many months and not be aware of it.

PELVIC INFLAMMATORY DISEASE (P.I.D.)

P.I.D. is and infection affecting the upper female genital tract. The adolescent age group has historically had the highest incidence of P.I.D. It can involve the fallopian tubes, ovaries, uterus, or peritoneum. Risk factors include sexual activity, multiple partners, use of an IUD for contraception, prior history of P.I.D., history of complicated S.T.D. (usually gonorrhea or chlamydia), and prior induced abortion. Signs and symptoms include dull abdominal pain (usually first), urinary tract infection, diarrhea or constipation, nausea, fever, and an inflammatory mass noted on pelvic examination.

At the slightest suspicion of P.I.D., the client should be treated with antibiotics until the tests are confirmed. If there is a high fever, hospitalization is required for further treatment. Complications of untreated P.I.D. include infertility and ectopic pregnancy due to strictures and adhesions in the fallopian tubes. Pain management and ensuring compliance with antibiotic regimen are the primary nursing functions associated with P.I.D.

CONTRACEPTION

With the increase in sexual activity among adolescents, the need has arisen to educate them about the types of contraceptives available. In order for a contraceptive to be effective, it must be suited to the individual. Proper use of the contraceptive is extremely important to help prevent any serious immediate and long-term consequences for the adolescent. The use of barrier contraception (as condoms with the addition of spermicide) helps prevent pregnancy and S.T.D.'s.

Match the method of contraception with the correct type of contraceptive on the right:

2. ____ Jellies, nonoxynol-9	A. condom
3. ____ Injectable progestin	B. diaphragm
4. ____ Implanted subcutaneously	C. spermicides
5. ____ Must be fitted to the individual	D. the pill
6. ____ Prevents sperm from being deposited	E. Depo-Provera
7. ____ Take by mouth on a daily basis	F. Norplant
8. ____ Small object placed in uterine cavity	G. IUD

ADOLESCENT PREGNANCY

Teenage pregnancy has become a prevalent issue in our society. The advancement of technology has decreased the incidence of mortality for the fetus of an immature mother, but adolescent pregnancy, usually out of wedlock, is still viewed as socially, emotionally, and psychologically handicapping to the mother. In addition, complications still exist that put both the pregnant teenager and her fetus at risk. Label the following statements about adolescent pregnancy either **true** or **false**:

9. _____ Adolescents are more likely than adults to give birth prematurely.

10. _____ Girls younger than 16 years old have a five times greater chance of developing pregnancy-induced hypertension.

11. _____ Iron-deficiency anemia is unusual during pregnancy.

12. _____ Labor in an adolescent is the same as in an adult.

13. _____ Teenagers need an additional 300 calories per day during the second and third trimesters.

14. _____ Teenagers do not have a high incidence of low birth weight infants.

15. _____ Initial signs of pregnancy include cessation of menstruation and enlarged breasts.

16. _____ Adolescents can diet during pregnancy.

EATING DISORDERS

Because the adolescent population is generally fixated on body image, eating disorders are a real concern during this developmental stage. They can result in severe consequences to the body of an adolescent. We discuss eating disorders in more detail in Part VI: Psychosocial Integrity, but quickly jog your memory by labeling the following characteristics as true for either **bulimia** or **anorexia nervosa**:

17. _____ Binge eating

18. _____ Denies hunger

19. _____ Person feels fat even when severely underweight

20. _____ Self-induced emesis

21. _____ Excessive exercise

22. _____ Absence of three or more consecutive menstrual cycles

23. _____ Self-imposed starvation

RAPE

Rape is a devastating act of sexual assault that affects a large number of adolescent girls and an increasing number of boys. The primary role of the nurse is to provide comfort and not induce further stress. Rape victims fear interrogation, injury, and the reaction of their parents and peers, so disclosure is difficult. The nurse should be alert to any additional cues, and initiate stress-reduction techniques to help the adolescent manage the experience.

OTHER PRINCIPLES OF ADOLESCENCE

Adolescence is Erikson's stage of identity vs. role confusion. The nurse can often help parents cope with their child's "rebellious" nature by carefully explaining the developmental need to exert independence. It is imperative, though, that parental rules and expectations be consistent and realistic.

CHAPTER 19: EXERCISE ANSWERS

1. "Hi, I'm Lisa. I am going to ask you some personal questions. This is not because I want to snoop, but it may be important to your **health**. I assure you that what we talk about is **confidential**, just between the two of us. Okay, how many **meals** do you eat daily and what types of **foods**? Do you have any difficulty **sleeping**, either **insomnia** or **frequent waking**, that would affect your daily life? When you drive do you wear your **seat belt**? What grade are you in in school? What are your long-term goals concerning your **career**? Do you use **tobacco** or **alcohol**? How often and what types? Have you ever experimented with **drugs**? Are you sexually active? Do you use any type of **contraception**? Do you perform **testicular self-examination** regularly?"

2. **C   spermicides**—Jellies, nonoxynol-9

3. **E   Depo-Provera**—Injectable progestin

4. **F   Norplant**—Implanted subcutaneously

5. **B   diaphragm**—Must be fitted to the individual

6. **A   condom**—Prevents sperm from being deposited

7. **D   the pill**—Take by mouth on a daily basis

8. **G   IUD**—Small plastic object placed in uterine cavity

9. **True**—Adolescents are more likely than adults to give birth prematurely.

10. **True**—Girls younger than 16 years old have a five times greater chance of developing pregnancy-induced hypertension.

11. **False**—Iron-deficiency anemia is unusual during pregnancy.

12. **False**—Labor in an adolescent is the same as in an adult.

13. **True**—Teenagers need an additional 300 calories per day during the second and third trimesters.

14. **False**—Teenagers do not have a high incidence of low birth weight infants.

15. **True**—Initial signs of pregnancy include cessation of menstruation and enlarged breasts.

16. **False**—Adolescents can diet during pregnancy.

17. **Bulimia**—Binge eating

18. **Anorexia nervosa**—Denies hunger

19. **Anorexia nervosa**—Person feels fat even when severely underweight

20. **Bulimia**—Self-induced emesis
21. **Anorexia nervosa**—Excessive exercise
22. **Anorexia nervosa**—Absence of three or more consecutive menstrual cycles
23. **Anorexia nervosa**—Self-imposed starvation

CHAPTER 19: NCLEX-RN STYLE QUESTIONS

1. An obese adolescent who is being counseled on weight reduction methods should be given which of these instructions?

   (1) "It's easier to lose weight if you eat low-calorie foods at mealtimes instead of eating what your family eats."
   (2) "Weight loss should be gradual—no more than one or two pounds a week."
   (3) "High-fiber foods add pounds to your weight so it's best not to eat them."
   (4) "We'll talk about complex carbohydrates because limiting them will make weight loss permanent."

2. When obtaining assessment data on an adolescent female client who admits to feeling "very depressed," the nurse should explore any losses related to

   (1) an ideal.
   (2) achievement of a goal.
   (3) termination of a close relationship.
   (4) an inability to perceive reality accurately.

3. When counseling an adolescent on the healthy means to achieve weight loss, it is important to

   (1) encourage the use of fat-free foods.
   (2) encourage increasing intake of diet sodas for fluid intake.
   (3) encourage losing no more than 1–2 pounds per week.
   (4) encourage increasing dietary intake of complex carbohydrates.

4. A client is admitted to the hospital with pelvic inflammatory disease (P.I.D.). A possible long-term effect that should be discussed with any adolescent with pelvic inflammatory disease is the risk of

   (1) bleeding.
   (2) infertility.
   (3) yeast infections.
   (4) cervical incompetency.

5. An adolescent client makes an unprovoked rude gesture to a staff member. In a staff conference the nurse explains that the reason for this is that

   (1) the client is exhibiting antisocial behavior.
   (2) the client is psychotic.
   (3) the client is testing limits the staff will set.
   (4) the client is a threat to others.

6. A 13-year-old child has a lateral curvature of the spine that disappears with forward bending. On assessment the nurse would record this as

   (1) a normal spine.
   (2) lordosis.
   (3) scoliosis.
   (4) kyphosis.

7. Though bracing can be highly effective in halting the progression of scoliosis, compliance by adolescents is a big issue. Which of the following interventions can increase compliance by an adolescent?

   (1) Minimize skin breakdown.
   (2) Teach the client what clothes might hide the brace.
   (3) Emphasize the importance of following orders about bracing with the parents.
   (4) Have the school nurse monitor the client.

8. The nurse learns from a 17-year-old adolescent client in the high school health office that she is sexually active. Which of the following interventions is appropriate for the nurse to do next?

   (1) Call her mother immediately.
   (2) Give her pamphlets regarding abstinence.
   (3) Find out who her boyfriend is.
   (4) Find out what measures are being taken to prevent the spread of communicable disease.

9. A 14-year-old female is to be admitted for the insertion of rods to straighten her spine. Because she is a 14-year-old female, you can predict which of the following about her postoperative course?

   (1) This client is likely to need some sense of control, but will want the nurse to do things for her.
   (2) This client will not cry.
   (3) Friends will probably be important to her recovery and return to school.
   (4) There will be physical, psychological, and social dimensions to her recovery.

CHAPTER 19: NCLEX-RN STYLE ANSWERS

1.   (2) CORRECT   Loss of one or two pounds per week is the maximum recommended loss.
    (1) *ELIMINATE*   The dieting adolescent should eat what the rest of the family eats.
    (3) *ELIMINATE*   High-fiber foods should be encouraged because they tend to be high in nutrients, low in calories, and satisfying.
    (4) *ELIMINATE*   Complex carbohydrates should be eaten.
    CATEGORY 04 PREVENTION AND EARLY DETECTION OF DISEASE

2.   **(3) CORRECT**   An important factor in female development is attachment within relationships.

        (1) *ELIMINATE*   Loss of an ideal is attributable to both males and females.

        (2) *ELIMINATE*   Loss of achievement of a goal is more attributable to males, especially in the workplace.

        (4) *ELIMINATE*   This has more to do with psychotic behavior.

CATEGORY 06 PSYCHOSOCIAL ADAPTATION

---

3.   **(3) CORRECT**   It is recommended that one should not lose more than 1–2 pounds per week while dieting.

        (1) *ELIMINATE*   Fat-free foods are expensive and do not provide proper nutrients for promoting weight loss.

        (2) *ELIMINATE*   Water, not diet sodas, is appropriate for fluid intake when dieting.

        (4) *ELIMINATE*   Increasing complex carbohydrates would not be appropriate.

CATEGORY 09 REDUCTION OF RISK POTENTIAL

---

4.   **(2) CORRECT**   Pelvic inflammatory disease can cause scarring and adhesions that can lead to infertility.

        (1) *ELIMINATE*   Bleeding is not a long-term effect.

        (3) *ELIMINATE*   Yeast infections are not a long-term effect.

        (4) *ELIMINATE*   Cervical incompetency is not a long-term effect of pelvic inflammatory disease.

CATEGORY 09 REDUCTION OF RISK POTENTIAL

---

5.   **(3) CORRECT**   Adolescents frequently test social limits as a normal manifestation of their process of individuation.

        (1) *ELIMINATE*   This is true, but not the reason for the behavior.

        (2) *ELIMINATE*   The action does not indicate the client is psychotic.

        (4) *ELIMINATE*   The gesture does not indicate the client is a threat to others.

CATEGORY 03 GROWTH AND DEVELOPMENT THROUGH THE LIFE SPAN

---

6.   **(3) CORRECT**   Scoliosis is a lateral curvature of the spine. In functional scoliosis, the spine curves to compensate for another condition.

        (1) *ELIMINATE*   This is not a normal spine.

        (2) *ELIMINATE*   Lordosis is the forward curvature of the lumbar spine.

        (4) *ELIMINATE*   Kyphosis is a hunchback spine.

CATEGORY 04 PREVENTION AND EARLY DETECTION OF DISEASE

7. (2) CORRECT The visibility of the brace can be minimized with certain clothing. Your client does not want to be different from her peers.

(1) *ELIMINATE* Minimizing skin breakdowns would not be related to compliance.

(3) *ELIMINATE* The parents might not have the greatest influence at this time. Peer group acceptance is most important to the adolescent.

(4) *ELIMINATE* The school nurse would be an influence and could not monitor the adolescent at all times.

CATEGORY 03 GROWTH AND DEVELOPMENT THROUGH THE LIFE SPAN

---

8. (4) CORRECT Collecting data is the first step of the nursing process. Making an assessment of the client's knowledge regarding safe sex and sexually transmitted diseases would be the priority.

(1) *ELIMINATE* A trusting nurse-client relationship will be jeopardized if a parent is contacted at this point against the adolescent's wishes.

(2) *ELIMINATE* Pamphlets regarding abstinence may be helpful later in providing information regarding S.T.D.'s and pregnancy, but the nurse must first find out what the client knows.

(3) *ELIMINATE* The boyfriend's name is not pertinent.

CATEGORY 04 PREVENTION AND EARLY DETECTION OF DISEASE

---

9. (4) CORRECT This is the more global statement, which incorporates the need for friends (peers).

(1) *ELIMINATE* The client at 14 years old will want some control while hospitalized. The nurse should encourage self-care.

(2) *ELIMINATE* Though many adolescents would prefer not to cry, surgery is a major stressor and this procedure is painful. The nurse cannot predict how the adolescent will react to this stress.

(3) *POSSIBLE* This is true but not the best response.

CATEGORY 03 GROWTH AND DEVELOPMENT THROUGH THE LIFE SPAN

20

CHRONIC HEALTH PROBLEMS OF CHILDHOOD

WHAT YOU NEED TO KNOW

Certain diseases span several developmental stages, so we have grouped them as chronic childhood diseases. As your review progresses, think about the nurse's role in addressing the special needs of children and families coping with chronic illness. The diseases are ordered according to the frequency with which you may see them on the NCLEX-RN. Remember the principles of development and the supposed "normal" physical characteristics of childhood.

ASTHMA

Asthma, an obstructive disease of the airways, is the most common childhood disease. It is characterized by irritability of the trachea and bronchi in the lungs that cause spasm and edema of the bronchial smooth muscle and increased mucous production. Asthma exacerbations are almost always reversible with immediate attention and medication. Thus education on prevention of attacks is imperative in the management of asthma. The cause of an asthma attack may be in the external environment, such as allergens or irritants, or it may be internal, such as infections.

The symptoms of an asthma attack may come on gradually, but they almost always include expiratory wheezing, anxiety, fear, and an uncontrollable cough. When a child with these symptoms is admitted to your emergency room, prepare to place him on oxygen (as per a provider's order) and then administer β-adrenergic agonists as ordered by the provider. These include albuterol, metaproterenol, and terbutaline. In acute exacerbations of asthma, a short course of steroids may be ordered to inhibit the inflammatory response.

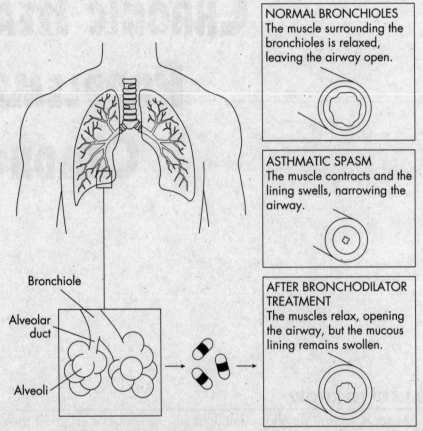

NORMAL BRONCHIOLES
The muscle surrounding the bronchioles is relaxed, leaving the airway open.

ASTHMATIC SPASM
The muscle contracts and the lining swells, narrowing the airway.

AFTER BRONCHODILATOR TREATMENT
The muscles relax, opening the airway, but the mucous lining remains swollen.

Bronchiole

Alveolar duct

Alveoli

The absence of wheezing and diminished breath sounds is not a good sign! Minimal air exchange is taking place and this child is on the brink of respiratory failure—act quickly!

CYSTIC FIBROSIS

Cystic fibrosis (C.F.) is a hereditary disease and one of the most common chronic illnesses. It affects multiple organ systems, although the primary difficulties are related to the mucus buildup in the lungs and pancreas. When the mucus builds up in the pancreas, the enzymes needed for the digestion of fats, proteins, and carbohydrates (**amylase**, **lipase**, and **trypsin**) are prevented from reaching the duodenum. This causes fatty stools (**steatorrhea**) and protein in the stools (**azotorrhea**), due to the impairment in nutrient digestion and absorption. It is necessary for these children to take pancreatic enzymes on a daily basis to increase the absorption and digestion of many foods.

The pulmonary complications of C.F. are the most serious and the most frequent reason for hospitalization for children with this disease. The thick and tenacious mucus causes patchy and chronic obstruction of the alveoli and contributes to frequent pulmonary infections. The goals of therapy are to provide adequate nutrition and prevent or lessen pulmonary complications. Nurses can assume a big role in assisting the family and child in adapting to their chronic disease. In the past these children rarely survived to adolescence, but now they often live into adulthood. Families should be encouraged to expect normal development. With recent advances in gene therapy in the treatment of C.F., their life spans will probably be further extended.

LEUKEMIA

Leukemia is a broad term given to a group of malignant diseases of the bone marrow and lymphatic system. Leukemia is the most common childhood cancer, affecting approximately 4 in 100,000 children. The cause is not known, although environmental, genetic, and immunologic factors have been associated with its onset. The diagnosis of leukemia is usually very upsetting for the child and family. Children and family members may associate leukemia with death, although the survival rate at 5 years is now close to 70 percent. The most common form of leukemia is **acute lymphocytic leukemia** (A.L.L.). Another form for you to recognize is **acute myelogenous leukemia** (A.M.L.).

In all forms of leukemia there is an abnormality in the white blood cells. The type of leukemia is determined by the morphology of the leukemic cells, which also determines the treatment the child will receive. The primary treatment is chemotherapy, usually given in three phases: **induction**, **maintenance**, and **consolidation**. There are numerous side effects associated with chemotherapy because many of the chemotherapeutic agents used kill any rapidly dividing cells, along with the leukemic cells. Therefore, cells of the GI tract, bone marrow, and integumentary system are commonly affected. Other modalities used in the treatment of leukemia may include radiation therapy (for central nervous system involvement or prophylaxis), immunotherapy, and/or bone marrow transplant.

Children with leukemia and their families require in-depth and frequent education regarding the child's status, particularly the treatment plan and the complete blood count results. Anemia, neutropenia, and thrombocytopenia are side effects almost always encountered in the child with leukemia receiving chemotherapy. Families of the children experiencing these side effects must be educated regarding the signs and symptoms of each condition and precautions that need to be taken when any of the counts are decreased.

Match the term on the left with the correct definition on the right:

1. ____ Thrombocytopenia   A. fatty stools

2. ____ Leukemia   B. low white blood cell count

3. ____ Anemia   C. low platelet count

4. ____ Neutropenia   D. healthy bone marrow is injected to replace diseased bone marrow

5. ____ Immunotherapy   E. low red blood cell count

6. ____ Bone marrow transplant   F. chemical treatment of disease

7. ____ Chemotherapy   G. passive immunization via serum or gamma globulin

8. ____ Steatorrhea   H. progressive disease of blood-producing organs; characterized by distorted leukocytes

It is also important for the nurse to educate and prepare the child for the painful procedures that are required for diagnosis and management of leukemia. The most common are venipuncture, bone marrow aspiration and/or biopsy, lumbar puncture, and the associated side effects of chemotherapy (nausea, vomiting, body image changes). They should be explained and demonstrated at a developmentally appropriate level.

In dealing with the child and family with leukemia, one crucial period that requires maximal support occurs if the child has a relapse. This is one of the most difficult times in caring for the child with leukemia. The family may be expected to experience many of the same emotions as they did at the time of initial diagnosis, including denial, acceptance, hopelessness, and anxiety.

Match the low blood count with the instructions that should be given to the child/family:

9. ____ Neutropenia   A. rest when needed; do not overexert

10. ____ Anemia   B. avoid contact sports; notify provider if any bleeding or bruising is noticed

11. ____ Thrombocytopenia   C. avoid crowded places; wash hands well

DIABETES MELLITUS

Diabetes mellitus (D.M.) is a chronic illness related to a deficiency in insulin. Diabetes is classified as either insulin dependent D.M. (Type I D.M.; I.D.D.M.), non–insulin dependent D.M. (Type II D.M.; N.I.D.D.M.), or maturity-onset diabetes of youth (M.O.D.Y.). The most common form that affects children is Type I. Its onset is usually during adolescence. Individuals with Type I D.M. require exogenous insulin to help control their serum glucose levels.

The child and family with D.M., as with the other chronic illnesses, require a considerable amount of education and support, particularly in regard to the daily requirements of monitoring and treatment needed with D.M. They must be educated regarding measurement of the blood glucose level by finger stick, administration of insulin, measurement of glucose in the urine, proper nutrition, and recognition of the signs and symptoms of hypoglycemia and hyperglycemia. Teaching is required regarding peripheral neuropathy and prevention of injury to extremities. The child should be encouraged to participate from the time of the initial diagnosis as much as is developmentally feasible.

For your review, match the different types of insulin with the appropriate time of action:

12. ____ Regular insulin, lente   A. intermediate acting, peaking in 6–12 hours

13. ____ NPH insulin, semilente   B. long acting, peaking in 14–24 hours

14. ____ Ultralente insulin   C. short acting, peaking in 2–4 hours

HEMOPHILIA

Hemophilia refers to a group of bleeding disorders in which there is a deficiency of one of the clotting factors in the blood. Hemophilia is transmitted as an X-linked recessive disorder. The primary therapy for hemophilia is preventing spontaneous bleeding by replacement of the missing factor (Factor VIII). Effective treatment of bleeding episodes depends on early detection. The nurse should teach the child and family that before clinical signs of internal bleeding are evident, the child will probably be instinctively aware that something is amiss. The clinical signs of internal tissue bleeding are:

- Headache
- Slurred speech
- Loss of consciousness from bleeding within the brain or gastrointestinal tract
- Black, tarry stools
- Hematemesis

SICKLE CELL ANEMIA

To begin your review of sickle cell anemia, label the following statements as **true** or **false**:

15. ____ The incidence of sickle cell anemia is greatest among African-Americans.

16. ____ Sickle cell anemia is an autosomal disorder.

17. ____ Sickle cell anemia is usually diagnosed in early infancy.

18. ____ Sickled cells differ from normal cells in their shape.

19. ____ Decreased blood viscosity and increased red blood cell destruction causes pathological changes to occur.

20. _____ The life span of a red blood cell is decreased with the formation of sickled erythrocytes.

21. _____ A child's sickle cell crisis will most likely be preceded by infection.

22. _____ During a sickle cell crisis, pain occurs as a result of the sickled cells obstructing the blood vessels, causing occlusion and ischemia.

23. _____ Sickle cell anemia is curable with the appropriate management.

24. _____ Enuresis is an early sign of renal failure in a child who has sickle cell anemia.

Sickle cell anemia is a chronic, autosomal recessive hemolytic anemia that is characterized by intensely painful episodes caused by the obstruction of blood vessels by red blood cells. These odd-shaped cells clog the small blood vessels and cause ischemia and, therefore, excruciating pain. Children with sickle cell anemia are almost always African-American and are homozygous for the trait, which means both parents must be at least carriers of the gene.

All babies born in the United States are tested for sickle cell disease before discharge from the hospital. A child's first sickle cell crisis is usually vaso-occlusive and probably won't occur until late in the first year of life. Precipitating factors for a crisis include:

- Dehydration
- Infection
- Exposure to the cold
- Trauma
- Strenuous physical activity and lack of oxygen
- Extreme fatigue

The nursing goals for the child with sickle cell anemia include prevention of infection and promotion of tissue oxygenation and hydration. To this end, interventions include:

- Teaching the importance of good nutrition
- Encouraging frequent medical exams
- Promoting completion of courses of antibiotics
- Teaching the child to avoid strenuous physical activity and emotional stress
- Teaching the child to avoid low-oxygen environments like non-pressurized airplanes and high altitudes
- Encouraging adequate fluid intake (100–125 cc/kg/day)
- Teaching the child and family the signs of dehydration (e.g., thirst, dry mucous membranes)

However, if the child develops signs of a sickle cell crisis (fever, acute abdominal pain, headache, hand-foot syndrome), treatment includes:

- Oxygen
- Bed rest to minimize energy expenditure and oxygen demand
- **Analgesics!**
- Hydration for hemodilution
- Electrolyte replacement
- Blood replacement
- Antibiotics

DOWN'S SYNDROME

Down's syndrome, or Trisomy 21, is the most common genetic disorder and is associated with a number of physical and mental abnormalities. It is caused by an extra chromosome on the 21st pair and is more common in infants born to mothers over age 35. The life expectancy of a child with Down's syndrome depends on the extent of physical complications present. Children with Down's syndrome can be expected to live at home and attend infant-stimulation programs and, later, schools with special education programs.

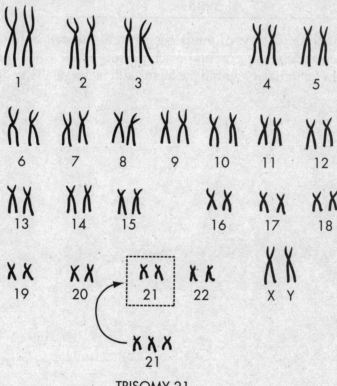

TRISOMY 21

This picture represents the 21 pairs of chromosomes with the extra (third) chromosome associated with Down's syndrome on the 21st pair.

Physical Characteristics of Children with Down's Syndrome	
Brachycephaly	A short, wide head
Epicanthic folds	Vertical skin fold on both sides of the nose, covers the canthus of the eye
Flat nasal bridge	Wide-set eyes
Simian crease	A continuous crease across the palm of the hand
Small, low-set ears	In the normal newborn, the top of the helix of the ear is on the same plane as the eye.
Possible congenital heart defect	Early identification and treatment can prevent congestive heart failure.
Mental retardation	Special education, infant-stimulation programs
Dry, scaly skin	Prevent cracking and infection!
Retarded physical growth	Plot growth on chart specific to Down's syndrome. Monitor onset of puberty.
Muscle hypotonicity	Physical, occupational, and speech therapy are imperative to maximize potential for muscular control.

Caring for the child with Down's syndrome poses physical, mental, and emotional challenges for parents. Nurses must lend support and teach parents about what they can expect from their child in order to minimize potential problems and facilitate life at home.

25. The following is a nursing care summary for the child with Down's syndrome. The nursing goals and associated rationales are provided. Your job is to decide the best nursing interventions:

Nursing Goals	Nursing Intervention	Rationales
Prevent physical complications caused by Down's syndrome		Hypotonicity and hyperextensibility of the joints complicate positioning and promote heat loss via greater body surface area.
Prevent respiratory infection		Decreased muscle tone compromises respiratory expansion. The underdeveloped nasal bone causes inadequate drainage of mucous. The constant "stuffy nose" forces the child to breathe by mouth, thereby drying the oropharyngeal membranes.
Minimize feeding difficulties in infancy		The large, protruding tongue associated with Down's syndrome interferes with feeding. Decreased muscle tone affects gastric motility, predisposing the infant to constipation. Excessive weight gain can slow motor development.
Prevent skin breakdown		The skin of a child with Down's syndrome can gradually become rough and dry and is prone to cracking and infection. Limited mobility can cause skin breakdown.

CEREBRAL PALSY

Cerebral palsy is a chronic, nonprogressive neurological disorder caused by malformation of the motor pathways of the brain. Factors that play a role in the development of cerebral palsy are either prenatal (maternal infection such as rubella, toxoplasmosis; maternal anoxia; genetics), perinatal (anoxia from anesthetics, prolonged labor, cerebral trauma during delivery), or postnatal (infections such as meningitis or encephalitis; vascular accidents).

Signs of Cerebral Palsy		
Early Signs	**Late Signs**	**Other Findings**
• Asymmetry of movement • Restlessness • Tongue thrust and poor sucking • High-pitched, feeble cry • Lack of head control • Long, thin babies	• Delayed motor development • Infantile reflexes do not go away • Hand preference visible before 12–15 months of age • Delayed speech development	• Seizures • Hearing and visual deficits • Mental retardation • Behavioral problems • Gastroesophageal reflux

If you are the nurse for a child recently diagnosed with cerebral palsy, educating the parents and assessing and maximizing the child's potential through appropriate referrals are imperative interventions. Parents must be encouraged to set limits with these children and to seek support from other parents with affected children.

REVIEW

To test your knowledge of **Down's syndrome** and **cerebral palsy**, identify which of the two disorders is characterized by each of the following statements:

26. _____ Usually diagnosed at birth.

27. _____ Most likely, diagnosis won't be confirmed until after 6 months of age.

28. _____ Incidence increases with infants born to mothers over age 35.

29. _____ An extra chromosome (21) has been identified in 95 percent of the children with this abnormality.

30. _____ Most common permanent disability of childhood.

31. _____ Children with this abnormality show a delay in all motor accomplishments.

32. _____ Observable physical characteristics of this disorder include Mongoloid slant to the eyes, a wide space between the big and second toes, and a protruding tongue.

33. _____ Signs of this abnormality include poor sucking, persistent tongue thrust, facial grimacing, and walking on toes.

34. _____ Characterized by abnormal muscle tone and decreased coordination.

35. _____ Complications of this disorder include attention deficit disorder (ADD), seizures, strabismus, and hearing loss.

36. _____ Anomalies associated with this disorder include congenital cardiac septal defects, transesophageal fistula, hip subluxation, and instability of the first and second vertebrae.

37. _____ As the nurse caring for a child with this disorder, you would assess for the persistence or hyperactivity of the Moro, plantar, and palmar grasp reflexes beyond the normal age.

38. _____ With this disorder, the child's developmental potential seems greatest during infancy, so parents should be involved in an infant-stimulation program.

39. _____ This disorder can be diagnosed in utero through amniocentesis.

40. _____ The drugs that may be prescribed for this disorder include anti-anxiety agents, muscle relaxants, and anticonvulsants.

41. _____ Infants at risk for this disease include low birth weight infants, preterm infants, and infants with low Apgar scores at 5 minutes. These children warrant careful assessment during early infancy.

1. **C** **Thrombocytopenia**—low platelet count
2. **H** **Leukemia**—progressive disease of blood-producing organs; characterized by distorted leukocytes
3. **E** **Anemia**—low red blood cell count
4. **B** **Neutropenia**—low white blood cell count
5. **G** **Immunotherapy**—passive immunization via serum or gamma globulin
6. **D** **Bone marrow transplant**—healthy bone marrow is injected to replace diseased bone marrow
7. **F** **Chemotherapy**—chemical treatment of disease
8. **A** **Steatorrhea**—fatty stools
9. **C** **Neutropenia**—avoid crowded places; wash hands well
10. **A** **Anemia**—rest when needed; do not overexert
11. **B** **Thrombocytopenia**—avoid contact sports; notify provider if any bleeding or bruising is noticed
12. **C** **Regular insulin, lente**—short acting, peaking in 2–4 hours
13. **A** **NPH insulin, semilente**—intermediate acting, peaking in 6–12 hours
14. **B** **Ultralente insulin**—long acting, peaking in 14–24 hours
15. **True**—The incidence of sickle cell anemia is greatest among African-Americans.
15. **True**—Sickle cell anemia is an autosomal disorder.
17. **False**—Sickle cell anemia is usually diagnosed in early infancy.
18. **True**—Sickled cells differ from normal cells in their shape.
19. **False**—Decreased blood viscosity and increased red blood cell destruction causes pathological changes to occur.
20. **True**—The life span of a red blood cell is decreased with the formation of sickled erythrocytes.
21. **True**—A child's sickle cell crisis will most likely be preceded by infection.
22. **True**—During a sickle cell crisis, pain occurs as a result of the sickled cells obstructing the blood vessels, causing occlusion and ischemia.
23. **False**—Sickle cell anemia is curable with the appropriate management.
24. **False**—Enuresis is an early sign of renal failure in a child who has sickle cell anemia.
25. The correct nursing interventions are listed in the following chart:

Nursing Goals	Nursing Intervention	Rationales
Prevent physical complications caused by Down's syndrome	Encourage parents to wrap the infant tightly in a blanket to provide warmth. Discuss with the parents that the child's positioning (lack of clinging or molding) is a physical characteristic, not a sign of detachment.	Hypotonicity and hyperextensibility of the joints complicate positioning and promote heat loss via greater body surface area.
Prevent respiratory infection	Teach the parents to clear the child's nose with a bulb syringe and to rinse the child's mouth with water after feedings. Encourage the use of a cool mist vaporizer. Stress the importance of changing the child's position frequently to promote drainage of mucous.	Decreased muscle tone compromises respiratory expansion. The underdeveloped nasal bone causes inadequate drainage of mucous. The constant "stuffy nose" forces the child to breathe by mouth, thereby drying the oropharyngeal membranes.
Minimize feeding difficulties in infancy	Inform the parents that the tongue thrust does not indicate food refusal. Feed solid food by pushing it to the back and side of the mouth with a long, straight spoon. Schedule small, frequent feedings with rest periods. Teach parents to include fiber and fluids in the child's diet to prevent constipation. Base the child's intake on his/her weight, not his/her chronological age.	The large, protruding tongue associated with Down's syndrome interferes with feeding. Decreased muscle tone affects gastric motility, predisposing the infant to constipation. Excessive weight gain can slow motor development.
Prevent skin breakdown	Teach the parents to keep the child's skin well lubricated. Minimize the use of soap. Apply lip balm when the child is outdoors.	The skin of a child with Down's syndrome can gradually become rough and dry and is prone to cracking and infection. Limited mobility can cause skin breakdown.

26. **Down's syndrome**—Usually diagnosed at birth.

27. **Cerebral palsy**—Most likely, diagnosis won't be confirmed until after 6 months of age.

28. **Down's syndrome**—Incidence increases with infants born to mothers over age 35.

29. **Down's syndrome**—An extra chromosome (21) has been identified in 95 percent of the children with this abnormality.

30. **Cerebral palsy**—Most common permanent disability of childhood.

31. **Cerebral palsy**—Children with this abnormality show a delay in all motor accomplishments.

32. **Down's syndrome**—Observable physical characteristics of this disorder include Mongoloid slant to the eyes, a wide space between the big and second toes, and a protruding tongue.

33. **Cerebral palsy**—Signs of this abnormality include poor sucking, persistent tongue thrust, facial grimacing, and walking on toes.

34. **Cerebral palsy**—Characterized by abnormal muscle tone and decreased coordination.

35. **Cerebral palsy**—Complications of this disorder include attention deficit disorder (ADD), seizures, strabismus, and hearing loss.

36. **Down's syndrome**—Anomalies associated with this disorder include congenital cardiac septal defects, transesophageal fistula, hip subluxation, and instability of the first and second vertebrae.

37. **Cerebral palsy**—As the nurse caring for a child with this disorder, you would assess for the persistence or hyperactivity of the Moro, plantar, and palmar grasp reflexes beyond the normal age.

38. **Down's syndrome**—With this disorder, the child's developmental potential seems greatest during infancy, so parents should be involved in an infant-stimulation program.

39. **Down's syndrome**—This disorder can be diagnosed in utero through amniocentesis.

40. **Cerebral palsy**—The drugs that may be prescribed for this disorder include antianxiety agents, muscle relaxants, and anticonvulsants.

41. **Cerebral palsy**—Infants at risk for this disease include low birth weight infants, preterm infants, and infants with low Apgar scores at 5 minutes. These children warrant careful assessment during early infancy.

CHAPTER 20: NCLEX-RN STYLE QUESTIONS

1. The primary nursing action in caring for an adolescent in sickle cell crisis is directed at
   (1) maintaining adequate hydration.
   (2) managing pain.
   (3) promoting adequate nutrition.
   (4) encouraging visitation by peers.

2. When caring for a child with cystic fibrosis, it is important to
   (1) administer pancreatic enzymes before all meals and snacks.
   (2) provide low-calorie, low-protein foods.
   (3) limit physical activity.
   (4) teach parents to administer cough suppressants as needed.

3. After teaching the parents of a child newly diagnosed with idiopathic thrombocytopenia purpura, you would know that they need further teaching if you observed the child
   (1) coloring in a book.
   (2) playing with putty.
   (3) playing football with his brother.
   (4) playing computer games with his sister.

4. If a child's platelet count is 1,000, you would not be surprised to see which of the following conditions?
   (1) Petechiae.
   (2) Oral *Candida*.
   (3) Contact dermatitis.
   (4) Pallor.

5. The nurse is aware that the primary pathophysiologic mechanism in cystic fibrosis is
   (1) respiratory failure.
   (2) inability to metabolize sodium.
   (3) malabsorption of nutrients.
   (4) viscous mucus obstructing organs and glands.

6. Children with some congenital heart defects are likely to be profoundly polycythemic. The nurse knows the reason for this is that
   (1) they are dehydrated and are trying to compensate.
   (2) they are anemic and the body overcompensates.
   (3) they are hypoxic and the body is trying to compensate.
   (4) they have high red cell concentrations for unknown reasons.

7. A 9-year-old client has sickle cell anemia and is being admitted because of sickle cell crisis. When assessing this client, the nurse is aware that
   (1) the sickling response is not reversible.
   (2) signs and symptoms are usually present during the neonatal period.
   (3) the spleen usually becomes enlarged due to congestion and engorgement with sickled cells.
   (4) it is transmitted as an autosomal dominant disorder.

8.	The nurse is aware that an important consideration in caring for a child with a Wilms' tumor is that	(1) the tumor is always very small.
		(2) the prognosis when discovered early is usually poor.
		(3) the presenting complaint is usually pain with difficulty voiding.
		(4) the abdomen should never be palpated.
9.	When caring for a child with a congenital cardiac defect, it is important to be aware of early signs of congestive heart failure. Which of the following changes is an early sign?	(1) Bradycardia
		(2) Hyperactivity
		(3) Weight loss
		(4) Tachycardia

CHAPTER 20: NCLEX-RN STYLE ANSWERS

1. (1) CORRECT   Dehydration promotes sickling, which will increase pain, decrease respiratory functioning, and further potentiate sickling.

(2) POSSIBLE   Pain management is an important component of care, but the prevention of sickling takes priority. However, if the patient is in tremendous pain during the crisis, pain management will work faster than fluid management in decreasing pain.

(3) POSSIBLE   Nutritional intake is important, but the prevention of sickling takes priority.

(4) POSSIBLE   Social contact is important, but the prevention of sickling takes priority.

CATEGORY 09 REDUCTION OF RISK POTENTIAL

2. (1) CORRECT   Pancreatic enzymes are necessary to digest food.

(2) ELIMINATE   High-calorie, high-protein foods should be a part of the child's diet.

(3) ELIMINATE   Physical exercise is necessary.

(4) ELIMINATE   Cough suppressants are contraindicated.

CATEGORY 09 REDUCTION OF RISK POTENTIAL

3. (3) CORRECT   Idiopathic thrombocytopenia purpura can cause easy bleeding. Football is a contact sport that involves a risk of injury.

(1) ELIMINATE   This is a normal activity for the child.

(2) ELIMINATE   This is a normal activity in which the child would not be prone to injury and/or bleeding.

(4) ELIMINATE   This is a normal activity in which the child would not be prone to injury and/or bleeding.

CATEGORY 09 REDUCTION OF RISK POTENTIAL

4. **(1) CORRECT** Petechiae or small capillary hemorrhages under the skin will often occur in children with low platelet counts.

(2) INCORRECT Oral candida is not associated with a low platelet count.

(3) INCORRECT Contact dermatitis is not associated with a low platelet count.

(4) INCORRECT Pallor is not associated with a low platelet count.

CATEGORY 10 PHYSIOLOGICAL ADAPTATION

---

5. **(4) CORRECT** Thick, tenacious mucus obstructs glands and organs, primarily in the respiratory and gastrointestinal systems.

(1) ELIMINATE Respiratory failure is not the primary pathophysiology in a client with cystic fibrosis.

(2) ELIMINATE Inability to metabolize sodium is not the primary pathophysiology.

(3) ELIMINATE Malabsorption of nutrients is not the primary pathophysiology.

CATEGORY 10 PHYSIOLOGICAL ADAPTATION

---

6. **(3) CORRECT** Polycythemia is an increased mass of red blood cells in the blood. In children with congenital heart defects, the body produces more red blood cells to compensate for the tissue hypoxia caused by the defect.

(1) ELIMINATE Dehydration is not associated with polycythemia.

(2) ELIMINATE Anemia is not associated with polycythemia.

(4) ELIMINATE The physiological reason for the polycythemia is known.

CATEGORY 10 PHYSIOLOGICAL ADAPTATION

---

7. **(3) CORRECT** The spleen does become enlarged due to congestion and engorgement with sickle cells.

(1) ELIMINATE Under conditions of adequate hydration and oxygenation, the sickling response is initially reversible.

(2) ELIMINATE Due to the presence of fetal hemoglobin at birth, the sickling phenomenon is usually not present until later infancy.

(4) ELIMINATE The disorder is inherited from both parents, who are carriers (autosomal recessive).

CATEGORY 10 PHYSIOLOGICAL ADAPTATION

8.   (4) CORRECT   A Wilms' tumor is very fragile, and palpating the abdomen may cause spreading
                         of cancer cells.
       (1) *ELIMINATE*   A Wilms' tumor is not always very small.
       (2) *ELIMINATE*   The prognosis when discovered early can be fair.
       (3) *ELIMINATE*   The presenting complaint is generally back pain.

CATEGORY 10 PHYSIOLOGICAL ADAPTATION

9.   (4) CORRECT   Tachycardia is the result of the heart trying to compensate early for the increased
                         fluid volume.
       (1) *ELIMINATE*   Tachycardia, not bradycardia, is an early sign of congestive heart failure.
       (2) *ELIMINATE*   Hyperactivity is not an early sign of congestive heart failure.
       (3) *ELIMINATE*   Weight gain, not weight loss, would be a sign of congestive heart failure.

CATEGORY 09 REDUCTION OF RISK POTENTIAL

21

THE CHILD AND FAMILY WITH SPECIAL NEEDS

WHAT YOU NEED TO KNOW

There are certain developmental tasks that children are expected to achieve based on their abilities and developmental age. The NCLEX-RN loves to use Erikson's theory of development to gauge if a child is developing within the expected time frame. As children with chronic illnesses and conditions develop, they may have special needs due to their illness or disability.

Match the possible effect hospitalization may have on a child with the appropriate age:

1. ___ Infant | A. may lose confidence in skills (e.g., walking, feeding, and toilet training)

2. ___ Toddler | B. may fear invasive procedures and feel that she caused her own illness

3. ___ Preschooler | C. may be very concerned about being different from peers

4. ___ School-age | D. may not have trust in the caregivers and environment

5. ___ Adolescent | E. may not experience a sense of accomplishment

During each stage of development it is important for the nurse to help the child and family focus on the positive aspects of the child's abilities, not only on the disabilities or things that make the child different from other children. Nurses need to remain nonjudgmental and supportive of the child and family at all times.

CHILDREN WITH CHRONIC ILLNESSES

Hospitalization is difficult for children and their families. A child with a chronic illness often spends much of her time in the hospital. It is ideal if nurses can help the child feel as if the hospital is a warm and welcoming place, almost like a second home. Nursing plays a vital role in preparing the child and family for repeated and sometimes unexpected hospitalizations. It is necessary for the nurse to assess the needs of both child and family on an ongoing basis. A key role of nursing is to help children maintain a sense of normalcy despite the challenges and interruptions related to their chronic illnesses.

6. From the list below, circle the diseases that are considered to be chronic illnesses:

   A. Hemophilia
   B. Congenital heart disease
   C. Chicken pox
   D. Leukemia and other childhood cancers
   E. Diabetes
   F. Croup
   G. Cystic fibrosis
   H. Asthma

With all of these illnesses, it is important to always treat the client as a developing child with individual needs and characteristics first, and not simply as a child with an illness or disability. The chronic diseases were discussed in more detail in Chapter 20.

When a family is told that a child has a chronic illness or disability, the news is usually very devastating. Nurses are often involved in both the initial and subsequent discussions regarding the child's diagnosis, illness, and prognosis. Acceptance and emotional support from the nurse are important elements that should be provided unconditionally to the family.

It is best to have both parents together for these discussions, if possible, or the single parent with a support person. Parents are often not able to remember what was said during this meeting and require ongoing education, support, and patience. It is best to end discussions with the family with information that is pertinent to what the child will be able to do, not what she will not be able to do.

There are three stages that may occur in families following a diagnosis of a chronic illness. The first is "shock and denial," a common defense mechanism. The denial can become maladaptive if it prevents the parents from recognizing the necessary treatment or if it interferes with rehabilitation goals. Shock and denial are often followed by "adjustment," which involves recognition of the illness. Then "reintegration and acknowledgment" should occur, which is demonstrated by the reintegration of the child into his family life and social environment. Realistic expectations of the child should be incorporated into daily life during this stage.

For more practice, match the following terms with the appropriate description on the right:

7. ____ Normalization	A.	provision of technical procedures and treatment in the home
8. ____ Mainstreaming	B.	helping the child and family maintain a normal pattern of living despite a given disability
9. ____ Home care	C.	identifying a child under 3 years old with an actual or potential disability and providing assistance to the family during this time to promote and support the child's development
10. ____ Early intervention	D.	integration of children with special needs into the classroom and child care centers

Label the following statements as either **true** or **false**:

11. _____ Siblings should never be informed of their sister or brother's diagnosis of a chronic illness.

12. _____ Siblings are not affected by the chronic illness or disability of their family member and, thus, do not require support or intervention.

13. _____ The child is usually affected if parents are having difficulty coping with their preschool-age child's diagnosis of a chronic illness.

ASSESSMENT

Assessment of the child and family with a chronic illness should include exploration of the following:

- Available support systems
- Their perception of the illness
- The effect of the illness on the child and family members
- Present and past coping mechanisms
- Observation of the interaction between the child and family members
- Additional stressors in the family
- Available resources

The assessment of the above factors should occur at the time of initial diagnosis and should be repeated on every subsequent hospital admission to optimally assist the family with their current needs.

CHILDREN WITH COGNITIVE IMPAIRMENTS

All hospitalized children present challenges to nurses because of the variations in developmental levels and needs, particularly children with cognitive impairments. In order for a child to be classified as having a cognitive impairment or mental retardation, the following must be present:

- Below-average intellectual functioning
- Limitations in adaptive behaviors
- Onset of the above prior to age 18

It is important to note that criteria other than a subaverage intelligence quotient (IQ) must be present. Children with mental retardation are further classified as having mild, moderate, severe, or profound mental retardation.

Match the degree of mental retardation to the IQ level and skills usually achieved:

14. ____ Mild mental retardation

    A. IQ < 25; gross retardation; requires complete care.

15. ____ Moderate mental retardation

    B. IQ 50–70; can usually achieve self-maintenance; has vocational and social skills.

16. ____ Severe mental retardation

    C. IQ 20–40; requires continuous supervision and direction; cannot live independently

17. ____ Profound mental retardation

    D. IQ 35–55; able to function independently with familiar, simple tasks; requires supervision in living

The etiology of severe mental retardation is primarily genetic, biochemical, or infectious. Nurses can be instrumental in the prevention of mental retardation. Primary prevention actions include maternal education regarding drug and alcohol use during pregnancy, rubella immunizations, and nutrition. Prenatal screening for neural tube defects and genetic counseling should be encouraged. Secondary prevention includes prenatal diagnosis or detection of carrier status of certain diseases and newborn screening for inborn errors of metabolism. Tertiary prevention is aimed at minimizing long-term sequelae in the child with mental retardation.

Two common chromosomal abnormalities that result in mental retardation are Down's syndrome and fragile X syndrome. In addition to the physical characteristics of children with Down's syndrome (see Chapter 20), these children also demonstrate deficits in intelligence, growth, sexual development, and social development. They also exhibit a greater propensity toward some congenital anomalies (congenital heart defects, atlantoaxial instability), sensory problems (hearing loss, strabismus), and other physical disorders (impaired immune function and an increased incidence of leukemia).

Fragile X syndrome is an inherited condition passed on via the X chromosome. Both boys and girls can be affected, although boys are affected more frequently. The clinical manifestations include long, wide, and/or protruding ears; a long, narrow face with a prominent jaw; increased head circumference; strabismus; mild to severe mental retardation; hyperactivity; and autistic-like behaviors. Although there is no cure for fragile X syndrome, these children are able to live a normal life span. Treatment may include phenothiazines to control behavioral outbursts and central nervous system stimulants to decrease hyperactivity.

18. List three health problems that children with Down's syndrome show an increased incidence of:

   A. _____

   B. _____

   C. _____

CHILDREN WITH SENSORY OR COMMUNICATION PROBLEMS

The most common sensory deficits encountered are those affecting vision and hearing. As you read, bear in mind the considerations we've discussed regarding children and families with special needs.

HEARING LOSS

Congenital deafness occurs in approximately 1 in 1,000 infants. There are many factors that contribute to hearing loss, both prenatal and postnatal, including maternal or neonatal infections, family history, childhood deafness, administration of ototoxic medications, chronic otitis media, and loud environmental noise. The precise level of sound that produces hearing loss is not known, although intense, very loud, brief noises, as well as lengthy exposure to somewhat loud noises, can cause irreversible and profound hearing loss.

Hearing loss is classified as conductive or sensorineural, or a mixture of both. Chronic otitis media infections may result in a conductive hearing loss, whereas the use of ototoxic drugs may result in sensorineural hearing loss.

VISUAL DEFICITS

Visual problems are usually classified under the guise of legally blind or partially sighted. A child with legal blindness has visual acuity of < 20/200 in one eye and a diminished visual field of < 20° in the better eye. Visual deficits, like vision loss, can also be caused by prenatal or postnatal conditions including infections and retinopathy of prematurity. A major cause of blindness is trauma. Vision can also be severely affected secondary to trauma of the eye or surrounding tissues (i.e., UV burns, chemical burns, foreign objects, or penetrating injuries). It is important to educate parents and children that one should never attempt to remove an object that has penetrated the eye.

Common visual impairments affecting children are strabismus, glaucoma, cataracts, amblyopia, refractory errors (myopia, hyperopia, and astigmatism), and infections. Review the terminology related to the eyes by matching the term on the left with the correct definition on the right:

19. ____	Hyperopia	A.	involuntary eye deviation
20. ____	Cataracts	B.	both eyes
21. ____	O.D.	C.	characterized by increased intraocular pressure; if untreated can lead to blindness
22. ____	Strabismus	D.	lens of the eye is opaque
23. ____	O.U.	E.	visual impairment due to a discrepancy between how each retina receives images
24. ____	O.S.	F.	a refractive error in which light falls diffusely over the eye; due to imperfectly shaped curves in the cornea and lens
25. ____	Glaucoma	G.	nearsightedness; vision for far objects is impaired
26. ____	Astigmatism	H.	left eye
27. ____	Amblyopia	I.	right eye
28. ____	Myopia	J.	farsightedness; vision for near objects is impaired

STRABISMUS

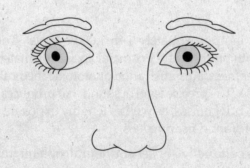

29. List two ways of communicating for a child with a hearing deficit:

    A. _____

    B. _____

30. **True** or **false**? _____ A 3-year-old who frequently stutters when speaking has a speech impairment that requires immediate assessment and intervention.

CHILDREN WITH LIFE-THREATENING ILLNESSES

The child experiencing a life-threatening illness poses an extreme challenge to the nurse. Whether the illness is acute or chronic, there is the reality that the condition may eventually result in death. Nurses are instrumental in supporting the child and family throughout this very difficult time. In order to do this they must have insight into their own feelings and views regarding death and dying, particularly in regard to children. They must also be considerate of the background of the family, including their ethical, religious, cultural, and social beliefs, and incorporate these into the care of the child. Recognition of these factors will help the nurse effectively communicate with the child and family who are experiencing a life-threatening illness.

THE CONCEPT OF DEATH

When dealing with dying children, it is particularly important to assess their cognitive development because it may relate to their concept of death. Dying children may actually be aware of much more than they are able to express and much more than is usually expected of a healthy child of the same age.

Piaget's cognitive developmental framework is helpful in the assessment of a dying child's awareness of death in that it provides a hierarchical sequence of developmental processes that a child is expected to experience. The most important factor in applying Piagetian concepts is that the child must master the tasks of each stage before advancing to the next stage. It is important for the nurse to remember that these stages are based on healthy children and that the dying child may actually advance through the stages at an accelerated rate.

Piaget's first stage, the **sensorimotor** period, occurs during infancy. The infant is not yet able to conceptualize death, but becomes aware of separation anxiety and object permanence. The infant defines anything that has any type of activity as living. During the next stage, the **preoperational** stage, from 2 to 7 years, the child sees death as temporary and reversible. Toddlers and preschool-age children's thought processes are dominated by egocentricity, magical thinking, and concrete thinking—they may know the words "death" and "dying", but not their meanings. The older child nearing the end of this stage (around 5 to 7 years old) equates living with all objects that have movement. He understands death as the cessation of movement. This child may see illness, and perhaps death, as a punishment for wrongdoing.

The next period of cognitive development is the **concrete-operational** period, during which the irreversibility of death is realized. The child begins to realize that all living things must die. The final stage is that of **formal-operational** thought processes. The child is now capable of abstract thought and her conception of death includes its irreversibility and universality. The child realizes that death is inevitable and that all functions of the living cease with death.

To practice, match the appropriate stage on the left to the appropriate concept of death on the right:

31. ____ Sensorimotor period   A. irreversibility of death is realized

32. ____ Preoperational period   B. death is seen as inevitable and irreversible

33. ____ Concrete-operational period   C. no concept of death

34. ____ Formal-operational period   D. illness or death is seen as punishment for wrongdoing

In communicating with the dying child, the siblings, and other family members, the needs of each person must be assessed and effectively addressed. The nurse should also encourage open communication between all members of the family. It is sometimes asked whether children should be told they are dying. For the most part, it is best to be open and honest, and share with the child the truth in terms that are developmentally appropriate. Even if a child is not directly told she is dying, she usually knows it.

CHAPTER 21: EXERCISE ANSWERS

1. **D** Infant—**may not have trust in the caregivers and environment**

2. **A** Toddler—**may lose confidence in skills (e.g., walking, feeding, and toilet training)**

3. **B** Preschooler—**may fear invasive procedures and feel that she caused her own illness**

4. **E** School-age—**may not experience a sense of accomplishment**

5. **C** Adolescent—**may be very concerned about being different from peers**

6. From the list below, circle the diseases that are considered to be chronic illnesses:
   - (A.) Hemophilia
   - (B.) Congenital heart disease
   - C. Chicken pox
   - (D.) Leukemia and other childhood cancers
   - (E.) Diabetes
   - F. Croup
   - (G.) Cystic fibrosis
   - (H.) Asthma

7. **B** Normalization—**helping the child and family maintain a normal pattern of living despite a given disability**

8. **D** Mainstreaming—**integration of children with special needs into the classroom and child care centers**

9. **A** Home care—**provision of technical procedures and treatment in the home**

10. **C** Early intervention—**identifying a child under 3 years old with an actual or potential disability and providing assistance to the family during this time to promote and support the child's development**

11. **False**—Siblings should never be informed of their sister or brother's diagnosis of a chronic illness.

12. **False**—Siblings are not affected by the chronic illness or disability of their family member and, thus, do not require support or intervention.

13. **True**—The child is usually affected if parents are having difficulty coping with their preschool-age child's diagnosis of a chronic illness.

14. **B** Mild mental retardation—**IQ 50–70; can usually achieve self-maintenance; has vocational and social skills**

15. **D** Moderate mental retardation—**IQ 35–55; able to function independently with familiar, simple tasks; requires supervision in living**

16. **C** Severe mental retardation—**IQ 20–40; requires continuous supervision and direction; cannot live independently**

17. **A** Profound mental retardation—**IQ < 25; gross retardation; requires complete care**

18. Health problems that children with Down's syndrome show an increased incidence of include:

atlantoaxial instability

congenital heart defects

frequent respiratory infections

hearing problems

leukemia

thyroid dysfunction

vision problems

19. **J** Hyperopia—**farsightedness; vision for near objects is impaired**

20. **D** Cataracts—**lens of the eye is opaque**

21. **I** O.D.—**right eye**

22. **A** Strabismus—**involuntary eye deviation**

23. **B** O.U.—**both eyes**

24. **H** O.S.—**left eye**

25. **C** Glaucoma—**characterized by increased intraocular pressure; if untreated can lead to blindness**

26. **F** Astigmatism—**a refractive error in which light falls diffusely over the eye; due to imperfectly shaped curves in the cornea and lens**

27. **E** Amblyopia—**visual impairment due to a discrepancy between how each retina receives images**

28. **G** Myopia—**nearsightedness; vision for far objects is impaired**

29. Ways of communicating for a child with a hearing deficit include:

sign language

lip reading

cued speech

30. **True**—A 3-year-old who frequently stutters when speaking has a speech impairment that requires immediate assessment and intervention.

31. **C** Sensorimotor period—**No concept of death**

32. **D** Preoperational period—**Illness or death is seen as punishment for wrongdoing**

33. **A** Concrete-operational period—**Irreversibility of death is realized**

34. **B** Formal-operational period—**Death is seen as inevitable**

1. In prioritizing nursing care for a terminally ill client, which of the following considerations needs to be addressed first?

   (1) Family support
   (2) Comfort measures
   (3) Spiritual well-being
   (4) Curative alternatives

2. Long-term care of a child with a seizure disorder usually involves which of the following?

   (1) Restricting the child from sports
   (2) Wearing a protective helmet
   (3) Informing the school nurse and the teacher
   (4) Modifying the amount of sugar in the diet

3. A 16-year-old client is having an acute asthma attack. Which of the following correctly describes the advice a nurse would give this client and the parents?

   (1) Take the client directly to the emergency room.
   (2) Take two puffs of the steroidal inhaler.
   (3) Drink extra fluids in order to liquefy secretions.
   (4) Use the home nebulizer with albuterol (Proventil).

4. The nurse should instruct the parents of a child with hemophilia to report which symptom immediately?

   (1) A swollen joint
   (2) Rhinitis
   (3) Fatigue
   (4) Fever

5. Which of the following statements would be helpful in teaching a family about caring for a HIV-positive infant at home?

   (1) The virus cannot be transmitted by casual contact.
   (2) Everyone in the house should receive an oral polio vaccine.
   (3) Sterilize all toys and utensils after the child has used them.
   (4) Wash the client's clothes separately from the rest of the family.

6. A child has a positive sweat test for cystic fibrosis. The nurse is teaching the family about the implications of the cystic fibrosis diagnosis on family life. Which of the following would the nurse include in the teaching plan?

   (1) The life expectancy is about 20 years.
   (2) Management of cystic fibrosis (CF) is aimed at preventing infection and promoting good nutrition.
   (3) Pregnancy will not be a possibility.
   (4) Parents should have genetic counseling so that they can make decisions about subsequent pregnancies.

7. After teaching the parents of a child who is newly diagnosed with leukemia, the nurse is sure that they thoroughly understand the discharge instructions when they say they will call the provider immediately if

(1) the child loses hair.
(2) the child wants to eat fast foods.
(3) a classmate develops chicken pox.
(4) the child eats a lot more than usual.

8. A mother asks what causes her child who has cystic fibrosis to be so sick. The nurse explains that the primary pathophysiologic mechanism in cystic fibrosis is

(1) respiratory failure and weakness.
(2) an inability to metabolize sodium.
(3) malabsorption of nutrients.
(4) viscous mucous obstructing organs

9. A 9-year-old sickle cell anemia client is requesting pain medication frequently during a painful sickle cell crisis and does not appear to get relief from intermittent dosing. What is your best nursing intervention?

(1) Suggest to the provider that a patient-controlled analgesia (PCA) machine be initiated.
(2) Discuss your concerns about the possible narcotic addiction with the parents.
(3) Reinforce the need for the client to learn deep-breathing techniques.
(4) Play soothing music.

10. A 17-year-old client has a brain tumor. This client has been through repeated treatment; however, it has become apparent that this client is very ill. While the nurse is taking midnight vital signs, the client asks, "Am I going to die?" What would be the most appropriate response by the nurse?

(1) "What do you think?"
(2) "Of course, we're all going to die sometime."
(3) "Go to sleep. I'll talk with you about it tomorrow."
(4) "You should ask your parents."

1.   (2) CORRECT   Utilizing Maslow's hierarchy of human needs, physiological and safety needs, especially pain control, are essential and must be satisfied prior to other concerns.

      (1) *POSSIBLE*   This is important but not a priority, based on Maslow's hierarchy of needs.

      (3) *ELIMINATE*   This is important but not a priority.

      (4) *ELIMINATE*   The goal of nursing care should focus on palliative interventions involving comfort and pain control, rather than curative alternatives, which are unrealistic for this client.

CATEGORY 01 MANAGEMENT OF CARE

2.   (3) CORRECT   The school nurse and the teacher should be informed of the child's condition and treatment regimen.

      (1) *ELIMINATE*   Children with seizure disorders may play sports as tolerated.

      (2) *ELIMINATE*   Wearing a protective helmet may damage the child's self-esteem and disrupt normalcy.

      (4) *ELIMINATE*   Sugar modification is not indicated.

CATEGORY 09 REDUCTION OF RISK POTENTIAL

3.   (4) CORRECT   Albuterol (Proventil) is the drug of choice for acute asthmatic attacks.

      (1) *ELIMINATE*   If nebulization is not sufficient, the client should be taken for emergency treatment.

      (2) *ELIMINATE*   Steroidal inhalers are not used to medicate acute attacks.

      (3) *ELIMINATE*   While fluids do help to loosen secretions, this will not benefit a client with an acute attack.

CATEGORY 08 PHARMACOLOGICAL AND PARENTERAL THERAPIES

4.   (1) CORRECT   Hemarthrosis is a potential complication of hemophilia and can cause hemorrhage and pain.

      (2) *ELIMINATE*   Rhinitis is not a common symptom of hemophilia.

      (3) *ELIMINATE*   Fatigue is not a complication of hemophilia.

      (4) *ELIMINATE*   Fever would not be specific to a complication of hemophilia.

CATEGORY 09 REDUCTION OF RISK POTENTIAL

5.   (1) CORRECT   The virus cannot be transmitted through casual contact. This must be reinforced
                                           so that the child is not deprived of touch.

       (2) ELIMINATE   Oral polio vaccine should not be taken by others in the household.

       (3) ELIMINATE   It is not necessary to sterilize toys and utensils after the child uses them.

       (4) ELIMINATE   The child's clothes do not have to be washed separately.

CATEGORY 04 PREVENTION AND EARLY DETECTION OF DISEASE

---

6.   (2) CORRECT   The goal of treatment of CF is to provide optimal nutrition and prevent infections
                                           that cause fatal complications of CF.

       (1) ELIMINATE   Life expectancy is now longer than 20 years.

       (3) ELIMINATE   This not a true statement.

       (4) ELIMINATE   This is true, but parents should initiate this possibility based on their religious
                                           values.

CATEGORY 04 PREVENTION AND EARLY DETECTION OF DISEASE

---

7.   (3) CORRECT   Exposure to chicken pox is serious in an immunocompromised child and requires
                                           prompt notification of the provider.

       (1) ELIMINATE   Alopecia (hair loss) is common with chemotherapy.

       (2) ELIMINATE   Food cravings are common with chemotherapy.

       (4) ELIMINATE   Steroids, which are usually part of the treatment for leukemia, can cause an
                                           increased appetite.

CATEGORY 09 REDUCTION OF RISK POTENTIAL

---

8.   (4) CORRECT   Excessive, thick secretions cause respiratory and digestive sequelae.

       (1) POSSIBLE   Respiratory failure and weakness are features of the disease, not pathophysiologic
                                           mechanisms.

       (2) ELIMINATE   Sodium metabolism is not impaired.

       (3) ELIMINATE   Nutrient malabsorption is a feature of the disease.

CATEGORY 10 PHYSIOLOGICAL ADAPTATION

9.   (1) CORRECT   The goal in caring for the client is prevention of pain. This is best achieved by use of patient-controlled analgesia (PCA). This method provides flexibility in dosing and gives the client control and responsibility.

     (2) ELIMINATE   Very few children who receive pain medication actually become addicted.

     (3) ELIMINATE   Deep breathing will most likely do little to help a child in pain.

     (4) ELIMINATE   Playing soothing music will most likely do little to help a child with sickle cell anemia in pain.

CATEGORY 07 BASIC CARE AND COMFORT

10. (1) CORRECT   In using this answer, the nurse would be evidencing a willingness to talk. Talking with a dying child about impending death is very difficult and should be done on the child's terms when the child wants to. These discussions or answers to questions should not be put off until what the nurse might believe is a better time.

     (2) ELIMINATE   This response would avoid the client's question and would cut off communication.

     (3) ELIMINATE   This response avoids the question and does not promote therapeutic communication.

     (4) ELIMINATE   The parents may not be able to handle the question unless they were prepared. Referral to the parents is another way to avoid the question and block therapeutic communication.

CATEGORY 05 COPING AND ADAPTATION

PART ◆ IV

HEALTH PROMOTION AND MAINTENANCE

"Health Promotion and Maintenance" comprises 17–23 percent of the actual test content. This is 50 questions out of the maximum number of questions possible on the CAT (265). When answering these questions, remember that the nurse is always trying to promote the accomplishment of milestones within the proper time frame.

These "client needs" include:

- Growth and development through the life span: physical, cognitive, and psychosocial factors
- Growth and development of the mother and newborn: antepartum, intrapartum, and postpartum
- Self-care and support systems
- Prevention and early treatment of disease

22

GROWTH AND DEVELOPMENT

WHAT YOU NEED TO KNOW

This is where your common sense can shine. After all, you've grown and developed yourself. If you are stumped on a question, think of yourself or a family member in the stage of development in question. What were you like at the age of 10? Probably your permanent teeth were coming in and you might have broken your arm. Most likely, the opposite sex had "cooties" and you were starting to enjoy your friends more than your family at this point. You were "normal"!

In this section, we are confronted with a lot of theory. Focus on Erikson; remember, the NCLEX-RN examiners love his developmental theory. We'll go over his ideas throughout our discussion of typical stages of growth and development and then go over the other main theorists' ideas towards the end of the chapter.

OVERVIEW OF GROWTH AND DEVELOPMENT

Growth and development (maturation) is an orderly and predictable process. While rates of maturation vary from person to person and from stage to stage within each person, there is a range of "normal" that we will discuss for the purposes of the NCLEX-RN. Before we begin the real crunch, match the words below with the appropriate definition:

1. _____ An increase in size (height and weight); seems to occur in cycles, tends to be most rapid in utero and during infancy, then increases again during adolescence

2. _____ The maturation of physiological, psychosocial, and cognitive systems to a more complex and differentiated state of being

3. _____ Skills and competencies associated with each developmental age that have an effect on the development of subsequent stages; there is a normal progression and sequence from which one cannot easily deviate

4. _____ A standard of reference by which to compare a child's behavior at specific ages; usually there is a range of normal; cultural differences may influence norms

5. _____ A variable of development in which one lags behind the range of a given age or stage of development

A. development

B. developmental delay

C. developmental milestones

D. developmental tasks

E. growth

STAGES OF GROWTH AND DEVELOPMENT

INFANCY (0–12/18 MONTHS)

- Birth weight doubles at 6 months.
- Birth weight triples at 12 months.
- Baby sits steadily, unsupported at 8 months.
- Baby walks with assistance, may attempt to stand, at 12 months.
- Teething begins at 3 to 6 months.

Erikson's stage of infancy is characterized by the conflict of trust vs. mistrust (0–12 months). Trust develops between the infant and his environment when his needs are met consistently and effectively. Mistrust develops when care is inconsistent and inadequate.

Developmental Milestones

Age	Gross Motor	Fine Motor	Language	Personal-Social
0–3 months	Head lags when pulled from supine to sitting	Sucking reflex; Moro (startle) reflex; rooting reflex; plantar and palmar reflexes; grasp reflex	Cries; pays most attention to voices	Gazes at surroundings; smiles responsively; makes no distinction between self and environment
3–6 months (may show signs of teething)	Begins to sit with support; holds head steady; rolls from side to side; no head lag	Holds hands open; holds moderate-sized objects; moves arms at sight of toys; hand to mouth movement; reaches for objects	Babbles; coos; gurgles; laughs; squeals; vocalizes displeasure	Initiates play by smiling; enjoys people; starts to recognize familiar faces
6–9 months (birth weight doubles at 6 months)	Lifts head when pulled to sitting; sits without support; crawls	Transfers toys from hand to hand; begins pincer grasp; holds own bottle; fixates on small objects	Puts two syllable sounds together without meaning (mama, dada); imitates sounds; cries when scolded	Initial stranger anxiety; prefers mom; enjoys affection; beginning awareness of separateness from environment
9–12 months	Creeps; sits steadily; stands and walks with support	Well-developed pincer grasp; can pick up and release toys; can hold and mark with a crayon; drinks from a cup; eats with fingers; hand preference demonstrated	Says a few words with meaning; knows own name; recognizes the meaning of "no!"	Plays simple games; shows wide range of emotions; explores environment, but still likes Mom
12 months (birth weight triples)	Walks with one hand held	Attempts to build tower but fails; throws, drops, scribbles, opens and pokes; spills food; sequential play	Vocabulary: 10 words; two words in phrases; names familiar objects; understands simple commands	Attention shifts quickly; throws temper tantrums; resists sleep; may control bowel movements; solitary play begins; searches for hidden objects where they were last seen

Appropriate toys for a 12-month-old child include large balls, teething beads, soft, cuddly toys, nested boxes, bright, dangling toys, and large blocks. Parental guidance at this point includes advice about child safety, as well as advice to not try to switch a child from left to right handedness or vice versa. The child should not be overstimulated and outdoor play should be encouraged.

TODDLER (12/18 MONTHS TO 3 YEARS)

- Birth weight quadruples by 3 years.
- Full set of baby teeth comes in by 30 months.
- Blood pressure 99/64 mmHg
- Pulse 110 beats per minute
- Grows 8–10 inches

Erikson's stage is autonomy vs. shame and doubt between 1 and 3 years of age. Autonomy develops when the child is permitted to assert himself. Shame and doubt develop if the child did not develop a sense of trust and/or learns that his assertiveness is not acceptable or that his actions are ineffective. The child has a sense of will and seeks and receives parental reassurances during this stage. Exploration and discovery of his environment is important to the toddler.

	12 Months	24 Months (2 years)
Gross motor skills	Walks; stoops and recovers; climbs, runs, and jumps; walks up stairs, one hand held; cannot zip, tie, or button yet but can unzip, untie, and take off gloves	Steady gait; walks up and down stairs; walks on tiptoes; stands on one foot; can ride a tricycle; runs well with wide base. Begins daytime control of bowel movement
Fine motor skills	Uses spoon, small glass; imitates in drawing; constructs 2–4 block tower	Constructs 5–8 block tower; puts cubes together to form a train; turns doorknobs; in drawing, imitates more specific strokes
Language	Vocabulary: 10 or more words	Vocabulary: about 300 words; knows full name; makes 3–4 word sentences
Psychosocial	Verbalizes wants; imitates; has attachment to security blanket; temper tantrums more evident	Obeys simple commands; helps undress self; toilet training possible during day; knows self as separate person
Play	Parallel play: Push/pull toys; riding toys; puzzles with large pieces; finger paints	Parallel play: "Snatch and grab" stage; molding clay, clothed dolls, books, balls; violently resists having toys taken away
Stresses	Separation anxiety: protest (inconsolable by anyone but parents) → despair (disinterested, clutches security blanket) → detachment (resigned, not content)	Separation anxiety continues; changing environment or routine causes insecurity
Parental guidance	Accidents are the leading cause of death due to clumsiness and increased mobility, independence, and curiosity	Present the child with choices; it is a domineering phase, use humorous subservience!

PRESCHOOL AGE (3–6 YEARS)

- Weight increases 4–6 pounds per year.
- Birth length doubles by 4 years.
- Permanent molars appear.
- Blood pressure 85–100/60 mmHg–70 mmHg
- Pulse 90–100 beats per minute
- Respirations 24–25 per minute
- Handedness is established.

Erikson's developmental stage for preschoolers is initiative vs. guilt. Initiative develops if the child is encouraged to initiate motor play, to ask questions, and engage in make believe and fantasy play. Guilt develops if the child is made to feel that his activity is bad, that he is asking too many questions, or that his play is silly or inappropriate. This child starts many tasks but completes few. She interacts more with parents and peers than before.

	3–6 Years
Motor skills	Rides tricycle Goes up (3 years) and down (4 years) stairs alternating feet Increased coordination Constructs tower of 10 blocks
Language	Vocabulary: 900–2,000 words Knows first name, then age, then last name Uses plurals and 3-word to complex sentences Talks in sentences Names 1–4 colors
Psychosocial	Fewer temper tantrums (child can understand simple reasoning) Rapid learning from experience Completely toilet trained Aware of sexual differences Asks questions Eager to please; morality and conscience develop
Play	Imaginary friends Passive to assertive Likes things that squish, move, talk, and make noise Books, crayons, transportation toys Imitative and dramatic play Magical thinking
Stresses	Illogical fears Separation from parents Intrusive procedures are threatening (child may say things such as, "The cut may not heal and my insides may fall out.")
Parental guidance	Encourage and promote interests, social contracts, exploration, imaginative outlets, and responsibility Group activity alternated with solitary play **Listen!** Praise and offer positive feedback! Naps are essential Kind but unmistakable discipline and consistent control are crucial Assist in learning to share and waiting for turns Apply criteria to carefully evaluate preschools

SCHOOL AGE (6–12 YEARS)

- Starts losing deciduous teeth
- Has all permanent teeth by age 12
- Slower growth
- Bone growth exceeds that of muscle and mineralization is not complete, thereby putting a child in this age group at high risk for fractures.

Erikson's stage at this point is industry vs. inferiority (6–12 years). Industry develops if the child is invited to make things, permitted to do things by himself, and praised for the efforts. Inferiority occurs if the child is not given encouragement and if his activities are belittled and deemed unimportant. The child wants to learn to do things well and to become more self-motivated. The child participates in a variety of activities and takes pride in accomplishments. Make-believe play is often a way to work through real-life situations.

	6–12 Years
Motor skills	Skips, skates, tumbles; always active Movement more coordinated and graceful, balance improving Deliberate hand-eye coordination Prints, cuts, and pastes Ties knots, then bows
Language	Vocabulary: 50,000 words More understanding of abstract relationships between words Language is used as a tool to share experiences, a vehicle for expression
Psychosocial	Assumes complete responsibility for personal care Develops modesty and morality Strict sense of right and wrong, cooperation and fair play Significant peer relationships; forms secret clubs Prefers friends of same sex over family Seeks praise and positive feedback
Play	**Group play** with leader and organized rules Team sports Jigsaw puzzles, building models
Stresses	Possible school phobia Fear of disease, injury, and punishment
Parental guidance	Decreased incidence of accidents except for sports injuries Child requires education on maintenance of equipment and on hazards of risk taking Child is able to understand the conservation of liquid, mass, number, length, area, and volume Child is learning that his actions have consequences

ADOLESCENCE (12–18 YEARS)

- Vital signs approach adult values.
- Wisdom teeth appear.
- Puberty (due to hormonal changes) is universal in pattern but variable in rate.
- Increased sweat production and body odor
- Acne

Boys	Girls
Height increases 4 inches/year starting at age 14, then slows in late teens.	Develop earlier than boys
Weight doubles between 12–18 years of age (increased muscle mass, broader chest).	Height increases 3 inches/year, then slows dramatically at age 16.
Increased genital size from age 13.	Fat deposits on thighs and hips; pelvis broadens.
Pubic, facial, axillary, and chest hair appear.	Breasts develop.
Voice deepens.	Axillary and pubic hair appear.
Production of functional sperm; nocturnal emissions of semen; masturbation	Menstruation begins around age 12 and is irregular for the first 1–2 years.

Erikson's developmental stage of adolescence is identity vs. role confusion. Identity develops when the adolescent is able to bring together life experiences into a whole and to integrate them into an acceptable self-image. Role confusion develops when the adolescent is not able to achieve this integration and therefore is not sure who he or she is, or what he or she can do. The adolescent views himself in a way similar to the way he is viewed by significant others. Adolescents begin to make long-range plans for an occupation, test social norms, and may try different lifestyles.

The adolescent period is characterized by rapid and dynamic physical and personality maturation (depending on gender and individual rate), characterized by emotional and family strife leading to redefinition of self and establishment of autonomy and independence. The stresses of this period include the threatened loss of control and fear of the changing body image. Parents should remember that accidents are the leading cause of death, and that many are related to alcohol and/or substance abuse.

Age	Psychosocial Behavior
12–14 years	Loud, boisterous behavior; mood swings Physical maturity comes before emotional maturity Vacillation between independence from and dependence on family Preoccupation with changing body
15–16 years	Decreased physical activity as talking becomes the pastime of choice Disengages from parents Intense relationships Sexual experimentation Rich fantasy life Deductive reasoning develops
17–18 years	Able to maintain stable relationships; highly values relations with opposite sex More independent Less conflict with family and peers; emotionally stable Future-oriented Thinks abstractly, develops life philosophy

Adolescent Suicide

Suicide threats are an acting-out behavior that represents a cry for help. These gestures are not uncommon in adolescence and are usually impulsive acts committed to force significant others to pay attention. The act of suicide is seldom planned because the teen does not really want to die. A prior suicide attempt is the largest risk factor for future attempts. Depression becomes the suicidal adolescent's most consistent mood, and seems to last an undue length of time. These mood swings become so disabling that teens cannot fulfill the normal tasks of daily living. Feelings of worthlessness are verbalized, and intervention is imperative.

Adolescent Substance Abuse

Identifying the drug being abused will help with a plan of care in relationship to dependency, withdrawal, tolerance, and related health hazards. A nonthreatening environment is imperative for establishing trust with an adolescent. Assess the function that the drug plays in the adolescent's life and help him identify his own role in self-destructive, inappropriate drug abuse behavior. Help the adolescent develop appropriate coping mechanisms through role playing.

EARLY ADULTHOOD (18–35 YEARS)

This is Erikson's stage of intimacy vs. isolation. It is characterized by the ability to develop a strong relationship with another without feeling isolated or alone. Love is mutual, not dependent as with parent and child. This developmental stage is characterized by self-sufficiency in pursuit of occupation/vocation and defined interpersonal relationships (most frequently, marriage).

MIDDLE ADULTHOOD (35–65 YEARS)

Erikson's stage of generativity vs. self-absorption is devoted to the creation and care of the next generation. Commitment to children is meaningful, although it does not have to be one's own children. Being unable to contribute in these ways, can bring about boredom, restlessness, stagnation, and a feeling that life is meaningless.

LATE ADULTHOOD (65 YEARS–DEATH)

This is Erikson's stage of ego integrity vs. despair. Each person develops a sense of integrity that results from satisfaction with the life she has lived. There is an acceptance of what has been; however, despair can arise from remorse for what might have been. The adult has a concern for life even though death appears more imminent. There is a general slowing of physical and cognitive functioning during late adulthood, and there is a need to establish the highest degree of independence (self-sufficiency) physically possible by adapting the environment to ability. The older adult reflects on life accomplishments, events, and experiences, and continues interpersonal relationships despite changes and losses.

ASSESSMENT OF GROWTH AND DEVELOPMENT

Height and head circumference are the most common measures to assess growth and development. Repeated measurements are necessary to ensure accuracy. These measurements should occur at least 5–6 times in the first year and then yearly at every well-child visit to establish patterns and to identify changes or deviations. A standardized growth chart must be utilized as the reference criterion. However, cultural and familial differences cannot be ignored.

Assessment of development evaluates current developmental function. Screening tools identify potential follow-up needs and help parents to understand their child's behavior and to prepare for new experiences. These tools also provide a basis for anticipatory guidance and teaching. Evaluation should include all the subsystems of development: gross and fine motor skills, cognitive skills, language, and social skills.

Developmental assessment tools include:

- Denver Developmental Screening Test (D.D.S.T.): Effective from birth to 6 years of age
- Motor screening: Proceed from head to toe (cephalocaudal), from trunk to periphery (proximodistal), and from gross to fine motor skills (mass to specific)
- Intellectual screening (IQ): Related to the person's genetic potential and environment; mental age $\times$ 100 = IQ

DEVELOPMENTAL THEORY

While the NCLEX-RN loves Erikson, it is important that you also recognize Piaget's and Freud's stages of development.

In the chart below, fill in Erikson's description of the developmental stage, and compare it with Piaget's and Freud's on the right.

Age	Erikson	Piaget	Freud
Infancy (0–18 months)		Sensorimotor (responds to environment through reflexes that are gradually replaced by voluntary activity; increasing awareness of object permanence)	Oral sensory (stimulation and pleasure through mouth)
Toddler (18–36 months)		Preoperational thought/preconceptual phase (symbols and figures stand for objects; egocentric)	Anal (pleasure in anal region; toilet training is mastered here)
Preschool (3–6 years)		Preoperational thought/ intuitive phase (thinking and learning is concrete; centers on one object at a time)	Genital/Phallic (intrusive behavior; Oedipal phase; identification with same-sex parent)
School age (7–12 years)		Concrete operations (increasingly rational in thinking; can sort, classify, collect information)	Latency (sexual drive is controlled and repressed; energy devoted to acquisition of new skills)
Adolescence (12–18 years)		Formal operations (hypothetical and theoretical thinking develop; can problem-solve and question)	Genitality (resurgence of sexual drive; adolescence is mastered when there is a concurrent ability to love and to work)

FACTORS AFFECTING GROWTH AND DEVELOPMENT

Most factors that affect growth and development are fairly obvious. They include the following:

- Environment (which may influence development more than genetic factors)
- Socioeconomic factors
- Interpersonal relationships
- Nutritional status
- Weather, climate, natural disasters
- Environmental hazards
- Heredity
- General state of health
- Emotional attitude or state of mind

GENETIC DEFECTS

Genetic defects can sharply affect growth and development. There are particular groups of people who exhibit greater risk for specific disorders. For example:

Group	Disorder
Blacks/African Americans	Sickle cell anemia
Northern European descendants of Ashkenazic Jews	Tay-Sachs disease
Caucasian/Non-Hispanic	Cystic fibrosis
Mediterranean descendants	Thalassemia

Couples who have produced a child with a defect and who have a family history of a structural abnormality or systemic disease that may be hereditary may be at increased risk for producing another child with a similar defect. This may also include couples who are closely blood-related and women over 40 years of age.

CHROMOSOMAL DEFECTS

Chromosomal defects may be numeric or structural. Down's syndrome (Trisomy 21) is the most common genetic disorder. There is an increased occurrence of Down's syndrome in babies born to women over age 35. These children are characterized by low-set ears; large fat pads at the nape of a short neck; a protruding tongue; inner epicanthic folds with slanted eyes; hypotonic muscles with hypermobility of joints; short, broad hands with an inward curved little finger; transverse simian palmar creases; mental retardation and cardiac defects; and increased susceptibility to upper respiratory infections and leukemia.

Turner's syndrome (females with only one X chromosome) is also a chromosomal defect. These girls lag in growth and are usually infertile, but have no intellect impairment. They occasionally exhibit immature, socially isolated behavior. Clients with Klinefelter's syndrome (males with an extra X chromosome) are usually of normal intelligence or have mild retardation, may have gross motor skill difficulties, and are most often infertile.

Autosomal defects are imperfections occurring in any chromosome pair other than the sex chromosomes. **Sex-linked transmission traits** are those in which the trait is present on a sex chromosome (typically, the X chromosome). They may be dominant or recessive, but recessive is more common. For example, hemophilia and color blindness are sex-linked recessive traits. **Autosomal dominant** traits are those in which the abnormal gene dominates the normal gene; thus, the condition is always demonstrated when the abnormal gene is present. The affected parent has a 50 percent chance of passing on the abnormal gene in each pregnancy. **Autosomal recessive** traits require transmission of the abnormal gene from both parents for demonstration of the defect in the child; however, each child has 50 percent chance of being a carrier of the disorder.

INBORN ERRORS OF METABOLISM

Inborn errors of metabolism are disorders caused by the absence of or a defect in enzymes that metabolize proteins, fats, or carbohydrates. Inborn errors of metabolism usually follow a recessive pattern of inheritance. Phenylketonuria (PKU) is an uncommon disorder caused by an autosomal recessive gene. There is a deficiency in the liver enzyme phenylalanine hydroxylase, which metabolizes the amino acid phenylalanine. The build-up of phenylalanine causes brain cell toxicity. Newborn PKU screening is best accomplished via blood sampling following protein ingestion. A special diet is the only way to control PKU. Tay-Sachs disease results from an autosomal recessive trait. There is a deficiency of hexosaminidase. By age 2, the child becomes inattentive, passive, and regresses in motor and social development. Life expectancy is only until early childhood.

CHILD ABUSE

Child abuse is a broad term that includes physical abuse or neglect, emotional abuse or neglect, and sexual abuse. Areas of a child's history that should arouse suspicions of abuse include:

- conflicting stories about the "accident" from the parents and the child
- injuries inconsistent with the history given
- complaints other than the one associated with the signs of abuse that are present
- inappropriate parental concern for the degree of injury, either exaggerated or absent
- refusal of parent to permit additional tests or agree to necessary treatment
- unavailability of parents for questioning

The nurse is required, by law, to report any **suspected** case of child abuse. It does not need to be confirmed in any way to be reported. Documentation must be factual and objective. Behavioral responses of the child to the parent and any interviews with the family must be recorded.

The extent of the physical injury to the child must be assessed. The child must be treated as though he or she has a physical problem, not as a victim of abuse. A safe, therapeutic environment is crucial to developing a trusting relationship, and the use of play can help work through a relationship. Praising the child's abilities helps relieve anxiety and promotes trust.

Nursing interventions for the abused child include, most importantly, preventing further abuse and identifying families at risk for child abuse. The nurse should promote attachment and bonding between the parent and the child. Educating parents about effective child-rearing principles using role-playing techniques helps prevent the use of physical force for discipline. The nurse should encourage families to use outside support systems to alleviate stressors that may contribute to abuse.

If the child is hospitalized for abuse, it is important that the parent(s) be included in the plan of care and that the nurse reinforces the positive skills the parent may already possess. Promotion of parental adequacy is the goal, and a consistent caregiver can best achieve this by reinforcing the healthy elements of the parent-child relationship.

IMMUNIZATIONS

The NCLEX-RN always asks a question on immunizations. Unfortunately, memorization is the only way to learn them. This 1998 schedule of immunizations is taken from the American Academy of Pediatrics recommendations.

Recommended Immunization Schedules Initiated During Infancy										
	Months								Years	
	0	1	2	4	6	12	15	18	4-6	11-12
Hepatitis B	#1		#2		#3					If not yet taken
Diphtheria Tetanus Pertussis (DTP)			#1	#2	#3		#4			
H. influenzae Type B			#1	#2	#3		#4			
Polio			#1	#2	#3				#4	
Measles Mumps Rubella (MMR)						#1			#2	
Varicella zoster virus						#1				If not yet taken and no history of chicken pox
Tuberculin test (Td)						Test				Frequency of testing depends on individual's risk of developing TB

The inactivated polio vaccine is recommended for routine infant vaccination.

CHAPTER 22: EXERCISE ANSWERS

1. **E** **growth**—An increase in size (height and weight); seems to occur in cycles, tends to be most rapid in utero and during infancy, then increases again during adolescence

2. **A** **development**—The maturation of physiological, psychosocial, and cognitive systems to a more complex and differentiated state of being

3. **D** **developmental tasks**—Skills and competencies associated with each developmental age that have an effect on the development of subsequent stages; there is a normal progression and sequence from which one cannot easily deviate

4. **C** **developmental milestones**—A standard of reference by which to compare a child's behavior at specific ages; usually there is a range of normal; cultural differences may influence norms

5. **B** **developmental delay**—A variable of development in which one lags behind the range of a given age or stage of development

Age	Erikson	Piaget	Freud
Infancy (0–18 months)	Conflict of trust vs. mistrust between infant and his environment	Sensorimotor (responds to environment through reflexes that are gradually replaced by voluntary activity; increasing awareness of object permanence)	Oral sensory (stimulation and pleasure through mouth)
Toddler (18–36 months)	Autonomy vs. shame and doubt	Preoperational thought/preconceptual phase (symbols and figures stand for objects; egocentric)	Anal (pleasure in anal region; toilet training is mastered here)
Preschool (3–6 years)	Initiative vs. guilt	Preoperational thought/ intuitive phase (thinking and learning is concrete; centers on one object at a time)	Genital/Phallic (intrusive behavior; Oedipal phase; identification with same-sex parent)
School age (7–12 years)	Industry vs. inferiority	Concrete operations (increasingly rational in thinking; can sort, classify, collect information)	Latency (sexual drive is controlled and repressed; energy devoted to acquisition of new skills)
Adolescence (12–18 years)	Identity vs. role confusion	Formal operations (hypothetical and theoretical thinking develop; can problem-solve and question)	Genitality (resurgence of sexual drive; adolescence is mastered when there is a concurrent ability to love and to work)

CHAPTER 22: NCLEX-RN STYLE QUESTIONS

1. A nurse is observing all of the following babies in a clinic. Which baby may be experiencing a developmental delay?

   (1) A 1-month-old who does not coo
   (2) A 3-month-old who does not crawl
   (3) An 8-month-old who does not walk
   (4) A 10-month-old who does not sit

2. The nurse is caring for a child suspected of being abused. The responsiblity of the nurse includes

   (1) reporting the parents to authorities.
   (2) caring for the physical wounds.
   (3) reporting the parents to her supervisor.
   (4) not allowing visitation.

3. In doing screening on preschool children a nurse knows that they usually reach normal vision acuity of 20/20 by what age?

   (1) 3 years of age
   (2) 4 years of age
   (3) 5 years of age
   (4) 6 years of age

4. In discussing what to expect in the development of a toddler with parents, which of the following behaviors would the nurse tell them would be typical of a 14-month-old toddler?

   (1) Turning on a television with the knob
   (2) Pulling a wagon
   (3) Saying that he or she knows where the toys are in the room
   (4) Building a tower with blocks

5. In terms of physical growth, at the age of 12 months, infants are expected to

   (1) double their birth weight.
   (2) triple their birth weight.
   (3) double their head circumference.
   (4) triple their head circumference.

6. An infant weighed 7 pounds at birth and is now 12 months old. In assessing this infant the nurse knows that the infant should now weigh

   (1) 14 pounds.
   (2) 19 pounds.
   (3) 21 pounds.
   (4) 32 pounds.

7. Which of the following toys is most appropriate for a 12-month-old infant?

   (1) Tricycle
   (2) Paints
   (3) Musical mobile
   (4) A push/pull toy

8.	Toddlers engage in parallel play. Which of the following best illustrates parallelism?	(1) Two toddlers playing with blocks, but building with them separately
		(2) A toddler playing with an adult
		(3) Two toddlers sitting together playing with separate toys
		(4) Two toddlers playing together alongside an infant

9.	The nurse is correct to assess a possible developmental delay in a 6-month-old child if that child	(1) is able to roll over.
		(2) demonstrates a social smile.
		(3) has a head lag.
		(4) does not demonstrate the Moro reflex.

CHAPTER 22: NCLEX-RN STYLE ANSWERS

1. (4) CORRECT An infant should be able to sit unsupported by 7 or 9 months. Therefore, further assessments should be made of the 10-month-old.
    (1) *ELMINATE* Cooing begins around 2 months of age.
    (2) *ELIMINATE* Crawling begins around 7 or 8 months of age.
    (3) *ELIMINATE* At about 9 months, infants begin to cruise and walk around furniture.

    CATEGORY 03 GROWTH AND DEVELOPMENT THROUGH THE LIFE SPAN

2. (1) CORRECT The nurse is responsible by law to report incidence of abuse, real or suspected.
    (2) *ELIMINATE* Caring for the physical wounds is important, but choice #1 is the best answer.
    (3) *ELIMINATE* The parents must be reported to the authorities, not to the supervisor.
    (4) *ELIMINATE* Parents will still be allowed to visit the child.

    CATEGORY 01 MANAGEMENT OF CARE

3. (4) CORRECT Normally a child reaches normal vision acuity (20/20) by 6 years of age.
    (1) ELIMINATE A 3-year-old normally has 20/50 vision.
    (2) ELIMINATE A 4-year-old has 20/40 vision.
    (3) ELIMINATE A 5-year-old has 20/30 vision.

    CATEGORY 03 GROWTH AND DEVELOPMENT THROUGH THE LIFE SPAN

4. (4) CORRECT A 14-month-old can generally hold and build with blocks.
    (1) *ELIMINATE* Fine motor skills are generally not developed enough to turn a knob.
    (2) *ELIMINATE* Gross motor skills are generally not perfected enough to walk and pull a wagon.
    (3) *ELIMINATE* 14-month-old children generally do not speak in complete sentences.

    CATEGORY 03 GROWTH AND DEVELOPMENT THROUGH THE LIFE SPAN

5.
(2) CORRECT   Infants are expected to triple their birth weight by the age of 12 months.

(1) *ELIMINATE*   Infants are expected to double their birth weight by the age of 6 months.

(3) *ELIMINATE*   The rate of growth for head circumference is an inch per month for the first 6 months, then an inch per month for months 6 through 12.

(4) *ELIMINATE*   The rate of growth for head circumference is an inch per month for the first 6 months, then an inch per month for months 6 through 12.

CATEGORY 03 GROWTH AND DEVELOPMENT THROUGH THE LIFE SPAN

6.
(3) CORRECT   An infant should triple its weight by 12 months of age.

(1) *ELIMINATE*   This infant would be undernourished, and diagnostic tests would be indicated.

(2) *ELIMINATE*   This infant also would be slightly underweight, and the nurse should review the diet with the mother.

(4) *ELIMINATE*   This infant is overweight for its stage of development, and nutritional counseling should be initiated.

CATEGORY 03 GROWTH AND DEVELOPMENT THROUGH THE LIFE SPAN

7.
(4) CORRECT   Toys that can be pushed or pulled along are most appropriate since they aid in walking and are enjoyed by children learning to walk.

(1) ELIMINATE   Tricycles are appropriate for 3–4-year-old children.

(2) ELIMINATE   Paints are better suited for older toddlers and preschoolers.

(3) ELIMINATE   Musical mobiles are best for young infants.

CATEGORY 03 GROWTH AND DEVELOPMENT THROUGH THE LIFE SPAN

8.
(3) CORRECT   Parallel play occurs while the toddlers are near each other but not sharing or playing together.

(1) *ELIMINATE*   Children do not share while engaging in parallel play.

(2) *ELIMINATE*   This is an example of interactive play behavior.

(4) *ELIMINATE*   Playing together does not fit the definition of parallel play.

CATEGORY 03 GROWTH AND DEVELOPMENT THROUGH THE LIFE SPAN

9.
(3) CORRECT   Head control should be achieved by 4 months of age.

(1) *ELIMINATE*   It is developmentally normal for children to roll over by 5–6 months of age.

(2) *ELIMINATE*   Social smiling is a normal developmental finding in a 6-month-old child.

(4) *ELIMINATE*   Primitive reflexes disappear by 3–4 months of age.

CATEGORY 03 GROWTH AND DEVELOPMENT THROUGH THE LIFE SPAN

Internal organs, contained within the bony pelvis, include the uterus, the fallopian tubes, the ovaries, and the vagina. Functions and structures of each organ are as follows:

Organ	Functions	Structure	Notes
Uterus	Menstruation and build-up of the endometrium; Pregnancy; Labor	Endometrium (innermost layer; placenta attaches here in pregnancy) Myometrium (middle layer of muscle) Parietal peritoneum (outermost layer)	The cervix is the lowest part of the uterus, protruding into the vagina. It creates an outlet for the fetus to be expelled from the uterus.
Fallopian tubes	Site of fertilization of the ovum with sperm	Pair of muscular tubes	Fallopian tubes transport the ova from the ovaries to the uterus.
Ovaries	Ovulation (the release of an ovum); Steroid hormone production	Pair of follicle-containing organs on either side of the uterus	The ovaries lie in the upper pelvic cavity.
Vagina	Organ for coitus; Birth canal; Conduit for menstrual flow	Tube extending from the introitus to the cervix	Fibromuscualr organ lined with mucous membrane

The menstrual cycle is defined as the 26- to 35-day cycle in which ovulation (release of an ovum) and menstruation take place. An egg is typically released 14 days before menstruation occurs. Menstruation is the shedding of the outer $\frac{2}{3}$ of the endometrium with bleeding. The menstrual cycle is divided into four phases. Events of each phase are listed in the chart below:

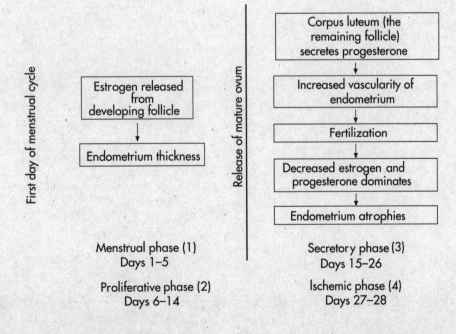

First day of menstrual cycle

Estrogen released from developing follicle
↓
Endometrium thickness

Release of mature ovum

Corpus luteum (the remaining follicle) secretes progesterone
↓
Increased vascularity of endometrium
↓
Fertilization
↓
Decreased estrogen and progesterone dominates
↓
Endometrium atrophies

Menstrual phase (1)
Days 1–5

Proliferative phase (2)
Days 6–14

Secretory phase (3)
Days 15–26

Ischemic phase (4)
Days 27–28

PREGNANCY

Assess your knowledge of terms related to reproduction by assigning the terms listed to the appropriate definitions below:

1. ____ Vaginal secretions; may increase during pregnancy

2. ____ Nausea and vomiting, a symptom of pregnancy

3. ____ A pregnant woman

4. ____ When the cervix takes on a bluish hue due to increased vascularity during pregnancy—a presumptive sign of pregnancy

5. ____ Toxoplasma, other (HIV, syphilis), rubella, cytomegalovirus, herpes; all of these except toxoplasma can cause abortion, fetal death, teratogenesis, or congenital disease

6. ____ The number of born, viable offspring of a woman

7. ____ The first perceivable movement of the fetus, usually at weeks 17–19; a presumptive sign of pregnancy

8. ____ Development of deformity in the developing embryo

9. ____ Irregular, painless, intermittent contractions during pregnancy

10. ____ Deeper pigmentation

11. ____ White-yellow fluid expressed from the nipples after childbirth

A. Braxton-Hicks contractions

B. Chadwick's sign

C. colostrum

D. gravida

E. leukorrhea

F. linea nigra

G. morning sickness

H. parity

I. quickening

J. teratogenesis

K. T.O.R.C.H. infections

The diagram below will refresh your memory with the chronology and terminology associated with fertilization and fetal development.

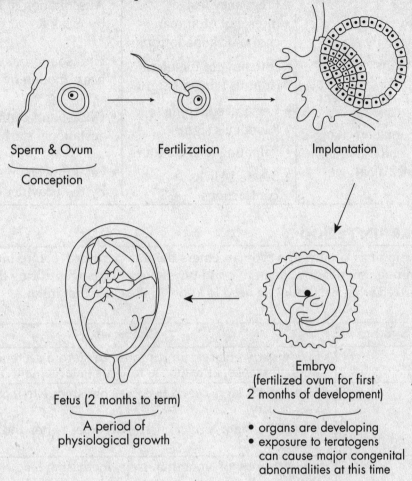

Sperm & Ovum   Fertilization   Implantation

Conception

Fetus (2 months to term)

A period of
physiological growth

Embryo
(fertilized ovum for first
2 months of development)

- organs are developing
- exposure to teratogens
  can cause major congenital
  abnormalities at this time

The placenta is the site of oxygen, nutrient, and waste exchange between the fetal and maternal blood supplies and is fully developed by 14 weeks of pregnancy. Materials that pass through the placenta into fetal circulation include oxygen, nutrients, small molecular-structured drugs, maternal antibodies (passive immunity), and viruses. Large particles such as bacteria and protozoa infect the placenta by causing lesions and then entering the fetal system, and large molecules pass through the placental barrier via pinocytosis. Human chorionic gonadotropin is produced by the placenta and is detected in maternal urine as early as 14 days after conception. Estrogen and progesterone produced by the placenta maintain the pregnancy, replacing the corpus luteum, the original source of steroid hormones.

ASSESSMENT FOR PREGNANCY

Subjective and objective signs of pregnancy may be divided into three categories: presumptive, probable, and positive.

Presumptive	Probable	Positive
• Amenorrhea • Nausea/vomiting • Breast sensitivity and increased size • Fatigue • Abdominal enlargement • Chadwick's sign • Skin pigmentation changes (melasma/chloasma, linea nigra & linea alba).	• Pregnancy test (presence of human chorionic gonadotropin) • Softening of the uterine isthmus (Hegar's sign) • Cervical softening (Goodell's sign) • Palpating fetal contours • Braxton-Hicks contractions	• Auscultation of fetal heart by week 8 • Ultrasound imaging of fetal heart motion by week 7 • Ultrasound confirmation of gestational sac by week 6 • Fetal movements palpated by the provider by week 20

THE ANTEPARTUM PERIOD

Once fertilization has occurred, a woman enters the antepartum ("before birth") period. Women go through tremendous anatomic and physiological changes during this time. We have summarized what we think you need to know in the chart that follows:

Organ/System	Changes
Uterus	• Size greatly enlarges in response to steroid secretion and, after 12 weeks, in response to fetus enlargement
Cervix	• Chadwick's sign: cervix becomes bluish due to increased vascularity • Goodell's sign: cervical tissue becomes softer and more elastic
Vagina	• Hypertrophy of smooth muscle, increasing length of vaginal vault
Breasts	• Increased sensitivity; nipple and areola pigmentation in the first trimester • Growth of mammary glands; increase in size and firmness • Colostrum (white-yellow fluid) is expressed from nipples at the termination of pregnancy
Cardiovascular system	• Increased blood volume due to increased metabolic demands and sodium and water retention • Physiological anemia due to dilution of red blood cells in increased plasma volume
Respiratory system	• Diaphragm pushed up due to enlarging fetus • Increased demand for oxygen to perfuse fetus
Basal metabolic rate	• Increases during pregnancy to meet increased demands for energy and oxygen and returns to normal within days after delivery
Renal system	• Urinary frequency due to pressure of fetus on bladder • Increased glomerular filtration rate to handle increased fluid volume

The goal of the nurse is to provide for the general well-being of the pregnant woman physically, socially, and psychologically. First, using Nägele's rule, correctly determine the client's estimated date of delivery (E.D.D.) or estimated date of confinement (E.D.C.):

Nägele's rule: E.D.D. = 1st day of last menstrual period + 7 days – 3 months + 1 year.

Your role, as the nurse, includes ensuring the optimal growth of the developing fetus, educating the client regarding her expected physiological changes resulting from the growing fetus and hormonal sequelae, and managing the pregnant state via adequate prenatal visits to assess maternal and fetal health. Early identification and intervention for maternal and fetal deviations from the norm minimize maternal and fetal morbidity and mortality.

After obtaining a thorough history of the client and performing a complete physical (including blood pressure and weight) on her, the nurse should obtain the following lab results:

- Rubella
- Blood type
- Rh factor
- Optional: HIV status, toxoplasma, and hepatitis B screen

In addition, tests for tuberculosis, gonorrhea, and chlamydia should be performed, as well as a Pap smear, urinalysis, and urine culture.

The nurse must counsel the client regarding nutrition, health, and exercise and also provide psychosocial support.

At later prenatal visits, the nurse should assess blood pressure and weight, fundal height, the fetal heartbeat (should be 120–160 beats per minute), and the woman's sensation of fetal movement and uterine contractions, and check for signs of infection and gestational diabetes. Other tests during the antepartum period include:

- one-hour glucose tolerance test—24–28 weeks

    This test is given to screen for gestational diabetes.
- maternal serum α-fetoprotein—15–18 weeks

    The AFP test is a routine screening blood test for certain fetal disorders.

All pregnant women are tested for the Rh factor early in pregnancy. If a woman is Rh positive or if both parents are negative, compatibility is not a concern. If the mother is Rh negative (lacks the factor) and the father is Rh positive (has the factor), there may be incompatibility problems. There is very little threat to the baby during the first pregnancy, but there may be serious problems for subsequent pregnancies. The Rh factor enters the Rh negative mother's circulatory system during delivery (also with miscarriage or abortion) of a child who has inherited the Rh factor from his or her father. The mother's immune system responds by producing antibodies against it, as it sees it as a foreign substance. During subsequent pregnancies the antibodies will cross the placenta and attack the fetal red blood cells and cause serious anemia in the fetus. To prevent the development of Rh antibodies in Rh incompatibility, **RhoGAM** (Rh immune globulin) is administered in the 28th week of pregnancy.

Later in the pregnancy, the nurse should engage in childbirth education and preparation. Birth control options for the postpartum period should be discussed.

DIAGNOSTIC TESTS DURING THE ANTEPARTUM PERIOD

Amniocentesis is used to diagnose potential genetic problems in the fetus (e.g., Down's syndrome), to estimate fetal lung maturity, or to diagnose fetal hemolytic disease. The procedure entails introduction of a needle through the abdomen and uterus into the amniotic sac and withdrawal of amniotic fluid for evaluation. Amniocentesis is performed with minimal risk after the 14th week of pregnancy. It is indicated for women over 35 years of age, for women with familial history of such diseases, or for women who themselves (or their spouses) have a chromosomal abnormality, to determine the presence of genetic or metabolic dysfunction in the fetus.

To determine fetal lung maturity, amniotic fluid is aspirated and the lecithin/sphingomyelin (L/S) ratio is determined. The normal L/S ratio is 2/1. If the L/S ratio is lower than 2/1, there is an increased incidence of respiratory distress syndrome in the newborn.

AMNIOCENTESIS

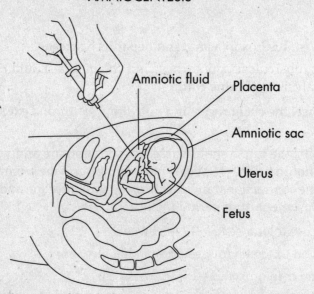

Ultrasonography is the use of high-frequency sound waves that resonate between the ultrasound wand and the fetus. It is noninvasive and there is no known risk to the fetus. It is used to confirm fetal viability, gestational age and growth, fetal anatomy, and placental location. It evaluates the quantity of amniotic fluid, as well as fetal physiological well-being, as in a biophysical profile.

POTENTIAL COMPLICATIONS DURING THE ANTEPARTUM PERIOD

A pregnancy is designated high-risk when there is an increased chance of maternal or fetal mortality or morbidity given specific known risk factors or those risk factors discovered during antepartum care. Risk factors that may be determined during the initial history include the following:

- age under 17 years
- AIDS
- diabetes
- drug abuse
- nullipara over age 35 years
- parity of 5 or more
- presence of T.O.R.C.H. infections
- previous hemorrhage

- heart disease
- history of premature labor
- hypertension
- malnutrition
- Rh negative
- sickle cell trait or disease
- thyroid disease
- massive obesity

Risk factors that can be discovered during antepartum care include:

- abnormal α-fetoprotein values
- anemia
- elevated glucose levels
- perinatal infection
- preeclampsia and eclampsia
- premature labor
- Rh isoimmunization problems
- T.O.R.C.H. infections

Risk factors should be identified as early as possible. This is only accomplished through routine prenatal care! You do not need to memorize the lists above. Just think about the physiological changes necessary for a healthy pregnancy and then think about conditions that would impede normal adaptation to those changes.

To determine the presence of complications as early as possible, assessment is done for vaginal bleeding, premature rupture of membranes, frequency and pattern of contractions before the 36th week, visual disturbances, headaches, noted facial and hand edema, continual and severe nausea and vomiting, decreased fetal movement per client's report, and the absence of fetal heart tone or fetal heart rate below 120 b.p.m. or above 160 b.p.m.

Client education in the antepartum period is vital to the nurse's success in preventing complications and promoting fetal well-being. Empower the woman to report anything abnormal and tell her what to watch for! Support the high-risk client in the control and management of her condition.

HIGH-RISK PREGNANCIES

Several conditions come under the category of high-risk pregnancy. The main nursing goals for all of them are maintaining maternal and fetal well-being, emotional support, and comprehensive client instruction.

Placenta Previa

Placenta previa occurs when the placenta develops within the lower uterine segment and covers all or part of the cervix, specifically the internal os (mouth of the uterus).

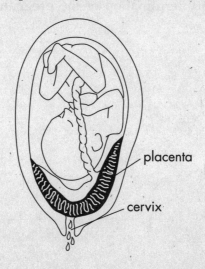

placenta

cervix

Risk Factors	Assessment	Nursing Considerations
• Multiparous woman • Increased age of the mother • Previous uterine surgery	Painless, bright red vaginal bleeding in gushes or intermittently, especially during the third trimester	• Client is hospitalized and put on bed rest. • Continually monitor fetal well-being. • Caesarean delivery is indicated.
• History of prior placenta previa	Soft, nontender uterus	• Measure blood loss through perineal pad counts. • **No** vaginal exams! • Provide **emotional support**.

Abruptio Placentae

Abruptio placentae is the premature separation of the placenta from its implantation site. Separation may be complete or partial. Hemorrhage from a placental abruption may be external (vaginal bleeding present) or concealed (visualized on sonogram), depending on the type of abruption.

Assessment	Nursing Considerations
• Blood is dark red, quantity varies • Intense, unremitting, cramp-like abdominal pain • Uterine tenderness • Fetal heart rate absent or slow (less than 120 b.p.m.)	• Bed rest in wedge position to prevent supine hypotension. • Continually monitor fetal well-being. • Treat signs of shock and hemorrhage. • Provide **emotional support**. • Prepare for delivery.

Abortion

Abortion is the termination of pregnancy before viability of the fetus, generally before 20 weeks gestation. Spontaneous abortion is involuntary delivery of the fetus, or miscarriage. Elective abortion is voluntary termination of the pregnancy for either therapeutic or nontherapeutic reasons.

Assessment	Nursing Consideration
• Vaginal bleeding (perineal pad count) • Contractions (frequency and intensity) • Passage of products of conception • Psychological state of client	• If abortion is threatened, bed rest, pelvic rest, and stress reduction are indicated; otherwise, assist with hemostasis and surgical intervention. • Provide **emotional support.**

Disseminated Intravascular Coagulation

Disseminated intravascular coagulation (D.I.C.) is a pathological clotting disorder that is diffuse and causes injury rather than protecting sites of coagulation. It is the consumption of clotting factors such as platelets and fibrinogen resulting in widespread external and/or internal bleeding. Uncontrolled uterine hemorrhage, bleeding from laceration sites, placental abruption, abortion, or shock can provoke the D.I.C. process.

Assessment	Nursing Consideration
• Spontaneous or uncontrolled bleeding	• Assist in correction of underlying cause of D.I.C. (delivery of fetus, removal of abrupted placenta, treatment of preeclampsia).
• Monitor labs for decreasing platelets, fibrinogen, and increasing prothrombin time.	• Replace blood and blood products as ordered. • Adminster heparin as ordered to prevent clot formation.
• Observe for signs of shock (tachycardia, anxiety, restlessness).	• Provide **emotional support.**

Match the complication of pregnancy on the left with the appropriate intervention on the right:

12. ____ Threatened abortion   A. administer fresh frozen plasma

13. ____ Abruptio placentae   B. bed rest, perineal pad count, and monitor fetal well-being

14. ____ Placenta previa   C. bed rest and pelvic rest

15. ____ D.I.C.   D. bed rest, monitor fetal well-being, and assess signs and symptoms of shock

Pregnancy-Induced Hypertension

Pregnancy-induced hypertension (P.I.H.) is categorized as follows:

Condition	Definition	Assessment
Gestational hypertension	Development of hypertension in normotensive client without proteinuria; blood pressure returns to normal by postpartum day 10	• Increased blood pressure • No proteinuria • Facial or hand edema
Preeclampsia	Acute hypertension specific to pregnancy; graded as mild or severe; onset after week 20; proteinuria present (differentiates preeclampsia from gestational hypertension)	• Increased blood pressure • Proteinuria • Sudden weight gain • Transient headache • If severe: oliguria, visual disturbances, abdominal pain, hyperreflexia, and epigastric pain
Eclampsia	Seizures (clonic = tonic) in a preeclamptic woman	• Increased blood pressure • Severe pitting edema • Oliguria • Visual disturbances • Severe abdominal pain • Hyperreflexia • Change in level of consciousness

Two of the following four symptoms must be present for a diagnosis of preeclampsia:

- Elevation of blood pressure
- Proteinuria
- Facial or hand edema
- Weight gain of more than 4.5 pounds per week

Nursing considerations to control the incidence of eclampsia and the associated morbidity include:

- Maintaining the client on bed rest in a left-lateral position in a quiet environment; limit visitors
- Monitor BP
- Administration of antihypertensive drugs as ordered
- Monitoring fetal heart rate and signs of labor
- Urine dipstick for protein every 4 hours
- Monitoring intake and output (oliguria means progression!)
- Daily weight
- Seizure precautions
- **Educate** and **support** the client!

- Measure and document any emesis
- Assess DTR (deep tendon reflexes)
- Assess for headaches or visual disturbances

Gestational Diabetes

Gestational diabetes is an abnormal glucose tolerance due to the decreased effectiveness of insulin during the second and third trimesters. Early identification of glucose intolerance is essential so that prompt therapy can be initiated. Untreated diabetes in pregnancy may lead to polyhydramnios (excessive amniotic fluid) or macrosomia (large fetus, can be 9 lbs or more). These conditions may lead to dystocia (difficult labor and delivery). Uncontrolled glucose metabolism is also associated with an increased incidence of preeclampsia, stillbirth, neonatal hypoglycemia, respiratory distress syndrome, and premature delivery.

Risk Factors	Assessment	Nursing Considerations
• Family history of diabetes in first-degree relatives • Poor obstetric history • Previous macrosomic infant • Previous newborn with congenital abnormalities • High parity	• Positive 1-hour glucose tolerance test confirmed by 3-hour glucose challenge test • Observe for signs of hyper- and hypoglycemia • Observe for signs of preeclampsia, polyhydramnios, and macrosomia	• Continually monitor fetal well-being. • Strict monitoring to maintain glucose in normal range. • Frequent antepartum visits for adequate supervision. • **Educate** client on blood glucose monitoring and diet guidelines, and about the effects of high blood sugar on the mother and the fetus. • Measure urine protein and ketones.

Hyperemesis Gravidarum

Hyperemesis gravidarum is excessive and persistent vomiting during pregnancy resulting in dehydration and starvation. The cause of hyperemesis is debatable, but may include both physical as well as psychological factors such as increased levels of estrogen and human chorionic gonadotropin (HCG), as well as stress. Dehydration leads to electrolyte imbalances, i.e., acidosis and starvation leads to dietary deficiency sequelae, such as maternal weight loss and fetal death.

Assessment	Nursing Considerations
• Monitor frequency of vomiting. • Measure weight loss. • Monitor urine for ketones. • Monitor pulse. • Evaluate fluid and electrolyte balance. • Assess for signs of metabolic acidosis (headache, stupor, disorientation).	• Intravenous hydration will be ordered. • Antiemetic administration as ordered. • Diet education (small, frequent meals starting with liquids and progressing to solids). • Encourage weight gain. • Provide **emotional support**.

THE INTRAPARTUM PERIOD

The intrapartum period starts with labor and ends with the delivery of the baby and the placenta. The onset of labor is attributed to several causes:

- Hormones from the fetal hypothalamus and maternal estrogen increase uterine contractility.

- Uterine distention, pressure, and the aging placenta are associated with uterine irritability.

- Oxytocin release from the maternal hypothalamus in response to uterine distention initiates uterine contractions.

Involuntary, intermittent muscle contractions of the uterus expel the fetus and placenta. These same contractions bring about cervical effacement (shortening and thinning) and dilatation (widening of the cervical os and canal). Abdominal muscles used during "bearing down" efforts of the client augment uterine forces of delivery. In true labor, contractions are regular in frequency and painful. They steadily increase in intensity and continue even with rest. Braxton-Hicks contractions, which usually start after the 20th week of pregnancy, are the uterus' way of flexing its muscles and preparing for true contractions. A client may feel her uterus bunch up and harden. These "practice" contractions may last from 30 seconds to as long as 2 minutes or more and usually stop with position change or rest.

Normal labor consists of regular contractions, cervical dilatation, effacement and descent, and delivery of the fetus. It is divided into four stages:

Stage	Phase	Assessment	Nursing Considerations
0	Latent	Onset of labor until cervical dilatation of 4 cm	• Monitor frequency, intensity, and pattern of uterine contractions • Monitor fetal status during labor by monitoring fetal heart rate • Assess bloody show (pink or blood-streaked mucus), perineal bulging, membrane status • Periodic vaginal exams • Monitor vital signs • Assess client's ability to cope with contractions • Provide emotional support
1	Active	Progression of dilatation from 4 cm to 10 cm Rapid dilatation and descent	• Assess progress of cervical effacement and dilatation • Assess need for analgesia • Observe for presenting part
2		From complete dilatation to delivery of the fetus	• Prep client for delivery • Immediate assessment of the newborn
3		From delivery of the fetus to delivery of the placenta, usually within 5–20 minutes of delivery	• Assess umbilical cord for 3 vessels (2 arteries, 1 vein) • Assess placenta for intactness • The fundus should be midline at or 2 cm below the umbilicus • The fundus should descend approximately 1–2 cm every 24 hours
4		The period of immediate recovery and observation after delivery of the placenta, approximately 2 hours	• Promote parent-infant bonding • Assess maternal vital signs, fundal height, lochia, and bladder distention • Assist breast-feeding efforts if indicated

CERVICAL EFFACEMENT AND DILATATION

PRIMIGRAVIDA

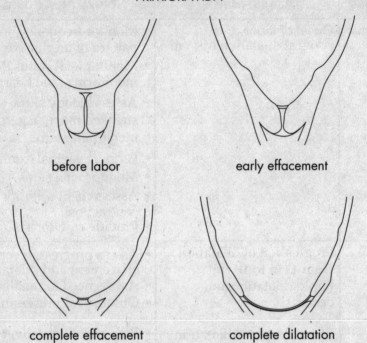

before labor

early effacement

complete effacement

complete dilatation

Effaced then dilated

MULTIGRAVIDA

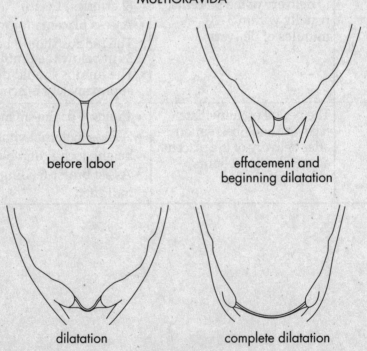

before labor

effacement and
beginning dilatation

dilatation

complete dilatation

Dilated then effaced

MECHANISM OF NORMAL LABOR

1. Engagement, descent, flexion

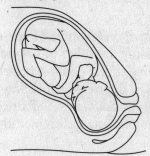

2. Internal rotation

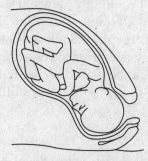

3. Extension beginning (rotation complete)

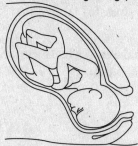

4. Extension complete

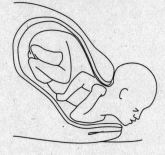

5. External rotation (restitution)

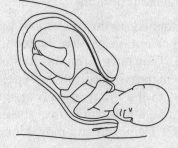

6. External rotation (shoulder rotation)

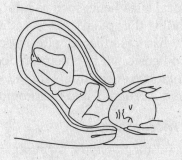

7. Expulsion

PHARMACOLOGICAL CONTROL OF LABOR PAIN

It is the nurse's responsibility to continually assess the laboring woman's contractions and her ability to cope with the associated pain. Ideally, she must be educated before labor about her pain management options.

Analgesia is defined as the alleviation of the sensation of pain or the elevation of one's threshold for perception of pain. Narcotic analgesics are effective for the relief of severe, persistent pain. They have no amnestic effect, but they do have adverse effects such as nausea and vomiting, maternal respiratory depression, and neonatal C.N.S. depression (blocking nerve impulses to the brain) requiring stimulation or resuscitation at delivery. Narcotics cross the placental barrier and affect the neonate. Examples of narcotic analgesics include meperidine HCl (Demerol) and morphine sulfate.

Anesthesia includes analgesia, amnesia, and relaxation. It abolishes pain perception by C.N.S. depression. An epidural block is the most commonly used method of anesthesia for labor. A local anesthetic, such as lidocaine or bupivacaine, is injected into the epidural space surrounding the spinal cord. A catheter is placed for continuous epidural anesthesia. The anesthetic has vasodilatory effects, so a fluid bolus is administered prior to insertion to prevent hypotension. If hypotension does occur, the woman should be placed on her left side, the rate of intravenous fluids should be accelerated as ordered, oxygen support should be administered if ordered, and the provider should be notified.

FETAL HEART MONITORING

Labor is stressful for the fetus; therefore, continual assessment of fetal well-being through fetal heart rate monitoring is essential. Fetal well-being is determined by the response of the fetal heart rate to uterine contractions. Fetal anoxia resulting from stressful labor must be avoided to prevent intrauterine death or neurological damage.

Fetal monitoring is either external (sonographic) or internal (fetal scalp electrode and intrauterine pressure catheter). The normal fetal heart rate is 120–160 b.p.m.

Fetal Heart Rate Patterns	Indicative of ...	Intervention
Tachycardia (>160 b.p.m.)	• Maternal or fetal infection • Fetal hypoxia (an ominous sign)	• Dependent upon cause
Bradycardia (<120 b.p.m.)	• Fetal hypoxia or stress • Maternal hypotension after epidural initiation	• Place client on left side. • Increase fluids (to counteract hypotension). • Stop oxytocin (Pitocin) if in use.
Early deceleration (deceleration begins and ends with uterine contraction)	• Head compression (not ominous) • Vagal stimulation	• None required
Late deceleration (H.R. decreases after peak of contraction and recovers after contraction ends)	• Fetal stress and hypoxia • Deficient placental perfusion • Supine position • Maternal hypotension • Uterine hyperstimulation	• Change maternal position. • Correct hypotension. • Increase IV fluid rate as ordered. • Discontinue oxytocin (Pitocin). • Administer oxygen as ordered.
Variable deceleration (transient decrease in H.R. any time during contraction)	• Cord compression • Hypoxia or hypercarbia	• Change maternal position. • Administer O_2.
Decreased variability (smooth baseline)	• Fetal sleep cycle • Depressant drugs • Hypoxia • C.N.S. anomalies	• Dependent upon cause

THE POSTPARTUM PERIOD

The **puerperium**, or postpartum period, begins after delivery of the placenta and ends at the beginning of the first menstrual cycle (usually 6–8 weeks). There are many anatomic and physiological adaptations that occur in this time frame:

Systems	Change
Uterus	• The fundus should not be palpable after the 9th postpartum day. • Involution process that results in a healed birth canal and the uterus returns to its prepregnant state
Urinary tract	• May become edematous and lose tone and sensation due to trauma • Anesthesia may cause urine retention • If the fundus is above the umbilicus, the probable reason is bladder distention, and the client should be catheterized
Vagina, cervix, ovaries	• Return to prepregnant state and functioning

Immediate nursing interventions during the postpartum period include:

- Monitoring for infection and signs of hemorrhage
- Evaluating the lochia (vaginal discharge after childbirth) for flow: Heavy clots or spurts of bleeding indicate uterine hemorrhage or cervical tear.

Lochia	Time	Characteristics
Rubra	Immediately after childbirth until 3 days after	Blood, fragments of residual and mucus
Serosa	3–10 days after delivery	Pink to brown in color; consists of old blood, tissue debris, and mucus
Alba	Final discharge, can last 2–6 weeks	Mostly yellow mucus, some blood

- Assessing the perineum for swelling and discoloration, as well as for the healing of the episiotomy (if performed)
- Assessing mother-infant bonding and the client's emotional status

ASSESSMENT OF THE NORMAL NEWBORN

This is the assessment of the newborn's immediate transition to extrauterine life.

Respiratory status	• Tachypnea (early sign of distress) • Retractions (use of accessory muscles to breathe) are indicative of respiratory distress. • Nasal flaring and expiratory grunting are early signs of respiratory distress. • Color may change from pink to circumoral pallor and cyanosis in respiratory distress.
Umbilical cord	• Should have 2 arteries and 1 vein
Physical appearance	• Birth trauma and congenital malformations

Apgar score	**0**	**1**	**2**
Color	Pale, blue	Body pink, extremities blue	Totally pink
Heart rate	Absent	Less than 100 b.p.m.	Over 100 b.p.m.
Reflex irritability	No response	Grimace	Vigorous cry
Muscle tone	Limp	Some flexion	Actively moves
Respiratory effort	Absent	Slow, irregular	Good cry

Neurological assessment (reflexes essential for life):

- Sucking (rooting): Stimulation of the cheek causes infant to turn head toward stimulus
- Swallowing: Swallowing caused by stimulation of the palate
- Extrusion: After stimulation of palate, tongue is pushed out when touched
- Tonic neck (fencing): Extension of arm and leg to side to which head is forcibly turned with flexion of opposite arm (should be absent by 3–4 months)
- Palmar (plantar): Fingers tighten around an object placed in the palm; similar response when the sole of the foot is stroked near the toes
- Moro (startle): Extension then flexion of arms and legs, fanning then clenching of fingers in response to startling stimulus
- Pull to sit: The infant's head lags until upright
- Babinski: Dorsiflexion of big toe and fanning of other toes when sole of the foot is stroked from heel to toe (should be absent after 1 year)

Thermogenic System

The neonate produces heat through metabolism of brown fat and an increased metabolic rate, not by shivering. The newborn is at great risk for hypothermia, and cold stress takes too much oxygen away from maintaining the brain and the heart. Heat loss occurs through convection, radiation, evaporation, and conduction.

PARENT-INFANT BONDING

After the newborn's physical stability is assured, assessment of parent-infant bonding is imperative. Facilitation of parent-infant bonding and intervention in situations that may detract from these efforts are nursing goals. The new mother may go through the stages of "taking in" and then "taking hold." While "taking in" the new situation, she may exhibit some passive behavior. Reassure her and her partner that exhaustion from labor and delivery plays a large part in this mood. She should advance to "take hold" of the situation and concern herself with providing food for her child. Postpartum blues may set in several days after delivery, and it is imperative that the nurse encourage the new mother to verbalize her feelings and to tap resources to facilitate coping.

CHAPTER 23: EXERCISE ANSWERS

1. **E** **leukorrhea**—Vaginal secretions; may increase during pregnancy
2. **G** **morning sickness**—Nausea and vomiting, a symptom of pregnancy
3. **D** **gravida**—A pregnant woman
4. **B** **Chadwick's sign**—When the cervix takes on a bluish hue due to increased vascularity during pregnancy
5. **K** **T.O.R.C.H. infections**—toxoplasma, other (HIV, syphilis), rubella, cytomegalovirus, herpes; all of these, except toxoplasma can cause abortion, fetal death, teratogenesis, or congenital disease
6. **H** **parity**—The number of born, viable offspring of a woman
7. **I** **quickening**—The first perceivable movement of the fetus, usually at weeks 17–19; a presumptive sign of pregnancy
8. **J** **teratogenesis**—Development of deformity in the developing embryo
9. **A** **Braxton-Hicks contractions**—Irregular, painless, intermittent contractions during pregnancy
10. **F** **linea nigra**—Deeper pigmentation
11. **C** **colostrum**—White-yellow fluid expressed from the nipples after childbirth
12. **C** Threatened abortion—**bed rest and pelvic rest**
13. **D** Abruptio placentae—**bed rest, monitor fetal well-being and assess signs and symptoms of shock**
14. **B** Placenta previa—**bed rest and perineal pad count and monitor fetal well-being**
15. **A** D.I.C.—**administer fresh frozen plasma**

CHAPTER 23: NCLEX-RN STYLE QUESTIONS

1. A multiparous client tells the nurse that she experienced afterbirth pains while breastfeeding her infant. The nurse should

   (1) Instruct the client to lie prone with a small pillow under her adbomen.
   (2) suggest that the client offer the infant a bottle at the next feeding.
   (3) encourage the mother to empty her bladder every 2 to 3 hours.
   (4) adminster the p.r.n. dose of simethicone (Mylicon).

2. A 35-year-old woman, at term, is admitted with a diagnosis of pregnancy-induced hypertension. The priority nursing assessment for the client should be

   (1) deep tendon reflexes.
   (2) gravida and para.
   (3) vital signs.
   (4) protein in urine.

3. Which of these adaptations is considered a positive sign of pregnancy?

   (1) Maternal nausea and vomiting
   (2) A positive pregnancy test
   (3) Ultrasound recognition of fetus
   (4) Braxton-Hicks contractions

4. Which sequence of cardinal fetal movements would be expected during a vertex delivery?

   (1) Flexion, descent, external rotation
   (2) Internal rotation, restitution, expulsion
   (3) Descent, engagement, extension
   (4) Engagement, descent, flexion

5. The nurse instructs the antepartal woman that preeclampsia in pregnancy is defined as the

   (1) occurrence of hypertension in the second half of pregnancy.
   (2) progression of pre-existing hypertension to include maternal seizures.
   (3) development of hypertension in pregnancy accompanied by proteinuria.
   (4) increase in pre-existing hypertension accompanied by edema.

6. A woman in her 38th week of pregnancy, diagnosed with a complete placenta previa, asks if she can still have a vaginal delivery. The nurse responds,

   (1) "Yes, if the fetal head descends enough to put pressure on the placenta."
   (2) "Probably, if bleeding can be kept under control."
   (3) "Maybe, you'll have to discuss this with your provider."
   (4) "Eighty percent of women with placenta previa require operative delivery."

7. A primiparous mother has just delivered an 8-pound baby. The nurse notes she appears anxious when the newborn is brought to her. What would be the priority in developing a nursing care plan for this mother?	(1) Explore whether the mother wanted the pregnancy. (2) Teach the mother how to feed and hold the baby. (3) Feed and hold the baby for the mother. (4) Explore what support system the mother has for caring for the infant at home.
8. A 29-year-old nulliparous woman who has been diagnosed with gestational diabetes has been offered serum α-fetoprotein testing. The nurse encourages her to have this done because	(1) diabetic mothers are more prone to placenta previa. (2) infants of diabetic mothers are ten times more likely than the general population to have a neural tube defect. (3) glucose intolerance in pregnancy predisposes the woman to oligohydramnios. (4) imperforate anus can be ruled out.
9. A 32-year-old primiparous woman who has had glucose intolerance during pregnancy is about to be discharged from the hospital. She asks the nurse when she can expect her blood sugar to return to normal. The nurse replies,	(1) "One to three weeks after delivery." (2) "Three to five weeks after delivery." (3) "It will never return to normal." (4) "About 3 months after delivery." 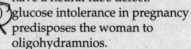

CHAPTER 23: NCLEX-RN STYLE ANSWERS

1.
    (1) CORRECT   Lying prone has been shown to decrease the discomfort associated with afterbirth pains.

    (2) ELIMINATE   The client should not be discouraged from breast feeding. The nurse would teach that afterbirth pains last only a few days.

    (3) ELIMINATE   While a full bladder may displace the uterus upward and to the right, afterbirth pains are associated with the release of oxytocin, not with a full bladder.

CATEGORY 07 BASIC CARE AND COMFORT

2.   **(3) CORRECT**   Baseline vital signs are essential to determine future changes in the client's condition. The vital signs are the priority because they form the baseline upon which therapy, including medications, will be based.

    (1) *ELIMINATE*   Not the priority nursing assessment.

    (2) *ELIMINATE*   Does not relate to the diagnosis of pregnancy-induced hypertension.

    (4) *ELIMINATE*   Not the priority for assessment of pregnancy-induced hypertension.

CATEGORY 04 PREVENTION AND EARLY DETECTION OF DISEASE

---

3.   **(3) CORRECT**   The adaptations considered to be positive signs of pregnancy include fetal heart tones, uterine sounds, observed fetal movement, and visualization of fetus by ultrasonography.

    (1) *ELIMINATE*   This is a presumptive sign of pregnancy.

    (2) *ELIMINATE*   This is a probable sign of pregnancy.

    (4) *ELIMINATE*   This is probably a sign of pregnancy.

CATEGORY 03 GROWTH AND DEVELOPMENT THROUGH THE LIFE SPAN

---

4.   **(4) CORRECT**   The usual sequence of fetal movements during a vertex delivery include engagement, descent, flexion, internal rotation, extension, restitution, external rotation, and expulsion.

    (1) *ELIMINATE*   Incorrect sequencing.

    (2) *ELIMINATE*   Incorrect sequencing.

    (3) *ELIMINATE*   Incorrect sequencing.

CATEGORY 03 GROWTH AND DEVELOPMENT THROUGH THE LIFE SPAN

---

5.   **(3) CORRECT**   When hypertension is accompanied by proteinuria and/or generalized edema, the disease is known as preeclampsia.

    (1) *ELIMINATE*   This adaptation would be classified as pregnancy-induced hypertension.

    (2) *ELIMINATE*   Preeclampsia develops in late pregnancy and is not characterized by pre-existing hypertension.

    (4) *ELIMINATE.*   Preeclampsia develops in late pregnancy and is not characterized by pre-existing hypertension.

CATEGORY 03 GROWTH AND DEVELOPMENT THROUGH THE LIFE SPAN

---

6.   **(4) CORRECT**   Vaginal delivery is considered only if the previa is marginal or if the fetus were dead or had severe malformations. Eighty percent of women require surgical intervention.

    (1) *ELIMINATE*   This statement would provide the client with inaccurate information.

    (2) *ELIMINATE*   This statement would provide the client with inaccurate information.

    (3) *ELIMINATE*   This statement would provide the client with inaccurate information.

CATEGORY 03 GROWTH AND DEVELOPMENT THROUGH THE LIFE SPAN

7.   (2) CORRECT   This would meet the physiological needs of the infant and would help the new mother with her coping skills.

       (1) *ELIMINATE*   This would not be a priority.

       (3) *ELIMINATE*   The nurse should encourage and assist the mother in order to allay anxiety, but should not take over care of the infant.

       (4) *ELIMINATE*   The nurse would want to include this in a plan, but this would not be a priority.

CATEGORY 05 COPING AND ADAPTATION

---

8.   (2) CORRECT   The frequency of neural tube defects in infants of diabetic mothers is more than ten times that of the general population. Maternal serum α-fetoprotein monitoring aids in the detection of this and other anomalies.

       (1) *ELIMINATE*   Placenta previa is not more prevalent in diabetic mothers.

       (3) *ELIMINATE*   Serum α-fetoprotein testing has no relationship to oligohydramnios.

       (4) *ELIMINATE*   This is not a test for imperforate anus.

CATEGORY 03 GROWTH AND DEVELOPMENT THROUGH THE LIFE SPAN

---

9.   (2) CORRECT   Blood sugar usually returns to prepregnancy levels approximately 3–5 weeks after delivery.

       (1) *ELIMINATE*   This would be too soon for the blood glucose levels to return to normal.

       (3) *ELIMINATE*   This is not a correct statement.

       (4) *ELIMINATE*   This is too long after delivery. Usually, the blood sugar returns to normal in 3–5 weeks.

CATEGORY 03 GROWTH AND DEVELOPMENT THROUGH THE LIFE SPAN

24

Nutrition Through the Life Cycle

WHAT YOU NEED TO KNOW

Nutrition is a large part of the NCLEX-RN—a part that often stumps nursing students. Here, we have a straightforward review to provide you with the essentials necessary to conquer the specific questions on the boards. After reviewing the basics of nutrition, we take a developmental approach to your client's specific needs, as this embraces the organization of the questions on the NCLEX-RN. This is a good place to use your common sense. Think of the friends and family you know who are going through the described developmental phases. What are they eating? What should they be eating?

THE FOOD GROUPS

Because nurses are holistic health care providers, they should be familiar with basic principles of nutrition. It is usually up to the nurse to obtain a dietitian consultation for clients with special needs, so he must know enough about nutrition to recognize those clients. The principles of nutrition are based on the food groups and the components listed below. You should familiarize yourself with these groupings and remember them as you review the developmental guide to nutrition. A variety of different food groups should be in each correct answer on the NCLEX-RN, and special physical conditions should be taken into account when choosing foods.

Food Group	Food Examples/Serving Size	Serving Information
Starch/bread	1 slice bread $\frac{1}{2}$ cup pasta, cereal, or potatoes $\frac{1}{3}$ cup rice	6–11 servings per day
Vegetables	1 cup raw $\frac{1}{2}$ cup cooked	3–5 servings per day Canned vegetables are high in sodium!
Fruits	1 small apple or orange $\frac{1}{2}$ banana	2–4 servings per day
Meats	3 ounces lean meat, poultry, or fish	2–3 servings per day
Dairy	1 cup (8 ounces) milk or yogurt	2–3 servings per day Major source of calcium Low-fat or non-fat is best
Fats	1 teaspoon oil, butter, or margarine	Use sparingly

The components listed on the following page are found within the foods in the appropriate food groups. Note that we have not listed each specific vitamin, mineral, and recommended dietary allowance (RDA), as the nurse does not need to know these for safe practice in the first year of working! Just familiarize yourself with general principles; any details you need to know can be found in the table.

Food Component	Function	Energy	Note
Protein	Tissue repair and maintenance Immunity	4 kcals/gram	Lean animal and low-fat dairy sources (e.g., lean meat, poultry, fish, low-fat yogurt) as well as dry beans and tofu are all good choices.
Carbohydrates	Energy source	4 kcals/gram	Choose complex carbohydrates such as whole grains, fruits and vegetables.
Fiber	Regulates intestinal transit Increases fecal bulk Examples include whole grains, fruits, and vegetables	Not an energy source	Reduce fiber in presence of diarrhea.
Lipids	Major storage form of energy Aids transport and absorption of fat-soluble vitamins (A, D, E, K)	9 kcals/gram	Fat is important for babies as it promotes nerve myelination.
Vitamins and minerals	Essential for normal growth and development Absorption (A, D, E, K) requires presence of bile and pancreatic juices Vitamin K is essential for clotting [the antidote for warfarin (Coumadin) overdose] Many vitamins function as co-enzymes	Not an energy source	Most vitamins are toxic in large quantities. Clients are rarely deficient in minerals. Green, leafy vegetables are high in vitamin K.
Water	A solvent (matter dissolves in water) Regulates body temperature Provides structure to cells	Not an energy source	Infants and the elderly are at high risk of dehydration.

1. **True** or **false**? Dietary fiber provides 4 kcals of energy per gram.

2. Along with _____, potassium helps to maintain water and acid-base balance in the body.

3. The fat-soluble vitamins are:
    A. _____
    B. _____
    C. _____
    D. _____

NUTRITIONAL NEEDS THROUGHOUT THE LIFE CYCLE

One of the best ways to assess a client's nutritional status is to ask him to keep a three-day diary of his food and beverage intake. (This question often comes up on the NCLEX-RN.) In addition, just by looking at your client you can determine certain nutritional needs. A client with poor skin turgor and dry mucous membranes may need hydration (water or IV hydration). An obese client may need to limit calorie and fat intake and start a supervised exercise routine as tolerated.

INFANCY (BIRTH TO 1 YEAR OF AGE)

The nurse is often in a position to educate new parents about their infant's nutritional needs. General feeding principles through 1 year of age are as follows:

Age	Feeding Guide
0–4 months	Breast feed or bottle feed (if possible, breast milk is best)
5 months	Introduce thinned rice cereal with breast milk or formula
6 months	Introduce semisolid, textured cereal with addition of fruits and vegetables
7 months	Thickened cereal; introduce meats and liquids via a cup; introduce diluted juices
8–9 months	Begin finger foods, and soft food in chunks
10–12 months	Soft, chopped table foods

In utero, fetal growth declines and almost stops just before birth. Full-term babies will lose weight shortly after birth and will regain their birth weight and resume growth by 2 weeks of age. By the age of 6 months, the infant should have doubled his birth weight. By the age of 1 year, infants should triple their body weight, increase their body length by 50 percent, and increase their head circumference by 40 percent.

Breast feeding is the feeding of choice for newborns, but this is not always possible. In some cases, (e.g., maternal HIV infection), bottle feeding is indicated. To remind yourself of terms related to infant feedings, fill in the blanks with the terms listed below:

at the end of feedings   during the day

colostrum   triple

double

4. By the end of the first year of life, a baby's weight should be _____ the birth weight.

5. _____ is the first milk expressed from the mother's breast after delivery.

6. Fat content of breast feedings is highest _____.

7. Milk production is greatest _____.

8. By the sixth month of life, a baby's weight should be _____ the birth weight.

Standard baby formulas are made from cow's milk that is altered by the removal of both butterfat and protein (e.g., Enfamil with iron, Similac with iron). Soy formula is fortified with proteins, carbohydrates, and vegetable oils (e.g., Isomil). Whole cow's milk is not recommended during the first year of life due to the high incidence of protein allergies and milk's low iron content.

At approximately 4–6 months of age, children's gross motor skills are developed to an extent that makes it possible for them to accept solid foods. The first solid food should be rice cereal thinned to a liquid comparable to breast milk or bottle formula. The infant's diet should slowly expand to include fruits, vegetables, and meats, with the introduction of new foods (one at a time) for 2–3 days at first to test for allergy or intolerance. In the absence of reactions (rashes, diarrhea, wheezing), feeding of new foods should continue. Initial resistance to spoon feedings is common, but choking or gagging indicates that, despite chronological age, the child is not ready for solid food.

9. A child is ready to accept solid foods at _____ due to the development of _____.

10. _____ and _____ indicate that an infant is not ready to accept solid food.

11. _____, _____, and _____ are signs of a food allergy. The causative food should be eliminated from the infant's diet.

Feeding Problems During Infancy

Common feeding problems during infancy include those listed below. The **boldfaced** words are those that you should associate with each problem.

Milk protein allergies	Often associated with eggs, nuts, peas, fish, citrus fruit, corn products, wheat, and chicken. This allergy **can resolve** with time.
Baby bottle tooth decay "bottle mouth"	Babies who are given **juice via bottle at bedtime** or while napping are at high risk.
Constipation	Infrequent, dry, or hard stooling is common in bottle-fed infants; **add water** in small amounts to the infant's diet in addition to, not as a substitution for, breast milk/formula.
Acute diarrhea	**Oral electrolyte formulas** are optimal to prevent dehydration and electrolyte imbalance caused by diarrhea; after four days, IV hydration is necessary to prevent/correct dehydration. **Infants are at a high risk for dehydration**. Gatorade and broth are **not** acceptable antidotes for diarrhea.
Gastroesophageal reflux (spitting up)	May cause failure to thrive, anemia, or aspiration. Ensure **upright feeding position**, prone position (on stomach) in bed with head elevated, and thickened feeds.
Food refusal	May be caused by physical or emotional stress; provide **relaxed atmosphere for eating**.

PRESCHOOL AGE (2–6 YEARS)

Growth between the ages of 2 and 6 is continuous and steady. Children prefer foods that are easy to pick up (with their fingers) as they are learning and practicing self-feeding skills. (Spills are frequent!) It is recommended that the preschool-aged child be served small meals with an initial offering of one tablespoon of each food for each year of life 4–6 times a day.

Children under 4 years of age are at the greatest risk for aspiration. This is especially pertinent for the nurse who is providing food for children in bed. The child should be upright for eating. Foods to be avoided include hot dogs, raw vegetables, whole grapes, popcorn, and hard candy. These can easily lodge in a child's throat and cause choking.

SCHOOL AGE (7–11 YEARS)

Between the ages of 7 and 11, children's growth is slow and steady. The child's appetite increases during these years, yet the structure of school life is not conducive to maintaining good nutrition for the following reasons:

- Skipping breakfast is common.
- School lunch programs do not always include a child's food of choice.
- After-school snacks are routine and are not always healthy.
- After-school activities lead to fewer balanced, family meals.

How can the nurse and/or parent optimize nutrition for the school-aged child? Careful food planning for the family is imperative. A few suggestions include scheduling enough time in the morning for a quick bowl of vitamin- and mineral-fortified cereal, packing lunches that include balanced foods that satisfy the child's food preferences, and encouraging fruits for after-school snacks. Nurses are often in an optimal position to educate children and their parents on healthy food habits that should be established during this developmental phase.

ADOLESCENCE (12–18 YEARS)

Adolescence is a period of rapid growth during which children are hungry all the time. Adolescents spend more time away from the home exerting their independence, so fewer balanced meals are served, and between-meal snacking is common. Ideally, the adolescent is already in the habit of grabbing a piece of fruit for a snack, but in reality nurses need to educate adolescents on good eating habits. As you probably recall from experience, the adolescent's body is rapidly changing shape, and body image has a large impact on self-esteem. These are factors that must be considered when educating and providing food for adolescents.

Substance use often begins during adolescence, having a negative effect on nutritional status. For example, cigarette smoking can decrease one's appetite and increase the body's metabolic rate. Therefore, the body's nutritional needs for growth and metabolism are probably not being met and a nutritional consultation should be ordered.

Nutrition is a big concern for pregnant adolescents. There is competition between the nutritional needs of the growing adolescent girl and the fetus. Pregnant adolescents need 14–16 more grams of protein daily than normal adolescent females. Weight gain of about 35 pounds leads to better pregnancy outcomes for adolescents.

12. Constipation is common in _____ infants.

13. Acute diarrhea that lasts for more than 4 days will require _____.

14. Finger food is preferred by _____ -aged children.

15. Foods that may cause aspiration include:

    A. _____

    B. _____

    C. _____

16. Pregnant adolescents should gain about ___ pounds to improve the outcome of the pregnancy.

ADULTS (19–60 YEARS)

"Adults" covers a broad age group. Factors to consider when counseling a nonpregnant adult about nutrition include:

- Familial history of heart disease
- Personal and familial history of high cholesterol
- Personal and familial history of obesity
- Daily schedules and routines
- Lifestyle factors including exercise regimen and/or sedentary lifestyle
- Food preferences (including cultural customs)
- Existing eating habits
- Financial status (ability to buy sufficient food)

When providing advice on food choices, it is important to be realistic in one's expectations of a client's ability to change. Compliance with suggestions often depends on the client's perception of his or her ability to realistically follow the suggestions of the nurse. Remember, obtaining a dietitian's consultation is always recommended.

Special Diets

While the nurse is concerned with both normal and abnormal nutritional needs of all adults, your focus in studying for the NCLEX-RN should be the special diets that an adult may require during a time of illness or to prevent certain conditions. We have simplified the diets you are most likely to encounter on the NCLEX-RN on the next page.

Diet	Indication	Examples
Clear liquid diet	Transition from NPO	Tea, apple juice, ginger ale, broth
Full liquid diet	Transition from clear liquid to soft foods; generally after surgery	Milk, cream soups
Soft foods	Useful if client has difficulty swallowing (dysphagia) or poor dentition Useful after esophageal surgery	Foods that are easy to chew (e.g., mashed potatoes, scrambled eggs)
Low-fiber (low-residue) diet	Used in intestinal obstruction, diarrhea, high-output ileostomy or colostomy, irritable bowel syndrome	Restrict dairy products (limit lactose) Minimize raw vegetables
High-fiber diet	Reduces constipation, increases fecal bulk	Vegetables, fruits, whole grain foods, fluid
Bland foods	Useful for clients with ulcers	Avoid caffeine and alcohol, spicy foods
Diabetic diet	For type 1 and 2 diabetes	Limit sugar, concentrated sweets Consistent timing and content of meals Achieve ideal body weight Use diabetic exchange lists (derived from food groups)
Post-gastrectomy diet	Prevent "dumping syndrome"	Avoid concentrated sweets Drink liquids between meals Increase protein intake, limit fat intake
Lactose-restricted diet	For clients with lactose intolerance	Avoid dairy foods
Protein-restricted diet	Liver encephalopathy Renal dysfunction	Limit to 40–60 grams/day Protein should come from meat, fish, eggs

Diet	Indication	Examples
Low-fat diet	Overweight Liver and gallbladder disease Heart disease	Avoid cream sauces, butter, fried food, whole milk, fatty meats
Low-fat/low-cholesterol diet	Heart disease High-cholesterol levels	Avoid organ meats; high-fat dairy foods; no more than three eggs/week
Sodium-restricted diet (can be 500–4,000 mg/day)	Congestive heart failure Hypertension Renal disease Edema Liver disease, ascites Adrenal corticoid therapy	Avoid processed, canned foods Do not add salt to foods **Be realistic to promote compliance**
Potassium-restricted diet	Renal disease (high serum potassium) Medication side effects	Avoid bananas, oranges, potatoes, tomatoes

17. Clients with high blood pressure should avoid foods high in _____.

18. Clients with difficulty digesting dairy products may have a _____ intolerance.

19. Clients with a history of heart disease should avoid foods high in _____ and _____.

20. Clients with kidney disease should avoid foods high in _____.

21. Foods high in potassium include:

    A. _____

    B. _____

    C. _____

22. Canned foods are high in _____ content.

Nutrition and Pregnancy

Nutrition plays an important role in the outcome of pregnancy. The client's nutritional status before pregnancy, the client's prepregnancy weight, and the client's weight gain during pregnancy **all** affect the outcome. For the NCLEX-RN, know that the **total** recommended weight gain during pregnancy is 25 pounds:

In the...	The client should gain...
1st trimester	approximately 5 pounds
2nd and 3rd trimesters	approximately 1 pound/week

Obese pregnant women should not diet, but instead should limit their weight gain to a total of approximately 15 pounds. Specific nutritional requirements during pregnancy include:

- An additional 300 kcals/day
- An additional 10 g protein/day
- An additional 30 mg iron/day
- 1,200 mg calcium/day throughout pregnancy and lactation

In general, the pregnant woman should avoid alcohol and limit caffeine and aspartame.

During lactation, the client should avoid severe kilocalorie restrictions. In fact, this client needs approximately **500 kcals/day extra** for the first 3 months following delivery for lactation. After that, she should not consume less than 1,500 kcals/day. The lactating woman also has increased protein, vitamin, and mineral requirements (the specifics of these additional requirements are not important for the NCLEX-RN).

23. During pregnancy, an average woman should gain approximately _____ pounds in the first trimester and approximately _____ pound(s) per week in the second and third trimesters.

24. Nutritional requirements during pregnancy include an additional _____ kcals/day, _____ grams of protein/day, and _____ mg calcium/day.

25. Energy requirements for lactation are an extra_____ kcals/day.

True or **false**?

26. _____ Women with PKU are allowed to consume aspartame in moderation.

27. _____ Gestational diabetics should try to lose weight while pregnant.

28. _____ RDAs for vitamins and minerals resume to prepregnancy requirements when a woman is postpartum and lactating.

GERIATRICS (OVER 60 YEARS)

Nutrition is a large concern in the geriatric population. There are many factors associated with aging that can affect nutrient intake. Each factor listed below should be examined when the nurse is assessing a client's nutritional status. Your common sense will lead you to consider many of these issues associated with aging, but for your review, a list follows:

- Decreased lean body mass (muscle atrophy)
- Decreased basal metabolic rate
- Increased adipose tissue (replaces muscle mass)
- Decreased total body water (**Dehydration is a risk!**)
- Decreased renal function
- Decreased cardiovascular function
- Decreased gastrointestinal function
- Increased oral pathology/poor dentition
- Decreased immune function

- Decreased taste, smell, and/or visual acuity (**food becomes less appealing**)
- Psychosocial changes (**fewer social outlets; eating alone is less appealing than eating with others**)
- Limited financial resources (e.g., retirement leads to fixed income)
- Alcohol/drug abuse
- Multiple medications (**This is extremely important for the NCLEX-RN!**)
- Drug/nutrient, drug/drug interactions
- Chronic disease (e.g., arthritis makes opening jars and packages difficult)

There are a few basic principles about nutrition for the geriatric population that you should know for the NCLEX-RN. The elderly are at risk for dehydration. The nurse should encourage fluids, monitor the client's daily intake and output, and assess renal function. Skin turgor and mucous membranes are good indicators of hydration. The nurse should ensure protein intake at normal or slightly increased levels unless renal disease is present. You should recall that protein is imperative in maintaining muscle mass and promoting tissue healing. Remember, energy needs are increased with sepsis, fever, and wounds.

29. List six factors that may affect an elderly person's nutritional status:
    A. _____
    B. _____
    C. _____
    D. _____
    E. _____
    F. _____

30. Elderly clients are at high risk for _____ and therefore require strict monitoring of intake and output and renal function.

KEEP IN MIND

Remember, dietitians specialize in nutrition and the NCLEX-RN loves it when the nurse makes referrals. Unfortunately, "consulting a dietitian" is not always an option on the exam, so you need to familiarize yourself with the principles described above. If you are stumped, use common sense and the test-taking principles we discussed in the beginning of the book: Process of Elimination, breaking down the question using what you know about the test structure, and using the roots of words to guide you to the answer.

1. **False**—Dietary fiber provides 4 kcals of energy per gram.
2. Along with **sodium**, potassium helps to maintain water and acid-base balance in the body.
3. The fat-soluble vitamins are: **A, D, E**, and **K**.
4. By the end of the first year of life, a baby's weight should be **triple** the birth weight.
5. **Colostrum** is the first milk expressed from the mother's breast after delivery.
6. Fat content of breast feedings is highest **at the end of feedings**.
7. Milk production is greatest **during the day**.
8. By the sixth month of life, a baby's weight should be **double** the birth weight.
9. A child is ready to accept solid foods at **5 months** due to the development of **gross motor skills**.
10. **Gagging** and **choking** indicate that an infant is not ready to accept solid food.
11. **Skin rash, wheezing,** and **diarrhea** are signs of a food allergy. The causative food should be eliminated from the infant's diet.
12. Constipation is common in **bottle-fed** infants.
13. Acute diarrhea that lasts for more than 4 days will require **IV hydration**.
14. Finger food is preferred by **preschool**-aged children.
15. Foods that may cause aspiration include **popcorn, hot dogs, raw vegetables, whole grapes, nuts,** and **hard candy**.
16. Pregnant adolescents should gain about **35** pounds to improve the outcome of the pregnancy.
17. Clients with high blood pressure should avoid foods high in **sodium**.
18. Clients with difficulty digesting dairy products may have a **lactose** intolerance.
19. Clients with a history of heart disease should avoid foods high in **fat** and **cholesterol**.
20. Clients with kidney disease should avoid foods high in **potassium**.
21. Foods high in potassium include **bananas, oranges,** and **tomatoes**.
22. Canned foods are high in **sodium** content.
23. During pregnancy, an average woman should gain approximately **5** pounds in the first trimester and approximately **1** pound per week in the second and third trimesters.
24. Nutritional requirements during pregnancy include an additional **300** kcals/day, **10** grams of protein/day, and **1,200** mg calcium/day.
25. Energy requirements for lactation are an extra **500 kcals/day**.
26. **False**—Women with PKU are allowed to consume aspartame in moderation.
27. **False**—Gestational diabetics should try to lose weight while pregnant.
28. **False**—RDAs for vitamins and minerals resume to prepregnancy requirements when a woman is postpartum and lactating.
29. Factors that may affect an elderly person's nutritional status include:

decreased lean body mass	decreased taste, smell, or visual acuity
decreased basal metabolic rate	physiological and metabolic changes
increased adipose tissue	psychosocial changes
decreased total body water	limited financial resources
decreased renal function	alcohol/drug abuse

decreased cardiovascular function   multiple medications

decreased gastrointestinal function   drug/nutrient, drug/drug interactions

increased oral pathology/poor dentition   chronic disease

decreased immune function

30. Elderly clients are at high risk for **dehydration** and therefore require strict monitoring of intake and output and renal function.

CHAPTER 24: NCLEX-RN STYLE QUESTIONS

1. Of the following foods, which is the best source of <u>phosphorus?</u>	(1) Raisins (2) Oranges (3) Milk (4) Molasses
2. The nurse is most correct to recommend which of the following foods for a child with iron-deficiency anemia?	(1) Apples (2) Bananas (3) Dried apricots (4) Carrots
3. The nurse is teaching a renal client how to restrict dietary potassium. The foods that are high in potassium include	(1) potatoes (2) caffeine (3) poultry (4) beef
4. A client's knowledge of foods lowest in both fat and sodium would be accurate if the client selected which of these menus?	(1) Tossed salad with blue cheese dressing, cold cuts, and vanilla cookies. (2) Split pea soup, cheese sandwich, and a banana. (3) Cold, baked chicken, lettuce with sliced tomatoes, and apple sauce. (4) Beans and frankfurters, carrot and celery sticks, and a plain cupcake.
5. How many calories are recommended daily for a girl, age 14, height 62 inches, weight 103 pounds, who is moderately active?	(1) 1,500 calories (2) 2,000 calories (3) 2,500 calories (4) 3,000 calories
6. The nurse can counsel a 16-year-old client that, as compared to previous pre-adolescent years, most normal adolescent boys need	(1) more calories but less protein. (2) more calories and more protein. (3) fewer calories but more protein. (4) fewer calories and less protein.

7. The nurse should counsel the parents of a child with iron deficiency anemia to include which of the following foods in the diet?	(1) Fish (2) Eggs (3) Roast beef ⟲ (4) Green beans
8. Which of the following menus is most appropriate for a client on a low-cholesterol diet?	(1) Chicken fried in hydrogenated oil, baked potato, fruit, coffee (2) Chicken salad sandwich, yellow cake, 2% milk (3) Broiled steak, fresh broccoli, baked potato with sour cream, diet soda (4) Flounder filet, baked potato, angel food cake, tea ⟲

CHAPTER 24: NCLEX-RN STYLE ANSWERS

1.
(3) CORRECT   Milk, along with cheese, meat, fish, egg yolk, nuts, grains and legumes, is a good source of phosphorus.
(1) *ELIMINATE*   Raisins are not a good source of phosphorus.
(2) *ELIMINATE*   Oranges are not a good source of phosphorus.
(4) *ELIMINATE*   Molasses is not a good source of phosphorus.
CATEGORY 07 BASIC CARE AND COMFORT

2.
(3) CORRECT   Dried fruit, meats, and leafy green vegetables are good sources of iron.
(1) *ELIMINATE*   Apples are not a good source of iron.
(2) *ELIMINATE*   Bananas are not a good source of iron.
(4) *ELIMINATE*   Carrots are not a good source of iron.
CATEGORY 07 BASIC CARE AND COMFORT

3.
(1) CORRECT   Potatoes are high in potassium.
(2) *ELIMINATE*   Caffeine does not contain potassium.
(3) *ELIMINATE*   Poultry does not contain potassium.
(4) *ELIMINATE*   Beef does not contain potassium.
CATEGORY 09 REDUCTION OF RISK POTENTIAL

4.
(3) CORRECT   These are all foods low in sodium and fat.
(1) *ELIMINATE*   The cheese and cold cuts are high in sodium and possibly fat.
(2) *ELIMINATE*   The pea soup and cheese contain sodium.
(4) *ELIMINATE*   Beans and frankfurters contain sodium and the frankfurters and cupcake are high in fat.
CATEGORY 04 PREVENTION AND EARLY DETECTION OF DISEASE

5.

(3)	CORRECT	2,500 calories would be appropriate for a normal 14-year-old girl who is moderately active.
(1)	*ELIMINATE*	1,500 calories would be too few.
(2)	*ELIMINATE*	2,000 calories would be too few.
(4)	*ELIMINATE*	3,000 calories would be too many.

CATEGORY 03 GROWTH AND DEVELOPMENT THROUGH THE LIFE SPAN

6.

(2)	CORRECT	Adolescent boys need more calories and protein to sustain growth.
(1)	*ELIMINATE*	Adolescent boys need high protein for muscle development as well as increased calories.
(3)	*ELIMINATE*	Adolescent boys need both more calories and protein than do pre-adolescent boys.
(4)	*ELIMINATE*	Adolescent boys need both more calories and protein than do pre-adolescent boys.

CATEGORY 03 GROWTH AND DEVELOPMENT THROUGH THE LIFE SPAN

7.

(3)	CORRECT	Red meats contain the highest levels of iron.
(1)	*ELIMINATE*	Fish does not contain high levels of iron.
(2)	*ELIMINATE*	Eggs do not contain high levels of iron.
(4)	*ELIMINATE*	Green beans do not contain high levels of iron.

CATEGORY 07 BASIC CARE AND COMFORT

8.

(4)	CORRECT	The flounder, baked potato, angel food cake, and tea is the most appropriate diet for this client.
(1)	*ELIMINATE*	Hydrogenated oils are high in cholesterol.
(2)	*ELIMINATE*	Chicken salad is often made with mayonnaise and yellow cake has egg yolks in it; both of these ingredients are high in cholesterol.
(3)	*ELIMINATE*	Sour cream and red meat are both high in cholesterol.

CATEGORY 07 BASIC CARE AND COMFORT

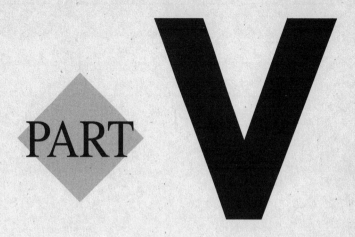

PART V

SAFE, EFFECTIVE CARE ENVIRONMENT

"Safe, Effective Care Environment" comprises 15–21 percent of the actual test content. This is 50 questions out of the maximum number of questions possible on the CAT. Keep the following tips in mind:

- When answering these questions, the client's safety is always your number one priority!
- The nurse is always the client's advocate!
- "Client needs" include:
  1. Coordinated care
  2. Environmental safety
  3. Safe and effective treatments and procedures

Factors that adversely affect the nurse's ability to provide a safe, effective care environment include substance abuse among professionals, practicing outside one's field of expertise, and working with faulty equipment.

Important principles to remember about ensuring a safe, effective care environment include:

- Stay current in your field. Read relevant literature and attend seminars. Ensure that your license is current and any other certifications necessary for practice are up-to-date.
- Adhere to your institution's policy and procedure standards when performing any intervention delegation issues.
- Seek help and ask questions if necessary.

25

CREATING A SAFE, EFFECTIVE CARE ENVIRONMENT FOR ADULTS

WHAT YOU NEED TO KNOW

One of the most important functions you will ever perform as a nurse is to provide a safe environment in which your clients can heal. Hospitals, clinics, emergency rooms, and people's homes are dangerous places with potential hazards everywhere! As a nurse, it is your responsibility to prevent your client from meeting any hazards, no matter what the setting. This professional responsibility includes careful discharge planning to ascertain a client's risks at home and in the community.

The nurse must be aware of potential problems, identify them, and take action to minimize risk for the client!

DOCUMENTATION

Documentation of each part of the nursing process is essential for communication, legal purposes, and continuity of care. It must be timely and objective, and include rationales for actions. Subjective documentation should be limited to direct quotes from the client.

Be concise, accurate, factual, and timely when charting.

Not charted = not done!

If you make a mistake in documentation, draw one line through it and then, according to your institution's policy, initial it and write "error" or "void."

MEDICATION ADMINISTRATION

1. The five rights of medication administration are:

   A. _____

   B. _____

   C. _____

   D. _____

   E. _____

These key words should guide you through the safe administration of any medication. The specific routes and techniques of medication administration are covered in Chapter 26, so we will not expound here. It is imperative that the nurse check and recheck the provider's order for the five rights of medication administration before administering any drug. In addition, a provider's order must be present **in writing** before the drug can be given. It is the nurse's responsibility to witness the client taking the drug. And remember, **not documented = not done!**

EQUIPMENT SAFETY

Technology is a huge part of every nurse's practice. Because the nurse is most often the professional actually using the equipment, it is his or her responsibility to assess its safety. Other equipment safety tips include the following:

- Assure bag and resuscitation equipment are present, if appropriate, and working properly.
- Locate the call light for the client upon admission and at the start of your shift. Confirm that it is within the client's reach at all times and that it works.
- Keep the client's side rails up if she is in bed.
- Assure a smoke-free environment.
- Know the facility's fire procedure, exits, and extinguisher locations.
- Lock all beds and wheelchairs when in a stationary position.
- Do not leave heating elements on or near a client's skin.

GENERAL SAFETY ASSESSMENT

Keep in mind that the elderly, the disabled, and the sensory impaired are at the greatest risk for accidents.

- Always check a client's identification band and compare it with the name on the chart and with any orders you are executing.

- Assess your clients at the beginning of every shift and document what you find. This is your baseline assessment, against which any changes will be compared.

- Assess if the side rails are up and the call light is in reach. **Document** that this is checked.

- When there is a complaint or deviation from the norm during an assessment, always document the way in which you intervene and how the client responds to your intervention.

- Take a client's complaint of generalized anxiety very seriously. Anxiety often precedes a serious condition, e.g., pulmonary embolism or angina. Vital signs should be taken immediately after the complaint. (Physical safety is your number one priority!)

- Observe the client's position and state in which you first receive him and document it!

- Observe client for any adverse effects to medications.

- Assess the physical environment: Is the path to the bathroom clear? Is the handrail in the hall blocked by furniture?

PLANNING FOR A CLIENT'S SAFETY

Once you have determined risk areas for your client, you must make every effort to involve the individual in formulating her plan of care. In this case, the plan is to prevent accidents.

- **Always** introduce yourself to your client. Use your first and last name and your position. Clients are much less likely to pursue legal retribution for wrongdoing if a personal relationship exists with the professionals.

- Planning for collaboration and good communication between the client, staff members, and disciplines is vital for the safety of your client. Confusion breeds accidents!

- In planning, recognize your own limitations. Assess the limits of your own education and experience and make timely referrals. Strive for comprehensive care.

- Frequently assess and revise your plan for safety. Keep it realistic!

INTERVENING TO ENSURE A CLIENT'S SAFETY

- Continuously monitor clients who are potential threats to themselves or to others.

- Inform clients of your actions and the reasoning behind them **before** intervening! This should be done in language the client can understand. The client should verbalize understanding before any procedure is initiated.

- Provide clear, concise instructions to the client, including discharge guidelines.

- Always use the **least** restrictive treatment first, one in which the client retains the most freedom.

Guidelines for using protective restraints:

1. A physician's order **must** be obtained before applying a restraint and must clearly state the type of restraint, the reason for its use, the length of time it can be used, and when and where it can be used. It also needs to be reordered every 24 hours.

2. Document the client's behavior, alternative measures must be tried first and carefully documented.

3. Assess the client's response to being restrained and document it.

4. Assess skin integrity, soft edges are placed against client.

5. Test for fit and comfort by inserting two fingers between restraint and the skin.

6. Monitor the client frequently and place call signal within reach.

7. For use of limb restraint (leg or arm), check for impaired circulation below restraint **every 15 minutes, remove every two hours and perform range of motion exercises.**

8. For use of jacket restraint, the solid part of the jacket goes in the back and the ties cross the front forming a V. Check frequently for impaired circulation and count respirations. **Must be removed every two hours and the client must be repositioned**.

9. Careful documentation is vital, the nurse is responsible for all actions performed or ignored.

- It is the duty of the nurse to be familiar with procedures and medications. Do not perform any action or treatment that may be contraindicated or harmful, regardless of a provider's order. Clarify any order with the physician which you suspect to be in error.

- Anticipate the effects of all treatments.

- The excuse that the provider ordered something and that the nurse "only carried out orders" is antiquated and not ethically or legally substantiated. The nurse is responsible for every action taken.

- Be knowledgeable of your client's history including allergies to prevent adverse reactions.

EVALUATION

It is the nurse's responsibility to assess and document the client's response to any and all interventions. **Be concise, accurate, factual, and timely when charting.** As a part of patient education, encourage a return demonstration of the instructed skill by the client to ensure accuracy in performance. In the event of adverse results, avoid contentious statements and blaming other members of the health care team. Professionalism should always be maintained.

Answer the following questions to enhance your understanding of planning for client safety:

A 62-year-old male client is newly diagnosed with noninsulin-dependent diabetes and is 10 days post coronary artery bypass surgery. The evening before he is to be discharged, he makes the following statement, "I can't wait to go home and eat my wife's apple pie. My grandson is waiting for me to play catch!"

2. What discharge teaching is essential for the client before he goes home?

   _____

3. How would you evaluate that the client understands his discharge instructions?

   _____

4. What statement by the client indicates a need for further discharge teaching?
   A. "If I feel light-headed I will take my glyburide (DiaBeta)."
   B. "I'll be sure to eat a balanced diet and gradually increase my activity."
   C. "If I begin to feel nauseated and weak, and notice I am urinating frequently, I will call my provider."
   D. "If I notice swelling and drainage from my incision, I will call my provider."

An 80-year-old male client has a history of rheumatoid arthritis. He had a lobectomy for lung cancer 7 days ago. On rounds this evening, the provider told him he would be discharged in the morning. His daughter, his primary caregiver at home, has not been to the hospital to see him for 5 days.

5. When should discharge planning have begun for the client?

   _____

6. With which professionals should the nurse consult in preparing for the client's discharge?

   _____

7. What items are essential for the client and his caregiver to understand before discharge?

   _____

8. On what basis is it indicated that a home health care agency referral is necessary for the client?

_____

A 70-year-old insulin-dependent female diabetic was discharged from the hospital after a left above-the-knee amputation. She is legally blind, hard of hearing, and in chronic renal failure. You are the visiting nurse assigned to her. On your initial home visit, you observe that she lives in a two-story home with poor lighting, narrow doors, and steep, narrow stairwells. Her refrigerator is stocked with soda and snack cakes. During your conversation with her, you discover that she has not checked her blood sugar in three days.

9. What are the potential physical hazards you assess in the client's home?

_____

10. List some reasons that the client may not have checked her blood sugar:

_____

11. Which statement by the client indicates that your teaching has been effective?
    A. "As long as I cut down on the sweets, I don't have to check my blood sugar."
    B. "When I notice that my finger stick supplies are running low, I will be sure to call the pharmacy to reorder."
    C. "If I take my insulin every day, my diabetes will eventually be cured."
    D. "I don't need any more lighting in my home. I'm blind anyway."

12. What types of community agencies might you tap to provide a safer home environment for the client?

_____

IDENTIFY THE UNSAFE FACTORS IN THIS HOME ENVIRONMENT

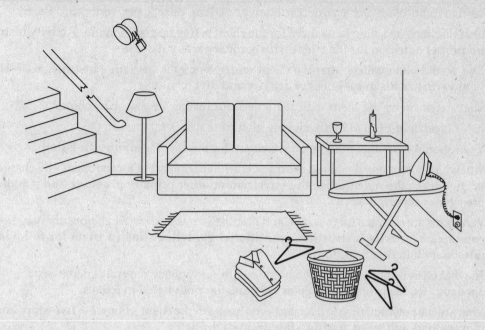

IDENTIFY THE POSITIVE SAFETY FACTORS IN THIS HOME ENVIRONMENT

1. The five rights of medicine administration are: **client, dose, drug, route,** and **time**.

2. What discharge teaching is essential for the client before he goes home?—**Activity instructions and proper nutrition for the client with coronary artery disease**

3. How would you evaluate that the client understands his discharge instructions?—**Have the client verbalize his guidelines for activity and diet to you**.

4. What statement by the client indicates a need for further discharge teaching?

   A. "If I feel light-headed I will take my glyburide (DiaBeta)."

5. When should discharge planning have begun for the client?—**upon admission**

6. With which professionals should the nurse consult in preparing for the client's discharge?—**The social worker, the nutritionist, the physician or other primary provider, and a home health care agency representative**

7. What items are essential for the client and his caregiver to understand before discharge?—**Proper wound care, activity instructions, nutritional guidelines, instructions for follow-up, and pulmonary toileting techniques**

8. On what basis is it indicated that a home health care agency referral is necessary for the client? **His daughter, his primary caregiver at home, has not visited in 5 days.**

9. What are the potential physical hazards you assess in the client's home?—**Two-story home with narrow doors and steep, narrow stairs; poor lighting**

10. List some reasons that the client may not have checked her blood sugar: —**She may not know how; she may not be able to find or read her machine; her machine may have been left out of her reach by the visiting nurse**

11. Which statement by the client indicates that your teaching has been effective?

    B. "When I notice that my finger stick supplies are running low, I will be sure to call the pharmacy to reorder."

12. What types of community agencies might you tap to provide a safer home environment for the client? **Home health care agency (if one has not already been tapped), home health aide, handyman services**

IDENTIFY THE UNSAFE FACTORS IN THIS HOME ENVIRONMENT

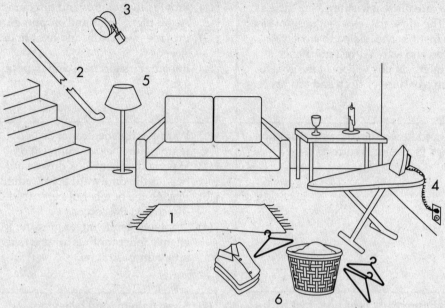

1. Throw rug 2. Broken hand rail 3. Nonfunctioning smoke detector
4. Iron left plugged in 5. Poor lighting 6. Clutter

IDENTIFY THE POSITIVE SAFETY FACTORS IN THIS HOME ENVIRONMENT

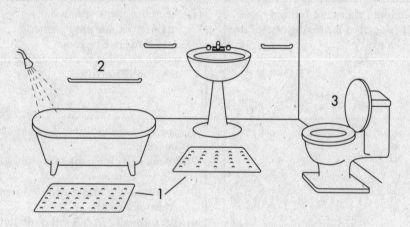

1. Nonskid bath mats 2. Hand rail 3. Raised toilet seat

1.	A home care nurse is visiting a geriatric client. The nurse makes a diagnosis of sleep pattern disturbance related to anxiety/confusion and activity/rest imbalance. Which interventions will meet the goal to maintain a balance of sleep and activity?	(1) Provide night lights and discourage naps. (2) Avoid night lights and encourage short naps. (3) Provide warm milk and tea 1 hour before sleep. (4) Encourage short naps and hypnotics.
2.	Which of these steps in the administration of eye drops to a client is correct?	(1) Warming the medication to body temperature before administering. (2) Having the client look downward as the head is tilted forward before administration. (3) Placing the number of perscribed drops directly on the cornea. (4) Applying gentle finger pressure to the client's inner canthus for one to two minutes after administration.
3.	A client has recently been admitted with a medical diagnosis of dementia, Alzheimer's type. When obtaining an assessment, the nurse should remember for safety purposes to ascertain what crucial information?	(1) Sleep patterns and behaviors (2) Skin turgor (3) The degree of memory impairment (4) The level of distractibility
4.	A 65-year-old blind client is admitted to a hospital. The priority for nursing care of this client would be to	(1) keep the client oriented. (2) maintain a safe environment. (3) assess for risk factors. (4) post a sign on the door stating that the client is visually impaired.
5.	When working with older clients, it is best for the nurse to	(1) speak very loudly, as they are usually hard of hearing. (2) speak in a cute baby talk style so they understand. (3) speak slowly and concisely to increase their comprehension. (4) perform all activities of daily living for them to optimize the care given.
6.	When planning care for the client with Parkinson's disease, teaching goals for the client and family should include an understanding of	(1) the contagiousness of the disease. (2) the safety risks due to symptomatology. (3) the need to schedule surgery as soon as possible. (4) the need to consider moving to a warm climate.

7. A nurse makes rounds at the start of a shift and finds a client in 4-point restraints with a left wrist abrasion. The nurse's priority action, after loosening the restraint, is to	(1) call the supervisor. (2) call the provider. (3) write an incident report. (4) report the nurse on the previous shift.
8. Discharge planning for clients with chronic obstructive pulmonary disease (C.O.P.D.) includes teaching them to maintain patency of their airway. This can be accomplished by teaching clients to	(1) take antibiotics. (2) increase their oxygen concentration. (3) use bronchodilators before coughing. (4) cough immediately after meals.
9. Which of these nursing diagnoses should the nurse give priority to for an elderly client who has impaired vision due to glaucoma?	(1) High risk for injury (2) Impaired physical mobility (3) Grooming self-care deficit (4) Feeding self-care deficit
10. A client intentionally overdoses on a salicylate preparation. Which complication should the nurse carefully monitor for and intervene promptly?	(1) Paralytic ileus (2) Hepatotoxicity (3) Pulmonary edema (4) Thrombus formation

CHAPTER 25: NCLEX-RN STYLE ANSWERS

1.
(1) CORRECT	Providing night lights will increase safety by reducing confusion. Naps should be discouraged so that the person will not be rested at bedtime.
(2) *ELIMINATE*	Night lights are to be encouraged, short naps discouraged.
(3) *ELIMINATE*	Warm milk will facilitate sleep, but tea contains caffeine and is more likely to keep the person awake.
(4) *ELIMINATE*	Short naps are to be avoided.

CATEGORY 07 BASIC CARE AND COMFORT

2.
(4) CORRECT	The major rationale for applying pressure to the inner canthus of the eye is to prevent systemic absorption of the eye drops. In addition, absorption in the eye is promoted, and drainage into the nose and throat is minimized.
(1) *ELIMINATE*	Eye drops do not need to be warmed.
(2) *ELIMINATE*	The client should tilt the head backwards and look upwards.
(3) *ELIMINATE*	The client's lower eyelids should be pulled downwards to form a conjunctival sac, where the drops should be placed.

CATEGORY 08 PHARMACOLOGICAL AND PARENTERAL THERAPIES

3. (1) CORRECT   All of the choices should be part of the assessment. However, knowing that the client seldom sleeps between 3 A.M. and 6 P.M. is critical for planning for the client's safety. It is important to know whether the client wanders at night.
    (2) *ELIMINATE*   This is not crucial to safety.
    (3) *ELIMINATE*   This is not crucial to safety.
    (4) *ELIMINATE*   This is not crucial to safety.

CATEGORY 02 SAFETY AND INFECTION CONTROL

---

4. (2) CORRECT   A safe environment is the priority goal for any client with a sensory impairment.
    (1) *ELIMINATE*   Although frequent orientation might also be a goal, the question does not indicate that the client is disoriented.
    (3) *ELIMINATE*   Choice #3 is an assessment, not a goal.
    (4) *ELIMINATE*   Posting a sign indicating impairment on the client's door violates his right to privacy.

CATEGORY 01 MANAGEMENT OF CARE

---

5. (3) CORRECT   Speaking slowly and concisely will help prevent misunderstanding and information overload.
    (1) *ELIMINATE*   Speaking loudly does not increase the comprehension by the client.
    (2) *ELIMINATE*   Baby talk would be demeaning.
    (4) *ELIMINATE*   The client should be encouraged to do as much as possible by himself.

CATEGORY 03 GROWTH AND DEVELOPMENT THROUGH THE LIFE SPAN

---

6. (2) CORRECT   It is important that clients/families are taught safety risks.
    (1) *ELIMINATE*   Parkinson's disease is not contagious.
    (3) *ELIMINATE*   Surgical intervention is not the mainstay of treatment, although the technology is improving.
    (4) *ELIMINATE*   Clients with Parkinson's disease are usually intolerant of excessive heat, as it can exacerbate symptoms.

CATEGORY 09 REDUCTION OF RISK POTENTIAL

---

7. (1) CORRECT   When an incident is discovered, a nurse should follow the chain of command, starting with the leadership person on that shift.
    (2) *ELIMINATE*   The supervisor would notify the provider.
    (3) *ELIMINATE*   An incident report would be written, but one would notify the supervisor first.
    (4) *ELIMINATE*   It would be the role of the supervisor to handle the situation with the nurse who was there when the restraints were applied.

CATEGORY 01 MANAGEMENT OF CARE

8.   (3) CORRECT   Bronchodilators are administered to open the airways and to potentiate coughing.

        (1) *ELIMINATE*   Antibiotics fight or prevent infection.

        (2) *ELIMINATE*   Increased oxygen levels will decrease the drive to breathe in a client with chronic obstructive pulmonary disease.

        (4) *ELIMINATE*   Coughing after meals can increase fatigue.

CATEGORY 09 REDUCTION OF RISK POTENTIAL

9.   (1) CORRECT   Clients who are visually impaired are at risk for injury or falls. Glaucoma alters depth perception and leads to more accidents.

        (2) POSSIBLE   Impaired physical mobility is of concern, but safety would be the priority.

        (3) ELIMINATE   Safety, not grooming, would be the priority.

        (4) ELIMINATE   Self-feeding is a concern, but risk for injury would be the priority.

CATEGORY 01 MANAGEMENT OF CARE

10.   (3) CORRECT   Severe metabolic acidosis is a complication of salicylate/aspirin overdose, which is a contributing factor to the development of pulmonary edema.

        (1) *ELIMINATE*   Paralytic ileus is not associated with a salicylate overdose.

        (2) *POSSIBLE*   Elevated hepatic enzymes can be evidenced with chronic salicylate ingestion.

        (4) *ELIMINATE*   More commonly, an increase in bleeding coagulation time, rather than a thrombus formation, results in salicylate ingestion.

CATEGORY 02 SAFETY AND INFECTION CONTROL

26

CREATING A SAFE, EFFECTIVE CARE ENVIRONMENT FOR CHILDREN

WHAT YOU NEED TO KNOW

Children present a different set of challenges when it comes to providing a safe environment to promote healing and prevent injury. Due to their ages and varying developmental stages, the nurse must possess knowledge of age-appropriate behaviors to intervene in this regard.

Accidents are the leading cause of death in children. In order to prevent accidents, the nurse needs to understand the developmental level at which children are operating and should plan accordingly. The leading accidental causes of injury or death in infancy and childhood include suffocation, drowning, falls, poisoning, choking, and burns. Avoid these common accidents, ensure a safe milieu in the hospital, and assist parents in providing a safe home environment.

The following are a few simple safety measures to maintain a safe environment and prevent injury:

- Infants and children in the hospital setting should always have an identification band and an allergy band, if applicable.
- Allergies should always be listed on the child's medication kardex.
- Keep crib rails up at all times when the child is unattended. Do not walk away from a bed or crib when a side rail is down!
- Wash your hands prior to and after caring for each client; teach parents to do the same.
- Examine toys and make sure that they are appropriate for the child's age.
- Keep medications and potentially hazardous materials out of the reach of children.
- The telephone number for Poison Control should be kept by the telephone. Parents should be instructed to call immediately in cases of accidental poisoning. Syrup of ipecac should be kept in the home to induce vomiting in cases where the ingested substance is not caustic (Poison Control will instruct).
- Ensure that children are always supervised when in the bathtub, high chair, and playpen.
- Evaluate appropriateness of foods for the child's developmental level; hot dogs, grapes, and peanuts are not appropriate for toddlers; they can easily become lodged in the toddler's throat.
- Never prop bottles!
- Do not warm formula, baby food, or warm compresses in the microwave (it heats unevenly).
- Place cribs away from electrical sockets and appliances; ensure that sockets are covered with outlet covers.
- Place cribs away from windows with shades that have cord pulls. Phone cords and shade pulls should be shortened out of reach. They can act like a noose around a toddler's neck.
- Clean up spills promptly to prevent slips.
- Make sure there is proper lighting in all client areas.
- Make a clear path to the bathroom and door.
- Teach car seat safety.
- Use safety gates on stairs.
- Teach the parent and child, if appropriate, where the call bell is and encourage them to use it!

As with adults, documentation of any safety measures you have implemented is vital.

Not charted = not done!

Parents should be encouraged to stay with their child whenever possible. The presence of a familiar face lessens the trauma of hospitalization or any procedure for a child. Between the parents and the nurse, the child will end up being supervised much of the time and the potential for accidents is minimized.

SAFE AND EFFECTIVE TREATMENTS AND PROCEDURES

Procedures and treatments during a child's hospitalization can be very traumatic experiences. All invasive or traumatic procedures should be performed in the treatment room, not in the child's room. In doing so, the child's room remains a safe place and the roommates are not disturbed or frightened by the proceedings. Parents should be offered the option of remaining with the child for the procedure, or leaving, whichever is more comfortable for them.

Every procedure must be explained to the child to the extent he or she is able to understand. Start teaching with the sensory details of what the child will **feel** during the procedure. Age-appropriate and nonthreatening phrases should be used, and questions should be encouraged. During the treatment, the child should be securely restrained if needed to provide safety and to maintain the desired position for the procedure.

RESTRAINTS

Label the following statements as **true** or **false**:

1. _____ Parents should restrain their child if they choose to remain with the child.

2. _____ Restraints should never be used as a form of punishment.

The use of restraints in the pediatric population is for safety only. There are various types of restraints, but all restraints need to be assessed frequently:

- Assess circulation to the restrained extremity often.
- Tie restraints to the actual bed or crib frame, not to the side rails.
- Release long-term restraints frequently to allow movement.
- Never substitute a restraint for observation; restraints are not baby-sitters!
- Remember to document the type of restraint used, the reason for the restraint, the peripheral vascular status of the restrained extremity, and the frequency at which the client was released from the restraints. Be concise, accurate, factual, and timely when charting. **Not charted = not done!**

MEDICATION ADMINISTRATION

Administering medications to the pediatric population is a dangerous task. Let's review before moving on:

3. The five rights of medication administration are:

    A. _____

    B. _____

    C. _____

    D. _____

    E. _____

Guidelines to follow when administering medications to children include:

- Allow choices if possible, but do not allow the child to choose whether or not to take the medicine.

- Be honest with the child; do not tell him that a sour medication tastes like candy.

- Praise the child for taking the medications.

- Take a history of drug allergies.

- Double-check the following medications with another nurse: digoxin, insulin, and heparin.

- Be aware of side effects and interactions with foods as well as other drugs.

- **Never** leave medications at the bedside!

- Document medications that are given.

- Medication teaching with parents and children, when appropriate, is very important and must be documented!

When administering medications to children, there are a few physiological principles you need to remember:

- Children's renal and liver functions are still immature, increasing the chance of drug toxicity due to decreased metabolism and excretion.

- A child's body is composed of more water and less fat than an adult's body, so fluid and electrolyte balance can fluctuate more easily.

- Dosages for pediatric medications are calculated by the child's body surface area (in square meters) or by weight (kilograms) to ensure that the dose is within a safe range.

There are many different routes for medication administration: oral, transdermal, subcutaneous, and intramuscular injections; intravenous through a peripheral catheter or through a more long-term central venous catheter; and eye, ear, and nose drops, to name a few. When possible, try to give medications through the least invasive method possible, but the route of administration must always match the provider's order!

In the following paragraphs, we have summarized the different routes and the points we think you need to know for the NCLEX-RN.

ORAL MEDICATION

Children receiving oral medications will most often put up a fight. Parents might be able to administer the medication more easily, but you must witness the parent actually administering the medication. Never leave medications at the bedside! To administer oral medications to children, follow these steps:

1. Check the five rights of medication administration (client, drug, dose, route, time).

2. Explain the procedure to the child and parents.

3. Wash your hands.

4. Choose the appropriate tool to administer the oral medication (a dropper or syringe).

5. If mixing medicine with juice, use a very small amount to ensure that the child will finish the medication.

6. If using a syringe or dropper, aim it toward the back and side of the child's mouth and administer slowly to allow for swallowing.

7. Wash your hands again.

8. Document that the medication was given.

INTRAMUSCULAR INJECTIONS

The nurse should expect some protest from children when the time comes for an injection. A child should be temporarily restrained by another nurse in order to administer the intramuscular medication safely and effectively. Remember, parents should never be asked to restrain their child! The proper intramuscular injection technique is as follows:

1. Check the five rights of medication administration.

2. Explain the procedure to the child and parents.

3. Wash your hands.

4. Restrain the child if needed.

5. Choose the proper site for injection:

Injection Sites and Their Indications	
Site	**Indication**
Vastus lateralis	Preferred for infants and toddlers
Ventrogluteal region	Second-most preferred for infants and toddlers; the primary site for children over the age of 12
Dorsogluteal region	Not recommended for children under 4 years old
Deltoid muscle	Use only for small volumes of medications that are not viscous

INTRAMUSCULAR INJECTION SITES

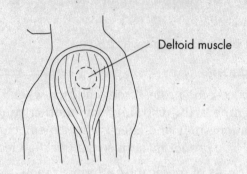

Deltoid muscle

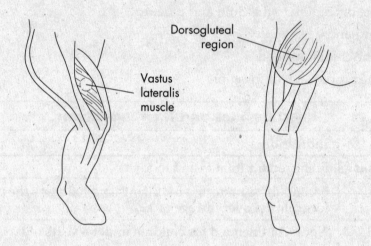

Dorsogluteal region

Vastus lateralis muscle

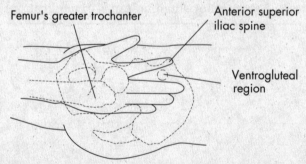

Femur's greater trochanter

Anterior superior iliac spine

Ventrogluteal region

There are certain parameters necessary for the needle you choose to administer an intramuscular injection:

Needle Choice for Intramuscular Injections			
Age	Needle Width	Needle Length	Maximum Volume
Infant	23–25 gauge	0.5–1 inch	0.5–1cc
Toddler	22 gauge	1–1.5 inch	1 cc
School–age	22 gauge	1–1.5 inch	1.5–2 cc
Adolescent	22 gauge	1–1.5 inch	1.5–2 cc

6. Put on gloves.

7. Clean the chosen site with alcohol, rubbing in a circle from inside to outside.

Locating Injection Sites	
Site	**To Find It . . .**
Vastus lateralis	Put one hand on the knee and one hand on the greater trochanter of the hip. Divide the space between your hands into thirds. Insert the needle into the middle third at a 45° or 90° angle toward the knee.
Ventrogluteal region	Place your index finger on the anterior, superior iliac spine and your second finger at the iliac crest. Inject the medication below the iliac crest at a 90° angle inside the triangle formed by these landmarks.

8. Stabilize the site (do **not** pinch skin; pull it taut) and insert the needle quickly using a dart-like motion and aseptic technique.

9. Aspirate, observing for blood return. If there is blood return, remove the needle and discard in the sharps container. **Do not administer the medication if there is blood return!**

10. If there is no blood return, inject the medication slowly and then withdraw the needle.

11. Rub the area with cotton and apply bandage.

12. Discard the needle in the sharps container. **Never break a needle!**

13. Praise the child.

14. Wash your hands again.

15. Document that you gave the medication and where you gave it.

INTRAVENOUS MEDICATION

Intravenous medication administration can pose particular challenges for the nurse, as children do not like to sit still to maintain an IV site. Continual assessment of the infusion and the catheter site are imperative to be sure that the child receives all of the medication.

1. Check the five rights of medication administration.

2. Explain the procedure to the child and parents.

3. Wash your hands.

4. Assess the area around the intravenous catheter for signs and symptoms of infiltration (redness, heat along the vein, swelling).

5. Determine the appropriate dilution and infusion rate for medication administration.

6. Administer the medication per provider's order.

7. Wash your hands again.

8. Throughout the infusion, continue to assess the IV site for redness, swelling, and/or pain.

9. When the infusion is complete, document that you gave the drug and how you gave it.

RECTAL MEDICATION

If children are vomiting but still need medications, some can be given per rectum (P.R.) if the provider orders this route.

1. Check the five rights of medication administration.
2. Explain the procedure to the child and parents.
3. Wash your hands and put on gloves.
4. Insert a lubricated suppository into the rectum using a gloved finger just until it passes the anal sphincter.
5. Withdraw the finger and press the child's buttocks together until the urge to expel the suppository subsides.
6. Praise the child.
7. Remove the gloves and wash your hands again.
8. Document that you gave the medication.

OPTIC MEDICATION

Holding a child's head still to instill optic medications requires a lot of patience.

1. Check the five rights of medication administration.
2. Explain the procedure to the child and parents.
3. Wash your hands.
4. Tell the child to look up; drop the medication into the medial aspect of the conjunctiva of the lower lid.
5. Tell the child to blink; apply gentle pressure to the inner aspect of the eye.
6. Praise the child.
7. Wash your hands again.
8. Document that you gave the medication.

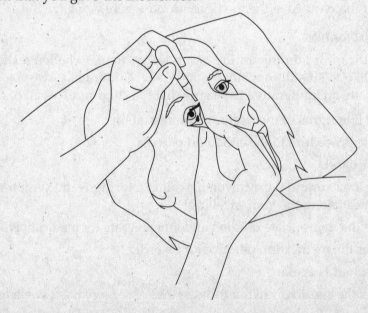

Instilling medication into the eye

Otic Medication

1. Check the five rights of medication administration.
2. Explain the procedure to the child and parents.
3. Wash your hands.
4. For children under 3 years old, pull the pinna of ear downward and straight back; for an older child, pull the outer ear up and back.
5. Administer the ordered number of drops of medication into the ear, and stabilize the child's head for 1 minute to prevent the drops from falling out.
6. If the other ear needs medication as well, wait 1 minute and repeat the procedure in the other ear.
7. Praise the child.
8. Wash your hands.
9. Document that you gave the medication.

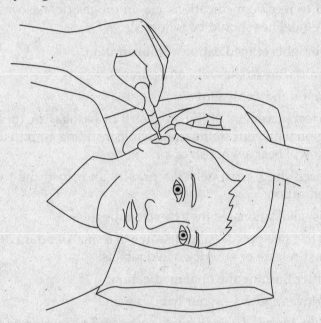

Instilling medication into the ear of
a child over 3 years of age

NASAL MEDICATION

1. Check the five rights of medication administration.

2. Explain the procedure to the child and parents.

3. Wash your hands.

4. Have the child tilt his head backward.

5. Instill the correct number of drops into each nostril.

6. Keep the child's head tilted back for at least 1 minute to prevent the medication from dropping out.

7. Praise the child.

8. Wash your hands again.

9. Document that you gave the medication.

MEDICATIONS BY TUBE

If a child is ordered to receive medications via an orogastric, nasogastric, or gastrostomy tube, the following guidelines should be followed:

1. Check the five rights of medication administration.

2. Explain the procedure to the child and parents.

3. Wash your hands and apply gloves.

4. Check for correct placement of the orogastric or nasogastric tube by auscultating the epigastric region with your stethoscope while instilling air into the tube. If placement is correct, you will hear a whoosh of air.

5. Administer each drug separately via gravity and flush the tube with clear water after each medication.

6. Avoid viscous medications, as they can clog the tube.

7. Crush tablets to a fine powder and dissolve in a small amount of warm water. Never crush sustained-release or enteric-coated tablets!

8. Clamp tube after flushing the final medication.

9. Remove the gloves and wash your hands again.

10. Document that the medication was given and that placement of the tube was checked.

COORDINATED CARE

Comprehensive and coordinated care is a very important aspect of a child's hospitalization. Although nurses are the primary caregivers, there are limits as to what we can do. It is important to make referrals in a timely fashion. In the following examples identify the correct professional to whom you would make a referral:

4. ____ A 7-year-old female client is admitted for ear surgery. During the admission assessment she is noted to have little round burn scars all over her back and on the backs of her hands. When asked how she got them, she states, "Daddy was mad one night because my toys were on the floor."

5. ____ A 5-year-old male client is admitted for minor surgery. It is his first time in the hospital and he is afraid of the blood pressure cuff and the other equipment.

6. ____ A 10-year-old boy, is status post a brain tumor resection. He has resulting left-sided weakness and is now unable to ambulate independently.

7. ____ The same client also has difficulty with his fine motor skills. Now he is unable to hold a fork in his hand.

8. ____ The client loses his gag reflex and is unable to swallow food. His speech becomes slurred.

9. ____ A gastrostomy tube is placed in the client because he still cannot swallow. He is now being fed enterally but is experiencing continuous diarrhea from this particular formula.

A. nutritionist

B. occupational therapist

C. physical therapist

D. play therapist

E. speech therapist

F. state authorities

CHAPTER 26: EXERCISE ANSWERS

1. **False**—Parents should not restrain their child if they choose to remain with the child.

2. **True**—Restraints should never be used as a form of punishment.

3. The five rights of medicine administration are: **client**, **dose**, **drug**, **route**, and **time**

4. **F** **state authorities**—A 7-year-old female client is admitted for ear surgery. During the admission assessment she is noted to have little round burn scars all over her back and on the backs of her hands. When asked how she got them, she states, "Daddy was mad one night because my toys were on the floor."

5. **D** **play therapist**—A 5-year-old male client is admitted for minor surgery. It is his first time in the hospital and he is afraid of the blood pressure cuff and the other equipment.

6. **C** **physical therapist**—A 10-year-old boy is status post a brain tumor resection. He has resulting left-sided weakness and is now unable to ambulate independently.

7. **B** **occupational therapist**—The same client also has difficulty with his fine motor skills. Now he is unable to hold a fork in his hand.

8. **E** **speech therapist**—The client gets progressively worse. He loses his gag reflex and is unable to swallow food. His speech becomes slurred.

9. **A** **nutritionist**—A gastrostomy tube is placed in the client because he still cannot swallow. He is now being fed enterally but is experiencing continuous diarrhea from this particular formula.

CHAPTER 26: NCLEX-RN STYLE QUESTIONS

1. When caring for a child in an oxygen mist tent, the nurse should

   (1) leave one side partially untucked to prevent suffocation.
   (2) discourage parents from placing toys in the tent.
   (3) keep the plastic away from the child's face.
   (4) keep the child's temperature cooler than usual.

2. A nurse on a pediatric unit is administering an antibiotic to a 3-year-old child who does not have an identification bracelet. What is the appropriate action by the nurse?

   (1) Have another staff member identify the child.
   (2) Withhold the medication until the nurse can get an ID bracelet.
   (3) Ask the child's mother, who is at the bedside, to state the child's name.
   (4) Ask the child to state her name.

3. A 4-year-old child has been diagnosed with iron-deficiency anemia. A liquid preparation is prescribed. When administering this liquid, the nurse should

   (1) ask the child if he wants to take the medicine.
   (2) mix the liquid in a bottle of milk and give it to the child at nap time.
   (3) allow the child to sip the medicine through a straw.
   (4) give the medicine after lunch with a sweet dessert.

4. Which of the following muscles is the best site for administering an injection of vitamin K to a normal newborn?	(1) Deltoid (2) Dorsogluteal (3) Gluteus maximus (4) Vastus lateralis
5. The nurse is aware that the proper method of administration of nystatin suspension (Mycostatin) to an infant is to	(1) put it in a bottle. (2) use a medicine dropper to instill the medication before feeding. (3) rub the nystatin in the cheek with a gloved finger after feeding. (4) have the infant suck the medication through a nipple or pacifier.
6. An 8-month-old infant will be admitted to a pediatric unit to rule out respiratory syncytial virus (RSV). In report, the nurse is told that the infant is wheezing, coughing, and has decreased breath sounds in the lower lobes. Which of the following actions is part of preparation by the nurse for the admission?	(1) Tape an extra tracheostomy tube above the bed. (2) Tell the caregiver that visiting will be restricted for the first 48 hours. (3) Set up an isolation room. (4) Ask what antibiotics to administer.
7. A baby with respiratory syncytial virus (RSV) is admitted to the hospital and the provider orders ribavirin (Virazole). Which of the following family members would the nurse restrict from visiting the infant while the child is on this medication?	(1) A sibling who is only 12 years old (2) A grandmother who has asthma (3) A pregnant aunt (4) A father who has a cold

CHAPTER 26: NCLEX-RN STYLE ANSWERS

1. (3) CORRECT   Keeping the plastic away from the child's face will prevent suffocation.
   (1) ELIMINATE   This will not prevent suffocation, which can still occur if plastic gets too close to the child's face.
   (2) ELIMINATE   Toys are allowable for children in a mist tent.
   (4) ELIMINATE   This will cause the child to lose body heat.

CATEGORY 10 PHYSIOLOGICAL ADAPTATION

2.   (3) CORRECT   Having the child's mother state the child's full name will enable the nurse to give the medication on time.

      (1) *ELIMINATE*   Another staff member may make a mistake in the identification.

      (2) *ELIMINATE*   The nurse would not want to withhold the antibiotic, as it should be given on time.

      (4) *ELIMINATE*   A 3-year-old may not give you her correct name.

CATEGORY 02 SAFETY AND INFECTION CONTROL

---

3.   (4) CORRECT   This would be the most pleasurable and would ensure that the child got the medication.

      (1) *ELIMINATE*   The child should not be permitted to refuse the medication.

      (2) *ELIMINATE*   The nurse would not mix the medication with milk because if the child didn't drink the bottle, the medication would not be taken.

      (3) *ELIMINATE*   Much of the medication might get stuck in the straw.

CATEGORY 03 GROWTH AND DEVELOPMENT THROUGH THE LIFE SPAN

---

4.   (4) CORRECT   Large, well-developed muscle with no important nerve or blood vessels exists in this location.

      (1) *ELIMINATE*   There is a small margin of safety there because of the small muscle mass and possibility of damage to the radial or axillary nerve.

      (2) *ELIMINATE*   This muscle is contraindicated in children who have not yet been walking for one year and thus would have small muscle mass.

      (3) *ELIMINATE*   This muscle would be contraindicated because of the possibility of injury to the sciatic nerve.

CATEGORY 09 REDUCTION OF RISK POTENTIAL

---

5.   (3) CORRECT   Mycostatin, an oral antifungal medication, should be applied after feeding and should not be mixed in or with anything.

      (1) *ELIMINATE*   Mycostatin should not be mixed with formula.

      (2) *ELIMINATE*   Mycostatin should be given after a feeding.

      (4) *ELIMINATE*   Mycostatin should not be put in a nipple or pacifier.

CATEGORY 08 PHARMACOLOGICAL AND PARENTERAL THERAPIES

6.

(3) CORRECT	RSV is highly contagious, and isolation should be maintained.
(1) *ELIMINATE*	A tracheostomy tube would not be taped to the bed.
(2) *ELIMINATE*	Isolation would be maintained, but parents should be with the child.
(4) *ELIMINATE*	This is not an appropriate nursing action.

CATEGORY 02 SAFETY AND INFECTION CONTROL

7.

(3) CORRECT	Whenever a client is receiving Virazole, there are precautions, such as wearing a gown, mask, and gloves when entering the room. Hand washing when leaving the room is essential. Anyone who is pregnant or has severe respiratory problems should not visit while the client is receiving ribavirin.
(1) *ELIMINATE*	The sibling can visit.
(2) *ELIMINATE*	The grandmother with asthma could visit.
(4) *ELIMINATE*	The father with a cold, as long as he does not have severe respiratory problems, may visit.

CATEGORY 02 SAFETY AND INFECTION CONTROL

27

PERIOPERATIVE NURSING

WHAT YOU NEED TO KNOW

The surgical nurse assists the client in dealing with the stressors of surgery, including pain management, minimizing complications, and the return to optimal functioning. Clients undergoing anesthesia are at the mercy of health care professionals. The nurse's job is to minimize stress through education, the establishment of trust, and advocacy.

Perioperative nursing is divided into three equally important phases: preoperative (before surgery), intraoperative (during surgery), and postoperative (after surgery).

THE PREOPERATIVE STAGE

The preoperative stage begins when surgery is chosen as the appropriate treatment for a client and ends when the client is brought to the operating room. Preparing your client for surgery requires an individualized plan and depends on the type of surgery planned. To remind yourself of the different rationales for surgery, match the type of surgery to its proper rationale on the right:

1. ____	Cosmetic	A.	to determine the cause of symptoms
2. ____	Diagnostic	B.	to remove diseased organ or parts
3. ____	Curative	C.	to strengthen weaknesses or correct a deformity
4. ____	Restorative	D.	to relieve symptoms without curing disease
5. ____	Palliative	E.	to improve appearance

Surgery can be defined as minor or major. Minor surgery frequently is performed under local anesthesia in a provider's office or ambulatory care setting. Major surgery is a procedure of greater risk, usually performed under general anesthesia in an inpatient setting. There is risk associated with all surgical procedures. Although a specific operation is termed "minor," to the client any surgery probably seems pretty **major**.

Regardless of whether surgery is deemed major or minor, surgery is a stressor to the body and induces both physiological and psychological stress reactions. Clients respond differently to the stress of surgery. However, there are common fears and concerns that can be anticipated. An important role of the nurse caring for the preoperative client is to identify and alleviate such fears. For example, common fears during the preoperative stage include fear of the unknown, fear of death, fear of pain, and fear of disfigurement.

CLIENT TEACHING

Client teaching is one of the most important aspects of nursing care for the preoperative client. Careful and thorough preoperative teaching of clients and their families can be the most important part of the perioperative experience. An informed, educated client participates in his or her healing process and can help decrease the incidence of postoperative complications.

Before initiating teaching, the nurse must assess the client's baseline knowledge of the upcoming events and the client's psychological readiness for surgery. Preoperative teaching typically begins in the surgeon's office and continues throughout the hospital stay. Effective teaching should include not only the client, but the family members if possible. Assessment of the client's teaching needs should be individualized, as there are many factors that can interfere with learning.

6. List five barriers to learning:

A. _____

B. _____

C. _____

D. _____

E. _____

A common nursing diagnosis for the preoperative client is knowledge deficit related to lack of education or lack of experience. Goals or expected outcomes for client teaching may include the following:

- The client verbalizes understanding of the procedure and has signed informed consent.

- The client can explain the activities expected in the early postoperative period.

- The client verbalizes that if the nurse does not offer pain medication, he or she must ask for it.

- The client verbalizes that pain medication is most effective when taken around the clock.

- The client demonstrates proper practice of postoperative exercises (use of incentive spirometer, coughing and deep breathing, and use of splinting pillow).

Surgery of any type requires informed consent from the client or legal guardian. The provider is responsible for having the consent signed before the surgery is performed and before the client has received any sedation. Informed consent implies that the client is aware of, or is informed by the provider of, the reason for and the nature of the surgery, all available alternatives, and the risks and benefits of each available treatment option. The role of the nurse in obtaining informed consent is to ensure that the client understands the above, to clarify the facts presented by the provider, and to dispel any myths the client or his/her family may have about the surgical experience. The nurse may be asked to serve as a witness to the signature of the client, spouse, or legal guardian.

Clients' fears can be decreased tremendously by providing information about the events that will occur. Information can be provided in many forms of client teaching: verbal, printed handouts, videotapes. The amount and type of detailed information provided to the client and family depends on their education, background, interest, and stress level. The nurse should judge the client's and family's responses to information as it is provided, and proceed as indicated. Return demonstration or verbalization is an important part of client teaching to evaluate the client's understanding of the information provided.

Information with which the client and family should be equipped includes:

- What will the client experience during preoperative testing and preparation?

- How will the client be transferred to the operating room?

- What will the client experience in the recovery room?

- Teaching about and rationale for expected postoperative therapies.

- Documentation of client teaching, including the type of information provided and client response is the nurse's responsibility.

- **Remember—not charted = not done!**

THE INTRAOPERATIVE STAGE

The intraoperative stage begins with the client's arrival in the operating room and ends with the client's transfer to the recovery room. Admission to the operating room can be an especially stressful time for a client as he or she is now separated from family members and the nurses with whom trust has been established. Being greeted by a friendly and supportive face can help decrease apprehension.

Teaching continues during the initial intraoperative phase. Explaining all preparation, answering last-minute questions, and explaining any delays to the client and family are imperative functions of the operating room nurse. The primary goal is to maintain client safety. This includes ensuring proper functioning of equipment and electrical devices, and maintaining aseptic technique.

The operating room nurse must verify the client's identity, verify that the informed consent is signed and in the chart, and observe the client for adverse effects of preoperative medications. It is the responsibility of the operating room nurse to be sure that both the surgeon and the anesthesiologist are aware of any client allergies and abnormalities in client test results.

POSITIONING

Determining the position of the client during surgery is a responsibility shared by the surgeon, the nurse, and the anesthesiologist. The nurse coordinates the position of the client for surgery and modifies the position based on the specific needs of the client. Many factors influence this position during surgery: the specific procedure being performed; the client's height, weight, and age; anesthesia administration and technique; and any limitations specific to the client, such as arthritis, emphysema, and deformities.

Positioning during surgery exposes the client to a number of possible preventable complications. Special attention must be given to prevent joint or nerve damage and muscle stretch or strain. Prolonged immobility during surgery may also lead to development of bruising or pressure sores. A careful assessment of the skin on admission to the operating room is critical, especially in the elderly or chronically ill client.

Match the operative position with the appropriate description:

7. _____ Supine

   A. flat on back with arms at side, and down, legs straight with feet slightly separated

8. _____ Prone

   B. on back with buttocks at edge of table, legs in stirrups

9. _____ Trendelenburg's position

   C. on side; table may be bent in middle

10. _____ Reverse Trendelenburg

   D. on abdomen, face turned to one side, arms at sides with palms up, feet elevated on pillow

11. _____ Lithotomy

   E. head elevated and feet lowered

12. _____ Lateral

   F. head and body lowered, shoulders placed in shoulder braces, knees flexed

For the following surgical procedures, fill in the most appropriate position:

13. Cholecystectomy   _____

14. Hemorrhoidectomy   _____

15. Renal surgery   _____

16. Vaginal surgery   _____

17. Brain surgery   _____

18. Lower abdominal surgery   _____

19. List three possible complications that can arise from improper positioning:

A. _____

B. _____

C. _____

SURGICAL PROCEDURES

Surgical procedures are most frequently given names that describe the type of procedure being performed and the site of the surgery. Match the surgical suffixes to the descriptions:

20. ____ -ectomy   A. plastic repair

21. ____ -rrhapy   B. suturing or stitching

22. ____ -ostomy   C. removal of an organ or gland

23. ____ -otomy   D. providing an opening or stoma

24. ____ -plasty   E. looking into

25. ____ -scopy   F. cutting into

Match the surgical prefixes with the site of the surgery on the right:

26. ____ Hyster-   A. lung

27. ____ Crani-   B. stomach

28. ____ Ocul-   C. breast

29. ____ Mamm-   D. eye

30. ____ Nephr-   E. uterus

31. ____ Gastr-   F. skull

32. ____ Salping-   G. gallbladder

33. ____ Chole-   H. liver

34. ____ Hepat-   I. fallopian tube

35. ____ Pneum-   J. kidney

THE POSTOPERATIVE STAGE

The postoperative stage begins as soon as the operation is finished. The client requires continuous monitoring for recovery from anesthesia and for complications resulting from surgery. Most postoperative nursing care is specific to the surgery performed. However, there are basic considerations that are the same for all clients. These include assessment of cerebral functioning, pulmonary ventilation, cardiac rhythm monitoring, circulation, acid-base balance, fluid and electrolyte balance, wound and skin integrity, and maintaining comfort and safety.

DISCHARGE FROM THE RECOVERY ROOM

Once the client has met the criteria for discharge from the recovery room, he or she will be transferred to the appropriate unit based on his or her specific needs.

36. From the following list choose the five criteria that suggest that the client is ready for discharge from the recovery room:

   A. Client is awake or easily aroused.
   B. Client moans when name is called, but does not open eyes.
   C. Client does not respond or cannot be aroused.
   D. Client is able to move four extremities.
   E. Client is able to move two extremities.
   F. Client is not moving extremities.
   G. Client's vital signs are stable.
   H. Client's temperature is 95.8°F (35.4°C) but climbing.
   I. Client's blood pressure is approximately 50 perent of pre-anesthesia blood pressure.
   J. Client's respiration is easy and unlabored; he is able to cough and breathe deeply.
   K. Client needs stimulation during periods of apnea.
   L. Client experiences intermittent labored breathing or dyspnea.
   M. Client's skin is pink, warm, and dry, with palpable peripheral pulses.
   N. Client's skin is pale, clammy, dusky, or blotchy.
   O. Client's peripheral pulses are not palpable.

When the client is transferred to the clinical unit, the accepting nurse should have prepared the client's room for transfer. Being prepared is the key component for facilitating a smooth and easy transfer. Preparations include:

- Assuring a clean, open bed with adequate lighting and a clear path for transferring the client from stretcher to bed

- Assuring that the necessary equipment is on hand, such as IV poles, a blood pressure cuff, a thermometer, a cardiac monitor or telemetry when indicated, oxygen setup, an irrigation setup, extra blankets, and IV pumps if indicated

As soon as the client is safely positioned in the bed, the nurse makes an initial assessment of the client's status. Frequency of continued assessments is based on the client's condition, the provider's orders, and the policy of the unit.

AIRWAY, BREATHING, AND CIRCULATION

Airway, breathing, and circulation (ABCs) are your priorities! Assess the client for signs of respiratory distress and hypoxemia and identify normal and abnormal (adventitious) breath sounds. Presence of adventitious breath sounds indicates the need for vigorous pulmonary toileting such as deep breathing, coughing, incentive spirometry, chest physiotherapy, and suctioning when indicated. In the following exercise, match the abnormal respiratory assessment findings to their possible causes:

37. ____	Loud snoring, grunting, or stridor	A.	leakage of air into subcutaneous tissue
38. ____	Crepitus	B.	drugs: anesthesia, sedatives, or narcotics
39. ____	Shallow respirations and/or apnea	C.	bronchospasm
40. ____	Crackles (fine rales)	D.	tracheal edema; narrowing of airway
41. ____	Absent breath sounds	E.	pulmonary edema
42. ____	Wheezes	F.	inflammation of pleura
43. ____	Pleural friction rub	G.	pneumothorax

After assuring airway patency, assess the client's vital signs, cardiac rhythm, and temperature. Assess for the presence and quality of peripheral pulses, as well as the client's skin color, temperature, texture, and turgor. In the following exercise, match the abnormal circulatory assessment findings to their possible causes:

44. ____	Increased pulse rate	A.	deep vein thrombosis
45. ____	Decreased blood pressure	B.	hypothermia
46. ____	Pulse deficit (difference between apical and peripheral pulses)	C.	fluid volume deficit
47. ____	Pain and warmth in lower extremity	D.	stress reaction of body to invasive surgery
48. ____	Increased temperature	E.	cardiac arrhythmia
49. ____	Decreased pulse rate	F.	pain and anxiety

NEUROLOGICAL ASSESSMENT

After the ABCs are assessed and protected, the neurological assessment is imperative. The nurse should be aware of the client's preoperative neurological status in order to know if there is any deviation from the client's baseline status postoperatively. In the following exercise, determine whether the statement is **true** or **false** regarding postoperative neurological status:

50. _____ Decreases in level of consciousness are normal after surgery and are nothing to be concerned about.

51. _____ Clients should not be expected to move extremities after surgery as effects of anesthesia can last for days.

52. _____ An appropriate nursing measure for a confused postoperative client would be to apply restraints, turn off all lights, and minimize interaction to promote rest.

FLUID VOLUME DEFICIT OR EXCESS

Fluid volume deficit and fluid volume excess are common postoperative complications. Fluid loss during and after the procedure, blood and fluid administration during and after the procedure, and a client's dietary restrictions before and after the procedure are all factors that can affect the client's fluid and electrolyte balance. Fluid and electrolyte imbalance compromises body systems and ultimately affects neurological status and the ABCs. It is important to take into account any pre-existing conditions the client may have or has a history of (e.g., CHF, renal insufficiency). These clients are at risk for fluid volume excess and need to be closely monitored for signs of increasing edema, adventitious breath sounds (rales), changes in lab values (BUN, Cr), decreased urine output. The rate of IV fluid therapy should be adjusted accordingly for each client.

Complete, continuous, and accurate measurement of intake and output in the postoperative client is a critical responsibility of the surgical nurse. To assess fluid status, the client should be weighed at the same time daily. Intake includes IV fluids, oral intake, enemas, and tube feeding. Output includes urine output, wound drainage, surgical drains, nasogastric tubes, ostomies, and bowel movements. Comparing intake with output is the best assessment of fluid status. Due to insensible fluid loss through the skin and lungs, output should equal only about two-thirds of intake over 24 hours.

SURGICAL WOUNDS

Surgical wound sites should be assessed upon receiving the client. Dressings should be inspected completely. Notation of the size and location of the surgical wound site as well as the color, consistency, amount, and odor of any drainage is important and should be documented. Drainage on the dressing should be outlined with a pen so that the rate of drainage may be easily determined. In addition, the nurse must inspect the bed underneath the client for drainage that escaped the dressing.

If a large amount of drainage from a surgical site is anticipated, the surgeon may place a drain into or close to the wound for accurate collection and measurement. The nurse is responsible for assessment of proper functioning and maintenance of such drains. In most cases, the surgeon will change the dressing the first time. Original dressings may be reinforced by the nurse as needed. Dressing changes should be done following a provider's orders or based on the policy and procedure of the specific unit. The client's wound should be inspected for any erythema and warmth (infection) or increases in swelling (may be indicative of a hematoma). Any changes in the approximation of the wound need to be monitored and reported to the physician (possible evisceration or dehiscence).

Healing of the surgical wound is a step-by-step process. Wounds heal by regeneration of tissue and scar formation. A client's individual physical condition, age, and size and the location of the wound all affect the rate of healing.

To maintain the conditions for optimal wound healing, the nurse institutes measures to maintain perfusion to the wound, prevent trauma, prevent infection, promote optimal nutritional status, and conserve the client's energy. List at least three nursing interventions for each of the following goals:

53. Promote circulation to wound

A. _____

B. _____

C. _____

54. Prevent trauma to wound

A. _____

B. _____

C. _____

55. Prevent infection of wound

A. _____

B. _____

C. _____

56. Promote optimal nutritional status

A. _____

B. _____

C. _____

57. Conserve energy

A. _____

B. _____

C. _____

PAIN MANAGEMENT

After the ABCs, pain management is the most vital function of the nurse. **Pain is whatever the client says it is!** Almost all postoperative clients experience pain as a result of the surgical wound, positioning during surgery, the presence of tubes or drains, and immobility. Assessment includes observing the client for signs of discomfort including facial grimacing, splinting, and/or restlessness. When possible, the nurse can ask the client to rate her pain on a scale of 1 to 10 before and after administering analgesics. Anxiety, muscle tension, and nausea may also contribute to discomfort in the postoperative client.

Pain medication is administered only according to the provider's orders. The effects of pain medication must be documented! These medications may need to be changed, with doses increased or decreased according to the client's response. As an adjunct to therapy, nonpharmacological comfort measures are encouraged to assist the client to rest and relax.

Good pain management is the most vital intervention to prevent postoperative complications. The absence of pain promotes early ambulation, pulmonary toileting, and a sense of well-being. This is a **major nursing priority** in real life and on the NCLEX-RN!

58. List five nursing interventions to promote comfort in the postoperative client:

A. _____

B. _____

C. _____

D. _____

E. _____

SAFETY

Maintaining a client's safety is, as you know, a nursing responsibility, surgery or not. Postoperative clients are at risk for falls due to weakness, fatigue, and effects of medications that may alter their sensory perception. Side rails are maintained in the raised position until it is determined that the client is fully awake, alert, oriented to person, place, and time and responds appropriately to commands. Instruct the client and his family members on the indicated activity restrictions, how to call for assistance, how to get out of bed, or how to change position. Instruct the client in the proper use of the call bell and keep it within reach! Position essential items such as tissues, urinal, the telephone, and the bedside table within reach of the client. Ensure proper functioning of all electrical equipment.

DISCHARGE PLANNING AFTER SURGERY

Preparing the client for discharge from the hospital and returning to independent living are the goals shared by all members of the health care team, as well as the client and her family. Discharge planning should begin on the **day of admission** and should include the client and her family! It begins with the admission assessment, which should include information regarding the client's living situation, support system, financial situation, and education. All of these factors influence the ability of the client to care for herself postoperatively.

The discharge teaching plan for postoperative clients and their caretakers is individualized depending on the client and the surgery performed (use your common sense on the NCLEX-RN). In general, it should include:

Activity	• A progressive increase in activity with adequate rest periods is appropriate.
Medications	• The client should be able to verbalize the purpose, dose, schedule, and pertinent side effects of each medication with which he is being discharged. • The client should be instructed to contact the provider if any adverse effects or questions develop. • Antibiotics must be taken for the entire prescribed course regardless of the presence or absence of symptoms.
Wound care	• The client should be instructed on specific dressing changes or bathing restrictions according to the provider and type of surgery; a return demonstration of the dressing change is appropriate. • The client and his family must be well versed in the importance of proper hand washing and the signs of wound infection.
Nutrition	• Specific diet restrictions must be addressed and adapted to the client's lifestyle and/or cultural preferences. • A nutrition consult is imperative if a client has special needs or questions that the nurse cannot answer. • Good nutrition is vital for wound healing!
Home care	• Refer the client to a social worker or visiting nurse, a home health aide, and/or the procurement of special equipment for the home. • Rehabilitation may be indicated before discharge to the home; a social worker is invaluable in arranging this, as well.
Follow-up	• The client must be aware of the importance of follow-up with the caretaker.

59. Signs of wound infection include:

    A. _____

    B. _____

    C. _____

    D. _____

60. A diet high in _____, _____, and _____ will promote wound healing.

61. Instructing clients and family members in the proper use of the _____ is a nursing measure to promote safety in the postoperative stage.

62. Referrals that the nurse can make for comprehensive discharge planning include:

    A. _____

    B. _____

    C. _____

63. Medication teaching requires that the client know each drug's:

A. _____

B. _____

C. _____

D. _____

E. _____

CHAPTER 27: EXERCISE ANSWERS

1. **E** **Cosmetic**—to improve appearance
2. **A** **Diagnostic**—to determine the cause of symptoms
3. **B** **Curative**—to remove diseased organ or parts
4. **C** **Restorative**—to strengthen weaknesses or correct a deformity
5. **D** **Palliative**—to relieve symptoms without curing disease
6. Barriers to learning include:

    anxiety

    education

    hearing impairment

    language

    pain

    past surgical experiences

    vision impairment
7. **A** Supine—**flat on back with arms at side and down, legs straight with feet slightly separated**
8. **D** Prone—**on abdomen, face turned to one side, arms at sides, with palms up, feet elevated on pillow**
9. **F** Trendelenburg's position—**head and body lowered, shoulders placed in shoulder braces, knees flexed**
10. **E** Reverse Trendelenburg—**head elevated and feet lowered**
11. **B** Lithotomy—**on back with buttocks at edge of table, legs in stirrups**
12. **C** Lateral—**on side; table may be bent in middle**
13. Cholecystectomy—**supine**
14. Hemorrhoidectomy—**prone**
15. Renal surgery—**lateral**
16. Vaginal surgery—**lithotomy**
17. Brain surgery—**reverse Trendelenburg**
18. Lower abdominal surgery—**Trendelenburg's position**
19. Possible complications that can arise from improper positioning include:

    cardiovascular compromise

    joint damage

    muscle strain

    peripheral nerve damage

respiratory compromise

skin necrosis

thromboses

20. **C** -ectomy—removal of an organ or gland

21. **B** -rrhapy—suturing or stitching

22. **D** -ostomy—providing an opening or stoma

23. **F** -otomy—cutting into

24. **A** -plasty—plastic repair

25. **E** -scopy—looking into

26. **E** Hyster- —uterus

27. **F** Crani- —skull

28. **D** Ocul- —eye

29. **C** Mamm- —breast

30. **J** Nephr- —kidney

31. **B** Gastr- —stomach

32. **I** Salping- —fallopian tube

33. **G** Chole- —gallbladder

34. **H** Hepat- —liver

35. **A** Pneum- —lung

36. From the following list choose the five criteria that suggest that the client is ready for discharge from the recovery room:

   A. Client is awake or easily aroused.

   D. Client is able to move four extremities.

   G. Client's vital signs are stable.

   J. Client's respiration is easy and unlabored; he is able to cough and breathe deeply.

   M. Client's skin is pink, warm, and dry with palpable peripheral pulses.

37. **D** Loud snoring, grunting, or stridor—**tracheal edema; narrowing of airway**

38. **A** Crepitus—**leakage of air into subcutaneous tissue**

39. **B** Shallow respirations and/or apnea—**drugs: anesthesia, sedatives, or narcotics**

40. **E** Crackles (fine rales)—**pulmonary edema**

41. **G** Absent breath sounds—**pneumothorax**

42. **C** Wheezes—**bronchospasm**

43. **F** Pleural friction rub—**inflammation of pleura**

44. **F** Increased pulse rate—**pain and anxiety**

45. **C** Decreased blood pressure—**fluid volume deficit**

46. **E** Pulse deficit (difference between apical and peripheral pulses)—**cardiac arrhythmia**

47. **A** Pain and warmth in lower extremity—**deep vein thrombosis**

48. **D** Increased temperature—**stress reaction of body to invasive surgery**

49. **B** Decreased pulse rate—**hypothermia**

50. **False**—Decreases in level of consciousness are normal after surgery and are nothing to be concerned about. **Changes in level of consciousness may indicate shock or neurological compromise!**

51. **False**—Clients should not be expected to move extremities after surgery as effects of anesthesia can last for days. **This data should be compared to the client's baseline. Changes could indicate nerve damage or a cerebrovascular accident.**

52. **False**—An appropriate nursing measure for a confused postoperative client would be to apply restraints, turn off all lights, and minimize interaction to promote rest. **Appropriate nursing interventions include frequent reorientation and monitoring; restraints are a last resort only!**

53. Nursing interventions to promote circulation to wound include:

    A. Maintain hydration.

    B. Use bandages or antiembolic stockings to prevent stasis.

    C. Monitor hemoglobin and hematocrit.

    D. Encourage early ambulation, if appropriate.

54. Nursing interventions to prevent trauma to wound include:

    A. Minimize use of tape on the skin.

    B. Use a pull sheet to reposition the client (to prevent friction).

    C. Institute fall-prevention measures.

55. Nursing interventions to prevent infection of wound include:

    A. Change dressings as soon as soiled or wet.

    B. Use aseptic technique when changing dressings.

    C. Keep client clean and well-groomed.

56. Nursing interventions to promote optimal nutritional status include:

    A. Advance diet as ordered.

    B. Obtain a nutritionist consultation as soon as indicated.

    C. Assess toleration of diet.

    D. Ensure intake to meet increased metabolic needs of wound healing.

    E. Determine and adhere to food likes and dislikes.

    F. Honor cultural needs related to food.

57. Nursing interventions to conserve energy include:

    A. Instruct the client to take frequent rest periods throughout the day.

    B. Administer medications as ordered to prevent pain or sleeplessness.

    C. Assist with activities of daily living if necessary.

    D. Maintain a quiet, comfortable environment.

58. Nursing interventions to promote comfort in the postoperative client include:

    A. Administer pain medications as ordered.

    B. Control or remove noxious stimuli.

    C. Position the client for comfort and in good body alignment for wound healing.

    D. Encourage participation in diversional activities (teach relaxation techniques).

    E. Facilitate adequate rest to increase pain tolerance.

59. Signs of wound infection include:

    redness
    swelling
    drainage
    fever

60. A diet high in **protein**, **calories**, and **vitamin C** will promote wound healing.

61. Instructing clients and family members in the proper use of the **call bell** is a nursing measure to promote safety in the postoperative stage.

62. Referrals that the nurse can make for comprehensive discharge planning include:

    social worker
    nutritionist
    home health care agency
    support groups
    community resources
    physical therapist

63. Medication teaching requires that the client knows each drug's:

    name
    purpose
    dose
    schedule
    side effects

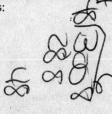

CHAPTER 27: NCLEX-RN STYLE QUESTIONS

1.	A client is 48 hours postoperative knee replacement surgery. There are surgical drains in place that reveal 300 cc of serosanguinous drainage. The nurse's intervention is to	(1) remove the drain. (2) call the provider. (3) empty the drain. (4) take no intervention.
2.	A nurse in the postanesthesia care unit is caring for a male client postcystoscopy who is complaining of urinary retention. To promote urination, the nurse should first	(1) administer pain medications to relax the sphincter. (2) pour warm water over the perineum. (3) teach bladder retraining to restore tone. (4) have the client stand up.
3.	A 5-year-old client has undergone a tonsillectomy. Following discharge from the hospital postoperatively, which instructions should be emphasized by the nurse to the parents?	(1) Notify the surgeon if bleeding occurs within the first 10 days. (2) The child should remain on bed rest for 48 hours. (3) The child should stay home from school for 2 weeks. (4) The child's contacts should be limited to family members.

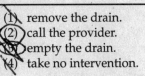

4. The nurse would know to check for which of the following laboratory test results for a child who is to undergo a tonsillectomy?

(1) Erythrocyte sedimentation rate (ESR)
(2) Urinalysis
(3) Serum potassium level
(4) Bleeding and clotting time

5. A client who is 2 hours post-appendectomy is complaining of intense incision pain. When assessing the client, the nurse notes the blood pressure is 170/90 mmHg, and the pulse is 140 beats per minute and regular. What action should the nurse take?

(1) Prepare for synchronized cardioversion.
(2) Administer p.r.n. nifedipine (Procardia) and assess the client's response.
(3) Reassure client that postoperative pain is normal.
(4) Administer p.r.n. meperidine HCl (Demerol) and assess the client's response.

6. A child has just had a tonsillectomy. Postoperative intervention would include

(1) having the child cough and deep breathe.
(2) having the child drink warm liquids.
(3) placing the child in a prone position.
(4) withholding analgesic administration to prevent bleeding.

7. When caring immediately postoperatively for a client who had an ileal conduit, the nurse would expect

(1) normal bowel sounds in all four quadrants.
(2) urine output of 30–60 cc/hour.
(3) a pale gray edematous stoma.
(4) constant bleeding in the urine for 24–48 hours.

8. A client undergoes an endoscopy for diagnostic purposes. The priority for administering nursing care following the procedure would include

(1) administering analgesics for pain.
(2) withholding food until a gag reflex is present.
(3) positioning the client on the right side.
(4) observing the client for rectal bleeding.

9. The nurse is assigned to do preoperative teaching for a blind client who is scheduled for surgery in the morning. The nurse's best teaching strategy would be

(1) to do the teaching verbally in short sessions.
(2) to provide a booklet in braille.
(3) to have another blind person do the teaching.
(4) to make an audiotape for the client.

28

LEGAL, ETHICAL, AND PROFESSIONAL ISSUES

WHAT YOU NEED TO KNOW

Legal, ethical, and professional issues are a vital component of maintaining a safe, effective care environment. The NCLEX-RN touches on the basic principles nurses should know and practice to provide optimal care for clients in any setting. In this chapter, we equip you with the knowledge to make educated decisions in the face of legal, ethical, and professional situations.

Some important concepts to remember for the NCLEX-RN include:

- Nurses must examine and recognize their own strengths, weaknesses, and values in order to provide comprehensive and competent care.
- Nurses must know and adhere to the policies and procedures of their institutions.
- The nurse must **document** everything. **Document, document, document!**
- Just following orders is not an excuse, legally or ethically.
- **All orders must be in writing before execution**.
- First and foremost, the nurse is a client advocate.
- The nurse must be accountable for all actions and be prepared to defend them.
- Nurses must ensure competence, confidence, collaboration, and confidentiality.
- A nurse's legal, ethical, and professional responsibilities are ongoing.
- Confidentiality.
- All patients have inherent rights.

SUBSTANCE ABUSE

Substance abuse among nurses violates a client's (and others') right to a safe environment and competent nursing care! The number of drug-addicted professionals is underestimated due to underreporting by abusers' colleagues.

If you know someone who is abusing drugs or alcohol:

- Understand that the person is compromising client care.
- Realize that the person is placing undue stress on the people who know about the abuse.
- Know that this person needs help; substance abuse is not isolated to one particular place or occasion.

To report the nurse who is a substance abuser:

- Be sure that a substance abuse problem exists and can be proven.
- Document incidents, specific times, dates, and/or inconsistencies.
- File a report according to policy and procedures of the institution and along the chain of command, i.e., head nurse, nursing supervisor, and director of nursing.
- Sign the document report and, if appropriate, request confidentiality.

Urging the substance-abusing colleague to quit is not enough and, in some cases, not appropriate. Disciplinary action is taken by the state board of nursing.

LEGAL TERMS

There are some terms you should recognize for the NCLEX-RN. Do this matching exercise to familiarize yourself with the legal and ethical terminology:

1. ____ An individual's right to make her own decisions regarding care and treatment; self-determination

2. ____ A wrongful, but unintended act against a person or his property

3. ____ To do good for clients

4. ____ The belief that another person knows what is best (and can make decisions) for another individual; conflicts with an individual's right to self-determination

5. ____ Client's permission to undergo a test or procedure after having had a full explanation of the procedure, its alternatives, its possible side effects, and risks involved with having or not having it done

6. ____ Laws that protect an individual from legal repercussions when providing emergency care to an individual who, without the care, would be in danger of imminent peril; encourages those in health care to respond to emergencies without fear of being sued

7. ____ Activities within the realm of a licensed nurse's education and experience that she may legally perform under the Nurse Practice Act of her state

8. ____ Rules and principles regarding what is right and wrong

9. ____ A willful act that violates another person's rights or property

10. ____ Legal responsibility

11. ____ Defines what a licensed nurse can do in a particular state

12. ____ The deviation from a standard of care that can be reasonably expected from a professional with the same education and experience in a similar situation; the negligent act results in injury or loss

13. ____ A breach in the duty of reasonable care that results in an injury

14. ____ A wrongful act committed against another person or his property; may be either intentional or unintentional; includes negligence and malpractice

A. autonomy

B. beneficence

C. ethics

D. Good Samaritan laws

E. informed consent

F. intentional tort

G. liability

H. malpractice

I. negligence

J. Nurse Practice Act

K. paternalism

L. Scope of Practice

M. tort

N. unintentional tort

INFORMED CONSENT

The nurse is not required to **obtain** the informed consent for a procedure, but he or she must ensure that it is present and that the client has signed an informed consent form or similar document before a procedure or treatment is done. It is the responsibility of the nurse to know and refer to state laws regarding informed consent. The process for obtaining informed consent requires that the client (or the legally appointed decision maker) understands the procedure or treatment thoroughly. A translator may be necessary.

A hospital cannot require a client or surrogate to sign an informed consent on days when the client's or surrogate's religious beliefs prohibit writing. Informed consent may be obtained from the spouse or a parent (if the client is under 18 years of age).

Clients should be informed of the following before signing the document:

- Nature and purpose of the procedure
- Any reasonable alternatives
- Risks, consequences, and benefits of the procedure and the alternative(s)
- Risk if the treatment is refused

HIV/AIDS

We touched on this in Chapter 13, but because it is such a vital component of nursing care in today's world, a short review in this section is imperative.

- An HIV-positive client may be discriminated against, fired, or dropped from his insurance carrier due to HIV status. Confidentiality must be maintained. **A breach of confidentiality is illegal and the health care provider can be sued for defamation of character!**
- It is illegal to disclose a client's HIV status **except** in response to a special release form or when required by law.
- Written informed consent must be signed before an HIV test can be performed.
- Pre- and posttest counseling must be provided to the client requesting the test.

PSYCHIATRIC CLIENTS

Psychiatric clients often present ethical challenges for the nurse. There are a few principles to remember when answering questions on the NCLEX-RN. These can guide your decision making when given a scenario on the exam.

- An informal, voluntary admission is initiated by the client, and the voluntarily admitted client initiates his discharge.
- Upon voluntary admission, the client retains all rights.
- Involuntary admission to a psychiatric unit limits a client's freedom and must be done in accordance with state laws.
- In order for an involuntary admission to occur, the client must be shown to be a potential and imminent harm to himself or others.
- After involuntary admission to a psychiatric unit, the client must have a psychiatric evaluation within 72 hours of admission by a certified examiner.

- Discharge of an involuntarily admitted client is initiated by the hospital or court, not by the client.

- The least restrictive interventions must be attempted initially.

- Being mentally ill does not mean that a client is incompetent.

- Providing a safe environment includes protecting the client from himself.

- In certain situations, confidentiality may be breached or restraints may be indicated.

- **Document, document, document,** taking care to note rationales for increasingly restrictive interventions.

CHAPTER 28: EXERCISE ANSWERS

1. **A** **autonomy**—An individual's right to make her own decisions regarding care and treatment; self-determination

2. **N** **unintentional tort**—A wrongful, but unintended, act against a person or his property

3. **B** **beneficence**—To do good for clients

4. **K** **paternalism**—The belief that another person knows what is best (and can make decisions) for another individual; conflicts with an individual's right to self-determination

5. **E** **informed consent**—Client's permission to undergo a test or procedure after having had a full explanation of the procedure, its alternatives, its possible side effects, and risks involved with having or not having it done

6. **D** **Good Samaritan laws**—Laws that protect an individual from legal repercussions when providing emergency care to an individual who, without the care, would be in danger of imminent peril; encourages those in health care to respond to emergencies without fear of being sued

7. **L** **Scope of Practice**—Activities within the realm of a licensed nurse's education and experience that she may legally perform under the Nurse Practice Act of her state

8. **C** **ethics**—Rules and principles regarding what is right and wrong

9. **F** **intentional tort**—A willful act that violates another person's rights or property

10. **G** **liability**—Legal responsibility

11. **J** **Nurse Practice Act**—Defines what a licensed nurse can do in a particular state

12. **H** **malpractice**—The deviation from a standard of care that can be reasonably expected from a professional with the same education and experience in a similar situation; the negligent act results in injury or loss

13. **I** **negligence**—Lack of reasonable care

14. **M** **tort**—A wrongful act committed against another person or his property; may be either intentional or unintentional; includes negligence and malpractice

1. You are a nurse on a crowded elevator with visitors and hospital staff. Two staff members begin to discuss a client. What would be the most appropriate action by the nurse?

   (1) Wait till you get off the elevator and tell the staff members that they should not openly discuss clients.
   (2) Report the situation to their supervisor.
   (3) Confront the staff immediately and divert their conversation.
   (4) Ignore the conversation, as this is probably the only time they would breach confidentiality.

2. The nurse recognizes that the client understands an informed consent form when

   (1) the client signs the form.
   (2) the client states that the physician explained the form to them.
   (3) the client states that the family read the form and said it was alright.
   (4) the client can give a verbal explanation of the informed consent.

3. A client refuses to take a 10 A.M. dose of phenytoin (Dilantin). The best action by the nurse would be to

   (1) document the refusal in the chart.
   (2) call the supervisor.
   (3) inform the client of the risks.
   (4) notify the provider.

4. A per diem nurse gave medications to the wrong client. The nurse asserted that the client responded to the name called. What is the nurse's appropriate documentation?

   (1) Note the client's orientation.
   (2) Complete a progress and incident report.
   (3) Record medications given on the drug form.
   (4) The client was not hurt. Forget it.

5. The psychiatric/mental health nurse should know which of the following is a violation of a client's rights?

   (1) A paranoid client is told that no one is trying to harm them.
   (2) The staff confiscates the letters that a psychotic client is writing to a local newspaper.
   (3) Upon admission, a client's gold watch is taken by staff and placed into the hospital safe.
   (4) Clients are rewarded for emptying ashtrays in the dayroom by getting to watch a requested video.

6. A client discharged the day before is readmitted with a possible wound infection. The client states that she was never taught the signs and symptoms for infection that she should be alert for. The main reason the nurse assigned to the client will obtain the past chart is to

(1) check what the wound appeared like at discharge.
(2) see if the client stated the signs and symptoms of a wound infection before discharge.
(3) see if the client had an infection during the last hospital stay.
(4) have the chart available for the provider to review.

7. Two nurses are not in violation of a client's right to confidentiality if they are discussing client information

(1) with a social worker in anticipation of discharge.
(2) in the cafeteria during their lunch hour.
(3) in the hallway outside the client's room.
(4) about a comatose person.

8. The nurse explains to a client that the Patient's Bill of Rights, created in 1973 by the American Hospital Association, was developed to

(1) provide standards of care for all clients.
(2) create policy and procedure guidelines.
(3) protect the client from civil liberties violations.
(4) ensure safe and competent medical care.

9. Upon arriving on the unit one morning, the nurse discovers a sign taped to the door of a client's room stating "PATIENT IS BLIND. PROVIDE ASSISTANCE." The nurse is aware that this violates the client's right to

(1) safe care.
(2) privacy.
(3) privileged communication.
(4) habeas corpus.

10. When documenting a client's response to pain medication, which of the following statements would the nurse document as part of her assessment?

(1) Client appears comfortable and is resting without complaints at this time.
(2) Client appears to tolerate pain poorly, even after medication was given.
(3) Pain medication given with relief of pain 30 minutes after injection.
(4) Client reports pain to be a 3 on a 1 to 10 scale, with 10 being most severe pain.

1. (3) CORRECT   The staff members should not continue the conversation. Visitors would be aware that confidentiality is respected within the institution. It is the nurse's ethical responsibility.

    (1) ELIMINATE   The damage would have been done in that visitors would have overheard confidential information.

    (2) POSSIBLE   You may wish to do this, but the visitors would have still overheard confidential information.

    (4) ELIMINATE   This would not be an appropriate action, as it is not ethical to discuss confidential information in public and the nurse has a responsibility to confront the staff.

    CATEGORY 01 MANAGEMENT OF CARE

2. (4) CORRECT   Having the client explain what they have been taught allows one to assess their knowledge.

    (1) ELIMINATE   Signing the form does not confirm that the client understands the contents.

    (2) ELIMINATE   Just having the client say someone explained the form does not indicate the client understands.

    (3) ELIMINATE   The fact that the family read the form does not indicate that the client who signs the form understands.

    CATEGORY 01 MANAGEMENT OF CARE

3. (4) CORRECT   As a refusal to take Dilantin may constitute a medical risk and be potentially dangerous, the provider should be notified.

    (1) ELIMINATE   The nurse would document the refusal on the chart, but this is not the best action.

    (2) ELIMINATE   In this case scenario, this would not be an appropriate action.

    (3) ELIMINATE   Informing the client of the risks may not motivate him to take his medication.

    CATEGORY 02 SAFETY AND INFECTION CONTROL

4. (2) CORRECT   It is most important for the nurse to complete a progress and incident report.

    (1) ELIMINATE   It is important to document the client's orientation, but this is not the best response.

    (3) ELIMINATE   The medications should be recorded, but this is not the most appropriate documentation.

    (4) ELIMINATE   The nurse should definitely record the error.

    CATEGORY 01 MANAGEMENT OF CARE

5.

(2) CORRECT	Clients have the right to communicate fully and privately with those outside of the facility.
(1) ELIMINATE	The staff is utilizing therapeutic communication to reinforce reality.
(3) ELIMINATE	This is a routine procedure to protect a client's valuables from loss or theft.
(4) ELIMINATE	This may be considered part of creating a therapeutic milieu.

CATEGORY 06 PSYCHOSOCIAL ADAPTATION

6.

(2) CORRECT	A client readmitted within 24 hours of discharge means that the case will be reviewed and possibly challenged by the insurance company. If there is no documentation stating that the client was taught and learned the signs and symptoms of a wound infection, the hospital may experience a financial loss.
(1) POSSIBLE	This is correct but not the priority.
(3) POSSIBLE	This is correct but not the priority.
(4) POSSIBLE	This is correct but not the priority.

CATEGORY 01 MANAGEMENT OF CARE

7.

(1) CORRECT	Client information may be discussed privately between health care workers when it is within the professional realm and without judgment or bias.
(2) ELIMINATE	This situation would breach client confidentiality.
(3) ELIMINATE	This situation would breach client confidentiality.
(4) ELIMINATE	This is not the best answer because you do not know where the conversation is taking place or who is present, although it may be a professional discussion.

CATEGORY 01 MANAGEMENT OF CARE

8.

(3) CORRECT	The Patient's Bill of Rights, which should be posted in all hospitals, was developed to protect the client from having their civil rights violated while in the hospital.
(1) ELIMINATE	This was not incorporated into the Bill of Rights but is covered in accreditation criteria.
(2) ELIMINATE	This is covered in accreditation criteria.
(4) ELIMINATE	Safe and competent medical care is covered under the Medical Examiners Board and Accreditation criteria.

CATEGORY 01 MANAGEMENT OF CARE

9. (2) CORRECT   A sign on the outside of a client's room is a violation of the right to privacy and
                     confidentiality.
    (1) *ELIMINATE*   The Bill of Rights does not relate to safe care.
    (3) *ELIMINATE*   This applies only in court proceedings.
    (4) *ELIMINATE*   Habeas corpus relates to the client's right to a speedy release.

CATEGORY 01 MANAGEMENT OF CARE

10. (4) CORRECT   The data are reported and measured based on assessment with measurable
                     outcomes.
    (1) *ELIMINATE*   This is an incomplete assessment not based on data provided by the client.
    (2) *ELIMINATE*   This statement is not based on client's report but rather on an assumption by the
                     nurse.
    (3) *ELIMINATE*   The parameters are not included when documenting relief.

CATEGORY 01 MANAGEMENT OF CARE

PART VI

PSYCHOSOCIAL INTEGRITY

"Psychosocial Integrity," comprises 8–16 percent of the actual test content. This is a maximum of 30 questions out of the total number of questions possible (265) on the CAT.

This part is divided into three chapters: basic concepts of psychiatric nursing and assessment; psychiatric disorders (analysis, planning, implementation, and evaluation); and psychopharmacology. We assume that you already possess basic knowledge in this specialty and, therefore, we focus on what you need to know to pass the test.

When answering "Psychosocial Integrity" questions, remember:

- Always promote the client's **self-care** and **adaptation** skills.
- **Never** ask a client **why** she is feeling a certain way!
- The NCLEX-RN always opts for the open-ended questions that validate feelings.
- In an emergency situation, your first priority is always your client's **airway**!
- In a **psychiatric** emergency, the first priority is always your client's **safety**!

29

Basic Concepts of Psychiatric Nursing and Assessment

WHAT YOU NEED TO KNOW

After ensuring a client's physical stability, all nurses attend to the bio-psychosocial needs of their clients. Ensuring psychosocial well-being includes managing the environment and acting as a health counselor and teacher, a group leader, and a family case worker. To meet client needs for psychosocial integrity, the nurse is guided by theory and the nursing process. Nurses, especially psychiatric nurses, must possess knowledge of the conceptual frameworks of psychiatric care, personality development, and psychopathology.

Psychiatric mental health nursing is concerned with actual or potential mental health problems and acute or chronic psychiatric disorders. Behavioral management techniques and crisis intervention are essential parts of psychiatric nursing. The focus is on anxiety and loss related to illness and stressful events. The goal of psychiatric nursing care is maintaining psychosocial integrity and safety through **self-care** and **adaptation.**

Psychiatric disorders may vary in their presentation owing to a client's cultural background, developmental stage, or gender. Spiritual and environmental factors must also be taken into consideration when assessing and treating clients with psychosocial needs.

1. Nursing to ensure a client's psychosocial integrity is grounded in theories of:

    A. _____

    B. _____

    C. _____

2. The goals of maintaining a client's psychosocial integrity and safety are

    A. _____

    B. _____

3. The focus of psychiatric nursing is on anxiety and loss related to:

    A. _____

    B. _____

4. Six factors that may influence the presentation of a client's psychosocial need or psychiatric disorder are:

    A. _____

    B. _____

    C. _____

    D. _____

    E. _____

    F. _____

CONCEPTUAL FRAMEWORKS FOR PSYCHIATRIC NURSING

A psychiatric nursing framework is an eclectic one that views the client as a bio-psychosocial entity. Remember, the NCLEX-RN loves Erikson's stages of development. Because you need to recognize other conceptual frameworks to help guide your nursing interventions, we will discuss key parts of the models deemed important for the NCLEX-RN while emphasizing Erikson's stages of development.

FREUD

Freud studied sexual and aggressive impulses and stated that these energies motivate behavior. Freud divided personality into three components: the id, ego, and superego.

Match each of Freud's personality components with its respective drive:

5. _____ superego   A. the realistic adult

6. _____ id   B. the conscience

7. _____ ego   C. the pleasure center

Freud also devised a theory of psychosexual development. There are five psychological stages from infancy to adulthood: the oral stage, the anal stage, the phallic (Oedipal) stage, the latency stage, and the genital stage.

Match each of Freud's stages of sexual development with its respective age:

8. _____ latency   A. adolescence and young adulthood

9. _____ oral   B. infancy

10. _____ genital   C. toddlerhood

11. _____ anal   D. preschool age

12. _____ phallic (Oedipal)   E. school age

ERIKSON'S THEORY OF PERSONALITY DEVELOPMENT

Erikson's theory of personality development builds on Freud's theory but is psychosocially focused. Erikson emphasized how external social forces, rather than internal sexual forces, influence personality development and span the life cycle from birth to death.

Match each of Erikson's eight stages of development with its appropriate age:

13. _____ trust vs. mistrust   A. adolescence (12–18 years)

14. _____ autonomy vs. shame and doubt   B. older adult (65 years to death)

15. _____ initiative vs. guilt   C. school age (6–12 years)

16. _____ industry vs. inferiority   D. early adulthood (18–35 years)

17. _____ identity vs. role confusion   E. middle adulthood (35–65 years)

18. _____ intimacy vs. isolation   F. preschool (3–6 years)

19. _____ generativity vs. stagnation and/or self absorption   G. toddlerhood (18 months to 3 years)

20. _____ integrity vs. despair   H. infancy (0–18 months)

Erikson theorized that the goal of each stage of development is to emerge with the positive trait, having mastered the developmental task. Clients who grow up in healthy, supportive environments with nurturing by significant others are more likely to successfully master these developmental tasks and move on to the next task (or developmental stage). Clients who lack age-appropriate interpersonal skills and behavior patterns have arrested development. They are stagnant in a developmental stage that does not correspond with their chronological age. Subsequent development is difficult for immature clients who lack requisite life skills. Nursing interventions should be tailored to enhance the client's developmental stage.

THE INTERPERSONAL FRAMEWORK

In the **interpersonal framework**, current social relationships are the concern as opposed to past, unresolved relationships. The relationship between the nurse and client is meant to serve as a model of a healthy, interpersonal relationship for the client. The nurse therapist functions as a participant-observer and attempts to provide a corrective interpersonal experience for the client. The nurse generalist modifies these principles to meet the psychosocial needs of the client.

THE BEHAVIORAL MODEL

The **behavioral model** states that behavior is learned and, hence, can be unlearned. Conditioning techniques, such as reinforcement and punishment, are employed to change behavior. Nurses are often involved in modifying client behavior, with the goal of increasing desirable behaviors and decreasing undesirable behaviors.

Following are examples of nursing interventions based on behavioral theory:

- Off-unit privileges can work as reinforcers in the following way: the client obtains privileges in response to positive behavior or loses privileges in response to negative behavior.

- Seclusion can be more or less effective depending on whether the client perceives it as a positive reinforcer or as an aversive punisher.

- Setting limits and behavioral expectations can be part of a contract the nurse and client agree on **together**. The client should assist in identifying what behavior will be targeted and what reinforcers will be manipulated.

Other examples of interventions based on behavioral theory include systematic desensitization, which slowly brings phobic clients in contact with the anxiety-producing object or situation; assertiveness training; problem solving; and relaxation exercises.

THE COGNITIVE FRAMEWORK

The **cognitive framework** is often related to the behavioral framework, as both models concentrate on learning and changing behavior. Cognitive work, however, focuses on a client's thoughts. Depressed clients with negative thoughts can be taught different ways to alter these negative thinking patterns. Thought stopping is a method of distracting and diverting a client's attention from disturbing ideas. Cognitive distortions are then replaced with accurate rational statements. Self-monitoring of behaviors and thoughts increases the client's responsibility for self-care.

THE BIOMEDICAL MODEL

The **biomedical model** is the disease model of emotional problems and deviant behavior. Bear in mind that deviant behavior is relative and culturally based. This biomedical framework assigns a physiological cause, symptoms, and treatment to mental disorders, labeling them as diagnosable illnesses. Somatic therapies are prescribed for the client by the provider.

However, the provider may not have a holistic perspective of the client, so the nurse must stay abreast of the intervening psychosocial variables.

Comparison of Nursing and Medical Models of Care

Discipline:	NURSING	MEDICINE
Etiology:	Vulnerability	Cause
Assessment:	Risk	Disease
Diagnosis:	Human Responses	Health Problems
Intervention:	Care	Cure

Reprinted with permission from *Principles and Practice of Psychiatric Nursing*, Fifth Edition. Copyright 1995, Mosby–Year Book, Inc.

Remember, the model utilized by nursing to ensure a client's psychosocial integrity is eclectic. It encompasses many theories, but the universal goals are **self-care** and **adaptation**.

21. Which of Freud's structures of the mind is harsh, moral, and rigid?

   A. Superego
   B. Id
   C. Ego

22. Toddlerhood is in what stage of Freud's psychosexual development?

   A. The anal stage
   B. The oral stage
   C. The phallic stage

23. At what age is a person struggling for identity, according to Erikson?

   A. Toddlerhood
   B. School age
   C. Adolescence

DEFENSE MECHANISMS

Defense mechanisms protect against anxiety caused by undesirable, unacceptable, and usually unconscious feelings. Defense mechanisms are similar to coping mechanisms but they are traditionally defined as being unconscious, intrapsychic processes. Both defense mechanisms and coping mechanisms serve the same protective purpose for clients. However, some defensive coping mechanisms are more adaptive than others. When any of these defenses are used exclusively or excessively by a client, this coping behavior becomes maladaptive and pathological. Defense mechanisms will provide the nurse with clues about a client's feelings, motives, and behavior. You should recognize the following defense mechanisms for the NCLEX-RN.

Defense Mechanisms		
Mechanism	**Definition**	**Example**
Compensation	An attempt to make up for real or fancied deficiencies	A high school student does poorly in his studies but becomes a talented artist.
Conversion	Expression of intrapsychic conflict symbolically through physical symptoms	A student develops diarrhea on the day of an important examination.
Denial	Disowning consciously intolerable ideas and impulses	A client with diabetes does not stay on her diet.
Displacement	Redirection of emotional feeling from one idea, person, or object to another	A principal berates a teacher, and when classes resume the teacher speaks harshly to the students.
Dissociation	Separation and detachment of emotional significance and effect from an idea or situation	A client grins and chuckles when telling about his automobile accident and its tragic consequences.
Fantasy	A conscious creation or distortion of unacceptable fears, wishes, and behaviors	A client daydreams during an intense group therapy session.
Identification	An attempt to fashion oneself to think, feel, and act like an idealized other	An adolescent dresses like a rock star and mimics his behavior.
Introjection	Unconsciously incorporating loved or hated wishes, values, and attitudes external to oneself	A little girl scolds and spanks her doll like her mother does to her.
Projection	Attributing intolerable wishes, emotional feelings, and motivations to other persons	A teenage girl blames her boyfriend for getting her drunk.
Rationalization	An attempt to make unacceptable feelings and behavior consciously tolerable and acceptable	A student fails an examination and says the lectures were poorly organized and presented unclearly.
Reaction formation	Attitudes, motives, and needs that are directly opposite of those consciously acknowledged	A mother, unaware of her anger toward her children, becomes overly protective.
Regression	Retreat to an earlier and more comfortable level of adjustment	A 4-year-old begins to wet his pants following the birth of his baby brother.

Mechanism	Definition	Example
Repression	Involuntary and unconscious forgetting of unbearable ideas and impulses	An accident victim does not remember the details of an accident.
Restitution	Going back or attempting to restore or repair unconscious guilt feelings	The head nurse is short-tempered toward a new nurse and then lets her leave early.
Sublimation	Diversion of consciously unacceptable instinctual drives into personally and socially accepted areas	A highly competitive man becomes a successful businessman.
Substitution	Replacement of an unacceptable need, attitude, or emotion with one that is more acceptable	A woman rushes into marriage following a breakup with her boyfriend.
Suppression	The intentional exclusion of material from consciousness	A young woman says she is not ready to talk about her abuse as a child.
Symbolization	Disguising an external object as the outward representation for another internal and hidden idea	A man sends his girlfriend a dozen roses.
Undoing	An attempt to actually or symbolically take away a previously consciously intolerable action or experience	A mother who has just punished her child gives him a cookie.

© Rawlins, Ruth Parmelee, RN, DSN, CS.; and Heacock, Patricia Evans, RN, PhD; *Clinical Manual of Psychiatric Nursing*, Second Edition; Mosby–Year Book, 1993; page 365

24. Which defense mechanism is involved when anger is taken out on some-one else?

    A. Denial
    B. Displacement
    C. Undoing

THERAPEUTIC NURSE-CLIENT RELATIONSHIPS

The nurse-client relationship is the heart of psychiatric nursing. It is a formal, professional relationship, though it can achieve a degree of spirituality and intimacy. The nurse-client relationship develops in three major stages: an orientation phase, a working phase, and a termination phase. Depending on the particular nurse and client, different functions and goals apply. The nurse is a teacher, role model, case manager, counselor, and advocate. He or she must use only healthy, growth-producing communications with the client.

THERAPEUTIC COMMUNICATION

The NCLEX-RN loves to ask for the appropriate response to a certain client. Rules apply that transfer across scenarios.

- Therapeutic communication is a priority, but only after a client is out of immediate physical danger.
- Never ask a client **why** he or she feels a certain way.

- Always consider developmental, cultural, and physical variables when responding to a client.
- Always ask open-ended questions and seek more information.
- Always stay in the here and now! Keep the client focused on the issues at hand.
- A therapeutic environment is essential for successful communication.
- Never assert your personal opinion about **anything** or **anyone**.

Label the following communication techniques or statements as **therapeutic** or **nontherapeutic**:

25. _____ Using silence

26. _____ Restating and/or reflecting

27. _____ Reassuring

28. _____ Advising

29. _____ Challenging

30. _____ Exploring

31. _____ Giving approval or disapproving

32. _____ Making observations

33. _____ "My name is . . . "

34. _____ "Don't be silly."

35. _____ "Go on."

36. _____ "Nice weather we're having."

37. _____ "I agree; that's right."

38. _____ "Describe how you feel about being here."

39. _____ "What would you like to do now?"

Assessment

As we have emphasized, effective interviewing, behavioral observation, and physical and mental health assessment are vital skills for all nurses to learn and use. These activities commence the data collection (assessment) phase of the nursing process and form the basis of the nurse's plan of care. Interviewing techniques using therapeutic communication are extremely important, since they allow the nurse to obtain the necessary information to make a diagnosis. These skills also help set the stage for developing a therapeutic relationship.

While the interview and history are taking place, the psychiatric nurse assesses the client's current status and level of functioning. This is referred to as a mental status examination and includes the following:

I. **General Description of the Client**

   A. Appearance (the nurse's overall physical impression of the client)

   B. Behavior and psychomotor activity

   C. Attitude toward the nurse examiner

II. Mood and Affect

A. Mood (the client's prevailing attitude and predominant emotion)

B. Affect (the client's outward expression of emotion at any one time)

C. Appropriateness

III. Speech

IV. Perceptual Disturbances

A. Assessment of the client's sensory awareness and interpretation of the environment

B. Examples of perceptual distortions to be aware of include:

1. Hallucinations (false perceptions of something that is not really there), which can be confused with illusions

2. Illusions (misinterpretations of real external sensory stimuli)

3. Depersonalization (extreme feelings of detachment from oneself)

4. Derealization (extreme feelings of detachment from the environment)

V. Thought

A. Process or form of thought (logical vs. illogical associations)

B. Content of thought (**Always** ask about suicidal ideation and self-destructive thoughts!)

VI. Sensorium and Cognition

A. Alertness and level of consciousness

B. Orientation

C. Memory

D. Concentration

E. Abstract thinking

F. Fund of information and intelligence

VII. Impulse Control

VIII. Judgment and Insight

(This information is collected in the initial interview but is also discerned throughout the therapeutic nurse-client relationship.)

IX. Reliability

(This is the nurse's judgment. Obtain information from any reliable source possible!)

You do not need to memorize the components of the mental status examination for the NCLEX-RN! We included this because it provides a solid framework for the nursing assessment of psychological and psychosocial factors.

NURSING DIAGNOSES

At this point, the nurse goes on to interpret data collected during the assessment phase and formulates nursing diagnoses.

40. A client hears the wind blowing into a room at night and thinks it's a voice. Is this an **illusion** or a **hallucination**? _____

Assign each of these impaired forms of thought to the proper definition below:

41. _____ Suddenly stopping in the stream of thought for no apparent reason, with no recall of the topic

42. _____ Free-flowing thoughts that seem to have little or no connection to one another

43. _____ An incoherent, incomprehensible mixture of words and phrases, consisting of both real and imaginary terms

44. _____ Talking in a continuous but fragmentary way, with extremely rapid speech

45. _____ Associating thought by double meaning

46. _____ Newly invented words, having no public, consensual meaning

47. _____ A rhythmic speech pattern in which sounds govern the choice of words

A. clang associations
B. flight of ideas
C. loosening of associations
D. neologisms
E. punning
F. thought blocking
G. word salad

Assign each of these disturbances in thought content to the proper definition below:

48. _____ False feeling that the self, part of the self, others, or the world does not exist

49. _____ False paranoid thoughts and beliefs

50. _____ Belief that thought can be inserted into one's head by another

51. _____ Beliefs involving another person or force controlling an aspect of one's behavior

52. _____ False belief involving a body's parts or functions changing

53. _____ Beliefs that a radio or television is speaking to or about oneself

54. _____ Exaggerated, unrealistic sense of importance and sense of self

55. _____ Belief that one's thoughts are being aired to the outside world

A. delusions of grandeur
B. delusions of persecution
C. ideas of influence
D. ideas of reference
E. nihilistic delusion
F. somatic delusion
G. thought broadcasting
H. thought insertion

CHAPTER 29: EXERCISE ANSWERS

1. Nursing to ensure a client's psychosocial integrity is grounded in theories of **psychiatric care**, **personality development**, and **psychopathology**.

2. The goals of maintaining a client's psychosocial integrity are **self-care** and **adaptation**.

3. The focus of psychiatric nursing is on anxiety and loss related to **illness** and **stressful events**.

4. Factors that may influence the presentation of a client's psychosocial need or psychiatric disorder include:

   spiritual
   environmental
   gender
   developmental and health status
   culture
   age

5. **B** superego—**the conscience**

6. **C** id—**the pleasure center**

7. **A** ego—**the realistic adult**

8. **E** latency—**school age**

9. **B** oral—**infancy**

10. **A** genital—**adolescence and young adulthood**

11. **C** anal—**toddlerhood**

12. **D** phallic (Oedipal)—**preschool age**

13. **H** trust vs. mistrust—**infancy (0–18 months)**

14. **G** autonomy vs. shame and doubt—**toddlerhood (18 months to 3 years)**

15. **F** initiative vs. guilt—**preschool (3–6 years)**

16. **C** industry vs. inferiority—**school age (6–12 years)**

17. **A** identity vs. role confusion—**adolescence (12–18 years)**

18. **D** intimacy vs. isolation—**early adulthood (18–35 years)**

19. **E** generativity vs. stagnation and/or self-absorption—**middle adulthood (35–65 years)**

20. **B** integrity vs. despair—**older adult (65 years to death)**

21. Which of Freud's structures of the mind is harsh, moral, and rigid?

    A. Superego

22. Toddlerhood is in what stage of Freud's psychosexual development?

    A. The anal stage

23. At what age is a person struggling for identity, according to Erikson?

    C. Adolescence

24. Which defense mechanism is involved when anger is taken out on someone else?

    B. Displacement

25. **Therapeutic**—Using silence

26. **Therapeutic**—Restating and/or reflecting

27. **Not therapeutic**—Reassuring

28. **Not therapeutic**—Advising

29. **Not therapeutic**—Challenging

30. **Therapeutic**—Exploring

31. **Not therapeutic**—Giving approval or disapproving

32. **Therapeutic**—Making observations

33. **Therapeutic**—"My name is . . . "

34. **Not therapeutic**—"Don't be silly."

35. **Therapeutic**—"Go on."

36. **Not therapeutic**—"Nice weather we're having."

37. **Not therapeutic**—"I agree; that's right."

38. **Therapeutic**—"Describe how you feel about being here."

39. **Therapeutic**—"What would you like to do now?"

40. A client hears the wind blowing into a room at night and thinks it's a voice. This is an **illusion**.

41. **F** **thought blocking**—Suddenly stopping in the stream of thought for no apparent reason, with no recall of the topic.

42. **C** **loosening of associations**—Free-flowing thoughts that seem to have little or no connection to one another

43. **G** **word salad**—An incoherent, incomprehensible mixture of words and phrases, consisting of both real and imaginary terms

44. **B** **flight of ideas**—Talking in a continuous but fragmentary way, with extremely rapid speech

45. **E** **punning**—Associating thought by double meaning

46. **D** **neologisms**—Newly invented words, having no public, consensual meaning

47. **A** **clang associations**—A rhythmic speech pattern in which sounds govern the choice of words

48. **E** **nihilistic delusion**—False feeling that the self, part of the self, others, or the world does not exist

49. **B** **delusions of persecution**—False paranoid thoughts and beliefs

50. **H** **thought insertion**—Belief that thought can be inserted into one's head by another

51. **C** **ideas of influence**—Beliefs involving another person or force controlling an aspect of one's behavior

52. **F** **somatic delusion**—False belief involving a body's parts or functions changing

53. **D** **ideas of reference**—Beliefs that a radio or television is speaking to or about oneself

54. **A** **delusions of grandeur**—Exaggerated, unrealistic sense of importance and sense of self

55. **G** **thought broadcasting**—Belief that one's thoughts are being aired to the outside world

1. A client who was recently diagnosed with terminal cancer states to the nurse, "I'm really scared...am I dying?" What would be the most appropriate response by the nurse?

   (1) "Why are you scared?"
   (2) "I'm sure you're scared. Other clients in your situation feel the same way."
   (3) "You really should be careful not to let your family know you're scared so they don't get upset."
   (4) "Tell me about what you are feeling."

2. A client who is a mother of three children is to undergo a breast biopsy. She says, "I know if I lose my breast my husband will no longer love me." What is the best response by the nurse?

   (1) "I know you are worried, but after surgery you can have reconstruction surgery."
   (2) "You feel your relationship with your husband will change if you have a breast removed?"
   (3) "Don't worry, most biopsies are negative, so wait until you see what happens."
   (4) "Why don't you wait and see what your husband's reaction is before you get upset?"

3. Which of the following independent nursing interventions would not be appropriate to implement with clients who are acutely psychotic?

   (1) Listening empathically to identify precipitants of their behavior
   (2) Conveying calmness by providing structure within the one-to-one interaction
   (3) Recognizing and dealing with their own feelings so as to not escalate the client's anxiety level
   (4) Encouraging the client to become involved with others in a psychotherapeutic group so as to lessen anxious feelings

4. The morning after admission to a psychiatric unit, a depressed client sits in the dining room staring blankly at the breakfast tray. The client has eaten very little since arriving at the unit. Which of the following comments by the nurse would be most appropriate?

   (1) "If you don't eat, we will have to resort to other methods of feeding you."
   (2) "If you don't eat your breakfast, you'll be hungry before lunchtime."
   (3) "The meals are planned to provide you with nutrients you need, so please eat."
   (4) "It's difficult to eat when you are sad. Let me put the milk on the cereal for you."

5. A nurse sees the wife of a client with end-stage AIDS crying outside the client's room. Which of the following is the most appropriate action for the nurse to take?	(1) Leave her alone, she needs time to grieve by herself. (2) Gently touch her arm, offer her some tissues, and encourage her to verbalize her feelings. (3) Tell her it's all right for her to cry, after all, her husband is about to die. (4) Tell her you appreciate how upset she is, but ask her to leave the hallway because her crying is upsetting the other clients.
6. One adjustment mechanism used by psychiatric clients is regression. Which one of the following best describes this mechanism?	(1) It is an immature way of responding. (2) It works most effectively to reduce anxiety. (3) It fosters dependence. (4) It provides attention through child-like behavior.
7. A combative and confused client is admitted to the gero-psychiatric unit with dementia, Alzheimer's type. His wife says to the nurse in a biting tone of voice, "Now let's see how well you can handle him." The nurse's most therapeutic response is	(1) "You could use some help yourself." (2) "What did you mean by that?" (3) "Why didn't you call someone to help you out at home?" (4) "It must have been difficult to take care of him by yourself."
8. An elderly man with dementia states to the nurse that he has to go to work or he'll be fired. The best response by the nurse that shows understanding of the aged is	(1) "You talk about your job frequently. Tell me about it." (2) "You can't go to work because you are in the hospital." (3) "If you continue talking like this, I'm going to have to restrain you." (4) "Your job called to say they gave you a holiday so you don't have to go in."
9. A 20-year-old college student is continuously pacing on the psychiatric unit and is muttering about how hopeless life is and how little there is to live for. What nursing intervention is most appropriate at this time?	(1) Walk with the client. (2) Ignore the behavior and it will be extinguished. (3) Ask the client to take the p.r.n. medication. (4) Reassure the client that life will be a lot better when the medication begins to work.
10. A 63-year-old client tells you that she doesn't want to know about tomorrow's surgery. She states, "My provider will take care of everything." The best response by the nurse would be	(1) "You're right; don't worry yourself tonight." (2) "I must go over certain information with you." (3) "Well, I could talk to your son about this instead." (4) "You really sound quite concerned about this."

1. (4) CORRECT   This is a therapeutic, open-ended response that encourages the client to explore his feelings.

(1) *ELIMINATE*   Never ask a "why" question, as this is a nontherapeutic response.

(2) *ELIMINATE*   This does not encourage verbalization by the client.

(3) *ELIMINATE*   This is nontherapeutic in that this response offers advice and doesn't encourage the client to verbalize feelings.

CATEGORY 05 COPING AND ADAPTATION

---

2. (2) CORRECT   This reflects the client's feelings and allows her to further explore what she is concerned about.

(1) *ELIMINATE*   This response avoids the client's concerns and gives advice.

(3) *ELIMINATE*   This is a nontherapeutic response that avoids the concerns of the client.

(4) *ELIMINATE*   This is a nontherapeutic response that dismisses the concerns of the client.

CATEGORY 05 COPING AND ADAPTATION

---

3. (4) CORRECT   Clients who are acutely psychotic are not appropriate for psychotherapeutic groups until they are stabilized.

(1) *ELIMINATE*   This is an appropriate nursing intervention with an acutely psychotic client.

(2) *ELIMINATE*   This is an appropriate nursing intervention.

(3) *ELIMINATE*   This is an appropriate nursing intervention.

CATEGORY 06 PSYCHOSOCIAL ADAPTATION

---

4. (4) CORRECT   With this comment the nurse is offering to stay with the client and is showing empathy.

(1) *ELIMINATE*   This comment is threatening and therefore not therapeutic.

(2) *ELIMINATE*   This comment is also threatening and would not motivate the client.

(3) *ELIMINATE*   This is giving advice and would not be therapeutic.

CATEGORY 06 PSYCHOSOCIAL ADAPTATION

---

5. (2) CORRECT   People who are grieving do not want to be left alone. They need to talk about their feelings with someone who understands and is empathetic. It is therapeutic to encourage clients to express their feelings, as it helps make the sensations associated with grief less frightening.

(1) *ELIMINATE*   This would show no empathy and would be abandoning the wife.

(3) *ELIMINATE*   Stating that the husband was about to die would be most insensitive.

(4) *ELIMINATE*   This response would not be accepting of her feelings.

CATEGORY 05 COPING AND ADAPTATION

6.
(2) CORRECT   Regression is a defense mechanism used by an individual to allay anxiety.

(1) *ELIMINATE*   Regression is a defense mechanism, not an immature way of responding.

(3) *ELIMINATE*   Regression is a defense mechanism.

(4) *ELIMINATE*   Regression is not meant to attract attention. It is a defense mechanism used to allay anxiety.

CATEGORY 06 PSYCHOSOCIAL ADAPTATION

7.
(4) CORRECT   The client's wife was probably feeling very guilty about admitting her husband. She has undoubtedly had a very hard time with him at home. The nurse should demonstrate an empathetic response that recognizes the feelings behind the wife's statement.

(1) *ELIMINATE*   This is derogatory and threatening.

(2) *ELIMINATE*   The client wouldn't be able to understand at this time why she made the comment.

(3) *ELIMINATE*   Never ask a "why" question. The client doesn't know why.

CATEGORY 05 COPING AND ADAPTATION

8.
(1) CORRECT   Encouraging the elderly client to reminisce provides an outlet for conversation and boosts self-esteem.

(2) *ELIMINATE*   Although this statement provides information, it also devalues the client.

(3) *ELIMINATE*   This is a threatening statement.

(4) *ELIMINATE*   This is not a truthful statement and therefore is not a therapeutic response.

CATEGORY 05 COPING AND ADAPTATION

9.
(1) CORRECT   Walking/moving with an agitated person is one way to begin to establish a therapeutic relationship.

(2) *ELIMINATE*   The behavior should not be ignored.

(3) *ELIMINATE*   Medication may not be appropriate.

(4) *ELIMINATE*   This is false reassurance and does not aid in the establishment of a therapeutic relationship.

CATEGORY 05 COPING AND ADAPTATION

10.
(4) CORRECT   This statement actually opens up the avenue to have a therapeutic conversation, thereby allowing the nurse to find out what may be troubling the client and then be able to give necessary information.

(1) *ELIMINATE*   This is false reassurance and blocks therapeutic communication.

(2) *ELIMINATE*   The nurse is more interested in providing information rather than listening to the client.

(3) *ELIMINATE*   This avoids the reaction of the client and allows them to give the nurse a response of "no."

CATEGORY 05 COPING AND ADAPTATION

30

PSYCHIATRIC DISORDERS

WHAT YOU NEED TO KNOW

Psychiatric nurses utilize nursing diagnoses and the standard classification of emotional disorders in the American Psychiatric Association's *Diagnostic and Statistical Manual of Mental Disorders* Fourth Edition (DSM-IV). "Major depression" is a medical diagnosis, whereas "hopelessness" and "spiritual distress" are comparative nursing diagnoses. This chapter outlines the psychiatric disorders classified in DSM-IV that are most likely to appear on the NCLEX-RN.

ANXIETY DISORDERS

Anxiety is a reaction to an unconscious internal conflict, in contrast to *fear*, which is an emotional response to consciously recognized external threat. Both anxiety and fear cause similar physiological reactions, including elevated vital signs, dry mouth, increased perspiration, gastrointestinal discomfort, restlessness, impaired sleep, difficulty concentrating, dizziness, frequency of urination, and muscular tension.

A small amount of anxiety is constructive, but too much can be disabling and overwhelming. Severity of anxiety is rated as mild, moderate, severe, or panic. Responses to anxiety can be behavioral, cognitive, and affective, as well as physical. Observe the anxious client for irritability; feelings of dread, guilt, or helplessness; change in communication level (increased or decreased); acting out behaviors; or withdrawal from others. Again, assess cultural factors that may contribute to or hide anxiety.

Specific anxiety disorders to recognize for the NCLEX-RN are:

- Panic disorder/panic attacks with or without agoraphobia
- Phobias with simple, specific subtypes
- Social phobia/social anxiety disorder (S.A.D.)
- Obsessive-compulsive disorder (O.C.D.)
- Post-traumatic stress disorder (P.T.S.D.)
- Acute stress disorder
- Generalized anxiety disorder (includes overanxious disorder of childhood)
- Anxiety disorder due to a medical condition
- Substance-induced anxiety disorder

In general, the body's reaction to anxiety is the same whether the stress is a positive or negative emotion or occurrence. First, the *fight or flight* mechanism is activated, causing biochemical changes in the body. Then, there's a *stage of resistance*, when physical and psychosocial adaptation is in operation. Finally, there's a *stage of exhaustion* when the body gives up its struggle against the stressor. Panic and crisis can result.

Initially, while the client's anxiety is very high, the nurse must remain calm; stay with the client; speak firmly, clearly, and simply; and provide a safe, protective environment. After this period of high anxiety, the client will likely be more receptive to the nurse and be ready for exploratory work and instruction.

General nursing interventions for the client with an anxiety disorder include reducing environmental stimuli (lights, noise, activity); administering medications as ordered and observing effects; using therapeutic communication skills to encourage the client to talk and express feelings; recommending physical activities as outlets for nervous energy and as distractions from anxiety; and teaching the client about diagnoses and treatments.

CRISIS INTERVENTION

The goal of crisis intervention is resolution of the immediate crisis with a return to the baseline level of functioning. Crises can be *situational* or *maturational*. Common examples of situational crises are child, spouse, or elder abuse; status and role changes, such as those that occur with a major illness, rape, or divorce; substance abuse and dependence; death and grief; and suicide. Maturational crises are those that occur during normal growth and development. These developmental crises include when a child first goes off to school or gets a new sibling; when an adolescent is torn between his parents and peers; or when a young female adult chooses between motherhood or a career. Maturational crises are more predictable than situational crises, but not all clients will have crises at times of life transitions.

Crises can have cumulative stressful effects on a client over the years, as well as when several crises occur simultaneously. A disequilibrium is caused when the client's defenses and supports are finally overwhelmed.

1. The three phases of adaptation to stress and anxiety are:

    A. _____

    B. _____

    C. _____

2. _____ is an apprehensive anticipation of an unknown danger.

3. Crises can be _____ or _____. Crises can have a _____ effect over the years.

4. List five physiological responses to anxiety and fear:

    A. _____

    B. _____

    C. _____

    D. _____

    E. _____

5. _____ is an emotional response to a consciously recognized threat.

MOOD/AFFECTIVE DISORDERS

The differences between a manic episode and a major depressive episode, the two largest components of mood disorders, appear in the table below.

Differences Between Mania and Depression	
Mania	Depression
Characterized by psychomotor activity (increased emotional and physical activity)	Characterized by psychomotor retardation (decreased emotional and physical activity)
Associated with the following signs and symptoms: • Restlessness • Flight of ideas • Inability to eat and sleep because of involvement in more important things	Associated with the following signs and symptoms: • Constipation • Slowed gait and activity • Inability to make decisions quickly • Sleep disturbance
Extroverted personality	Introverted personality
Initiation of activity	Lack of initiative
Delusional self-confidence	Lack of self-confidence (feelings of worthlessness, inadequacy, and inferiority)
Directing hostility onto environment; aggressively finding fault with others; seeking out and picking on others' sensitive areas; showing open hostility	Internalizing hostility; feeling completely at fault; suicidal ideation
Elated mood	Melancholy mood
Tendency to dress in bright, bizarre colors and clothing combinations; use of too much makeup	Loss of interest in appearance; tendency to dress in somber colors; no makeup
Apparent unlimited energy	Lack of energy; easily fatigued
Involved in groups; enjoys being the center of activity	Withdrawn from groups
Higher muscle tone; possibly appearing younger than age	Low muscle tone; possibly appearing older than age
Possible increase in sexual interest	Possible lack of sexual interest

© Springhouse Clinical Rotation Guides: *Mental Health and Psychiatric Nursing*;
Laura Aromando, RN, MSN; Springhouse Corporation, 1995; page 37

SUICIDE

Violence and suicide are major complications of mood disorders. The suicidal client demands emergency evaluation and attention. Nursing priorities include suicide precautions, one-on-one supervision, and a restrictive, safe environment.

The depressed client feels desperately hopeless, and may think about dying or actually plan to end it all. On the other hand, owing to hyperactivity, poor impulse control, and lack of judgment, the euphoric client may unintentionally hurt himself or someone else. A client with a mood disorder can also become psychotic, possibly intensifying any destructive tendencies or impulses. All hazardous objects are to be removed from the client, and a no-harm contract is to be instituted. **Only** after the client is **physically safe** should the nurse facilitate expression of the client's feelings. When the risk of suicide has passed, the nurse explores with the client more adaptive ways of dealing with conflict and losses in the future.

Certain risk factors are associated with suicide potential. Fill in the blanks with the word **men** or **women** to complete the following sentences:

6. _____ more often attempt suicide; however, ...

7. _____ more often succeed at suicide.

8. _____ choose more lethal methods of suicide, such as hangings, shootings, or jumps, whereas...

9. _____ choose less lethal methods, such as overdoses and self-mutilation.

Substance intoxication disinhibits a person to a point of increasing the likelihood of risky behavior. A psychotic client may commit suicide or homicide because voices of a command hallucination said to. Remember, a previous suicide attempt is the single best indicator that a client will engage in such an activity again.

ELECTROCONVULSIVE THERAPY

Electroconvulsive therapy (E.C.T.) is a treatment for mood disorders. E.C.T. is primarily used to treat depression; however, it can also be used for mania.

The nurse's role in E.C.T. is mostly educative and supportive for both the client and family. After a client has signed a consent for E.C.T., the nurse follows specific steps to orient and prepare the client:

- The client must be N.P.O. from midnight the evening before.
- The client should void immediately before the treatment.

During E.C.T., the nurse:

- Assists the psychiatrist and anesthesiologist
- Monitors the client's vital functions, including E.C.G., pulse, blood pressure, and oxygen saturation

The psychiatrist is responsible for administering the electric shock that induces grand mal seizure activity. The anesthesiologist is responsible for administering all IV medications and oxygen. The client is supported physically and emotionally through the entire course of E.C.T. (6–12 treatments can be given). Any restlessness, agitation, confusion, or disorientation after E.C.T. is managed palliatively and symptomatically.

One side effect of E.C.T. is memory deficits. The short-term memory loss experienced as a result of E.C.T. can be distressing to clients and their significant others. The nurse needs to provide reassurance that this is only temporary. Mild symptoms of tiredness, nausea, and headache can also occur postanesthesia.

10. The biggest risk factor for suicide is _____.

11. The one and only side effect of E.C.T. is _____. It is a (temporary, permanent) effect.

12. _____ and _____ are major complications of mood/affective disorders.

13. Clients (require, do not require) consent for E.C.T.

14. The _____ delivers the E.C.T. shock that produces a _____ seizure.

SCHIZOPHRENIA AND OTHER PSYCHOTIC DISORDERS

Schizophrenic and psychotic clients have disturbances in mood, affect, behavior, and thought. In the past, schizophrenia was believed to be caused solely by the psychosocial environment; however, more recent studies have suggested and even shown biological correlates of this illness. For the NCLEX-RN, you should recognize different types of schizophrenia and related disorders:

- Schizophrenia
  1. Paranoid
  2. Disorganized
  3. Catatonic
  4. Undifferentiated
  5. Residual
- Schizophreniform disorder
- Schizoaffective disorder
- Delusional disorder
- Brief psychotic disorder
- Shared psychotic disorder
- Psychotic disorder due to a general medical condition
- Substance-induced psychotic disorder

The predominant problematic and disabling behaviors of these clients become the basis of the nursing care plan. Difficult behaviors exhibited by psychotic clients include delusions, hallucinations, hostility and suspicion, and social withdrawal with poor self-care.

Delusions and hallucinations are the client's disorganized way of attempting to adapt to the environment and to satisfy unmet needs. Therefore, the client's day needs to be highly structured with diversionary, stress-reducing activities. This decreases the time the client has for being alone with disturbed thoughts and perceptions.

Physical problems can also result when psychotic clients are unable to sleep or eat owing to the messages in delusions or hallucinations. Clients may be preoccupied with their psychotic experiences to the extent that they regress and withdraw. Psychomotor symptoms may also interfere with the clients' ability to participate in normal activities of daily living or attending to self-care activities.

Nursing Interventions for Psychotic Disorders

The nurse must establish a trusting relationship slowly, especially if the client is paranoid. At first, make only brief supportive contact and speak to the client in a clear, reality-oriented way. Do not dwell on the client's delusional material so as not to reinforce these ideas, but do not challenge this thinking, either. The nurse can attempt to decode the content in a delusion or hallucination in order to better understand the client's fears and underlying feelings. Only when the client feels safe within a protected environment should delusions and hallucinations be questioned by the nurse.

A client who is paranoid and/or hallucinating may be suspicious and hostile. The content of hallucinations is frequently threatening and contributes to a client's guardedness and anger. These behaviors can occasionally escalate to the point of agitation and loss of control. Seclusion or restraints may be necessary if other, less restrictive interventions are unsuccessful.

There are legal, medical, and ethical rules to follow when applying restraints or placing a client in seclusion in a psychiatric setting. Clients can only be restrained or confined when dangerous to themselves or others. The safety of everyone involved is of utmost importance. The client is monitored closely for pulses distal to the restraints and for range of motion in the restrained extremities. Medication is also used in a humane, dignified manner to control the client's behavior. (There must be a provider's written order to permit administration of a medication.) Accurate documentation is essential. Additionally, staff and other clients should be given the opportunity to express emotions after an upsetting event has occurred on a psychiatric unit.

15. _____ contributes most to psychotic behavior.

16. Initial communication between the nurse and the psychotic client should be (brief, lengthy).

17. Seclusion and restraints are (first, last) choice interventions for the psychotic client.

18. _____ and _____ are the client's disorganized way of adapting to the environment.

19. Intervention for the psychotic client is (highly structured, without structure) to reduce anxiety.

PERSONALITY DISORDERS

Clients with personality disorders are often victims of childhood trauma in dysfunctional family systems. Because of inappropriate parental role models and due to environmental stressors, these clients are manipulative, needy, and unable to form close, stable relationships. Some general principles of personality disorders are as follows:

General Diagnostic Criteria for a Personality Disorder

A. An enduring pattern of inner experience and behavior that deviates markedly from the expectations of the individual's culture. This pattern is manifested in two (or more) of the following areas:
 	
  (1) cognition (i.e., ways of perceiving and interpreting self, other people, and events)
 	
  (2) affectivity (i.e., the range, intensity, lability, and appropriateness of emotional response)
 	
  (3) interpersonal functioning
 	
  (4) impulse control

B. The enduring pattern is inflexible and pervasive across a broad range of personal and social situations
C. The enduring pattern leads to clinically significant distress or impairment in social, occupational, or other important areas of functioning
D. The pattern is stable and of long duration and its onset can be traced back at least to adolescence or early adulthood
E. The enduring pattern is not better accounted for as a manifestation or consequence of another mental disorder
F. The enduring pattern is not due to the direct physiological effects of a substance (e.g., a drug of abuse, a medication) or a general medical condition (e.g., head trauma)

Reprinted with permission from the *Diagnostic and Statistical Manual of Mental Disorders*; Fourth Edition. Copyright 1994, American Psychiatric Association.

NURSING INTERVENTIONS FOR PERSONALITY DISORDERS

Nursing interventions reflect the specific personality disorder of the client and relevant nursing diagnoses and goals. The best nursing approach to take with difficult clients with personality disorders is a firm, consistent one. For example, the client with borderline personality disorder will test limits and attempt to split staff. A comprehensive treatment plan, coordinated with the other involved disciplines, helps prevent this. Role playing and/or group therapy can be used to help these clients develop healthier interpersonal skills. Assertiveness training teaches the difference between passive, aggressive, and assertive behaviors. Since clients with borderline personalities are angry and tend to blame and devalue others, psychiatric nurses may have strong personal reactions to these clients. The emotional feelings the nurse has in response to these clients and their behaviors are called **countertransference**.

Countertransference can be productive if the nurse identifies these feelings and does not let them interfere with the therapeutic relationship. This can be hard to do since not all countertransferential feelings are conscious. Psychiatric nurses should be open about their feelings toward clients so that these feelings do not have a negative impact on their relationships with clients.

Assign the ten personality disorders to their main descriptive characteristics:

20. ____ Patient with this disorder is impulsive and unpredictable; he engages in acting out and self-mutilation.

21. ____ Patient with this disorder is overly dramatic and intensely expressive and has tantrums to be the center of attention.

22. ____ Patient with this disorder has an exaggerated sense of self-importance, and is exhibitionistic and preoccupied with fantasies.

23. ____ Patient with this disorder is passive and helpless and has low self-confidence and low self-esteem.

24. ____ Patient with this disorder is perfectionistic, rigid, stubborn; indecisive, and anxious.

25. ____ Patient with this disorder is suspicious and distrustful of others, hostile, cold, and defensive.

26. ____ Patient with this disorder is aloof, indifferent, and reclusive; he engages in excessive daydreaming.

27. ____ Patient with this disorder is odd and eccentric and interested in unusual beliefs and habits.

28. ____ Patient with this disorder has a deceitful attitude, displays a lack of remorse, exploits others, and exhibits "con artist" behavior.

29. ____ Patient with this disorder is hypersensitive to rejection and socially withdrawn, despite a desire for affection and interaction.

A. antisocial personality disorder

B. avoidant personality disorder

C. borderline personality disorder

D. dependent personality disorder

E. histrionic personality disorder

F. narcissistic personality disorder

G. obsessive-compulsive personality disorder

H. paranoid personality disorder

I. schizoid personality disorder

J. schizotypal personality disorder

DELIRIUM, DEMENTIA, AND OTHER COGNITIVE DISORDERS

Delirium and dementia are mental disorders caused by neurophysiological, neurochemical, or structural alterations or abnormalities of the brain. Specific etiologies of delirium and dementia include brain infection or trauma, systemic infections, medications and poisons, withdrawal from drugs, endocrine dysfunction, electrolyte imbalance, organ system diseases, nutritional deficiencies, postoperative adverse reactions, or genetics.

Dementia must be distinguished from depression (depression can also coincide with dementia). Dementia can be difficult to distinguish from delirium as well. Delirium is a life-threatening emergency that can be medically treated and reversed, if identified quickly. Note that demented patients are more susceptible to delirium, and delirium superimposed on dementia is common.

Delirium is also called acute brain syndrome. As the name implies, it is an acute, treatable, and reversible disease. It can be caused by a multitude of conditions, including infection, metabolic and endocrine disorders, poisons, and tumors. The client with delirium will most likely be anxious, with intermittently impaired orientation and varying levels of consciousness, from hazy to alert. This client's thought processes will be disorganized.

Dementia, on the other hand, is a chronic, progressive disease that slowly impairs one's orientation and thought processes. In dementia, brain damage is irreversible and there is gradual deterioration of neurons.

NURSING INTERVENTIONS FOR COGNITIVE DISORDERS

Nursing care encompasses the acute medical needs of the delirious client and the chronic medical needs of the demented client. Psychotropic medications can be used carefully to treat the symptoms of anxiety, restlessness, agitation, depression, or insomnia that can be associated with delirium or dementia. Medication doses must be very small, considering that the client's brain is already compromised and that the client may be elderly, on other medications, or in a debilitated state.

A safe, structured environment is a priority for clients with cognitive deficits. The nurse must provide routine schedules, reorientation cues, and a balance in sensory stimulation for confused clients. Promote memory function, but do not challenge or confront a forgetful client. Reminiscence therapy is becoming increasingly popular with older and demented clients since their past remote memory remains intact longer. Clients are assisted, directed, or supervised with activities of daily living and self care, depending on their level of functioning. Clients are encouraged to be as independent as possible without frustrating them.

The family of the demented client will require a lot of support and teaching about the client's limitations and what can realistically be expected. Coping skills training, family therapy, and support groups may be beneficial for family members of a client with a progressive dementia.

30. List five characteristics of dementia:

    A. _____

    B. _____

    C. _____

    D. _____

    E. _____

31. List four characteristics of delirium:

    A. _____

    B. _____

    C. _____

    D. _____

32. Delirium and dementia are _____ disorders.

33. The _____ is of utmost importance in ensuring the safety of clients with cognitive disorders.

SUBSTANCE-RELATED DISORDERS

Substance disorders are classified as **substance use** disorders and **substance-induced** disorders. Substance use on a continuum becomes more serious and lethal as one goes from substance abuse to substance dependence. Not everyone who takes a substance develops a problem or addiction. A client may be using more than one substance at a time (polysubstance use), and may be abusing over-the-counter or prescription medication.

Substance **use** becomes substance **abuse** when the substance begins to interfere in the user's ability to take care of himself, work, and maintain relationships. As substance use increases in amount, frequency, and duration, problems in the person's life escalate to the point of being out of control. Compulsive maladaptive use of the substance replaces family, friends, work, and interests. Physiological dependence as evidenced by tolerance and/or withdrawal occurs with some, but not all, drugs, as the person becomes psychologically dependent on the substance. Dependent clients use the mechanisms of denial, projection, and rationalization to protect their secret: substance abuse is minimized, related conflicts are externalized, and others are blamed. After multiple psychosocial losses, physiological integrity is compromised. Substance dependence, intoxication, and withdrawal can be life threatening.

Substance intoxication and withdrawal are referred to as **substance-induced** disorders. Substance intoxication includes all the symptoms caused by ingestion of a drug. For example, a psychoactive drug causes impairments in mood, perception, judgment, cognition, and coordination.

Substance Withdrawal

Substance withdrawal is demonstrative of physical dependence. Withdrawal of the drug causes a complex of symptoms such as generalized body aches, nausea and vomiting, increased perspiration, and shaking or tremors. Withdrawal symptoms can develop when a drug that has been used frequently and regularly is stopped or reduced. Psychological dependence is more common with drugs, but physical dependence is more dangerous, partly because of the physical symptoms of withdrawal.

The symptoms of intoxication and withdrawal are reversible and substance specific. Once the nurse understands the concepts of substance abuse, dependence, intoxication, and withdrawal, specific interventions can be applied to the specific client and drug.

Delirium tremens (D.T.s) is an acute and sometimes fatal complication of alcohol withdrawal. Signs and symptoms include elevations in vital signs, gross tremors, ataxia, restlessness and agitation, convulsions, illusions, and hallucinations. D.T.s is a medical emergency in which maintaining an airway is the priority!

Detoxification and rehabilitation are usually necessary for substance dependence. Detoxification encompasses the medical management of the acute withdrawal. This is followed by a longer period of rehabilitation, family/marital therapy, group therapy, and 12-step self-help programs.

Dual Diagnosis

Many clients with substance-related disorders also have another psychiatric diagnosis. Clients self-medicate symptoms of depression, anxiety, agitation, and hallucinations with alcohol or other drugs. The most prevalent group of clients with dually diagnosed psychiatric disorders are young adults. It is essential to address the substance problem first. Detoxification medically stabilizes the client and restores adequate cognitive functioning. At this point, the coexisting psychiatric disorder is easier to diagnose because it is more clearly evident. Both diagnoses must be attended to in order for treatment to succeed. Noncompliance is a nursing challenge for clients with a dual diagnosis, so the plan should be coordinated with a strong behavioral focus on abstinence and coping skills management.

EATING DISORDERS

There is a vital overlap between the psychosocial and physiological needs of clients with eating disorders. On the NCLEX-RN, your primary concern is physical stability; these clients can die if left untreated. Although they are often thought of as disorders affecting only females, males are also affected by eating disorders.

Anorexia nervosa is characterized by a preoccupation with being thin and a distorted body image. It is primarily a disorder of adolescence and is caused by both biological and psychodynamic factors. The client with anorexia nervosa refuses to eat or eats very little because of an internal fear of getting fat. Fasting and starvation lead to emaciation, amenorrhea, and other medical complications.

Bulimic clients engage more regularly in bingeing and purging. Purging behaviors include heavy use of laxatives, emetics, diuretics, and self-induced vomiting. Purging activities compensate for compulsive overeating and bingeing. Bulimics need to do this because they are obsessed with being thin like anorectics are, but anorexic clients only occasionally resort to bingeing and purging.

Clients with eating disorders may also have medical problems such as constipation, dental caries, gum disease, and skin changes. Nursing care is focused on the client's anxiety, low self esteem, maladaptive behaviors, and issues of control, as well as on the client's nutritional status and weight. Behavior modification techniques along with a mutually formulated and agreed-upon contract can set target weight gain or loss.

A dietitian and peer support groups can provide an educative environment. A trusting and consistent therapeutic relationship with these clients is extremely important in order to explore perfectionistic, helpless, and sexual feelings. Family involvement and education are essential in the successful treatment of clients with eating disorders.

ABUSE

Abuse can be physical (including neglect), sexual, emotional, intellectual, or spiritual. The victims can be children, adults, elders, women, and men. Nurses are legally required to report **any suspected child abuse**. Prevention, early detection, crisis intervention, treatment, and rehabilitation is the continuum of care. Again, physical safety is always your number one nursing priority.

A few of these clients, especially rape victims, may go on to develop post-trauma syndromes. Post-traumatic stress disorder (P.T.S.D.) is an anxiety disorder characterized by emotional numbing, irritability, hypervigilance, difficulty concentrating, increased startle reactions, and reliving of the trauma through flashbacks, intrusive memories or thoughts, and dreams or nightmares. Victims of trauma usually benefit from support groups.

BEREAVEMENT

Bereavement occasionally develops into one of the psychiatric disorders, such as depression. The diagnosis of depression should not be given unless the symptoms continue for longer than 2 months after the loss. Sometimes grieving individuals will seek out medical or psychological attention for depressive symptoms before that time. Grief is a personal experience, the expression of which can be culturally influenced, so it is impossible to define a normal grief reaction. However, gross psychotic symptoms, active suicidal ideation, or major deteriorations in functioning should always be taken seriously by the nurse. Crisis intervention is indicated if grieving and/or anticipatory grieving progresses to a dysfunctional level.

OTHER PSYCHIATRIC DISORDERS

The NCLEX-RN may contain disorders we did not discuss at length. Hopefully, you will apply the general nursing knowledge you have acquired throughout this review to break down and answer the questions correctly. You should recognize some other psychiatric diagnoses, so do the following matching exercise and become familiar with the terminology. Use the roots of the words to help you define the disorder.

34. ____ Preoccupation with somatic concerns, and a fear of having a serious medical illness

35. ____ Maladaptive fire-setting behavior

36. ____ A psychotic state characterized by some impairment in reality testing due to a non-bizarre, circumscribed delusion

37. ____ When an unconscious wish is expressed in a functional somatic way

38. ____ An obsessive-compulsive pulling out of one's own hair

39. ____ The occurrence of schizophrenic symptoms with and without mood symptoms

40. ____ A disturbance in sleep behavior, e.g., walking or talking while sleeping

41. ____ Alteration in sexual desire accompanied by psychophysiological changes in the sexual response cycle

42. ____ Partial or total inability to recall upsetting, stressful information

43. ____ Chronic low-level depression

44. ____ Chronically seeking out medical treatment for multiple somatic problems of different organ systems with no physiological basis

45. ____ Having spontaneous, episodic, and intense periods of anxiety

A. body dysmorphic disorder

B. conversion disorder

C. cyclothymia

D. delusional disorder

E. dissociative amnesia

F. dissociative fugue

G. dissociative identity disorder

H. dyssomnia

I. dysthymia

J. hypochondriasis

K. kleptomania

L. panic disorder

M. paraphilia

N. parasomnia

O. phobia

P. pyromania

Q. schizoaffective disorder

R. sexual dysfunction

S. somatization disorder

T. trichotillomania

46. ____ Problematic sleep process, like insomnia or early morning awakenings

47. ____ An unexpected leaving of one's home area to relocate, without recollection of past experiences and identity

48. ____ A cyclical mood disturbance, not as severe as bipolar disorder

49. ____ Pathological impulses to steal that cannot be resisted

50. ____ An irrational fear leading to a conscious avoidance of the specific anxiety-provoking object or situation

51. ____ A disorder characterized by an irrational preoccupation with a real or imagined bodily defect

52. ____ Engaging in sexually arousing behavior of an unusual nature

53. ____ Splitting of personality usually related to traumatic past events

GENERAL INTERVENTIONS TO PROMOTE PSYCHOSOCIAL INTEGRITY

Group intervention modalities are therapeutic because of factors such as universality, altruism, instillation of hope, and group cohesion. The goals of a group are agreed upon by the members of the group, and the functions of the group leader will vary depending on the group purpose, philosophy, and framework.

Group psychotherapy goes through developmental stages just as individual psychotherapy does. First, there is a pre-group stage when the nurse makes the physical and administrative arrangements for the group, and interviews and prepares the clients. The group then has an orientation stage that is characterized by anxiety, questions, testing the leader, and establishing similarities and group norms among the members. Assurance of confidentiality is a vital function of the nurse in this stage. In the working stage, group members may become challenging, confrontational, and aggressive toward each other and the leader but they eventually accept each other's differences and work on their problems together. Finally, the group enters the termination stage. Feelings elicited by separation are expressed when either the whole group ends or a particular member leaves the group.

Intervention with the **family** is vital in the promotion of psychosocial integrity. The identified client in a family is a symptom of a family problem, crisis, or disequilibrium. The whole family is affected by an ill member. A family is more than the sum of its parts, and change in any one part creates change in all the other parts. The nurse assesses system-related issues and explores family relationships in the here and now, though it helps to be aware of intergenerational influences.

GENERAL PRINCIPLES OF EVALUATION

The nursing process is cyclical and ongoing. The nurse is continually evaluating outcomes, reassessing data, observing new phenomena, modifying goals and diagnoses, and adjusting the treatment plan. As with the other phases of the nursing process, the nurse proceeds in an organized and systematic manner. The client, the client's significant others, and varied health care disciplines are also involved in every stage of nursing care. The nurse wants feedback from clients and staff to improve care delivery. Evaluation of treatment outcomes and client responses helps assure good quality of care.

CHAPTER 30: EXERCISE ANSWERS

1. The three phases of adaptation to stress and anxiety are:

   fight or flight

   resistance

   exhaustion

2. **Anxiety** is an apprehensive anticipation of an unknown danger.

3. Crises can be **situational** or **maturational**. Crises can have a **cumulative** effect over the years.

4. List five physiological responses to anxiety and fear: **restlessness, GI upset, insomnia, difficulty concentrating, perspiration, dry mouth, increased vital signs, urinary frequency, muscle tension**.

5. **Fear** is an emotional response to a consciously recognized threat.

6. **Women** more often attempt suicide; however, . . .

7. **Men** more often succeed at suicide.

8. **Men** choose more lethal methods of suicide, such as hangings, shootings, or jumps, whereas...

9. **Women** choose less lethal methods, such as overdoses and self-mutilation.

10. The biggest risk factor for suicide is **a previous suicide attempt**.

11. The one and only side effect of E.C.T. is **memory loss**. It is a **temporary** effect.

12. **Violence** and **suicide** are the major complications of mood/affective disorders.

13. Clients **require** consent for E.C.T.

14. The **physician** delivers the E.C.T. shock that produces a **grand mal** seizure.

15. **Anxiety** contributes most to psychotic behavior.

16. Initial communication between the nurse and the psychotic client should be **brief**.

17. Seclusion and restraints are **last** choice interventions for the psychotic client.

18. **Delusions** and **hallucinations** are the client's disorganized way of adapting to the environment.

19. Intervention for the psychotic client is **highly structured** to reduce anxiety.

20. **C   borderline personality disorder**—Patient with this disorder is impulsive and unpredictable; he engages in acting out and self-mutilation.

21. **E   histrionic personality disorder**—Patient with this disorder is overly dramatic and intensely expressive and has tantrums to be the center of attention.

22. **F** **narcissistic personality disorder**—Patient with this disorder has an exaggerated sense of self-importance, and is exhibitionistic and preoccupied with fantasies.

23. **D** **dependent personality disorder**—Patient with this disorder is passive and helpless and has low self-confidence and low self-esteem.

24. **G** **obsessive-compulsive personality disorder**—Patient with this disorder is perfectionistic, rigid, stubborn; indecisive, and anxious.

25. **H** **paranoid personality disorder**—Patient with this disorder is suspicious and distrustful of others, hostile, cold, and defensive.

26. **I** **schizoid personality disorder**—Patient with this disorder is aloof, indifferent, and reclusive; he engages in excessive daydreaming.

27. **J** **schizotypal personality disorder**—Patient with this disorder is odd and eccentric and interested in unusual beliefs and habits.

28. **A** **antisocial personality disorder**—Patient with this disorder has a deceitful attitude, displays a lack of remorse, exploits others, and exhibits "con artist" behavior.

29. **B** **avoidant personality disorder**—Patient with this disorder is hypersensitive to rejection and socially withdrawn, despite a desire for affection and interaction.

30. Characteristics of dementia include:

chronic

insidious onset

orientation intact at first

normal psychomotor skills

not reversible

31. Characteristics of delirium include:

acute

rapid onset

changing level of consciousness and psychomotor abilities

reversible

32. Delirium and dementia are **cognitive** disorders.

33. The **environment** is of utmost importance in ensuring the safety of clients with cognitive disorders.

34. **J** **hypochondriasis**—Preoccupation with somatic concerns, and a fear of having a serious medical illness

35. **P** **pyromania**—Maladaptive fire-setting behavior

36. **D** **delusional disorder**—A psychotic state characterized by some impairment in reality testing due to a non-bizarre, circumscribed delusion

37. **B** **conversion disorder**—When an unconscious wish is expressed in a functional somatic way

38. **T** **trichotillomania**—An obsessive-compulsive pulling out of one's own hair

39. **Q** **schizoaffective disorder**—The occurrence of schizophrenic symptoms with and without mood symptoms

40. **N** **parasomnia**—A disturbance in sleep behavior, e.g., walking or talking while sleeping

41. **R** **sexual dysfunction**—Alteration in sexual desire accompanied by psychophysiological changes in the sexual response cycle

42. **E** **dissociative amnesia**—Partial or total inability to recall upsetting, stressful information

43. **I** **dysthymia**—Chronic low-level depression

44. **S** **somatization disorder**—Chronically seeking out medical treatment for multiple somatic problems of different organ systems with no physiological basis

45. **L** **panic disorder**—Having spontaneous, episodic, and intense periods of anxiety

46. **H** **dyssomnia**—Problematic sleep process, like insomnia or early morning awakenings

47. **F** **dissociative fugue**—An unexpected leaving of one's home area to relocate, without recollection of past experiences and identity

48. **C** **cyclothymia**—A cyclical mood disturbance, not as severe as bipolar disorder

49. **K** **kleptomania**—Pathological impulses to steal that cannot be resisted

50. **O** **phobia**—An irrational fear leading to a conscious avoidance of the specific anxiety-provoking object or situation

51. **A** **body dysmorphic disorder**—A disorder characterized by an irrational preoccupation with a real or imagined bodily defect

52. **M** **paraphilia**—Engaging in sexually arousing behavior of an unusual nature

53. **G** **dissociative identity disorder**—Splitting of personality usually related to traumatic past events

CHAPTER 30: NCLEX-RN STYLE QUESTIONS

1.	A client is hospitalized with obsessive-compulsive disorder. The nurse notes the client is vigorously washing his or her hands. Which response by the nurse would be the most appropriate?	(1) "Your hands look clean. Why are you still washing them?" (2) "You should stop washing your hands because they will get chapped." (3) "It's time to go to the dining room. I'll walk with you." (4) "I'll go get some lotion for your hands so they won't get chapped."
2.	A client is admitted with the diagnosis of paranoid schizophrenia. Which of the following behaviors can the nurse anticipate with this client?	(1) Negative cognitive distortions (2) Impaired psychomotor development (3) Delusions of grandeur and hyperactivity (4) Alteration of appetite and sleep patterns
3.	A client is admitted to the hospital. During the assessment, the nurse notes that the client has not slept for a week. The client is talking rapidly and throwing his arms around randomly. What would be the highest priority in formulating a nursing care plan for this client?	(1) Isolate the client until he or she adjusts to the hospital. (2) Provide nutritious food and a quiet place to rest. (3) Protect the client and others from harm. (4) Create a structured environment.

4. Which nursing diagnosis would be the priority with a client's DSM-IV Axis 1 diagnosis of schizophrenia, paranoid type?

(1) Altered protection
(2) Risk of loneliness
(3) Altered thought processes
(4) Ineffective individual coping

5. A client is scheduled for electroconvulsive therapy (E.C.T.) in the morning. It is most important that the evening nurse ensures that the client does which of the following?

(1) Signs an informed consent
(2) Is placed on seizure precautions
(3) Remembers to take morning medications
(4) Has a family member bring home any valuables

6. A client is admitted with a diagnosis of paranoid schizophrenia. Recognizing the common behaviors exhibited by a client with schizophrenia, the nurse can anticipate which of the following?

(1) Grandiosity, arrogance, and distractability
(2) Slumped posture and feelings of despondency
(3) Disorientation, anxiety, and panic reactions
(4) Withdrawal, regressed behavior, and problems with social skills

7. While caring for a client diagnosed with schizophrenia, the nurse knows that the client may have trouble with

(1) staff who are cheerful.
(2) simple direct sentences.
(3) multistage commands.
(4) violent behaviors.

8. When writing an assessment of a client with mood disorder, the nurse should specify

(1) how flat the client's affect is.
(2) how suicidal the client is.
(3) how grandiose the client is.
(4) how the client is behaving.

9. Which nursing diagnosis is most likely to be associated with a person who has a medical diagnosis of schizophrenia, paranoid type?

(1) Fear of being alone related to suspiciousness
(2) Perceptual disturbance related to delusions of persecution
(3) Social isolation related to impaired ability to trust
(4) Impaired social skills related to inadequately developed superego

CHAPTER 30: NCLEX-RN STYLE ANSWERS

1. (3) CORRECT   This would distract the client by offering an alternate activity.
    (1) *ELIMINATE*   Never ask a "why" question. The client is unable to explain this behavior.
    (2) *ELIMINATE*   This response is threatening and implies misbehavior by the client.
    (4) *ELIMNATE*   This does not distract the client from the behavior and leaves her in the room alone to continue washing her hands.

    CATEGORY 06 PSYCHOSOCIAL ADAPTATION

2. (4) CORRECT   The client with paranoid schizophrenia may feel everyone is against them, believe food is poisoned, and may remain watchful and vigilant so as not to be harmed during their sleep.
    (1) *ELIMINATE*   Clients with paranoid schizophrenia do not have negative cognitive distortions.
    (2) *ELIMINATE*   These symptoms are seen more frequently with the depressive symptoms of schizophrenia.
    (3) *ELIMINATE*   Delusions and hyperactivity are seen more frequently with manic episodes of bipolar disorder.

    CATEGORY 05 COPING AND ADAPTATION

3. (2) CORRECT   Using Maslow's hierarchy of needs, the physiological needs of the client would take priority.
    (1) *ELIMINATE*   The nurse would want to decrease stimulation, but isolation would be an extreme measure.
    (3) *ELIMINATE*   The client may experience some destructive behavior, but using Maslow's hierarchy of needs, physiological needs would take priority over safety needs.
    (4) *ELIMINATE*   A structured environment allows the client to use energy in constructive ways. However, the first priority would be to meet physiological, not psychosocial, needs.

    CATEGORY 05 COPING AND ADAPTATION

4. (3) CORRECT   The client preoccupied with delusions of persecution, grandeur, ideas of reference, and auditory hallucinations is predisposed to suicidal and violent behavior.
    (1) *ELIMINATE*   Not applicable, as this would reinforce the client's delusions of persecution.
    (2) *ELIMINATE*   This is another area of concern, but safety must first be addressed.
    (4) *ELIMINATE*   This would be an area of concern once safety has been addressed.

    CATEGORY 06 PSYCHOSOCIAL ADAPTATION

5.   (1) CORRECT   Major aspects of the pre-E.C.T. stage are: obtaining lab and diagnostic data, getting an informed consent, and reinforcing client and family education.

   (2) *ELIMINATE*   Not applicable.

   (3) *ELIMINATE*   The client is NPO after midnight.

   (4) *ELIMINATE*   This is important, but not necessarily the nurse's responsibility.

CATEGORY 01 MANAGEMENT OF CARE

6.   (4) CORRECT   Although some persons with schizophrenia are distractable, despondent, and anxious, they almost all exhibit withdrawal, lack of social skills, and regressed behavior. Therefore this is the best response.

   (1) *ELIMINATE*   Only some clients with a diagnosis of paranoid schizophrenia are distractable.

   (2) *ELIMINATE*   Only some schizophrenics are despondent.

   (3) *ELIMINATE*   Only some schizophrenics are disoriented and anxious.

CATEGORY 06 PSYCHOSOCIAL ADAPTATION

7.   (3) CORRECT   Clients who are diagnosed with schizophrenic disorders have difficulty handling complex information, so it is best to keep communication simple.

   (1) *ELIMINATE*   The mood of the staff is not significant.

   (2) *ELIMINATE*   The client deals best with simple direct sentences.

   (4) *ELIMINATE*   Clients in general do not have trouble with violent behaviors.

CATEGORY 06 PSYCHOSOCIAL ADAPTATION

8.   (4) CORRECT   An assessment and description of the client's specific behaviors are important in formulating an overall picture of target symptoms for intervention.

   (1) *ELIMINATE*   Vague comments about the client's affect are not helpful.

   (2) *ELIMINATE*   Suicidal behavior may be documented but this is not the best response.

   (3) *ELIMINATE*   Vague documentation of the client's grandiosity is not helpful.

CATEGORY 06 PSYCHOSOCIAL ADAPTATION

9.   (3) CORRECT   Clients with paranoid schizophrenia frequently seclude themselves from others because of their suspiciousness, which results in their reluctance to trust people.

   (1) *ELIMINATE*   Fear of being alone is not the appropriate nursing diagnosis.

   (2) *ELIMINATE*   This response has to do with suspiciousness and persecutory feelings but it is incorrect because it is an example of circular reasoning.

   (4) *ELIMINATE*   Impaired social skills is not the appropriate nursing diagnosis.

CATEGORY 06 PSYCHOSOCIAL ADAPTATION

31

PSYCHOPHARMACOLOGY

WHAT YOU NEED TO KNOW

There are certain psychotropic drugs you must know about in detail and others you should recognize on the NCLEX-RN. The test writers want to make sure you know the major classifications, side effects, and indications for drugs. They want you to know the proper methods of drug administration and the importance of educating your client about medications. We think the following information is most likely to appear on your exam. But first, a little review.

1. Review the five rights of medication administration:

    A. _____

    B. _____

    C. _____

    D. _____

    E. _____

Remember the following points about medication administration:

- You need a **written** order from a provider to administer any medication.
- Client education pertaining to medications is vital.
- If you withhold a medication because of a side effect, you must notify the provider.

ANTIPSYCHOTIC AGENTS

The following tables summarize the most important aspects of antipsychotic medications:

Class	Other Nomenclature	Indication	Main Effects
Antipsychotic agents	Major tranquilizers Neuroleptic drugs Antischizophrenic drugs	Schizophrenia Psychotic disorders Tourette's syndrome Organic mental disorders	Treatment of psychotic symptoms: thought disorders, perceptual disturbances, hostility, agitation, anxiety, control of tics and vocal utterances; can be used in combination with analgesics for pain management

Summary of Antipsychotic Medications

Classification	Generic Name (Trade Name)	Adult Daily Dosage Range	Therapeutic Notes
Phenothiazines	chlorpromazine (Thorazine)	30–2000 mg	Potent hypotensive effect
	thioridazine (Mellaril)	150–800 mg	May cause retinitis pigmentosa in doses above 800 mg
	mesoridazine (Serentil)	30–400 mg	
	perphenazine (Trilafon)	12–64 mg	
	trifluoperazine (Stelazine)	2–40 mg	
	fluphenazine (Prolixin)	1–40 mg	Available in long-acting form; may be used in clients with a history of noncompliance
Thioxanthenes	thiothixene (Navane)	8–30 mg	
Butyrophenone	haloperidol (Haldol)	1–100 mg	Available in long-acting form; may be used in clients with a history of noncompliance
Dihydroindolone	molindone (Moban)	15–225 mg	
Dibenzoxazepine	loxapine (Loxitane)	20–250 mg	
Dibenzodiazepine	clozapine (Clozaril)	300–900 mg	Increased risk for agranulocytosis; higher incidence of seizures reported
Benzisoxazole	risperidone (Risperidal)	2–6 mg	
Thienobenzodiazepine	olanzapine (Xyprexa)	5–20 mg	Weight gain

Antipsychotic drugs have a high incidence of troublesome side effects. The nurse must be aware of these potential side effects, make ongoing assessments of a client's condition, and intervene to alleviate or minimize these symptoms.

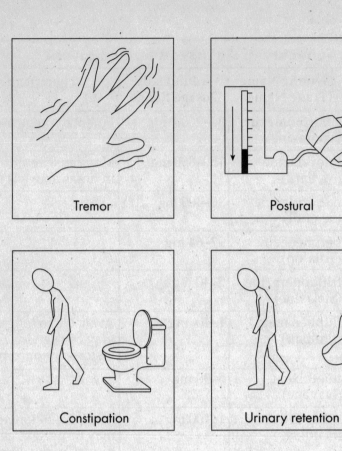

Tremor

Postural

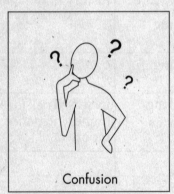

Constipation

Urinary retention

Confusion

Sexual

COMMON SIDE EFFECTS OF ANTIPSYCHOTICS

Nursing Process Related to Side Effects of Antipsychotic Drugs		
Adverse Reaction	**Assessment/Evaluation**	**Interventions**
Anticholinergic Symptoms		
Dry mouth	Subjective statement Dry, cracked lips	Encourage frequent sips of water, good oral hygiene, chew sugarless gum, artificial saliva preparations
Blurred vision	Subjective statement Use antipsychotic drugs with caution in clients with glaucoma.	Reassure client of transient nature of blurred vision.
Retinitis pigmentosa	Impaired acuity, pigmentary deposits on retina on ophthalmic exam	Stop or change drug. Mellaril (thioridazine) should never be given in doses greater than 800 mg.
Urinary retention or hesitancy	Subjective complaint Percuss bladder for distention. Observe for symptoms of infection. Review history for underlying causes.	Instruct client to report any difficulty urinating. Record intake and output. Withhold medication pending medical evaluation.
Constipation	Subjective complaint Record bowel movements. Observe for abdominal distention. Assess for pain.	Encourage diet high in fiber. Increase fluid intake and increase exercise. Discuss possibility of stool softener with provider.
Paralytic ileus	Auscultate for bowel sounds. Assess for pain.	Withhold medication pending medical evaluation.
Sedation	Complaints of fatigue, sleepiness Increased number of hours asleep Reaction time slowed Decreased dexterity in performing tasks	Client teaching regarding need to restrict driving or operation of machinery while feeling sedated. Promote environmental safety; prevent falls due to lethargy.
Orthostatic hypotension	Complaints of palpitations, dizziness, syncope, decreased blood pressure Get a baseline sitting and standing blood pressure when antipsychotic medication is initiated.	Instruct client to rise slowly from a lying or sitting position. Take blood pressure lying and standing; if more than 20 mm drop in pressure, withhold dose, take blood pressure again, and if no change, notify provider prior to giving dose.
Tachycardia	Review history of cardiac disease, concurrent medications for other hypotensives.	Notify provider for pulse above 120 b.p.m.

...essment/Evaluation	Interventions
Dermatologic Effects	
...for maculopapular ...olving most of the body.	Hold medication dose, notify provider. Treat symptoms.
...on exposed areas of	Instruct the client to wear protective sunscreens, clothing and sunglasses, and to limit exposure time in the sun.

	Hormonal Effects	
Decreased libido Failure to achieve orgasm	Subjective complaints	Explain that this may be transient. Notify provider: drug may be stopped, decreased, or changed.
Amenorrhea	Serum test for pregnancy if indicated.	Explain that this is reversible. Instruct client not to discontinue the use of birth control as ovulation is continuing and pregnancy is possible.
Weight gain	Baseline and periodic weights	Encourage proper diet and exercise.
Extrapyramidal Effects		
Dystonia (involuntary muscular movements of face, arms, legs, and neck)	Observe client closely during acute treatment. Check tendons for "cogwheel" jerkiness.	Teach client to recognize onset of dystonic symptoms. Respond to symptoms of dystonia immediately, pursue dose reduction and/or antiparkinsonian drug order. Severe dystonic reactions may be treated with diphenhydramine (Benadryl) 25–100mg or benztropine (Cogentin) 1mg IM IV.
Oculogyric crisis (uncontrolled rolling back of the eyes)	Observe client closely. Side effect may become psychiatric emergency as it can be a precursor to muscular/respiratory collapse.	Notify provider. Prepare to administer antiparkinsonian drug; may be given IM or IV. Anticipate need for respiratory/emergency support p.r.n.
Akinesia (muscular weakness and fatigue-like symptoms)	Subjective complaints of muscle weakness, lethargy	Pursue dose reduction and/or administer antiparkinsonian drug.

Adverse Reaction	Assessment/Evaluation	Interventions
Extrapyramidal Effects *cont.*		
Akathesia (restlessness, fidgeting, pacing beyond the conscious control of the client)	Insomnia, pacing, constant movement	Pursue dose reduction and/or administer antiparkinsonian drug.
Pseudoparkinsonism (mimics symptoms of parkinsonism)	Observe for tremor, shuffling gait, drooling, rigidity.	Pursue dose reduction and/or administer antiparkinsonian drug.
Tardive dyskinesia (characterized by bizarre facial and tongue movements, stiff neck, difficulty swallowing)	Observe for changes in gait and facial and extremity movements. Be aware of risk factors: elderly females, extended treatment on high dose antipsychotic drugs	Notify provider immediately if signs are observed. Antipsychotic may be discontinued or changed.
Neuroleptic malignant syndrome (NMS): (characterized by muscular rigidity, hyperthermia, altered consciousness, and autonomic dysfunction)	Regularly monitor vital signs of clients taking antipsychotic medication. Be alert to signs of possible development of neuroleptic malignant syndrome: elevated temperature, severe extrapyramidal rigidity, diaphoresis, tachycardia, or an altered level of consciousness.	Withhold antipsychotic medication until discussion with provider. Monitor vital signs. Initiate supportive measures to lower temperature. Monitor electrolytes and intake and output.
Other Effects		
Reduced seizure threshold	History of seizures	Closely observe client with a history of seizures.
Agranulocytosis	Periodic complete blood counts Observe clients for bruising, bleeding, mouth sores, lethargy.	Stop medication if red blood count is below 3000 mm or if granulocytes fall below 1500 mm.

ANTIPARKINSONIAN AGENTS

Because antiparkinsonian agents are often administered to control the extrapyramidal side effects of antipsychotic medications, we'll now focus on this classification of drugs.

Class	Other Nomenclature	Indication	Main Effects
Antiparkinsonian agents	Anti-extrapyramidal agents	Treatment of side effects of antipsychotic medications	Decrease in side effects of blurred vision, dry mouth, tremors, shuffling gait, muscle spasms or rigidity, and restlessness

SIDE EFFECTS OF THE ANTIPARKINSONIAN DRUGS

Side effects of the antiparkinsonian drugs are most often associated with high dosages in middle-aged and young adults; the elderly may experience side effects with moderate or even low doses.

Potential side effects of antiparkinsonian drugs include constipation, urinary retention, paralysis of bowel or bladder, lethargy, blurred vision, dry mouth, dilated pupils, confusion, tachycardia, decreased sweating, elevated temperature, dizziness, gastrointestinal disturbances, and dry, flushed skin.

Assign each of the following side effects to the correct definition:

2. ____ Irreversible side effect of antipsychotic medication causing a syndrome characterized by bizarre facial and tongue movements, stiff neck, and difficulty swallowing.

3. ____ Potentially fatal blood disorder in which the client's white blood cells drop to dangerously low levels. Associated with antipsychotic medications, in particular clozapine (Clozaril).

4. ____ Involuntary movement or spasms of the face, arms, legs, and neck; usually an acute side effect of antipsychotic medication.

5. ____ Uncontrollable upward or rolling back movement of the eyes; may occur as an extrapyramidal side effect of antipsychotic drugs.

6. ____ Rare but potentially fatal complication of treatment with neuroleptic drugs. Symptoms include severe muscle rigidity, high fever, tachycardia, fluctuating blood pressure, diaphoresis, and rapid deterioration of mental status into stupor and coma.

A. agranulocytosis

B. akathesia

C. dystonia

D. neuroleptic malignant syndrome

E. oculogyric crisis

F. pseudoparkinsonism

G. tardive dyskinesia

7. _____ Sensation of restlessness or a feeling of the need to move; shifting from one foot to the other. An extrapyramidal side effect of antipsychotic medications.

8. _____ Symptoms of drooling, shuffling gait, tremor and rigidity, mask-like face, pill-rolling of the fingers, and cogwheel rigidity that may occur early in treatment with antipsychotic medications.

ANTIANXIETY AGENTS

Class	Other Nomenclature	Purpose	Main Effects
Antianxiety agents	Minor tranquilizers Anxiolytic drugs	To treat anxiety, panic, phobias, insomnia, obsessive-compulsive disorders, post-traumatic stress disorders Some benzodiazepines may be used as muscle relaxants and anticonvulsants.	Buspirone has been used to treat psychotic symptoms. Decrease in anxiety Increase in sleep Decrease in nervous system activation Decrease in skeletal spasms Produces anticonvulsant activity

SUMMARY OF COMMONLY USED ANTIANXIETY DRUGS

Chemical Group	Generic Name (Trade name)	Daily Dosage Range
Antihistamines	hydroxyzine (Vistaril, Atarax)	100–400 mg
Benzodiazepines	alprazolam (Xanax)	0.75–4 mg
	chlordiazepoxide (Librium)	10–100 mg
	clonazepam (Klonopin)	1.5–10 mg
	diazepam (Valium)	7.5–60 mg
	lorazepam (Ativan)	2–9 mg
	temazepam (Restoril)	15–30 mg
	triazolam (Halcion)	0.125–0.5 mg
Miscellaneous	buspirone (BuSpar)	15–60 mg

Side Effect	Nursing Implication
Drowsiness, confusion, and lethargy	Instruct client not to drive or operate dangerous machinery while taking medication.
Orthostatic hypotension	Monitor vital signs; instruct client to change positions slowly.
Nausea and vomiting	Advise that this medication may be taken with meals.
Dry mouth	Frequent sips of water, sugarless gum, or candy.
Potentiates the effects of other C.N.S. depressants	Instruct client to avoid alcohol and to check with provider before taking other medications.
Blood dyscrasias	Symptoms of sore throat, fever, malaise, easy bruising, or unusual bleeding should be reported to the provider immediately.
Paradoxical excitement	Report to provider immediately.
Tolerance	Instruct clients on long-term therapy not to discontinue drug abruptly.
Liver dysfunction	Symptoms of nausea, upper abdominal pain, jaundice, fever, rash; monitor liver function tests.

Remember, antianxiety drugs:

- Should not be taken with other C.N.S. depressants
- Are strictly contraindicated in clients with narrow-angle glaucoma, shock, or coma, and during pregnancy or lactation
- May exacerbate depression

BENZODIAZEPINES

DURATION OF ACTION OF BENZODIAZEPINES

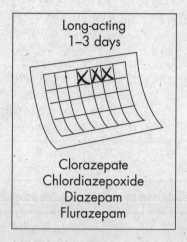

Long-acting
1–3 days

Clorazepate
Chlordiazepoxide
Diazepam
Flurazepam

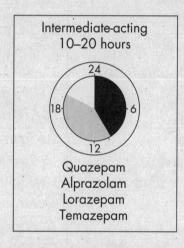

Intermediate-acting
10–20 hours

Quazepam
Alprazolam
Lorazepam
Temazepam

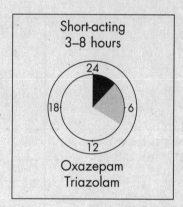

Short-acting
3–8 hours

Oxazepam
Triazolam

Benzodiazepine Withdrawal Syndrome

- Withdrawal from benzodiazepines begins within 12 to 48 hours after the last dose.
- Withdrawal may last from 12 to 48 hours.
- Some symptoms persist for weeks.
- Medication dosages must be reduced gradually to avoid the possibility of seizures.
- Symptoms of withdrawal include anxiety, agitation, tremors, insomnia, dizziness, headaches, tinnitus, blurred vision, diarrhea, hypotension, hyperthermia, neuromuscular irritability, psychosis, and seizures.

BUSPIRONE

BuSpar (buspirone) lacks the anticonvulsant and muscle relaxant properties of the benzodiazepines, causes minimal sedation, and has a lower interactive effect with other C.N.S. depressants. Headache, dizziness, nervousness, and lightheadedness are common side effects of BuSpar.

ANTIDEPRESSANTS

Class	Other Nomenclature	Purpose	Main Effects
Antidepressant agents	Mood elevators Energizers	To treat dysthymia, major depression with melancholia or psychotic symptoms, depression associated with organic disease, bipolar disorder, dual diagnoses	Decrease depressive symptoms, improve mood, improve sleep, increase ability to experience pleasure, decrease psychomotor retardation

Summary of Common Antidepressant Medications		
Classification	**Generic Name (Trade name)**	**Daily Dose Range**
Tricyclics	amitriptyline (Elavil)	20–300 mg
	desipramine (Norpramin)	25–200 mg
	doxepin hydrochloride (Sinequan)	25–300 mg
	imipramine (Tofranil)	30–300 mg
	nortriptyline (Pamelor)	50–150 mg
Monoamine oxidase (MAO) inhibitors	isocarboxazid (Marplan)	10–30 mg
	phenelzine sulfate (Nardil)	15–75 mg
	tranylcypromine sulfate (Parnate)	10–30mg
Selective reuptake inhibitors (SSRIs)	fluoxetine (Prozac)	40–80 mg
	paroxetine (Paxil)	10–50 mg
	sertraline (Zoloft)	50–200 mg
Miscellaneous	bupropion (Wellbutrin)	300–450 mg
	trazodone (Desyrel)	200–600 mg

Here are a few things you should keep in mind about antidepressants for the NCLEX-RN:

- Antidepressants affect the actions of norepinephrine, dopamine, or serotonin in the brain.
- Response time to the antidepressants varies, but in general it takes from 2 to 3 weeks to see therapeutic effects.

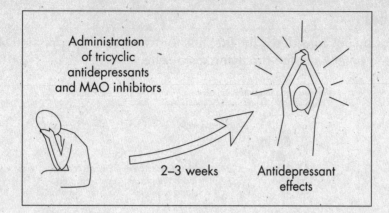

Administration
of tricyclic
antidepressants
and MAO inhibitors

2–3 weeks

Antidepressant
effects

- SSRIs are generally seen as the first line of treatment because of their lower side effect profile and decreased potential for overdose.

- Tricyclic and tetracyclic antidepressants have anticholinergic side effects: dry mouth, blurred vision, constipation, urinary hesitancy, orthostatic hypotension, and drowsiness.

- Adverse effects include exacerbation of psychosis and cardiac arrhythmias.

MAO Inhibitors

MAO inhibitors are not considered the first line for treatment of depression because of their more serious and potentially life-threatening side effects.

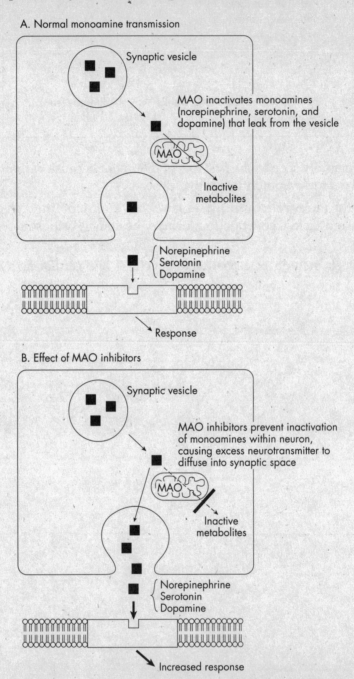

A. Normal monoamine transmission

Synaptic vesicle

MAO inactivates monoamines (norepinephrine, serotonin, and dopamine) that leak from the vesicle

MAO

Inactive metabolites

Norepinephrine
Serotonin
Dopamine

Response

B. Effect of MAO inhibitors

Synaptic vesicle

MAO inhibitors prevent inactivation of monoamines within neuron, causing excess neurotransmitter to diffuse into synaptic space

MAO

Inactive metabolites

Norepinephrine
Serotonin
Dopamine

Increased response

The most serious side effect of the MAO inhibitors is the hypertensive crisis, which is considered a medical emergency with potential for producing intracranial hemorrhage or death. The MAO inhibitors produce hypertension in combination with foods that are tyramine-rich. (Clients taking MAO inhibitors should avoid the tyramine-rich foods listed below.) Several medications are also contraindicated in combination with the MAO inhibitors.

Symptoms of Hypertensive Crisis	General Nursing Interventions
Headaches	Hold next MAO inhibitor dose.
Elevated blood pressure	Monitor vital signs.
Palpitations and chest pain	Cooling techniques for fever.
Sweating	Maintain hydration/electrolyte balance.
Nausea/vomiting	
Fever	
Neck stiffness	
Photophobia	
Nosebleed	

In order to avoid a hypertensive crisis, a client taking MAO inhibitors must consult his provider before taking any over-the-counter medication or any other prescription medication.

Foods to Avoid Include	Use in Moderation
Aged or mature cheese (e.g., cheddar, parmesan)	Soy sauce
Aged protein and fermented foods (e.g., salami, sausage)	Chocolate
Broad beans	Caffeine drinks
Pickled herring; beef or chicken livers	
Beer, red wine	
Yeast or protein extracts (Marmite, Oxo, Bovril)	
Yogurt	
Overripe fruit	

Therapeutic Uses
- Moderate to severe depression: Use of MAO inhibitors is indicated for depressed patients who are unresponsive or allergic to tricyclic antidepressants or who experience strong anxiety.
- Treatment of hypersomnia.
- Treatment of phobic states.

ANTIMANIC AGENTS OR MOOD STABILIZERS

Class	Other Nomenclature	Purpose	Main Effects
Antimanic agents	Mood stabilizer	To treat bipolar disorder, mania, depression, or schizoaffective disorder	Stabilization of mood, decrease in and prevention of manic episodes, decrease in depression

LITHIUM CARBONATE

Lithium carbonate is the drug of choice for acute manic symptoms, as well as for prophylactic treatment of cyclical mood swings. Lithium's mode of action is not known, but it takes 7–10 days for the medication to work. During that time, antipsychotic drugs are often used to control the acute symptoms of mania until lithium takes effect. Serum lithium blood levels are used to titrate the dose, with therapeutic levels ranging from 0.5 to 1.5 mEq/L. Dose stabilization usually takes 1 year.

ANTICONVULSANTS

The second line of treatment for mood stabilization in bipolar disorder is anticonvulsants. These drugs are usually prescribed for those who do not respond to lithium or for whom lithium may be contraindicated.

Anticonvulsant Drugs to Treat Bipolar Disorder		
Drug	**Daily 1 Dose/Therapeutic Blood Level**	**Side Effects**
carbemazapine (Tegretol)	300–1,200 mg Serum level of 6–12 mg/L	Skin rash, sore throat, low-grade fever, mucosal ulceration, ataxia, vertigo, nausea, vomiting, hepatotoxicity, benign < WBC, agranulocytosis
valproic acid/valproate (Depakene/Depakote)	500–1,000 mg Serum level of 50–125 mcg/mL	Anorexia, nausea, vomiting, diarrhea, tremor, sedation, ataxia
clonazepam (Klonapin)	4–24 mg	Ataxia, drowsiness, increased salivation
lamotrigine (Hamictal)	200–500 mg	Dizziness, sedation, headache, diplopia, ataxia. Rash occurs in about 10% of all cases.

CHAPTER 31: EXERCISE ANSWERS

1. Review the five rights of medication administration: **client**, **dose**, **drug**, **route**, and **time**

2. **G** **tardive dyskinesia**—Irreversible side effect of antipsychotic medication causing a syndrome of symptoms characterized by bizarre facial and tongue movements, stiff neck, and difficulty swallowing.

3. **A** **agranulocytosis**—Potentially fatal blood disorder in which the client's white blood cells drop to dangerously low levels. Associated with antipsychotic medications, in particular clozapine (Clozaril).

4. **C** **dystonia**—Involuntary movement or spasms of the face, arms, legs, and neck; usually an acute side effect of antipsychotic medication.

5. **E** **oculogyric crisis**—Uncontrollable upward or rolling back movement of the eyes; may occur as an extrapyramidal side effect of antipsychotic drugs.

6. **D** **neuroleptic malignant syndrome**—Rare but potentially fatal complication of treatment with neuroleptic drugs. Symptoms include severe muscle rigidity, high fever, tachycardia, fluctuating blood pressure, diaphoresis, and rapid deterioration of mental status into stupor and coma.

7. **B** **akathesia**—Sensation of restlessness or a feeling of the need to move; shifting from one foot to the other. An extrapyramidal side effect of antipsychotic medications.

8. **F** **pseudoparkinsonism**—Symptoms of drooling, shuffling gait, tremor and rigidity, mask-like face, pill-rolling of the fingers, and cogwheel rigidity that may occur early in treatment with antipsychotic medications.

CHAPTER 31: NCLEX-RN STYLE QUESTIONS

1. A nurse is conducting an in-service program on psychotropic medications for other staff nurses. In discussing the mechanism of action (MOA) for benzodiazepines versus nonbenzodiazepines, the nurse needs to emphasize that the nonbenzodiazepines

   (1) have a decreased risk of dependency.
   (2) cause central nervous system depression.
   (3) are categorized as a controlled substance.
   (4) activate γ-aminobutyric acid (GABA).

2. A client who has schizoaffective disorder has been taking haloperidol (Haldol) for several months. Recently, lithium (Lithane) was added to the medication regime. The nurse in the outpatient program should carefully monitor which of the following due to the combination of these two drugs?

   (1) Decreased need to sleep and a surge of energy
   (2) Increased appetite and a weight gain of 5 pounds
   (3) Fluctuating level of consciousness, confusion, disorientation
   (4) Complaints of flu-like symptoms, including a temperature of 100°F

3. A client who is diagnosed with obsessive compulsive disorder is taking clomipramine (Anafranil). The nurse is aware that the most common side effects of this drug are

   (1) insomnia and weakness.
   (2) incontinence and muscle twitching.
   (3) urinary retention and fatigue.
   (4) memory loss and depressed appetite.

4. A psychiatric client is receiving temazepam (Restoril). The client tells the nurse, "I'm feeling dizzy, and I can't think right." What would be an appropriate response by the nurse?

(1) "Try to get some rest and you will feel better."
(2) "That is because you're not eating. With the medication you're taking you must eat to feel better."
(3) "The dizziness and confusion you are experiencing are common side effects of the drugs you are taking."
(4) "Don't worry, the dizziness will go away in a few days."

5. A client is prescribed haloperidol (Haldol) 10 mg po hs. In teaching the client about self-administration, for which of the following side effects should the nurse emphasize that the client seek immediate medical attention?

(1) Drowsiness
(2) Increased urine output
(3) Metallic taste and diarrhea
(4) Restlessness and muscle spasms

6. A client has been very despondent, withdrawn, and apathetic for about 6 months. Recently, the client began to attend an outpatient clinic for treatment of depressive disorder. Fluoxetine HCl (Prozac) is prescribed, and after 3 days the client shows improvement. What is the most appropriate nursing intervention at this time?

(1) Assess the client's knowledge about the medication.
(2) Encourage the client to interact with other clients.
(3) Discuss long-term plans for discharge and follow-up.
(4) Evaluate the potential for self-destructive behaviors.

7. In evaluating a client's compliancy to lithium therapy, the nurse would assess an improved clinical response and a therapeutic lithium level of

(1) 0.1–0.3 mEq/L
(2) 0.3–0.5 mEq/L
(3) 1.0–1.2 mEq/L
(4) 1.5–1.8 mEq/L

8. A client has been attending the partial hospitalization program for several weeks. Clozapine (Clozaril) 100 mg po tid is prescribed. Today the client did not come for a scheduled appointment and when the nurse telephoned the client, it was stated that he had a "fever and sore throat." The nurse interprets these complaints as the client experiencing

(1) allergic reaction.
(2) agranulocytosis.
(3) conversion disorder.
(4) serotonin syndrome.

9.	A client is receiving fluphenazine (Prolixin). During a scheduled appointment to the outpatient unit, the client complains of an inability to sit still and a need to pace. The nurse, in evaluating this client, expects that he may be experiencing	(1) akathesia. (2) akinesia. (3) anticholinergic crisis. (4) another episode of his psychiatric symptoms.
10.	A client has just been placed on haloperidol (Haldol) for a psychosis. When doing an assessment, the nurse finds that the client is displaying tongue thrusting and jerky movements of the extremities. The client asks why this is happening. The nurse's best response is	(1) "You have developed Huntington's chorea, which is a side effect of the drug you're taking." (2) "You're having extrapyramidal side effects." (3) "You're having tardive dyskinesia, which is a side effect of the drug you're taking." (4) "You're having akathesia, which is a side effect of the drug you're taking."

CHAPTER 31: NCLEX-RN STYLE ANSWERS

1.
(1) CORRECT	There is no indication that physical or psychological dependence develops with the nonbenzodiazepine class of drugs.
(2) ELIMINATE	True of the benzodiazepine class of drugs.
(3) ELIMINATE	True of the benzodiazepine class of drugs.
(4) ELIMINATE	True of the benzodiazepine class of drugs.

CATEGORY 08 PHARMACOLOGICAL AND PARENTERAL THERAPIES

2.
(3) CORRECT	Potential encephalopathic syndrome can occur with this combination.
(1) ELIMINATE	More characteristic of a manic episode.
(2) ELIMINATE	Not applicable.
(4) ELIMINATE	More characteristic of agranulocytosis.

CATEGORY 08 PHARMACOLOGICAL AND PARENTERAL THERAPIES

3.
(3) CORRECT	These are side effects of Anafranil. Other side effects are dry mouth, dizziness, seizures, and sexual dysfunction.
(1) ELIMINATE	Not the most common side effects of Anafranil.
(2) ELIMINATE	Not the most common side effects of Anafranil.
(4) ELIMINATE	Not the most common side effects of Anafranil.

CATEGORY 08 PHARMACOLOGICAL AND PARENTERAL THERAPIES

4.   (3) CORRECT   Dizziness, confusion, drowsiness, and euphoria are common side effects of Restoril.

       (1) *ELIMINATE*   This response ignores the concerns the client has expressed.

       (2) *ELIMINATE*   The symptoms expressed by the client have nothing to do with food intake.

       (4) *ELIMINATE*   This response ignores the concerns the client has expressed.

CATEGORY 08 PHARMACOLOGICAL AND PARENTERAL THERAPIES

---

5.   (4) CORRECT   These are characteristics of the extrapyramidal reactions (akathesia and dystonia) for which the client should be administered a stat dose of an anticholinergic medication.

       (1) *ELIMINATE*   Drowsiness may occur when initially taking haloperidol. The client should be informed about postural changes and taking the scheduled doses at bedtime. It does not require immediate medical attention.

       (2) *ELIMINATE*   Increased urine output is not associated with Haldol.

       (3) *ELIMINATE*   Metallic taste and diarrhea are not associated with Haldol.

CATEGORY 08 PHARMACOLOGICAL AND PARENTERAL THERAPIES

---

6.   (4) CORRECT   Antidepressant therapy may take 1–6 weeks for the client to demonstrate an improvement and reduction of suicidal behaviors.

       (1) *POSSIBLE*   This should be done, but only after the risk of suicide has been evaluated.

       (2) *POSSIBLE*   This is not the most appropriate nursing intervention at this time.

       (3) *POSSIBLE*   This would be done at a later date.

CATEGORY 06 PYSCHOSOCIAL ADAPTATION

---

7.   (3) CORRECT   An improved clinical response usually corresponds with this therapeutic range.

       (1) *ELIMINATE*   Not an appropriate level.

       (2) *ELIMINATE*   Not an appropriate level.

       (4) *ELIMINATE*   Not an appropriate level.

CATEGORY 08 PHARMACOLOGICAL AND PARENTERAL THERAPIES

8.
(2)	CORRECT	A side effect of Clozaril is agranulocytosis.
(1)	*ELIMINATE*	Signs of allergy include rash, hives, and a lump in the throat.
(3)	*ELIMINATE*	A conversion disorder occurs when a client manifests symptoms of an illness, but with this medication the symptoms indicate a severe adverse effect.
(4)	*ELIMINATE*	The symptoms described do not relate to serotonin syndrome.

CATEGORY 08 PHARMACOLOGICAL AND PARENTERAL THERAPIES

9.
(1)	CORRECT	This is a subjective feeling of restlessness and agitation due to the antipsychotic medication.
(2)	*ELIMINATE*	This is a slowing or absence of movement often associated with pseudoparkinsonism.
(3)	*ELIMINATE*	Not applicable.
(4)	*ELIMINATE*	The complaints are specific and relate directly to the client receiving the antipsychotic medication.

CATEGORY 08 PHARMACOLOGICAL AND PARENTERAL THERAPIES

10.
(3)	CORRECT	Tardive dyskinesia is an unwanted and disfiguring side effect that occurs in some people who take neuroleptics.
(1)	*ELIMINATE*	The client has not developed Huntington's chorea.
(2)	*ELIMINATE*	These are not extrapyramidal side effects.
(4)	*ELIMINATE*	This is not akathesia.

CATEGORY 08 PHARMACOLOGICAL AND PARENTERAL THERAPIES

APPENDIX 1

LIST OF STATE BOARDS AND ADDITIONAL REQUIREMENTS FOR LICENSURE

In most states, licensure depends on the state board's receipt of the candidate's final academic transcript from an accredited, registered nursing program and the candidate's passing the NCLEX-RN. Some states require continuing education credits soon after licensure. There are constant changes in what each state requires, so be sure you continue to get updated information from your state board of nursing.

Alabama

Alabama Board of Nursing
PO Box 303900
Montgomery, AL 36130
334-242-4060

Alaska

Alaska Board of Nursing
Dept. of Comm. and Econ. Development
Div. of Occupational Licensing
3601 C Street, Suite 722
Anchorage, AK 99503
907-269-8161

American Samoa

American Samoa Health Service
  Regulatory Board
LBJ Tropical Medical Center
Pago Pago, AS 96799
011-684-633-1222

Arizona

Arizona State Board of Nursing
1651 E. Morten Avenue, Suite 150
Phoenix, AZ 85020
602-255-5092

Arkansas

Arkansas State Board of Nursing
University Tower Building
1123 S. University, Suite 800
Little Rock, AR 72204
501-686-2700

California

California Board of Registered Nursing
PO Box 944210
Sacramento, CA 94244
916-322-3350
Additional Requirements: Fingerprinting

Colorado

Colorado Board of Nursing
1560 Broadway, Suite 670
Denver, CO 80202
303-894-2430

Connecticut

Connecticut Board of Examiners for
  Nursing/Dept. of Public Health Nurse
  Licensure
150 Washington Street
Hartford, CT 06106
860-509-7624

Delaware

Delaware Board of Nursing
Cannon Building, Suite 203
PO Box 1401
Dover, DE 19903
302-739-4522

District of Columbia

District of Columbia Board of Nursing
614 H Street, NW
Washington, DC 20001
202-727-7454

Florida

Florida Board of Nursing
4080 Woodcock Drive, Suite 202
Jacksonville, FL 32207
904-858-6940

Georgia

Georgia Board of Nursing
166 Pryor Street, SW
Atlanta, GA 30303
404-656-3943

Guam

Guam Board of Nurse Examiners
PO Box 2816
Agana, GU 96910
011-671-475-0251

Hawaii

Hawaii Board of Nursing
PO Box 3469
Honolulu, HI 96801
808-586-2695

Idaho

Idaho Board of Nursing
PO Box 83720
Boise, ID 83720-0061
208-334-3110

Illinois

Illinois Department of
  Professional Regulation
320 West Washington Street, 3rd Floor
Springfield, IL 62786
217-785-9465

Indiana

Indiana State Board of Nursing
Health Professions Bureau
402 W. Washington Street, Room 041
Indianapolis, IN 46204
317-232-2960

Iowa

Iowa Board of Nursing
State Capitol Complex
1223 East Court Avenue
Des Moines, IA 50319
515-281-3255

Kansas

Kansas State Board of Nursing
Landon State Office Building
900 SW Jackson, Suite 551-S
Topeka, KS 66612
913-296-4929

Kentucky

Kentucky Board of Nursing
312 Wittington Parkway, Suite 300
Louisville, KY 40222
502-329-7000
Additional Requirements: Two hours of
  Kentucky Cabinet for Health Services-
  approved HIV/AIDS education

Louisiana

Louisiana State Board of Nursing
912 Pere Marquette Building
150 Baronne Street
New Orleans, LA 70112
504-838-5332

Maine

Maine State Board of Nursing
State House Station, #158
Augusta, ME 04333
207-624-5275

Maryland

Maryland Board of Nursing
4140 Patterson Avenue
Baltimore, MD 21215
410-764-5124

Massachusetts

Massachusetts Board of Registration
  in Nursing
Leverett Saltonstall Building
100 Cambridge Street, Room 1519
Boston, MA 02202
617-727-9961

Michigan

Bureau of Occupational and
  Professional Regulation
Michigan Department of Commerce
Ottawa Towers N., 611 W. Ottawa
Lansing, MI 48933
517-373-1600

Minnesota

Minnesota Board of Nursing
2700 University Avenue West, #108
St. Paul, MN 55114
612-642-0567

Mississippi

Mississippi Board of Nursing
239 N. Lamar Street, Suite 401
Jackson, MS 39201
601-359-6170

Missouri

Missouri State Board of Nursing
PO Box 656
Jefferson City, MO 65102
573-751-0681

Montana

Montana State Board of Nursing
111 North Jackson
PO Box 200513
Helena, MT 59620
406-444-2071

Nebraska

Division of Professional and Occupational
  Licensure
Nebraska Department of Health
PO Box 95007
Lincoln, NE 68509
402-471-2115

Nevada

Nevada State Board of Nursing
PO Box 46886
Las Vegas, NV 89114
702-739-1575
Additional Requirements: Fingerprinting

New Hampshire

New Hampshire Board of Nursing
Health and Welfare Building
6 Hazen Drive
Concord, NH 03301
603-271-2323

New Jersey

New Jersey Board of Nursing
PO Box 45010
Newark, NJ 07101
201-504-6493

New Mexico

New Mexico Board of Nursing
4206 Louisiana Boulevard, NE, Suite A
Albuquerque, NM 87109
505-841-8340

New York

New York State Board of Nursing
State Education Department
Cultural Education Center, Room 3023
Albany, NY 12230
518-474-3843
Additional Requirements: Course in
  recognition and reporting of child abuse

North Carolina

North Carolina Board of Nursing
PO Box 2129
Raleigh, NC 27602
919-782-3211

North Dakota

North Dakota Board of Nursing
919 South 7th Street, Suite 504
Bismarck, ND 58504
701-328-9777

North Mariana Islands

Commonwealth Board of Nurse Examiners
Public Health Center
PO Box 1458
Saipan, MP 96950
011-670-234-8950

Ohio

Ohio Board of Nursing
77 South High Street, 17th Floor
Columbus, OH 43266
614-466-3947

Oklahoma

Oklahoma Board of Nursing
2915 N. Classen Boulevard, Suite 524
Oklahoma City, OK 73106
405-525-2076

Oregon

Oregon State Board of Nursing
800 NE Oregon Street, Box 25, Suite 465
Portland, OR 97232
503-731-4745

Pennsylvania

Pennsylvania State Board of Nursing
PO Box 2649
Harrisburg, PA 17105
717-783-7142

Puerto Rico

Commonwealth of Puerto Rico
Board of Nurse Examiners
Call Box 10200
Santurce, PR 00908
809-725-8161

Rhode Island

Rhode Island Board of Nurse Registration
and Nursing Education
Cannon Health Building
Three Capitol Hill, Room 104
Providence, RI 02908
401-277-2827

South Carolina

South Carolina State Board of Nursing
220 Executive Center Drive, Suite 220
Columbia, SC 29210
803-731-1648

South Dakota

South Dakota Board of Nursing
3307 South Lincoln Avenue
Sioux Falls, SD 57105
605-367-5940

Tennessee

Tennessee State Board of Nursing
283 Plus Park Boulevard
Nashville, TN 37217
615-367-6232

Texas

Texas Board of Nurse Examiners
PO Box 140466
Austin, TX 78714
512-305-7400

Utah

Utah State Board of Nursing
Division of Occupational and Professional
Licensing
PO Box 45805
Salt Lake City, UT 84145
801-355-5009

Vermont

Vermont State Board of Nursing
109 State Street
Montpelier, VT 05609
802-828-2396

Virginia

Virginia Board of Nursing
6606 W. Broad Street, 4th Floor
Richmond, VA 23230
804-662-9909

Virgin Islands

Virgin Islands Board of Nurse Licensure
PO Box 4247
Veterans Drive Station
St. Thomas, VI 00803
809-776-7397

Washington

Washington State Nursing Care Quality
   Assurance Commission
Department of Health
PO Box 47864
Olympia, WA 98504
360-753-2686

West Virginia

West Virginia Board of Examiners for
   Registered Professional Nurses
101 Dee Drive
Charleston, WV 25311
304-558-3596

Wisconsin

Wisconsin Department of Regulation
   and Licensing
1400 E. Washington Avenue
PO Box 8935
Madison, WI 53708
608-266-0257

Wyoming

Wyoming State Board of Nursing
2020 Carey Avenue, Suite 110
Cheyenne, WY 82002
307-777-7601

APPENDIX 2

PREFIXES AND SUFFIXES

No matter how much you prepare for the NCLEX-RN, you will no doubt be faced with words you've never seen. This is normal. You can help yourself out on the test by learning the meanings of parts of the words. Medical terminology can often be broken down to help you understand the word and make the best guess on a multiple choice exam, or at least eliminate a few choices, giving yourself a better chance of finding the best answer. Making flashcards is helpful in memorizing the list below.

The following list was taken from *Introduction to Medical Science on a Basis of Pathology*, by Charles G. Darlington, MD, and Grace G. Appleton, MA, RN (JB Lippincott Company, Philadelphia, 1942).

acr- pertaining to extremity: acrodermatitis, a dermatitis of the limbs

aden- pertaining to a gland: adenitis, inflammation of a gland

bio- pertaining to life: biopsy, inspection of living organism (or tissue)

bleph- pertaining to the eyelids: blepharitis, inflammation of an eyelid

cardi- pertaining to the heart: cardialgia, pain in the heart

cephal- pertaining to the head: cephalalgia, headache

cheil- pertaining to the lip: cheilitis, inflammation of the lip

cheir- pertaining to the hand: cheirospasm, writer's cramp

chole- pertaining to bile: cholecyst, the gallbladder

chondr- pertaining to the cartilage: chrondrectomy, removal of cartilage

cleid- pertaining to the clavicle: cleidocostal, pertaining to the clavicle and ribs

colp- pertaining to the vagina: colporrhagia, vaginal hemorrhage

cost- pertaining to the ribs: costalgia, pain in the ribs

crani- pertaining to the skull: craniotomy, surgical opening in the skull

crypt- pertaining to anything hidden: cryptogenic, of hidden or unknown origin

cyst- pertaining to any fluid-containing sac: cystitis, inflammation of the bladder

cyt- pertaining to a cell: cytometer, a device for counting and measuring cells

dacry- pertaining to lachrymal glands: dacryocyst, tear sac

derm- (dermat-) pertaining to skin: dermatoid, skin-like

encephal- pertaining to the brain: encephalitis, inflammation of the brain

enter- pertaining to the intestines: enteroptosis, falling of intestine

galact- pertaining to milk: galactose, a milk sugar

gastr- pertaining to the stomach: gastrectomy, excision of the stomach

gynec- pertaining to woman: gynecology, science of diseases pertaining to women

hem- (hemat-) pertaining to blood: hemopoiesis, forming blood

hyster- pertaining to the uterus: hysterectomy, excision of the uterus

kerat- pertaining to horn, cornea: keratitis, inflammation of the cornea

kopr- (copr-) pertaining to feces: coprolith, a fecal concretion

leuk- (leuc-) pertaining to anything white: leukocyte, white cell

mer- part: merotomy, division into segments

metr- pertaining to the uterus: metritis, inflammation of the uterus

my- pertaining to muscle: myoma, tumor made of muscular elements

myc- pertaining to fungi: mycology, science and study of fungi

neo- new: neoplasm, any new growth or formation

nephr- (nephro-) pertaining to the kidney: nephrectomy, surgical excision of the kidney

odont- pertaining to tooth: odontology, dentistry

omo- pertaining to the shoulder: omohyoid, pertaining to shoulder and hyoid bone

oo- pertaining to egg: oocyte, original cell of the egg

oophor- pertaining to the ovary: oophorectomy, removal of an ovary

ophthalm- pertaining to the eye: ophthalmometer, an instrument for measuring the eye

oss- pertaining to bone: osseous, bony

oste- pertaining to bone: osteitis, inflammation of a bone

ot- (oto-) pertaining to the ear: otorrhea, discharge from the ear

ovar- pertaining to the ovary: ovariorrhexis, rupture of an ovary

path- pertaining to disease: pathology, science of disease

ped- pertaining to feet: pedograph, imprint of the foot

ped- (pedia-, pedo-) pertaining to children: pediatrician, child specialist

pneum- (pneumon-) pertaining to lung (pneum = air): pneumococcus, organism causing lobar pneumonia

polio- gray: poliomyelitis, inflammation of the gray substance of the spinal cord

proct- pertaining to the anus: proctectomy, surgical removal of the rectum

psych- pertaining to the soul or mind: psychiatry, treatment of mental disorders

py- pertaining to pus: pyorrhea, discharge of pus

pyel- pertaining to the pelvis: pyelitis, inflammation of the pelvis or kidney

rach- pertaining to the spine: rachicentesis, puncture into the vertebral canal

rhin- pertaining to the nose: rhinology, knowledge concerning noses

salping- pertaining to a tube: salpingitis, inflammation of a tube

sapr- pertaining to pus or decomposition: saprophyte, vegetable organism living on dead or decaying vegetable matter

septic- pertaining to poison: septicemia, poisoned condition of blood

tox- (toxic-) pertaining to poison: toxemia, poisoned condition of blood

trache- pertaining to the trachea: tracheitis, inflammation of the trachea

trich- pertaining to the hair: trichosis, any disease of the hair

zoo- pertaining to animal: zooblast, an animal cell

PREFIXES

a- (ab-) away, lack of: abnormal, departing from normal

a- (an-) from without: asepsis, without infection

ab- away; abduction

ad- to, toward, near: adrenal, near the kidney

ambi- both: ambidextrous, referring to both hands

ante- before: antenatal, occurring—or formed—before birth

anti- against: antiseptic, against or preventing sepsis

auto- self: auto-intoxication, poisoning by toxin generated in the body

bi- (bin-) two: binocular, pertaining to both eyes

brady- slow: bradycardia, abnormal slowness of heartbeat

circum- around: circumocular, around the eyes

contra- against, opposed: contraindication, opposing usually indicated treatment

counter- against: counter-irritation, an irritation to relieve some other irritation (as a liniment)

di- two: diphasic, occurring in two stages or phases

dis- apart: disarticulation, taking a joint apart

dys- pain or difficulty: dyspepsia, impairment of digestion

ecto- outside: ectoretina, outermost layer of the retina

em- (en-) in: encapsulated, enclosed in a capsule

end- (endo-) within: endothelium, layer of cells lining heart, blood, and lymph vessels

epi- above or upon: epidermis, outermost layer of skin

erythro- red: erythrocyte, red blood cell

eu- well: euphoria, well feeling or feeling of good health

ex- (e-) out: excretion, material thrown out of the body or an organ

exo- outside: exocrine, excreting outwardly (opposite of endocrine)

extra- outside: extramural, situated or occurring outside a wall

glyco- sugar: glycosuria, sugar in the urine

hemi- half: heminephrectomy, excision of half the kidney

hetero- other (opposite of homo-): heterotransplant, skin grafting using skin from a member of another species

homo- same: homotransplant, skin grafting using skin from a member of the same species

hyper- above, excess of: hyperglycemia, excess of sugar in the blood

hypo- under, deficiency of: hypoglycemia, deficiency of sugar in the blood

im- (in-) in: infiltration, accumulation of abnormal substances in tissue

im- (in-) not: immature, not mature

infra- below: infraorbital, below the orbit

inter- between: intermuscular, between muscles

intra- within: intramuscular, within the muscle

macro- large: macroblast, abnormally large red cell

meg- (megal-, megalo-) great: megacolon, abnormally large colon

mesa- middle: mesaortitis, inflammation of the middle coat of the aorta

micro- small: microplasia, dwarfism

mycet- fungus: mycetona, tumor caused by fungus

olig- little: oligemia, deficiency in volume of blood

para- wrong, irregular; in the neighborhood of, around: paradenitis, inflammation of tissue in the vicinity of a gland

per- through, excessively: percutaneous, through the skin

peri- around, immediately around (in contradistinction to para-): periapical, surrounding the apex of a root to a tooth

poly- many: polydactylism, many fingers, i.e., more than the usual five

post- after: postpartum, after childbirth

pre- before: prenatal, occurring before birth

pro- (prol-, prog-) before: prognosis, forecast as to the result of disease

pseud- false: pseudoangina, false angina

retro- backward: retroversion; turned backward (usually, of uterus)

semi- half: semicoma, mild coma

sub- under: subdiaphragmatic, under the diaphragm

super- above, excessively: superacute, excessively acute

supra- above, upon: suprarenal, above or upon the kidney

sym- (syn-) with, together: symphysis, a growing together

tachy- fast: tachycardia, fast beating heart

trans- across: transplant, transfer tissue from one place to another

tri- three: trigastric, having three bellies (muscle)

uni- one: unilateral, affecting one side

SUFFIXES

-algia pain: cardialgia, pain in the heart

-asis (-osis) affected with: leukocytosis, excess number of leukocytes

-asthenia weakness: neurasthenia, nervous weakness

-blast an immature cell: myeloblast, bone marrow cell

-cele tumor, hernia: enterocele, any hernia of the intestine

-clysis injection: hypodermoclysis, injection under the skin

-coccus round bacterium: *Pneumococcus*, bacteria of pneumonia

-cyte cell: leukocyte, white cell

-ectasis (-asis, -osis) dilatation, stretching: angiectasis, dilatation of a blood vessel (the word for stretching comes from the Greek, ekt or ect)

-ectomy excision: adenectomy, excision of the adenoids

-emia blood: glycemia, sugar in the blood

-esthesia relating to sensation: anesthesia, absence of feeling

-genic producing: pyogenic, producing pus

-iatric pertaining to a physician or the practice of healing (medicine): pediatrics, science of medicine for children

-itis inflammation: tonsillitis, inflammation of the tonsils

-logy science: pathology, science of disease

-lysis losing, flowing, dissolution: autolysis, dissolution of tissue cells

-malacia softening: osteomalacia, softening of bone

-megaly enlarged: splenomegaly, enlarged spleen

-oma tumor: myoma, tumor made up of muscle elements

-osis (-asis) disease or condition: arteriosclerosis, a condition of the arterial walls

-(o)stomy creation of an opening: gastrostomy, creation of an artificial gastric fistula

-(o)tomy cutting into: laparotomy, surgical incision into the abdomen

-pathy disease: myopathy, disease of a muscle

-penia lack of: leukopenia, lack of white blood cells

-pexy to fix: proctopexy, fixation of rectum by suture

-phagia eating: polyphagia, excessive eating

-phasia speech: aphasia, loss of power of speech

-phobia fear: hydrophobia, fear of water

-plasty molding: gastroplasty, molding or re-forming the stomach

-poiesis making, forming: hematopoiesis, forming blood

-pnea air or breathing: dyspnea, difficult breathing

-ptosis falling: enteroptosis, falling of intestine

-rhythmia rhythm: arrhythmia, variation from normal rhythm of the heart

-rrhagia excessive flow or bursting forth: otorrhagia, hemorrhage from ear

-rrhaphy suture of: enterorrhaphy, act of sewing up a gap in the intestine

-rrhea profuse discharge: otorrhea, discharge from the ear

-rrhexis rupture: cardiorrhexis, rupture of the heart

-sthen (**-sthenia**, **-sthenic**) pertaining to strength: asthenia, loss of strength

-taxia (**-taxis**) order, arrangement of: ataxia, failure of muscular coordination

-trophia (**-trophy**) nourishment: atrophy, wasting or diminution

-ultation act of: auscultation, listening for sound in body

-uria to do with urine: polyuria, excessive secretion of urine

INDEX

A

Abdominal cavity
    assessment of, infant, 311, 322
    disorders of, 121-122
    x-ray, 155
Abducent nerve, 29, 309, 321
Abduction, 165, 312
ABO incompatibility, 286
Abortion, 430
Abruptio placentae, 430, 442
Absence seizures, 38
Abuse
    child, 333-334, 338, 552
    types of, 552
Acetaminophen (Tylenol), 92, 261
Acetylcholine, 26
Acetylcysteine (Mucomyst), 92
Acid-base balance, 82-83, 94
    diarrhea and, 318
Acidosis, 83, 93
    newborn, 278
Acinar cells, 211
Acne vulgaris, 194, 355, 358
Acrocyanosis, 298
Actelectasis, 86
Active transport, 153

Acute brain syndrome, 549-550
Acute diarrhea, 318
Acute lymphocytic leukemia (A.L.L.), 371
Acute myelogenous leukemia (A.M.L.), 371
Acute renal failure, 146-147
Acyclovir (Zovirax), 361
Adaptation, 529
Addison's disease, 211, 213
Adduction, 165, 312
Adenosarcoma, 231
ADH, 154
Adolescence, 353-367
    assessment in, 354-358, 366
    cognitive development in, 393, 395
    common health problems of, 358-359
    defined, 254, 353
    as developmental stage, 254, 259, 409, 412, 535
    eating disorders in, 364, 365, 552
    health promotion during, 358-359
    intramuscular injections in, 483, 484
    nutrition in, 452-453, 452
        eating disorders and, 363, 364, 552
        pregnancy and, 453, 459
    pregnancy in, 363, 365, 453, 459
    rape, 364
    sexual activity in, 361-362, 366
    substance use in, 408, 409, 453

suicide in, 410
vital signs in, 257, 409
Adrenal cortex, 202
Adrenal glands, 203, 210-211
    disorders of, 210-211
        Addison's disease, 211, 213
        Conn's syndrome, 211, 213
        Cushing's syndrome, 211, 213
    function of, 210
Adrenocorticotropic hormone (ACTH), 202
Adulthood
    early, 254, 410
    late, 410, 411, 457-458
    middle, 410, 411
    nutrition in, 453-458
    young, 254, 411
Adult respiratory distress syndrome (A.R.D.S.), 84-85, 284
Adventitious breath sounds, 79-80, 93
Afferent arterioles, 153
Afferent neurons, 27
Afterload, 68
Agnosia, 33, 48
Agranulocytosis, 566, 577
Airway, breathing, and circulation (ABC), 501, 507
Akathisia
    from antipsychotic medication, 566, 577
    in oncology clients, 231-232
Akinesia, 565
Albuterol (Proventil), 92
Alkalosis, 82, 93
Allergy
    food, 314, 450, 451, 459
    to medication, 482
    skin allergy testing, 196
Alopecia, 348
Alprazolam (Xanax), 570
Altered level of consciousness, 38, 39, 48, 508
Aluminum hydroxide (amphogel), 147
Alveolocapillary membrane, 93
Amblyopia, 395
Ambulation aids, 174
Amenorrhea, 566
American Academy of Pediatrics, 314-315, 415
American Burn Association, 190
American Psychiatric Association, 541
Aminophylline (Amoline), 92
Amitriptyline (Elavil), 572
Amniocentesis, 427-428
Amputation, 169
Analgesic medication, 122, 228-229, 232, 243, 261-262, 264, 438
Anal stage, 412, 527, 535
Anemia, 231, 380
    of newborn, 287
    in pregnancy, 364
    sickle cell, 373-374, 380

Anergy, 245
Anesthetic medication, 438, 545
Aneurysms, 41
Angina, 63
Anorexia nervosa, 363, 364, 532
Antacids, 106, 111, 123-124, 147
Antepartum period, 426-435
    assessment in, 427-428
    diagnostic tests during, 287, 426, 429
    physical changes during, 427
    potential complications during, 429-435
    risk factors, 430
Antianxiety medication, 569-572
    benzodiazepines, 570, 572
    BuSpar, 570, 572, 577
    side effects of, 571
    summary of, 570
Antibiotics, 85, 142-149, 317, 319, 334, 346, 361, 362
Anticholinergics, 91, 124
Anticholinesterase medication, 43
Anticonvulsant medication, 38, 576
Antidepressant medication, 572-575
    characteristics of, 573-574
    MAO inhibitors, 573, 574-577
    summary of, 573
Antidiarrheal medication, 124
Anti-DNA, 176
Antiemetics, 124
Antifungal medication, 287
Antihistamines, 91-92, 571
Antihypertensive medication, 147
Antiinflammatory agents, 91
Antimanic medication, 575-576, 578
    anticonvulsants, 576
    lithium carbonate, 575-576
Antinausea medication, 231
Antiparkinsonian agents, 568-569, 577
Antipsychotic medication, 562-567, 577
    side effects of, 564-566
    summary of, 562-563
Antiretroviral medication, 244
Antisocial personality disorder, 557
Antituberculosis medication, 92
Antitussive medication, 92
Antiviral medication, 361
Anus, imperforate, 294
Anxiety, 467, 556
Anxiety disorders, 542-543, 556
    antianxiety agents, 569-572, 577
    crisis intervention for, 543, 556
    nursing interventions for, 542
Anxiolytic medication, 569
Aortic insufficiency, 73
Aortic valve, 68
Apgar scoring, 273-274, 297, 441
Aphasia, 33, 48

Apnea, 93
  infant, 316, 322
  newborn, 278, 297
Apneustic breathing, 34, 48
Appendicitis, 117
Apraxia, 33, 48
Arterial blood gases (A.B.G.'s), 82-83
Arteries, 70
  arteriovenous (A-V) fistula, 148
  renal, 153, 156
Arthrography, 177
Arthroscopy, 177
Ascites, 114
Aspartame, 456
Associations, loosening of, 536
Asthma, 84
  childhood, 370-371, 382, 394
Astigmatism, 395
Ataxic breathing, 34, 48, 94
Atelectasis, 70
Atonic seizures, 37
Atopic dermatitis (eczema), 316
Atria, 68
Atrial septal defect (A.S.D.), 290, 291
Atrioventricular node, 57, 68
Atrioventricular valves, 60
Atropine sulfate, 91
Attention deficit disorder, 349
Auscultation, 310
Autoimmune disorders, myasthenia gravis, 42-43
Autonomic nervous system (A.N.S.), 26
  newborn, 276
  See also Nervous system
Autonomy, 517
Autonomy vs. shame and doubt, 254, 337, 535
Autosomal defects, 414
Avoidant personality disorder, 557
Azathioprine (Imuran), 158
Azotorrhea, 371
AZT. See ZDV (Retrovir)

B

Babinski reflex, 298, 441
Bacterial infections
  brain abscess, 40
  cancer and, 225, 227
  cardiovascular system, 72
  encephalitis, 40
  epiglottitis, 317, 335-336, 339
  infant, 319
  meningitis, 39
  newborn, 287-288
  pneumonia, 85
  respiratory system, 85
  urinary tract, 142-143, 319

Balanced suspension traction, 171, 179
Barbiturates, 37
Barium enema/swallow, 125, 318
Barrier contraception (safe sex), 221, 362, 364
Basal cell carcinoma, 195
Basal metabolic rate, during pregnancy, 427
Beclomethasone (Vanceril, Beclovent), 91
Behavioral model, 528
Behavioral problems. See Psychosocial development
Bell's palsy, 44
Beneficence, 517
Benign prostatic hypertrophy (B.P.H.), 151, 222
Benzodiazepines, 569, 571
Bereavement, 553
Beta-adrenergic agonists, 370
Bilirubin, 287
Biomedical model, 528-529
Biopsy, 193
  liver, 126
  renal, 156
Biot's (ataxic) breathing, 34, 48, 94
Bladder, 138
Blepharitis, 316
Blood
  hemolytic disease, 287
  hemophilia, 371-372
  leukemia, 230, 372-374, 380
  sickle cell anemia, 373-374, 380
Blood glucose, 231
Blood transfusions, 244, 287
Blood type, pregnancy and, 428
Blood urea nitrogen (BUN), 155
Blood vessels, cancer of, 230
Body dysmorphic behavior, 558
Bonding, parent-newborn, 283, 293, 442
Bone marrow suppression, 231, 372
Bone marrow transplants, 380
Bones, 176
  biopsy of, 176
  cancer of, 230
Bone scans, 177
Borderline personality disorder, 556
Brace, spinal, 359-360
Brachial artery, 70
Bradycardia
  fetal, 439
  infant, 322
  newborn, 278
Bradypnea, 322
Brain
  abscess to, 40
  anatomy of, 27
  cancer of, 214
  cerebral palsy, 376-378
  surgery on, 506
  tumors of, 40

Brain stem, 48
Braxton-Hicks contractions, 424, 434, 442
Breast feeding, 289-290, 419, 426
Breasts
    adolescent, 355
    cancer, 231
        examination for, 222
        surgical care plan, 226-228
        tumor staging, 222
    changes during pregnancy, 426
    newborn, 274
Bronchial asthma, 84, 370, 394
Bronchitis, 84
Bronchodilators, 92
Bronchoscopy, 94
Bronchospasm, 507
Brudzinski's sign, 40
Buck's traction, 171, 179
Bulimia, 363, 364, 552
Bundle of His, 57, 67
Bupivacaine, 438
Burns, 189-193, 195, 197, 338
    assessment of, 189-191, 195
    injury intervention, 191-193
BuSpar (buspirone), 570, 571, 577
Buspirone (BuSpar), 570, 571, 577
Butyrophenone, 563

C

Calcium
    levels of, 155, 176, 210, 230
    serum, 213
    supplements, 210
Calcium gluconate, 432
Call bell, 509
Calories, postoperative, 509
Cancer, 219-238
    complications of, 233
    emergencies in, 230
    pain management for, 228-229
    screening guide for, 222
    treatment of
        chemotherapy, 224-226, 232, 371, 380
        radiation therapy, 223-224, 232
        surgery, 226-228
    tumor staging, 222
    types and locations of, 231, 371-372, 380, 384-386, 395
        bone, 231
        breast, 222, 226-228, 231
        cervical, 222, 245
        colorectal, 119, 127, 222, 231
        liver, 222, 231
        lung, 88, 231
        lymphatic, 231
        ovarian, 222

    pancreatic, 115
    prostate, 222, 231, 232
    skin, 188-189, 195
    testes, 222
Candidiasis infection, 245, 287, 307, 316
Canes, 174
Cantor tubes, 119
Caput succedaneum, 297
Carbamazepine (Tegretol), 38, 576
Carbohydrates
    in diet, 127, 449
    metabolism of, 211
Carcinoembryonic antigen (CEA), 222
Carcinogen, 231
Cardiac arrhythmia, 507
Cardiac catheterization, 62
Cardiac glycosides (digoxin), 63, 64, 65, 70, 71
Cardiac output, 68
Cardiogenic shock, 66
Cardiomyopathy, 72
Cardiovascular system, 55-76
    anatomy and physiology of, 56-58
    assessment of, 59-67
        infant, 310
        newborn, 278, 290-292
    disorders of, 63-67
        newborn, 290-292
    heart disease and, 67
    nutrition and, 67
    poisoning and, 333
    during pregnancy, 426
Cartilage, 176
    cancer of, 231
    newborn, 280
Casts, 173
Cataracts, 395
Catheters
    cardiac, 62
    for delivering anesthesia, 438
CAT scans, 125
Central nervous system (C.N.S.), 25
    poisoning and, 333
    See also Nervous system
Central neurogenic hyperventilation, 34, 48
Cephalohematoma, 297
Cerebral aneurysms, 41
Cerebral palsy, 378-379, 381-382
    development of, 378
    signs of, 378
Cerebrospinal fluid (C.S.F.), 285
Cerebrovascular accidents (C.V.A.'s), 41
Cervical halters, 171, 179
Cervical tongs, 171, 179
Cervix
    cancer of, 222, 245
    cervical effacement in labor, 434, 435, 436
    changes during pregnancy, 426

dilatation, 434, 435, 436
postpartum, 440
Chadwick's sign, 442
Chalazion, 322
Chancre, 361
Chemoreceptors, 93
Chemotherapy, 224-226, 232, 371, 380
side effects of, 225, 232, 371
Chest, infant, 311
Cheyne-Stokes respirations, 37, 48, 69, 94
Chicken pox, 194, 245, 336, 339
immunization for, 315, 415
Child abuse, 333-334, 338, 414
reporting, 334, 339, 414, 490
Childhood, 253-351
developmental stages of, 254, 258-261, 264, 388, 394. *See also* Preschool period; School-aged period; Toddlerhood
hospitalization in, 254-269, 387-400
chronic illness and, 388-391, 394, 395
cognitive impairments and, 390-391, 394, 395
developmental considerations and, 258-261, 260, 388, 394
discharge planning and, 257, 264-265
informed consent in, 256-257, 264
life-threatening illnesses and, 393, 395
medication administration and, 482-488, 489
nutrition and, 262
pain medication and, 261-262
parental reaction to, 254
parent and child teaching in, 255-256
play therapy and, 256, 264
prioritizing interventions during, 263, 265-266
restraints in, 481, 489
safety considerations during, 479-480
sensory and communication problems and, 391-393, 394-395
vital signs and, 258
nutrition in, 262
pain medication in, 261
Child maltreatment. *See* Child abuse
Chlamydia, 361, 362
Chlordiazepoxide (Librium), 570
Chlorpromazine (Thorazine), 563
Choking, 339, 459
Cholecystectomy, 126, 506
Cholecystitis, 111
Cholesterol, and heart disease prevention, 67
Chondrosarcoma, 231
Chromosomal defects, 413-414
autosomal, 414
diagnostic tests for, 427-428
Down's syndrome, 375-377, 385, 390, 413
fragile X syndrome, 390-391

Klinefelter's syndrome, 413
Turner's syndrome, 413
See also Genetic defects
Chronic bronchitis, 84
Chronic childhood illnesses, 369-386
asthma, 370-371, 377, 394
cerebral palsy, 377-379, 377
cystic fibrosis, 371-372, 377, 394
diabetes mellitus, 372-373, 380, 394, 375
Down's syndrome, 375-377, 390
hemophilia, 373, 394
hospitalization and, 388-390, 394
leukemia, 371-372, 380, 394
sickle cell anemia, 373-375, 380, 413
Chronic diarrhea, 318
Chronic obstructive pulmonary disease (C.O.P.D.), 84
Chronic renal failure, 148
Cimetidine (Tagamet), 106, 124
Circumcision, 284
Cirrhosis, 107, 114
Clang associations, 536
Cleft lip, 293, 299
Cleft palate, 293, 299
Clonazepam (Klonopin), 569, 576
Clozapine (Clozaril), 563
Clubbing, 84, 94
Cluster breathing, 34, 48
Coarse crackles, 93
Cognitive development
concept of death and, 393, 395
intelligence quotient (IQ), 390-391, 394, 411
Cognitive disorders, 549-550, 556
Down's syndrome, 375-377, 381-382, 390
hospitalization of children with, 390-391, 394
mental retardation. *See* Mental retardation
nursing interventions for, 550, 556
types of, 549-550
Cognitive framework, 528
Colic, 287, 318, 323
Collecting ducts, 154
Colon, 116-121
anatomy of, 116-117, 125
colorectal cancer, 119, 126, 222, 231
disorders of, 117-121
Colostomy, 120, 125
Colostrum, 441, 459
Coma, diabetic, 212
Communication, in psychiatric nursing, 531-532, 535-536
Compensation, as defense, 530
Computed tomography (CT), 177
Computer adaptive testing (CAT), 3, 6-7
Concrete operational period
characteristics of, 412
concept of death and, 393, 395
Concussion, 44

Condoms, 364
Conduction, heat loss from, 278, 442
Conductive hearing loss, 391
Congenital chordae, 299
Congenital heart disease, 394
Congenital hip dysplasia, 280-282, 322
Congestive heart failure, 63-64
Conjunctivitis, 337, 340
Conn's syndrome, 211, 213
Constipation
    infant, 452, 459
    from medication, 244, 565
    from radiation therapy, 224, 232
Contact dermatitis, 345
Contraception, 363-364, 364
    barrier methods, 221, 362, 364
Contusion, 43, 177
Convection, heat loss from, 278, 442
Conversion, as defense, 530
Conversion disorder, 556
Coordinated care, 489-490
Coronary artery disease, risk factors, 68
Cortex
    adrenal, 202
    brain, 32
    kidney, 153
Cough, 94
    antitussive medication, 92
    reflex, 278
Countertransference, 548
Cradle cap, 316
Cranial nerves
    assessment of, 307-309
    described, 29, 309, 321
    disorders of, 43
Crawl reflex, 298
Creatinine, 155
    clearance test, 138
    normal range, 232
Crohn's disease, 118
Croup (laryngotracheobronchitis), 317, 335-336, 339
Crutches, 174
Crying
    colic and, 287, 318, 323
    infant mouth examination and, 307
    vital signs and, 258
Cryptococcus meningitis, 245
Cryptorchidism (undescended testicles), 280, 295, 299, 322
Cultures, skin, 194
Cushing's syndrome, 211, 213
Cyanosis, 94
    infant, 322
    newborn, 282
Cyclosporine (Sandimmune), 158
Cyclothymia, 556
Cystic fibrosis (C.F.), 371, 382, 394, 413

Cystitis, 142
Cystoscopy, 156
Cystourethrogram, 156
Cytomegalovirus (CMV), 245

D
Dairy products
    as food group, 448
    for infants, 450, 451
DDC (dideoxycytidine), 244
DDI (dideoxyinosine), 244
Death
    children and concept of, 393, 395
    sudden infant death syndrome (S.I.D.S.), 315
    from suicide, 410, 544-545, 555
Decerebration, 32
Decortication, 32
Deep tendon reflexes, 36
Deep vein thrombosis, 44, 507
Defense mechanisms, 530-531, 551
Deformity, bone, 167, 178
Dehydration, 449, 450, 458
    diarrhea and, 318
    in hyperemesis gravidarum, 433-434
    newborn, 278, 279
Delirium, 549, 556
Delirium tremens (D.T.'s), 551
Delusional disorder, 536, 546, 555, 556
Delusions of grandeur, 536
Delusions of persecution, 536
Dementia, 549, 556
Denial
    as defense, 530, 551
    and hospitalization of child, 389
Denver Developmental Screening Test (D.D.S.T.), 411
Dependent personality disorder, 555
Depolarization, 67
Depo-Provera, 364
Depression, 409
    antidepressant medication, 572-575
    dementia vs., 549
    mania vs., 544
    postpartum, 442
Dermatome map, 36
Dermititis, 246, 347
Desipramine (Norpramin), 573
Detoxification and rehabilitation, 551, 552
Developmental delay, 417
Developmental disorders, 287-298
    cardiac, 290-292
    cognitive. See Cognitive disorders; Mental retar
      dation
    failure to thrive (F.T.T.), 318-319
    gastrointestinal, 293-295

genitourinary, 295-296
nervous system, 288-289
Developmental milestones, 416
Developmental stages, 403-419
cognitive, 393, 395
considerations in, 258-261
developmental disorders, 288-296
Erikson's classification of, 254, 337, 348, 364, 404-412
Freud's classification of, 412, 527, 535
hospitalization and, 254, 258-261, 264, 388, 394
Piaget's classification of, 393, 395, 412
play therapy and, 256, 264
teaching methods and, 255-256
vital signs and, 258
See also Adolescence; Infancy; Preschool period; School-aged period; Toddlerhood
Developmental tasks, 416
Dextromethorphan (Pertussin), 92
d4T, 244
Diabetes mellitus (D.M.), 205-207
assessment of, 205
childhood, 372-373, 380, 394
complications of, 206-207
diet for, 455
gestational, 433, 459
insulin administration in, 205-206
maternal, 287
types of, 205-206, 211-212, 372-373
Diabetic ketoacidosis, 212
Diagnostic and Statistical Manual of Mental Disorders (DSM-IV), 541
Dialysis, 148-150, 157-158
Diaper dermititis, 316
Diaphragm (chest), 93, 311
Diaphragm (contraceptive), 364
Diarrhea
antidiarrheals, 124
infant, 318, 452, 449
from medication, 128
in oncology clients, 224, 232
Diastole, 67
Diazepam (Valium), 570
Dibenzodiazepine, 563
Dibenzoxazepine, 563
Diets
phenylketonuria (PKU), 297, 414, 459
special, 207, 221, 454-456
See also Food; Nutrition
Digital rectal exam, 222
Digoxin therapy, 63, 64, 65, 70, 71
Dihydroindolone, 563
Dilantin (phenytoin sodium), 38
Diphtheria, immunization for, 315, 415
Discharge planning
for children, 257, 264
postoperative, 504-506

safety and, 472
Dislocation, 177
Displacement, as defense, 530, 535
Disseminated intravascular coagulation (D.I.C.), 233, 431
Dissociation, as defense, 530, 557
Dissociative amnesia, 557
Dissociative fugue, 557
Dissociative identity disorder, 557
Distal tubules, 154
Diuretic medication, 39, 64, 70, 147
Diverticula, 117
Diverticulitis, 117
Diverticulosis, 117
Documentation
importance of, 466, 467, 468
mistakes in, 466
for psychiatric clients, 516-517
of response to intervention, 467
of restraint use, 481
of safety measures, 480
Dopamine, 26, 42, 147
Dopamine antagonists, 106
Down's syndrome, 375-377, 381-382, 413
characteristics of children with, 376, 391, 413
nursing interventions for, 381
Doxepin hydrochloride (Sinequan), 572
Doxycycline, 361
Dressings
occlusive, 194
open, wet, 194
postoperative, 502-503, 508-509
Drowning, 338
"Dumping syndrome," 110, 455
Duodenal ulcers, 109-110
Dysphagia, 455
Dyspnea, 81, 84, 93
Dyssomnia, 557
Dysthymia, 557
Dystonia, 566, 577
Dysuria, 142, 361

E

Early adulthood, 254, 410
Early childhood. *See* Preschool period; Toddlerhood
Early intervention, 394
Ears
anatomy of, 46
hearing loss, 391, 395
infant, 306
newborn, 274, 275
otic medication, 487
otitis media, 334, 339, 346, 391
Eating disorders, 363, 364, 552

anorexia nervosa, 363, 364, 552
  bulimia, 363, 364, 552
Ecchymosis, 348
Eclampsia, 432
Eczema, 322
Edema, 323
  myxedema, 212-213
  during pregnancy, 429, 432
  pulmonary, 63, 87, 507
  of respiratory mucosa, 317
  tracheal, 507
Efferent (motor) neurons, 27
Ego, 535
Ego integrity vs. despair, 413
Ejection fraction, 68
Electrocardiograms (E.C.G.'s), 60, 69
Electroconvulsive therapy (E.C.T.), 545-546, 555
Electrolytes, 194
  in hyperemesis gravidarum, 433-434
  newborn, 278
  postoperative, 502
Electromyography, 176
ELISA (enzyme-linked immunosorbent assay), 244
Embolism, pulmonary, 87
Emergencies
  oncology, 229-233
  psychiatric crisis intervention, 543, 555-556
Emotional neglect, 333-334, 338, 414
Emphysema, 84
Encephalitis, 40
Endocarditis, 72
Endocardium, 67
Endocrine system, 201-218
  anatomy and physiology of, 202-203
  newborn, 280, 283
Endometrium, 423
Endoscopic retrograde cholangiopancreatography
  (E.R.C.P.), 125
Endoscopic sclerotherapy, 107
Enuresis, 348
Enzymes
  muscle, 176
  pancreatic, 124, 371
Epicardium, 67
Epiglottitis, 317, 335, 339
Epinephrine, 27
Epinephrine HCl (Adrenalin), 92
Equipment, safety of, 467
Eriksonian approach to development, 254, 337, 348,
  364, 404-411, 527, 535
Erythema, 348
Erythema toxicum, 298
Erythromycin, 362
Esophageal hernia (hiatal hernia), 105, 121, 126
Esophageal neoplasms, 106
Esophageal varices, 107, 114, 126
Esophagectomy, 126

Esophagogastrectomy, 126
Esophagus, 105-108, 125-126
  disorders of, 105-106, 125-126
    esophageal hernia, 105, 121-122, 126
    esophageal neoplasms, 106
    esophageal varices, 107, 114, 126
    tracheoesophageal fistula (T.E.F.), 293
Estimated date of confinement (E.D.C.), 427
Estimated date of delivery (E.D.D.), 427
Ethacrynic acid (Edecrin), 71
Ethical issues, 517
  concerning HIV/AIDS, 240
  for psychiatric clients, 516
  rights of drug administration, 95, 232, 466, 472
  substance abuse among nurses, 514
Evaporation, heat loss from, 278, 442
Exercise, for clients with HIV/AIDS, 243
Exophthalmus, 213
Expectorants, 92
Exploratory thoractomy, 94
Extension, 312
External rotation, 312
Extrusion reflex, 313, 441
Eyes
  adolescent, 355
  anatomy of, 45
  chalazion, 322
  conjunctivitis, 336, 339
  exophthalmus, 213
  infant, 322, 323
  newborn, 275-276, 283, 323
  nystagmus, 307, 323
  optic medication, 486
  red retinal reflex, 323
  retinopathy, 212
  visual deficits, 392, 394-395

F

Face shields, as protective gear, 244
Facial nerve, 29, 309, 321
Failure to thrive (F.T.T.), 318-319
Fallopian tubes, 423
Falls, 338
Family intervention, 554
Famotidine (Pepcid), 105, 124
Fantasy, as defense, 530
Fasting blood glucose, 212
Fat, dietary, 127, 231, 449, 450, 456
Fear, 555
Fecal impaction, 232
Federal Americans with Disabilities Act (1990), 240
Femoral artery, 70
Fertilization, 423, 425, 426
Fetal development, 425, 450

Fiber
  chemotherapy and, 226
  colon disorders and, 117, 231
  in diet, 449, 455
Fiberoptic colonoscopy, 125
Fibrosarcoma, 231
Fine crackles, 93
FK506 (Prograf), 158
Flail chest, 86
Flexion, 312
Flight of ideas, 536
Fluid volume, postoperative, 502, 507, 509
Fluoxetine (Prozac), 572
Fluphenazine (Prolixin), 563
Follow up, postoperative, 505
Fontanels
  infant, 306, 321, 323
  newborn, 275, 280, 285
Food
  allergy to, 313-314, 450-451, 459
  hypertensive crisis and, 575
  regurgitation of, 318
  spitting up, 318
  See also Diets; Nutrition
Food groups, 448-450, 459
Formal operational period
  characteristics of, 412
  concept of death and, 393-394, 395
Fracture
  from head injury, 44
  interventions for, 170-177, 179-180
  musculoskeletal system, 169-170, 176-177
Fragile X syndrome, 391
Freudian approach to development, 412, 526-527, 535
Friction rubs, 69
Fundoplication, 106
Furosemide (Lasix), 70

G

Gagging, 459
Gallbladder, 111
  anatomy of, 111
  disorders of, 111, 127
Gallops, 69
Gastric ulcers, 109-110
Gastritis, 108, 126
Gastroduodenostomy (Billroth I), 127
Gastroesophageal reflux disease (G.E.R.D.), 108, 126-127, 452
Gastrointestinal system, 101-132
  anatomy and physiology of, 102-104, 125
  assessment of, 102-104, 125
    infant, 311
    newborn, 280, 293-295
  burns and, 195

disorders of
    abdominal cavity, 121
    colon, 117-120
    esophagus, 105-107
    gallbladder, 111
    infant, 318
    liver, 113-114
    mouth, 94
    newborn, 293-294
    pancreas, 115-116
    stomach, 107-110
  medication for, 123-124
  poisoning and, 333
  postoperative nursing care for, 122-123
  radiation therapy impact on, 224
Gastrojejunostomy (Billroth II), 127
Gastroschisis, 311
Gastrostomy, 126
Gastrostomy tubes, 128
  for children, 489
Gastrourinary system, postpartum, 440
Generalized anxiety, 467
Generativity vs. self-absorption, 411, 535
Genetic counseling, 390
Genetic defects, 412
  cystic fibrosis (C.F.), 371-372, 378, 394, 413
  diagnostic tests for, 428-429
  sickle cell anemia, 373-374, 380, 413
  Tay-Sachs disease, 413, 414
  thalassemia, 413
  See also Chromosomal defects
Genitalia
  adolescent, 355-356
  anatomy of, 422-423
  newborn, 275, 280, 283
  Tanner staging of, 355-356
Genital stage, 412, 527, 531
Genitourinary system, 133-162
  anatomy and physiology of, 134-136, 422-423
  assessment of
    infant, 312
    newborn, 279
  diagnostic studies of, 138-142, 154-156
  disorders of, 142-151
  during pregnancy, 427
Geriatrics. See Late adulthood
German measles. See Rubella
Gestational diabetes, 433, 459
Gestational hypertension, 432-433
Glasgow Coma Scale, 32-33
Glaucoma, 395
Glial tissue cancer, 230
Glioma, 230
Glomerular filtration rate, 153
Glomeruli, 153, 154
Glomerulonephritis, 143-144
Glossopharyngeal nerve, 29, 309, 321
Gloves, as protective gear, 244

Glucagon, 127
Glucose, 147, 230
    blood, 231
Glucose tolerance test, 231
Glycogen, 230
Glycolysated hemoglobin, 231
Gonads, 231
Gonorrhea, 361, 362
Good Samaritan laws, 517
Gout, 167, 176
Gowns, as protective gear, 244
Grand mal (tonic-clonic) seizures, 38, 545
Granisetron (Kytril), 231
Grasping reflex, 277, 280, 298
Graves' disease, 232
Gravida, 442
Grief
    cancer and, 227
    dysfunctional, 553
Group intervention, 554
Growth and development, 403-419
    assessment of, 411
    developmental theory of, 254, 337, 348, 363, 404-
        412, 413
    factors affecting, 413-415
    immunizations and, 314-315, 415
    stages of. See Developmental stages; specific devel
        opmental stages
Guaifenesin (Robitussin), 92
Guillain-Barré syndrome, 49
Gynecomastia, 355

H

H. influenzae Type B
    epiglottitis and, 317
    immunization for, 315, 415
Hair
    in adolescence, 355-358
    pubic, Tanner staging of, 355, 357-358
Hair follicles, 231
Hallucinations, 546, 556
Haloperidol (Haldol), 563
Hands, newborn, 277, 280, 298
Harlequin sign, 298
Head
    circumference, 274, 411
    infant, 306-307
    injuries to, 44, 286
    newborn, 274, 275-276
        intracranial pressure, 286, 299
        molding, 297
Head, eyes, ears, nose, and throat (HEENT), 306-307
Headaches, 39
Hearing loss, 391, 395, 396
Heart
    anatomy of, 56-57, 68, 272, 297

fetal heart monitoring, 438-439
    newborn, 272, 297
    See also Cardiovascular system
Heart sounds, 60
Heat loss, newborn, 278, 442
Heel creases, newborn, 274
Height, measuring, 411
Hemangiosarcoma, 230
Hematocrit levels, 155
Hematology, 193
Hemodialysis (HD), 148-150, 157-158
Hemoglobin, 94
Hemolytic disease, 287
Hemophilia, 373-374, 394
Hemoptysis, 70, 94
Hemorrhage
    from head injury, 44
    intracranial, 286
    postpartum, 440
    during pregnancy, 431, 432
Hemorrhoidectomy, 506
Hemorrhoids, 112-113
Hepatic encephalopathy/coma, 114
Hepatitis, 112-113
    immunization for, 314, 315, 415
Hepatitis virus, 112-113
Hernias
    diaphragmatic, 311
    gastroschisis, 311
    hiatal (esophageal), 105, 121-122, 126
    inguinal, 295
    omphaloceles, 311
Herpes simplex, 245, 361
Herpes zoster (shingles), 187, 245
Hiatal (esophageal) hernia, 106, 121-122, 126
Histamine antagonists (H2-blockers), 106, 124
Histrionic personality disorder, 556
Home care, 394
    postoperative, 505
    safety evaluation, 471
Hospitalization
    childhood, 254-599
        child abuse and, 414
        chronic illness and, 388-391, 394
        cognitive impairments and, 391-392, 394, 396
        developmental stages and, 254, 258-262, 264,
            388, 394
        discharge planning and, 257, 263-264
        emotional stress in, 254, 263
        informed consent in, 256-257, 263
        life-threatening illnesses and, 393-394, 395
        nutrition in, 261
        pain management and, 260-261, 264
        parents and, 254-256
        play therapy in, 255-256, 263
        prioritizing interventions in, 262, 264-265

restraints in, 481-482, 490
  safety considerations and, 479-493
  sensory and communication problems and,
    391-394, 394-395
  special needs and, 387-399
  vital signs and, 258
discharge planning and, 257, 263-264, 472
informed consent and, 256-257, 263
single-day, 255
Human chorionic gonadotropin, 425, 426
Human immunodeficiency virus (HIV)/acquired immunodeficiency syndrome (AIDS), 239-249
  health maintenance for, 222-244
  legal and ethical issues concerning, 240
  medications for, 241-242
  opportunistic infections with, 241-242, 244-245
  pain management for, 243
  screening for, 244
  transmission of, 361
  universal precautions against, 240-241
Human papillomavirus (H.P.V.), 361
Huntington's chorea, 43
Hydrocele, 280, 299, 312
Hydrocephalus, 285, 286, 299
  infant, 322
Hydrochlorothiazide (Esidrix), 70
Hydrocortisone (Solu-cortef), 92
Hydrogen, 93
Hydroxyzine (Vistaril, Atarax), 570
Hyperactivity, 348
Hyperbilirubinemia, 287
Hypercalcemia, 53, 230
Hypercalciuria, 210
Hyperemesis gravidarum, 433-434
Hyperglycemia, 211, 212
Hyperglycemic, hyperosmolar, nonketotic coma, 212
Hyperinflation, 84
Hyperinsulinism, 287
Hyperkalemia, 155
Hypermagnesemia, 155
Hypernatremia, 155
Hyperopia, 394
Hyperparathyroidism, 210
Hyperphosphaturia, 210
Hypertension
  antihypertensive medication, 147
  hypertensive crisis, 535
  pregnancy-induced, 432-433
Hyperthyroidism, 209-210, 213
Hypertonia, 307
Hyperventilation, 94
  central neurogenic, 37, 48
Hypocalcemia, 155
Hypochondriasis, 556
Hypoglossal nerve, 29, 308, 321

Hypoglycemia, 206-207, 212
Hypokalemia, 64-65, 71
Hypomagnesemia, 155
Hyponatremia, 64, 155
Hypoparathyroidism, 210
Hypospadias, 299, 322, 296
Hypotension, during labor, 438
Hypothalamus, 202, 203, 213
Hypothermia, 507
  newborn, 278, 442
Hypothyroidism, 208-209, 210, 212
Hypotonia, 365
Hypoventilation, 94
Hypoxemia, 84
Hypoxia, 84

I

Id, 535
Ideas of influence, 536
Ideas of reference, 536
Identification, as defense, 530
Identity of patient, 467, 498
Identity vs. role confusion, 254, 364, 409, 534
Ileostomy, 121, 127
Illusion, 536
Imipramine (Tofranil), 572
Immobilization, 170
  casts in, 173
  in postoperative care, 227-228
  traction in, 171-173, 179-180
Immunization
  infant, 314-315, 415
  schedule, 415
Immunoglobulin G (IgG), 283
Immunosuppressive medication, 158
Immunotherapy, 380
Imperforate anus, 294
Impetigo, 194
Inborn errors of metabolism, 414
Industry vs. inferiority, 254, 348
Infancy, 305-327
  assessment in, 306-307, 320-322
  cognitive development in, 393, 395
  common health problems of, 315-321, 322-325
  defined, 254, 305
  as developmental stage, 254, 259, 305, 404-405,
    412
  health promotion during, 313-315
  immunizations in, 314-315, 415
  injury prevention in, 315
  intramuscular injections in, 485, 486
  motor function, 412, 451
  nutrition during, 313-315, 450-452
  sleep in, 315
  vital signs in, 258
  See also Neonatal period

Infections
    antibiotics to prevent, 85, 142-143, 317, 319, 334, 346, 361, 362
    bacterial. *See* Bacterial infections
    Candidiasis, 245, 287, 307, 316
    opportunistic, 85, 241-242, 244-245
    viral. *See* Viral infections
    wound, prevention of, 502-503, 505, 508-509
Infective endocarditis, 66
Informed consent, 256-257, 263, 497, 517
Inguinal hernias, 295
Initiative vs. guilt, 254, 337, 407, 535
Injections
    immunization, 314-315, 415
    insulin, 205
    intramuscular, 483-485
    needle size for, 483-484
    sites for, 206, 483-484
Injuries
    in early childhood, 333, 339
    in infancy, 315
Insulin, 127, 147, 204-207
    administration of, 206, 212
    functions of, 204, 211
    of newborns, 287
    types of, 212, 380
Integrity vs. despair, 535
Integumentary system, 185-200
    assessment of
        in adolescence, 354-357
        infant, 310
        newborn, 282
    diagnostic studies of, 186
    disorders of, 187-189, 194-195
        infant, 316
    functions of, 186
    interventions for disorders of, 188-189, 196
    See also Skin
Intelligence quotient (IQ), 390-392, 395, 411
Internal rotation, 312
Interpersonal framework, 528
Intestinal obstructions, 118-119, 233, 279
Intimacy vs. isolation, 254, 410, 535
Intracranial hemorrhage, 285
Intracranial pressure (I.C.P.), increased, 39
    newborn, 285, 288-289, 298-299
Intraoperative stage, 498-499, 506-507
    positioning in, 498-499, 506
    procedures in, 499
Intrapartum period, 434-439
    delivery, 435-437
    labor, stages of, 434, 436
Intravenous cholangiogram, 125
Intravenous medication, 485-486
Intravenous pyelogram, 155
Introjection, as defense, 530
Intussusception, 318, 323

Ipratropium (Atrovent), 92
Iron
    infants and, 450
    in pregnancy, 363
Islets of Langerhans, 204
Isocarboxazid (Marplan), 572
Isoniazid (INH), 85, 93
IUDs, 362

J

Jackson-Pratt reservoir, 127
Jaundice
    infant, 322
    newborn, 279, 282, 286
Jejunostomy tube, 127
Joints, 176

K

Kaposi's sarcoma, 231, 245
Kayexalate, 133
Kernicterus, 286
Kernig's sign, 40
Kidneys
    anatomy of, 134-137, 153-154
    disorders of, 142-150, 155-157, 455
    newborn, 278, 279
    during pregnancy, 427
    transplantation of, 152, 158
Kleptomania, 553
Klinefelter's syndrome, 413
Kock pouch, 127
Kussmaul's respiration (hyperpnea), 93

L

Labor
    fetal heart monitoring in, 438-439
    mechanism of, 437
    pain management during, 438
    stages of, 434-436
Labored respirations, 94
Lactose intolerance, 455, 459
Language development
    infant, 405
    preschooler, 407
    school-aged period, 408
    toddler, 406
Lanugo, 298, 322
Late adulthood, 412, 413
    nutrition in, 457-458, 459
Latency stage, 412, 528, 535
Lateral position, 506
Laxatives, 124
Lecithin/sphingomyelin (L/S) ratio, 427
Legal issues, 513-522
    concerning HIV/AIDS, 240

documentation. *See* Documentation
informed consent, 256-257, 263, 497, 516
legal terminology, 516
reporting of child abuse, 333, 334, 388
Leiomyosarcoma, 231
Leukemia, 231, 380
childhood, 371-373, 380, 394
types of, 371
Leukorrhea, 442
Levine tube, 128
Levothyroxine (T4), 208
Liability, 517
Lidocaine, 438
Ligaments, 164
Linea nigra, 442
Lipids, in diet, 449
Liposarcoma, 221
Lithium carbonate, 576
Lithotomy, 506
Liver, 112-114
anatomy of, 112
disorders of, 107, 112-114, 455
biopsy for, 125
cancer, 222, 231
newborn, 279, 282, 286
Lobectomy, 93
Lochia, 440
Loop of Henle, 137
Loosening of associations, 534
Lorazepam (Ativan), 569
Lou Gehrig's disease, 49
Lower urinary tract infections, 142-143
Loxapine (Loxitane), 563
Lungs
anatomy of, 78-79, 87
cancer of, 88, 231
mucus buildup from cystic fibrosis, 371, 381
See also Respiratory system
Lyme disease, 347
Lymphangiosarcoma, 231
Lymph nodes
adolescent, 355
removal of, 227, 228
tumor migration and, 231
in tumor staging, 223
Lymphoma, 231, 245
Lymph vessels, cancer of, 231

M

Macrocephaly, 306
Macules, 322
Magnesium
levels of, 155
renal insufficiency and, 128
Magnesium sulfate, 432
Magnetic resonance imaging (MRI), 174
Mainstreaming, 394

Malignant melanoma, 194
Malpractice, 517
Mammography, 223
Mania, 544
antimanic medication, 569-570
Mannitol (Osmitrol), 147
MAO (monoamine oxidase) inhibitors, 575, 576-577
Masks
in oxygen administration, 89
as protective gear, 244
Mastectomy, 226
Measles, 322
immunization for, 315, 415
Meconium, 278, 294, 297
Meconium aspiration syndrome, 285
Medication
administration of
injection, 206, 483-485
postoperative, 505, 506
rights of, 95, 232, 466, 472
analgesics, 122, 228-229, 233, 243, 261, 264, 438
anesthetics, 438, 545
antacids, 106, 110, 123-124, 147
antianxiety, 570-571
antibiotics, 85, 143, 317, 319, 333, 366-347, 361, 362
anticholinergics, 92, 124
anticholinesterase, 43
anticonvulsant, 38, 576
antidepressants, 572-575
antidiarrheals, 123-124
antiemetics, 124
antifungal, 287
antihistamines, 92, 570
antihypertensives, 147
antiinflammatory agents, 92
antimanic agents, 569-570
antinausea, 232
antiparkinsonian agents, 568, 577
antipsychotics, 565-567, 577
antiretroviral, 241, 244
antituberculosis, 85, 92
antitussives, 92
antiviral, 361
beta-adrenergic agonists, 370
bronchodilators, 92
cardiac glycosides, 63, 64, 65, 70
chemotherapeutic, 227-229, 232
diuretic, 39, 64, 70, 147
expectorants, 92
histamine antagonists (H2-blockers), 106, 124
immunosuppressants, 158
insulin, 147, 205-207, 212, 215
laxatives, 123
mucolytics, 93
narcotics, 261, 265, 438
pancreatic enzymes, 124

potassium-lowering agents, 147
protease inhibitors, 244
psychotropic, 550
sodium bicarbonate, 147
tranquilizers, 569
vasodilators, 64, 65, 71
xanthines, 92
Medulla
cluster breathing and, 48
kidney, 153
Menarche, 355, 409
Meningitis, 39
Meningomyelocele, 288, 299
Menstruation, 355, 409, 423
Mental retardation
classification of, 390-391, 395
in Down's syndrome, 375-377, 381-382, 391
in fragile X syndrome, 391
Mesoridazine (Serentil), 563
Metabolism
carbohydrate, 211
inborn errors of, 297, 414
pancreatic enzymes and, 124, 371
during pregnancy, 426
Metaproterenol sulfate (Alupent), 92
Metastasis, 231
Methylprednisolone (Solu-Medrol), 92
Methylxanthines (theophylline, caffeine), 316
Metoclopramide (Reglan), 106, 124, 232
Microcephaly, 306
Middle adulthood, 410
Middle childhood. *See* School-aged period
Milia, 298, 322
Miller-Abbott tubes, 119
Mitral stenosis, 72
Mitral valve, 67
Molindone (Moban), 563
Mongolian spots, 298, 322
Monoamine oxidase (MAO) inhibitors, 572-575
Mood/affective disorders, 544-546, 555
depression, 410, 544, 549
electroconvulsive therapy, 545-546, 555
mania, 544, 576
suicide, 410, 544-545, 555
Mood stabilizers, 576
Morning sickness, 442
Moro reflex, 277, 298, 441
Morphine sulfate, 261
Motor function
assessment of, 35-36
infant, 405, 451
preschooler, 407
range of motion, 165, 312-313
school-aged period, 408
screening, 411
toddler, 406

Mouth
disorders of, 104, 125
infant, 307
oral medication, 482, 483
Mucolytics, 93
Mucositis, 226
Multiple sclerosis, 42
Mumps, immunization for, 315, 415
Murmurs, 69, 310, 322
Muromonab-CD3 (OKT3), 158
Muscle enzymes, 176
Muscles, 176
cancer of, 231
intramuscular injections, 483-485
Musculoskeletal system, 163-183
adolescent, 355
anatomy and physiology of, 164-165
assessment of
infant, 312-313
newborn, 280-282
diagnostic studies of, 165-167, 176, 177
disorders of, 167-170
interventions for disorders of, 170-175
Musculoskeletal trauma, 168-170
Myasthenia gravis, 42-43
Myelography, 176
Myelomeningocele, 289, 299
Myocardial infarction, 63
Myocardium, 67
Myoclonic seizures, 38
Myometrium, 423
Myopia, 395
Myxedema, 212-213

N

Nägele's rule, 427
Narcissistic personality disorder, 556
Narcotics, 261, 265, 438
Nasal cannula, 89
Nasal medication, 488
Nasogastric tubes, for children, 261, 488
National Council of State Boards of Nursing (NC-SBN), 4
Nausea
burns and, 192
medication for, 232
in morning sickness, 442
in oncology clients, 233
NCLEX-RN, 3-22
computer adaptive testing (CAT), 6
content of, 5-6
described, 4
maximum number of questions completed, 12
minimum number of questions completed, 12
preparation for, 11-22
strategy for taking, 11-22

common sense, 15
  first impression, 12
  pacing in, 21
  pre-exam tips, 22
  prefixes and suffixes in, 15-16
  process of elimination (POE), 12
  test structure and, 13-14
  timing, 21
Necrotizing enterocolitis (N.E.C.), 295
Needle size, 484
Neglect, child, 333-334, 338
Negligence, 517
Neologisms, 536
Neonatal period, 271-303
  assessment in, 273-283, 297-298, 441-442
  bonding and, 259, 284, 293, 442
  common health problems of, 284-287, 298-299
  defined, 254, 271
  developmental disorders of, 288-296, 299
    cardiac, 290-292
    gastrointestinal, 293-295
    genitourinary, 295-296
    nervous system, 288-289
  HIV/AIDS and, 244
  nursing care of, 283-284
  nutrition in, 450
  respiratory system in, 278, 284-285, 441
  stools of, characteristics of, 279
  thermoregulation in, 278, 442
  vital signs of, 258
  See also Infancy
Neoplasms, esophageal, 106
Nephrectomy, 157
Nephrolithotomy, 157
Nephrons, 153
Nerve sheath, cancer of, 231
Nervous system, 25-54
  anatomy and physiology of, 25-31
  assessment of, 31-37
    cerebral dysfunction, 33-34, 48
    Glasgow Coma Scale, 32
    infant, 307-309
    motor function, 35-36
    newborn, 273-274, 276, 441
    postoperative, 501-502, 508
    respiratory patterns, 34, 48
    sensory function, 36
  disorders of, 37-43, 288-289, 378-379
  injuries to, 44
  newborn, 288-289
Neural tube defects, 391
Neurolemic sarcoma, 231
Neuroleptic malignant syndrome (NMS), 567, 577
Neurons, 26-27
Neurotransmitters, 26
Neutropenia, 380
Newborns. See Neonatal period

Nihilistic delusion, 536
Nitroglycerin, 65
Nocturia, 142
Nodules, 358
Norepinephrine, 26
Normalization, 394
Norplant, 364
Nortriptyline (Pamelor), 572
Nose
  infant, 307
  nasal medication, 488
Nurse Practice Act, 517
Nutrition, 447-463, 490
  burns and, 195
  for clients with HIV/AIDS, 243
  eating disorders, 363, 364, 552
  food groups in, 448-450, 459
  gastrointestinal problems and, 122
  gout and, 167
  for heart disease prevention, 67
  parenteral, 106, 122
  in pediatric hospitalization, 261, 262
  postoperative, 505
  during pregnancy, 453, 456-457, 459
  radiation therapy and, 223-224
  respiratory disorders and, 84
  through the life cycle, 450-462
    adolescence, 358, 363-365, 453, 459
    adulthood, 454-460
    geriatric, 457-460
    infancy, 313-314, 450-452
    newborn, 313-314, 450-452, 457
  See also Diets; Food
Nystagmus, 307, 323
Nystatin (Mycostatin), 287, 321

O

Oatmeal baths, 195
Obesity, during pregnancy, 457
Obsessive-compulsive personality disorder, 556
Obstruction
  chronic obstructive pulmonary disease (C.O.P.D.), 84
  intestinal, 118-119, 232, 279
  respiratory, 317
Occipital-frontal circumference (OFC), 306
Occlusive dressings, 194
Occupational therapy, 490
Oculogyric crisis, 566, 577
Oculomotor nerve, 29, 309, 321
Olfactory nerve, 29, 309, 321
Omeprazole (Prilosec), 106, 124
Omphaloceles, 311
Oncology. See Cancer
Ondansetron (Zofran), 232
Ophthalmia neonatorum, 283

Optic medication, 486
Optic nerve, 29, 309, 321
Oral cholecystogram, 125
Oral medication, 482-483
Oral stage, 412, 527, 535
Organic mental disorders, 562
Orogastric tubes, for children, 261, 488
Orthopnea, 93
Orthostatic hypotension, 565
Ortolani's click, 280-281, 322, 323
Osmolality, 154
Osteitis deformans (Paget's disease), 167, 178
Osteoarthritis, 167
Osteomalacia, 167
Osteomyelitis, 167
Osteoporosis, 167
Osteosarcoma, 231
Ostomies, 120-121, 127
Otic medication, 487
Otitis externa, 316
Otitis media, 334-339, 346, 391
Ovaries, 203, 423
    cancer of, 222
    postpartum, 440
Overhead 90-90 traction, 171, 179
Oxygen, 94
Oxygenation, 70
Oxygen therapy, 89
Oxytocin, 434

P

Pacifiers, 261, 293
Paget's disease (osteitis deformans), 167, 178
Pain management
    angina, 63
    cancer, 228-229, 232
    childhood, 261, 264
    for clients with HIV/AIDS, 243
    labor, 438
    leukemia, 372
    lung, 94
    medication in, 438, 545
        analgesics, 122, 228-299, 232, 243, 261, 264, 438
        anesthetics, 438, 545
    postoperative, 122, 503-504, 508
Pancreas, 114-116, 202, 204-207
    anatomy of, 114-115, 204
    diabetes mellitus, 205-207, 212
    disorders of, 115-116
    mucus buildup from cystic fibrosis, 371
Pancreatic enzymes, 124, 371
Pancreatin, 124
Pancreatitis, 115
Pancreatoduodenectomy, 115-116
Pancrelipase (Viokase), 124

Panic disorder, 557
Pap smear, 222, 245, 427
Papules, 322, 358
Parallel play, 406
Paralytic ileum, 565
Paralytic poliomyelitis, 315, 316, 415
Paranoid personality disorder, 556
Paraphilia, 557
Parasomnia, 556
Parasympathetic nervous system, 26
Parathyroid glands, 202, 203, 210
    disorders of, 210
            hyperparathyroidism, 210
            hypoparathyroidism, 210
    function of, 210
Paroxetine (Paxil), 572
Parents
    bonding with newborn, 259, 283, 293, 442
    and child abuse, 333-334, 338, 414-415
    preschoolers and, 407
    reaction to child's hospitalization, 254, 388-390
    school-aged children and, 408
    teaching, hospitalization of child, 255-256
    toddlers and, 406
Parity, 442
Parkinson's disease, 42
    antiparkinsonian agents, 568-569
Parotitis, 104
Passive transport (diffusion), 153
Patent ductus arteriosus, 290, 291, 320
Paternalism, 517
Pathological reflexes, 36
Pavlik harness, 281-282
Pedialyte, 318
Pelvic belt traction, 171, 179
Pelvic examination, 222
Pelvic inflammatory disease (P.I.D.), 362
Penicillin, 361, 362
Penrose drain, 128
Peptic ulcer disease, 109, 110
Percutaneous lithotripsy, 157
Percutaneous transhepatic cholangiogram (P.T.C.), 125
Pericardial tamponade, 230
Pericarditis, 72
Pericardium, 67
Perineal (radical) resection, 151
Peripheral nervous system (P.N.S.), 25
    cranial nerves and, 29, 43, 307-309, 321
    See also Nervous system
Peripheral parenteral nutrition (P.P.N.), 106
Peripheral pulses, 310
Peristalsis, 26
Peritoneal dialysis (P.D.), 148-150, 157-158
Peritonitis, 121
Perphenazine (Trilafon), 563
Personality disorders, 547-549, 555-556

diagnostic criteria for, 548
    nursing interventions for, 548-549, 555-556
Pertussis, immunization for, 315, 415
Petechiae, 348
Petit mal (absence) seizures, 38
Phallic (Oedipal) stage, 412, 527, 535
Phenazopyridine HCl (Pyridium), 142-143
Phenelzine sulfate (Nardil), 572
Phenobarbital, 38
Phenothiazines, 563
Phenylketonuria (PKU), 297, 414, 457, 459
Phenytoin sodium (Dilantin), 38
Phimosis, 322
Phobia, 557
Phosphate, serum, 210, 213
Phosphorus, levels of, 155, 210
Photosensitivity, 566
Phototherapy, 286
Physical abuse, 333-334, 338, 414-415
Physical neglect, 333-334, 338, 414
Physical therapy, 489-490
Pituitary gland, 202, 203
Placenta, 425
    abruptio placentae, 430, 442
    delivery of, 435
    placenta previa, 429-430, 442, 443
Planning
    discharge, 257, 264, 472
    safety, 467
Plantar reflex, 298, 441
Platelets, normal range, 232
Play
    in hospital setting, 256, 263, 489
    in infancy, 405
    parallel, 406
    in preschool period, 332, 407
    solitary, 405
    in toddlerhood, 332, 406
Pleural drainage, 89-91
Pleural effusion, 86, 93
Pleural friction rub, 93
Pneumocystis carinii, 85, 245
Pneumo/hemothorax, 86-87
Pneumonectomy, 95
Pneumonia, 85
Pneumothorax, 507
Poisoning, 333, 338
Polio, 314, 315, 415
Polydipsia, 212
Polyphagia, 212
Polyuria, 212
Pons, 48
Portal hypertension, 107, 114
Postnatal care
    hearing loss and, 391
    visual deficits and, 392
Postoperative stage, 500-506
    airway, breathing, and circulation in, 507

breast surgery, 227-228
    discharge from recovery room, 500, 507
    discharge planning after, 504-406
    fluid volume and, 502, 507, 509
    neurological assessment in, 501-502, 508
    pain management in, 503-504, 508
    safety in, 504
    surgical wounds and, 502-503, 505, 508-509
Postpartum period, 440-442
Posttraumatic stress disorder (P.T.S.D.), 552
Potassium
    dietary, 456, 459
    levels of, 155
    sources of, 71
Potassium iodide (SSKI), 93
Potassium-lowering agents, 147
Prednisone, 92
Preeclampsia, 431, 442
Prefixes
    medical, 499
    in taking NCLEX-RN, 15-16
Pregnancy, 424-446
    adolescent, 363, 364, 453, 459
    antepartum period, 426-434
    assessment for, 425-426
    cardiovascular system during, 426
    complications of, 428-434
        abortion, 430-431
        abruptio placentae, 430, 442
        assessment for, 429
        disseminated intravascular coagulation
            (D.I.C.), 431
        gestational diabetes, 433, 459
        hyperemesis gravidarum, 433-434
        obesity, 457
        placenta previa, 429-430, 442, 443
        pregnancy-induced hypertension, 432-433
        Rh incompatibility, 286, 427
        risk factors, 428-429
        sexually transmitted diseases, 361-362, 442
    diagnostic tests during, 286, 426, 428
    endocrine system in, 434
    intrapartum period, 434-439
    nutrition during, 453, 456-457, 459
    postpartum period, 440-442
    prenatal screening and, 491
    prevention of, 221, 362, 364
    renal system during, 426
    respiratory system during, 426
    RhoGAM in, 286
    syphilis during, 362
    urinary system during, 426
    validation of, 425-426
Preload, 68
Prenatal care
    hearing loss and, 391
    HIV/AIDS transmission in, 244

mental retardation and, 391
visual deficits and, 392
Preoperational period
characteristics of, 412
concept of death and, 393-394, 395
Preoperative stage, 496-497, 506
breast surgery, 227
client teaching and, 496-497
major surgery, 496
minor surgery, 496
Preschool period, 329-343
assessment in, 331-332, 337-338
child maltreatment in, 333-334, 338
cognitive development in, 393-394, 395
common health problems of, 334-337, 338-339
defined, 254, 329, 337
as developmental stage, 254, 259, 407, 412, 416
health promotion during, 333-334
immunization in, 415
injuries in, 333, 338-339
poisoning in, 333, 338
vital signs in, 258, 406
See also Chronic childhood illnesses
Pressure ulcers (decubiti), 193, 196, 498
Priority setting, in pediatric hospitalization, 262- 263, 264-265
Process of elimination (POE), for NCLEX-RN, 12
Prochlorperazine (Compazine), 232
Projection, as defense, 530, 551
Pronation, 312, 323
Prone position, 506
Propranolol HCl (Inderal), 107
Prostate
benign prostatic hypertrophy (B.P.H.), 150-151, 222
cancer of, 222, 231
Protease inhibitors, 244
Protein
allergies to, 451
in diet, 127, 449, 455
postoperative, 509
in pregnancy, 457
Proteinuria, 432
Proton pump inhibitors, 106
Proximal tubules, 154
Pseudoparkinsonism, 567, 577
Psoriasis, 348
Psychiatric nursing, 525-540
clients, 516-517
conceptual frameworks for, 526-528, 535
behavioral, 528
biomedical, 528-529
cognitive, 528
Eriksonian, 527-528, 535
Freudian, 527, 535
interpersonal, 528
defense mechanisms and, 530-531, 551

diagnoses in, 534, 536, 551-552
nurse-client relationships in, 531-533, 535-536
assessment in, 532-533
communication in, 531-532, 535-536
psychiatric disorders, 541-560
abuse and, 333-334, 338, 552
anxiety disorders, 542-543, 555
bereavement, 553
cognitive disorders, 549-550, 556
eating disorders, 363, 364-365, 552
interventions to promote psychosocial integrity, 554
mood/affective disorders, 544-546, 555
other disorders, 556-557
personality disorders, 547-549, 555-556
principles of evaluation, 555
psychotic disorders, 546-547, 555
schizophrenia, 546-547, 555
substance-related disorders, 551-552
psychopharmacology, 561-581
antianxiety agents, 569-571, 577
antidepressants, 572-575
antimanic agents, 576
antiparkinsonian agents, 568-569, 577
antipsychotic agents, 562-567, 577
Psychogenic problems, 349
Psychosocial development
adolescent, 409-410
infant, 405
preschool period, 407
school-aged period, 347-349, 408
toddler, 406
See also Psychiatric nursing
Psychotic disorders, 546-547, 555
antipsychotic agents, 562-567, 577
delusions, 546
hallucinations, 546
nursing interventions for, 547, 555
Psychotropic medication, 550
PTU (propylthiouracil), 209
Puberty, 353, 355, 408
Puerperium, 440-442
See also Neonatal period
Pulmonary bronchioles, 26
Pulmonary edema, 63, 87, 507
Pulmonary emboli, 87
Pulmonary function test, 94
Pulmonary toileting, 88, 122, 501
Pulmonary valve, 67
Pulses, peripheral, 310
Punning, 536
Purified protein derivative, 85
Purkinje's fibers, 57, 68
Pustules, 358
Pyelolithotomy, 157
Pyelonephritis, 143
Pyloric stenosis, 294
Pyloroplasty, 127

Pyromania, 556
Pyuria, 142

Q

Quickening, 442

R

Radiation, heat loss from, 278, 442
Radiation therapy, 223-224, 371
  side effects of, 223-224, 231-232
Radiological studies, genitourinary, 140-142, 154-156
Rales, 69, 311
Range of motion, infant, 312-313
Ranitidine (Zantac), 106, 124
Rape, 364
Rationalization, as defense, 530, 551
Reaction formation, as defense, 530
Rebound hypoglycemia, 287
Recovery room, 500, 507
Rectum
  colorectal cancer, 119, 127, 222
  rectal medication, 486
Red retinal reflex, 323
Reflexes
  in assessment of cerebellar function, 36
  newborn, 277, 280, 297-298, 441
Regression, as defense, 530
Regurgitation, 318
Relaxation techniques, 264
Reminiscence therapy, 550
Renal arteriogram, 155
Renal biopsy, 156
Renal calculi (urinary stones), 144-145, 157
Renal capsule, 153
Renal pyramids, 153
Renal surgery, 506
Renal ultrasound, 156
Repolarization, 68
Repression, as defense, 531
Respiration, 93
Respiratory distress syndrome (R.D.S.), 85-86, 284-285
Respiratory system, 77-79
  airway, breathing, and circulation (ABC) after surgery, 501, 507
  anatomy and physiology of, 78
  assessment of, 79-81, 93-94
    infant, 311
    newborn, 278, 284-285, 441
  breathing patterns, 34, 48, 62, 68, 93-94, 278, 311
  care of client with dysfunction of, 88-91
  diagnostic studies of, 82-83, 94
  disorders of
    with cerebral dysfunction, 34

early childhood, 334-335
  infancy, 315-316, 317
  neonate, 284-285
  types of, 84-88
medication for, 91-93
poisoning and, 333
during pregnancy, 426
surgery for, 91, 94-95
Restitution, as defense, 531
Restraints, 481, 490
Restricted breathing, 93
Retinitis pigmentosa, 565
Retinopathy, 212
Retropubic resection, 150-151
Retrovir, 241, 244
Reverse Trendelenburg's position, 506
Rhabdomyosarcoma, 231
Rheumatic endocarditis, 72
Rheumatoid arthritis, 167
Rheumatoid factor, 176
Rh incompatibility, 286, 427
RhoGAM, 286, 427
Rhonchi, 93, 311, 323
Rice cereal, 314, 451
Rifabutin (Mycobutin), 245
Rifampin (Rifadin), 85, 92
Romberg's test, 36
Rooting reflex, 277, 297, 441
Rubella
  immunization for, 315, 415
  pregnancy and, 427
Russel's traction, 171, 179

S

Safe sex (barrier contraception), 221, 362, 364
Safety, 463-493
  of children, 479-493
    coordinated care, 489-490
    documentation and, 480, 482
    medication administration, 481-488, 490
    restraints in, 481, 490
  documentation and, 446-468, 480, 482
  equipment, 466
  evaluation of, 468-471, 472, 473
  general assessment of, 467
  injury prevention, 468-471, 472, 473, 480
  intervening to ensure, 467-468
  in medication administration, 95, 232, 466, 471, 481-488, 490
    guidelines, 482
    injection, 206, 483-485
    intravenous, 485
    nasal, 488
    optic, 486
    oral, 482-483
    otic, 487
    rectal, 486

rights, 95, 232, 466, 472
   via tube, 488
  planning for, 467
  postoperative, 503-504
Salem sump, 128
Schizoaffective disorder, 556
Schizoid personality disorder, 556
Schizophrenia, 546-547, 556
  antipsychotic agents, 562-567
Schizotypal personality disorder, 556
School-aged period, 345-351
  assessment in, 346, 348
  cognitive development in, 393-394, 395
  common health problems of, 346-347
  defined, 254, 345
  as developmental stage, 254, 260, 348, 408, 411-412
  health promotion during, 333-334
  immunization in, 415
  intramuscular injections in, 483, 484
  vital signs in, 258, 408
  See also Chronic childhood illnesses
School phobia, 349
Scoliosis, 359
Scope of Practice, 517
Scrotum, newborn, 280
Seborrheic dermititis, 316
Sedation
  from antipsychotic medication, 565
  in oncology clients, 232
Segmental resection, 95
Seizure disorders, 38-39, 567
  anticonvulsant medication, 38, 567
Selective serotonin reuptake inhibitors (S.S.R.I.'s),
  572, 573
Self-care, 529
Sengstaken-Blakemore tubes, 107
Sensorimotor period
  characteristics of, 411-412
  concept of death and, 393-394, 395
Sensorineural hearing loss, 391
Sensory function
  assessment of, 36
  childhood sensory and communication problems,
    391-393, 394-395
    hearing loss, 391, 395
    visual deficits, 392-393, 395
  cranial nerves in, 29
Separation anxiety, toddler, 259, 264, 331, 406
Septic shock, 233
Serotonin, 26
Serotonin antagonists, 232
Sertraline (Zoloft), 572
Serum studies, 139-140
Sex-linked transmission traits, 414
Sexual dysfunction, 566
Sexuality, in school-aged period, 348
Sexually transmitted diseases (S.T.D.'s), 295, 361-362,
  427

Shingles (herpes zoster), 187, 245
Shock
  cardiogenic, 66
  and hospitalization of child, 389
  septic, 233
Sickle cell anemia, 373-374, 380, 413
Side rails, 504
Sigmoidoscopy, 222
Sinoatrial node, 57, 67
Skeletal traction, 171, 179
Skin
  in adolescence, 355, 358
  breakdown of
    after radiation therapy, 231
    in Down's syndrome, 381
    with HIV/AIDS, 242
    pressure ulcers, 193, 196, 498
    traction and, 171, 179
  cancer of, 188-189, 195, 231
  in school-aged period, 347, 348
  See also Integumentary system
Skin grafts, 193
Skin traction, 171, 179
Sleep
  infant, 314
  newborn, 314
  sudden infant death syndrome (S.I.D.S.), 315
Sleepwalking, 348
Smoking, 231, 339, 453
Sodium
  dietary, 456, 459
  and heart disease prevention, 67
  levels of, 154-155
Sodium bicarbonate, 147
Sodium levothyroxine (Synthroid), 209
Sodium nitroprusside (Nipride), 65
Solitary play, 405
Somatic delusion, 536
Somatization disorder, 557
Somatostatin, 121
Spectinomycin, 361
Speech therapy, 490
Spermicides, 364
Spina bifida, 288
Spinal accessory nerve, 29, 309, 321
Spinal cord
  anatomy of, 28
  compression of, 233
  injuries to, 44
Spine
  assessment of, infant, 313
  scoliosis, 359
Spironolactone (Aldactone), 70
Spitting up, 318
Sprain, 177
Sputum, 94
Squamous cell carcinoma, 195, 231

Startle reflex, 277, 298, 441
State authorities, and child abuse, 335, 340, 414-415, 990
Steatorrhea, 371, 380
Step reflex, 277, 298
Steroids, 92, 370
Stomach, 107-110
    anatomy of, 107
    disorders of, 108-110, 126-127
    pyloric stenosis, 294
Stomatitis, 104
Stones
    gallbladder, 111
    urinary tract, 144-145, 157
Stool occult blood, 222
Stools
    infant, 318
    newborn, 279
Strabismus, 323, 392, 395
Strain, 177
Streptococcus, 346
Stresses
    of hospitalization, 254
    preschooler, 407
    school-aged period, 408
    of surgery, 496
    in toddlerhood, 406
Striae, 322
Stridor, 94
Strokes, 41
Stroke volume, 68
Sublimation, as defense, 531
Substance use and abuse
    in adolescence, 409, 410, 453
    among nurses, 514
    disorders related to, 551-552
        dual diagnosis, 551-552
        withdrawal and, 551
    in prenatal period, 391
    risky behavior and, 545
Substitution, as defense, 531
Subtotal gastrectomy, 127
Sucking (rooting) reflex, 277, 297, 441
Sucralfate (Carafate), 110, 124
Sudden infant death syndrome (S.I.D.S.), 315
Suffixes
    medical, 499
    in taking NCLEX-RN, 15-16
Suicide, 410, 544-545, 555
Superego, 535
Superficial reflexes, 36
Superior vena cava syndrome, 233
Supination, 312
Supine position, 506
Suppression, as defense, 531
Suprapubic resection, 150-151
Surfactants, 93, 284

Surgery, 495-512
    amputation, 170
    for benign prostatic hypertrophy (B.P.H.), 150-151
    for cancer, 226-228
    gastrointestinal system, 110, 116, 119-121, 122-123, 126-127
    for genitourinary system, 157
    informed consent for, 256-257, 263, 497
    intraoperative stage, 498-499, 506-507
    postoperative stage, 227-228, 500-506
    preoperative stage, 227, 496-497, 506
    respiratory system, 91-92, 94-95
    thyroidectomy, 209
    tonsillectomy, 346-347
Symbolization, as defense, 531
Sympathetic nervous system, 26
Syphilis, 245, 362
Systemic lupus erythematosus, 187
Systole, 57, 67

T

Tachycardia
    from antipsychotic medication, 565
    fetal, 439
    infant, 322
    newborn, 278
Tachypnea, 69, 322, 441
Tardive dyskinesia, 567, 577
Tar preparations, 194
Tay-Sachs disease, 413, 414
Teeth, decay of, 452
Temazepam (Restoril), 570
Tendons, 176
Tenesmus, 142
Tensilon test, 42
Teratogenesis, 442
Terbutaline sulfate (Brethine), 92
Testes, 202
    cancer of, 222
    hydrocele, 280, 299, 322, 323
    undescended (cryptorchidism), 280, 295, 299, 322
Tetanus, immunization for, 315, 415
Tetracyclic antidepressants, 573
Tetracycline, 362
Tetralogy of Fallot (T.O.F.), 290, 292
Thalassemia, 413
Theophylline (Theo-dur), 92
Thermoregulation, 278, 442
Thioridazine (Mellaril), 563
Thiothixene (Navane), 563
Thioxanthene, 563
Thoracentesis, 94
Thorax, newborn, 278
Thought blocking, 536
Thought broadcasting, 536
Thought insertion, 536
3TC (Zerit), 244

Thrombocytopenia, 380
Thrombosis, deep vein, 44, 507
Thrush, 287, 307, 321
Thyroidectomy, 209
Thyroid glands, 202, 203, 208-210
    disorders of, 208-210
        hyperthyroidism, 209-210
        hypothyroidism, 208-209, 210, 212
    function of, 208
Thyroid releasing hormone (TRH), 212
Thyroid stimulating hormone (TSH), 202
Thyroid storm, 213
Tissue infiltration, cancer and, 232
Tissue perfusion, cancer and, 228
Toddlerhood, 329-343
    assessment in, 331-332, 337-339
    child maltreatment in, 333-334, 338
    cognitive development in, 393, 395
    common health problems of, 334-337, 338-339
    defined, 254, 329, 338
    as developmental stage, 254, 259, 406, 411-412,
      416
    health promotion during, 333-334
    injuries in, 333, 338
    intramuscular injections in, 483, 484
    poisoning in, 333, 338
    separation anxiety in, 259, 264, 331, 406
    vital signs in, 258, 406
    See also Chronic childhood illnesses
Tonic-clonic seizures, 38
Tonic neck reflex, 277, 298, 441
Tonsillectomy, 346-347
Tonsillitis, 346-347
T.O.R.C.H. infections, 442
Tort
    intentional, 517
    unintentional, 517
Total parenteral nutrition (T.P.N.), 106, 122
Tourette's syndrome, 562
Toxoplasmic encephalitis, 245
Toxoplasmosis, 245, 442
Tracheal edema, 507
Tracheoesophageal fistula (T.E.F.), 293
Traction, 170-173, 179-180
Tranquilizers, 569
Transcutaneous shock wave lithotripsy, 157
Transfusions, 244
    exchange, 286
Transplants
    bone marrow, 380
    kidney, 152, 158
Transurethral resection of the prostate (T.U.R.P.), 151
Tranylcypromine sulfate (Parnate), 572
Trendelenburg's position, 506
Triamcinolone acetonide (Azmacort), 92
Triamterene (Dyrenium), 71
Triazolam (Halcion), 570

Trichotillomania, 556
Tricuspid valve, 67
Tricyclic antidepressants, 572, 573
Tricyclics, 572
Trifluoperazine (Stelazine), 563
Trigeminal nerve, 29, 309, 321
Trigeminal neuralgia, 43
Triiodothyronine, T3, 208
Trisomy 27
    See Down's syndrome
Trochlear nerve, 29, 309, 321
Trust vs. mistrust, 254, 404, 535
Trypsin, 371
T-tube, 128
Tuberculosis (TB), 85, 245
    immunization for, 315, 415
Tubular reabsorption, 153
Tumors
    brain, 41
    migration of, 231
    staging of, 222, 231
    See also Cancer
Turner's syndrome, 413
Tylenol (acetaminophen), 93, 261

U

Ulcerative colitis, 118
Ulcers
    diet for, 455
    peptic, 109-110, 124
    pressure (decubiti), 193, 196, 498
Ultrasound, 125
    fetal, 426, 428
Umbilical cord, 284, 441
Undescended testicles (cryptorchidism), 280, 295,
    299, 322
Undoing, as defense, 531
Universal precautions, 240-241
Upper urinary tract infections, 143
Ureterolithotomy, 157
Ureters, 138
Urethra, 138
Urethritis, 142
Uric acid, 167, 176
Urinalysis, 138, 427
Urinary tract infection (U.T.I.), 142-144
    infant, 315
Urine, 138
Urine culture and sensitivity, 138, 427
Urine ketone levels, 212
Uterus, 423
    changes during pregnancy, 426
    in labor, 434
    postpartum, 440
Uticaria, 348

V

Vagina, 423
    changes during pregnancy, 426
    postpartum, 440
Vaginal surgery, 506
Vagotomy, 126
Vagus nerve, 29, 126, 309, 321
Valproic acid/valproate (Depakene/Depakote), 576
Varicella zoster (chicken pox), 194, 245, 336, 339
    immunization for, 315, 415
Vasodilator therapy, 64, 65, 71
Vasopressin (Pitressin), 107
Vein
    arteriovenous (A-V) fistula, 148-149
    in chemotherapy, 232
    intravenous medication, 485
Ventilation, 93
Ventricles, 67
Ventricular septal defect (V.S.D.), 290, 292
Vernix caseosa, 282
Vesicular, 93
Vestibulocochlear nerve, 29, 309, 321
Viral infections
    chicken pox, 245, 315, 336, 339
    croup (laryngotracheobronchitis), 317, 334-335, 339
    hepatitis, 113
    meningitis, 39, 245
    viral pneumonia, 85
    See also Human immunodeficiency virus (HIV)/
        acquired immunodeficiency syndrome (AIDS)
Virchow's triad, 87
Visual deficits, 392-393, 395
Vital signs
    adolescent, 258, 408
    developmental stage and, 258
    fetal heart monitoring, 438-439
    infant, 258
    newborn, 258, 278, 297
    in postoperative stage, 501
    during pregnancy, 427
    preschooler, 258, 407
    respiratory patterns, 34, 48, 62, 69
    school-age, 258, 408
    toddler, 258, 406
Vitamin A, 459
Vitamin C, 314
    postoperative, 509
Vitamin D, 167, 210, 459
Vitamin E, 459
Vitamin K, 107, 285, 297, 459

Vomiting
    antiemetics, 124
    burns and, 196
    in hyperemesis gravidarum, 433-434
    in morning sickness, 442
    in oncology clients, 232
    rectal medication and, 486

W

Walkers, 174
Water, in diet, 449, 450
Weaning, 314
Wedge resection, 95
Weight
    antipsychotic medication and, 566
    birth, 450-451, 459
    gain during pregnancy, 432, 456-457
Western Blot test, 244
Wheezes, 69, 93, 311, 370
Whipple, 115-116, 127
White blood cells
    in leukemia, 371
    normal range, 232
Word salad, 536
Wounds, surgical, 502-503, 505, 508-509

X

Xanthines, 92
X-rays
    genitourinary system, 155-156
    lung, 94
    musculoskeletal system, 176-177
    See also Radiation therapy

Y

Young adulthood, 254, 412

Z

ZDV (Retrovir), 241, 244
Zidovudine, 241

Using the NCLEX-RN Diagnostic Software

ABOUT THE SOFTWARE

The sample tests on the CD-ROM were designed to help you practice for all areas of the NCLEX-RN, while also allowing you to adjust to a computer testing environment. Although the format of a real exam is now Computer Adaptive, the linear tests on the disc should still be very useful as you study. We advise making good use of the review features—look at the explanations for questions you missed, and determine which question types are giving you the most trouble.

SYSTEM REQUIREMENTS

Windows™

- IBM PC or 100% Compatible (486/66 MHz or higher)
- Windows 95, 98
- 8 MB RAM
- 10MB Hard Disk space
- SVGA Monitor (256 Colors)
- Double-speed CD-ROM or faster
- Mouse

Macintosh©

- Power PC
- System 7.1 or higher
- 8 MB RAM
- 10MB Hard Disk space
- Double-speed CD-ROM or faster
- Mouse

INSTALLATION AND START-UP

Windows:

Close all other applications

Check that your monitor is set to 256 colors

1. Insert the CD-ROM in your CD-ROM drive
2. From your Start Menu select **Run**
3. Type D:setup and press **Enter.** If your CD-ROM drive is not drive D:, type the appropriate letter)
4. Follow the onscreen instructions until installation is complete.
5. Once setup is complete, if you want to begin immediately, you can check "Yes, I want to run NCLEX Diagnostic now" and select **Finish.** Otherwise, just select Finish.

To run the software later, make sure the CD is in your CD-ROM drive, and simply select **NCLEX-RN Diagnostic** from the *Princeton Review* folder in Programs from the Start Menu.

MACINTOSH:

1. Insert the CD in your CD-ROM drive.
2. Double click the NCLEX-RN Diagnostic Installer icon.
3. Follow the onscreen instructions until installation is complete.

To run the software, make sure the CD is in your CD-ROM drive, and simply double click the *Tester* icon located in the *NCLEX Diagnostic* folder on your hard drive.

USING NCLEX DIAGNOSTIC TESTS

Each time you launch you NCLEX Diagnostic, you will begin with the Main Menu. This screen contains two sections: **Start a Test** and **Review a Test.** Once a test has been taken, it will move from **Start** to **Review.**

TAKING A TEST

You have your choice of eight different tests. Click on the test you want, then click on **Begin.** Each sample NCLEX contains about 160 questions and provides 160 minutes to complete it. In an actual NCLEX, you will answer between 75 and 265 questions in up to five hours, but these sample tests will help you pace yourself.

The Score Report

When you have completed a test, you will see a screen that asks you to wait while your exam is scored. Then you will see your **SCORE REPORT**. Although an actual score is not provided, you can view your results for each question as well as your performance on each type of question. You can also print the full report by clicking the **Print** button. The **SCORE REPORT** can be viewed at another time by selecting the test from the **Review a Test** section of the Main Menu.

Reviewing Your Test

You may review any question from your test by clicking on the question number in the **SCORE REPORT**. The review mode will show you a green checkmark to indicate the credited response, and show your answer as the darkened oval. To view an explanation for an answer choice, click on the answer (the words in the answer, not on the oval). These explanations do not print. To return to the **SCORE REPORT**, click on the **STOP SECTION** button.

If you have any questions, please call our Technical Support Center at (800) 546-2102.

ABOUT THE AUTHOR

Jennifer Meyer graduated magna cum laude from the University of Pennsylvania School of Nursing, where she was an Alex Hillman Family Foundation Scholar. After passing the NCLEX-RN, she worked at New York University Medical Center in NYC.

NOTES

NOTES